Praise for Romantic Poetry: An An...

"Romantic Poetry is the ideal anthology for students and specialists alike, defining a new canon of ten Romantic poets and reflecting the full diversity of Romantic poetic forms. All readers will welcome the freshly edited texts, the authoritative headnotes and annotations, and the thought-provoking introduction. Edited by two leading scholars of Romanticism, the new Blackwell anthology of Romantic poetry will be the first choice for the classroom, library, and private study."

Nicholas Roe, University of St. Andrews

"This is a welcome and usefully up-to-date new anthology, providing, in a concise and manageable selection, a genuinely representative overview of the canon of romantic poetry, as it is comprised today by the works of poets of both sexes. O'Neill's excellent introduction pulls off the difficult feat of offering, to the first-time reader or student, a coherent and accessible summary of its subject without being reductive or overly simplifying. The introduction is nicely complemented by the thematically divided list of texts, particularly user-friendly from the undergraduate point of view. Prefaces, which address both individual poems as well as each poet more generally, are critical rather than merely informative; the annotations too, are more detailed and explanatory than the more minimal glosses usually provided in comparable publications."

Uttara Natarajan, Goldsmiths College, University of London

BLACKWELL ANNOTATED ANTHOLOGIES

Advisory Editors
Robert Cummings, University of Glasgow; David Fairer, University of Leeds; Christine Gerrard, University of Oxford; Andrew Hadfield, University of Sussex; Angela Leighton, University of Hull; Michael O'Neill, University of Durham; Duncan Wu, University of Oxford.

This new series of mid-length anthologies is devoted to poetry and the provision of key texts, canonical and post-canonical, with detailed annotation, sufficient to facilitate close reading, for use on specialist and appropriate survey courses. Headnotes and foot-of-page notes are designed to provide contexts for poets and poems alike, elucidating references and pointing to allusions. Selected variants may be given, where these provide vitally illuminating clues to a work's evolution and editorial history, and there are cross-references between poems.

Sixteenth-century Poetry: An Annotated Anthology
Edited by Gordon Braden

Seventeenth-century Poetry: An Annotated Anthology
Edited by Robert Cummings

Eighteenth-century Poetry: An Annotated Anthology, Second Edition
Edited by David Fairer and Christine Gerrard

Romantic Poetry: An Annotated Anthology
Edited by Michael O'Neill and Charles Mahoney

Victorian Poetry: An Annotated Anthology
Edited by Francis O'Gorman

Romantic Poetry

An Annotated Anthology

Edited by
Michael O'Neill and Charles Mahoney

Blackwell Publishing

Editorial material and organization © 2008 by Michael O'Neill and Charles Mahoney

BLACKWELL PUBLISHING
350 Main Street, Malden, MA 02148-5020, USA
9600 Garsington Road, Oxford OX4 2DQ, UK
550 Swanston Street, Carlton, Victoria 3053, Australia

The right of Michael O'Neill and Charles Mahoney to be identified as the authors of the editorial material in this work has been asserted in accordance with the UK Copyright, Designs, and Patents Act 1988.

All rights reserved. No part of this publication may be reproduced, stored in a retrieval system, or transmitted, in any form or by any means, electronic, mechanical, photocopying, recording or otherwise, except as permitted by the UK Copyright, Designs, and Patents Act 1988, without the prior permission of the publisher.

Designations used by companies to distinguish their products are often claimed as trademarks. All brand names and product names used in this book are trade names, service marks, trademarks, or registered trademarks of their respective owners. The publisher is not associated with any product or vendor mentioned in this book.

This publication is designed to provide accurate and authoritative information in regard to the subject matter covered. It is sold on the understanding that the publisher is not engaged in rendering professional services. If professional advice or other expert assistance is required, the services of a competent professional should be sought.

First published 2008 by Blackwell Publishing Ltd

1   2008

Library of Congress Cataloging-in-Publication Data

Romantic poetry : an annotated anthology / edited by Michael O'Neill and Charles Mahoney.
    p. cm.—(Blackwell annotated anthologies)
  Includes bibliographical references and index.
  ISBN 978-0-631-21316-1 (hb.: alk. paper)—ISBN 978-0-631-21317-8 (pbk. : alk. paper)
  1. English poetry—19th century. 2. English poetry—18th century.
  3. Romanticism—England. I. O'Neill, Michael, 1953– II. Mahoney, Charles, 1964–

PR1222.R653 2007
821'.708—dc22
                        2007001660

A catalogue record for this title is available from the British Library.

Set in 9.5 on 11 pt Ehrhardt
by SNP Best-set Typesetter Ltd., Hong Kong
Printed and bound in Singapore
by Markono Print Media Pte Ltd

The publisher's policy is to use permanent paper from mills that operate a sustainable forestry policy, and which has been manufactured from pulp processed using acid-free and elementary chlorine-free practices. Furthermore, the publisher ensures that the text paper and cover board used have met acceptable environmental accreditation standards.

For further information on
Blackwell Publishing, visit our website at
www.blackwellpublishing.com

Contents

(Titles, or portions of titles, within square brackets are editorial. Poems are printed in order of publication and, on occasions, composition. Details of initial publication and relevant textual history are provided in headnotes to the individual poems.)

Selected Contents by Theme	viii
List of Plates	xv
Note on Texts and Editorial Method	xvi
Chronology of Events and Poetic Landmarks	xvii
Introduction: Romantic Doubleness	xxi
Acknowledgements	xxx
Anna Laetitia Barbauld, *née* Aikin (1743–1825)	1
The Rights of Woman	3
Inscription for an Ice-House	4
To Mr. S. T. Coleridge	6
Charlotte Smith, *née* Turner (1749–1806)	9
Sonnet I ['The partial Muse, has from my earliest hours']	11
Sonnet VII: On the departure of the nightingale	12
Sonnet XII: Written on the sea shore. – October, 1784	13
Sonnet XXX: To the River Arun	14
Sonnet XXXII: To Melancholy	15
Sonnet XXXIX: To Night	16
Sonnet XLIV: Written in the church-yard at Middleton in Sussex	17
William Blake (1757–1827)	19
from Songs of Innocence and of Experience	20
(*from* Innocence)	21
Introduction	21
The Ecchoing Green	22
The Lamb	24
The Little Black Boy	25
The Chimney Sweeper	27
Holy Thursday	28
Nurse's Song	29
(*from* Experience)	30
Introduction	30
The Clod and the Pebble	31
Holy Thursday	32
The Sick Rose	33
The Fly	34
The Tyger	34
Ah! Sun-flower	36
London	37
A Poison Tree	39

Visions of the Daughters of Albion	40
The First Book of Urizen	50
The Mental Traveller	68
The Crystal Cabinet	71

William Wordsworth (1770–1850) — 73

Lines written at a small distance from my House, and sent by my little Boy to the Person to whom they are addressed	75
Simon Lee, The Old Huntsman, With an incident in which he was concerned	76
Anecdote for Fathers, Shewing how the practice of Lying may be taught	79
Lines written in early Spring	81
The Thorn	82
The Last of the Flock	88
The Idiot Boy	91
Expostulation and Reply	102
The Tables Turned; An Evening Scene, on the same subject	103
Lines written a few miles above Tintern Abbey, on revisiting the banks of the Wye during a Tour, July 13, 1798	105
The Ruined Cottage	110
Strange fits of passion I have known	121
Song: 'She dwelt among th'untrodden ways'	122
A slumber did my spirit seal	123
The Two April Mornings	124
The Fountain, A Conversation	126
Nutting	128
Michael, A Pastoral Poem	129
The Prelude, 1805, Book 1	140
Resolution and Independence	156
The world is too much with us	160
Composed upon Westminster Bridge, Sept. 3, 1803	161
Ode (from 1815 entitled 'Ode: Intimations of Immortality from Recollections of Early Childhood')	162
The Solitary Reaper	169
Elegiac Stanzas, Suggested by a Picture of Peele Castle in a Storm, Painted by Sir George Beaumont	170

Samuel Taylor Coleridge (1772–1834) — 173

The Eolian Harp. Composed at Clevedon, Somersetshire	175
Reflections on Having Left a Place of Retirement	177
This Lime-Tree Bower My Prison	180
Kubla Khan	183
The Rime of the Ancient Mariner	187
Christabel	205
Frost at Midnight	221
France: An Ode	224
The Nightingale: A Conversation Poem, April, 1798	228
The Pains of Sleep	232
Dejection: An Ode	234

George Gordon, Lord Byron (1788–1824)	240
Stanzas to [Augusta]	243
[Epistle to Augusta]	246
Stanzas to the Po	251
Don Juan	254
Dedication	257
Canto I	263
Percy Bysshe Shelley (1792–1822)	316
Alastor; Or, The Spirit of Solitude	318
Hymn to Intellectual Beauty	338
Mont Blanc. Lines written in the Vale of Chamouni	342
Prometheus Unbound, Act I	348
Ode to the West Wind	376
Adonais, An Elegy on the Death of John Keats, Author of 'Endymion', 'Hyperion' Etc.	381
Felicia Hemans, *née* Browne (1793–1835)	400
Properzia Rossi	401
The Homes of England	405
The Spirit's Mysteries	407
The Graves of a Household	409
The Image in Lava	410
Casabianca	412
The Lost Pleiad	413
The Mirror in the Deserted Hall	415
John Keats (1795–1821)	417
On First Looking into Chapman's Homer	420
The Eve of St Agnes	421
La Belle Dame Sans Merci	436
Ode to Psyche	439
If by dull rhymes our english must be chain'd	442
Ode to a Nightingale	443
Ode on a Grecian Urn	448
Ode on Melancholy	451
Ode on Indolence	453
To Autumn	456
Bright star, would I were stedfast as thou art	458
Letitia Elizabeth Landon (L. E. L.) (1802–38)	459
Lines Written under a Picture of a Girl Burning a Love-Letter	460
A Child Screening a Dove from a Hawk. By Stewardson	461
Lines of Life	462
Felicia Hemans	465
Index of Titles and First Lines	469

Selected Contents by Theme

(Many poems appear under more than one heading; short titles are used.)

1   Innocence and Childhood

William Blake, *Introduction (from Songs of Innocence)*	21
The Ecchoing Green	22
The Lamb	24
The Little Black Boy	25
The Chimney Sweeper (from Songs of Innocence)	27
Holy Thursday (from Songs of Innocence)	28
Nurse's Song (from Songs of Innocence)	29
William Wordsworth, *Anecdote for Fathers*	79
The Idiot Boy	91
Michael	129
The Prelude, Book 1	140
Ode: Intimations of Immortality	162
Samuel Taylor Coleridge, *Frost at Midnight*	221
The Nightingale	228
Lord Byron, *Don Juan, Canto 1*	263
Percy Bysshe Shelley, *Hymn to Intellectual Beauty*	338

2   Death

William Blake, *The Fly*	34
A Poison Tree	39
William Wordsworth, *The Thorn*	82
Strange fits of passion I have known	121
Song: 'She dwelt among th'untrodden ways'	122
A slumber did my spirit seal	123
The Two April Mornings	124
The Fountain	126
Nutting	128
Elegiac Stanzas	170
Samuel Taylor Coleridge, *Christabel*	205
Percy Bysshe Shelley, *Alastor*	318
Adonais	381
Felicia Hemans, *Properzia Rossi*	401
The Homes of England	405
The Graves of a Household	409
The Image in Lava	410
Casabianca	412
The Lost Pleiad	413
John Keats, *The Eve of St Agnes*	420
Bright Star	458
Letitia Elizabeth Landon, *Felicia Hemans*	465

3 GOD, RELIGION, ATHEISM

William Blake, *Introduction (from Songs of Experience)*	30
The Tyger	34
The First Book of Urizen	50
William Wordsworth, *Resolution and Independence*	156
Ode: Intimations of Immortality	162
Samuel Taylor Coleridge, *The Eolian Harp*	175
Reflections on Having Left a Place of Retirement	177
Frost at Midnight	221
The Pains of Sleep	232
Percy Bysshe Shelley, *Hymn to Intellectual Beauty*	338
Mont Blanc	342
Prometheus Unbound, Act I	348
Felicia Hemans, *The Homes of England*	405
The Spirit's Mysteries	407
The Graves of a Household	409

4 IMAGINATION

Anna Laetitia Barbauld, *Inscription for an Ice-House*	5
To Mr. S.T. Coleridge	6
William Blake, *Introduction (from Songs of Innocence)*	21
The Tyger	34
Visions of the Daughters of Albion	40
William Wordsworth, *Lines written a few Miles above Tintern Abbey*	105
The Prelude, Book 1	140
Resolution and Independence	156
The world is too much with us	160
Ode: Intimations of Immortality	162
The Solitary Reaper	169
Samuel Taylor Coleridge, *This Lime-Tree Bower*	180
Kubla Khan	183
Frost at Midnight	221
Dejection: An Ode	234
Lord Byron, *Don Juan, Canto 1*	263
Percy Bysshe Shelley, *Alastor*	318
Prometheus Unbound, Act I	348
Adonais	381
Felicia Hemans, *The Spirit's Mysteries*	407
The Lost Pleiad	413
John Keats, *On First Looking into Chapman's Homer*	420
The Eve of St Agnes	421
Ode to Psyche	439
Ode to a Nightingale	443

5 WRITING POETRY AND ARTISTIC CREATION

William Blake, *The First Book of Urizen*	50
William Wordsworth, *The Idiot Boy*	91
The Prelude, Book I	140
Elegiac Stanzas	170

Samuel Taylor Coleridge, *The Eolian Harp* — 175
Kubla Khan — 183
Dejection: An Ode — 234
Lord Byron, *Don Juan, Canto 1* — 263
Percy Bysshe Shelley, *Alastor* — 318
Hymn to Intellectual Beauty — 338
Mont Blanc — 342
Prometheus Unbound, Act I — 348
Ode to the West Wind — 376
Felicia Hemans, *Properzia Rossi* — 401
John Keats, *On First Looking into Chapman's Homer* — 420
If by dull rhymes our english must be chain'd — 442
Ode to Psyche — 439
Ode to a Nightingale — 443
Ode on a Grecian Urn — 448
Ode on Indolence — 453
Letitia Landon, *Lines Written under a Picture of a Girl Burning a Love-Letter* — 460
A Child Screening a Dove from a Hawk. By Stewardson — 461
Lines of Life — 462
Felicia Hemans — 465

6 EXPERIENCE

William Blake, *Introduction (from Songs of Experience)* — 30
The Clod and the Pebble — 31
Holy Thursday (from Songs of Experience) — 32
The Sick Rose — 33
The Fly — 34
The Tyger — 34
Ah! Sun-flower — 36
London — 37
A Poison Tree — 39
William Wordsworth, *Anecdote for Fathers* — 79
Samuel Taylor Coleridge, *Christabel* — 205
The Pains of Sleep — 232
Dejection: An Ode — 234
Lord Byron, *Stanzas [to Augusta]* — 243
[Epistle to Augusta] — 246
Don Juan, Canto 1 — 263
John Keats, *Ode on Melancholy* — 451
Letitia Landon, *A Child Screening a Dove from a Hawk. By Stewardson* — 461
Lines of Life — 462

7 LOVE AND SEXUALITY

William Blake, *The Clod and the Pebble* — 31
The Sick Rose — 33
Ah! Sun-flower — 36
Visions of the Daughters of Albion — 40
The Mental Traveller — 68
The Crystal Cabinet — 71

William Wordsworth, *Strange fits of passion I have known*		121
Song: 'She dwelt among th'untrodden ways'		122
A slumber did my spirit seal		123
Samuel Taylor Coleridge, *Christabel*		205
Dejection: An Ode		234
Lord Byron, *Stanzas [to Augusta]*		243
[Epistle to Augusta]		246
Stanzas to the Po		251
Don Juan, Canto 1		263
Percy Bysshe Shelley, *Alastor*		318
Felicia Hemans, *Properzia Rossi*		401
The Graves of a Household		409
John Keats, *The Eve of St Agnes*		421
La Belle Dame Sans Merci		436
Ode to Psyche		439
Ode on a Grecian Urn		448
Ode on Melancholy		451
Bright Star, would I were stedfast as thou art		458
Letitia Landon, *Lines Written under a Picture of a Girl Burning a Love-Letter*		460

8 POLITICS AND SOCIETY

William Blake, *Holy Thursday (from Songs of Experience)*		32
London		37
William Wordsworth, *Simon Lee*		76
Lines written in early Spring		81
The Last of the Flock		88
The Prelude, Book 1		140
The world is too much with us		160
Samuel Taylor Coleridge, *France: An Ode*		224
Lord Byron, *Don Juan, Dedication and Canto 1*		263
Percy Bysshe Shelley, *Hymn to Intellectual Beauty*		338
Prometheus Unbound, Act I		348
Ode to the West Wind		376
Adonais		381
John Keats, *To Autumn*		456
Letitia Landon, *Lines of Life*		462

9 SELF AND SOLITUDE

Charlotte Smith, *Sonnet I ['The partial Muse, has from my earliest hours']*		11
Sonnet VII: On the departure of the nightingale		12
Sonnet XII: Written on the sea shore. – October, 1784		13
Sonnet XXXII: To Melancholy		15
Sonnet XXXIX: To Night		16
Sonnet XLIV: Written in the church-yard at Middleton in Sussex		17
William Wordsworth, *Lines written at a small distance from my House*		75
Lines written in early Spring		81
The Thorn		82
Expostulation and Reply		102

The Tables Turned	103
Lines written a few miles above Tintern Abbey	105
The Ruined Cottage	110
The Two April Mornings	124
The Fountain	126
Nutting	128
Michael	129
The Prelude, Book 1	140
Resolution and Independence	156
The world is too much with us	160
Composed upon Westminster Bridge	161
Ode: Intimations of Immortality	162
The Solitary Reaper	169
Samuel Taylor Coleridge, *The Ancient Mariner*	187
France: An Ode	224
Dejection: An Ode	234
Lord Byron, *Stanzas [to Augusta]*	243
[Epistle to Augusta]	246
Percy Bysshe Shelley, *Alastor*	318
Mont Blanc	342
Ode to the West Wind	376
Felicia Hemans, *Properzia Rossi*	401
The Mirror in the Deserted Hall	415
John Keats, *La Belle Dame Sans Merci*	436
Ode to a Nightingale	443
Ode on Indolence	453
Letitia Landon, *Lines of Life*	462

10 NATURE

Anna Laetitia Barbauld, *Inscription for an Ice-House*	5
William Wordsworth, *Lines written at a small distance from my House*	75
Lines written in early Spring	81
The Thorn	82
Expostulation and Reply	102
The Tables Turned	103
Lines written a few miles above Tintern Abbey	105
The Ruined Cottage	110
The Two April Mornings	124
The Fountain	126
Nutting	128
Michael	129
The Prelude, Book 1	140
Composed upon Westminster Bridge	161
Ode: Intimations of Immortality	162
Samuel Taylor Coleridge, *Reflections on Having Left a Place of Retirement*	177
This Lime-Tree Bower	180
Frost at Midnight	221
France: An Ode	224
The Nightingale	228
Lord Byron, *Don Juan, Canto 1*	263

Percy Bysshe Shelley, *Hymn to Intellectual Beauty*	338
Mont Blanc	342
Ode to the West Wind	376
Felicia Hemans, *The Homes of England*	405
John Keats, *To Autumn*	456

11 SLAVERY AND FEMINISM

Anna Laetitia Barbauld, *The Rights of Woman*	3
William Blake, *The Little Black Boy*	25
The Chimney Sweeper (from Songs of Innocence)	27
Visions of the Daughters of Albion	40
Percy Bysshe Shelley, *Prometheus Unbound, Act I*	348
Felicia Hemans, *Properzia Rossi*	401
Letitia Landon, *Lines of Life*	462

12 DREAM

William Wordsworth, *Strange fits of passion I have known*	121
Elegiac Stanzas	170
Samuel Taylor Coleridge, *Kubla Khan*	183
Christabel	205
Frost at Midnight	221
Percy Bysshe Shelley, *Alastor*	318
Mont Blanc	342
Adonais	381
John Keats, *The Eve of St Agnes*	421
La Belle Dame Sans Merci	436
Ode to Psyche	439
Ode to a Nightingale	448

13 ORIENTALISM

William Wordsworth, *The Solitary Reaper*	169
Samuel Taylor Coleridge, *Kubla Khan*	183
Percy Bysshe Shelley, *Alastor*	318

14 SUFFERING

Charlotte Smith, *Sonnet I ['The partial Muse, has from my earliest hours']*	11
Sonnet VII: On the departure of the nightingale	12
Sonnet XII: Written on the sea shore. – October, 1784	13
Sonnet XXXII: To Melancholy	15
Sonnet XXXIX: To Night	16
Sonnet XLIV: Written in the church-yard at Middleton in Sussex	17
William Blake, *Visions of the Daughters of Albion*	40
The First Book of Urizen	50
The Mental Traveller	68
The Crystal Cabinet	71
William Wordsworth, *Simon Lee*	76
The Thorn	82
The Last of the Flock	88

Lines written a few miles above Tintern Abbey	105
The Ruined Cottage	110
Michael	129
Resolution and Independence	156
Elegiac Stanzas	170
Samuel Taylor Coleridge, Christabel	205
The Pains of Sleep	232
Dejection: An Ode	234
Lord Byron, [Epistle to Augusta]	243
Percy Bysshe Shelley, Alastor	318
Prometheus Unbound, Act I	348
Ode to the West Wind	376
Adonais	381
Felicia Hemans, Properzia Rossi	401
The Image in Lava	410
Casabianca	412
John Keats, La Belle Dame Sans Merci	436
Ode to a Nightingale	443
Ode on a Grecian Urn	448
Ode on Melancholy	451
Letitia Landon, Lines of Life	462
Felicia Hemans	465

15 WAR

William Blake, London	37
William Wordsworth, The Ruined Cottage	110
Samuel Taylor Coleridge, Kubla Khan	183
France: An Ode	224
Lord Byron, Don Juan, Dedication	263
Percy Bysshe Shelley, Prometheus Unbound, Act I	348
Felicia Hemans, The Graves of a Household	409
Casabianca	412

Plates

Plate 1	The Ecchoing Green	23
Plate 2	The Little Black Boy	26
Plate 3	The Tyger	36
Plate 4	London	38
Plate 5	A Poison Tree	39

Illustrations are all by William Blake, from his *Songs of Innocence and of Experience*, printed by kind permission from copy in King's College, Cambridge, UK.

Note on Texts and Editorial Method

Copy-texts derive from first or early printed editions. We have varied our policy according to poets and poems: thus Coleridge's poems are taken from the 1834 edition, in which they appear to achieve final form and by which they are best known and most often studied, but Wordsworth's poems are taken, where possible, from the first printed collection in which they appeared, again in accordance with much recent editorial practice. Readers need to be aware that such decisions are of considerable significance in that they necessarily give prominence to a particular version of a poem. We have corrected printing errors (such as the omission of lines from *Michael* in the *Lyrical Ballads* [1800]), and we have drawn attention to some significant revisions in our notes. We have followed a policy of minimal editorial intervention. Thus we do not usually modernize spelling, though we expand ampersands and abbreviated forms such as 'thro' (for 'through') in poems, or on occasions introduce speech marks, where they are absent from our copy-text, or eliminate them when they are redundant. We modernize where serious obstacles to understanding may be presented: thus 'it's' for the possessive adjective 'its' is altered to the modern form. Most of our intervention concerns punctuation, where we have cautiously modernized when it is in the interests of understanding the poetry to do so. Blake, something of a special case, punctuates in a way that requires considerable attention. He strews his poems with full stops or he fails to punctuate at all; here, as we have tried tactfully to intervene, the practice of previous editors, especially Geoffrey Keynes, has been of great assistance. Shelley, too, presents particular problems, because of the error-ridden nature of the 1820 volume; in editing *Prometheus Unbound*, we have used 1820 as our copy-text, but we have consulted other relevant authorities, including manuscripts and Mary Shelley's 1839 editions. A further editorial issue is the challenge presented by posthumous first appearance (examples include the Dedication to Byron's *Don Juan* or his [*Epistle to Augusta*]). In cases where errors occurred in the poem's first appearance and have been corrected by later editors, those corrections are inserted and acknowledged in the notes.

Note that all definitions in quotation marks in the notes to the poems are taken from the *Oxford English Dictionary*.

Chronology of Events and Poetic Landmarks

Selective List of Poetic Landmarks in the Romantic Period

Selective List of Historical and Cultural Events in the Romantic Period

(Unless otherwise indicated, dates refer to publication of the work in question.)

1784	Charlotte Smith, *Elegiac Sonnets* (7th edn, 1795)	
1785	William Cowper, *The Task*	
1786	Robert Burns, *Poems Chiefly in the Scottish Dialect*	
1789	William Blake, *Songs of Innocence*	Fall of the Bastille
1790		Edmund Burke, *Reflections on the Revolution in France*
		Mary Wollstonecraft, *Vindication of the Rights of Man*
1791	Anna Laetitia Barbauld, *An Epistle to William Wilberforce*	Thomas Paine, *The Rights of Man*
1792		Mary Wollstonecraft, *Vindication of the Rights of Woman*
		Percy Bysshe Shelley born (Aug)
1793	William Blake, *Visions of the Daughters of Albion*	Execution of Louis XVI (Jan)
		England declares war on France (Feb)
		William Godwin, *Political Justice*
		Execution of Marie Antoinette (Oct)
1794	William Blake, *Songs of Innocence and of Experience*	*Habeas Corpus* suspended (May)
	William Blake, *The First Book of Urizen*	Robespierre arrested, end of the Terror (July)
		William Godwin, *Caleb Williams*
1795		John Keats born (Oct)
		Passage of 'Two Bills', outlawing unlawful assembly and treasonable practice (Dec)
1796	Samuel Taylor Coleridge, *Poems on Various Subjects*	Napoleon's Italian campaign
		Robert Burns dies (July)
1797		Wordsworth's and Coleridge's *annus mirabilis* (July 1797–July 1798)
		Edmund Burke dies (July)
		Mary Wollstonecraft dies (Sept)
		Mary Godwin (Shelley) born.
1798	William Wordsworth and Samuel Taylor Coleridge, *Lyrical Ballads*	France invades Switzerland (Jan)
		Irish rebellion, United Irish leaders arrested
		Battle of the Nile (Aug)
		Joanna Baillie, *Plays on the Passions*
1799		Napoleon becomes First Consul (9 Nov)
1800	William Wordsworth and Samuel Taylor Coleridge, *Lyrical Ballads* (enlarged edition with Preface; Preface is expanded in the 1802 edn)	William Cowper dies (April)

1800–04	William Blake, poems in the so-called Pickering Manuscript	
1802		Peace of Amiens (March 1802–May 1803) Napoleon becomes Life Consul (Aug) *Edinburgh Review* founded (ed. Francis Jeffrey)
1805	William Wordsworth, *The Prelude* (13-book version finished; poem only published, in a 14-book version, after Wordsworth's death in 1850; title given to the poem was not Wordsworth's, but his executors')	
1806		Elizabeth Barrett (Browning) born (March)
1807	William Wordsworth, *Poems, in Two Volumes* Charlotte Smith, *Beachy Head, Fables, and Other Poems* Thomas Moore, *Irish Melodies* Sir Walter Scott, *Marmion*	Abolition of British slave trading and importation of slaves Charles and Mary Lamb, *Tales from Shakespeare*
1808	William Blake, *Milton* (dated 1804 on title page)	France invades Spain and Portugal Convention of Cintra (Aug) *Examiner* founded (eds John and Leigh Hunt)
1809		Napoleon captures Vienna (May) *Quarterly Review* founded (ed. William Gifford) Alfred Tennyson born (Aug)
1811	Leigh Hunt, *The Feast of the Poets* (reissued with notes in 1814)	Prince of Wales made Regent (Feb) Luddite uprisings (machine-breakings) in Nottingham (until 1816)
1812	Lord Byron, *Childe Harold's Pilgrimage*, Cantos I and II	United States declares war on Britain Napoleon invades Russia, retreats (Oct)
1813		Napoleon defeated at Leipzig (Oct) Jane Austen, *Pride and Prejudice*
1814	William Wordsworth, *The Excursion*	Allied armies enter Paris, Napoleon exiled to Elba Congress of Vienna (restoration of European monarchies) Peace of Ghent (ends war between United States and Britain) Sir Walter Scott, *Waverley* (published anonymously)
1815	William Wordsworth, *Poems*	The Hundred Days: Napoleon returns to Paris Napoleon defeated by Wellington at Waterloo (June), exiled to St Helena
1816	Percy Bysshe Shelley, *Alastor and Other Poems*; composed 'Hymn to Intellectual Beauty' and 'Mont Blanc', the former first published in 1817 in Leigh Hunt's *The Examiner*, the latter first published in 1817 in Mary and P. B. Shelley, *History of a Six Weeks' Tour* Lord Byron, *The Prisoner of Chillon and Other Poems* Lord Byron, *Childe Harold's Pilgrimage*, Canto III	Lord Byron leaves England (April) Lord Byron and Shelleys spend summer together in Switzerland Spa Fields riots (Dec)

Chronology of Events and Poetic Landmarks xix

	Samuel Taylor Coleridge, 'Christabel'; 'Kubla Khan: A Vision'; 'The Pains of Sleep' Leigh Hunt, *The Story of Rimini*	
1817	Samuel Taylor Coleridge, *Sibylline Leaves* Lord Byron, *Manfred* John Keats, *Poems* Percy Bysshe Shelley, *Laon and Cythna* published, then reissued in revised form as *The Revolt of Islam* (dated 1818)	Robert Southey, *Wat Tyler* (written 1794) Samuel Taylor Coleridge, *Biographia Literaria* William Hazlitt, *Characters of Shakespeare's Plays* *Blackwood's Magazine* founded
1818	William Blake, *Jerusalem* (dated 1804 on title page) Lord Byron, 'Beppo' Lord Byron, *Childe Harold's Pilgrimage*, Canto IV John Keats, *Endymion*	*Habeas Corpus* restored Mary Shelley, *Frankenstein*
1819	Lord Byron, *Don Juan*, Cantos I and II Percy Bysshe Shelley, *The Mask of Anarchy* (not published until 1832)	Queen Victoria born (May) Peterloo Massacre, St Peter's Fields, Manchester (Aug) William Hazlitt, *Political Essays*
1820	Percy Bysshe Shelley, *Prometheus Unbound; with Other Poems* (includes 'Ode to the West Wind') John Keats, *Lamia, Isabella, The Eve of St Agnes, and Other Poems* John Clare, *Poems Descriptive of Rural Life and Scenery*	George III dies (Jan); Prince Regent succeeds to throne as George IV John Keats sails for Italy (Sept)
1821	Percy Bysshe Shelley, *Epipsychidion* Percy Bysshe Shelley, *Adonais* Lord Byron, *Don Juan*, Cantos III–V	John Keats dies at Rome (Feb) Napoleon dies on St Helena (May) Thomas De Quincey, *Confessions of an English Opium-Eater*
1822	Lord Byron, 'The Vision of Judgment'	*The Liberal* founded (Shelley, Hunt, Byron) Percy Shelley drowns off coast of Livorno, Italy (July) Matthew Arnold born (Dec)
1823	Felicia Hemans, *The Vespers of Palermo* Lord Byron, *Don Juan*, Cantos VI–X	Lord Byron sails for Greece (July) to fight for Greek independence from Turks William Hazlitt, *Liber Amoris* Charles Lamb, *Essays of Elia*
1824	Percy Bysshe Shelley, *Posthumous Poems*, ed. Mary Shelley (first publications of 'Julian and Maddalo', 'The Witch of Atlas', 'Letter to Maria Gisborne', and 'The Triumph of Life') Letitia Landon, *The Improvisatrice and Other Poems*	Lord Byron dies at Missolonghi (April) James Hogg, *Private Memoirs and Confessions of a Justified Sinner*
1825	Felicia Hemans, *The Forest Sanctuary: with Other Poems* (2nd edn in 1829) Letitia Landon, *The Troubadour; Catalogue of Pictures, and Historical Sketches*	William Hazlitt, *The Spirit of the Age*

1827	John Clare, *The Shepherd's Calendar with Village Stories and Other Poems*	William Blake dies (Aug)
1828	Felicia Hemans, *Records of Woman: with Other Poems*	Duke of Wellington becomes Prime Minister Repeal of Test and Corporation Acts Leigh Hunt, *Lord Byron and Some of His Contemporaries*
1829	Letitia Landon, *The Venetian Bracelet and Other Poems*	Catholic Emancipation Act
1830	Felicia Hemans, *Songs of the Affections, with Other Poems*	George IV dies, succeeded by his brother, William IV William Hazlitt dies (Sept) Alfred Tennyson, *Poems, Chiefly Lyrical*
1831		Charles Darwin's first voyage in the Beagle
1832		First Reform Act passed
1834	Samuel Taylor Coleridge, *Poetical Works*	Coleridge dies (July)
1835	John Clare, *The Rural Muse*	
1837	*Fisher's Drawing Room Scrap Book, 1838* (contains Landon's 'Felicia Hemans')	
1843		Southey dies (March) Wordsworth accepts Laureateship
1848	*Life, Letters, and Literary Remains of John Keats* by Richard Monkton Milnes (first publication of 'La Belle Dame sans Merci')	
1850	Wordsworth, *The Prelude* (July)	Wordsworth dies (April)

Introduction: Romantic Doubleness
Michael O'Neill

Romanticism and the Romantic Period

Romanticism is a notoriously difficult term to define. Indeed, in a famous article Arthur O. Lovejoy counselled in favour of using the term only in the plural, to do justice to its multiple strands.[1] Concept and period can pull in different directions. For many, 'Romanticism' is one thing, the 'Romantic period' quite another. You can speak of 'Romanticism' as if it were an ethos, even an essence, sometimes of a kind that is present across history. By this token Wallace Stevens, celebrant in 'Evening without Angels' of 'the voice that is great within us', is as Romantic as is Coleridge.[2] But you might define 'the Romantic period' as running roughly between 1780 and 1830 and might wish to suggest that the period contains a great variety of works, some of which, such as George Crabbe's poetry or Jane Austen's novels, seem to give the idea of 'Romanticism' a wide berth.[3]

We might square the definitional circle as follows. Yes, the force of the Romantic movement ensures that it persists in related cultures beyond the period of its initial manifestation, transmuting itself as various legacies work themselves out. But it is clear that, during the 'Romantic period' as just defined, a new power pervades British literature. At the same time, the nature of that newness resists being constructed as an essence. Or, if it has to have an essence, that essence involves a fundamental bias in favour of doubleness, multiplicity, tension and division. For example, the discoveries of science animate some of the finest writing of the Romantic period. New thinking about magnetism, electricity, geology, astronomy, the workings of the cosmos, and the nature of life itself course through the veins of Romantic poetry. At the same time, there is a suspicion of science when it is at the service of the merely mechanistic; then, in Wordsworth's line, 'We murder to dissect' ('The Tables Turned', l. 28).[4]

Certainly some emphases remain constant in most accounts of the Romantic. There is the quietly revolutionary sense, apparent in the philosophy of the German thinker Immanuel Kant and gradually affecting British thought, of human beings as shapers of the meanings they encounter. This sense is hardly straightforward, however; Kant, as helpfully glossed by Stanley Cavell, informs us that our 'categories of understanding' allow us to know only of 'appearances' which, in turn, make up 'experience'; there is, for Kant in his *Critique of Pure Reason* (1781), what Cavell calls 'something else – that of which appearances are appearances' which 'cannot be known'. Where the mind recovers its authority and power, as at the end of Shelley's 'Mont Blanc' (p. 342), is its recognition of 'limitation'. In Cavell's words, 'In discovering this limitation of reason, reason proves its power to itself, over itself'.[5] In other words, the Romantic

---

1 Arthur O. Lovejoy, 'On the Discrimination of Romanticisms', *PMLA* 39 (1924), pp. 229–53.
2 Quoted from *The Collected Poems of Wallace Stevens* (London: Faber, 1955).
3 For the suggestion that Austen, in fact, had much in common with other Romantics, such as Keats, see Beth Lau, 'Jane Austen and John Keats: Negative Capability, Romance and Reality', *Keats-Shelley Journal* 55 (2006), pp. 81–110. Lau persuasively finds parallels between Keats's idea and practice of Negative Capability, and Austen's 'inability to ignore qualifications and alternative perspectives' (p. 99).
4 For more on Romanticism and science, see Tim Fulford, Debbie Lee and Peter J. Kitson, *Literature, Science and Exploration in the Romantic Era: Bodies of Knowledge* (Cambridge, UK: Cambridge University Press, 2004), and Sharon Ruston, *Shelley and Vitality* (Basingstoke, UK: Palgrave Macmillan, 2005).
5 Stanley Cavell, *In Quest of the Ordinary: Lines of Skepticism and Romanticism* (Chicago: University of Chicago Press, 1988), p. 30.

mind discovers its limits as much as its power, and indeed the latter is bound up with the former; it is often in confronting the limits of reason that the Romantics assert, as in Blake's work, the force of the imagination or, as in Shelley's 'Mont Blanc', the necessary resourcefulness of the 'human mind's imaginings' (l. 143). Shelley inherits from eighteenth-century philosophy a scepticism about the mind's capacity to know, a scepticism embodied most radically in David Hume's *Treatise of Human Nature* (1739). But at the close of 'Mont Blanc' he shows how 'imaginings' can work with, yet reach beyond the limits of sense-impressions to evoke the possibility of a 'secret strength of things' (l. 139). At the same time the poetry is aware that this possibility may only be an 'imagining'.

It is significant that 'things' and 'imaginings' should rhyme in 'Mont Blanc' since the poem tussles to establish a relationship between inner and outer. More generally, poetry of the Romantic period displays a reconception of the relationship between human beings, nature and God, the last two nouns coming closer together than ever before in a poem such as Wordsworth's 'Tintern Abbey' (p. 105). Wordsworth no longer speaks of deity; he refers, simply or complexly, to 'a sense sublime / Of something far more deeply interfused' (ll. 98–9), where 'something' speaks of a reluctance to pin down, and where 'sublime' alludes to a tradition of 'sublime' experience, codified by Edmund Burke in his treatise, *A Philosophical Enquiry into the Origins of Our Ideas of the Sublime and the Beautiful* (1757), a tradition which values the experience of all that challenges and overpowers rational comprehension.[6] Wordsworth adds to Burke a renewed conviction of a creative and receptive imaginative power, and Romantic writers often see the capacity to feel overwhelmed as evidence of the mind's greatness, a greatness which resides, for Wordsworth, in an ability to reach out towards 'something ever more about to be' (*The Prelude*, 1805, VI, l. 542). In this passage Wordsworth speaks of 'the light of sense' going out 'in flashes that have shown to us / The invisible world' (ll. 534–6). He becomes aware of the 'Imagination' (l. 527), addressed in an apostrophe, as leading beyond sense-impressions, of the breakdown of 'sense' as allowing for a visionary breakthrough.

Accordingly, there is, too, in the period an unprecedented view of poetry as a form of knowledge that is the match for and challenges, albeit with unease and self-doubt, the claims of rival modes of understanding. Poetry of the period displays a novel fascination with process, the historical, the dynamic, provisionality, the mysterious. Crucially, as outlined above, there is an impulse to reject or express dissatisfaction with empirical explanations of how knowledge is arrived at, and an accompanying sense of the imagination as a creative, God-like faculty. Arguably, one theme of Coleridge's 'Kubla Khan' (p. 183) is its exploration of how this faculty might arise, function and be received. As the Romantic poets assert the force and function of poetry, they seek to rework and reshape poetic forms and genres. Wordsworth's *The Prelude* rewrites Milton's *Paradise Lost*; it makes of 'the might of Souls' 'heroic argument' (*Prelude*, 1805, II, ll. 178, 182) every bit as important as the 'argument / Heroic' (IX, ll. 28–9) which Milton depicts. Again, Shelley's 'Hymn to Intellectual Beauty' (p. 338) casts the hymnal form in a new, distinctly non- or post-Christian guise. Shelley uses language that sounds religious, but he attacks traditional Christian concepts, such as 'God [. . .] and heaven' (l. 27), as 'Frail spells' (l. 29). His own belief in 'Intellectual Beauty' is itself riven with anxiety and suppressed fear. As a result the poem is no mere exercise in heterodox nose-tweaking; it becomes an intense and expressively unstable inner drama. The poem's figurative activity speaks volumes about Shelley's sense that his 'light' might be a form of shadowy 'darkness', when he says that the 'nourishment' it gives 'human thought' (l. 44) is 'Like darkness to a dying flame' (l. 45). The presence of doubt is inseparable from Shelleyan and often from Romantic hope.

---

6 Unless indicated otherwise, poems in this Introduction are quoted from the present volume or from Duncan Wu (ed.), *Romanticism: An Anthology*, 3rd edn (Oxford: Blackwell, 2006).

Such doubt does not detract from the significance attached by Romantic poets to their activity. Indeed, it is in the Romantic period that the poetic career, or even the poetic vocation, emerges as a major theme: Keats's letters and *Hyperion* poems, or Wordsworth's *The Prelude* typify the seriousness that attaches itself to the process of becoming a poet. So, the opening of 'The Fall of Hyperion' closes with the lines, 'Whether the dream now purposed to rehearse / Be poet's or fanatic's will be known / When this warm scribe my hand is in the grave' (ll. 16–18). Posterity will decide whether the poem now being written is that of an authentic poet.[7] The fact that composition turns into a theme for poetry suggests how much is at stake. In Byron's *Childe Harold's Pilgrimage*, canto 3, stanza 6, a comparable appeal is made to the process of creation: the reason for writing, Byron asserts, is to 'live / A being more intense', 'gaining as we give / The life we image – even as I do now'. The 'now' of writing' permits living to enjoy a second, intensified existence.

Despite Byron's own intermittent scepticism about his contemporaries, Romantic poets display consciousness of participating in a period when poetry itself had taken on 'A being more intense'. 'We live', wrote Shelley towards the end of *A Defence of Poetry*, 'among such philosophers and poets as surpass beyond comparison any who have appeared since the last national struggle for civil and religious liberty'.[8] Shelley alludes to the English Civil War, and he has in mind the mighty achievement of Milton's *Paradise Lost*. For him, as for others, the period in which he lived and wrote represented a recovery and an extension of imaginative power and political hope. The Romantics may not have seen themselves as 'Romantics' ('Romanticism', as Seamus Perry points out, 'is a posthumous invention'),[9] but they were aware of their participation in 'a new and great age of poetry', as Leigh Hunt called it.[10] Cyclical, evolutionary and progressive ideas of literary development fascinate Romantic writers; so, too, does the parallel between such development and larger historical and political changes. At the same time, they recognized and wrote about despondency, dejection, the failure of creativity: all that shadowed their brightest wishes.

For all the challenges to definition it poses, the poetry of the Romantic period incontrovertibly represents one of the greatest and most influential achievements of literature in English. It flourishes in the period between the aftermath of the War of American Independence and the accession of Queen Victoria. It accompanies a period of social transformation and political instability in England and Europe, the chief embodiment of which is the French Revolution. 'Bliss was it in that dawn to be alive', wrote Wordsworth retrospectively of his feelings at the outset of the Revolution, 'But to be young was very Heaven!' (*The Prelude*, 1805, X, ll. 692–3). Yet, for Wordsworth and other liberals of his generation, the Revolution proved to be a false dawn; for them, it descended all too quickly into a political nightfall – and nightmare: the barbarities of the Reign of Terror, instigated by Robespierre and the Jacobins, followed by an expansionist militarism, most significantly after Napoleon seized power. The result was a long and bitter war between France on the one hand and Britain, Austria, Prussia and Russia on the other. This war was only ended in 1815 after Napoleon was finally defeated at the Battle of Waterloo, and the whole unhappy experience is briefly sketched in the semi-choral taunts directed at Prometheus by the Furies in Act I, ll. 567–77 of Shelley's lyrical drama.

---

7 For a discussion of Romantic appeals to posterity, see Andrew Bennett, *Romantic Poets and the Culture of Posterity* (Cambridge, UK: Cambridge University Press, 1999).
8 Quoted from *Percy Bysshe Shelley: The Major Works*, ed. Zachary Leader and Michael O'Neill (Oxford: Oxford University Press, 2003), p. 700.
9 Seamus Perry, 'Romanticism: The Brief History of a Concept', in *A Companion to Romanticism*, ed. Duncan Wu (Oxford: Blackwell, 1998), p. 4.
10 Leigh Hunt, notes to *The Feast of the Poets* (1814); *The Selected Writings of Leigh Hunt*, 6 vols, general editor Robert Morrison (London: Pickering & Chatto, 2003), vol. 5, *Poetical Works: 1801–21*, ed. John Strachan, p. 65.

Revolution, War, Nature, Poetic Form

Throughout the greater part of the period, then, Britain was a country at war.[11] Moreover, it was divided against itself ideologically. Many former admirers of the Revolution turned against it when it lurched towards violent aggression: Coleridge's 'France: An Ode' (p. 224) is the finest expression in poetry of the changed sentiments experienced by former sympathizers with the Revolution who were appalled by the French Republic's invasion of Switzerland in 1798. In his poem's last stanza, Coleridge asserts that the one place where he can be sure of still experiencing 'Liberty' (l. 105) is the natural world; it is when 'he shot [his] being through earth, sea, and air' (l. 103) that his 'spirit felt thee [Liberty] there!' (l. 105). The poem locates Liberty in a 'there' that exists in imaginative space, one that is conjured up out of an 'earth, sea, and air' informed by the poet's 'being'. In this poem and in poems such as 'Fears in Solitude' (published with 'France: An Ode'), Coleridge does something characteristic of Romantic poetry: he invests a traditional genre, in this case pastoral, with a fresh urgency. In 'Fears in Solitude' Coleridge uses solitude in nature as a point of vantage from which to offer a critique of war-mongering, even as he lends support belatedly to anti-French feeling; it is solitude that makes possible the final mood of 'Love, and the thoughts that yearn for humankind' (l. 229).

'Nature' is a term that undergoes a religious and philosophical sea-change in the period. In their poetry of the late 1790s Wordsworth and Coleridge appreciate it in new terms as a guarantee of the essential goodness and benignity of the material universe. It provides a point of departure for a deep belief in the goodness of 'natural' instincts, often celebrated in poems about human feeling in *Lyrical Ballads* (1798 and 1800). It is the basis for the adoption of a poetic 'language near to the language of men' (Preface to *Lyrical Ballads* [1802]). And yet even in *Lyrical Ballads* Coleridge's Ancient Mariner encounters a nature that seems hostile, while the idea of the 'language of men' would prove elusive. By the time of Wordsworth's 'Ode: Intimations of Immortality', nature has, it would seem, unwittingly betrayed the heart that loved her, and Wordsworth arrives at a complex resolution that values the human heart and the faith that looks through death as much as his bond with the natural world. In 'Dejection: An Ode' (p. 234), Coleridge asserts that 'in our life alone does Nature live' (l. 48). He does not quite say that the notion of life in nature is a fiction, but he does stress that human response and creativity is the catalyst for the discovery of harmonizing 'Joy' (l. 64). It is striking that Wordsworth's and Coleridge's finest odes offer imaginative responses to the fear of loss. Certainly, the sense of nature as ethically neutral or indifferent to human beings is a strong and anxious presence in second-generation Romantic poetry. Even in a first-generation poet such as Blake material nature is a delusion, while in Shelley's *The Triumph of Life* the 'shape all light' (l. 352), bewitchingly emerging from and entangled with the natural world, induces a decidedly ambivalent response in the reader. Byron, in his grimly sardonic and multi-toned account of the shipwreck in *Don Juan*, Canto 2, ascribes the sailors' recourse to cannibalism thus: 'None in particular had sought or planned it, / 'Twas nature gnawed them to this resolution' (stanza 75). This 'nature' is far removed from the beneficent power that presides over 'Tintern Abbey', and yet, reminding us again of Romantic doubleness, Nature's potential goodness re-emerges towards the close of Canto 2 in *Don Juan*, when Byron affirms the innate innocence of Haidee's sexuality: 'Haidee was Nature's bride' (st. 202). Byron finds a poetic form, a comic epic written in *ottava rima*, that can accommodate swerves and complications of thought, but all the Romantics conceive of the natural as both the mind's finest ally and its rival, sometimes its most dan-

---

11 Duncan Wu writes that 'By the time Wordsworth was in his mid-twenties, Britain was embroiled in nothing less than world war which, unlike those in the twentieth century, would last not for years but decades', *Romanticism: An Anthology*, 3rd edn, p. xxxii.

gerous adversary. Wordsworth insists at the end of *The Prelude* that he and Coleridge, in their very role as 'Prophets of Nature' (1805, XIII, l. 442), will instruct others 'how the mind of man becomes / A thousand times more beautiful than the earth / On which he dwells' (ll. 446–8).

It is in their use of poetic form that the Romantics incorporate their uniquely double vision – whether of nature, politics, society, or the self. Such a doubleness complicates any account of Wordsworth's political development as that of revolutionary turned apostate: the caricaturing tale narrated with glee and hostility by many writers (such as William Hazlitt). When in 1802 Wordsworth apostrophizes Milton, 'Milton! thou should'st be living at this hour', he uses enjambments and shapes the sonnet in ways that recall Miltonic practice, claiming for his own writing the heroic or epic mantle bequeathed by Milton. This formal freedom finds a figurative analogue in the claim made about Milton that 'Thou hadst a voice whose sound was like the sea' (l. 10), a line that rhymes with the assertion that Milton was 'Pure as the naked heavens, majestic, free' (l. 11). At the same time, he commits himself (and Milton) to celebration of 'The lowliest duties' (l. 14). Romantic writers exalt the humble and question empty pomp. Wordsworth's patriotism in the sonnet is clear, but even as late as the 1805 *Prelude* he records with that authenticity which is a hallmark of the Romantic his siding with France in the battles of the mid-1790s, unable, at church, to add his voice to prayers said for British soldiers.

William Blake, meanwhile, was following his own spiritual trajectory, one marked by the individualism characteristic of his temperament and genius. For Blake, war began at home, with what in a famous lyric he calls 'mental fight' (Preface to *Milton*, l. 13) undertaken against the ruination of innocence and goodness he found on his doorstep. In a poem such as 'London' (p. 37) he attacks religious hypocrisy and social abuses; more than this, he uses metaphors to suggest a system of interlocking ills: marriage licenses prostitution; the greed and social inequity of which 'palace walls' are the symbol are shown up by the accusatory sigh of the 'hapless soldier'. That very image shows how Blake's poetic powers cannot simply be ascribed to his desire for social change; he communicates his vision through metaphors of great power that haunt the reader's imagination as well as assailing his or her conscience. Later poems show Blake responding to the increasing repression of William Pitt's government through poems that compose home-made, heterodox versions of the early books in the Bible, especially Genesis. In terms that include but transcend parodic mockery, they present, in their updating of a narrative about creation and the fall, a despotic authoritative figure Blake calls 'Urizen'. Indeed, a poem such as *The First Book of Urizen* (included in this volume) explores far reaches of religious and philosophical thought, even as it is rooted in a deep if oblique response to the lived historical experience of the 1790s.

Women Poets, Conflict, Genre, and Gender

Female poets of the period such as Anna Barbauld, Charlotte Smith, Felicia Hemans and Letitia Landon offer individual variations on a wide variety of Romantic themes. The question of the relationship between gender and genre is intricate. No easy correlations will survive close inspection. Anna Barbauld, for example, emerges as one of the more explicitly political poets of the Romantic period. Her 'Epistle to William Wilberforce' (1791) uses its couplets to lend coruscating rhetorical support to Wilberforce's work on behalf of the Society for the Abolition of the Slave Trade. A chief target in Barbauld's mixture of indignant satire and admiring panegyric is 'pale Beauty' (l. 57) whom we are invited to see 'Contriving torture and inflicting wounds' (l. 70). Limits of space have also prevented us from including Barbauld's *Eighteen Hundred and Eleven* (1812), in which she addresses, in sombre, admonitory tones, the state of the nation, including imminent war with America and the consequences of the long conflict with France. '[T]hy Midas dream is o'er; / The golden tide of commerce leaves thy shore' (ll. 61–2), she writes.[12] The poem, which met with a denunciatory reception at the hands of Tory reviewers, illustrates her capacity for impassioned argument and independent thought.

Barbauld demonstrates the presence in women's poetry of firm conviction and a public voice. Charlotte Smith, though never unaware of politics (as is clear from *The Emigrants* [1793]), shows a female poet at the very heart of the lyric turn which is one powerful energy in Romantic poetry. Smith exercised a major formal and emotional influence as a result of her recovery, in *Elegiac Sonnets* (1784), of the sonnet form as a vehicle for consolation in the face of disappointment and sorrow (Smith, led into financial ruin by her husband, was obliged to maintain her family through literary work). Her self-presentation in the sonnets is expertly full of art and contrivance, yet her recognition in Sonnet 1 (p. 9) that poetry is, at best, a half-hearted comforter alerts us to the new connection in Romantic poetry between expression and confession. Smith speaks of the muse's 'dear delusive art' (l. 6) and concludes: 'Ah then, how dear the muse's favours cost / *If those paint sorrow best who feel it most!*' (ll. 13–14). Cleverly, the italicized words are presented only as a possibility, and the connection that is posited here between 'sorrow' and 'painting' it in words can be mimicked, marketed (as to some degree it was Byron), and vulgarized in the period; but the self's exposed position in Romantic poetry means that a cult of authenticity and sincerity is never far away. Yet poets of the period refuse to be imprisoned within a poetics of self-expression. Smith's own allusion here in the last line of her sonnet to Pope's *Eloisa to Abelard* (ll. 365–6) demonstrates how poets of the period keep the doors and windows of their poetic houses open: past literature enters, often to undergo change; posterity is frequently evoked. Male and female poets are alike in this respect. Keats reworks Spenser, playing his own variations on the clash between aesthetic appeal and moral judgement central to the Renaissance poet. These variations can be enigmatic; Madeline may have to leave her Bower of Bliss in *The Eve of St Agnes*, but Keats's refusal to moralize his song is striking.

Awareness of violence and conflict pervades the poetry of female Romantic writers, giving short shrift to any notion that their work is confined to the spheres of the house and hearth. Felicia Hemans writes in poems such as 'Casabianca' (p. 412) of constancy of purpose and self-sacrificing bravery, as one might expect of a poet whose brothers and errant husband were soldiers. And yet 'Casabianca' problematizes as much as it praises. Beneath Hemans's seeming praise for courage and valour a disquieting questioning voice makes itself heard, debating the worth of traditional masculine virtues. Her speakers in *Records of Woman* (1828) lament lovelessness and desertion; at the same time, they affirm (in, say, 'Properzia Rossi', p. 400) their own creative potential. In Hemans's work, fracture lines in the porcelain beauty of her stanzas alert us to one of the most intriguingly ambivalent voices in Romantic poetry. Gender issues are prompted by that voice's accents, the more fascinatingly so because Hemans is not overtly radical as (say) Mary Wollstonecraft is in her *Vindication of the Rights of Woman*; her feminism is less polemical than a product of her dramatizing imagination.

Hemans's chief inheritor is Letitia Landon, a poet who was at once manipulator and victim (in her social life) of the cult of self. In Landon, the fate of the female poet emerges as a full-blown and tautly gendered topic. Landon speaks with affecting insight of the hidden cost exacted by a poetics of the self, when, elegizing Hemans, she seems to speak of herself as well as the deceased poet: 'We say, the song is sorrowful, but know not / What may have left that sorrow on the song; / However mournful words may be, they show not / The whole extent of wretchedness and wrong' ('Felicia Hemans', ll. 41–4). And yet these lines offer a sense of depths beyond the beholder, implying an ultimate release from the voyeuristic reading culture of the 1820s. The Romantics write, not just for their time, but for all time.

---

[12] Quoted from Wu (2006).

First- and Second-Generation Romantic Poetry

This is not to deny that the transhistorical ambitions of Romantic poetry emerge from specific temporal frames. Indeed, nothing is more central to English Romantic poetry than the fact that it divides into at least two generations. In the first generation, Wordsworth, Coleridge, Blake, Barbauld, Smith and others write in response to particular historical events; their work is quickened by hope, beset by disappointment. By the time of the second-generation Romantics, who came to maturity as poets during the period of the Regency (1811–20), the cycle of hope and disappointment continues, but the later writers have the example of the older poets before them: an example which is matter for admiration (as in Keats's and Shelley's response to Wordsworth's and Coleridge's poetic achievements) and reservation (chiefly centred on the young poets' feeling that the older poets had embraced reactionary politics in a too hasty response to the apparent failure of the French Revolution). In his sonnet 'To Wordsworth' (published in his 1816 *Alastor* volume), Shelley elegizes the 'Poet of nature' (l. 1), who he feels has deserted his true calling as a poet who wrote 'Songs consecrate to truth and liberty' (l. 12). Consciously Shelley turns Wordsworthian form and cadence against him; Wordsworth in his sonnet to Milton (quoted above) hailed Milton in these terms, 'Thy soul was like a Star' (l. 9); Shelley says of Wordsworth, 'Thou wert as a lone star' (l. 7). Yet Shelley's past tense strikes a note of loss absent in Wordsworth, and he allows Wordsworth's accents of loss in 'Ode: Intimations of Immortality' to rebound against the older poet.

It is in the second generation of male Romantic poets that the most politically daring voices of the period can be heard. Byron lamented Napoleon's defeat at Waterloo (as did William Hazlitt), even as he saw the French Emperor as a fatally flawed and 'antithetically mixed' figure (*Childe Harold's Pilgrimage* III, 36, l. 317). The political settlement that followed Waterloo dampened stirrings of nationalist libertarianism throughout Europe, much to Byron's disgust: he was actively involved in supporting the Carbonari in Italy and died, in support of Greece, at the outset of that country's War of Independence against the Turks.

Byron's radicalism represents a Romantic aristocratic contempt for social conformity. Percy Bysshe Shelley, with whom he enjoyed a close but taxingly difficult relationship, was also born into a high social position. More so than Byron, his politics were part of an overarching Utopian vision, a wish to imagine a world other than that in which he lived. Shelley exemplifies a fundamental feature of Romantic poetry, its desire for freedom. Compatible with artistic control in complex ways, this desire took the form in Shelley of rebellion against any attempt to impose restrictions on thought in political, religious and personal matters. He was expelled from Oxford for refusing to deny co-authorship of a provocative short pamphlet *The Necessity of Atheism*. He eventually chose a life of exile in Italy, where he wrote powerful poetic denunciations in works such as 'The Mask of Anarchy'. In this poem Shelley ironically mocks and denounces the political repression which resulted in a massacre at St Peter's Fields in 1819, when a peaceful demonstration in Manchester in favour of parliamentary reform was broken up by local yeomanry riding, sabres bared, on the defenceless crowd. 'Peterloo' was the ironic name given to this event, suggesting that the armed power which had been victorious against Napoleon was now being used by the government against its own people. Much of Shelley's work could not be published, given the threat of imprisonment. At the same time, Shelley is far more than a poetic journalist; his greatest works, poems such as *Adonais* (included in this volume), may be unafraid to engage in contemporary literary and political controversy, but their imagining of an alternative extends the reach of his reader's imagination in transformative and highly creative ways.

Keats and Byron illustrate the variety of imaginative modes produced by second-generation writers. Keats breathed his own life into the ode and narrative poem, making both forms the arena for imaginative discovery and debate, and often thriving on changes of direction. In his very different way, Byron, too, perfected a poetry that relied on sudden transition and instability of tone; his mode of freedom in a poem involves never allowing his reader to sum him up. Drawn in *Childe Harold's Pilgrimage* to figures who exemplify inconsistency and a mixture of greatness and imperfection, he embodies in his own work a refusal to fit anyone's ideological programme, even as his antipathy to reactionary governments remains consistent. It is the comic use of *ottava rima* that proved to be the key that unlocked his poetic genius. In 'Beppo' (1818) and *Don Juan*, he brings a seemingly casual, nonchalant irony into Romantic poetry, an ability to discomfort the single point of view that has much in common with ideas of 'Romantic irony', associated with Friedrich Schlegel, the German theorist and Romanticist.

Romantic Doubleness

Romantic irony exalts the poetic capacity simultaneously to create and undercut, and represents, not a commitment to sardonic pessimism, but a joyous delight in creative freedom and possibility. Something of its twofold spirit links with the doubleness that this anthology stresses is a principal feature of much Romantic poetry. One thinks of Blake's *Songs of Innocence and of Experience*, with their interest in clashing perspectives; or of Wordsworth's 'Tintern Abbey', moving between gain and loss, past, present and future; or of Coleridge's 'Christabel', deeply if obscurely preoccupied by sin and goodness. Keats, too, in his odes and narrative poems explores the dualities of the imaginative and emotional life: the tug of dreams and imagination against the fear that they may be merely illusory; the claims of poetic enchantment against those of rationalizing clarity; the disconcerting discovery that melancholy and delight are inseparable companions. Like other Romantic poets, he establishes, as noted at the beginning of this introduction, the individual writer's poetic career as a central subject of his work. The result is not solipsism, but an intensified self-consciousness about the purposes of poetry. John Clare is one of a number of poets (others include Hemans, Landon and Thomas Lovell Beddoes) who inherited the example of Blake, Shelley and Keats. Clare brings an innovative voice into Romantic poetry by virtue of his first-hand knowledge of peasant life; at the same time, he shares with other Romantics a conviction of the imagination's power and an awareness of the price that may have to be paid for exercise of that power. Apparent most notably in his asylum poems, such an awareness beats away throughout his fine 'I Am'. Clare writes beautifully about belonging and desolatingly about alienation. In doing so, he reminds us of the riven but remarkable achievement of the English Romantic poets.

The Present Edition: Romantic Form

Flowing from the editors' conviction that it is in the use of poetic shaping that Romantic poetry conveys most authoritatively its variety and high quality, the present edition sets itself to illustrate and explore anew the nature and workings of what might be called Romantic form. The range of forms and genres encompassed by its major practitioners is immense, including odes, ballads, sonnets (including elegiac sonnets), blank verse, updated epic, pastoral, romance, lyrics in many stanzaic shapes, the greater Romantic lyric, couplets, Spenserian stanzas, elegies, *ottava rima*, *terza rima*, and composite forms such as lyrical drama or lyrical ballads. English poets renew and reinvent the possibilities of poetry with virtuosity, power, truthfulness to feeling, and sophisticated self-awareness. The poets, moreover, respond to one another in a ceaseless dialogue of affinity and difference. *Romantic Poetry: An Annotated Anthology* seeks to provide readers with freshly edited and fully annotated texts of a carefully selected group of Romantic poems. Annotation is unusually detailed for an anthology, taking the form of an introductory headnote to each of our poets, followed by headnotes and annotations to the poems that provide relevant contextual information, but give pride of place to features such as form, theme, genre, structure, rhyme, line-endings, imagery, and allusions to other poems. The intention is to open up debate about interpretations and modes of valuing the poetry by demonstrating ways of reading the poems. Formal analysis is offered in the interests of stimulating a sense of the imaginative and affective force of the original.

The volume is the product of what the editors have found to be enjoyable and rewarding dialogue and collaboration. Michael O'Neill wrote the introduction and assembled the selected contents by theme (both with input from Charles Mahoney), and wrote and edited the material on Blake, Wordsworth, Coleridge, Shelley, Hemans and Landon; Charles Mahoney wrote and edited the material on Barbauld, Smith, Byron and Keats. The chronology of poetic landmarks and events is a collaborative effort.

Further Reading

M. H. Abrams, *The Mirror and the Lamp: Romantic Theory and the Critical Tradition* (Oxford: Oxford University Press, 1953).

M. H. Abrams, *Natural Supernaturalism: Tradition and Revolution in Romantic Literature* (New York: Norton, 1971).

M. H. Abrams, *The Correspondent Breeze: Essays on English Romanticism* (New York: Norton, 1984).

W. H. Auden, *The Enchafèd Flood: or, The Romantic Iconography of the Sea* (London: Faber, 1951).

Marilyn Butler, *Romantics, Rebels and Reactionaries: English Literature and its Background 1760–1830* (Oxford: Oxford University Press, 1981).

Stanley Cavell, *In Quest of the Ordinary: Lines of Skepticism and Romanticism* (Chicago: University of Chicago Press, 1988).

Philip Cox, *Gender, Genre and the Romantic Poets: An Introduction* (Manchester: Manchester University Press, 1996).

Stuart Curran, *Poetic Form and British Romanticism* (New York: Oxford University Press, 1986).

Marilyn Gaull, *English Romanticism: The Human Context* (New York: Norton, 1988).

Jerome J. McGann, *The Romantic Ideology: A Critical Investigation* (Chicago: University of Chicago Press, 1983).

Jerome J. McGann (ed.), *The New Oxford Book of Romantic Period Verse* (Oxford: Oxford University Press, 1993).

Jerome J. McGann, *The Poetics of Sensibility: A Revolution in Literary Style* (Oxford: Oxford University Press, 1996).

Anne K. Mellor, *English Romantic Irony* (Cambridge, MA: Harvard Oxford University Press, 1980).

Anne K. Mellor, *Romanticism and Gender* (New York: Routledge, 1993).

Michael O'Neill and Mark Sandy (eds), *Romanticism: Critical Concepts in Literary and Cultural Studies*, 4 vols (London: Routledge, 2006).

Seamus Perry, 'Romanticism: The Brief History of a Concept', in *A Companion to Romanticism*, ed. Duncan Wu (Oxford: Blackwell, 1998), pp. 3–11.

Arden Reed (ed.), *Romanticism and Language* (London: Methuen, 1984).

Nicholas Roe (ed.), *Romanticism: An Oxford Guide* (Oxford: Oxford University Press, 2005).

Jane Stabler, *Burke to Byron: Barbauld to Baillie* (Basingstoke, UK: Palgrave, 2002).

Charles Taylor, *Sources of the Self: The Making of the Modern Identity* (Cambridge, UK: Cambridge University Press, 1989).

Duncan Wu (ed.), *Romanticism: An Anthology*, 3rd edn (Oxford: Blackwell, 2006).

Acknowledgements

The editors are grateful to the editorial staff at Blackwell, especially Andrew McNeillie who commissioned the volume, and Emma Bennett, who has patiently and helpfully presided over its development. They are indebted to the work of innumerable editors and critics of Romantic poetry, debts indicated in the Notes and the lists of Further Reading. Volumes appearing in this series to date have been an inspiring model.

For encouragement and advice, Michael O'Neill would like to thank Professor Duncan Wu and the anonymous readers of his original proposal. He would also like to thank Durham University and the Department of English at Durham for terms of research leave when he has been able to work on the volume. He owes a particular debt of gratitude to Dr Anita O'Connell, who worked as his research assistant during the summer and autumn of 2006, and spring of 2007. Her sharp-eyed accuracy and concern for detail have significantly improved his contributions. She has taken primary responsibility for assembling the Index. He is also grateful to Charles Mahoney for advice and exchange of ideas, and to staff at the National Library of Scotland.

Charles Mahoney would like to thank Michael O'Neill both for the opportunity to collaborate on this project and for his guidance throughout its course. He would also like to thank the staffs at the Homer Babbidge Library, University of Connecticut, and the Beinecke Rare Book and Manuscript Library, Yale University.

The editors owe an immeasurable debt to Jenny Roberts, whose interventions and suggestions as copy-editor have been unfailingly precise, helpful and erudite. The editors are grateful to King's College, Cambridge, for permission to include a number of black and white versions of designs from its copy of Blake's *Songs of Innocence and of Experience*. They are also grateful to the Wordsworth Trust, Grasmere, and to the Bodleian Library, University of Oxford, for permission to consult in photographic form manuscripts in their possession.

Anna Laetitia Barbauld, *née* Aikin (1743–1825)

Anna Laetitia Barbauld was born in 1743 into a prominent dissenting family in Leicestershire. In 1758, her father, Dr John Aikin, became a teacher at the Warrington Academy for Dissenters (those Protestants who refused to subscribe to the articles of the Church of England and thus were consequently refused admission to the universities) in Lancashire. Shortly thereafter, he was succeeded as tutor in languages and *belles lettres* by Joseph Priestley (the discoverer of oxygen and, with Richard Price, one of the founding members of the Unitarian Society). She was immediately influenced by Priestley, who, along with her father, encouraged her voracious reading as well as the study of Latin and Greek (traditionally only open to boys), and modern romance languages. With her younger brother John (b. 1747), also a tutor at the Academy, she published *Miscellaneous Pieces, in Prose* (1773) – the same year as her own *Poems* (which were successful enough to go through three editions in the first year).

In 1774, she married Rochemont Barbauld, a dissenting minister who had been educated at the Warrington Academy, and together they opened a school for boys in Palgrave, Suffolk. It was here that she wrote her popular *Lessons for Children* (1778) and *Hymns in Prose for Children* (1781). Following the death of her mother in 1775, and the strain on her husband from running the school, they left the Palgrave School for France, eventually returning to Hampstead (then on the outskirts of London) in 1786. Her proximity to the literary and political life of London gave Barbauld increased opportunities to intervene – with both poetry and pamphlets – in the pressing debates of the day: amongst her numerous publications during this fertile period are *An Address to the Opposers of the Repeal* (1790; occasioned by the failure of Parliament to repeal the Corporation and Test Acts, which prevented Dissenters from holding civil or military office); *An Epistle to William Wilberforce* (1791; written in response to Parliament's refusal to abolish the slave trade); *Remarks on Mr. Gilbert Wakefield's Enquiry into the Expediency and Propriety or Public or Social Worship* (1792; Wakefield was a fellow Dissenter and a classicist); and *Sins of the Government, Sins of the Nation* (1793; a critique of the British government's rationale for prosecuting the war against France). When, in 1796, her brother John became the editor of the influential periodical *The Monthly Magazine*, she contributed a number of poems (see, for instance, *To Mr. S.T. Coleridge*; below, p. 6), as she did later to *The Annual Review* during the editorship of her nephew Arthur Aikin (1803–9).

The Barbaulds moved to Stoke Newington (then a village to the north of London) in 1802, where Rochemont Barbauld became the dissenting minister. His already unreliable mental health, however, became an increasing concern for them both. In 1808, after an assault on his wife, Rochemont Barbauld was placed under restraints and the couple were obliged to separate; later that same year, he drowned himself in the New River, Stoke Newington. After her husband's death, Barbauld took on ever more miscellaneous literary work, establishing her reputation as perhaps the most versatile *femme des lettres* of the period. In addition to editing the poetry of Mark Akenside and William Collins, as well as Samuel Richardson's correspondence, Barbauld began to write for the *Monthly Review* (1809–15), oversaw the publication (writing all the introductions and prefaces) of the exhaustive 50-volume *British Novelists* (1810), edited the popular anthology *The Female Speaker* (1811), and wrote what is generally considered to be her greatest poem, *Eighteen Hundred and Eleven* (1812), a remorseless indictment of the state of Britain after nearly 20 years of war with France. She died at Stoke Newington in 1825.

As noted by the editors of the standard edition of her poetry, 'the critical neglect of Barbauld's poetry is baffling'.[1] The first volume of her poetry was greeted with excitement (so much so that her subsequent marriage was viewed as a loss to English *belles lettres*); her subsequent productivity was such as to place her at the forefront of the literary landscape in the 1790s and 1810s; and critics from Johnson to Roger Lonsdale have esteemed her as a major innovator in both the themes and forms of early Romantic poetry.[2] Integral to both the explanation for Barbauld's relative neglect and to her restoration to her 'rightful place' in literature is an understanding of her relegation to the anecdotal in standard accounts of Romanticism and the Romantic canon. Representative is the oft-repeated vignette in Coleridge's *Table-Talk* apropos 'Mrs' Barbauld's concern that *The Rime of the Ancyent Marinere* (1798) had no moral, to which Coleridge represents himself as having wittily responded that 'in

---

1 *The Poems of Anna Laetitia Barbauld*, ed. William McCarthy and Elizabeth Kraft (Athens, GA and London: University of Georgia Press, 1994), p. xxi.
2 Lonsdale goes so far as to position Barbauld as arguably 'the most versatile of women poets in the period'; cited in *The Poems of Anna Laetitia Barbauld*, p. xxii.

my judgment the chief fault of the poem was that it had too much moral'. Positioned thus in such an overdetermined exchange, 'Mrs Barbauld' is equated with the pedagogic concerns of the school-marm while 'Coleridge' stands for the daring freedom of the Romantic poet.[3] (It must be noted, however, that 35 years before Coleridge quipped at Barbauld's expense, he had walked 40 miles, from Stowey to Bristol and back, for the opportunity to meet the poet and radical, Anna Barbauld.) Hazlitt provides an altogether different sort of anecdote in the *Lectures on the English Poets* (1818). Professing himself a 'great admirer of the female writers of the present day', he proceeds to single out Barbauld:

> The first poetess I can recollect is Mrs. Barbauld, with whose works I became acquainted before those of any other author, male or female, when I was learning to spell words of one syllable in her storybooks for children. I became acquainted with her poetical works long after in Enfield's *Speaker*; and remember being much divided in my opinion at that time, between her *Ode to Spring* and Collins's *Ode to Evening*. I wish I could repay my childish debt of gratitude in terms of appropriate praise. She is a very pretty poetess; and, to my fancy, strews the flowers of poetry most agreeably round the borders of religious controversy.[4]

Hazlitt's memory and his praise are interesting not least for the ways in which they simultaneously reinforce and complicate certain received habits of thinking about Barbauld. While identifying her as a children's writer and a 'pretty poetess' would seem to mitigate any claims regarding her stature as, first-and-foremost, a highly literary 'poet', the inclusion of the *Ode to Spring* and the comparison with Collins undo any such easy categorization. Along with Thomas Gray's own 'sublime odes', those of Collins are of undisputed importance to the development of the Romantic ode. And, Hazlitt suggests, Barbauld's own deserves the same commendation – as George Dyer agreed when, in 1800, he had included Barbauld's ode (and two others) in his anthology of English odes. Though the terms of 'appropriate praise' for Barbauld's poetry may not yet be established, her inclusion in this volume will, we hope, provide another occasion to make the attempt.

The texts here have been taken from the two-volume *Works of Anna Laetitia Barbauld*, edited by her niece, Lucy Aikin, and published in 1825, the year of her death.

Further Reading

Primary Texts

The Works of Anna Laetitia Barbauld, 2 vols (London: Longman, 1825) [hereafter *1825*].

Memoir of Mrs Barbauld, including letters and notices of her family and friends, by Anna L. Le Breton (London, 1874).

The Poems of Anna Laetitia Barbauld, ed. William McCarthy and Elizabeth Kraft (Athens, GA and London: University of Georgia Press, 1994).

Selected Poetry and Prose, ed. William McCarthy and Elizabeth Kraft (Peterborough, ONT: Broadview Press, 2002).

Secondary Texts

Isobel Armstrong, 'The Gush of the Feminine: How Can We Read Women's Poetry of the Romantic Period?', in *Romantic Women Writers: Voices and Countervoices*, ed. Paula R. Feldman and Theresa M. Kelley (Hanover, NH: University Press of New England, 1995), pp. 13–32.

William Keach, 'A Regency Prophecy and the End of Anna Barbauld's Career', *Studies in Romanticism* 33 (1994), pp. 569–77.

William McCarthy, '"We Hoped the *Woman* Was Going to Appear": Desire, Repression, and Gender in Anna Barbauld's Early Poems', in *Romantic Women Writers: Voices and Countervoices*, ed. Paula R. Feldman and Theresa M. Kelley (Hanover, NH: University Press of New England, 1995), pp. 113–37.

Marlon Ross, 'Configurations of Feminine Reform: The Woman Writer and the Tradition of Dissent', in *Revisioning Romanticism: British Women Writers, 1776–1837*, ed. Carol Shiner Wilson and Joel Haefner (Philadelphia: University of Pennsylvania Press, 1994), pp. 91–110.

---

3   For a fuller account of this and other aspects of Barbauld's anecdotal status in literary history, see *Selected Poetry and Prose*, ed. McCarthy and Kraft (Peterborough, ONT: Broadview Press, 2002), pp. 27–30.
4   *The Complete Works of William Hazlitt*, 21 vols, ed. P. P. Howe (London and Toronto: J. M. Dent, 1930–4), vol. 5, p. 147.

The Rights of Woman

This poem was apparently written in 1792 in response to Mary Wollstonecraft's pejorative comments on Barbauld in the *Vindication of the Rights of Woman* (though it was not published until 1825). In Chapter 4 of the *Vindication* ('Observations on the State of Degradation to which Woman is Reduced by Various Causes'), Wollstonecraft laments the 'sensual error' that distinguishes the sexual from the human character of women, an error which has led in turn to a 'false system of female manners ... which robs the whole sex of its dignity'. Not only has this ever been the propensity of men, she continues, but 'the fear of departing from a supposed sexual character, has made even women of superior sense adopt the same sentiments'. In support of her point, she then cites Barbauld:

Pleasure's the portion of th'*inferior* kind;
But glory, virtue, Heaven for *man* design'd.
 (*To Mrs. P[riestley], with some
 Drawings of Birds and Insects*, ll. 101–02;
 emphasis Wollstonecraft)

After writing these lines, how could Mrs Barbauld write the following ignoble comparison?

 To a Lady, with some painted flowers.
Flowers to the fair: to you these flowers I bring,
And strive to greet you with an earlier spring.
*Flowers SWEET, and gay, and DELICATE LIKE
 YOU;*
Emblems of innocence, and beauty too.
With flowers the Graces bind their yellow hair,
And flowery wreaths consenting lovers wear.
Flowers, the sole luxury which nature knew,
In Eden's pure and guiltless garden grew.
To loftier forms are rougher tasks assign'd;
The sheltering oak, resists the stormy wind,
The tougher yew repels invading foes,
And the tall pine for future navies grows;
But this soft family, to cares unknown,
Were born for pleasure and delight ALONE.

Gay without toil, and lovely without art,
They spring to CHEER THE SENSE, and *GLAD
 the heart.*
Nor blush, my fair, to own you copy these;
Your *BEST, your SWEETEST empire* is – to
 PLEASE.
 (emphasis and upper case Wollstonecraft)

So the men tell us; but virtue, says reason, must be acquired by *rough* toils, and useful struggles with worldly *cares*.
 (*Vindication of the Rights of Woman*, ch. 4)

Barbauld, then, is positioned by Wollstonecraft as a woman of 'superior sense' who has succumbed to the insulting conceit according to which women are but 'sweet', 'gay', 'delicate' flowers, 'born for pleasure and delight' and to be, as Wollstonecraft condemns it, 'the solace of man'. Her comparison is thus doubly 'ignoble' in that it does not do justice either to her own 'sense' or to the capacity for women generally to be 'rational companions' to men (two categories constantly valorized by Wollstonecraft). While presumably a response to Wollstonecraft's criticism, Barbauld's poem should not be construed as in any way a reliable reading of Wollstonecraft's own arguments in the *Vindication*. (Nowhere, for instance, does Wollstonecraft urge women to resume their 'empire o'er the breast' [l. 4] or to usurp the reign of man [ll. 7–8].) Consequently, the poem's tone is difficult to gauge: occasionally mocking and elsewhere in earnest, Barbauld nonetheless ennobles 'injured Woman' throughout the poem before urging her, in the poem's closing lines, to renounce 'separate rights' for 'mutual love'. The one constant in the poem (and a potential indicator of its tone) is its form. Barbauld's use here of the heroic stanza (an iambic pentameter quatrain rhyming *abab*) suggests that she is indeed girding 'degraded, scorned, opprest' woman in an appropriately heroic form, one befitting the seriousness of her undertaking in these lines.
 Text follows *1825*.

Yes, injured Woman! rise, assert thy right!
Woman! too long degraded, scorned, opprest;
O born to rule in partial Law's despite,
Resume thy native empire o'er the breast!

Go forth arrayed in panoply divine; 5
That angel pureness which admits no stain;

---

5 *panoply* 'A complete suit of armour'; figuratively, any kind of complete defence or clothing, any splendid array or covering for warfare.

Go, bid proud Man his boasted rule resign,
And kiss the golden sceptre of thy reign.

Go, gird thyself with grace; collect thy store
Of bright artillery glancing from afar; 10
Soft melting tones thy thundering cannon's roar,
Blushes and fears thy magazine of war.

Thy rights are empire: urge no meaner claim,—
Felt, not defined, and if debated, lost;
Like sacred mysteries, which withheld from fame, 15
Shunning discussion, are revered the most.

Try all that wit and art suggest to bend
Of thy imperial foe the stubborn knee;
Make treacherous Man thy subject, not thy friend;
Thou mayst command, but never canst be free. 20

Awe the licentious, and restrain the rude;
Soften the sullen, clear the cloudy brow:
Be, more than princes' gifts thy favours sued;—
She hazards all, who will the least allow.

But hope not, courted idol of mankind, 25
On this proud eminence secure to stay;
Subduing and subdued, thou soon shalt find
Thy coldness soften, and thy pride give way.

Then, then, abandon each ambitious thought,
Conquest or rule thy heart shall feebly move, 30
In Nature's school, by her soft maxims taught,
That separate rights are lost in mutual love.

---

8 *golden sceptre of thy reign* See Wollstonecraft: 'I love man as my fellow; but his scepter, real, or usurped, extends not to me, unless the reason of an individual demands my homage' (*Vindication of the Rights of Woman*, ch. 2); see also ch. 3: 'Taught from their infancy that beauty is a woman's sceptre, the mind shapes itself to the body, and, roaming round its gilt cage, only seeks to adorn its prison'.
12 *magazine of war* Building for the storage of arms, ammunitions, gunpowder, and other explosives.
24 *hazards* To expose oneself to risk; in eighteenth-century writing, with particular emphasis on putting something at risk in a game of chance.
32 *That separate rights . . . mutual love* Compare Milton, *Paradise Lost*:

> Among *unequals* what society
> Can sort, what harmony or true delight?
> Which must be mutual, in proportion due
> Giv'n and receiv'd; but in *disparity*
> The one intense, the other still remiss
> Cannot well suit with either, but soon prove
> Tedious alike: of *fellowship* I speak
> Such as I seek, fit to participate
> All rational delight –
> (VIII, ll. 383–91; cited by Wollstonecraft, *Vindication of the Rights of Woman*, ch. 2)

Inscription for an Ice-House

In Barbauld's poem, probably written in the early 1790s (1793–5), the ice-house represents two things, one material and the other metaphorical: a structure (often partly underground) in which ice is stored in winter for use throughout the year; and a dwelling which captures the spirit of winter, the 'genius' of frigidity. While 'ice-house' names the location where these verses are to be seen and read, the term 'inscription' indicates their generic status: verses conscious of their location that have been engraved or otherwise traced upon a surface (for the sake of durability). In this regard, Barbauld's poem may be understood as a variant on the locodescriptive inscription (poetry about a particular place), in which the inscribed verses are to be understood as calling out to passing travellers to stop and consider the landscape (or in this case, building) before them. In the case of Barbauld's inscription, the poem moves quickly from a description of the ice-house itself to a consideration of the ways in which the giant, 'stern Winter', is subjugated and housed by 'man, the great magician'. It is in this regard a multi-faceted meditation on the 'genius' of place.

Text follows *1825*.

> Stranger, approach! within this iron door
> Thrice locked and bolted, this rude arch beneath
> That vaults with ponderous stone the cell; confined
> By man, the great magician, who controuls
> Fire, earth and air, and genii of the storm, 5
> And bends the most remote and opposite things
> To do him service and perform his will,—
> A giant sits; stern Winter; here he piles,
> While summer glows around, and southern gales
> Dissolve the fainting world, his treasured snows 10
> Within the rugged cave.—Stranger, approach!
> He will not cramp thy limbs with sudden age,
> Nor wither with his touch the coyest flower
> That decks thy scented hair. Indignant here,
> Like fettered Sampson when his might was spent 15
> In puny feats to glad the festive halls
> Of Gaza's wealthy sons; or he who sat
> Midst laughing girls submiss, and patient twirled
> The slender spindle in his sinewy grasp;
> The rugged power, fair Pleasure's minister, 20
> Exerts his art to deck the genial board;
> Congeals the melting peach, the nectarine smooth,
> Burnished and glowing from the sunny wall:
> Darts sudden frost into the crimson veins
> Of the moist berry; moulds the sugared hail: 25
> Cools with his icy breath our flowing cups;
> Or gives to the fresh dairy's nectared bowls
> A quicker zest. Sullen he plies his task,

1 *Stranger, approach!* The poem's initial apostrophe to the passing traveller, urging the stranger to come closer and read the inscription, is a variation on the traditional *Siste Viator* ('Wait, Traveller') found inscribed on Roman tombstones. Compare the opening of Wordsworth, *Lines left upon a Seat in a Yew-tree*, 'Nay, Traveller! rest'.
5 *genii* The plural of 'genius', to be understood here not so much in terms of characteristic disposition or inclination, but as the interfering spirit(s) of the storm.
8 *stern Winter* The spondee here (*stern Win-*ter) underscores the hard, rough spirit of winter (despite the fact that, in the 'cell' of the ice-house, Winter is disciplined by 'man' rather than the other way round).
11 *Stranger, approach!* The poem's second apostrophe to the passing stranger (see above, l. 1) reassures the stranger that, in the ice-house, the 'giant' winter is sufficiently controlled by 'man' that he will not 'cramp' or 'wither' any who approach; such is the power of 'man' as 'magician' over the 'genius' of winter.
15–17 *like fettered Sampson . . . Gaza's wealthy sons* Compare Judges 16: 21, 'But the Philistines took him, and put out his eyes, and brought him down to Gaza, and bound him with fetters of brass; and he did grind in the prison house'; see also Judges 16: 25, 'And it came to pass, when their [the lords of the Philistines] hearts were merry, that they said, Call for Samson, that he may make us sport'.
17–19 *or he who sat . . . his sinewy grasp* As McCarthy and Kraft (2002) note (*Poems*, p. 294), these lines appear to allude to the plight of Hercules; compare Ovid, *Heroides* 9, *Deianira to Hercules*, 'They say that you have held the wool-basket among the girls of Ionia, and been frightened at your mistress' threats' (ll. 73–5) and 'Ah, how often, while with dour finger you twisted the thread, have your too strong hands crushed the spindle!' (ll. 79–80).
20 *The rugged power, fair Pleasure's minister* 'Rugged' and powerful though winter is, it is here subordinated (across the medial caesura) to 'fair' pleasure – precisely the predicament of Samson and Hercules in the similes above.
21 *board* 'A table used for meals'.
28 *zest* 'Something which furnishes a relish or provides a savoury addition to a meal'; cold though winter's ice is, it 'quickens' the tastes of all those foods with which it comes in contact.

And on his shaking fingers counts the weeks
Of lingering Summer, mindful of his hour
To rush in whirlwinds forth, and rule the year.
                                                                30

31   *whirlwinds forth* Similar to the spondee in line 8, the three consecutive stresses of *whirl-winds forth* (resulting in a spondee in the third foot) underscore the rough impetuosity of winter – especially in this closing line, poised as winter is to 'rush' forth and 'rule' the year.

To Mr. S. T. Coleridge

Probably written in September 1797, *To Mr. C—ge* was published (unsigned) in *The Monthly Magazine* 7 (April 1799). Writing to John Thelwall from Bridgewater in August 1797, Coleridge was preoccupied with his futile attempts to arrange for Thelwall to take up residence with his family and the Wordsworths near Nether Stowey. What he did not mention is that, on the same trip, he had met Anna Barbauld in Bristol (Coleridge, *Collected Letters of Samuel Coleridge*, ed. E. L. Griggs, 6 vols (Oxford: Clarendon Press, 1956–61), vol. i., p. 341n). Written shortly after this meeting, Barbauld's poem thus captures her impressions of him at the height of his lyrical powers during the 1797–8 *annus mirabilis* spent in the company of Wordsworth. In her address, Barbauld allegorically places Coleridge midway on his journey through this life and up the 'hill of Science', in order to admonish him not to settle for the pleasures presented by the grove of 'tangled mazes' filled with 'strange enchantment' but, rather, to follow those 'noble aims' of his which will lead him away from torpor to 'active scenes' and 'fair exertion'. By all accounts, Coleridge concurred with the assessment and respected the temper of Barbauld's own mind; as he wrote in a letter after the publication of the poem,

> The more I see of Mrs Barbauld the more I admire her – that wonderful *Propriety* of Mind! – She has great *acuteness*, very great – yet how steadily she keeps it within the bounds of practical Reason. This I almost envy as well as admire – My own Subtleties too often lead me into strange (tho' God be praised) transient Out-of-the-waynesses. Oft like a winged Spider, I am entangled in a new Spun web – but never fear for me, 'tis but the flutter of my wings – & off I am again!
> (Coleridge *Letters*, vol. i., p. 578)

(For Coleridge's later, less generous appraisals of Barbauld, see for example *Lectures 1808–1819: On Literature*, ed. R. A. Foakes (Princeton, NJ: Princeton University Press, 1987), vol. i., p. 407 and note.)

Text follows *1825*.

Midway the hill of Science, after steep
And rugged paths that tire th' unpractised feet
A Grove extends, in tangled mazes wrought,
And fill'd with strange enchantment:—dubious shapes
Flit through dim glades, and lure the eager foot
                                                                5

1   *hill of Science* Latin, *scientia*, knowledge. 'The Hill of Science' is also the title of an allegory of Barbauld's collected in *Miscellaneous Pieces in Prose* (1773). Compare the hill named 'Difficulty' in Bunyan's *Pilgrim's Progress*, midway up the ascent of which Christian falls asleep: 'Now about the midway to the top of the Hill, was a pleasant *Arbour*, made by the Lord of the Hill, for the refreshing of weary Travailers. Thither therefore *Christian* got, where also he sat down to rest him'. Compare also Coleridge, *The Eolian Harp*:

> And thus, my Love! as on the midway slope
> Of yonder hill I stretch my limbs at noon
> Whilst thro' my half-clos'd eyelids I behold
> The sunbeams dance, like diamonds, on the main,
> And tranquil muse upon tranquillity . . .
> (ll. 26–30)

Whereas for Barbauld the midway point on the hill is replete with dangerous distractions from the 'road' to knowledge, for Coleridge it represents a sublime opportunity to become one of innumerable living, 'organic' eolian harps 'That tremble into thought, as o'er them sweeps, / Plastic and vast, one intellectual breeze' (ll. 38–9). See below, note to l. 19.
3   *tangled mazes wrought* Compare Milton, *Paradise Lost*, 'And found no end in wand'ring mazes lost' (II, l. 561).
4   *enchantment* 'the action . . . of employing magic or sorcery'. From Latin, *incantare*, to sing or chant; hence, a product of poetry (rather than 'science').
5   *dim glades* Compare Coleridge's description of the dell in *This Lime-Tree Bower My Prison*:

> And there my friends,
> Behold the dark-green file of long lank weeds,
> That all at once (a most fantastic sight!)
> Still nod and drip beneath the dripping edge
> Of the dim clay-stone.
> (ll. 16–20)

Of youthful ardour to eternal chase.
Dreams hang on every leaf; unearthly forms
Glide through the gloom, and mystic visions swim
Before the cheated sense. Athwart the mists,
Far into vacant space, huge shadows stretch 10
And seem realities; while things of life,
Obvious to sight and touch, all glowing round
Fade to the hue of shadows. *Scruples* here
With filmy net, most like th' autumnal webs
Of floating Gossamer, arrest the foot 15
Of generous enterprize; and palsy hope
And fair ambition, with the chilling touch
Of sickly hesitation and blank fear.
Nor seldom *Indolence* these lawns among
Fixes her turf-built seat, and wears the garb 20
Of deep philosophy, and museful sits,
In dreamy twilight of the vacant mind,
Soothed by the whispering shade; for soothing soft
The shades, and vistas lengthening into air,
With moon beam rainbows tinted. Here each mind 25
Of finer mold, acute and delicate,
In its high progress to eternal truth
Rests for a space, in fairy bowers entranced;
And loves the softened light and tender gloom;
And, pampered with most unsubstantial food, 30
Looks down indignant on the grosser world,
And matter's cumbrous shapings. Youth belov'd

---

13 Scruples 'A thought or circumstance that troubles the mind or conscience'; figuratively, any cause of uneasiness. In the tangled grove that threatens to stall those who ascend the 'hill of Science' (according to Barbauld's allegory here), 'scruples' name those fundamentally insubstantial reservations which cause one to hesitate rather than proceed boldly. Compare (in the headnote above) Coleridge's use of 'Subtleties'.
15 *Gossamer* 'A fine filmy substance, consisting of cobwebs, spun by small spiders, which is seen floating in the air in calm weather'; hence insubstantial, and an appropriate image for the 'scruples' mentioned above. See the headnote above for Coleridge's depiction of himself as often 'entangled in a new Spun web'.
16 *palsy* Here deployed as a verb: to render powerless, ineffectual or inert.
19 *Indolence* Literally, 'freedom from pain' (see headnote to Keats, *Ode on Indolence*, p. 453). Akin to the 'scruples' identified in line 13, 'indolence' similarly threatens to distract and delude those ascending the 'hill of Science' – in this case, with its 'soothing', 'dreamy', and 'museful' enticements. In his own musings on indolence in *The Eolian Harp*, Coleridge posits indolence not as an impediment to knowledge but in fact as a necessary state if the mind is to resemble such a harp:

> Full many a thought uncall'd and undetain'd,
> And many idle flitting phantasies,
> Traverse my indolent and passive brain
> As wild and various, as the random gales
> That swell or flutter on this subject Lute!
> (ll. 31–5)

Finally, see Thomson, *The Castle of Indolence* (stanzas 39–40).
25–32 *Here each mind . . . matter's cumbrous shapings* In a transition between describing the grove and directly addressing Coleridge ('Youth belov'd / Of Science', ll. 32–3 below), the speaker concedes that 'each mind / Of finer mold' will want to rest here, but ought not to 'build' on this dangerous ground (ll. 35, 36 below).
26 *acute* 'having nice or quick discernment; penetrating'; see Coleridge's letter (cited in the headnote above) for his praise of Barbauld's own acuteness of mind.
28 *in fairy bowers entranced* Similar to 'strange enchantment' (l. 4), the grove is here described as a Spenserian bower, an idealized abode which could never be realized in the 'grosser world' (l. 31).
29 *and tender gloom* Compare Byron, *Hebrew Melodies*, 'And the wild cypress wave in tender gloom' ('Oh! snatch'd away in beauty's bloom', l. 5).
31 *grosser world* The material world, as opposed to the ethereal, unsubstantial world of the 'fairy bowers' (l. 28).
32 *cumbrous* 'Troublesome from bulk or heaviness; burdensome'; cumbersome.
32 *Youth belov'd* Barbauld's most direct admonition to Coleridge begins here.

Of Science—of the Muse belov'd, not here,
Not in the maze of metaphysic lore
Build thou thy place of resting; lightly tread 35
The dangerous ground, on noble aims intent;
And be this Circe of the studious cell
Enjoyed, but still subservient. Active scenes
Shall soon with healthful spirit brace thy mind,
And fair exertion, for bright fame sustained, 40
For friends, for country, chase each spleen-fed fog
That blots the wide creation—
Now Heaven conduct thee with a Parent's love!

34 *maze of metaphysic lore* See line 3 above and note. More comprehensively, the 'maze of metaphoric lore' is the entirety of the tangled grove midway up the 'hill of Science', as described in lines 3–25.
37 *Circe* In Homer, *Odyssey* X, Circe is an enchantress who turns Odysseus' men into swine, though Odysseus himself is able to resist her spells. She eventually restores his men and, after Odysseus lives with her for a year, gives him directions for his journey home.
37 *cell* Dwelling consisting of a single room, often associated (as here) with students, hermits and monks.
38–9 *Active scenes . . . brace thy mind* Compare Coleridge, *Reflections on Having Left a Place of Retirement*:

> Was it right,
> While my unnumber'd Brethren toil'd and bled,
> That I should dream away the trusted Hours
> On rose-leaf Beds, pamp'ring the coward Heart
> With feelings all too delicate for use?
> . . .
> I therefore go, and join head, heart, and hand,
> Active and firm, to fight the bloodless fight
> Of Science, Freedom, and the Truth in Christ.
> (ll. 44–8, 60–2)

Published in *The Monthly Magazine* in October 1796, Coleridge's poem presents its author as already 'active and firm', fully disengaged from the Circe that Barbauld imagines enticing him.
41 *spleen-fed fog* In eighteenth-century poetry (e.g. Anne Finch's 'The Spleen' and Pope's *The Rape of the Lock*, Canto V), the spleen named both an organ and an illness, one characterized by melancholia, moodiness and irritability. It was also productively, if spasmodically, affiliated with wit and poetic inspiration.

Charlotte Smith, *née* Turner (1749–1806)

In 1835, 29 years after the death of Charlotte Smith, Wordsworth remarked that she was in fact a poet 'to whom English verse is under greater obligations than are likely to be either acknowledged or remembered'.[1] This obligation, in which Wordsworth's poetry certainly participated, has only recently begun to be adequately acknowledged. Not only as the author of the popular *Elegiac Sonnets* (nine editions between 1784 and 1800), but also as the poet of the blank verse poems *The Emigrants* (1793) and *Beachy Head* (1807), and 11 novels (between 1788 and 1802), Smith exerted an astonishing degree of influence over the forms, themes and sensibilities of British Romanticism. Formally, her achievement is perhaps most pronounced when we recognize her for having revived the sonnet tradition in English (fundamentally dormant from 1642 until 1784) and for having produced (in *The Emigrants*) the most significant blank verse between Cowper and Wordsworth. In her meditations on the relationship between landscape and imagination – her highly subjective responses to the forces at work in the natural world – she had, as Wordsworth also observed, 'true feeling for rural nature, at a time when nature was not much regarded by English poets'.[2] Indeed, in form as well as sensibility, Charlotte Smith is arguably (as Stuart Curran has noted) 'the first poet in England whom in retrospect we would call Romantic'.[3]

Smith was the daughter of Nicholas Turner, of London and Bignor Park, Sussex (on the banks of the River Arun), and split her youth between the sophistication of a lavish London life and the idyllic retreat provided by a Sussex estate. When her father remarried in 1764 (having been earlier widowed in 1752), he arranged for his daughter (only 15) to be married to Benjamin Smith, the son of a prosperous West Indies merchant. Abusive, violent and financially careless, Smith effectively destroyed his wife's prospects and condemned her to what she considered a life of personal slavery. By the time they finally separated in 1788, he had saddled Charlotte with 12 children and insoluble debts. It was in fact Benjamin's Smith's imprisonment for debt in 1783 that led Charlotte to write for commercial gain, and when the first edition of *Elegiac Sonnets* appeared in 1784 (with some assistance from the popular and prolific poet William Hayley), she was living with him in a London debtor's prison. For the remainder of her life, she wrote to support herself and her children, with translations, subsequent editions of *Elegiac Sonnets* (notably, the highly successful edition, published by subscription, of 1789), and the lucrative novels beginning with *Emmeline* (1788) and including *Desmond* (1792) as well as *The Old Manor House* (1793).

In her preface to both the first and second editions of *Elegiac Sonnets*, Smith modestly characterizes her 'little Poems' less in terms of form than of feeling:

> The little Poems which are here called Sonnets, have, I believe no very just claim to that title: but they consist of fourteen lines, and appear to me no improper vehicle for a single Sentiment. I am told, and I read it as the opinion of very good judges, that the legitimate Sonnet is ill calculated for our language. The specimen Mr. Hayley has given, though they form a strong exception, prove no more, than that the difficulties of the attempt vanish before uncommon powers.
>
> Some very melancholy moments have been beguiled by expressing in verse the sensations those moments brought. Some of my friends, with partial indiscretion, have multiplied the copies they procured of several of these attempts, till they found their way into the prints of the day in a mutilated state; which, concurring with other circumstances, determined me to put them into their present form. I can hope for readers only among the few, who, to sensibility of heart, join simplicity of taste.

Smith's sonnets are not 'elegiac' in the sense of being a series of lamentations over the dead, but because of their abiding aura and tone of pensive sadness and melancholy. While each sonnet may indeed be the vehicle for 'a single sentiment', the sentiment here which prevails throughout is the poet's elegiac melancholy, which she repeatedly would 'beguile' not simply by 'expressing [it] in verse' but, equally important, by

---

1 *The Poetical Works of William Wordsworth*, ed. Ernest de Selincourt and Helen Darbishire, 5 vols (Oxford: Clarendon Press, 1947), vol. 4, p. 403.
2 ibid.
3 *The Poems of Charlotte Smith*, ed. Stuart Curran (Oxford and New York: Oxford University Press, 1993), p. xix.

controlling and confining it within the fixed form of the sonnet. Thus it is that, though she is wary of the 'legitimate Sonnet' in English – she habitually favours an easier, more malleable arrangement of rhymes – Smith is attentive nonetheless to the ramifications of her formal decisions. (The 'legitimate' sonnet, otherwise called the Italian sonnet, consists in just two rhymes in the octave, with a turn after the eighth line, compared with the 'illegitimate' or English sonnet, with six rhymes over three quatrains and a turn after the 12th line.)

Throughout the career of the *Elegiac Sonnets*, Smith consciously attends to the interplay between form and feeling in relation to the tradition of the sonnet in English. Compare her preface to the third edition of *Elegiac Sonnets* (1786):

> The reception given by the public, as well as my particular friends, to the two first editions of these poems, has induced me to add to the present such other Sonnets as I have written since, or have recovered from my acquaintance, to whom I had given them without thinking well enough of them at the time to preserve any copies myself. A few of those last written, I have attempted on the Italian model; with what success I know not, but I am persuaded that to the generality of readers those which are less regular will be more pleasing.
>
> As a few notes were necessary, I have added them at the end. I have there quoted such lines as I have borrowed; and even where I am conscious the ideas were not my own, I have restored them to their original possessors.

Expanding her range from the English to the Italian model (she would later add an epigraph from Petrarch),[4] Smith now presents herself not merely as a woman who has written a handful of 'little poems', but as a poet who is both taking her place within the august English tradition of the sonnet and remaking the mode as well as the mood of that tradition (all the while doing so with conscious attention to her predecessors). In her wake, poets such as William Lisle Bowles, Anna Seward, Mary Robinson, Coleridge, Wordsworth, and Keats would continue the revitalization of the sonnet in English.

Indeed, the obligations of British Romantic poetry to Charlotte Smith are nowhere more legible than in this revivification. Years before Wordsworth (who had a copy of the 1789 fifth edition of *Elegiac Sonnets*) consciously took up the sonnet in 1802, Coleridge acknowledged the indebtedness of contemporary poets and readers to Smith (even more than to William Lisle Bowles, who didn't publish his *Fourteen Sonnets* until 1789, Coleridge's great model in this form) when he introduced the sonnets in *Poems* (1797) with the simple declaration that 'Charlotte Smith and Bowles are they who first made the Sonnet popular among the present English: I am justified therefore by analogy in deducing its laws from *their* compositions'.[5] And the 'laws' of the sonnet, as adduced by Coleridge, have far less to do with form than with feeling – less to do, in other words, with Petrarch or Shakespeare than with Smith:

> In a Sonnet then we require a developement of some lonely feeling, by whatever cause it may have been excited; but those Sonnets appear to me the most exquisite, in which moral Sentiments, Affections, or Feelings, are deduced from, and associated with, the scenery of Nature. Such compositions generate a habit of thought highly favourable to delicacy of character. They create a sweet and indissoluble union between the intellectual and the material world. Easily remembered from their briefness, and interesting alike to the eye and the affections, these are the poems which we can 'lay up in our heart, and our soul,' and repeat them 'when we walk by the way, and when we lie down, and when we rise up'.[6]

That Coleridge's primary criterion for a sonnet should be its cultivation of 'some lonely feeling' (in other words, Smith's 'melancholy moments') is remarkable not only for its lack of interest in any formal criteria but also for the degree to which it underscores the poetic association of individual sentiment and sensibility with natural scenes – a direct inheritance from Smith's numerous sonnets located, say, on the seashore or the banks of the River Arun, during a tempestuous night or whilst passing over a dreary tract of country, on a cliff or in a churchyard. (Writing over 50 years later, Leigh Hunt also seized on the power of sentiment in the *Elegiac Sonnets* when he wrote that 'everybody likes the sonnets because nobody doubts their being in earnest, and because they furnish a gentle voice to feelings that are universal'.[7]) Such is the deeply felt 'union between the intellectual and the material world' that marks Smith's poetry as so perspicaciously 'Romantic'.

---

4 'Flee serenity and renewal; approach not, my song, where there be smiles or singing, no, only tears: it will not do for you to remain among happy people, disconsolate widow, clothed in black'; as translated in *The Poems of Charlotte Smith*, ed. Stuart Curran (Oxford and New York: Oxford University Press, 1993), p. 3.
5 Samuel Taylor Coleridge, *Poems*, 2nd edn (Bristol: Joseph Cottle, 1797), p. 71.
6 Coleridge, *Poems*, 72.
7 Leigh Hunt, 'An Essay on . . . the Sonnet' (1867) in *Later Literary Essays*, ed. Charles Mahoney (vol. 4 of *Selected Writings of Leigh Hunt*, London: Pickering & Chatto, 2003), p. 316.

The texts here have been taken from the two-volume seventh edition of *Elegiac Sonnets* (1795). Smith provided her notes (beginning with the third edition of 1786) in one section of end-matter entitled 'Quotations, Notes, and Explanations', but they have here been inserted at the appropriate line and assigned to her parenthetically.

Further Reading

Primary Texts

Smith, Charlotte, *Elegiac Sonnets* (London: Cadell and Davies, 1784).

Smith, Charlotte, *Elegiac Sonnets*, 5th edn (1789), facsimile edition, ed. Jonathan Wordsworth (Oxford and New York: Woodstock Books, 1992).

Smith, Charlotte, *Elegiac Sonnets*, 7th edn, 2 vols (London: Cadell and Davies, 1795). [hereafter *1795*]

The Poems of Charlotte Smith, ed. Stuart Curran (Oxford and New York: Oxford University Press, 1993).

The Letters of Charlotte Smith, ed. Judith Phillips Stanton (Bloomington, IN: Indiana University Press, 2003).

Secondary Texts

Curran, Stuart, 'The I Altered', in *Romanticism and Feminism*, ed. Anne K. Mellor (Bloomington, IN: Indiana University Press, 1988), pp. 185–207.

Pinch, Adela, 'Sentimentality and Experience in Charlotte Smith's Sonnets', in *Strange Fits of Passion: Epistemologies of Emotion, Hume to Austen* (Stanford, CA: Stanford University Press, 1996), pp. 51–71.

Robinson, Daniel, 'Reviving the Sonnet: Women Romantic Poets and the Sonnet Claim', *European Romantic Review* 6 (1995), pp. 98–127.

Sonnet I

The first sonnet in the first (1784) and all subsequent editions of *Elegiac Sonnets*, Smith's opening sonnet is representative both of her habitual form in the first two editions (the English or 'illegitimate' sonnet, with six rhymes over three quatrains, followed by a concluding couplet) and of her penchant for developing a 'single sentiment' over 14 lines. In this instance, the sentiment is one to which she returns throughout the sonnets: the intransigence of the poet's sorrow despite the 'fantastic garlands' and beguiling charms of poetry. In her preface to the sixth edition of *Elegiac Sonnets* (1792), Smith explains to the reader that when she was asked to add some additional poems to the collection, she asked a friend for his opinion as to what to include. As Smith restages their exchange, he responded that

> I am far from supposing that *your* compositions can be neglected or disapproved on whatever subject: but perhaps 'toujours Rossignols, toujours des chansons tristes' [always nightingales, always sad songs], may not be so well received as if you attempted, what you would certainly execute as successfully, a more cheerful style of composition.

In turn, Smith represents herself as reacting to this suggestion with two questions, 'Alas! . . . Are grapes gather'd from thorns, or figs from thistles? Or can the *effect* cease, where the *cause* remains?' Identifying herself as the mythic Philomel (turned into a nightingale after her seduction and betrayal by her brother-in-law, Tereus, the King of Thrace, then left, according to Ovid, with a thorn in her breast, which in turn produced her melancholy music; see note to lines 7–8 below), Smith suggests that she is more or less condemned to sing *les chansons tristes*. (For further details pertaining to Smith's identification with the nightingale, see below, headnote to 'Sonnet VII: On the departure of the nightingale'.)

Text follows *1795*.

> THE partial Muse, has from my earliest hours
> Smil'd on the rugged path I'm doom'd to tread,
> And still with sportive hand has snatch'd wild flowers,
> To weave fantastic garlands for my head:

1 *partial* 'favouring a particular person or thing excessively or especially'.
4 *fantastic garlands* The garlands woven by the muse are 'fantastic' insofar as they are capricious (wild flowers snatched sportively) and merely decorate her head without addressing the pains in her heart (see note to lines 7–8 below). Compare the similarly vulnerable garlands of flowers in 'Sonnet II: Written at the Close of Spring', 'fond visions' subject to the power of 'tyrant Passion, and corrosive Care, / [To] Bid all thy fairy colours fade away!' (ll. 11–12).

> But far, far happier is the lot of those 5
> Who never learn'd her dear delusive art;
> Which, while it decks the head with many a rose,
> Reserves the thorn, to fester in the heart.
> For still she bids soft Pity's melting eye
> Stream o'er the hills she knows not to remove, 10
> Points every pang, and deepens every sigh
> Of mourning friendship, or unhappy love.
> Ah! then, how dear the Muse's favours cost,
> *If those paint sorrow best—who feel it most!*

6 *dear delusive art* Again, the art of the muse is delusive, Smith laments, because its beauties are merely superficial – the intertwined 'garlands' of rhyme (*abab cdcd efef gg*) may decorate but they do nothing to soften the 'rugged path' (l. 2) or remove the pangs (l. 11) of the speaker. This art is furthermore 'dear' because its price is so high.

7–8 *Which, while it decks . . . fester in the heart* In juxtaposing the speaker's heart with her head (see also l. 4), the head is decorated with the rose's flower while the heart receives the rose's thorn – the attribute of Philomel (see the headnote above).

13–14 *Ah! then . . . who feel it most!* 'The well-sung woes shall soothe my pensive ghost; / He best can paint them, who shall feel them most. *Pope's Eloisa to Abelard, 366th line*' (Smith's note). Though not particularly dramatic, the sonnet's turn may be said to occur here, with the plaintive, exclamatory 'Ah!' and the subsequent estimation of the price of the muse's favours.

Sonnet VII: On the departure of the nightingale

From the first edition of *Elegiac Sonnets* (1784), this is one of two sonnets on the nightingale (see also 'Sonnet III, To a Nightingale') included in the first edition of *Elegiac Sonnets* (1784), later supplemented by a third, 'Sonnet LV, The Return of the Nightingale'. In writing a sonnet on such a mythopoeic songbird, Smith would have been able to draw on a range of literary influences, including sonnets by Petrarch ('*Quel rosignioul, che si soave piagnê*' ['That nightingale so tenderly lamenting']), which she cites apropos 'To a Nightingale') and Milton (see note to line 7 below), for whom the nightingale was that 'most musical, most melancholy' of birds (*Il Penseroso*, l. 62). In turn, her own sonnets in this vein may be heard to resonate in Mary Robinson's 'Ode to the Nightingale' and 'Second Ode to the Nightingale', Coleridge's 'To the Nightingale' and 'The Nightingale: A Conversation Poem', as well as Keats's 'Ode to a Nightingale' (see individual notes below). The structure of the sonnet follows the 'illegitimate' or English model, with three heroic quatrains (*abab cdcd efef*) followed by a concluding couplet (*gg*) after the turn.

Text follows *1795*.

> SWEET poet of the woods—a long adieu!
> Farewell, soft minstrel of the early year!
> Ah! 'twill be long ere thou shalt sing anew,
> And pour thy music on 'the night's dull ear.'
> Whether on Spring thy wandering flights await, 5

1 *a long adieu!* Compare Keats, 'Ode to a Nightingale', 'Adieu! adieu! Thy plaintive anthem fades' (l. 75). It is characteristic of Smith's elegiac address that her apostrophe to the nightingale should begin at the end, at the moment of the bird's departure (a moment at which Keats does not arrive for nearly 80 lines).

2 *soft minstrel* Compare Robinson, 'Second Ode to the Nightingale', 'Lorn minstrel of the lonely vale!' (l. 2) and Coleridge, 'To the Nightingale', 'Minstrel of the Moon!' (l. 16).

4 *'the night's dull ear.'* 'Shakespeare' (Smith's note). Compare *Henry V*, 'in high and boastful neighs / Piercing the night's dull ears' (IV, Prologue, ll. 10–11).

5 *thy wandering flights await* 'Alludes to the supposed migration of the Nightingale' (Smith's note).

>   Or whether silent in our groves you dwell,
>   The pensive muse shall own thee for her mate,
>   And still protect the song she loves so well.
>   With cautious step, the love-lorn youth shall glide
>   Through the lone brake that shades thy mossy nest;
>   And shepherd girls, from eyes profane shall hide
>   The gentle bird, who sings of pity best:
>   For still thy voice shall soft affections move,
>   And still be dear to sorrow, and to love!

7 *The pensive muse shall own thee for her mate* " 'Whether the Muse of Love call thee his mate, / Both of them I serve, and of their train am I.' Milton's 'First Sonnet' " (Smith's note). See Milton, 'Sonnet I, O Nightingale', ll. 13–14. In placing the nightingale under the lyric protection of the 'pensive muse', Smith further inflects its song as elegiac and prone to melancholy.
10 *brake* 'fern, bracken'.
11 *eyes profane* Uninitiated eyes, or those which might somehow desecrate the sacredness of the nightingale.

12 *who sings of pity best* Compare Coleridge, 'To the Nightingale', 'Thy warblest sad thy pity-pleading strains' (l. 11) and 'The Nightingale: A Conversation Poem', 'Philomela's pity-pleading strains' (l. 39).
13 *For still thy voice* The turn occurs here with the consolidation of the nightingale's song in 'still' – here implying not only its motionless retreat in its nest (in the third quatrain), but also the continuity of its song both in moving the affections (l. 13) and in its allegiance to Smith's melancholy poetics (l. 14).

Sonnet XII: Written on the sea shore. – October, 1784

Added for the third edition of *Elegiac Sonnets* (1786), this sonnet was the first to include Smith's experiments with sonnets 'on the Italian model' – that is to say, two rhymes in the octave (*abba abba*) preceding a turn after the eight line rather than after the twelfth. Although Smith uses four rhymes in the octave here (*abba cddc*), and in many ways seems only to develop its gloomy musings over all 14 lines, a turn may nonetheless be glimpsed in the sestet's depiction of the speaker as a shipwrecked mariner. As is the case with numerous other of Smith's sonnets placed amidst savage and sublime natural scenery (compare XLIV below, LI, LIX, LXVI, LXVII and LXX), the speaker dramatically represents the 'awful' external scene before turning inward to observe her own state in similar (if not greater) terms of dereliction and dismay.

Text follows *1795*.

>   On some rude fragment of the rocky shore,
>   Where on the fractured cliff the billows break,
>   Musing, my solitary seat I take,
>   And listen to the deep and solemn roar.
>
>   O'er the dark waves the winds tempestuous howl;
>   The screaming sea-bird quits the troubled sea:
>   But the wild gloomy scene has charms for me,
>   And suits the mournful temper of my soul.

1 *rude* 'rugged, rough, uncultivated, wild'.
8 *And suits the mournful temper of my soul* 'Young' (Smith's note). As Stuart Curran notes, 'Zanga, the hero of Edward Young's once-popular tragedy, *The Revenge* (1721), begins the play in high-pitched soliloquy: "Rage on, ye winds, burst clouds, and waters roar! / You bear a just resemblance of my fortune, / And suit the gloomy habit of my soul" (I.i.5–7)' (*The Poems of Charlotte Smith*, ed. Stuart Curran, 1993, p. 20).

> Already shipwreck'd by the storms of Fate,
>   Like the poor mariner methinks I stand,
>   Cast on a rock; who sees the distant land
> From whence no succour comes—or comes too late.
> Faint and more faint are heard his feeble cries,
> 'Till in the rising tide the exhausted sufferer dies.

10

9 *Already shipwreck'd* The turn begins here, as the speaker begins an extended comparison of her state and that of the distressed mariner – both of them shipwrecked, one by the 'storms of Fate' and the other by the 'troubled sea'.

14 *the exhausted sufferer dies.* Compare the concluding couplet of 'Sonnet XLIV: Written in the church-yard at Middleton in Sussex' (included below) for a similarly dramatic representation of 'life's long storm'.

Sonnet XXX: To the River Arun

Added for the third edition of *Elegiac Sonnets* (1786), this sonnet is one of many of Smith's either located by or addressed to the Arun, the river which flowed through her father's estate at Bignor Park in Sussex (see also sonnets XXVI, XXXII below, XXXIII, and XLV). Smith habitually affiliates the Arun with 'the mournful muse' ('Sonnet XXVI: To the River Arun', l. 3) as well as with the English poets Thomas Otway, William Collins and William Hayley (see notes to ll. 9, 11 and 12 below). Though it is not particularly dramatic, the sonnet's turn here may be read in its shift, with line 9, from describing the poetic attributes of the riverbank in terms of hopeless love and drooping sorrow, to celebrating these specific poets of Smith's local pantheon. Here and elsewhere, Smith's preoccupation with the Arun is furthermore significant for the numerous ways in which it anticipates later sonnets such as Coleridge's 'To the River Otter', which similarly mingles detailed natural observations with highly personalized reflections.

Text follows *1795*.

> BE the proud Thames, of trade the busy mart!
>   Arun! to thee will other praise belong;
> Dear to the lover's, and the mourner's heart,
>   And ever sacred to the sons of song!
>
> Thy banks romantic, hopeless. Love shall seek,
>   Where o'er the rocks the mantling bindwith flaunts;
> And Sorrow's drooping form and faded cheek,
>   Choose on thy willow'd shore her lonely haunts!

5

1 *mart* 'public place for buying and selling'; 'periodical gathering of people for the purposes of buying and selling'.
2 *Arun* See headnote above.
6 *the mantling bindwith* 'The plant Clematis, Bindwith, Virgin's Bower, or Traveller's Joy, which towards the end of June begins to cover the hedges and sides of rocky hollows with its beautiful foliage, and flowers of a yellowish white of an agreeable fragrance; these are succeeded by seed pods, that bear some resemblance to feathers or hair, whence it is sometimes called Old Man's Beard' (Smith's note).

> Banks! which inspir'd thy Otway's plaintive strain!
>   Wilds!—whose lorn echoes learn'd the deeper tone   10
> Of Collins' powerful shell! yet once again
>   Another poet—Hayley is thine own!
> Thy classic stream anew shall hear a lay,
> Bright as its waves, and various as its way!

9 *Otway's plaintive strain* Thomas Otway (1652–85), British dramatist and poet remembered now for two powerful tragedies in blank verse: *The Orphan* (1680) and *Venice Preserv'd* (1681). He was celebrated by the Romantics as a poet of the passions. In a note to 'Sonnet XXVI: To the River Arun', Smith writes:

> Otway was born at Trotten, a village in Sussex. Of Woolbeding, another village on the banks of the Arun (which runs through them both), his father was rector. Here it was, therefore, that he probably passed many of his early years. The Arun is here an inconsiderable stream, winding in a channel deeply worn, among meadow, heath, and wood.
> (Smith's note)

Compare an apostrophe to the Arun in Collins, 'Ode to Pity':

> There first the wren thy myrtles shed
>   On gentle Otway's infant head,
>   To him thy cell was shown;
> And while he sung the female heart,
> With youth's soft notes unspoiled by art,
>   Thy turtles mixed their own.
> (ll. 19–24)

10 *lorn* forlorn; 'abandoned, left alone, bereft'.
11 *Collins's powerful shell* Collins, as well as Otway [see note to l. 9 above], was a native of this country, and probably at some period of his life an inhabitant of this neighbourhood, since in his beautiful 'Ode on the Death of Colonel Ross', he says:

> The muse shall still, with social aid,
> Her gentlest promise keep,
> E'en humble Hearting's cottag'd vale
> Shall learn the sad repeated tale,
> And bid her shepherds weep. [ll. 56–60; Hearting, or Harting, is a village in Sussex.]

And in the 'Ode to Pity':

> Wild Arun too has heard thy strains,
> And Echo, midst my native plains,
> Been sooth'd with Pity's lute. [ll. 16–18]
> (Smith's note)

Collins's 'shell' is to be understood here as a poeticism for lyre; see Collins, 'Ode to Pity': '. . . thou again delight / To hear a British shell!' (ll. 41–2). The poet of *Odes on Several Descriptive and Allegoric Subjects* (1746), William Collins (1721–59) was admired by Smith and other Romantic poets for both the melancholic sensibility and the lyrical intensity that pervade his best-known odes (e.g. 'Ode to Pity', 'Ode to Fear', 'Ode on the Poetical Character').
12 *Hayley* William Hayley (1745–1820) was a popular, prolific poet and a friend of Smith's. He aided her in publishing *Elegiac Sonnets* (he also patronized William Cowper and William Blake), and she dedicated *Elegiac Sonnets* to him. Smith also cites Hayley in her Preface to the first and second editions as an accomplished sonneteer.
13 *lay* 'short lyric poem intended to be sung'.

Sonnet XXXII: To Melancholy.
Written on the banks of the Arun, October 1785

Added for the third edition of *Elegiac Sonnets* (1786), this is another of Smith's attempts 'on the Italian model' of two rhymes in the octave (*abba abba*) and three in the sestet (here, *cdecde*). The turn occurs in this instance as the speaker shifts the setting from the time of an appropriately autumnal evening to a specific place, the 'Here' (l. 9) on the banks of the Arun, which cues her conjuring of Thomas Otway (see headnote to 'Sonnet XXX: To the River Arun' above and note to l. 10 below), whose plaintive 'deep sighs' mark him as another poet of the abstracted 'Melancholy' to whom the poem is addressed. Smith's sense of melancholy may be instructively compared with Keats's in the 'Ode on Melancholy'. In a characteristic meditation on the interwoven relations of joy and sorrow, Keats locates melancholy in the 'temple of Delight' (l. 25) and affiliates it there with beauty, joy, and pleasure:

16 *Charlotte Smith (1749–1806)*

She dwells with Beauty – Beauty that must die;
And Joy, whose hand is ever at his lips
Bidding adieu; and aching Pleasure nigh,
Turning to poison while the bee-mouth sips.
                                    (ll. 21–4)

While Smith does not associate melancholy only with death and oblivion – it is after all the 'magic power' of melancholy that it can 'soothe the pensive visionary mind' – there is no Keatsian elation in her address. As she writes in the preface to the sixth edition of *Elegiac Sonnets* (1792), her 'melancholy lyre' is so strung due to her 'unaffected sorrows': 'I wrote mournfully because I was unhappy – And I have unfortunately no reason yet, though nine years have since elapsed, to *change my tone*'.

Text follows *1795*.

WHEN latest Autumn spreads her evening veil,
   And the grey mists from these dim waves arise,
   I love to listen to the hollow sighs,
Through the half-leafless wood that breathes the gale:
For at such hours the shadowy phantom, pale,   5
   Oft seems to fleet before the poet's eyes;
   Strange sounds are heard, and mournful melodies,
As of night-wanderers, who their woes bewail!
Here, by his native stream, at such an hour,
   Pity's own Otway I methinks could meet,   10
   And hear his deep sighs swell the sadden'd wind!
O Melancholy!—such thy magic power,
   That to the soul these dreams are often sweet,
   And sooth the pensive visionary mind!

1–4 *When latest Autumn . . . breathes the gale* The first quatrain puts in play a pattern of both visual and aural 'images' – the veil of grey mists rising off the river, followed by the hollow sighs breathed by the woods – which will be simultaneously reinforced and complicated in the second quatrain.
4 *breathes* Poetically, the wood here inspires (*inspirare*, to breathe into) the gale, itself in turn the 'breath' of the wood.
5–8 *For at such hours . . . their woes bewail!* Moving from the natural, externally recognizable forms of the river and the woods, the second quatrain depicts the visual in terms of the strange apparition before the poet's eyes, and the aural in terms of the equally strange sounds that the poet hears.

6 *to fleet* 'to float; to drift or be carried by'.
9 *Here, by his native stream* The turn occurs 'here', as the persona (closely affiliated with the poet of l. 6) consolidates the sights and sounds of the octave in the phantom of Otway, himself a poet closely affiliated with pathos (see below, note to l. 10).
10 *Otway* See above, 'Sonnet XXX: To the River Arun', note to line 9.
14 *pensive visionary mind* That the speaker's mind is pensive due to its melancholy is evident enough; that it should be visionary as well is due to the 'magic power' of melancholy to conjure phantoms and produce dreams (in this particular instance, that of Otway).

Sonnet XXXIX: To Night

This sonnet was added for the fifth edition of *Elegiac Sonnets* (1789), after having originally appeared in Smith's first novel, *Emmeline* (1788). Writing to Alexander Dyce in 1830, Wordsworth suggested that, should Dyce's *Specimens of British Poetesses* (1825) go into a second edition, he might add several more of Smith's sonnets, 'particularly "I love thee, mournful, sober-suited night"'. Though Wordsworth says nothing more specifically about this sonnet, there may in fact be an echo of Smith's use of 'viewless wind' [l. 5] in Book 5 of *The Prelude* (see note to l. 8 below). Enmeshed within the sonnet's loose rhyme scheme (*abab cbbc cddc ee*) is a turn at line 9 to what the speaker 'finds' (significantly, the *c* rhyme as it carries over to the sestet), to the solace of resignation in an otherwise 'cheerless' night.

Text follows *1795*.

I LOVE thee, mournful, sober-suited Night!
 When the faint Moon, yet lingering in her wane,
And veil'd in clouds, with pale uncertain light
 Hangs o'er the waters of the restless main.
In deep depression sunk, the enfeebled mind
 Will to the deaf cold elements complain,
 And tell the embosom'd grief, however vain,
To sullen surges and the viewless wind.
Though no repose on thy dark breast I find,
 I still enjoy thee—cheerless as thou art;
 For in thy quiet gloom the exhausted heart
Is calm, though wretched; hopeless, yet resign'd.
While to the winds and waves its sorrows given,
May reach—though lost on earth—the ear of Heaven!

1 *sober-suited Night* Compare Shakespeare, *Romeo and Juliet*, 'Come, civil night, / Thou sober-suited matron, all in black' (III. ii. 10–11).
2 *wane* 'gradual decrease of the visible illuminated area of the moon'.
4 *main* Poeticism for the high sea or open ocean.
7 *And tell* Here, in the sense of to divulge or to disclose (something secret or private).
7 *however vain* The complaints of the 'enfeebled mind' are vain in the sense that they are ineffectual: it is but a vain surmise that the elements (specifically, the 'sullen surges and the viewless wind') will comprehend and, furthermore, sympathize with the speaker's depression and grief.
8 *viewless wind* Compare Wordsworth, *The Prelude* (1850), 'Visionary power / Attends the motions of the viewless winds, / Embodied in the mystery of words' (V, ll. 595–7).
9–14 *Though . . . ear of Heaven!* Repeating 'though' (and the related 'yet') four times in the sestet, the speaker underscores the sonnet's paradoxical comfort: although the night provides 'no repose', 'I still enjoy thee' for the possibility of calm and quiet gloom that is otherwise not even a possibility.

Sonnet XLIV: Written in the church-yard at Middleton in Sussex

Added for the fifth edition of *Elegiac Sonnets* (1789), this sonnet describes a churchyard which also provides the backdrop for Smith's later poem in heroic stanzas, 'Elegy' ('Dark gathering clouds involve the threatening skies . . .'). Elegiac both in its setting and its meditation on the appeal of the 'gloomy rest' of the dead, Smith's sonnet is organized in three envelope quatrains (*abba cddc effe*) followed by a concluding couplet (*gg*). As a result, though it relies on the same number of rhymes as a standard English sonnet, it exploits the framing possibilities inherent in the envelope pattern commonly associated with the structure of the octave in an Italian sonnet (*abba abba*). Especially in the first quatrain, the external rhymes enclose the internal sounds and unify the quatrain's statement: thus the 'tides' ride over the 'shrinking land' and consequently 'confine' it according to the power of their own 'swelling surge'.

Text follows *1795*.

PRESS'D by the Moon, mute arbitress of tides,
 While the loud equinox its power combines,
 The sea no more its swelling surge confines,
But o'er the shrinking land sublimely rides.

Title 'Middleton is a village on the margin of the sea, in Sussex, containing only two or three houses. There were formerly several acres of ground between its small church and the sea, which now, by its continual encroachments, approaches within a few feet of this half-ruined and humble edifice. The wall, which once surrounded the church-yard, is entirely swept away, many of the graves broken up, and the remains of the bodies interred washed into the sea: whence human bones are found among the sand and shingles on the shore' (Smith's note).
1 *arbitress* The feminine of 'arbiter', one who settles disputes; in this instance, the 'mute' moon, which presides over the tidal patterns most pressingly at the time of the 'loud equinox'. See Milton, *Paradise Lost*, 'while overhead the moon / Sits arbitress' (I, ll. 784–5).
4 *sublimely* A critical heading of Romantic aesthetics, the 'sublime' here denominates the categorically irresistible power with which the sea overwhelms the vulnerable mainland.

The wild blast, rising from the Western cave, 5
    Drives the huge billows from their heaving bed;
    Tears from their grassy tombs the village dead,
And breaks the silent sabbath of the grave!
With shells and sea-weed mingled, on the shore
    Lo! their bones whiten in the frequent wave; 10
    But vain to them the winds and waters rave;
They hear the warring elements no more:
While I am doom'd—by life's long storm opprest,
To gaze with envy on their gloomy rest.

12 *no more* Though their bones 'whiten in the frequent wave', the churchyard dead are impervious to the waves which 'rave' across the dwindling shore; thus the 'no more' which concludes this quatrain manages to enclose and close down the power of the 'wave / rave' rhyme.

13 *While I am doom'd* The turn occurs here, as the speaker shifts from '*They*' to 'I' and juxtaposes, however paradoxically, the 'gloomy rest' of the dead (despite the violence visited upon their bodily remains) with her own conviction of being 'doom'd—by life's long storm opprest'.

William Blake (1757–1827)

William Blake is a poet-painter who combines visionary intensity with a fierce, vigilant alertness to the politics of his time. Like a number of figures in English Romanticism, he hailed from a Dissenting background. For the typical Dissenting emphasis on conscience, Blake substitutes what is, in effect a religion based on art; he brings to his work a strong if at times embattled trust in his own creativity. His alter-ego, Los, a blacksmith and poetic surrogate, asserts in *Jerusalem*, a complex epic poem concerned with sustaining an imaginative vision in a dark time, 'I must Create a System, or be enslav'd by another Mans / I will not Reason & Compare: my business is to Create' (10, ll. 20–1).[1] Blake's 'System' has been the subject of much analysis. Essentially it consists of a growing trust in the Imagination as a means of renewing a sense of human possibility in an age preoccupied with physical warfare, industrial development and an acceptance of a Lockean–Newtonian view of the mind and the world. However, Blake sees human beings and societies as involved in continual 'Mental Fight' (Preface to *Milton*, l. 13; *E*, p. 95), so in a sense he does not wish to repose in or on a 'System', but rather to be engaged continually in the process of creating. His adversaries were external: the epistemology of Locke which restricted knowledge to that received through the corporeal senses, until, as Blake has it in *The Marriage of Heaven and Hell* (1793), 'man has closed himself up, till he sees all things thro' narrow chinks of his cavern' (*E*, p. 39); the cosmology of Newton, which resulted in a separation between the human and a universe now conceived as running like clockwork on determining laws; and the cruelties of an increasingly urbanized and mercantilist culture which sent young children out to clean chimneys and usually to succumb to early death, turned in many instances a blind eye to the barbaric practice of slavery (at the heart of which were the great ports of Bristol and Liverpool), and glossed over its faults with an unctuous, hypocritical appeal to religion.

However, Blake's adversaries were also internal; he possessed to an extraordinary degree the ability to hear and represent different viewpoints. As Michael Mason points out, Blake is 'the great anti-simplifier, always probing for contradiction, especially self-contradiction'.[2] For Los to prevail in *Jerusalem*, he must subdue and work with his Spectre, that side of him which doubts and questions. The Spectre is never wholly banished, and Blake's invention of him is testimony to his ability to shape a homespun myth that does justice to the complexity of the artist's task. Indeed, Blake involves his readers and viewers in a constantly active engagement with his words and designs. From his first major collection, *Songs of Innocence* (1789), through to his late engravings, *The Book of Job* (1821), and his illustrations to Dante's *The Divine Comedy* (1824), Blake invites us to wrestle with possible interpretations. He reminds us that meaning is always inter-subjective, that it is always made, constructed by the mind; at the same time, he draws our attention to the many traps into which we can fall when assigning meaning. As a result he is not only a visionary but also a satirist and an ironist, in works such as *The Marriage of Heaven and Hell*, where his dazzling dialectic rarely allows us to pin down his tones. That interest in dialectic extends to his practice of producing illuminated books, which gave him total control over the production and dissemination of his work, and allowed him to set texts and images into sometimes intricate relationship with one another.

Blake spent most of his life in London, where he was born in 1757, the son of a hosier. He married Catherine Boucher, daughter of a poor market gardener, in 1782, and worked as an artist, being apprenticed to James Basire, an engraver, in 1772 before he was admitted in 1779 as a student to the Royal Academy. He knew leading artists of the time, including John Flaxman, but he developed a unique visual style, neoclassical in its sweeping lines, arresting in its representation of deep primary feeling. His work reflects the ferment of the revolutionary age. After meeting the Swiss painter Henry Fuseli around 1787, Blake probably met various political radicals of the time such as Mary Wollstonecraft, author of *A Vindication of the Rights of Woman* (1792). Politically the mood of the country darkened after the execution of Louis XVI in 1793, the commencement of the Reign of Terror in France, and France's invasion of Switzerland. Blake's own political mood in the mid-1790s can be gauged by the tonalities of his later so-called Lambeth Prophecies, the poems written in 1794 and 1795, including *The First Book of Urizen* (included below), a poem which deals with the subject of tyranny, employs a coded satirical method, and articulates pessimism about the possibility of escape from restriction. The figure of Orc, a flaming spirit of

---

1   Quoted from *The Complete Poetry and Prose of William Blake*, ed. David V. Erdman, newly rev. edn. (New York: Doubleday, 1988); hereafter *E*.
2   *William Blake*, ed. Michael Mason (Oxford: Oxford University Press, 1985), p. xv.

rebellion in a work such as *America*, seems to turn into the repressive character of Urizen, and Blake is haunted, henceforward, by the ease with which desire can be restrained. The topic, with all its intra-psychic, religious and political implications, is central to the three great poems of his maturity: the never finished *Vala* or *The Four Zoas* (c. 1796–1807), *Milton* (c. 1804–1810), and *Jerusalem* (1804–20).

Blake found it difficult at times to earn a living through the commercial engravings for which he sometimes received commissions. In 1800 he and Catherine left London to live in a cottage near the home of William Hayley in Felpham, near Chichester. Hayley was a wealthy man of letters who would act as Blake's patron for a number of years, a patronage that soon grew intolerable for Blake. Characteristically alluding to the Gospels in support of his understanding of the importance of the imaginative life, Blake sums up the relationship thus: 'Christ is very decided on this Point. "He who is Not With Me is Against Me" There is no Medium or Middle state & if a Man is the Enemy of My Spiritual Life while he pretends to be the Friend of my Corporeal. he is a Real Enemy' (*E*, p. 728). Blake's Pickering Manuscript poems (two of which, 'The Mental Traveller' and 'The Crystal Cabinet', are included below) may date from this period, a period made more stressful for the poet in 1803 by an accusation brought by a soldier, John Scholfield, whom Blake had thrown out of his garden, that led to a charge of sedition (Blake was acquitted in 1804). After Felpham, Blake and Catherine returned to London where they lived in 17 South Moulton Street, near Oxford Street. Blake made some attempts to exhibit his visual work, but with little success, though figures such as Coleridge and Wordsworth began to learn about and admire his poetry and designs, especially the *Songs of Innocence and of Experience*. In his later years, Blake enjoyed the support of a group of younger artists such as Samuel Palmer, whom he strongly influenced.

Further Reading

Primary Texts

The Complete Poetry and Prose of William Blake, ed. David V. Erdman, commentary by Harold Bloom (1965; rev. edn, New York: Doubleday, 1982).

The Poems of William Blake, ed. W. H. Stevenson, Longman Annotated English Poets (1971; 3rd edn, London: Longman, 2007).

The Illuminated Books of William Blake, gen. ed. David Bindman (Tate Gallery/Princeton University Press, 1991–): vol. 1, *Songs of Innocence and of Experience*, ed. Andrew Lincoln (1991); vol. 3, *The Early Illuminated Books*, ed. Morris Eaves, Robert N. Essick and Joseph Viscomi (1993); vol. 6, *The Urizen Books*, ed. David Worrall (1995).

Selected Poetry and Prose, ed. David Fuller (Harlow, UK: Longman, 2000).

Secondary Texts

David V. Erdman, *Prophet Against Empire* (1954; 3rd edn, Princeton, NJ: Princeton University Press, 1977).

Michael Ferber, *The Poetry of William Blake* (Princeton, NJ: Princeton University Press, 1991).

Northrop Frye, *Fearful Symmetry. A Study of William Blake* (Princeton, NJ: Princeton University Press, 1947).

David Fuller, *Blake's Heroic Argument* (London: Croom Helm, 1988).

Heather Glen, *Vision and Disenchantment: Blake's 'Songs' and Wordsworth's 'Lyrical Ballads'* (Cambridge, UK: Cambridge University Press, 1983).

Christopher Heppner, *Reading Blake's Designs* (Cambridge, UK: Cambridge University Press, 1995).

Edward Larrissy, *William Blake* (Oxford: Blackwell, 1985).

Zachary Leader, *Reading Blake's 'Songs'* (London: Routledge, 1981).

John Lucas (ed.), *William Blake*, Longman Critical Readers (London: Longman, 1998).

Morton D. Paley, *Energy and the Imagination: A Study of the Development of Blake's Thought* (Oxford: Clarendon Press, 1970).

Morton D. Paley, *The Continuing City: William Blake's 'Jerusalem'* (Oxford: Clarendon Press, 1983).

Jon Mee, *Dangerous Enthusiasm: William Blake and the Culture of Radicalism in the 1790s* (Oxford: Oxford University Press, 1992).

Michael O'Neill, 'And I stain'd the water clear: Blake', in *Romanticism and the Self-Conscious Poem* (Oxford: Oxford University Press, 1997), pp. 3–24.

Kathleen Raine, *Blake and Tradition*, 2 vols (Princeton, NJ: Princeton University Press, 1968).

Songs of Innocence and of Experience

Songs of Innocence (26 copies surviving) was published as a separate volume in 1789, though versions of three poems had already appeared in Blake's often satirical work *An Island in the Moon* (1784). *Songs of Experience* (four copies surviving) was being advertised for sale in 1793. *Songs of Innocence and of Experience* (24 copies surviving) was published in 1794. The order of the poems varies considerably, and two poems – 'The

School Boy' and 'The Voice of the Ancient Bard' – shift from *Innocence* to *Experience*. The book is produced according to Blake's method of illuminated printing, which probably involved Blake working directly on a copper plate in an acid-resistant medium. Immersion in acid left the design in relief, and this design was used to produce the final image on an etching press. The method resulted in different colouring in each copy; it gave Blake control over the means of producing his work. The defining purpose of the joint volume is 'Shewing the Two Contrary States of the Human Soul'. States of soul are enacted and explored in the poetry which, for all its apparently instructive, even hymn-like, simplicity, is always challengingly open to interpretation. One reason for this is that the poetry is fascinated by 'point of view'. This fascination underlies the existence of a number of poems with the same title in *Innocence* and *Experience*. The title-page shows a male figure and a female figure wearing fig-leaves engulfed in flame, resembling Adam and Eve after the Fall, driven out of Eden; the woman lies on the floor; the man is bent down, head in hands, but sheltering the woman. Above them, more suggestive of hope, a bird flies upwards.[3]

Songs of Innocence

Frontispiece design   A bare-footed youth wearing a blue-violet, flesh-tight costume and with a pipe held in his hands walks between a frame of two trees, looking upward at a child who, naked but for a loincloth, floats overhead. The child is haloed by gold cloud and smiles down at the piper (who does not smile). Behind the piper a flock of sheep grazes. The picture illustrates the harmony of Innocence and the inspiration afforded the piper by the child.

Title-page design   To the left of a tree a nurse or mother with a white bonnet and in a red-violet dress sits on an upright chair, with a book open on her lap; a boy and a girl stand at her lap, the girl seeming to turn a page. The theme of instruction of the young by the adult is to the fore. It is difficult to read the woman's expression, but her posture, though straight-backed, is not unkind in appearance; the children appear eager to learn. Uncertainty about what the future holds hovers over the design.

Introduction

The poem, five quatrains of trochaic tetrameters rhyming *abab*, introduces the *Songs of Innocence* by addressing explicitly the process of 'Piping songs' (l. 2) or making poetry. The tone is largely joyful, but the poem begins by separating the speaker from 'a child' (l. 3) as though to concede, however quietly, the gap between adulthood and childhood. These are songs *of* innocence, sometimes voiced, it seems, by a poet who knows of considerations that challenge innocence. The child's initial weeping in response to the 'song about a Lamb' (l. 5) is unexplained until 'he wept to hear' (l. 8) is rephrased as 'he wept with joy to hear' (l. 12): the momentary doubt about the cause of the weeping hangs in the poem's air, never fully dispelled, since it links with other suggestions that the writing down of songs involves loss as well as the granting of relative permanence. After the injunctions to the speaker, first to pipe his songs, then to sing them without musical accompaniment, and then to 'sit thee down and write / In a book' (ll. 13–14), the child 'vanish'd from my sight' (l. 15), a vanishing preceded by the word 'So', as if to imply that the vanishing of the child was connected with the writing of a book. As always with *Songs of Innocence*, the reader has to decide how much weight to attach to shadows that chase across the sunny surfaces of the poetry; should we, for instance, make much, or anything, of the fact that the pen with which the poet writes is made from a 'hollow reed' (l. 16)? Is the hollowness merely literal? Again, does the fact that the speaker 'stain'd the water clear' (l. 18), probably alluding to the poet's mode of producing his illuminated manuscripts, have any further suggestions of sullying (or enriching) an original clarity? Overall, the mood is celebratory, one of 'merry chear' (l. 6); yet, despite the assertively positive close, the questions and suggestions noted above may remain in the reader's mind.

Design   The title is written and underlined in gold. It is framed by coils and loops on either side in a Tree of Jesse style that form in each case four full oval-shaped windows. The Tree of Jesse depicts the descent of Christ from Jesse, father of David; the allusion to this motif may lend support to the Christian resonances in *Songs of Innocence*. Depicted in each window are scenes appropriate to Innocence: an exuberant figure dancing (left, second from top), for example, or a bird flying upward (right, top). A streams flows at the foot of the design.

---

3   References to the designs are to those in the King's College, Cambridge copy of *Songs* as presented in facsimile in William Blake, *Songs of Innocence and of Experience*, ed. with intro. and notes Andrew Lincoln (Princeton, NJ: The William Blake Trust/Princeton University Press, 1991).

William Blake (1757–1827)

Piping down the valleys wild,
Piping songs of pleasant glee
On a cloud I saw a child
And he laughing said to me.

Pipe a song about a Lamb: 5
So I piped with merry chear,
Piper, pipe that song again—
So I piped, he wept to hear.

Drop thy pipe, thy happy pipe,
Sing thy songs of happy chear; 10
So I sung the same again
While he wept with joy to hear.

Piper, sit thee down and write
In a book that all may read—
So he vanish'd from my sight, 15
And I pluck'd a hollow reed,

And I made a rural pen,
And I stain'd the water clear,
And I wrote my happy songs
Every child may joy to hear. 20

4 *laughing* Laughter is a common feature of the *Songs of Innocence*.
5 *Lamb* Blake's capital letter, in the context of *Songs of Innocence*, might justify the discovery of an allusion to Christ as a 'Lamb' (see 'The Lamb' below).
6 *So* The first use of a conjunction that grows in importance in the poem, since it implies a casual link between events: see also lines 8, 11, and, most significantly, 15.
15–20 *So he vanish'd . . . to hear* The lines involve a series of strongly active verbs, but conclude with the more conditional 'may joy to hear'.

The Ecchoing Green

The poem is among those lyrics in *Songs of Innocence* which seem to look across the fence that divides Innocence from Experience. The 'darkening Green' (l. 30) of the close might simply herald the inevitable end of a daily cycle which will restart again next morning when 'The Sun does arise, / And make happy the skies' (ll. 1–2). But it might hint in a more sombre way at the end of innocence and childhood, and imply the onset of a more troubled phase of life. The poem typifies the suggestiveness of Blake's lyric manner. In three stanzas, each of 10 lines (five short-lined couplets, each line made up of two feet, normally an iamb followed by an anapaest), 'The Ecchoing Green', spoken by a child, moves from welcoming the start of the day, through recording the recollections of 'the old folk' (l. 14), to the coming of bedtime and night. The poem's temporal shifts are significant and can be charted with reference to the refrain-like final couplet of the three stanzas. In the first stanza, the child looks forward to the new day in which 'our sports shall be seen / On the Ecchoing Green' (ll. 9–10); in the second, the old folk look back to their youth when their 'joys' (17) 'were seen / On the Ecchoing Green' (19–20); and in the last stanza the children's sport is 'no more seen / On the darkening Green' (ll. 29–30).

The switch from 'Ecchoing' implying modes of harmony to 'darkening' in the final line has a potentially chilling impact; whereas 'Ecchoing' locates its activity in a secure present, 'darkening' leans forward into the future, suggesting an ongoing process of getting darker. The semantic content of the final rhyme – saying that sports were no longer seen on the darkening green – is at odds with the previous sense, betokened by the chime of 'seen' and 'Green', that all is well in the child's world.

Design There are two plates. In the first, containing the opening stanza and the first four lines of the second, the plate divides into two halves. The lower half contains the text and title. There are boyish figures either side of the text; on the left hand a boy holds a bat; on the right hand a boy rolls a hoop. Budding vegetation, possibly sexual in implication, is also present. The upper half shows a dense oak tree. To the left two boys are playing with a bat and ball; on the right, three youthful figures are standing, seeming to watch the game. Seated below the tree (from left to right) are a youthful mother or nurse with a child at her knee, a white-haired male figure wearing a blue hat who is presumably 'Old

John' (l. 11), one further mother or nurse with children at her knee, and a final mother or nurse who wears a purple dress and has a child on her lap as well as one at her knee. The scene suggests continuity between the generations and a collective harmony under the protective dark-green shade of the tree. In the second plate, containing in its top half the remaining six lines of stanza 2 and all of stanza 3, Blake depicts two boys; one (on the left), standing, picks grapes; the other one (on the right), reclining, hands a bunch of grapes to a girl in a red-pink bonnet below who reaches up her left arm to take them. There is a suggestion in these images of adolescent sexuality. The girl is the last in a train of youthful figures including a boy with a kite and a boy with a bat guided home by 'old John' who is at the centre of the design, his right arm pointing towards the setting sun. A stream flows at the foot of the design. The picture is extremely attractive in its mixture of colours, and does not wholly tally with the foreboding mood conjured up in the text's final lines.

Plate 1   The Ecchoing Green. Reproduced courtesy of King's College, Cambridge.

> The Sun does arise,
> And make happy the skies.
> The merry bells ring,
> To welcome the Spring.
> The sky-lark and thrush,   5
> The birds of the bush,
> Sing louder around,
> To the bells' chearful sound,
> While our sports shall be seen
> On the Ecchoing Green.   10

4   *To welcome* Governed by 'ring' (l. 3), this infinitive suggests a purposefulness; the human and the natural are allied.
9   *While* The word intimates a present tense; in so doing, it contrasts with the words used in the same position in the next two stanzas: 'In our youth time' (l. 19), where 'In' places us in the past, and the enigmatic 'And' in line 29, which may or may not indicate a straightforward connection with the fact that the children 'Are ready for rest' (l. 28).

24 William Blake (1757–1827)

>Old John with white hair
>Does laugh away care,
>Sitting under the oak,
>Among the old folk.
>They laugh at our play, 15
>And soon they all say,
>Such such were the joys
>When we all, girls and boys,
>In our youth time were seen
>On the Ecchoing Green. 20
>
>Till the little ones weary
>No more can be merry;
>The sun does descend,
>And our sports have an end:
>Round the laps of their mothers 25
>Many sisters and brothers,
>Like birds in their nest,
>Are ready for rest;
>And sport no more seen
>On the darkening Green. 30

11–12 *Old John . . . care* The notion of 'care' is brought into the poem, even as it is 'laughed away'.
15 *laugh at* Presumably in a good-natured, friendly way.
17 *Such such . . . joys* Turns the present 'joys' into something more representative and typical, and, therefore, subject to adult awareness of the passage of time.
21–2 *Till . . . merry* The rhyme of 'weary' and 'merry' might almost pinpoint the relationship between innocence and experience; at the same time, the weariness is the natural consequence of a day spent in play.
25–6 *Round . . . brothers* Evokes the security of the family group.
27 *Like . . . nest* Recalls the first stanza's reference to 'The birds of the bush' (l. 6), though here for the only time in the poem Blake uses a simile, a form of speech that often implies difference in the act of asserting a connection.

The Lamb

The poem is written in two stanzas of 10 lines, each stanza containing five rhyming couplets, the first and last couplets rhyming on themselves. The metre is trochaic, with four stresses to the line. Blake asks questions about the creation of the Lamb, giving the answer in the second stanza which alludes to God's incarnation as a human being and his identity in Christian thought as a 'Lamb', betokening his sacrifice on behalf of humanity. If there is an allusion to Christ's suffering, it is made very delicately. The poem uses apparently simple devices of repetition and identification to bind together speaker, lamb, and God in a vision of unity that has its own intricacy. The poem's 'opposite' in *Songs of Experience* is 'The Tyger'.

Design The design largely supports the text's trust in a protective universe. At the foot is a stream; above it a young boy holds out his right hand and possibly his left hand, too, to a lamb for it to lick; sheep nestle behind them. To the right is a yellow-thatched barn or cottage; just right of centre, offering the animals shade when they need it, is a low, wide-spreading oak tree. Overarching the poem and the scene are two thin trees, circled by vines, which rise from left and right and interweave their branches at the top of the picture. Bluish shade above the cottage or barn might suggest gathering clouds, but the mood is mainly serene.

>Little Lamb, who made thee?
>Dost thou know who made thee,
>Gave thee life and bid thee feed
>By the stream and o'er the mead;
>Gave thee clothing of delight, 5

Softest clothing, wooly bright;
Gave thee such a tender voice.
Making all the vales rejoice?
   Little Lamb, who made thee?
   Dost thou know who made thee?   10

Little Lamb, I'll tell thee,
Little Lamb I'll tell thee;
He is called by thy name,
For he calls himself a Lamb:
He is meek and he is mild,   15
He became a little child:
I a child and thou a lamb,
We are called by his name.
   Little Lamb, God bless thee,
   Little Lamb, God bless thee.   20

7–8 *voice ... rejoice* Another example in the *Songs of Innocence* of rhyme as a means of creating a sense of harmony.

11–12 *I'll tell thee ... I'll tell thee* The speaker does identify the lamb's creator, but he does so indirectly. 'God' is named only in the last two lines, and then it is understood, not stated, that he is the creator.

13–14 *called ... calls* The circularity here is noteworthy; the lamb's creator 'calls himself' the name by which he is 'called'. The lines look ahead to line 18 when 'We are called by his name'.

The Little Black Boy

The poem is spoken by a black child; though it never mentions slavery by name, it depends for its effect on the knowledge that trafficking in people was still lawful. In this poem, the child's innocence cannot disguise the cruelty of a world that judges humans in terms of the colour of their skin. Blake suggests that the child has interiorized socially generated feelings of inferiority, and displays 'a state of the soul' that is both impressive and touching; the child's innocence shows in his capacity for trust in his mother's teaching and admiration for the 'little English boy' (l. 22); his openness to exploitation is equally evident, however. In effect, the child's mother indoctrinates her son into accepting the trials of this life because of a belief in God's goodness. For the mother, skin-colour, for which it is hinted she, too has suffered, is part of a system of binaries: black/white, body/soul, earth/heaven. On this view of things, bodies are but clouds which will 'vanish' (l. 18) when we are ready to rejoin God in an afterlife. Though there is the suggestion that black bodies are better able than white ones to withstand the 'beams of love' (l. 14) emitted by a sun-like God, it is clear from the opening stanza that the boy has learned to regard his blackness as inferior; he is 'black as if bereav'd of light' (l. 4). By locating the action of the poem in the child's speech, Blake allows us to see the kinds of language use to which the boy has already been subjected. At the same time, innocence is clearly also a quality highly valued by the poem: innocence has an intrinsic goodness, conveyed through the even-paced movement of the quatrains. Their air of trusting exposition serves as a balm for feelings of hurt. Our view of the boy's modes of understanding and the mother's forms of comfort is sympathetic, even if we feel they are the subject of restrained critique on Blake's part.

Design There are two plates, the first containing stanzas one to four and including in its top third a scene that illustrates the second stanza in particular; it depicts the little black boy (naked) and his partially dressed mother sitting beneath a tree that shades them from the rays of a fiery rising sun, surrounded by a purple aurora and golden rays. In the second plate, containing the final three stanzas, there is in the lower half a scene that focuses in particular on the poem's last six lines: a Christ-like figure with white robes and a shepherd's crook sits beneath a willow tree at the edge of a stream; before him, hands raised in prayer, is the little white boy; behind the white boy is the little black boy in the act of presenting the white boy to the Christ-like figure. In this plate the colours are cool; in the former plate they are fiery. The plates can be read in different ways, thus supporting the interpretative activity set going by the plate: the fiery sun might, for example, be read as 'hell-like', from one (a false) perspective; the fact that both boys still have bodies in the second plate might bear on our understanding of what it means to be 'free' (l. 23).

Plate 2 The Little Black Boy. Reproduced courtesy of King's College, Cambridge.

> My mother bore me in the southern wild,
> And I am black, but O! my soul is white.
> White as an angel is the English child:
> But I am black as if bereav'd of light.
>
> My mother taught me underneath a tree   5
> And sitting down before the heat of day,
> She took me on her lap and kissed me,
> And pointing to the east began to say.
>
> Look on the rising sun: there God does live
> And gives his light, and gives his heat away.   10
> And flowers and trees and beasts and men recieve
> Comfort in morning, joy in the noon day.
>
> And we are put on earth a little space,
> That we may learn to bear the beams of love;

1 *southern wild* Suggests that the mother and child have been transported from their native land, presumably as slaves.
2 *And ... white* The opposition between 'black' and 'white' corresponds to a further split between body and soul. The exclamation ' but O!' speaks eloquently of the boy's acculturated sense that 'whiteness' is superior to 'blackness'.
3–4 *White ... light* The stanza ends with the boy's feeling of inferiority to 'the English child' on the grounds of skin-colour; the attempted assertion in line 2 has failed to reassure him. Indeed, lines 2 to 4 form a chiasmus that brings the boy back to the fact of his blackness: 'I am black' (A); but 'my soul is white' (B); the English child is 'White as an angel' (B); 'But I am black' (A).
5 *underneath a tree* As often in Blake, the 'tree' provides a shade that shades into shadiness, mystification.
7 *She ... kissed me* The line suggests that the mother's motive for her teaching, however contestable that teaching is, is love for her child.
13 *And ... space* For the mother, life is essentially preparation; it seems probable that Blake is sympathetically ironizing a particular form of accommodating oneself to the injustices of existence.

And these black bodies and this sunburnt face 15
Is but a cloud, and like a shady grove.

For when our souls have learn'd the heat to bear
The cloud will vanish; we shall hear his voice,
Saying: Come out from the grove, my love and care,
And round my golden tent like lambs rejoice. 20

Thus did my mother say and kissed me.
And thus I say to little English boy,
When I from black and he from white cloud free,
And round the tent of God like lambs we joy,

I'll shade him from the heat till he can bear 25
To lean in joy upon our father's knee.
And then I'll stand and stroke his silver hair,
And be like him and he will then love me.

17–20 *For when ... rejoice* The stanza evokes a biblical sense of God as speaking words of comfort and hope to those who believe in him; the 'golden tent' serves as a metaphor for the heavenly state. It is hard to provide precise biblical parallels, but one might compare Luke 3:22: 'and a voice came from heaven, which said, Thou art my beloved Son; in thee I am well pleased'.
22 *And thus ... English boy* 'Thus' appears to mean that the little black boy spoke to the English boy in the way that his mother spoke to him. But it could also mean that the following lines (22–8) are the substance of what he says.

The line uses a linguistic device characteristic of non-standard English in its omission of an article before 'little English boy'.
25–8 *I'll shade ... love me* The stanza, enjambed from its predecessor, focuses on the future; despite the attempt in line 23 to imply equality, the little black boy is evidently in need of a sign from the white boy that the latter loves him. The final line has much pathos as it expresses the black boy's wish to 'be like him' and the hope that he 'will then love me', where 'then' expresses the black boy's current sense of not being loved.

The Chimney Sweeper

This is another song of innocence that clearly knows about harsh realities: in this case, the realities of children working in appalling conditions as chimney sweeps. Again, the lyric is not a simple protest poem, though contemporary readers would have been aware of Porter's petition of 1788, which attempted to make the conditions of sweeps less inhumane; it was accepted by Parliament but the proposed Act was, in the end, never passed. The name Tom Dacre may allude, possibly with ironic intent, to the Lady Ann Dacre Houses for foundlings in Westminster. The first stanza spells out the oppression involved in a child being sold, but like the poem as a whole it concentrates on the speaker's state of mind. Despite the hint of criticism in the fourth line, the speaker describes what has happened to him without bitterness or recrimination; the 'When' of the first line suggests that the early death of the mother and the being sold by the father in early boyhood are events that do not require an embittered gloss. His focus is on caring for others; hence the comfort he offers Tom Dacre in the second stanza. In fact, the poem's method of presentation is layered; from the speaker's own kind of innocence it moves to Tom's, embodied in his dream (communicated to us by the older sweep) of release and liberation. Tom's vision has at its centre a boyish longing caught in the vitality of phrases such as 'leaping, laughing' (l. 15), but we note that the speaker is at a distance from it: 'they run' (l. 15) excludes him. As elsewhere the process of acculturation is captured, Tom or the speaker on his behalf repeating words in lines 19 and 20 whose controlling force is apparent. The gap between speaker and Tom is especially noticeable in the final stanza, where the speaker says that, despite the cold morning, 'Tom was happy and warm' (l. 23); this gap does not imply, however, that the speaker has a cynical or detached view of Tom. The speaker's innocence takes the form of concerning himself with others (here the contrast with the *Experience* poem 'The Chimney-Sweeper' is marked). The poem's final assertion of a moral may suggest both a further example of adult indoctrination and the speaker's innocence, his trust in a world where the performance of 'duty' (l. 24) is rewarded by a benevolent God. At the same time, 'they need not fear harm' (l. 24) speaks out of the chimney sweep's knowledge of 'harm'. Throughout, Blake uses rhythm and tone with admirable restraint and eloquence. The rhythm is a blend of anapaests and iambs, and is responsible for nuanced effects: the fourth line's approach to condemnation, for example, in the half-stressed use of 'your' in 'your chimneys'; or the pathos of the comfort offered by the speaker to the shaven-headed 'Tom' in lines 7 to 8; or the lilt of line 10 with the colloquial 'such a sight' suited both to the speaker and to Tom.

Design Most of the design consists of the text surrounded by vines and leaves. At the bottom, evidently illustrating stanza 4, is a picture of a haloed figure in pale blue raising a child from a coffin; to the left pairs of naked boys play on the green bank of a river. The boys are touched with gold, especially the head of the child freed from the coffin.

When my mother died I was very young,
And my father sold me while yet my tongue
Could scarcely cry weep weep weep weep,
So your chimneys I sweep and in soot I sleep.

There's little Tom Dacre, who cried when his head   5
That curl'd like a lamb's back, was shav'd, so I said
Hush Tom, never mind it, for when your head's bare,
You know that the soot cannot spoil your white hair.

And so he was quiet, and that very night
As Tom was a sleeping he had such a sight,   10
That thousands of sweepers, Dick, Joe, Ned and Jack,
Were all of them lock'd up in coffins of black,

And by came an Angel who had a bright key
And he open'd the coffins and set them all free.
Then down a green plain leaping, laughing, they run   15
And wash in a river and shine in the Sun.

Then naked and white, all their bags left behind,
They rise upon clouds, and sport in the wind;
And the Angel told Tom, if he'd be a good boy,
He'd have God for his father and never want joy.   20

And so Tom awoke and we rose in the dark
And got with our bags and our brushes to work.
Though the morning was cold, Tom was happy and warm;
So if all do their duty, they need not fear harm.

1 *When . . . young* Much of the poem's effect derives from this line, which would read more stridently or self-pityingly if Blake had written: 'My mother died when I was very young'.
2–3 *And . . . weep* 'Weep weep' is the child's version of the sweeper's cry for business ('sweep sweep'); it also suggests that his plight is a matter of tears (his and ours), and yet the grave expository tone holds tears at bay; this speaker is decidedly not breaking up his lines to weep.
5–6 *There's . . . said* Tom does cry, and Blake's use of the long line allows us to see the beauty ('his head / That curl'd like a lamb's back') that has been brutally cropped; 'so I said' uses 'so' to convey the speaker's instinct to comfort and protect.
9 *And so* Again, 'so' implies a comforting causal chain, as it will do, a little more disturbingly, at line 21.
13 *And . . . key* The line, like the stanza of which it is part, runs on from the previous stanza, in keeping with Tom's dream of freedom.
19–20 *And . . . joy* Here the child's dream of freedom criss-crosses with a social discourse that uneasily combines the prospect of hope with the hint of something more punitive.

Holy Thursday

The poem, which has a darker counterpart in *Songs of Experience*, describes a speaker's response to the sight of children from charity schools in London entering St Paul's Cathedral. This service, introduced in 1782, was held on the first Thursday of May. The children would be led in by beadles (parish officers). The speaker sees the children as 'innocent' (l. 8), implying his adult vantage-point, and there has been debate about how to characterize his response: is he percep- tively sympathetic or complacent? Much depends on one's sense of the final line, where, as in 'The Chimney Sweeper', a moral injunction is offered. Does Blake, elsewhere critical of 'pity' since it involves unequal power relations, believe that the command to 'cherish pity' (l. 12) is, in context, an admirable maxim? Or does he suggest the latent injustice of a social and educational system where children are in need of charity and pity? The poem evokes both the regimented nature of the procession (the children are 'walking two and two', l. 2), and the almost awe-inspiring power of the children's presence: they are associated figuratively with a natural force in line 4 and in lines 9 and 10; though 'Seated in companies', they possess 'radiance all their own' (l. 6). In the first stanza they enter St Paul's; in the second they are described sitting in the cathedral; in the third they are depicted singing. The poem's rhythm has a majestic but subtle impressiveness, deriving from a long line that uses two- and three-stress feet, and often begins with stressed feet, thus making the line more emphatic.

Design The plate contains the poem; above it two beadles in blue garments, one carrying a stick ('wand'), lead regimented pairs of boys wearing blue, green and red clothes; below it, pairs of girls, walking in the opposite direction (right to left), follow a matronly figure who wears black and holds a book.

> Twas on a Holy Thursday, their innocent faces clean,
> The children walking two and two in red and blue and green,
> Grey-headed beadles walk'd before with wands as white as snow,
> Till into the high dome of Paul's they like Thames' waters flow
>
> O what a multitude they seem'd, these flowers of London town!   5
> Seated in companies they sit with radiance all their own.
> The hum of multitudes was there, but multitudes of lambs,
> Thousands of little boys and girls raising their innocent hands.
>
> Now like a mighty wind they raise to heaven the voice of song
> Or like harmonious thunderings the seats of heaven among.   10
> Beneath them sit the aged men, wise guardians of the poor;
> Then cherish pity, lest you drive an angel from your door.

1 *innocent faces clean* The children have been well-scrubbed for the day's outing, the first hint of their institutionalized status.
3 *Grey-headed beadles ... snow* A differentiation between the appearance of children and their beadles is brought out, but any implication of moral difference is left unstated.
5 *O what ... town* The speaker's exclamation makes clear his admiration for the children's beauty; whether he is guilty of simply seeing them in aesthetic terms, as 'flowers of London town', is another interpretative issue.
9 *Now ... song* The line has the more force for building on yet redirecting the description of 'Thousands of little boys and girls' (l. 8); here the children's genuine power emerges as their song is compared to 'a mighty wind', often linked in Romantic poetry with inspiration. Blake might also have been influenced by Acts 2: 2, where the coming of the Holy Spirit is described 'as of a rushing mighty wind'. The wording of 'raise to heaven' may momentarily provoke the question whether the children not only pray, but also challenge the arrangements seemingly countenanced by 'heaven'.
11 *Beneath ... poor* The 'guardians' are said to be 'wise', surely an unironic judgement on the speaker's part; but he does note that they sit 'Beneath' the children, a preposition which may have a moral as well as a physical meaning.
12 *Then cherish ... door* Offered, it would seem, with well-meaning sincerity by the speaker, but Blake may invite us to think that it suits the speaker to discharge any latent discomfort induced by the scene in this rather than in a more questioning way.

Nurse's Song

One of the *Songs of Innocence* that has a counterpart in the *Songs of Experience*, 'Nurse's Song' is another poem that makes use of adult and childish voices. In this poem, the opening speaker is the nurse who takes pleasure in the children's enjoyment of their games; in Andrew Lincoln's words, 'The relationship between the nurse and the children seems at once close and remote' (1991, p. 167). The children's pleas to be allowed to play for longer enter the poem in the third stanza. The Nurse responds positively to these pleas in the fourth and final stanza. Age and youth are in harmony in this poem; her 'still' (l. 4) state is in concord with the children's vigour and activity, brought out in the three verbs of the penultimate line. The poem trembles on the edge of what it excludes: a world where adults give authoritarian commands and age is envious of youth. It achieves a decisive yet faintly imperilled happiness in the last stanza in which the rhyme (of 'bed' (l. 14) and 'ecchoed' (l. 16)) reinforces the idea of reciprocity central to Innocence. The fact that the Nurse's state of mind is not straightforward complicates the poem. She asserts that her 'heart is at rest within my breast' (l. 3), but she seems, as a result of the passive voice used in the first two lines, slightly removed from the scene she describes. In tune with the poem's fusion of moods, the rhythm is at once lilting and lively, and capable in its shorter second and fourth lines of a more curbed impact.

End-rhyme occurs only in the second and fourth lines, though unrhymed lines (see ll. 3, 7, 9, 11 and 13) make use of internal rhyme. The poem has a contrary in *Experience* (not included in this anthology): in that poem, the nurse feels jealousy for her charges' youth, and suggests that their life will be 'wasted' (l. 7); adult life, for her, is a question of 'disguise' (l. 8), a state that is repressed and full of frustration.

Design A nurse sits below a tree reading a book, while a group of children play in a ring on an area of grassy rising ground; delicately coloured willow-like foliage branches profusely out of the text. The children are playing a game that involves running underneath a piece of material held by two children on the left; the ring of hands is broken at the point where the nurse's figure occurs, suggesting that she is included in the scene. The yellow of a setting sun can be glimpsed to the lower left of the picture. There is a weeping willow at the lower right of the picture, possibly a portent of sorrows to come.

> When the voices of children are heard on the green
> And laughing is heard on the hill,
> My heart is at rest within my breast
> And everything else is still.
>
> Then come home, my children, the sun is gone down   5
> And the dews of night arise;
> Come, come, leave off play, and let us away
> Till the morning appears in the skies.
>
> No, no, let us play, for it is yet day
> And we cannot go to sleep;   10
> Besides in the sky, the little birds fly
> And the hills are all covered with sheep.
>
> Well, well, go and play till the light fades away
> And then go home to bed.
> The little ones leaped and shouted and laugh'd   15
> And all the hills ecchoed.

6 *dews of night arise* A suggestion of forces at odds with Innocence.
7 *let us away* The nurse persuades, she does not command; and she speaks of herself and the children as a united group.
9 *No no ... day* The children respond directly to the nurse's words, but find an alternative rhyme for 'play' ('it is yet day' rather than 'let us away'). In line 13, the nurse, yielding to the children's request, will respond with the same rhyme, this time 'till the light fades away'. Blake skilfully introduces these effects of dialogue through internal rhymes in lines that have no end rhyme.
14 *go home* The command shifts from the earlier 'come home' (l. 5); a fractional degree of distance has opened up in the nurse's relation with the children; the door between innocence and experience is now slightly ajar.

Songs of Experience

Frontispiece design A naked winged cherub sits on the shoulders of a red-costumed young man (similar in appearance to the piper in the Frontispiece to *Innocence*); the youth walks towards the viewer; sheep graze behind him. Some of the trunk and a branch of a tree are apparent to the right of the design; in the middle distance stands a conifer. A dark blue hill dominates the background. There is a purposefulness about the design, an air of confronting life.

Title-page design The design is divided into two related halves. In the lower half a youth in blue and a girl in red, both with hands raised beside their faces in prayer, stand either side of a blue-violet bed or tomb on which the corpses of a bearded man and a woman (presumably their parents) lie like sculpture. Above, figures of a girl and a boy dance in an air full of birds and budding flowers and vegetation. There is a balance of grief and joy in the design.

Introduction

The poem begins with a command to 'Hear the voice of the Bard!' (l. 1), and just as the Piper presided over the world of Innocence, so the Bard asserts his status as the principal poetic voice of the world of Experience. Experience is a place or state of lament, protest, sullen or defeated acquiescence, angry resistance, thwarted energy; it is by no means a condition that is necessarily worse than Innocence. Indeed, it may represent in some ways an advance on Innocence. The Introduction claims access to a powerful poetic voice, but as the poem progresses the Bard's authority appears to falter. A subtly disintegrating syntax ensures that his identity blurs into that of the 'Holy Word' (l. 4) and 'the lapsed Soul' (l. 6). The poem seeks a voice that might call to the 'lapsed Soul', which, in turn, 'might control / The starry pole' (ll. 8–9). But a fall of some kind seems to have occurred, as the allusions to Genesis indicate. In the last two stanzas a voice – presumably the Bard's or the Holy Word's – urges 'Earth' (l. 11) to 'return', as though she were a lover who has grown indifferent. The cadences of the last stanza are pleading and moving, and the speaker claims to have given Earth some stability by providing her with a 'starry floor' (l. 18) and 'wat'ry shore' (l. 19). In 'Earth's Answer', however, the next poem in the sequence, the 'wat'ry shore' (l. 6) is interpreted as a prison and 'Starry Jealousy' (l. 7) as a gaoler, a reversal which shows Blake's fascination with warring perspectives. 'Introduction' is written in four five-line stanzas, and makes lyrically beguiling but enigmatic use of short lines and a rhyme scheme (*abaab*) which mimics the tugs and pulls of the poem. As mentioned above, it shows Blake's ability to use syntax in memorably non-logical ways.

Design Among Blake's most striking designs, the plate shows a naked figure (presumably Earth), back turned to the viewer, lying on a couch-cum-robe, which in turn is supported by a cloud-like structure; round the blue edges of the poem stars are strewn. The rising sun behind her head may suggest that 'the break of day' (l. 20) is imminent, but the overall impact of the image is less one of optimistic hope than of coldly beautiful uncertainty.

> Hear the voice of the Bard!
> Who Present, Past, and Future sees,
> Whose ears have heard
> The Holy Word,
> That walk'd among the ancient trees,   5
>
> Calling the lapsed Soul
> And weeping in the evening dew:
> That might controll
> The starry pole;
> And fallen, fallen light renew!   10
>
> O Earth, O Earth, return!
> Arise from out the dewy grass;
> Night is worn,
> And the morn
> Rises from the slumberous mass.   15
>
> Turn away no more:
> Why wilt thou turn away?
> The starry floor,
> The wat'ry shore,
> Is giv'n thee till the break of day.   20

1 *Hear* The imperative is used with an urgency lacking in the child's playful commands to the Piper in the 'Introduction' to *Innocence*.
4–7 *The Holy Word . . . evening dew* Compare Genesis 3: 8: 'And they heard the voice of the Lord God walking in the garden in the cool of the day: and Adam and his wife hid themselves from the presence of the Lord God amongst the trees of the garden.' Blake shifts the scene of the poem to the 'evening dew', and draws on the original for emotions of guilt and repression, and the scenario of a 'fall'.
9 *The starry pole* In *Experience*, the world of nature is less domesticated and intimate than in *Innocence*; here the reference is to the larger movement of the earth in relation to the stars.
10 *fallen, fallen* As in later lines (see 'O Earth, O Earth' (l. 11) and the double use of 'turn away' (ll. 16, 17), repetition conveys the intensity of the appeal to Earth.
20 *Is giv'n . . . day* The physical universe is represented as a stay against the fall with which it is bound up; the 'break of day' might indicate the hope that the 'fall' will be remedied.

The Clod and the Pebble

The poem is one of the purest examples of Blake's interest in dialectic, opposites, contrasts. It places a seemingly selfish view of love – 'Warbled' (l. 8) by a 'Pebble' – against a seemingly selfless view of love –

'sung' by a 'little Clod of Clay' (l. 5). The poem's lucidity is at one with an enigmatic refusal to take sides. It is tempting to see the clod of clay as the voice of innocence and the pebble as the voice of experience. However, it is also possible to see both views as the product of experience, in which case the clod of clay's view may be read less idealistically, masking a potential manipulativeness, one that would deny the self's legitimate longing for joy and delight, possibly with a view to trapping others into supposed selfishness. When the clod, therefore, is described as 'Trodden' (l. 6) the verb may describe its actual or its fantasized fate. The pebble's case may emerge from the desire to counter or unmask the apparent altruism of the clod, and expose the element of self-gratification that drives 'love'. Its 'metres meet' (l. 8) crush the self-sacrifice extolled by the clod of clay. Much depends on the meanings of 'Hell' and 'Heaven', words which may admit both of orthodox and of heterodox interpretations: thus, 'Hell' may point to a 'bad', immoral side of human nature, or it may be the word which those who would repress desire use for energy and instinct.

Design The design consists of the poem, above which there is a scene in which four sheep and two oxen drink at a 'brook' (l. 7); below the poem Blake depicts a finely painted duck swimming in a river; on the river bank there are two frogs (one of which is leaping) either side of a worm, plus a burgeoning vine. The top half represents a gentle harmony; the lower half a more instinctual scene.

> Love seeketh not Itself to please,
> Nor for itself hath any care;
> But for another gives its ease,
> And builds a Heaven in Hell's despair.
>
> > So sung a little Clod of Clay, 5
> > Trodden with the cattle's feet;
> > But a Pebble of the brook
> > Warbled out these metres meet.
>
> Love seeketh only Self to please,
> To bind another to Its delight; 10
> Joys in another's loss of ease,
> And builds a Hell in Heaven's despite.

11 *Joys* The stress on the line's first syllable imparts a fierce energy to the verb.
12 *And . . . despite* Just as the first line of the third stanza reverses the first line of the first stanza, so the poem's last line reverses line 4; "Heaven's despite' might mean: 'in order to spite Heaven' or it might mean 'in the face of Heaven's spite'.

Holy Thursday

The poem is directly contrary in its attitudes to the same subject as 'Holy Thursday' in *Songs of Innocence*. This time the speaker finds nothing of beauty in the children's song, hearing in its 'trembling cry' (l. 5) evidence only of an unjust society in which children are 'reduced to misery, / Fed with cold and usurous hand' (ll. 3–4). Instead of evoking a particular scene, as in the poem's *Innocence* counterpart, here the poet asks searing ethical questions and paints a more generalized picture of a 'land of poverty' (l. 8). The mood is one of bitterness and protest; only in the final stanza does the poet sketch the possibility of a utopian 'there' where hunger and poverty are absent. To place this poem against its contrary in *Innocence* is to be made aware of Blake's dialectical vision; both poems serve as critiques of one another. If, from the perspective of the *Experience* poem, the *Innocence* poem seems unquestioningly complicit with injustice, from the perspective of the *Innocence* poem, the *Experience* poem wilfully refuses to take delight in the children's vitality and joy, and the efforts made to look after those in need of charity. The longer lines of the *Innocence* poem are replaced by curtly angered tetrameters in the *Experience* poem.

Design The design reinforces the poem's bleak vision. In the top half a well-dressed woman standing beneath a leafless tree looks down at a child lying (presumably dead) on the ground; the woman may be a spectator of rather than an actor in the tragic scene; below this picture is an image of a mother dressed in red with a child in blue standing beside her, hands raised to his head, while another child (naked) clings to her; and below this a child lies outstretched (again, one presumes, dead) on ground covered with leaves.

Is this a holy thing to see,
In a rich and fruitful land,
Babes reducd to misery,
Fed with cold and usurous hand?

Is that trembling cry a song? 5
Can it be a song of joy?
And so many children poor?
It is a land of poverty!

And their sun does never shine,
And their fields are bleak and bare, 10
And their ways are fill'd with thorns:
It is eternal winter there.

For where-e'er the sun does shine,
And where-e'er the rain does fall,
Babe can never hunger there, 15
Nor poverty the mind appall.

3–4 *Babes . . . hand* The initial stresses in both lines allow the voice to fall on 'Babes' and 'fed' with scornful power.
5–6 *Is that . . . joy?* The first question asks whether the 'cry' can be a 'song'; the second concedes that it may be a 'song' but implies it cannot be one 'of joy'.
7–8 *And . . . poverty!* The movement of the lines is swift and generalizing; much of the poem's force derives from its compression and speed.

9–11 *And . . . thorns* The triple use of 'their' – 'their sun', 'their fields' and 'their ways' – suggests the 'land' is divided into 'two nations': that of the well-off and that of the poor.
16 *appall* Might imply a state of ineffectual indignation, in which the 'mind' (l. 16) is 'appalled' but does nothing to change an unjust social order.

The Sick Rose

This poem of two quatrains, each rhyming *abcb*, mixes two- and three-stress feet in its evocation of the rose's 'destruction' (see l. 8) by the 'invisible worm' (l. 2); 'worm' probably has the archaic sense of 'dragon'. Blake's symbols resist easy translation, but one suggestion of the poem is that the worm's 'dark secret love' (l. 7) is provoked by and a match for the rose's 'bed / Of crimson joy' (ll. 5–6). That is, the rose's attempt at concealed self-gratification, involving a luxurious, quasi-masturbatory 'crimson joy', has drawn to it the worm's phallic power to 'destroy'. The opening exclamation leaves unstated what the cause of the rose's sickness is. Has the sickness been caused by the worm's 'dark secret love'? Or was it this sickness that attracted that love? The opening line may sympathize; or it may diagnose with some disgust. The language of the poem is full of erotic implications.

Design A large crimson many-petalled rose occupies the foot of the design; emerging from it arms outstretched (possibly in fright) is a young woman. Coiled round her (possibly penetrating her heart) is a snake-like worm. At the top of the picture a caterpillar is about to eat a leaf; on the branch below it are two abject-looking figures. The general impression reinforces the poem's mood of erotic corruption.

O Rose thou art sick.
The invisible worm,
That flies in the night
In the howling storm,

Has found out thy bed 5
Of crimson joy:
And his dark secret love
Does thy life destroy.

The Fly

In 'The Fly' Blake uses short lines, hypotheses and questions to riddle his way in and out of large issues. The poem appears to explore questions of human responsibility for and comparability with the animal kingdom. Indeed, a draft began, 'Woe alas my guilty hand'. The second stanza's questions imply a likeness between man and fly, a likeness furthered by the third stanza's suggestion that the speaker is himself a fly waiting to be brushed aside by 'some blind hand'. Yet rather than accepting the grim view that human beings are so many flies at the mercy of a force like that of a wanton boy, to adapt *King Lear*'s famous simile, the poem concludes with a sentence that dances with some irony away from pessimism. The fourth stanza proposes an identification between 'life' and 'thought' (l. 13), and 'death' (l. 16) and 'the want / Of thought' (ll. 15–16); in either case, the fifth stanza asserts, the speaker is 'A happy fly' (l. 18). If he thinks, happiness lies in thought; if he cannot think, because dead, then he has the happiness that derives from lack of consciousness. With its air of constructing gossamer-thin syllogisms, the poem's manner is jauntily at odds with its weighty subject matter; it gives the sense of blowing like thistledown across an abyss.

Design To the left, a girl in white plays on her own with bat and shuttlecock. Beside her, an unsmiling mother or nurse in purplish red holds a child's arms with her arms, teaching it to walk. The picture is framed by leafless trees. As though imitating the poem's circles of thought, two circles catch the eye: one formed by the mother's and child's arms; one (not fully closed) by the girl's arm and bat. The text is set against clouds. The mood is solitary; a sense of joyless play and instruction is conveyed.

Little Fly,
Thy summer's play,
My thoughtless hand
Has brush'd away.

Am not I   5
A fly like thee?
Or art not thou
A man like me?

For I dance
And drink and sing;   10
Till some blind hand
Shall brush my wing.

If thought is life
And strength and breath;
And the want   15
Of thought is death;

Then am I
A happy fly,
If I live,
Or if I die.   20

3 *thoughtless* Replaces 'guilty' in the draft.
5 *Am not I* The poem rhymes only the second and fourth lines of each quatrain. This chime with the first line reinforces the poem's concern with possible affinities between the two rhyme-words, 'fly' (l. 1) and 'I' (l. 5).

8 *A man like me* The poem proceeds as though its equations were evident, but the questions challenge traditional distinctions between humans and the rest of the created world.
17 *Then am I* As in line 5, the additional rhyme (here with ll. 18 and 20) underlines a preoccupation with identity.

The Tyger

This poem, the contrary of 'The Lamb' in *Innocence*, deploys the driving rhythm of its six quatrains written in trochaic tetrameters to 'frame' (l. 4) a series of questions about the nature of the tiger's enigmatic creator. The speaker may be Blake; he may be a student of the sublime, that is, the awe-inspiring or incomprehensible. The poem also asks questions provoked by the orthodox appeal to 'design' as proof of the existence of a benevolent first cause. If God can create a lamb, did he also create a tiger? Is he, the implication goes, an embodiment of terror as well as loveliness, rage along with peace, energy and love – and, crucially evil as well as good? Indeed, is what we think of as evil, bodied forth in the form of a tiger, really evil? Or is it, rather, a manifestation of what the orthodox think of as evil, but which, from another perspective, may be the welcome energies of revolution? After all, Blake rebukes the orthodox angel in *The Marriage of Heaven and Hell* with the statement that 'All that we saw was owing to your metaphysics' (*E*, p. 42); and the 'Proverbs of Hell' in the same work include the maxim, 'The tygers of wrath are wiser than the horses of instruction' (*E*, p. 37). In 'The Tyger' the creature is invested with a fiery power which burns 'In the forests of the night' (l. 2), where the phrasing edges towards the symbolic; this is not a literal forest, but 'forests of the night', 'the night' taking on suggestive force. The tiger is 'in' these 'forests', part of the darkness yet blazing out against it, like repressed energy. The poem shifts between two words, 'could' and 'dare'. The first provokes questions about the scope of the creator's power, the second about the creator's resolve, his readiness to unleash forces of which the tiger is an emblem. 'Could' (l. 4) is picked up in stanza 3 (l. 10); 'dare' (ll. 7, 8) is introduced in stanza 2, where the focus switches (as it does in stanza 1) from the tiger to his creator: a creator not like the God of Genesis, able to create by means of an absolute fiat, but like a figure from Greek mythology – Icarus, for instance (l. 7), or the fire-stealing Prometheus (l. 8). The poem's incantatory rhythms build to a crescendo of excitement in the third and fourth stanzas, in which incomplete questions evoke the speaker's intensifying dread. In stanza 4, attention is given to the means of creation, culminating in the question, 'What dread grasp / Dare its deadly terrors clasp?' (ll. 15–16). The sound-effects there, especially the rhyme between 'dread' and 'deadly', bind creature and creator in a mutual embrace. Stanza 5 breaks away from the two verbs 'could' and 'dare', as it evokes a scenario of celestial submission, and asks questions that pivot on 'Did' (ll. 19, 20). The stanza's last question, 'Did he who made the Lamb make thee?' (l. 20), addresses the major question at the heart of any attempt to justify the idea of a good God, namely, *unde malum?* (whence evil?). In the last stanza Blake returns to the wording of the opening quatrain, except that for 'Could' he substitutes 'Dare'. The poem matches in its design something of the 'fearful symmetry' (ll. 4, 24) which is attributed to the tiger.

Design The tiger of the design seems not quite to square with the terrifying creature of the poem. Set in front of a tree it presents a somewhat lugubrious profile. It has a long tail and thin haunches; the anatomy of its legs is strikingly four-square and rigid, almost a satire on the idea of 'fearful symmetry'. In one copy, however, the tiger is represented in a way more consonant with the text; this is the startlingly coloured and altogether less lumbering image in copy T (see Andrew Lincoln (ed.), p. 136).

> Tyger, Tyger, burning bright,
> In the forests of the night,
> What immortal hand or eye
> Could frame thy fearful symmetry?
>
> In what distant deeps or skies 5
> Burnt the fire of thine eyes?
> On what wings dare he aspire?
> What the hand dare sieze the fire?
>
> And what shoulder, and what art,
> Could twist the sinews of thy heart? 10
> And when thy heart began to beat,
> What dread hand? and what dread feet?
>
> What the hammer? what the chain?
> In what furnace was thy brain?
> What the anvil? what dread grasp 15
> Dare its deadly terrors clasp?

5–8 *In what . . . fire?* The tiger is not created from nothing, as the traditional Christian God creates, but from pre-existent and not unterrifying materials.
12 *What . . . feet?* The 'dread hand' and 'dread feet' seem to belong to the creature as well as the creator; the speaker expresses his 'dread' of both. The line's effect of increased anxiety derives from its omission of a verb corresponding to 'twist' (l. 10).
15 *dread grasp* Echoes the two uses of 'dread' in line 12, but in this case the 'dread grasp' belongs clearly to the creator.

When the stars threw down their spears
And water'd heaven with their tears,
Did he smile his work to see?
Did he who made the Lamb make thee? 20

Tyger, Tyger, burning bright,
In the forests of the night,
What immortal hand or eye
Dare frame thy fearful symmetry?

Plate 3 The Tyger. Reproduced courtesy of King's College, Cambridge.

17–20 *When ... make thee?* The stanza shows Blake's ability to use symbolic effects that are not easily translatable. One may sense an allusion to Lucifer's revolt against God. Yet if 'threw down' (l. 17) is interpreted as 'gave up' rather than as 'hurled', the revolt does not end in proud defiance, of the kind depicted by Milton in *Paradise Lost*, but in hypocritical surrender. On this reading, 'water'd heaven with their tears' means 'surrendered with an exaggerated display of remorse'. What emerges clearly is the speaker's fascination with the power of the tiger's creator, now seen as possibly triumphing in his achievement (l. 20).

24 *symmetry* Here, as in line 4, the word seems to allude ironically to the Christian and Deist idea of beautiful and benevolent design.

Ah! Sun-flower

The poem's single sentence brings out the fact that the opening exclamation is expressive of sympathy and critique. Through a cunning use of syntax, the poem articulates longing for an attractive but illusory 'sweet golden clime' (l. 3). The participle 'Seeking' (l. 3) is the poem's pivot: what the sunflower seeks is a place to which the 'Youth' (l. 5) and 'pale Virgin' (l. 6) – figures who repress present desire in the hope of future fulfilment – 'aspire' (l. 7). In turn, bringing the poem round full circle, the Youth and Virgin 'aspire / Where my Sun-flower wishes to go' (ll. 7–8). The poem's structure thus mimics a process of endless and almost certainly futile aspiration.

Design The poem is the central text on a single plate that contains, above it, 'My Pretty Rose Tree' and, below it, 'The Lilly'. The text is set against a cloud, which may be suggestive of mental confusion; to the left, a small yellow-gold figure, recognizably human but also flower-like with petals and roots, dances above and just to the right of a coiled tendril. This figure presumably represents the 'sun-flower', the word above which it is placed.

> Ah Sun-flower! weary of time,
> Who countest the steps of the Sun,
> Seeking after that sweet golden clime
> Where the traveller's journey is done:
>
> Where the Youth pined away with desire, 5
> And the pale Virgin shrouded in snow
> Arise from their graves and aspire
> Where my Sun-flower wishes to go.

1 *weary of time* The phrase edges the poem into an allegorical dimension; the sunflower is weary of the temporal aspect of existence.
2 *the Sun* Serves as an image for the object of desire.
3–4 *that ... done* 'That' conveys the fact that belief in such a 'clime' is strong. Blake evokes the near-archetypal nature of the desire and the probability that it is an illusion.
5 *pined ... desire* Blake cheats us into thinking that 'pined away' is a main verb, before it becomes clear that the phrase serves as a past participle; the effect is to turn even the pining away into a less active condition than it at first appeared to be.

London

The poem is among the most impressive examples in the *Songs* of Blake's concentrated verbal power as he communicates his vision of contemporary London. 'London' detects in the wrongs it apprehends evidence both of wasted potential and of a system of interlocking and inhumane institutions. In stanzas three and four, for example, after the wandering speaker has set himself at odds with his world, a world of 'mind-forg'd manacles' (l. 8), he observes, in writing of visionary daring, how the exploitation of chimney sweeps is implicitly condoned by the Established Church; how the suffering of soldiers indicts the rulers who are its instigators; and how prostitution with its horrors of disease and corruption depends for its existence on a code of sexual repression that exalts marriage. 'How' (ll. 9 and 14) is a key word in these two stanzas; it implies the speaker's capacity to piece together connections and patterns of causality. Attempts have been made to read the poem as telling us more about the speaker's supposed paranoid state of mind than about the truth of his vision. But this line of interpretation seems strained, given the power with which that vision is conveyed. In the first two stanzas, the speaker is said to 'mark in every face I meet / Marks of weakness, marks of woe' (ll. 3–4), and to hear 'mind-forg'd manacles' (l. 8), and Blake persuades us that these generalized responses have force and value. The repetition of 'mark' and 'Marks' offers less a suggestion that the speaker projects his assumptions on to those he sees than that there is a consonance, a rhyme, between his mode of seeing and what is there to be seen. 'Mind-forg'd manacles' is a major metaphor. It implies manacles forged by and for the mind, and it ushers in the metaphorical method of stanzas three and four. In stanza three, the speaker hears how a cry (the chimney sweeper's) 'appalls' (l. 10), where the verb means 'whitens', 'casts a pall over', and 'induces a state of horror that is hypocritically assumed'. That the Church is 'black'ning' (l. 10) even as it is appalled, as though adding to the sweeper's task, is grimly effective. Again, the movement from the 'hapless Soldier's sigh' (l. 11) to 'Runs in blood down Palace walls' (l. 12) converts passive plight into a thunderous accusation. Stanza four displays a comparable compression and pointing up of hidden links: the 'Harlot', herself 'youthful' (l. 14) and scarcely beyond childhood, destroys infancy and marriage by transmitting venereal diseases. The compacting of 'Marriage' and 'hearse' (l. 16), traditional emblems of undying love and the solemn container of death, in the poem's final phrase speaks volumes about Blake's embittered disillusion in 'London'. The metre is tetrameter, trochaic in places, iambic in others; each quatrain rhymes *abab*.

Design Above the poem, in a reversal of the usual roles found in *Innocence*, a child in a green gown leads a white-bearded, stooped old man in blue-grey; the backdrop is a brick wall and shut door, suggestive of the claustrophobic city. However, a slant of light introduces a more optimistic intimation. To the right of the poem a figure kneels before a fire at which he warms his hands; smoke rises above the fire. The design's colour suggests a warmth – that of creative energy, perhaps – at odds with the wretchedness depicted in the poem.

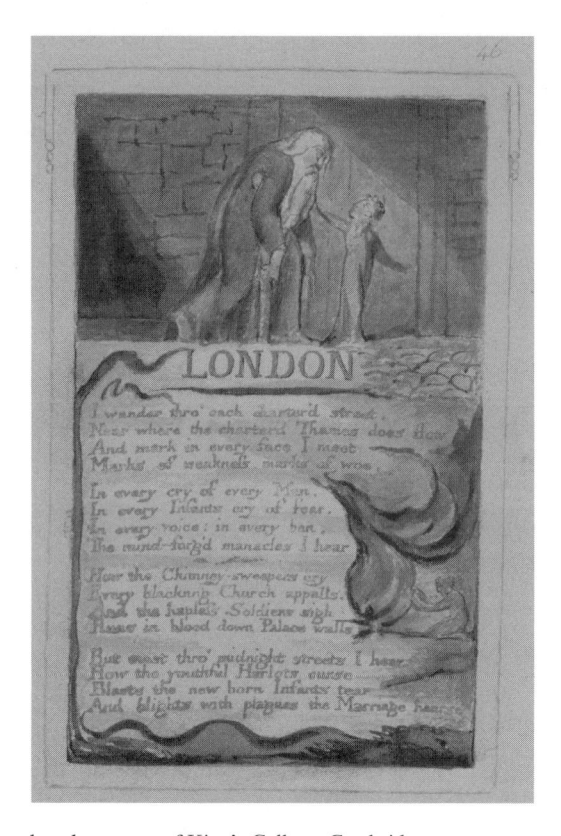

Plate 4 London. Reproduced courtesy of King's College, Cambridge.

> I wander through each charter'd street,
> Near where the charter'd Thames does flow,
> And mark in every face I meet
> Marks of weakness, marks of woe.
>
> In every cry of every Man, 5
> In every Infant's cry of fear,
> In every voice, in every ban,
> The mind-forg'd manacles I hear.
>
> How the Chimney-sweeper's cry
> Every black'ning Church appalls; 10
> And the hapless Soldier's sigh
> Runs in blood down Palace walls.
>
> But most through midnight streets I hear
> How the youthful Harlot's curse
> Blasts the new-born Infant's tear 15
> And blights with plagues the Marriage hearse.

1–2 *I . . . flow* The lines point up the speaker's nomadic wandering through 'charter'd streets'. The repetition of 'charter'd' ironizes the notion of a charter as a guarantee of liberty.
4 *Marks . . . woe* The alliterative binding together of 'weakness' and 'woe shows Blake's sense that human 'weakness' is, at least in part, responsible for human 'woe'.
7 *ban* 'Formal or authoritative prohibition (*on*)', but also '(arch.) angry execration'. There may be a concealed suggestion, especially given the content of the fourth stanza, of a pun on marriage 'banns', 'notice in church etc. of intended marriage, read on three Sundays to give opportunity of objection'.
8 *mind-forg'd manacles* In the draft this read 'german-forged links', an allusion to the Hanoverian monarchy ruling England.
12 *Runs . . . walls* May allude to the writing 'upon the plaister of the wall of the king's palace' in Daniel 5: 5.

14 *curse* A swear-word, but also a 'curse' in a stronger sense, 'consigning person or thing to destruction', possibly an unwanted child.

15 *Blasts* Withers, infects. *Infant's tear* A baby born to a mother with gonorrhoea can suffer from blindness.

A Poison Tree

'A Poison Tree' was entitled 'Christian Forbearance' in manuscript, a title which, to the degree that the poem is a moral satire, indicates its target. The poem uses its couplet rhymes, gathered into four stanzas, to tell a psychological story about the subterfuges involved in the deferral of anger and delayed revenge. The speaker obeys the injunction to keep your friends close, but your enemies closer as he describes the effect of not communicating his anger to his 'foe' (l. 3). From the start, Blake is concerned with consequences, a concern relayed through the barest of syntactical means, that of appositional statement: 'I told my wrath, my wrath did end' (l. 2); 'I told it not, my wrath did grow' (l. 4). That last verb 'grow' sets going the poem's dominant metaphor of a poison-tree, whose burgeoning is the subject of the second stanza, where a crucial word is 'and', a conjunction that allows the speaker to link events without describing his latent motives. Blind as he may be to these motives, his language betrays his thinking as born out of hypocrisy and guile. In the third stanza, a reprise of the Temptation in the Garden of Eden takes place, as the tree bears 'an apple bright' (l. 10), which lures the foe to steal it *because* (not the poem's word but its implication) 'he knew that it was mine' (l. 12). The consequence, caught in the opening couplet of the last stanza, is a transgression on the part of the foe, which results in his death after (we assume) eating the fruit of the poison tree. Blake's references to the Fall and the Garden of Eden widen the poem's scope without taking it out of the territory – peculiarly his – of psychic entanglement. The final couplet describes the speaker's 'gladness' (see l. 15) at the fate of his foe, and brings out how Blake's eye is less on moral disapproval than on the dramatizing of corrupt yet deeply human feelings of dissimulation and the desire for revenge.

Design In one of Blake's most striking images, a foreshortened figure in grey lies, arms outstretched, below the boughs of a leafless tree whose branches almost lasso the title. The picture has a chilling pallor in its colouring.

Plate 5   A Poison Tree. Reproduced courtesy of King's College, Cambridge.

I was angry with my friend;
I told my wrath, my wrath did end.
I was angry with my foe:
I told it not, my wrath did grow.

And I water'd it in fears,   5
Night and morning with my tears:
And I sunned it with smiles,
And with soft deceitful wiles.

And it grew both day and night,
Till it bore an apple bright;   10
And my foe beheld it shine,
And he knew that it was mine,

And into my garden stole
When the night had veil'd the pole;
In the morning glad I see   15
My foe outstretchd beneath the tree.

1 *I . . . friend* The line, like the poem, illustrates Blake's use of the first-person pronoun to act as a lens which focuses a 'state' of the 'human soul'. Gillian Beer speaks of 'the desolate privacy of the Romantic ego' (*Darwin's Plots*, Cambridge University Press, 2nd edn, 2000, p. 163), but Blake, along with other Romantic poets, diagnoses rather than exalts such a 'desolate privacy'.
10 *Till* The word implies an intention (hidden until now) on the part of the tree's cultivator.
11 *beheld* Implies a looking on that is prolonged, full of longing.

12 *mine* The rhyme word brings out the fact that the major appeal of the apple to the foe is that it belongs to the speaker.
13 *stole* Means 'entered stealthily', but, in context, suggests the act of stealing about to occur.
14 *When . . . pole* Returns to the cosmic images of the 'Introduction' to *Experience*, this time to suggest that the 'pole' or fixed star is hidden from view, thus encouraging the foe to suppose that his transgression will go undetected.
15 *glad I see* Connects and contrasts with the foe's 'beholding' in line 11: 'I see' is both 'glad' and unsurprised in its tone.

Visions of the Daughters of Albion

This illuminated book was printed by Blake in 1793; 11 copies survive of the first print run; there were also three copies printed in 1818. The copy text for this anthology is large-paper copy G, the copy used as copy text in the relevant volume (3) of *Blake's Illuminated Books*, namely *The Early Illuminated Books* (1993; ed. with intro and notes Morris Eaves, Robert N. Essick and Joseph Viscomi). Some editorial intervention has been thought desirable, especially with regard to Blake's idiosyncratic punctuation (often he uses exclamation marks where modern convention would dictate a question mark). Written in septenaries, or seven-stress iambic lines, the poem features three main characters, organizing their interaction in ways that point up gendered and ideological conflict. At the same time, the poem makes us aware of Blake's avoidance of easy allegory in his visionary narratives; we must enter the tumultuous and changeable world of the poem itself in order to appreciate its 'Visions'.

The three characters are Oothoon, Theotormon and Bromion. Oothoon is a female figure who contrasts with the earlier figure of Thel in *The Book of Thel*. Thel, treated with delicate, ruthless sympathy by Blake, flees from the challenges of experience and sexuality. Oothoon embraces these challenges, and is clearly held up for our admiration with her conviction that 'every thing that lives is holy!' (11: 10). She embodies a female independence probably associated for Blake with Mary Wollstonecraft, author of *Vindication of the Rights of Woman* (1792). Wollstonecraft knew and fell in love with Blake's friend, the artist Henry Fuseli; this was not reciprocated but Wollstonecraft appears to have suggested that she lived with Fuseli and his wife in a platonic relationship, an arrangement that Mrs Fuseli was not prepared to countenance. Wollstonecraft's *Vindication* is concerned that women should establish themselves as free and above all rational beings. Blake's engagement with Wollstonecraft's feminism involves critique as well as admiration; for Blake, true freedom involves acceptance of the centrality to life of sexuality. Oothoon's name derives from James Macpherson's Ossian poem, *Oithona* (1762); 'Oithona' means, Macpherson tells his reader in a note, 'the virgin of the waves' (quoted in *The Early Illuminated Books*, p. 229). Macpherson's heroine is also seized by a captor and taken to his cave on the island of Tromathan (which may have prompted the name of 'Theotormon' in Blake's poem). Blake's Oothoon has something in common with mythological figures: an eagle tears her flesh (5: 17), much as Prometheus' liver is eaten by an eagle; and like Persephone before she is snatched by Pluto, Oothoon is picking flowers before she is seized by Bromion. But Blake introduces differences: unlike Prometheus, Oothoon asks that the eagle 'Rend away this defiled bosom' (5: 15), and, unlike Persephone, she seeks to rescue herself (see *Early Illuminated Books*, p. 230 for this last point). A key question asked by some modern commentators is whether Oothoon achieves mental liberation. Is she, or is Blake, still governed by the assumption that the meaning of a woman's life is shaped by her relationship with a man? Is her offer to Theotormon to 'catch for thee girls of mild silver, or of furious gold' (10: 24) evidence of freedom from possessive jealousy, or merely her author's male fantasy? Or is it the case that Blake shows us a female character caught between male oppression and a longing for a freedom as yet unavailable to her, but surmised through bold flights of metaphorical imagining?

The two male characters, Bromion (stress on the first syllable) and Theotormon, anticipate in their respective qualities the different male characters at the centre of Thomas Hardy's *Tess of the D'Urbevilles*, Alec d'Urbeville and Angel Clare. Like Alec, Bromion would achieve mastery through force. Bromion's act of violence against Oothoon is unmotivated and sudden (see 4: 16–17). When he speaks we hear the accents of the slave-owner and colonial exploiter of others, 'Stampt with my signet' (4: 21), who believes, as Sylvia Plath puts it in her poem 'Daddy', that 'Every woman adores a Fascist'. Blake's attitude to Bromion as a slave-owner is influenced by his work illustrating (at its author's request) John Gabriel Stedman's *Narrative, of a Five Years' Expedition, against the Revolted Negroes of Surinam*. Stedman, a mercenary soldier, was shocked by the Dutch colonialists' treatment of their slaves, but he was at the same time involved in the slaves' oppression. Blake's 16 designs to Stedman's narrative (published in 1796) register the cruelty of slavery with great power, and suggest his insight into the psychological processes of oppression, how they run between private and public arenas. Bromion treats Oothoon as a possession sullied by his own sexual aggression and addresses Theotormon tauntingly: 'Now thou maist marry Bromion's harlot' (5: 1). Later Bromion will ask questions about knowing, emphasizing human limitations but stressing the existence of an all-powerful 'one law for both the lion and the ox' (7: 22). Theotormon, like Angel Clare, is repressively concerned with purity, to judge by Oothoon's laments 'That Theotormon hears me not!' (5: 37). When he breaks his silence, in Plates 6 and 7, it is to ask a range of questions, but to do without the exuberant openness to experience apparent in Oothoon's preceding litany of questions (6: 2–13). Instead, Theotormon is trapped in 'the present moment of affliction' (7: 9), tormented by thoughts of how he might escape it. Only Oothoon, especially in her remarkably wide-ranging and tonally varied final speech (8: 3 to 11: 10), is able to confront experience without anxiety or fear. Bromion drops away from the text of the poem; Theotormon remains 'conversing with shadows dire' (11: 12). Oothoon is audible to the 'Daughters of Albion' (11: 13), Blake bringing out again, at the poem's close, her female representativeness. The poem places questions of female liberation in the context of different modes of oppression and of the implications for freedom of different ways of perceiving and responding to life. *Visions* is a forerunner of more complex presentations of conflicting perspectives in works such as *The Four Zoas*. But its focus on three characters gives it the power of an operatic aria sustained by several voices. The poem gives the sense of being at once compressed and spacious, caught up in the traumatic aftermath of Oothoon's rape but on the verge, in her speeches, of a breakthrough in awareness. In this respect, the title page's enigmatic motto – 'The Eye sees more than the Heart knows' – is suggestive; there are more things in human experience than can properly be assimilated by any individual's particular affective bias.

Plate 1 design In the copy text, Plate I is the title page. Below the word 'Albion' a naked woman runs, pursued by a creature with huge bat-like purplish wings and a human face that resembles that of Urizen in *The [First] Book of Urizen*, and may stand for a blend of Bromion and Urizen. To the left a trio of acrobat-like naked dancers whirls round. Above, to the left a naked woman reaches down from a branch-like squiggle to another naked woman lying on her back; to the right, a naked man with legs crossed reaches his long arms in a downwards gesture as though hurling down the rain that pours into the waters over which Oothoon runs. A rainbow arcs from the group of dancers to the crossed-leg man. The design is full of promise and terror, conflict and possibility, and thus forms an appropriate introduction to the work. The motto is placed below Oothoon's right foot.

VISIONS of the Daughters of Albion

The Eye sees more than the Heart knows.
Printed by Will:^m Blake : 1793.

Plate 2 design In the copy text, Plate 2 is the frontispiece. It illustrates Plate 5, lines 3–5, in which Theotormon 'folded his black jealous waters round the adulterate pair' (5: 4). Blake depicts Bromion and Oothoon bound back to back; to the left, Theotormon is depicted, sitting on a rock, head in hands; possibly the image we behold is one he has conceived. The expression on Bromion's face, his hair standing on end, is one of terror or rage. His left foot is manacled, the slave-owner himself chained. Oothoon, head bowed, wears a more accepting look. The figures are set in an opening of a cave from which a blood-red sun is visible. There have been suggestions that all three figures could be thought of as occupying a skull-like space, with the sun as the skull's eye (see *Early Illuminated Books*, p. 236). Alternatively it might be thought that we look beyond the torments of the three figures to a sun rising.

Plate 3 design Eight lines of text, composing 'The Argument' are set above an image of a naked woman, hands held to her breasts, kneeling and kissing a naked form that arises from a flower in the midst of a green field; the image illustrates 4: 11–13, and is flooded with a gold and red light that rays out from the two figures, and which mixes with the green and blue hints of sky to sustain the rainbow-like effect of Plate 1.

The Argument

I loved Theotormon
And I was not ashamed
I trembled in my virgin fears
And I hid in Leutha's vale!

I plucked Leutha's flower, 5
And I rose up from the vale;
But the terrible thunders tore
My virgin mantle in twain.

1–2 *I... ashamed* 'The Argument' is told from Oothoon's point of view.
3–4 *I... vale* Refers to Thel-like 'fears' which Oothoon overcomes. 'Leutha's vale' is a place of virginal safety, a little like Blake's conception of Innocence.
5–6 *I... vale* Describes Oothoon's active decision to leave the vale and (implicitly) to embrace sexuality.
7 *terrible thunders* Bromion.
8 *virgin mantle* Hymen.

Plate 4 design At the foot of the page, two naked figures sprawl in post-coital exhaustion, Bromion on the right with right arm outstretched, left knee bent and right knee raised, Oothoon a green sylph-like figure on the left, arms outstretched. Above the word 'Visions' at the top of the page two archers to the right fire or prepare to fire arrows; below them, a liquid seems to drip from the hand held out by a woman. To their left a woman rides a cloud shaped like a horse. To her left a naked cupid-like figure sits on the 'V' of 'Visions', possibly blowing a horn.

Visions

Enslav'd, the Daughters of Albion weep; a trembling lamentation
Upon their mountains; in their valleys, sighs toward America.

For the soft soul of America, Oothoon wander'd in woe,
Along the vales of Leutha seeking flowers to comfort her;
And thus she spoke to the bright Marygold of Leutha's vale 5

1 *Enslav'd ... weep* Slavery is a major theme of the poem (hereafter *V*); here it is applied to the condition of women in Blake's England ('the Daughters of Albion').
2 *sighs toward America* Because Oothoon is 'the soft soul of America' (l. 3), from which England is now separated (after the American War of Independence). America figures in *V* as a place of potential renewal, but as a place that has been affected adversely by forms of exploitation such as slavery brought to it by the Old World.
5 *Marygold* Blake's spelling of 'marigold' humanizes the flower and may allude to Mary Wollstonecraft.

Art thou a flower? art thou a nymph? I see thee now a flower;
Now a nymph! I dare not pluck thee from thy dewy bed!

The Golden nymph replied; pluck thou my flower Oothoon the mild.
Another flower shall spring, because the soul of sweet delight
Can never pass away; she ceas'd and clos'd her golden shrine. 10

Then Oothoon pluck'd the flower saying, I pluck thee from thy bed
Sweet flower, and put thee here to glow between my breasts
And thus I turn my face to where my whole soul seeks.

Over the waves she went in wing'd exulting swift delight;
And over Theotormon's reign, took her impetuous course. 15

Bromion rent her with his thunders, on his stormy bed
Lay the faint maid, and soon her woes appall'd his thunders hoarse.

Bromion spoke. Behold this harlot here on Bromion's bed.
And let the jealous dolphins sport around the lovely maid:
Thy soft American plains are mine, and mine thy north & south: 20
Stampt with my signet are the swarthy children of the sun;
They are obedient, they resist not, they obey the scourge:
Their daughters worship terrors and obey the violent:

6–7 *Art . . . nymph!* Illustrates Blake's fascination with modes of perception that show the mind's capacity to transcend sense-perception.
8 *Oothoon the mild* Blake stresses Oothoon's initial gentleness and mildness; she will develop into a bold and imaginative thinker.
13 *And thus . . . seeks* Conveys Oothoon's commitment to what her 'whole soul seeks' in a line of great rhythmic elegance, partly created by the omission of a foot (most lines have 14 syllables, this has 12).
15 *Theotormon's reign* Theotormon's realm (the Atlantic Ocean).
16–17 *Bromion . . . hoarse* The major event of the poem occurs in two swift, even brutal lines; yet 'appall'd' speaks of an element of immediate revulsion on Bromion's part.
18 *harlot* Bromion's description, one which Oothoon repudiates (see 5: 28, 'I am pure').
19 *jealous dolphins* The dolphins are jealous because they have been unable to protect Oothoon; Bromion is asserting his mastery over her.
20 *Thy soft American plains* Bromion's rape of Oothoon serves as a prelude to his speaking in aggressively colonialist terms: she is at once a woman and a conquered country.
21 *Stampt . . . signet* His slaves are branded with Bromion's private seal. Blake engraved a plate showing an African branded with Stedman's initials.

Plate 5 design In the middle of the Plate, an African slave lies face down; to his right his pickaxe lies in the ground.

Now thou maist marry Bromion's harlot, and protect the child
Of Bromion's rage, that Oothoon shall put forth in nine moons time.

Then storms rent Theotormon's limbs; he roll'd his waves around,
And folded his black jealous waters round the adulterate pair.
Bound back to back in Bromion's caves terror and meekness dwell. 5

At entrance Theotormon sits wearing the threshold hard
With secret tears; beneath him sound like waves on a desart shore
The voice of slaves beneath the sun, and children bought with money,
That shiver in religious caves beneath the burning fires
Of lust, that belch incessant from the summits of the earth. 10

3 *Then storms . . . limbs* Bromion 'rent' Oothoon (4: 16); Theotormon is 'rent' by psychological conflict, inner 'storms'.
6–10 *At entrance . . . earth* Theotormon's 'secret tears' sound corruptly self-regarding; Blake also associates him with Bromion's world slavery, 'children bought with money', and religious hypocrisy.

Oothoon weeps not; she cannot weep! her tears are locked up;
But she can howl incessant writhing her soft snowy limbs.
And calling Theotormon's Eagles to prey upon her flesh.

I call with holy voice! kings of the sounding air,
Rend away this defiled bosom that I may reflect, 15
The image of Theotormon on my pure transparent breast.

The Eagles at her call descend and rend their bleeding prey;
Theotormon severely smiles, her soul reflects the smile;
As the clear spring mudded with feet of beasts grows pure and smiles.

The Daughters of Albion hear her woes, and eccho back her sighs. 20

Why does my Theotormon sit weeping upon the threshold:
And Oothoon hovers by his side, perswading him in vain?
I cry arise O Theotormon for the village dog
Barks at the breaking day, the nightingale has done lamenting,
The lark does rustle in the ripe corn, and the Eagle returns 25
From nightly prey, and lifts his golden beak to the pure east;
Shaking the dust from his immortal pinions to awake
The sun that sleeps too long. Arise my Theotormon I am pure,
Because the night is gone that clos'd me in its deadly black.
They told me that the night and day were all that I could see; 30
They told me that I had five senses to inclose me up.
And they inclos'd my infinite brain into a narrow circle,
And sunk my heart into the Abyss, a red round globe hot burning
Till all from life I was obliterated and erased.
Instead of morn arises a bright shadow, like an eye 35
In the eastern cloud: instead of night a sickly charnel house;
That Theotormon hears me not! to him the night and morn
Are both alike: a night of sighs, a morning of fresh tears;

18 *severely smiles* Theotormon's unattractive severity is shown in his unwillingness to accept Oothoon's essential 'purity', an unwillingness to which she draws attention in the speech which follows.

30–4 *They told me ... erased* Oothoon begins to generalize her predicament; she has been misled by voices of authority to which she refers as 'They' into believing that she was limited by sense experiences; the strong verbs of line 34 capture her sense of having been 'obliterated and erased'. The attack on theories that lay stress on the mind's debt to sense-impressions has to do with Blake's quarrel with the philosophical empiricism of John Locke. Lines 32–3 anticipate in their depiction of the limits of the senses *The First Book of Urizen* 11: 1–4 and 25: 28–30. A major text for understanding Blake's opposition to Locke is *There is no Natural Religion* [*b*] (printed c. 1795), Plate 1 of which reads: 'Mans perceptions are not bounded by organs of perception. he percieves more than sense (tho' ever so acute) can discover' (*E*, p. 2).

35–6 *Instead ... house* Touches with its own irony on a crucial idea in Blake, that of visionary subjectivity, developed in a letter to Rev. Dr Trusler of August 1799: 'I see Every thing I paint In This World, but Every body does not see alike. . . . The tree which moves some to tears of joy is in the Eyes of others only a Green thing that stands in the way. . . . As a man is So he Sees' (*E*, p. 702).

Plate 6 Illustrates 5: 13–17. An eagle, predominantly brown in colouring, but with flashes of yellow on its extremely wide wings and with a black tail, thrusts its beak towards the midriff of Oothoon, who lies, naked, on a gold-yellow cloud, arms outstretched, thighs wide apart and legs bent at the knee. Her posture is one of sexual openness, and the design is highly erotic.

And none but Bromion can hear my lamentations.

With what sense is it that the chicken shuns the ravenous hawk?
With what sense does the tame pigeon measure out the expanse?
With what sense does the bee form cells? have not the mouse and frog

2–4 *With what sense ... With what sense* Here and elsewhere Blake builds momentum by using the rhetorical device known as anaphora, the repetition of a word or phrase at the beginning of successive clauses. Throughout her speech, Oothoon evinces a fascination with the diversity of different species which heralds Darwin's *On the Origin of Species* (1859).

Eyes and ears and sense of touch? yet are their habitations 5
And their pursuits, as different as their forms and as their joys:
Ask the wild ass why he refuses burdens: and the meek camel
Why he loves man: is it because of eye ear mouth or skin
Or breathing nostrils? No, for these the wolf and tyger have.
Ask the blind worm the secrets of the grave, and why her spires 10
Love to curl round the bones of death! and ask the rav'nous snake
Where she gets poison: and the wing'd eagle why he loves the sun
And then tell me the thoughts of man, that have been hid of old.

Silent I hover all the night, and all day could be silent,
If Theotormon once would turn his loved eyes upon me; 15
How can I be defil'd when I reflect thy image pure?
Sweetest the fruit that the worm feeds on, and the soul prey'd on by woe,
The new wash'd lamb ting'd with the village smoke and the bright swan
By the red earth of our immortal river: I bathe my wings,
And I am white and pure to hover round Theotormon's breast. 20

Then Theotormon broke his silence, and he answered.

Tell me what is the night or day to one o'erflow'd with woe?
Tell me what is a thought? and of what substance is it made?
Tell me what is a joy? and in what gardens do joys grow?
And in what rivers swim the sorrows? and upon what mountains 25

13 *And then ... old* The paragraph concludes with a suggestion that 'the thoughts of man' are as peculiar to him and perhaps as instinctual as the idiosyncrasies observable throughout the animal kingdom. Oothoon's intention is the celebration of variety.
17 *Sweetest ... woe* A major assertion of the value of experience.

22 *Tell ... woe?* Theotormon's questions do not relish the variety of life, as do Oothoon's. Rather, they seek anxiously to define. Lines 24–5, in particular, sound as though their speaker is cut off from his own experiences of 'joys' (24) and 'sorrows' (25).

Plate 7 design A naked Oothoon, left ankle manacled, curves in a black-green wave over the head of an unresponsive Theotormon, who sits at the edge of a sea, dressed in a blue gown, head bowed against his drawn-up knees. Oothoon's hands are joined in prayer; her expression is one of pleading love. In the background a sun appears above the horizon, emitting a blaze of red and yellow light.

Wave shadows of discontent? and in what houses dwell the wretched
Drunken with woe forgotten, and shut up from cold despair?

Tell me where dwell the thoughts forgotten till thou call them forth?
Tell me where dwell the joys of old? and where the ancient loves?
And when will they renew again and the night of oblivion past, 5
That I might traverse times and spaces far remote and bring
Comforts into a present sorrow and a night of pain?
Where goest thou O thought? to what remote land is thy flight?
If thou returnest to the present moment of affliction
Wilt thou bring comforts on thy wings, and dews and honey and balm; 10
Or poison from the desart wilds, from the eyes of the envier?

6–7 *That I ... pain* Theotormon longs for a solution to what he perceives as 'the present moment of affliction' (l. 9).
10–11 *Wilt thou ... envier?* 'Thou' is 'thought', invoked in line 8; Theotormon is mistrustful of what thought might bring with it, unsure whether it will deliver 'comforts' or 'poison'. He is ineffectual in his response to Oothoon's and his own predicament because he is unable to advance beyond a dithering questioning.

Then Bromion said: and shook the cavern with his lamentation

Thou knowest that the ancient trees seen by thine eyes have fruit;
But knowest thou that trees and fruits flourish upon the earth
To gratify senses unknown? trees beasts and birds unknown:
Unknown, not unperciev'd, spread in the infinite microscope,
In places yet unvisited by the voyager, and in worlds
Over another kind of seas, and in atmospheres unknown.
Ah! are there other wars, beside the wars of sword and fire?
And are there other sorrows, beside the sorrows of poverty?
And are there other joys, beside the joys of riches and ease?
And is there not one law for both the lion and the ox?
And is there not eternal fire, and eternal chains
To bind the phantoms of existence from eternal life?

Then Oothoon waited silent all the day, and all the night,

15

20

25

13–24   Thou knowest . . . eternal life? Taunting Theotormon, Bromion puts the case for experiences beyond those 'seen by thine eyes'. But he, too, is unable to conceive of human experience in anything like Oothoon's visionary terms, and he concludes by emphasizing the need for 'one law', hell, and 'eternal chains', as though rejecting his surmises of otherness as so many 'phantoms of existence'.

Plate 8 design   A figure, probably female, lies on a pillow; Blake appears to be illustrating the condition of masturbatory fantasies described in 10: 3–7.

But when the morn arose, her lamentation renewd,
The Daughters of Albion hear her woes, and eccho back her sighs.

O Urizen! Creator of men! mistaken Demon of heaven;
Thy joys are tears! thy labour vain, to form men to thine image.
How can one joy absorb another? are not different joys
Holy, eternal, infinite? and each joy is a Love.

Does not the great mouth laugh at a gift? and the narrow eyelids mock
At the labour that is above payment, and wilt thou take the ape
For thy councellor? or the dog for a schoolmaster to thy children?
Does he who contemns poverty, and he who turns with abhorrence
From usury feel the same passion or are they moved alike?
How can the giver of gifts experience the delights of the merchant?
How the industrious citizen the pains of the husbandman?
How different far the fat fed hireling with hollow drum;
Who buys whole corn fields into wastes, and sings upon the heath:

5

10

15

3   O Urizen . . . heaven The line begins Oothoon's final speech which will continue to 11:10. The speech brims with ideas and insights, often phrased in the form of thought-prompting questions, about the widest implications of her predicament. It recommends openness to experience, the embracing of sexuality, and the recognition of unique value; it condemns the restrictive ethic that governs the institution of marriage. It begins with an invocation of 'Urizen', embodiment of tyrannical rule-giving in Blake's mythic imaginings, and a crucial figure in many later prophetic books, including *The First Book of Urizen*. Oothoon sees him as equivalent both to the God of the Old Testament, the 'Creator of men', and as a 'Demon of heaven', seeking to deny the 'Holy, eternal, infinite' (l. 6) nature of 'joys' (l. 5).

10–11   Does he . . . alike? Many of Oothoon's questions are rhetorical; this one, however, seems genuinely open-ended.

14–15   How different . . . heath Oothoon's vision takes in contemporary social abuses; here, she may indict military recruiters (the 'fat fed hireling with hollow drum'), or gamekeepers who turn farmland into hunting-grounds for prosperous hunters (see *Early Illuminated Books*, p. 277).

How different their eye and ear! how different the world to them!
With what sense does the parson claim the labour of the farmer?
What are his nets and gins and traps, and how does he surround him
With cold floods of abstraction, and with forests of solitude,
To build him castles and high spires, where kings and priests may dwell. 20
Till she who burns with youth, and knows no fixed lot, is bound
In spells of law to one she loaths? and must she drag the chain
Of life, in weary lust? must chilling murderous thoughts obscure
The clear heaven of her eternal spring; to bear the wintry rage
Of a harsh terror driv'n to madness, bound to hold a rod 25
Over her shrinking shoulders all the day; and all the night
To turn the wheel of false desire: and longings that wake her womb
To the abhorred birth of cherubs in the human form
That live a pestilence and die a meteor and are no more;
Till the child dwell with one he hates, and do the deed he loaths 30
And the impure scourge force his seed into its unripe birth
E'er yet his eyelids can behold the arrows of the day?

Does the whale worship at thy footsteps as the hungry dog?
Or does he scent the mountain prey, because his nostrils wide
Draw in the ocean? does his eye discern the flying cloud 35
As the raven's eye? or does he measure the expanse like the vulture?
Does the still spider view the cliffs where eagles hide their young?
Or does the fly rejoice because the harvest is brought in?
Does not the eagle scorn the earth and despise the treasures beneath?
But the mole knoweth what is there, and the worm shall tell it thee. 40
Does not the worm erect a pillar in the mouldering church yard

17 *With ... farmer?* Alludes to the practice of 'tithes', whereby a tenth of a farmer's annual produce or income deriving from it had to be paid to the church. Lines 18–20 make clear Oothoon's hostility to this practice and her sense of a system of connected abuses linking 'kings and priests' (l. 20).
21–32 *Till she ... day* Oothoon moves from attacking 'kings and priests' to indicting the institution of marriage, seen as resulting in loveless unions for women, unions that expose women to physical abuse and enforced, joyless sex; their children, in turn, experience further misery. The writing has a subtle inwardness with processes of loathing and linked, reactive desire. Desire itself is poisoned in the circumstances delineated by Oothoon.

Plate 9 design A naked man (possibly Bromion since he holds a whip in his left hand, though possibly Theotormon if his intent is self-flagellation) lies to the left on a couch of what seems black cloud; to his right a naked woman moves forward, her head held in her hands. In the copy text, there is the suggestion that the head held in the woman's hands is a mask since above the woman's right shoulder is what seems to be a small head.

And a palace of eternity in the jaws of the hungry grave?
Over his porch these words are written, Take thy bliss O Man!
And sweet shall be thy taste and sweet thy infant joys renew!

Infancy, fearless, lustful, happy! nestling for delight
In laps of pleasure; Innocence! honest, open, seeking 5
The vigorous joys of morning light; open to virgin bliss.
Who taught thee modesty, subtil modesty? child of night and sleep

2 *Take ... Man!* Oothoon's reflections and questions lead to this restatement of a *carpe diem* theme.
5 *Innocence* This celebration of 'Innocence' sees it as wholly compatible with the 'vigorous joys' (l. 6) of sexuality. Oothoon attacks 'hypocrite modesty' (l. 16) in the remaining lines of the paragraph.

When thou awakest wilt thou dissemble all thy secret joys
Or wert thou not awake when all this mystery was disclos'd?
Then com'st thou forth a modest virgin knowing to dissemble   10
With nets found under thy night pillow, to catch virgin joy,
And brand it with the name of whore: and sell it in the night,
In silence, ev'n without a whisper, and in seeming sleep.
Religious dreams and holy vespers light thy smoky fires:
Once were thy fires lighted by the eyes of honest morn   15
And does my Theotormon seek this hypocrite modesty,
This knowing, artful, secret, fearful, cautious, trembling hypocrite?
Then is Oothoon a whore indeed! and all the virgin joys
Of life are harlots: and Theotormon is a sick man's dream
And Oothoon is the crafty slave of selfish holiness.   20

But Oothoon is not so, a virgin fill'd with virgin fancies
Open to joy and to delight where ever beauty appears;
If in the morning sun I find it, there my eyes are fix'd

18–20 *Then ... holiness* If one accepts that sexuality involves dissembled modesty, entrapment, and moral righteousness, then Theotormon would be right to proclaim the views set out here, views refuted by Oothoon in line 21.

22 *Open ... appears* Among the central assertions made by Oothoon, the line gains in emphasis from the reversed stress at its start.

Plate 10 design Three women (Daughters of Albion) sit in postures of consternation and concern at the top of the plate. One, to the right, wears red and has her head bowed; a second wears yellow, and sits in the front, sideways on, again hiding her head; a third wearing green, her hair streaming out as though blown by a wind, gazes with a stricken look into the middle distance. A much smaller figure in green huddles at the left of the group in a sideways posture.

In happy copulation; if in evening mild, wearied with work,
Sit on a bank and draw the pleasures of this free born joy.

   The moment of desire! the moment of desire! The virgin
That pines for man shall awaken her womb to enormous joys
In the secret shadows of her chamber; the youth shut up from   5
The lustful joy, shall forget to generate, and create an amorous image
In the shadows of his curtains and in the folds of his silent pillow.
Are not these the places of religion? the rewards of continence?
The self enjoyings of self denial? Why dost thou seek religion?
Is it because acts are not lovely, that thou seekest solitude,   10
Where the horrible darkness is impressed with reflections of desire?

Father of Jealousy, be thou accursed from the earth!
Why hast thou taught my Theotormon this accursed thing?

---

1 *In happy copulation* Extends the poem's dominant concern with sexuality to describe the ideal relationship between viewer and reality, a relationship akin to that of 'copulation'.

3–11 *The moment of desire! ... desire?* The repeated opening phrase may seem poised to introduce an ecstatic account of sexual rapture. Instead, what follows is a depiction of desire turned into masturbatory fantasy, which, for Blake, results from the influence of 'religion'. It should be said that 'The self enjoyings of self denial' are evoked with sympathy rather than disgust, as the inevitable consequence of sexual prohibition and the belief that 'acts are not lovely' (l. 10). The poetry owes its power to its ability to enter into the feelings of, say, the youth driven 'to create an amorous image', where 'create' is ironic and yet compassionate in its inflection.

12 *Father of Jealousy* Oothoon addresses Urizen.

Till beauty fades from off my shoulders darken'd and cast out,
A solitary shadow wailing on the margin of non-entity. 15

I cry, Love! Love! Love! happy happy Love! free as the mountain wind!
Can that be Love, that drinks another as a sponge drinks water?
That clouds with jealousy his nights, with weepings all the day:
To spin a web of age around him, grey and hoary! dark!
Till his eyes sicken at the fruit that hangs before his sight? 20
Such is self-love that envies all! a creeping skeleton
With lamplike eyes watching around the frozen marriage bed.

But silken nets and traps of adamant will Oothoon spread,
And catch for thee girls of mild silver, or of furious gold;
I'll lie beside thee on a bank and view their wanton play 25
In lovely copulation bliss on bliss with Theotormon;
Red as the rosy morning, lustful as the first born beam,
Oothoon shall view his dear delight, nor e'er with jealous cloud
Come in the heaven of generous love; nor selfish blightings bring.

Does the sun walk in glorious raiment, on the secret floor 30

14 *cast out* Picks up on the sounds of 'accursed' in the two previous lines, but moves away from anger towards a sense of inner desolateness.

15 *A solitary ... non-entity* A striking line, versions of which Blake uses in later works, because it suggests how 'entity' or being is, for Blake, bound up with subjective emotional states.

16–22 *I cry ... bed* Follows the same trajectory as lines 3–11, in that it begins with an affirmative cry, before passing into an account of the opposite of what Blake, like Keats in 'Ode on a Grecian Urn' (l. 25), calls 'happy happy Love!' (l. 16), namely, jealousy, envy, and 'self-love' (l. 21). Again, as is often the case in Blake, he reserves some of his finest writing for a shudder-inducing recoil from things as they are, as in the simile in lines 21–2, where the 'lamplike eyes watching' operate in the opposite way from Oothoon's at the end of the previous plate and beginning of this one.

23–9 *But ... bring* In her revolt against jealous possessiveness, Oothoon articulates an ethic of free love, an ethic tainted for some commentators by its reliance on an imagery of entrapment ('silken nets and traps' recalls the 'nets and gins and traps' of 8: 18) and its element of voyeurism ('Oothoon shall view his dear delight'). Perhaps the speech is best read as an attempt to imagine an alternative to the constraining sexual status quo, an attempt that involves considerable daring on the part of the female speaker. Psychologically, it might be seen as an effort on Oothoon's part to win back Theotormon (who shows no sign of budging from his own version of 'self-love').

26 *lovely copulation* Blake reuses words employed earlier in the plate: here 'lovely' affirms that acts are 'lovely' (see l. 10), while 'copulation' gives a specifically sexual sense to the all-inclusive 'happy copulation' described in line 1.

29 *heaven of generous love* Oothoon's humanist alternative to the traditional Christian heaven.

Plate 11 design At the bottom right is a group of three women (Daughters of Albion); one dressed in yellow looks down, but the other two figures – dressed in red and blue, respectively – look up to where a naked Oothoon flies in mid-air, arms stretched wide; flames float below her; a bank of brown-yellow cloud billows behind her. The sea remains dark and stormy at her feet, as does the blue horizon in the distance. Her posture recalls that of her attacker in Plate 1, but whereas he was bent on aggression Oothoon flies above like an angel of hope for the watching women.

Where the cold miser spreads his gold? or does the bright cloud drop
On his stone threshold? does his eye behold the beam that brings
Expansion to the eye of pity? or will he bind himself
Beside the ox to thy hard furrow? does not that mild beam blot
The bat, the owl, the glowing tyger, and the king of night? 5
The sea fowl takes the wintry blast for a cov'ring to her limbs:
And the wild snake, the pestilence to adorn him with gems and gold.
And trees and bird and beasts, and men behold their eternal joy.
Arise you little glancing wings, and sing your infant joy!
Arise and drink your bliss for every thing that lives is holy! 10

8 *And trees. ... joy* This 'beholding' conveys Oothoon's sense that the universe, if seen aright, is a place of dynamic, mutually interволving 'joy' for all elements of creation.

Thus every morning wails Oothoon, but Theotormon sits
Upon the margin'd ocean conversing with shadows dire.

The Daughters of Albion hear her woes, and eccho back her sighs.

The End

13 *The Daughters . . . sighs* Oothoon's words are left suspended by the poem's end; they speak in their sorrows and hopes to a readership whom Blake imagines still awaiting true liberation.

The First Book of Urizen

Printed by Blake in 1794, *The First Book of Urizen* [*U*] exists in a number of illuminated copies, eight in all, seven of which are extant. In each copy the plates are in a different order. In a letter to Dawson Turner of 9 June 1818, Blake speaks of *U* as having '28 Prints' (*E*, p. 771). Plates 4 and 16 are missing in four of the extant copies of the poem (and also from copy E, now untraced). The present text follows that of copy D, the basis for the relevant volume (vol. 6, ed. David Worrall, 1995) in the *Blake's Illuminated Books* series (see p. 26), but adds to it the two plates missing from D, plates 4 and 16: these plates can be found in Worrall (ed.), pp. 114–17. The consequent adjustment to the plate numbering in Worrall's edition is indicated in the headnote and notes by showing his edition's numbering in square brackets where it differs from the text supplied in this edition. For details of the ways in which the plates were ordered in different copies, see Worrall, pp. 148–9.

The fact that the plate-ordering of *U* varies from copy to copy is appropriate for a work that emphasizes confusion and disorder, the ironic consequences of Urizen's attempt to impose order. And yet *U* illustrates Blake's understanding of himself as a poet-prophet, ironizing the vision of earlier creators. In the Preludium he calls not on 'God' but on 'Eternals' (2: 2). Whereas Milton invokes the Holy Spirit at the start of his epic attempt to 'justify the ways of God to men' (*Paradise Lost*, I. 26), Blake is intent on revealing 'dark visions of torment' (2: 7) as he replaces the benevolent God of traditional Christianity with the repressive figure of Urizen. Foreshadowing Freud's notion of the tyrannous superego, Urizen embodies limits and the desire for limiting forms of order. His name is pronounced with a stress on the first syllable; yet it may derive from 'Your Reason', a mockingly polite form of address. It may also derive from the Greek word that lies behind 'horizon'. Urizen's futile attempts to establish 'a solid without fluctuation' (4: 11 [Additional Plate 1]) implicate Los, or the poetic imagination, delegated by the Eternals to 'confine, / The obscure separation alone' (5: 39–40 [4: 39–40]). Indeed, the very awareness by the Eternals of Urizen's 'obscure separation' indicates that they, too have been caught up in, even as they seek to hold at bay, the Urizenic compulsion to fence off and define. Much of

U reads as a satire on God's work in the first chapter of Genesis. The God of Genesis 'saw every thing that he had made, and behold, it was very good' (1: 31). Blake looks at the creation – including the construction of the human body and of the different sexes – and sees a hideous monstrosity. Creation is a kind of Fall in *U*, a falling away from the 'unquenchable burnings' (4: 13 [Additional Plate 1]) of Eternity. Formally the poem reflects its satiric and ironic intent, being divided into quasi-biblical chapters and arranged in the original in double columns as though it were a Bible. Blake departs from the long line (normally septenaries, or seven-feet lines) used in previous Lambeth prophecies (such as *Visions*) and employs a shorter line suited to harsh alienations of perspective and scenarios of 'unseen conflictions' (3: 14). It is a style that captures vividly the illusory nature of Urizen's conflictions, and yet enters the workings of his mind. Urizen is the hero of his own epic struggle: the poem presents views of his acts and thoughts both from outside and inside (especially in Plate 4). From outside, Urizen is a 'soul-shudd'ring vacuum' (3: 5), engaged in futile if 'enormous labours' (3: 22). Even his identity is insecure, an introspective delusion; he is 'A selfcontemplating shadow' (3: 21), himself the embodiment of the 'petrific abominable chaos' (3: 26) which he fears. From the inside, especially as depicted through the monologue of Plate 4, Urizen is the hero of his attempt to establish order; he is the conqueror of chaos after perilous adventures in which he was 'self-balanc'd stretch'd o'er the void. / I alone, even I' (4: 18–19 [Additional Plate 1]). Blake's tone is at once satirical and adapted to Urizen's self-conception. Urizen's outlook is embodied in his 'Book / Of eternal brass, written in my solitude' (4: 32–3 [Additional Plate 1]), in which he prescribes prohibitions and dictates, all in the service of a crushing uniformity, 'One King, one God, one Law' (4: 40 [Additional Plate 1).

One of Urizen's functions, then, is to suggest the repressive power of the written. His writings enshrine not merely the workings of reason, however, but also the dire consequences of misapplied imagination. Los enters the poem as an alternative form of imaginative activity, but in *U* he is a less developed figure than in the later prophetic books, *Milton* and *Jerusalem*. In

U Los must bind and confine in order to limit the damage caused by Urizen's defection from eternal life; but he risks being caught up in the plight he deplores, dragged down into the fall to which he attempts to set limits. This setting of limits results in a series of 'changes' (8: 12 [7: 12]) that lead to the binding of 'The eternal mind' (10: 19 [9: 19]); these changes include the creation of the human body, of different genders and of the child, Orc, born to Los and his partner Enitharmon, all represented as horrific catastrophes from the perspective of Eternity. The consequences are emotional division and conflict, of which the fitting emblem is 'the Chain of Jealousy' (20: 24 [18: 24]), as well as the emergence of a material universe in which, in a striking anticipation of Charles Darwin's theories, Urizen 'saw that life liv'd upon death' (23: 27 [21: 27]), and the creation of a mind-manacling 'Net of Religion' (25: 22 [23: 22]). In the final chapter, in a parody of Genesis, human beings decline into something like their current form (though they are still of 'seven feet stature', 25: 38 [23: 38]), before one of Urizen's sons, Fuzon, a fire-god, leaves 'the pendulous earth' (28: 21 [26: 21]), concluding the poem with a faint hope of future rebellion (the subject of *The Book of Ahania*, in which Fuzon's revolt is crushed by Urizen). *U* is a work of astonishing power, full of often parodic inventiveness and marked by a harshly expressive use of three- and four-stress lines. The designs are among Blake's most vivid pictorial works; they give overpowering expression to visions of entrapment and struggle.

Plate 1: Title-page design The design shows a white-bearded Urizen whose eyes are closed writing with both hands on open books. His left foot is placed on a book. A tree grows overhead. Behind him are two tablets of stone without writing. The design is the start of many references to writing in *U*.

Plate 2 design Above the text, bordered by flame-like shoots, floats a woman in a swirling white gown, holding her left hand out towards a young child whose right hand touches the woman's left hand. The plate is the only one in *U* where the writing is not divided into two columns, and has a gentle positiveness often lacking in the text and designs elsewhere in the poem. In Blake's *A Small Book of Designs* (1796) this design is entitled 'Teach these souls to fly'.

Preludium to The First Book of *Urizen*

Of the primeval Priest's assum'd power,
When Eternals spurn'd back his religion;
And gave him a place in the north,
Obscure, shadowy, void, solitary.

Eternals I hear your call gladly, 5
Dictate swift winged words and fear not
To unfold your dark visions of torment.

1 *Of . . . power* The opening alludes to and parodies the opening of *Paradise Lost*, 'Of man's first disobedience'.
2 *spurn'd back . . . religion* Makes clear that at stake in the poem is an exploration of 'religion': Blake satirizes what he sees as a 'false' religion; the idea of 'true' religion remains implicit.

Plate 3 design Above the double-columned text a naked figure with arms and legs extended whirls round in the midst of dark-red flames, possibly illustrating the energy of eternal life.

Chap: I.

1. Lo, a shadow of horror is risen
In Eternity! Unknown, unprolific!
Self-clos'd, all-repelling; what Demon
Hath form'd this abominable void
This soul-shudd'ring vacuum? Some said 5
"It is Urizen". But unknown, abstracted
Brooding secret, the dark power hid.

3–5 *what . . . vacuum?* The perspective enjoined on the reader is doubt and wonder.
7 *Brooding secret* Echoes but contrasts ironically with Milton's Holy Spirit, described in *Paradise Lost* as having 'sat'st brooding on the vast abyss / And mad'st it pregnant' (I. 21–2).

2. Time on times he divided, and measur'd
Space by space in his ninefold darkness
Unseen unknown: changes appeard 10
Like desolate mountains rifted furious
By the black winds of perturbation.

3. For he strove in battles dire
In unseen conflictions with shapes
Bred from his forsaken wilderness, 15
Of beast, bird, fish, serpent and element,
Combustion, blast, vapour and cloud.

4. Dark revolving in silent activity:
Unseen in tormenting passions;
An activity unknown and horrible; 20
A self-contemplating shadow,
In enormous labours occupied.

5. But Eternals beheld his vast forests;
Ages on ages he lay, clos'd, unknown,
Brooding shut in the deep; all avoid 25
The petrific abominable chaos.

6. His cold horrors silent, dark Urizen
Prepar'd: his ten thousands of thunders
Rang'd in gloom'd array stretch out across
The dread world, and the rolling of wheels 30
As of swelling seas, sound in his clouds,
In his hills of stor'd snows, in his mountains
Of hail and ice; voices of terror,
Are heard, like thunders of autumn,
When the cloud blazes over the harvests. 35

Chap: II.

1. Earth was not, nor globes of attraction;
The will of the Immortal expanded
Or contracted his all flexible senses.
Death was not, but eternal life sprung.

2. The sound of a trumpet the heavens 40
Awoke and vast clouds of blood roll'd
Round the dim rocks of Urizen, so nam'd
That solitary one in Immensity.

3. Shrill the trumpet: and myriads of Eternity

18–21 *Dark revolving ... shadow* Blake's short line and appositional syntax capture the process of self-contemplation which marks Urizen's solipsistic self-creation; the lines seem to 'revolve' round one another without advancing much as Urizen's 'enormous labours' (l. 22) solve nothing.
26 *petrific* Stony. See *Paradise Lost* 10. 294 which describes 'Death with his mace petrific'.
28 *Prepar'd* The holding-back of the verb conveys Urizen's secrecy in making his preparation.
28–35 *his ten thousand ... harvests* The language is that of the sublime, possibly parodically so.

36 *globes of attraction* Associated by Blake with Newton's gravitational system, a system at odds with Blake's own visionary understanding of reality.
40 *The ... trumpet* Recalls various biblical trumpets, including the trumpet which precedes the issuing to Moses by God of the Ten Commandments on Mount Sinai (Exodus 19: 16) and the 'seven trumpets' of Revelation (8: 6). Blake's poem mocks the law-giving of the Old Testament, but it has its own apocalyptic ambitions.
43 *That ... Immensity* Again Urizen is described in terms usually applied to the God of the Bible.

Plate 4 [Additional Plate 1] design In this plate, which Blake omitted from four of the seven extant copies, possibly to 'de-heroicize' Urizen or possibly because of technical problems (see Robert N. Essick, 'Variation, Accident, and Intention in Blake's *Book of Urizen*', *Studies in Bibliography* 39 (1986), pp. 230–5), the design is difficult to interpret because its outlines verge on the abstract. Drizzling greens and browns seem to indicate a permanent rain, falling on what appears to be a shapeless naked man, head bowed, left leg bent in front of him, right leg stretched out.

Muster around the bleak desarts
Now fill'd with clouds, darkness and waters
That roll'd perplex'd labring and utter'd
Words articulate, bursting in thunders
That roll'd on the tops of his mountains.   5

4. From the depths of dark solitude, from
The eternal abode in my holiness,
Hidden, set apart in my stern counsels
Reserv'd for the days of futurity,
I have sought for a joy without pain,   10
For a solid without fluctuation.
Why will you die O Eternals?
Why live in unquenchable burnings?

5. First I fought with the fire; consum'd
Inwards, into a deep world within: 15
A void immense, wild, dark and deep
Where nothing was; Nature's wide womb
And self balanc'd stretch'd o'er the void.

I alone, even I! the winds merciless
Bound; but condensing in torrents   20
They fall and fall; strong, I repell'd
The vast waves, and arose on the waters
A wide world of solid obstruction.

6. Here alone I in books form'd of metals
Have written the secrets of wisdom,   25
The secrets of dark contemplation
By fightings and conflicts dire
With terrible monsters Sin-bred:
Which the bosoms of all inhabit;
Seven deadly Sins of the soul.   30

4–5 *Words ... mountains* Recalls God's appearance to Moses in Exodus 'on the top of the mount' (Exodus 19: 20).
6 *From ... from* The prepositions indicate Urizen's sense of his own fathomless inwardness.
7 *my holiness* Urizen's self-praise betrays his arrogance.
9 *days of futurity* Urizen tyrannically suppresses the present in favour of some supposed religious reward in the future.
10–13 *I ... burnings?* Urizen again betrays the faultlines in his thinking; he wishes for an impossible consistency of experience and rejects the 'unquenchable burnings' which constitute eternal life. His question in line 12 echoes Ezekiel 18: 31, 'why will ye die, O house of Israel?'
15 *a deep world within* A Urizenic equivalent to Miltonic Chaos. As throughout this plate, the writing enters Urizen's mode of thinking with intense, if intensely ironic, empathy.

22–3 *arose ... obstruction* Blake's word-ordering allows the 'wide world of solid obstruction' a line to itself, after a series of lines with conflict-ridden pauses and caesurae. Urizen pronounces the line with satisfaction, but the reader notices that his achievement is to have become an 'obstruction'.
24 *Here ... metals* It is perhaps worthy of note, as Nelson Hilton has noted ('Blakean Zen,' *Studies in Romanticism* 24 (1985), pp. 183–2000), that Blake printed 'metals' on two lines ('me- / tals'). As a result, an especially egotistical line ends with the word 'me'. However, Blake hyphenated many words because of the space limitations created by the double-columned presentation of text.
28 *terrible ... Sin-bred* These 'monsters' are themselves begotten by Urizen's sense of sin, as are the 'Seven deadly Sins of the soul' (l. 30).

7. Lo! I unfold my darkness: and on
This rock, place with strong hand the Book
Of eternal brass, written in my solitude.

8. Laws of peace, of love, of unity;
Of pity, compassion, forgiveness, 35
Let each chuse one habitation;
His ancient infinite mansion;
One command, one joy, one desire,
One curse, one weight, one measure
One King, one God, one Law. 40

Chap: III.

1. The voice ended, they saw his pale visage
Emerge from the darkness; his hand
On the rock of eternity unclasping
The Book of brass. Rage siez'd the strong.

2. Rage, fury, intense indignation 45
In cataracts of fire, blood and gall,
In whirlwinds of sulphurous smoke:
And enormous forms of energy;
All the seven deadly sins of the soul

---

31 *Lo!* Compare the opening of Plate 3; here Urizen unveils what he regards as his 'secrets of wisdom' (l. 25).
32–3 *the Book / Of eternal brass* For the tablets of stone on which God gives Moses in Exodus (24: 12), Urizen supplies his book made of brass. The mockery runs both ways.
34–5 *Laws...forgiveness* The abstractions may appeal, but Urizen's determination to impose 'Laws' upon them suggests that they will participate in his will to power over others.
40 *One King...one Law* Such unity for Blake will result in oppression.
41 *they saw* Presumably the Eternals, who are also 'the strong' alluded to in line 44.
45–9 *Rage...soul* The energies of the Eternal are interpreted by Urizen as 'seven deadly sins'.

Plate 5 [Plate 4] design A white-haired figure, presumably Urizen, with arms at full stretch holds open a large book, made of some hard material (probably brass); the book contains coloured daubs, possibly satirizing the idea of a sacred book.

In living creations appear'd
In the flames of eternal fury.

3. Sund'ring, dark'ning, thund'ring!
Rent away with a terrible crash
Eternity roll'd wide apart 5
Wide asunder rolling
Mountainous all around
Departing; departing: departing:
Leaving ruinous fragments of life
Hanging frowning cliffs and all between 10
An ocean of voidness unfathomable.

1–2 *In...fury* The lines recall the 'unquenchable burnings' (4: 13) from which Urizen recoils.
3 *Sund'ring...thund'ring!* The participles here and in the lines following capture a process of disintegration.

4. The roaring fires ran o'er the heav'ns
In whirlwinds and cataracts of blood
And o'er the dark desarts of Urizen
Fires pour through the void on all sides 15
On Urizen's self-begotten armies.

5. But no light from the fires, all was darkness
In the flames of Eternal fury.

6. In fierce anguish and quenchless flames
To the desarts and rocks he ran raging 20
To hide, but he could not: combining
He dug mountains and hills in vast strength,
He piled them in incessant labour,
In howlings and pangs and fierce madness,
Long periods in burning fires labouring 25
Till hoary, and age-broke, and aged,
In despair and the shadows of death.

7. And a roof vast petrific around,
On all sides he fram'd: like a womb;
Where thousands of rivers in veins 30
Of blood pour down the mountains to cool
The eternal fires beating without,
From Eternals; and like a black globe
View'd by sons of Eternity, standing
On the shore of the infinite ocean 35
Like a human heart struggling and beating
The vast world of Urizen appear'd.

8. And Los round the dark globe of Urizen
Kept watch for Eternals to confine
The obscure separation alone; 40
For Eternity stood wide apart

12–27 *The roaring ... shadows of death* Eternity crashes its fires down upon Urizen in an outpouring of 'fury' (l. 18); Urizen attempts to take refuge from these fires, seeking to hide underneath 'mountains and hills' (l. 22) as when in Revelation human beings call upon the 'mountains and rocks' to 'Fall on us, and hide us from the face of him that sitteth on the throne' (6: 16). Thus Urizen is momentarily identified with those who would hide from God's wrath.
29 *fram'd* Compare the 'framing' of 'The Tyger'. Urizen is now a creator, but his creation takes the form of a protection against, that is a denial of, 'eternal fires' (l. 32).

37 *The vast ... appear'd* Compare 4: 23. Urizen's world has about it qualities of our material universe; it is 'like a black globe' (l. 33) and 'Like a human heart' (l. 36), features which mark it, for Blake, as fallen.
38 *And Los ... Urizen* Los appears as working on behalf of the Eternals, a precursor of the poet-prophet he will become in later prophetic works by Blake.
41 *For ... wide apart* Earlier 'Eternity roll'd wide apart' (l. 5); now as the fires cool and solidification takes over, it is said to have 'stood wide apart': an example of Blake's control of tempo in *U*.

Plate 6 [Plate 5] design Arms outstretched, a youthful figure is positioned upside down, as though falling, in a sea of flames; a dark, speckled serpent coils round his body, its open mouth close to his head. (In other copies there are three such figures.) The design calls to mind the crucifixion (upside down, as tradition has it that Saint Peter was crucified), and there may be an allusion to the design in Plate 3. There, a similar figure delights in the flames of Eternity; here, a figure enters the Urizenic world of law and judgement.

As the stars are apart from the earth.

9. Los wept howling round the dark Demon:
And cursing his lot for in anguish
Urizen was rent from his side.
And a fathomless void for his feet; 5
And intense fires for his dwelling.

10. But Urizen laid in a stony sleep
Unorganiz'd, rent from Eternity.

11. The Eternals said: What is this? Death.
Urizen is a clod of clay. 10

1 *As... earth* Blake mimes the apartness of which he speaks by separating this comparison from the previous plate to which it belongs syntactically.
2 *dark Demon* Urizen as viewed by Los.
4 *rent... side* Urizen and Los are now divided from one another; the implication is that, in Eternity, they shared in one another's being as 'The will of the Immortal expanded / Or contracted his all flexible senses' (3: 37–8).
8 *Unorganiz'd* Ironic, since Urizen's efforts have been bent on establishing 'A solid without fluctuation'.

Plate 7 [Plate 6] design A foreshortened naked figure set against flames dominates the design; his eyes start, his mouth is agape and he hugs himself in horror; his hands hold or cup each ear. Presumably the representation is of Los, appalled by his task.

12. Los howl'd in a dismal stupor,
Groaning! gnashing! groaning!
Till the wrenching apart was healed.

13. But the wrenching of Urizen heal'd not.
Cold, featureless, flesh or clay. 5
Rifted with direful changes
He lay in a dreamless night,

14. Till Los rouz'd his fires affrighted
At the formless unmeasurable death.

2 *Groaning... groaning!* Again, Blake gives participles an independent life, thrusting the reader into the immediacy of the experience.
4 *But... not* The previous line's hope – of a healed wrenching – is denied.
6 *Rifted* Implies the process of gaps or rifts involved in Urizen's 'direful changes' (l. 6).

Plate 8 [Plate 7] design A skeleton curls up in a near-foetal position, sitting on what looks like a coral ground, its spine curved against what looks like a blue aqueous solution, its skull held between its hands. This is the human form bequeathed by Urizen's 'changes'.

Chap: IV.
1. Los smitten with astonishment
Frighten'd at the hurtling bones

2. And at the surging sulphureous
Perturbed Immortal mad raging

3. In whirlwinds and pitch and nitre 5
Round the furious limbs of Los.

4 *Immortal* Urizen.

4. And Los formed nets and gins
   And threw the nets round about.

   5. He watch'd in shuddring fear
   The dark changes and bound every change
   With rivets of iron and brass;

   6. And these were the changes of Urizen:

9–11 *He ... brass* Giving form to Urizen's 'dark changes' (l. 10), Los employs Urizenic tactics of entrapment ('nets and gins', l. 7) and binding.

12 *And ... Urizen* Has a mock-biblical ring, like many of the locutions in *U*.

Plate 9 [Plate 8] design A naked white-bearded figure, Urizen, kneels on his left knee beneath a cavern whose roof seems to press against his hunched shoulders.

Plate 10 [Plate 9] design A naked young man, back to the viewer and head hidden by an overhanging ledge of rock, forces his way through an opening in a cave-like structure, coloured as though covered with lichen. His left leg is bent, his right outstretched.

Chap: IV.

   1. Ages on ages roll'd over him!
   In stony sleep ages roll'd over him!
   Like a dark waste stretching, chang'able,
   By earthquakes riv'n, belching sullen fires
   On ages roll'd ages in ghastly
   Sick torment; around him in whirlwinds
   Of darkness the eternal Prophet howl'd
   Beating still on his rivets of iron,
   Pouring sodor of iron; dividing
   The horrible night into watches.

   2. And Urizen (so his eternal name)
   His prolific delight obscur'd more and more
   In dark secresy hiding in surging
   Sulphureous fluid his phantasies.
   The Eternal Prophet heav'd the dark bellows
   And turn'd restless the tongs; and the hammer
   Incessant beat; forging chains new and new,
   Numb'ring with links hours, days and years.

   3. The eternal mind bounded began to roll
   Eddies of wrath ceaseless round and round
   And the sulphureous foam surging thick
   Settled, a lake, bright, and shining clear
   White as snow on the mountains cold.

1 *him* Urizen.
2 *ages* Blake's language gives the sense of the speeding-up of millennia of geological processes.
7 *eternal Prophet* Los.
9 *sodor* Blake's coinage for 'solder' ('fusible alloy used to join edges of less fusible metals').
9 *dividing* Division here is necessary if the 'horrible night' (l. 10) is to be given a form which will make it endurable.
11 *And ... name* Blake reminds us of Urizen's 'eternal' nature.
12–14 *His prolific ... phantasies* Urizen's 'prolific delights' in Eternity have turned into secretive 'phantasies',
a queasy metamorphosis rendered by Blake's 'fluid' syntax.
17 *chains new and new* The repetition conveys the succession of 'new' chains being created.
18 *Numb'ring ... years* In the fallen state units of time and processes of numbering dominate.
19–23 *The eternal ... cold* Blake uses devices of internal rhyme ('bounded', l. 19, with 'round and round', l. 20, and 'bright', l. 22, with 'White', l. 23) as well as strong initial stresses (see ll. 20 and 22) to convey the binding and stilling of 'eternal' energies.

4. Forgetfulness, dumbness, necessity!
In chains of the mind locked up
Like fetters of ice shrinking together
Disorganiz'd, rent from Eternity.
Los beat on his fetters of iron:
And heated his furnaces and pour'd
Iron sodor and sodor of brass.

5. Restless turn'd the immortal inchain'd
Heaving dolorous! anguish'd! unbearable
Till a roof shaggy wild inclos'd
In an orb his fountain of thought.

6. In a horrible dreamful slumber;
Like the linked infernal chain;
A vast Spine writh'd in torment
Upon the winds; shooting pain'd
Ribs, like a bending cavern,
And bones of solidness froze
Over all his nerves of joy.
And a first Age passed over
And a state of dismal woe.

24 *Forgetfulness . . . necessity!* 'Necessity' is a major term in 1790s philosophical discourse, describing an inexorable causal link set in motion by events; it could give comfort to those libertarians who, disappointed by the development of the French Revolution, hoped that ultimately reform would prevail. For Blake, here, the word describes an aspect of a fallen condition and evokes 'the Philosophy of Causes & Consequences' (*E*, p. 601) which he attacks in his Annotations to Lavater.
25 *chains of the mind* Compare with 'The mind-forg'd manacles' (l. 8) of 'London'.
27 *Disorganiz'd* The 'disorganization' is the more felt by the reader because of the lack of a stated antecedent for 'Disorganiz'd'; we assume Urizen is meant, but Los may be referred to as well.

31 *Restless turn'd the immortal* Again Blake makes identification less than straightforward; Urizen is the prime candidate for 'the immortal', but 'restless' is a word that has, earlier in this plate, been applied to Los (see l. 16).
37 *A vast Spine* The beginnings of humanized form, said to resemble the 'linked infernal chain' (l. 36) which Los has been constructing as a means of setting a limit to Urizen's chaotic state. Ironically, 'necessity' turns out to be the ruler of the fallen world, as events and acts form links in a chain.
42 *And a first Age* Compare the relating of creation in Genesis where each day is marked off (1: 5, 8, 13, 19, 23, 31, 2: 2). In *U* Blake's allusion works ironically.

Plate 11 [Plate 10] design Depicts two naked figures in anguished states, both crouching with knees raised. On the left a gaunt, skeleton-like figure is set against a wave of flame with a black chain in front of him; his head twists upward. On the right a more substantial male figure, represented as though his arms were leg-like limbs, holds in his right hand a hammer; his expression is one of sorrow and possibly extreme fatigue. The former figure is likely to be Urizen, the latter Los.

7. From the caverns of his jointed Spine
Down sunk with fright a red
Round globe hot burning deep
Deep down into the Abyss:
Panting: Conglobing, Trembling,
Shooting out ten thousand branches
Around his solid bones.
And a second Age passed over
And a state of dismal woe.

5 *Panting . . . Trembling* Again participles plunge the reader into a process, here one of horrific metamorphosis as nerves ('branches', l. 6) shoot out through the newly forming body.

8. In harrowing fear rolling round,
His nervous brain shot branches
Round the branches of his heart
On high into two little orbs
And fixed in two little caves
Hiding carefully from the wind,
His Eyes beheld the deep,
And a third Age passed over:
And a state of dismal woe.

9. The pangs of hope began,
In heavy pain striving, struggling,
Two Ears in close volutions.
From beneath his orbs of vision
Shot spiring out and petrified
As they grew. And a fourth Age passed
And a state of dismal woe.

10. In ghastly torment sick;
Hanging upon the wind,

---

14 *two little caves* Blake's term for the eye-sockets communicates his wariness of knowledge derived from the senses.
23 *petrified* The ear takes on solid form; 'petrified' may allude to the 'petrous', a bone in the inner ear. More generally, 'petrified' conveys Blake's sense that the material body involves a petrification, a hardening, of possibilities of awareness.

Plate 12 [Plate 11] design A naked old man with white-flowing beard (Urizen), knees bent and arms outstretched, hangs vertically in blue-green water. It is difficult to tell whether he is actively swimming.
Plate 13 [Plate 12] design A graceful naked female figure in the middle of a plate with much writing appears against a blue-black sky, her outstretched arms holding apart two clusters of cloud. She may represent 'Pity' (l. 51) which in the plate is seen as 'dividing and dividing' (l. 52).

Two Nostrils bent down to the deep.
And a fifth Age passed over,
And a state of dismal woe.

11. In ghastly torment sick,
Within his ribs bloated round,
A craving Hungry Cavern;
Thence arose his channel'd Throat
And like a red flame a Tongue
Of thirst and of hunger appear'd
And a sixth Age passed over:
And a state of dismal woe

12. Enraged and stifled with torment
He threw his right Arm to the north,
His left Arm to the south
Shooting out in anguish deep,
And his Feet stamp'd the nether Abyss
In trembling and howling and dismay.

---

1 *Two ... deep* Again there is an expressive carry-over of sense from the previous plate, prolonging the first experience of smell.
6 *Hungry Cavern* The stomach.
8 *like a red flame* The simile links the 'Tongue' (l. 8) with previous flame-imagery; this flame stands in contrast, however, with those that characterize the condition of the Eternals.
12–16 *Enraged ... Abyss* Blake achieves his grotesquely mythic effects through powerful verbs and a sublime geography in which definite articles are significant ('*the* north', l. 13, '*the* south' l. 14, '*the* nether Abyss', l. 16).

And a seventh Age passed over
And a state of dismal woe.

Chap: V.

1. In terrors Los shrunk from his task:
His great hammer fell from his hand.
His fires beheld, and sickening
Hid their strong limbs in smoke.
For with noises ruinous loud,
With hurtlings and clashings and groans
The Immortal endur'd his chains
Though bound in a deadly sleep.

2. All the myriads of Eternity
All the wisdom and joy of life
Roll like a sea around him
Except what his little orbs
Of sight by degrees unfold.

3. And now his eternal life
Like a dream was obliterated.

4. Shudd'ring, the Eternal Prophet smote
With a stroke, from his north to south region.
The bellows and hammer are silent now;
A nerveless silence his prophetic voice
Siez'd; a cold solitude and dark void
The Eternal Prophet and Urizen clos'd.

5. Ages on ages roll'd over them,
Cut off from life and light, frozen
Into horrible forms of deformity.
Los suffer'd his fires to decay;
Then he look'd back with anxious desire
But the space undivided by existence
Struck horror into his soul.

6. Los wept obscur'd with mourning,
His bosom earthquak'd with sighs;
He saw Urizen deadly black
In his chains bound and Pity began

7. In anguish dividing and dividing,
For pity divides the soul
In pangs eternity on eternity,
Life in cataracts pour'd down his cliffs.
The void shrunk the lymph into Nerves
Wandring wide on the bosom of night

---

21 *His . . . hand* This detail may be partly represented in Plate 11's design.
28 *myriads* The meaning of the word ('tens of thousands') is given fresh life in context, reminding us of the shutting-down of eternal life.
33–4 *And now . . . obliterated* Arguably these lines are at the elegiac heart of *U*, as of other Romantic poems.
40 *The Eternal Prophet and Urizen* Los has now succumbed to a fallen state; he has, as a later line in the plate puts it, 'suffer'd his fires to decay' (l. 44).
45 *anxious desire* With the fall come emotions of longing and pity which further confirm the isolation of the self.
53 *For pity . . . soul* The generalization shows how Blake makes the events of *U* suit larger purposes. Pity 'divides the soul' for Blake because it separates the person pitying from the person pitied and introduces mingled feelings – of superiority as well as compassion.

> And left a round globe of blood
> Trembling upon the void.

58–9 *And left . . . void* Part of the poetry's impact comes from Blake's ability to move between frames of reference: an image – the 'globe of blood' (l. 58) – that appears to belong within the human body is related to cosmic space. Blake captures a state where division between inner and outer is itself only beginning to take on solid form.

Plate 14 [Plate 13] design Upside down, a naked young male figure, immersed in water or air, pushes with both arms against blue rocks or clouds. There are links and contrasts between the image and the designs in Plate 10 [9], in which a figure explores an opening in a cave, and in Plate 12 [11] in which an old man, right side up, is immersed in water.

Plate 15 [Plate 14] design The design shows the upper bodies of three figures who look down at the rim of a dark globe edged with flame. The central figure, a young male, trails the fingers of his left hand over the globe, leaving a track of white; he is flanked by two white-bearded older figures. The picture may represent the Eternals looking down at 'The Abyss of Los' (15 [14]: 5).

> Thus the Eternal Prophet was divided
> Before the death image of Urizen,
> For in changeable clouds and darkness
> In a winterly night beneath
> The Abyss of Los stretch'd, immense,   5
> And now seen, now obscur'd, to the eyes
> Of Eternals the visions remote
> Of the dark separation appear'd.
> As glasses discover Worlds
> In the endless Abyss of space   10
> So the expanding eyes of Immortals
> Beheld the dark visions of Los,
> And the globe of life blood trembling.

1 *was divided* As elsewhere in *U* division has occurred.
6 *now . . . obscur'd* That is, the 'visions remote' (l. 7) are sometimes visible, sometimes not, to the Eternals.

9 *As . . . Worlds* The glasses are astronomical instruments; the Newtonian universe has materialized. The simile captures the 'separation' (l. 8) of the Eternals from 'the dark visions of Los' (l. 12).

Plate 16 [Additional Plate 2] design This design, found only in three copies of *U*, shows a naked figure, with his knees drawn up to his chin and his hands joined behind his head; he sits or squats in a shower of flames. The figure may be Los.

Plate 17 [Plate 15] design A kneeling figure bends his or her head above a globe of blood; red filaments connect the globe to the hair of the figure. The base of the figure's naked back reveals a network of veins and arteries, which run along the thighs.

Plate 18 [Plate 16] design A naked male figure, Los, stands, arms outstretched, against a background of dark-red flames; from his left hand hangs a black hammer.

> 8. The globe of life blood trembled
> Branching out into roots:
> Fibrous, writhing upon the winds:
> Fibres of blood, milk and tears:
> In pangs, eternity on eternity.   5
> At length in tears and cries imbodied
> A female form trembling and pale
> Waves before his deathy face.

4 *Fibres . . . tears* Again Blake depicts the human body with anatomical fascination; the writing wavers between abhorrence for the physicality of the human being, seen as involving 'pangs' (l. 5) in its creation, and deep preoccupation with it.

7 *A female form* The female is the result of Los's inner division.

9. All Eternity shudder'd at sight
Of the first female now separate, 10
Pale as a cloud of snow
Waving before the face of Los.

10. Wonder, awe, fear, astonishment
Petrify the eternal myriads
At the first female form now separate. 15

9 *shudder'd* The initial response of the Eternals appears to be one of horror, but as line 13 suggests this passes into something more complex.
12 *Waving* Owes its peculiarly hallucinatory quality to the fact that it picks up on 'Waves' in line 8.
14 *Petrify* A further instance of 'petrifaction' in *U*.

Plate 19 [Plate 17] design A naked woman stands, her body bent away from a naked man who sits, curled up, head in his hands. The design represents Enitharmon and Los,

They call'd her Pity, and fled.

11. "Spread a Tent with strong curtains around them.
Let cords and stakes bind in the Void
That Eternals may no more behold them."

12. They began to weave curtains of darkness, 5
They erected large pillars round the Void,
With golden hooks fasten'd in the pillars;
With infinite labour the Eternals
A woof wove, and called it Science.

Chap: VI.

1. But Los saw the Female and pitied; 10
He embrac'd her, she wept, she refus'd;
In perverse and cruel delight
She fled from his arms, yet he follow'd.

2. Eternity shudder'd when they saw,
Man begetting his likeness, 15
On his own divided image.

3. A time passed over, the Eternals
Began to erect the tent;
When Enitharmon sick, 20
Felt a Worm within her womb.

4. Yet helpless it lay like a Worm
In the trembling womb
To be moulded into existence.

1 *They call'd her Pity* Naming is a preoccupation of *U*; it forms part of the process of giving shape to experience, a giving shape that may limit.
2–9 *"Spread... Science* Now the Eternals shield themselves from 'the Void' (ll. 3, 6). Their 'Science' is, for Blake, a form of objective knowing that wards off the possibility of visionary apprehension. Blake himself 'weaves' image and abstraction with great skill in this passage.
12 *perverse... delight* Relations between male and female in Blake are often characterized by a pattern of male pursuit and female evasiveness.
19 *Enitharmon* Named for the first time in the poem, she appears in other Blakean prophetic books as Los's partner or emanation and as an embodiment of what Blake calls 'Female will'.
20 *Worm* The word, suggestive of the poem's quasi-Gnostic distaste for processes of sexual reproduction, is sometimes used in the Old Testament to express humanity's degradation (Job 25: 6 'How much less man, that is a worm' and Psalm 22:6 'I am a worm and no man').

5. All day the worm lay on her bosom, 25
All night within her womb
The worm lay till it grew to a serpent
With dolorous hissings and poisons
Round Enitharmon's loins folding.

6. Coil'd within Enitharmon's womb 30
The serpent grew casting its scales;
With sharp pangs the hissings began
To change to a grating cry;
Many sorrows and dismal throes,
Many forms of fish, bird and beast 35
Brought forth an Infant form
Where was a worm before.

7. The Eternals their tent finished
Alarm'd with these gloomy visions
When Enitharmon groaning 40
Produc'd a man Child to the light.

8. A shriek ran through Eternity:
And a paralytic stroke;
At the birth of the Human shadow.

9. Delving earth in his resistless way, 45
Howling, the Child with fierce flames
Issu'd from Enitharmon.

10. The Eternals closed the tent;
They beat down the stakes, the cords

---

34 *Many forms* Blake repeats an idea from contemporary embryology, that the foetus recapitulates in its development different forms of animal life.
38 *gloomy visions* Suggests that the Eternals see 'visions'; to some extent, they create what they see.
40 *man Child* Orc, who appears as a youthful figure of revolt in other 1790s poems by Blake such as *America*.
44–6 *Delving . . . Issu'd* Three lines in succession begin with an initial stress, emphasizing the energy associated with Orc.

Plate 20 [Plate 18] design A naked boy dives downwards against a backdrop of blossoming flames. The design is typical of the interpretative challenges posed by Blake's pictorial illustrations. At first sight it suggests delight in energy and plays against the grimmer view of Orc's birth offered by the text. However, the downward dive may be a hapless tumble and the outstretched arms may also convey a degree of helplessness.

Stretch'd for a work of eternity;
No more Los beheld Eternity.

11. In his hand he siez'd the infant,
He bathed him in springs of sorrow,
He gave him to Enitharmon. 5

Chap: VII.

1. They named the child Orc, he grew
Fed with milk of Enitharmon.

---

6 *named* A further instance of 'naming'; among other things, these instances reintroduce and offer new perspectives on characters who have appeared in earlier works by Blake.

2. Los awoke her; O sorrow and pain!
A tight'ning girdle grew,
Around his bosom. In sobbings
He burst the girdle in twain,
But still another girdle
Oppress'd his bosom. In sobbings
Again he burst it. Again
Another girdle succeeds.
The girdle was form'd by day;
By night was burst in twain.

3. These falling down on the rock
Into an iron Chain
In each other link by link lock'd.

4. They took Orc to the top of a mountain.
O how Enitharmon wept!
They chain'd his young limbs to the rock
With the Chain of Jealousy
Beneath Urizen's deathful shadow.

5. The dead heard the voice of the child
And began to awake from sleep;
All things heard the voice of the child
And began to awake to life.

6. And Urizen craving with hunger
Stung with the odours of Nature
Explor'd his dens around.

7. He form'd a line and a plummet
To divide the Abyss beneath.
He form'd a dividing rule:

8. He formed scales to weigh;
He formed massy weights;
He formed a brazen quadrant;
He formed golden compasses
And began to explore the Abyss
And he planted a garden of fruits.

9. But Los encircled Enitharmon
With fires of Prophecy
From the sight of Urizen and Orc.

10. And she bore an enormous race.

9–17 *A tight'ning ... twain* The writing has a nightmarish quality; we do not know exactly what the endlessly reformed and broken girdles betoken, but we are taken into Los's state of fevered struggle to be rid of them. Soon it transpires that they compose links in a 'Chain of Jealousy' (l. 24).
23 *They chain'd ... rock* Blake suggests an Oedipal complex in reverse: not that the son envies the father, but that the father envies the son. Various sources for this chaining suggest themselves, including Prometheus' fate.
25 *Urizen's deathful shadow* Urizen reappears at this point, the presiding guilt-inducing presence of the world that, between them, he and Los have made.

29 *And began ... life* In another poem, this line would have a positive inflection; here it is harder to be sure.
32 *Explor'd ... around* Urizen now becomes an explorer, charting, dividing and measuring.
33 *He form'd* The repetition of this phrase in subsequent lines on this plate gives a strong sense of Urizen's compulsion to order.
39 *golden compasses* Compare the frontispiece to *Europe* in the famous design often known as 'The Ancient of Days' where Urizen sets golden compasses over the deep.
42–4 *But Los ... Orc* Los's shielding of Enitharmon may spring from jealousy, yet it may serve a nobler purpose since it employs 'fires of Prophecy'.

Chap: VIII.

1. Urizen explor'd his dens,
Mountain, moor, and wilderness,
With a globe of fire lighting his journey;
A fearful journey, annoy'd
By cruel enormities: forms 50

---

46 *Urizen ... dens* Urizen's journey may recall Satan's through Chaos in *Paradise Lost*, yet it serves a would-be benign purpose.

Plate 21 [Plate 19] design Shows three naked forms, those of a woman and man (Enitharmon and Los), and that of a young boy (Orc) holding the woman. A red-linked chain hangs in front of the man and seems to fall from his chest. Los rests his right hand on a large black hammer to the right of the design. The adult figures bow their heads towards one another; the impression is of deep emotional and physical interlocking.

Plate 22 [Plate 20] design A white-bearded old man, Urizen, sits, with eyes upturned but closed; his legs are drawn up at the knees and his arms rest by his legs; both feet and hands are manacled.

Plate 23 [Plate 21] design Urizen, white-bearded and in a long gown, strides towards the right, his left hand held out, his right hand holding a red globe with spikes raying out; in his path is a lion, of which the head, mane, and left foreleg are visible. The picture illustrates 20: 48 [18: 48] in which Urizen explores his dens 'With a globe of fire lighting his journey'. Above him is the outline of a rock or a valley slope.

Of life on his forsaken mountains.

2. And his world teem'd vast enormities
Frightning; faithless; fawning
Portions of life; similitudes
Of a foot, or a hand, or a head 5
Or a heart, or an eye, they swam mischevous,
Dread terrors! delighting in blood.

3. Most Urizen sicken'd to see
His eternal creations appear,
Sons and daughters of sorrow on mountains 10
Weeping! wailing! first Thiriel appear'd
Astonish'd at his own existence
Like a man from a cloud born, and Utha
From the waters emerging, laments!
Grodna rent the deep earth howling 15
Amaz'd! his heavens immense cracks
Like the ground parch'd with heat; then Fuzon
Flam'd out! first begotten, last born;
All his eternal sons in like manner;
His daughters from green herbs and cattle, 20
From monsters, and worms of the pit.

---

4 *similitudes* Likenesses, either because yet fully to develop human form or because copies of some better versions of themselves. For the use of 'similitude' in *Paradise Lost*, in a relevant context (the entrance of disease and suffering into human existence after the Fall), see XI. 512.

6 *swam mischevous* The verb resonates with a sickening sense of pullulating life; see also 'teem'd' (l. 2) and 'delighting in blood' (l. 7).

8 *sicken'd to see* The alliterative bond is significant. Typically, to 'see' in *U* is to be 'sicken'd'.

11–18 *first Thiriel ... Flam'd out!* Urizen's 'eternal sons' (l. 19) represent the four elements: Thiriel represents air, Utha represents water, Grodna represents earth, and Fuzon represents fire.

4. He in darkness clos'd, view'd all his race
And his soul sicken'd! he curs'd
Both sons and daughters; for he saw
That no flesh nor spirit could keep   25
His iron laws one moment.

5. For he saw that life liv'd upon death.

24–6 *for ... moment* Blake holds back his explanation of Urizen's sickened response to the end of the plate; sensuous seeing gives way to an act of Urizenic understanding: 'he saw' (ll. 24, 27) that his 'iron laws' could not be kept by denizens of the material world he has helped to create.

27 *For ... death* A strikingly proto-Darwinian line, showing Blake's understanding of the relentlessly competitive nature of existence.

Plate 24 [Plate 22] design Illustrates the elements created by Urizen, though two copies, including copy D, show only two figures; others have four. In copy D one figure (Tharmas) floats in mid-air, below stormy clouds and above a sinking red sun emitting gold rays; he is naked and holds his hands in front of him, as if half-way through a swimming stroke or as if warding off something; below the setting sun, in a choppy sea, the black-haired head of another figure (Utha) rises above the waves.

Plate 25 [Plate 23] design The image shows at its centre the upper half of a naked women round whose breasts the fold of a serpentine creature wraps itself; behind the creature the heads of two further blonde-haired women can be found; these women, too, seem to be trapped by serpentine folds.

The Ox in the slaughter house moans,
The Dog at the wintry door;
And he wept, and he called it Pity
And his tears flowed down on the winds.

6. Cold he wander'd on high, over their cities   5
In weeping and pain and woe
And where ever he wanderd in sorrows
Upon the aged heavens
A cold shadow follow'd behind him
Like a spider's web, moist, cold and dim,   10
Drawing out from his sorrowing soul
The dungeon-like heaven dividing
Where ever the footsteps of Urizen
Walk'd over the cities in sorrow.

7. Till a Web dark and cold throughout all   15
The tormented element stretch'd
From the sorrows of Urizen's soul.
And the Web is a Female in embrio.
    None could break the Web, no wings of fire.

8. So twisted the cords and so knotted   20
The meshes: twisted like to the human brain.

1–2 *The Ox ... door* Emblems of the cruelties involved in material existence. Blake telescopes times and phases of emergent human history; the 'slaughter house' is already in existence.

3 *called it Pity* A further example of the poem's quasi-deconstructive concern with unmasking the business of naming. Urizen transforms his response to creation into one that he can approve of morally by giving it the title 'Pity'.

5–14 *Cold ... in sorrow* Blake's syntax is subtly expressive of a circular process: wherever Urizen wanders he is followed by 'A cold shadow' (l. 9); the shadow is drawn from his 'sorrowing soul' (l. 11) wherever he wanders.

9. And all call'd it The Net of Religion.

Chap: IX.

1. Then the Inhabitants of those Cities
Felt their Nerves change into Marrow
And hardening Bones began 25
In swift diseases and torments,
In throbbings and shootings and grindings
Through all the coasts; till weaken'd
The Senses inward rush'd, shrinking
Beneath the dark net of infection. 30

2. Till the shrunken eyes clouded over
Discern'd not the woven hypocrisy
But the streaky slime in their heavens
Brought together by narrowing perceptions
Appear'd transparent air; for their eyes 35
Grew small like the eyes of a man
And in reptile forms shrinking together
Of seven feet stature they remain'd.

3. Six days they shrunk up from existence
And on the seventh day they rested. 40
And they bless'd the seventh day, in sick hope
And forgot their eternal life.

4. And their thirty cities divided
In form of a human heart.
No more could they rise at will 45
In the infinite void, but bound down
To earth by their narrowing perceptions

22 *And . . . Religion* Blake sees a cultural process – the development of religion – in powerfully metaphorical terms; it is noticeable that the 'Web' (l. 15) from which the 'Net of Religion' is formed is 'a Female in embrio' (l. 18) – Blake's sense of the baleful consequences of sexual division is evident. Again, we are told that 'all *call'd* it the Net of Religion' (emphasis added); the possibility of a misunderstanding of the true nature of religion is thus introduced.
26 *diseases and torments* Recalls the post-lapsarian vision given by Michael to Adam of 'Diseases dire' in *Paradise Lost*, XI. 474.
30 *dark net of infection* Coming so soon after 'The Net of Religion' (l. 22), this new 'net' seems causally linked to the earlier one.
31–6 *Till . . . man* Blake skilfully suggests how in the fallen state 'narrowing perceptions' create a false sense of reality; humans are at the mercy of the misleading evidence proffered by 'The Senses' (l. 29).
40 *And . . . rested* Echoes ironically Genesis 2: 3 in which God 'rested from all his work'.

Plate 26 [*Plate 24*] *design* A child in a white gown stands at the left, hands clasped as if begging or in prayer; behind him looms a dark prison-like door; behind the child a large brown dog reclines, his head lifted as if howling. The design suddenly removes us from *U*'s mythic world; we are now close to the contemporary horrors of Blake's 'London'.

Plate 27 [*Plate 25*] An old man (Urizen), white-gowned and bare-footed, with his back to the viewer, moves away from us, his held-up and held-out hands seeming to push at the edge of a black rim of rock or cloud, below which there is a reddened opening. The gown, which may represent the 'cold shadow' (25: 9 [23: 9]) following Urizen, billows out behind him.

Plate 28 [*Plate 26*] Urizen, white-bearded, sits, his arms raised to the level of his shoulders, his hands holding cable-like ropes which seem to bind him, as though he were himself caught in the 'Net of Urizen' (28: 13 [26: 13]). The design recalls the poem's opening design, and suggests that Urizen has been trapped in his own net. His eyes are open, and his ability to see his predicament possibly offers a glimmer of hope; though fallen, Urizen was once an Eternal, and may contain within himself the possibility of return to eternal life. The later prophetic books explore the possibility of this return.

They lived a period of years,
Then left a noisome body
To the jaws of devouring darkness.

5. And their children wept, and built
Tombs in the desolate places,
And form'd laws of prudence, and call'd them
The eternal laws of God.

6. And the thirty cities remain'd
Surrounded by salt floods, now call'd
Africa: its name was then Egypt.

7. The remaining sons of Urizen
Beheld their brethren shrink together
Beneath the Net of Urizen:
Perswasion was in vain
For the ears of the inhabitants
Were wither'd, and deafen'd, and cold!
And their eyes could not discern
Their brethren of other cities.

8. So Fuzon call'd all together
The remaining children of Urizen:
And they left the pendulous earth:
They called it Egypt, and left it.

9. And the salt ocean rolled englob'd.

The End of the first book of Urizen

6–7 *And ... laws of God* The law-giving tendencies of Urizen have now been taken up at large. Human history, for Blake, has been terrifyingly distorted by the Urizenic.
13 *the Net of Urizen* Possibly a renaming of the 'Net of Religion'.
19–22 *So ... left it* Fuzon, embodiment of fire, remains as a rebellious force; he leads an attempted break-out from 'the pendulous earth', called 'Egypt' because Egypt was the land of bondage from which Moses led the Israelites in Exodus. Again, the process of naming or 'calling' (see l. 22) is emphasized.
23 *And ... englob'd* Suggests the rolling up of material creation into a globe or ball, always for Blake a sign of narrowed perceptions.

The Mental Traveller

This poem, like 'The Crystal Cabinet', survives in the Pickering Manuscript, so called after a nineteenth-century owner. The poems seem to have been written in the early years of the nineteenth century, 1800–4, possibly during Blake's period in Felpham (1800–3) where he worked under the patronage of William Hayley. 'The Mental Traveller', composed in a ballad metre, octosyllabic quatrains rhyming *abcb*, offers in shockingly lucid and yet enigmatic outline the essence of Blake's vision in his prophetic books, or, at least, of its negative aspects. Blake moves towards affirmation in *Milton* and *Jerusalem*, yet much of the writing in the books is concerned with conflict. In 'The Mental Traveller' the speaker is like an Eternal visiting Urizen's creation, a world in which (see l. 2) sexual division has occurred, and gives a report on what he sees. Moral judgement is absent from his account of the vicious cycles he describes, in which a boy is tormented by an old woman, before he grows into a youth and she becomes a virgin whom he 'binds ... down for his delight' (l. 24). He grows old, an 'aged Shadow' (l. 29); she grows young, metamorphosing into the 'little Female Babe' of line 44, who is said, oxymoronically, to be 'all of solid fire' (l. 45): energy solidified. She grows up, takes a partner; they 'drive out the aged Host' (l. 51). He turns to a young maid, who beguiles him to 'Infancy' (l. 72). He grows young; she grows old. He becomes 'the frowning Babe' (l. 93), recalling Orc in the earlier prophecies; she becomes the 'Woman Old' (l. 102) who restricts Orc's powers, nailing him down, and the poem ends where it began. The poem gives in condensed and distilled form the essence of Blake's disillusioned sense of the endless conflict between male and female, energy and restraint. It owes its power to the relentless tracing of cycles and its pathos to rare moments when break-out from the cyclical seems possible, as in the movement closer to human life of 'The Sun and Stars' (l. 88). In 'The Mental Traveller' Blake subjects our time-bound, sexually driven condition to an unsparing imaginative X-ray. His verbal powers are at their height in this magnificent lyric of near-despair, by turns mocking, cruelly pointed, aphoristic, cosmic, reworking words, always suggesting that human existence is governed remorselessly 'By various arts of Love and Hate' (l. 81).

> I travel'd through a Land of Men,
> A Land of Men and Women too,
> And heard and saw such dreadful things
> As cold Earth wanderers never knew.
>
> For there the Babe is born in joy 5
> That was begotten in dire woe;
> Just as we Reap in joy the fruit
> Which we in bitter tears did Sow.
>
> And if the Babe is born a Boy
> He's given to a Woman Old, 10
> Who nails him down upon a rock,
> Catches his Shrieks in Cups of gold.
>
> She binds iron thorns around his head,
> She pierces both his hands and feet,
> She cuts his heart out at his side 15
> To make it feel both cold and heat.
>
> Her fingers number every Nerve,
> Just as a Miser counts his gold;
> She lives upon his shrieks and cries
> And She grows young as he grows old. 20
>
> Till he becomes a bleeding youth,
> And she becomes a Virgin bright;
> Then he rends up his Manacles
> And binds her down for his delight.
>
> He plants himself in all her Nerves, 25
> Just as a Husbandman his mould;
> And She becomes his dwelling place
> And Garden fruitful Seventy fold.

1 *travel'd* The 'Mental Traveller' travels, distinguishing him from 'cold Earth *wanderers*' (l. 4, emphasis added).
2 *Men and Women too* Division into the two sexes is a novel feature, for the Traveller, of the world he visits.
3 *such dreadful things* The tone is complex; it half-mocks its own shudder at what, from one perspective, is our world seen down the wrong end of a telescope.
5–8 *For . . . sow* This stanza implies a likeness between the blend of 'joy' and 'woe' in human existence and in the Mental Traveller's world, but in the latter's world there is a purposeful embracing of contraries, an acceptance that 'we' (they) reap what they sow, which is lacking in human existence.
5 *there* That is, 'here': human existence.
11–12 *Who .. gold* The shock lies in the writing's expository nature and sudden suggestion of a mythic dimension. The 'babe' is brought into association with Christ by way of the sufferings he endures, crowned with 'iron thorns' (l. 13). At the same time, he belongs to a pre-Christian era; nothing transcendental or even compassionate has any place in his world.
18 *Just as* Typical of the poem's use of repetition to support its cyclical vision, the phrase recalls 'Just as' in line 7 and anticipates its use in line 26.
19 *lives upon* The poem suggests that this 'living upon' each other is a feature of the 'land' (l. 1) visited by the Traveller.
21 *Till* Another of the small words crucial to the poem's effect, 'Till' implies an inevitability about the process described. See also lines 43, 54, 56, 82, 85, and 91.
27 *becomes his dwelling place* Any positive suggestion is complicated by 'becomes', turning this into yet another stage on the turning wheel.

An aged Shadow soon he fades,
Wandring round an Earthly Cot, 30
Full filled all with gems and gold
Which he by industry had got.

And these are the gems of the Human Soul,
The rubies and pearls of a lovesick eye,
The countless gold of the akeing heart, 35
The martyr's groan and the lover's sigh.

They are his meat, they are his drink;
He feeds the Beggar and the Poor
And the wayfaring Traveller:
For ever open is his door. 40

His grief is their eternal joy;
They make the roofs and walls to ring;
Till from the fire on the hearth
A little Female Babe does spring.

And she is all of solid fire 45
And gems and gold that none his hand
Dares stretch to touch her Baby form,
Or wrap her in his swaddling-band.

But She comes to the Man she loves,
If young or old or rich or poor; 50
They soon drive out the aged Host,
A Begger at another's door.

He wanders weeping far away,
Untill some other take him in;
Oft blind and age-bent, sore distrest, 55
Untill he can a Maiden win.

And to Allay his freezing Age
The Poor Man takes her in his arms;
The Cottage fades before his Sight,
The Garden and its lovely Charms. 60

The Guests are scatter'd through the land,
For the Eye altering alters all;
The Senses roll themselves in fear,
And the flat Earth becomes a Ball;

The Stars, Sun, Moon, all shrink away, 65
A desart vast without a bound,
And nothing left to eat or drink,
And a dark desart all around.

The honey of her Infant lips,
The bread and wine of her sweet smile, 70

---

31 *Full filled* But not, Blake suggests ironically, 'fulfilled'.
33–6 *And these . . . sigh* Blake alters the metre here, introducing a number of trisyllabic feet, which gives the stanza the air of a digressive pause.
41 *His grief . . . joy* Returns us to the oppositions of stanza 2.
45–6 *solid . . . gold* The 'gems and gold' echo the same phrase in line 31, and suggest the female babe's association with material acquisitions.
61–8 *The Guests . . . around* An especially bleak phrase of the cycle, in which the 'altering' eye turns outward creation into a post-Newtonian 'Ball' (l. 64) and human beings inhabit 'a dark desart'. In this state, the man is especially vulnerable to the female wiles described in the next stanza.

The wild game of her roving Eye,
Does him to Infancy beguile.

For as he eats and drinks he grows
Younger and younger every day;
And on the desart wild they both 75
Wander in terror and dismay.

Like the wild Stag she flees away,
Her fear plants many a thicket wild;
While he pursues her night and day,
By various arts of Love beguil'd, 80

By various arts of Love and Hate,
Till the wide desart planted oer
With Labyrinths of wayward Love,
Where roams the Lion, Wolf and Boar,

Till he becomes a wayward Babe, 85
And she a weeping Woman Old.
Then many a Lover wanders here;
The Sun and Stars are nearer roll'd.

The trees bring forth sweet Extacy
To all who in the desart roam; 90
Till many a City there is Built,
And many a pleasant Shepherd's home.

But when they find the frowning Babe,
Terror strikes through the region wide:
They cry the Babe, the Babe is Born 95
And flee away on Every side.

For who dare touch the frowning form,
His arm is wither'd to its root;
Lions, Boars, Wolves, all howling flee,
And every Tree does shed its fruit. 100

And none can touch that frowning form,
Except it be a Woman Old;
She nails him down upon the Rock,
And all is done as I have told.

77–80 *Like the wild . . . beguil'd* This stanza captures a pattern of male pursuit and female coyness which Blake describes in many places.
81 *Love and Hate* The rephrasing of the previous line, and introduction of 'hate', are striking.
87–8 *Then .. roll'd* At this stage of the cycle the possibility of harmony and creativity is at its strongest; this is the phrase in which cities are built (see next stanza).

95 *the Babe . . . born!* Hails the Babe's birth, a hailing that recalls the heralding of Christ's birth, except that this hailing is terrified rather than joyous. The Babe is a force that destroys – whether this destruction is necessary or even beneficial is left open.
104 *And . . . told* Blake signs off his extraordinary ballad with a laconic use of a storyteller's formula, repeating a rhyme sound that has pounded away through the poem.

The Crystal Cabinet

The poem, a ballad of seven quatrains, each quatrain rhyming *abcb* and written in iambic tetrameters with variations, represents Blake's mature and haunting view of desire's illusory insufficiency; in this poem desire leads to entrapment and disappointment.

Blake's idea of Beulah – the third of his four stages of vision – is relevant to the poem. Beulah is a state where the mind is both comforted and beguiled: it will destroy if mistaken for a final resting-place. Blake writes in a verse-letter to Thomas Butts: 'a fourfold vision is given to me / Tis fourfold in my supreme delight, / And three fold in soft Beulahs night' (ll. 84–6; *E* p. 722). 'Beulah' is 'soft', but also, by comparison with the poet's 'supreme delight', a place which forms a 'night'. The poem involves us in the speaker's differing phases of feeling: unthinking surrender to capture; entranced delight in the secondary 'World' (l. 7) to which he is taken by the 'Maiden' (l. 1); the sense that the maiden herself has a double; and the final movement towards disappointed apprehension after the speaker has striven to 'sieze the inmost Form' (l. 21) only to destroy the 'Crystal Cabinet' (l. 23). The poem has a figurative suggestiveness that will not be allegorized straightforwardly; but the fact that the speaker ends up in 'the outward Air again' (l. 27) intimates that the maiden's cabinet serves as a seeming refuge from the travails of experience. The cabinet appears to be a place or space where erotic fantasy and aesthetic dream meet.

> The Maiden caught me in the Wild,
> Where I was dancing merrily;
> She put me into her Cabinet
> And Lock'd me up with a golden Key.
>
> This Cabinet is form'd of Gold   5
> And Pearl and Crystal shining bright,
> And within it opens into a World
> And a little lovely Moony Night.
>
> Another England there I saw,
> Another London with its Tower,   10
> Another Thames and other Hills,
> And another pleasant Surrey Bower,
>
> Another Maiden like herself,
> Translucent, lovely, shining clear,
> Threefold each in the other clos'd –   15
> O, what a pleasant trembling fear!
>
> O, what a smile! a threefold Smile
> Fill'd me that like a flame I burn'd;
> I bent to Kiss the lovely Maid,
> And found a Threefold Kiss return'd.   20
>
> I strove to sieze the inmost Form
> With ardor fierce and hands of flame,
> But burst the Crystal Cabinet,
> And like a Weeping Babe became –
>
> A weeping Babe upon the wild,   25
> And Weeping Woman pale reclin'd,
> And in the outward Air again
> I fill'd with woes the passing Wind.

1 *the Wild* It is to 'the wild' that the speaker, this time a 'weeping Babe' (l. 25), will return at the poem's end; 'wild' implies a state of nature, beyond art.
2 *dancing merrily* The syntax is arranged so that the dancing merrily seems to continue after the capture, indicating the speaker's less than full awareness of the significance of the capture.
5–6 *Gold / And Pearl and Crystal* The precious stones bring to mind (but as an ironic contrast) the 'new Jerusalem' of Revelation 21, a city of 'pure gold, like unto clear glass' (21: 18) associated with a 'pure river of water of life, clear as crystal' (22: 1).

8 *a little . . . Night* The slightly fey diction suggests limitations, even as it expresses delight.
16 *pleasant trembling fear* The response is like that induced by a safely predictable art-work.
19–20 *I bent . . . return'd* In the virtual world of the cabinet reciprocal kisses seem possible; it is only when the speaker seeks to turn the virtual into the actual that the cabinet is destroyed.
25–6 *A weeping . . . reclin'd* The speaker reverts to the condition of a 'weeping Babe'; the maiden is now a 'Weeping Woman'. There are suggestions of a cycle such as is described in 'The Mental Traveller'.

William Wordsworth (1770–1850)

William Wordsworth was born on 7 April 1770 in Cockermouth, son of a legal agent for the landowner, Sir James Lowther, later Earl of Lonsdale. Both his parents died when he was young: his mother Ann in 1778 and his father John in 1783, traumatic events which meant that Wordsworth and his siblings (Richard, Christopher, John and Dorothy) were dependent from an early age on relatives. Wordsworth attended Hawkshead Grammar School from May 1779, and it was while at this school, encouraged by two fine teachers, William Taylor and Thomas Bowman, that he began writing poetry, completing a long poem, 'The Vale of Esthwaite', before he went to St John's Cambridge. At Cambridge he appears to have enjoyed himself but not to have studied very hard. In the long vacation of 1790 he went with a friend, Robert Jones, on a walking tour to France, then in the early days of revolutionary fervour. He returned to France in 1791–2, staying in Blois, where he met Michel Beaupuy, a French soldier and supporter of the Revolution, and Annette Vallon, a young French woman, with whom he had a relationship and a child, Caroline, born in December 1792. Wordsworth was then back in London, unable to return to France after the outbreak of war between Britain and France early in 1793.

Wordsworth's early poems, *An Evening Walk* and *Descriptive Sketches*, are written in couplets and in an ornate diction against which he would react in *Lyrical Ballads*, which he co-authored with Coleridge, whom he met in Racedown, Dorset, in 1797 where he was staying with his sister Dorothy. The poetry produced in this period by the two poets is among the finest work of the Romantic period. In the Preface to *Lyrical Ballads*, Wordsworth charts the tenets which at this time he and Coleridge appear to have shared: principally that poetry should not use an artificial language, but should deploy a language mimicking that used by ordinary people when in states of strong feeling. In particular, Wordsworth's purpose was 'to follow the fluxes and refluxes of the mind when agitated by the great and simple affections of our nature'; as a result, in his poems, 'the feeling therein developed gives importance to the action and situation and not the action and situation to the feeling' (Preface to *Lyrical Ballads*, 1800, p. xvii). The poetry focuses on states of emotion rather than on making political points. Wordsworth's earlier revolutionary sympathies have, arguably, modulated into a deeper, less ideologically categorizable feeling for human suffering. The poet has turned decisively away from the Godwinian rationalism which briefly attracted him after the publication of *Enquiry Concerning Political Justice* (1793). 'The Ruined Cottage', not included in *Lyrical Ballads*, is an excellent example of the tragic compassion apparent in Wordsworth's work of the period. Underpinning this compassion was a belief, explored in 'Tintern Abbey', in the power of nature to give access to joy and love. 'Tintern Abbey' is a critical poem in Wordsworth's career, since it views his earlier self from the perspective of the precarious calm and happiness achieved in 1798, and affectingly weighs a sense of 'loss' (l. 88) against a new belief that the years have brought 'Abundant recompence' (l. 89). The earlier Wordsworth, in love with nature but also at odds with Britain's foreign policy, haunts 'Tintern Abbey', and yet the poem alludes only obliquely if hauntingly to 'what I was' (l. 67). Throughout the poem, an undercurrent of sadness makes itself felt, surfacing at moments such as the poet's reference to 'The still, sad music of humanity' (l. 92). The sadness amplifies rather than undercuts the poem's overall mood of happiness, and reminds us that remnants of millennial hope pervade some poems in *Lyrical Ballads*. Indeed, Wordsworth was encouraged by Coleridge to think of writing a major philosophical poem, *The Recluse*, which would describe the ideas and experiences underpinning the two poets' conception of the good life. In the end, Wordsworth never wrote *The Recluse*, though he made heroic efforts to do so; efforts resulting in (among other poems) 'Home at Grasmere' and *The Excursion* (1814), a long poem involving different speakers and employing 'something of a dramatic form' (Preface to *The Excursion*, 1814) which Wordsworth saw as contributing with *The Prelude* to *The Recluse*. It is important to remember that the second-generation Romantic poets, including Byron, Shelley and Keats, knew Wordsworth as the author of *The Excursion*, not as the poet of *The Prelude*, only published in 1850 after his death.

Lyrical Ballads was reissued as a second edition in 1800, by when Wordsworth had moved to Grasmere, close to which, in a number of houses (principally Dove Cottage and Rydal Mount), he was to live for the rest of his life, first with Dorothy, then with Dorothy and his wife Mary Hutchinson, sister of Sara Hutchinson, for whom Coleridge wrote the epistolary version of 'Dejection: An Ode'. 'Fools have laughed at, wise men scarcely understand them':[1] Hazlitt's

---

1 *The Complete Works of William Hazlitt*, ed. P. P. Howe, 21 vols (London: Dent, 1930–4), vol. xi, p. 87.

comment suggests the layered subtlety of the collection, in which questions of voice and perspective jostle with challenges to the reader. The title *Lyrical Ballads* hints at a blend of genres in Wordsworth's poems in the collection, and at the impulse to turn story into something more inward and lyrical. Poems such as 'Simon Lee' and 'The Idiot Boy' confront and tease the reader's desire for sensational plot, and lure us towards a more considered response. Wordsworth also contributed some magnificent poems in blank verse to the collection, especially 'Tintern Abbey' and 'Michael', a narrative poem which shows his fascination with silent suffering. In 1798–9, while staying in Goslar, Germany, with Dorothy, Wordsworth began writing autobiographical lines which turned rapidly into *The Two-Part Prelude* (1799), and then, after further work and revision, into the 13-book *Prelude* finished in 1805. Wordsworth began the poem in guilt and completed it with dissatisfaction, but it remains one of the major creations of English Romantic writing, describing in evocative poetry experiences which formed the poet's imagination and confirmed him in his vocation as a poet. Alongside work on *The Prelude*, during the period up to 1807, when he published *Poems, in Two Volumes*, Wordsworth wrote some of his major shorter poems, including sonnets inspired by his reading of Milton's poems in the same form and poems that embody his response to different crises in his life. Of these the chief are 'Resolution and Independence', part of a dialogue involving Coleridge's 'Dejection: An Ode', 'Ode' (from 1815 'Ode: Intimations of Immortality'), and 'Elegiac Stanzas, Suggested by a Picture of Peele Castle, in a Storm'. 'Resolution and Independence' responds to fears about the loss of joy by reasserting the poet's imaginative strength, a reassertion catalysed by his meeting with a leech-gatherer. 'Ode: Intimations of Immortality' dwells on the loss of vision and the fading of 'glory' (l. 5), and finds consolation in two things: the fact that memory takes the poet back to a time in childhood of 'obstinate questionings / Of sense and outward things' (ll. 144–5), and the conviction that time not only takes away visionary intensity, but also brings with it increased understanding of 'the human heart by which we live' (l. 203) as well as 'the faith that looks through death' (l. 188). Central to the poem's complex emotional impact is its movement between feelings and the sense of loss that clings to the poet's uncomplacent consolations. 'Elegiac Stanzas' is an explicit example of the elegiac impulse close to the heart of Wordsworth's imagination. Written in the aftermath of the death at sea of Wordsworth's brother, John, it replays the dialectic of loss and recompense found in 'Tintern Abbey' and the Ode. This time, Wordsworth laments the loss of 'A power . . . which nothing can restore' (l. 35), but he states that 'A deep distress hath humaniz'd my Soul' (l. 36).

Although Wordsworth continued to write much fine poetry after 'Elegiac Stanzas', poetry for which in recent years there has been increasing admiration, there is little doubt that his greatest work was composed between 1797 and 1807, the so-called 'Great Decade'. The poetry composed in this period reveals a poet of diverse voices and moods: a poet of consciousness and inwardness, but also a writer sympathetic to others and deeply concerned with social, historical and political questions.

Further Reading

Primary Texts

Lyrical Ballads (1798, 1800)
Poems, in Two Volumes (1807)
Poems (1815)
Lyrical Ballads, ed. Michael Mason (London: Longman, 1992) [Based on the 1805 text.]
The Prelude, 1799, 1805, 1850, ed. Jonathan Wordsworth, M. H. Abrams and Stephen Gill (New York: Norton, 1979).
The Prelude: The Four Texts (1798, 1799, 1805, 1850), ed. Jonathan Wordsworth (London: Penguin, 1995).
'The Ruined Cottage' and 'The Pedlar', ed. James Butler, Cornell Wordsworth Series (Ithaca, NY: Cornell University Press, 1979).
The Thirteen-Book 'Prelude', ed. Mark L. Reed, Cornell Wordsworth Series, 2 vols (Ithaca, NY: Cornell University Press, 1991).

Secondary Texts

M. H. Abrams, *Natural Supernaturalism: Tradition and Revolution in Romantic Literature* (New York: Norton, 1971).
Harold Bloom, *The Visionary Company: A Reading of English Romantic Poetry* (rev. edn, Ithaca, NY: Cornell University Press, 1971).
David Ellis, *Wordsworth, Freud and the Spots of Time: Interpretation in 'The Prelude'* (Cambridge, UK: Cambridge University Press, 1985).
Stephen Gill, *William Wordsworth: A Life* (Oxford: Oxford University Press, 1989).
Stephen Gill (ed.), *A Cambridge Companion to Wordsworth* (Cambridge, UK: Cambridge University Press, 2003).
Mary Jacobus, *Tradition and Experiment in Wordsworth's 'Lyrical Ballads'* (Oxford: Clarendon Press, 1976).
Zachary Leader, *Revision and Romantic Authority* (Oxford: Clarendon Press, 1996). Ch. 1.
Brennan O'Donnell, *The Passion of Meter: A Study of Wordsworth's Metrical Art* (Kent, OH: Kent State University Press, 1995).

Stephen Parrish, *The Art of the 'Lyrical Ballads'* (Cambridge, MA: Harvard University Press, 1973).
Nicholas Roe, *Wordsworth and Coleridge: The Radical Years* (Oxford: Clarendon Press, 1988).
Jonathan Wordsworth, *The Music of Humanity* (London: Nelson, 1969).
Jonathan Wordsworth (ed.), Beth Darlington (assistant ed.), *Bicentenary Wordsworth Studies* (Ithaca, NY: Cornell University Press, 1970).
Jonathan Wordsworth, *William Wordsworth: The Borders of Vision* (Oxford: Clarendon Press, 1982).
Duncan Wu, *Wordsworth: An Inner Life* (Oxford: Blackwell, 2002).

Lines written at a small distance from my House, and sent by my little Boy to the Person to whom they are addressed

The poem was composed in March 1798; the 'House' in the title is Alfoxden House; the 'little boy' is Basil Montague Jr, who was staying with William and Dorothy at the time; the 'person' to whom the lines 'are addressed' is Dorothy Wordsworth. The poem is among Wordsworth's most effective celebrations of 'blessing' (l. 5) in the natural world, of a 'sense of joy' (l. 6), of 'Love, now an universal birth' (l. 21), of a 'blessed power' (l. 33). The poem is clear and direct, affectionately insistent in its address to Dorothy, at ease in its surprising transition from one form of declaration ('It is the first mild day of March', l. 1) to another ('There is a blessing in the air', l. 5), daring in its widening of significance in the stanza starting 'Love, now an universal birth' (l. 21). In its own way, the poem is revolutionary in its commitment to 'the hour of feeling' (l. 24) in which the poet and his sister can make 'silent laws' (l. 29) of their own; but the revolution that dispenses with 'joyless forms' (l. 17) is pantheistic rather than politically radical.

Text from *Lyrical Ballads 1798*.

It is the first mild day of March:
Each minute sweeter than before,
The red-breast sings from the tall larch
That stands beside our door.

There is a blessing in the air, 5
Which seems a sense of joy to yield
To the bare trees, and mountains bare,
And grass in the green field.

My Sister! ('tis a wish of mine)
Now that our morning meal is done, 10
Make haste, your morning task resign;
Come forth and feel the sun.

Edward will come with you, and pray,
Put on with speed your woodland dress,
And bring no book, for this one day 15
We'll give to idleness.

No joyless forms shall regulate
Our living Calendar:
We from to-day, my friend, will date
The opening of the year. 20

---

7 *bare trees, and mountains bare* The poem repeats 'bare' in a way that reminds the reader of Wordsworth's attraction to the unadorned and simple; the writing shows a marked avoidance of adjectives.

20 *The opening of the year* This 'opening' is a new beginning that owes much to millennial imaginings in the period, but puts those imaginings at the service of an individual vision.

Love, now an universal birth,
From heart to heart is stealing,
From earth to man, from man to earth,
—It is the hour of feeling.

One moment now may give us more 25
Than fifty years of reason;
Our minds shall drink at every pore
The spirit of the season.

Some silent laws our hearts may make,
Which they shall long obey; 30
We for the year to come may take
Our temper from to-day.

And from the blessed power that rolls
About, below, above;
We'll frame the measure of our souls, 35
They shall be tuned to love.

Then come, my sister! come, I pray,
With speed put on your woodland dress,
And bring no book; for this one day
We'll give to idleness. 40

33–6 *And from . . . to love* Wordsworth and his sister are not merely acted on by the 'blessed power'; they will actively 'frame the measure' of their souls in accordance with it.

Simon Lee, The Old Huntsman, With an incident in which he was concerned

'Simon Lee' recounts the effect of age upon Simon Lee, who used to serve as a huntsman in the 'hall of Ivor' (l. 22). Yet it does in a way that, for much of the poem, trembles on the edge of the seemingly maladroit. It is only 'seemingly maladroit': the poem works skilfully to compel a new and first-hand perspective on the part of the reader. The first stanza establishes a tone that flirts with the banal: we are told that Simon is 'a little man' (l. 3), before being informed, 'I've heard he once was tall' (l. 4); and the feminine rhyme that concludes each stanza works, here, in a disconcerting fashion when the 'burthen weighty' (l. 6) of years is calculated as a possible 'eighty' (l. 8). The rhyme implies a jaunty indifference to the actuality of age, as though the narrator were unable to focus on the pathos of Simon's predicament; again, the difference between 'little' and 'tall' tells us – apparently against the intention of the speaker – about the impact on Simon of age and a life of punishing physical labour in the service of his masters, which has bowed his once tall frame. Wordsworth uses his narrator to puzzle the reader into guessing at the poet's view of his subject. Details such as Simon's swollen 'ancles' (l. 35) do not elicit straightforward compassion so much as a bald sense of the indignities of age. At the same time, running through the poem is a recollection of Simon's former vigour, recollection which can grow elegiac. The turning-point of the poem comes when Wordsworth and narrator no longer act at cross-purposes, and Wordsworth addresses the 'gentle reader' (l. 69), teasing our desire that the poem will turn itself into a 'tale' (l. 72). It does, but not into a story of exciting events. Instead, the poem closes with a thought-provoking encounter between Simon and the narrator, who helps Simon cut the 'root of an old tree' (l. 87). Wordsworth's enigmatic conclusion – 'Alas, the gratitude of men / Has oftner left me mourning' (ll. 103–4) – may take issue with Godwin's objections to gratitude in his *Enquiry Concerning Political Justice*.

Text from *Lyrical Ballads 1798*.

In the sweet shire of Cardigan,
Not far from pleasant Ivor-hall,
An old man dwells, a little man,
I've heard he once was tall.
Of years he has upon his back, 5
No doubt, a burthen weighty;
He says he is three score and ten,
But others say he's eighty.

A long blue livery-coat has he,
That's fair behind, and fair before; 10
Yet, meet him where you will, you see
At once that he is poor.
Full five and twenty years he lived
A running huntsman merry;
And, though he has but one eye left, 15
His cheek is like a cherry.

No man like him the horn could sound,
And no man was so full of glee;
To say the least, four counties round
Had heard of Simon Lee; 20
His master's dead, and no one now
Dwells in the hall of Ivor;
Men, dogs, and horses, all are dead;
He is the sole survivor.

His hunting feats have him bereft 25
Of his right eye, as you may see:
And then, what limbs those feats have left
To poor old Simon Lee!
He has no son, he has no child,
His wife, an aged woman, 30
Lives with him, near the waterfall,
Upon the village common.

And he is lean and he is sick,
His little body's half awry
His ancles they are swoln and thick 35
His legs are thin and dry.
When he was young he little knew
Of husbandry or tillage;
And now he's forced to work, though weak,
– The weakest in the village. 40

He all the country could outrun,
Could leave both man and horse behind;
And often, ere the race was done,
He reeled and was stone-blind.
And still there's something in the world 45
At which his heart rejoices;

---

1 *Cardigan* On the west coast of Wales.
9 *livery-coat* A distinctive coat given to Simon (and other servants) by his master.
15 *but one eye left* This loss is announced casually (mock-casually) in a subordinate clause.

24 *survivor* The feminine rhyme (with 'Ivor', l. 22) has pathos here, following the stress-shift in the previous line, which opens with a strong spondee (a foot with two successive stresses).
26 *as . . . see* In context, a grim joke.

For when the chiming bounds are out,
He dearly loves their voices!

Old Ruth works out of doors with him,
And does what Simon cannot do;
For she, not over stout of limb,
Is stouter of the two.
And though you with your utmost skill
From labour could not wean them,
Alas! 'tis very little, all
Which they can do between them.

Beside their moss-grown hut of clay,
Not twenty paces from the door,
A scrap of land they have, but they
Are poorest of the poor.
This scrap of land he from the heath
Enclosed when he was stronger;
But what avails the land to them,
Which they can till no longer?

Few months of life has he in store,
As he to you will tell,
For still, the more he works, the more
His poor old ancles swell.
My gentle reader, I perceive
How patiently you've waited,
And I'm afraid that you expect
Some tale will be related.

O reader! had you in your mind
Such stores as silent thought can bring,
O gentle reader! you would find
A tale in every thing.
What more I have to say is short,
I hope you'll kindly take it;
It is no tale; but should you think,
Perhaps a tale you'll make it.

One summer-day I chanced to see
This old man doing all he could
About the root of an old tree,
A stump of rotten wood.
The mattock totter'd in his hand
So vain was his endeavour
That at the root of the old tree
He might have worked for ever.

'You're overtasked, good Simon Lee,
Give me your tool' to him I said;
And at the word right gladly he
Received my proffer'd aid.
I struck, and with a single blow
The tangled root I sever'd,

---

69 *gentle reader* 'gentle' suggests the reader's social status as well as potential for compassion.

78 *kindly* As well as 'with sympathy, benevolence', the word has something of its older meaning of 'naturally'.

> At which the poor old man so long 95
> And vainly had endeavour'd.
>
> The tears into his eyes were brought,
> And thanks and praises seemed to run
> So fast out of his heart, I thought
> They never would have done. 100
> – I've heard of hearts unkind, kind deeds
> With coldness still returning.
> Alas! the gratitude of men
> Has oftner left me mourning.

103 *gratitude* Something of a loaded term, given the attack on this emotion by William Godwin in *Enquiry Concerning Political Justice*.

Anecdote for Fathers, Shewing how the practice of Lying may be taught

In this poem, composed in the first half of 1798, Wordsworth explores the ways in which the young can be coerced by their elders. The well-meaning narrator evidently loves his 'boy of five years old' (l. 1), probably modelled on Basil Montagu Jr., the son of Basil Montague; Wordsworth and his sister Dorothy were looking after the child for a while in 1798. The narrator is highly Wordsworthian in his capacity for 'happiness' (l. 15), and in his pleasure in nature. However, the poem ironizes his adult insistence on comparison, his inability wholly to live in the present, shown in his demand that the child should tell him whether he prefers Kilve or Liswyn Farm. The poem works through dialogue and gesture. We realize that the boy is being made to think in terms foreign to him ('There surely must some reason be', l. 42) and slightly bullied ('And five times did I say to him', l. 47). The boy's reply – he invents a reason to support his preference for Kilve (a preference that may, we feel, be merely assumed to humour the narrator) – is both spirited and an example of how the young are taught to 'lie'. Happily, the narrator recognizes the folly of his demands in the final stanza, a stanza in which he cedes primacy to 'what from thee I learn' (l. 60). Like 'Simon Lee', the poem enacts a scene of oblique instruction. The poem is light in manner and tone; the result is an undidactic, lyrical comedy with serious implications.

Text from *Lyrical Ballads 1798*.

> I have a boy of five years old,
> His face is fair and fresh to see;
> His limbs are cast in beauty's mould,
> And dearly he loves me.
>
> One morn we stroll'd on our dry walk, 5
> Our quiet house all full in view,
> And held such intermitted talk
> As we are wont to do.
>
> My thoughts on former pleasures ran;
> I thought of Kilve's delightful shore, 10
> My pleasant home, when spring began,
> A long, long year before.

4 *dearly he loves me* One might expect the line to tell of the narrator's feeling for the boy; Wordsworth's wording suggests the narrator's streak of egotism (not incompatible with genuine love for the boy).

10 *Kilve's delightful shore* A village on the Somersetshire coast, not far from Alfoxden.
12 *long, long* Like the repetition of 'think' in line 14, the doubling of 'long' implies a pressure of emotion.

A day it was when I could bear
To think, and think, and think again;
With so much happiness to spare, 15
I could not feel a pain.

My boy was by my side, so slim
And graceful in his rustic dress!
And oftentimes I talked to him,
In very idleness. 20

The young lambs ran a pretty race;
The morning sun shone bright and warm;
'Kilve,' said I, 'was a pleasant place,
'And so is Liswyn farm.

'My little boy, which like you more,' 25
I said and took him by the arm –
'Our home by Kilve's delightful shore,
'Or here at Liswyn farm?'

'And tell me, had you rather be,'
I said and held him by the arm, 30
'At Kilve's smooth shore by the green sea,
'Or here at Liswyn farm?

In careless mood he looked at me,
While still I held him by the arm,
And said, 'At Kilve I'd rather be 35
'Than here at Liswyn farm.'

'Now, little Edward, say why so;
My little Edward, tell me why;'
'I cannot tell, I do not know.'
'Why this is strange,' said I. 40

'For, here are woods and green-hills warm;
'There surely must some reason be
'Why you would change sweet Liswyn farm
'For Kilve by the green sea.'

At this, my boy, so fair and slim, 45
Hung down his head, nor made reply;
And five times did I say to him,
'Why? Edward, tell me why?'

His head he raised – there was in sight,
It caught his eye, he saw it plain – 50
Upon the house-top, glittering bright,
A broad and gilded vane.

Then did the boy his tongue unlock,
And thus to me he made reply;
'At Kilve there was no weather-cock, 55
'And that's the reason why.'

---

20   *idleness* A valuable state, yet one in which the speaker's happiness creates the need to talk, which in turn leads to the comic imbroglio at the poem's heart.
50   *caught his eye* The boy clutches for an answer to the speaker's question through something that attracts his gaze.
52   *gilded vane* Weather-cock (as in l. 55), but 'vane' and gilded' also suggest 'vanity'.

Oh dearest, dearest boy! my heart
For better lore would seldom yearn,
Could I but teach the hundredth part
Of what from thee I learn.   60

58 *lore* 'body of traditions and knowledge on a subject or held by a group'. A word of some significance; in context, it implies a knowledge that cannot be gained from books, a knowledge guided by right feeling.

Lines written in early Spring

In this poem, composed in April 1798, Wordsworth offers a darker vision than in 'Lines Written at a small distance' as he contrasts his sense of nature's goodness and harmony with his awareness of 'What man has made of man' (l. 8). However, this contrast is not pointed up by the poem, in which 'pleasant thoughts' (l. 3) glide easily into 'sad thoughts' (l. 4), and in which 'And' rather than 'But' introduces the description of the poet's grief at the human condition in line 7 after he has described the harmonious union between 'nature' (l. 5) and the 'human soul' (l. 6). The effect is of a poetic state in which happiness dominates, and yet does not exclude recognition of the need to 'lament / What man has made of man' (ll. 23–4). Wordsworth paints a vivid picture of nature as alive, in accord with contemporary science; and there is even an indication that his 'faith' (l. 11) is involuntary, borne in upon him irresistibly by the evidence of his senses. It is, in fact, the conviction of nature as full of 'pleasure' (l. 20) that brings to the poet's mind sadness at human folly. Formally, the poem uses a typical ballad metre, three octosyllabic lines followed by a line of six syllables, rhyming *abab*, but it achieves surprises through a shorter second line in stanzas four and five.

Text from *Lyrical Ballads 1798*.

I heard a thousand blended notes,
While in a grove I sate reclined,
In that sweet mood when pleasant thoughts
Bring sad thoughts to the mind.

To her fair works did nature link   5
The human soul that through me ran;
And much it griev'd my heart to think
What man has made of man.

Through primrose-tufts, in that sweet bower,
The periwinkle trail'd its wreathes;   10
And 'tis my faith that every flower
Enjoys the air it breathes.

The birds around me hopp'd and play'd:
Their thoughts I cannot measure,
But the least motion which they made,   15
It seem'd a thrill of pleasure.

The budding twigs spread out their fan,
To catch the breezy air;

1 *blended notes* The different songs of the birds, but also a clue to the poem's overall effect.
6 *The human . . . ran* Phrased to suggest the poet's participation in a general 'human' state.
7–8 *And much . . . man* Echoes the end of Robert Burns's 'Man Was Made to Mourn': 'Man's inhumanity to man / Makes countless thousands mourn' (ll. 55–6). The original, one of Burns's most famous poems, dwells powerfully on 'Man's inhumanity' and the echo reinforces Wordsworth's sense of being 'griev'd'.
12 *Enjoys* Wordsworth attributes feeling to 'every flower' (l. 11), not as a poetic conceit, but literally.

And I must think, do all I can,
That there was pleasure there.

If I these thoughts may not prevent,
If such be of my creed the plan,
Have I not reason to lament
What man has made of man? 20

19 *And I must think, do all I can* The wording implies that the poet finds the next line's assertion unavoidable.

22 *plan* Design.

The Thorn

Composed between March and April 1798, the poem, according to the later Fenwick Note, was prompted by Wordsworth's wish to commemorate in words a thorn he had often passed on Quantock Hill 'in calm and bright weather without noticing it', but which caught his attention 'on a stormy day'. 'I said to myself', Wordsworth is reported as asking, 'Cannot I by some invention do as much to make this thorn permanently an impressive object as the storm has made it to my eyes this moment?' In his later reflections, then, on his creative work in the poem, Wordsworth represents himself as seeking to rival the effects of nature. There is a further appeal to the natural in the 'Note to *The Thorn*' included in the 1800 version of *Lyrical Ballads*. Here, after an account of the poem's 'credulous and talkative' narrator, likened to 'a Captain of a small trading vessel' (vol. 1, p. 211), Wordsworth draws attention to the use of 'tautology' or repetition of the same words in this and other poems in *Lyrical Ballads*; this use is justified by the view that 'Poetry is passion' and that it is difficult to 'communicate impassioned feelings without something of an accompanying consciousness of the inadequateness of our own powers, or the deficiencies of language' (vol. 1, p. 213). The poem itself depends on indirections. At its centre is Martha Ray, the woman with her cry, 'Oh misery!

oh misery! / Oh woe is me! oh misery!' (ll. 65–6), of whom it is suggested strongly (see, e.g., l. 52) that she has killed her baby and buried it in a grave beside the thorn which she haunts; she does so, it is implied, because she has been driven mad after being jilted by her fiancé Stephen Hill who has married another woman and left Martha pregnant. But the poem's speaker is reluctant – half-bumblingly, half-tactfully – to go beyond gossip, rumour and hearsay. Much of the poem's effect depends on our being led by the narrator to form conclusions from which he himself half-wishes to withdraw. The poem returns over and over to the surmises that are prompted by the cluster of objects including and surrounding the thorn. Its climax occurs when the narrator tells us of a time when he saw Martha face to face beside the thorn and glimpses her suffering for himself: 'I did not speak – I saw her face, / Her face it was enough for me' (ll. 199–200), where the emphasis on 'face' conveys the narrator's 'impassioned feelings' of something close to sympathy. Written in simple language yet a complex 11-line stanza form (in which the first, third, and fifth lines do not rhyme), 'The Thorn' remains one of Wordsworth's most emotionally enigmatic poems.

Text from *Lyrical Ballads 1798*.

I

There is a thorn; it looks so old,
In truth you'd find it hard to say,
How it could ever have been young,
It looks so old and grey.
Not higher than a two-years' child, 5
It stands erect this aged thorn;
No leaves it has, no thorny points;
It is a mass of knotted joints,
A wretched thing forlorn.
It stands erect, and like a stone 10
With lichens it is overgrown.

5 *two-years' child* The first of many comparisons between the landscape and childhood.

9 *wretched thing forlorn* Prepares the reader, by association, for the introduction of Martha Ray.

II

Like rock or stone, it is o'ergrown
With lichens to the very top,
And hung with heavy tufts of moss,
A melancholy crop: 15
Up from the earth these mosses creep,
And this poor thorn they clasp it round
So close, you'd say that they were bent
With plain and manifest intent,
To drag it to the ground; 20
And all had joined in one endeavour
To bury this poor thorn for ever.

III

High on a mountain's highest ridge,
Where oft the stormy winter gale
Cuts like a scythe, while through the clouds 25
It sweeps from vale to vale;
Not five yards from the mountain-path,
This thorn you on your left espy;
And to the left, three yards beyond,
You see a little muddy pond 30
Of water, never dry;
I've measured it from side to side:
'Tis three feet long, and two feet wide.

IV

And close beside this aged thorn,
There is a fresh and lovely sight, 35
A beauteous heap, a hill of moss,
Just half a foot in height.
All lovely colours there you see,
All colours that were ever seen,
And mossy network too is there, 40
As if by hand of lady fair
The work had woven been,
And cups, the darlings of the eye
So deep is their vermilion dye.

V

Ah me! what lovely tints are there! 45
Of olive-green and scarlet bright,
In spikes, in branches, and in stars,
Green, red, and pearly white.
This heap of earth o'ergrown with moss
Which close beside the thorn you see, 50

---

18 *you'd say* This idiomatic use of 'you' (meaning myself, anyone, yourself) does much to involve the reader in the process of surmise central to the poem.
32–3 *I've measured . . . two feet wide* A much-mocked couplet and revised by Wordsworth in later editions, the lines follow on from the measurements conducted earlier in the stanza, and suggest the narrator's anxious care in the presence of a natural object that creates in him a subliminal disquiet (at some level, he may be wondering whether the pool is deep enough to drown a child).
40 *network* Embroidery.

So fresh in all its beauteous dyes,
Is like an infant's grave in size
As like as like can be:
But never, never any where,
An infant's grave was half so fair. 55

VI

Now would you see this aged thorn,
This pond and beauteous hill of moss,
You must take care and chuse your time
The mountain when to cross.
For oft there sits, between the heap 60
That's like an infant's grave in size,
And that same pond of which I spoke,
A woman in a scarlet cloak,
And to herself she cries,
'Oh misery! oh misery! 65
'Oh woe is me! oh misery!'

VII

At all times of the day and night
This wretched woman thither goes,
And she is known to every star,
And every wind that blows; 70
And there beside the thorn she sits
When the blue day-light's in the skies,
And when the whirlwind's on the hill,
Or frosty air is keen and still,
And to herself she cries, 75
'Oh misery! oh misery!
'Oh woe is me! oh misery!'

VIII

'Now wherefore thus, by day and night,
'In rain, in tempest, and in snow,
'Thus to the dreary mountain-top 80
'Does this poor woman go?
'And why sits she beside the thorn
'When the blue day-light's in the sky,
'Or when the whirlwind's on the hill,
'Or frosty air is keen and still, 85
'And wherefore does she cry? –
'Oh wherefore? wherefore? tell me why
'Does she repeat that doleful cry?'

IX

I cannot tell; I wish I could;
For the true reason no one knows, 90

53–5 *As like . . . fair.* The simile posits, pulls away from and cannot let go of the idea that the 'heap of earth' (l. 49) is 'An infant's grave'.

But if you'd gladly view the spot,
The spot to which she goes;
The heap that's like an infant's grave,
The pond – and thorn, so old and grey,
Pass by her door – 'tis seldom shut –
And if you see her in her hut,
Then to the spot away! –
I never heard of such as dare
Approach the spot when she is there.

X

'But wherefore to the mountain-top
'Can this unhappy woman go,
'Whatever star is in the skies,
'Whatever wind may blow?'
Nay rack your brain – 'tis all in vain,
I'll tell you every thing I know;
But to the thorn, and to the pond
Which is a little step beyond,
I wish that you would go:
Perhaps when you are at the place
You something of her tale may trace.

XI

I'll give you the best help I can:
Before you up the mountain go,
Up to the dreary mountain-top,
I'll tell you all I know.
'Tis now some two and twenty years,
Since she (her name is Martha Ray)
Gave with a maiden's true good will
Her company to Stephen Hill;
And she was blithe and gay,
And she was happy, happy still
Whene'er she thought of Stephen Hill.

XII

And they had fix'd the wedding-day,
The morning that must wed them both;
But Stephen to another maid
Had sworn another oath;
And with this other maid to church
Unthinking Stephen went –
Poor Martha! on that woful day
A cruel, cruel fire, they say,
Into her bones was sent:
It dried her body like a cinder,
And almost turn'd her brain to tinder.

XIII

They say, full six months after this,
While yet the summer-leaves were green,
She to the mountain-top would go,

And there was often seen.
'Tis said, a child was in her womb,
As now to any eye was plain;
She was with child, and she was mad,
Yet often she was sober sad 140
From her exceeding pain.
Oh me! ten thousand times I'd rather
That he had died, that cruel father!

XIV

Sad case for such a brain to hold
Communion with a stirring child! 145
Sad case, as you may think, for one
Who had a brain so wild!
Last Christmas when we talked of this,
Old Farmer Simpson did maintain,
That in her womb the infant wrought 150
About its mother's heart, and brought
Her senses back again:
And when at last her time drew near,
Her looks were calm, her senses clear.

XV

No more I know, I wish I did, 155
And I would tell it all to you;
For what became of this poor child
There's none that ever knew:
And if a child was born or no,
There's no one that could ever tell; 160
And if 'twas born alive or dead,
There's no one knows, as I have said,
But some remember well,
That Martha Ray about this time
Would up the mountain often climb. 165

XVI

And all that winter, when at night
The wind blew from the mountain-peak,
'Twas worth your while, though in the dark,
The church-yard path to seek:
For many a time and oft were heard 170
Cries coming from the mountain-head,
Some plainly living voices were,
And others, I've heard many swear,
Were voices of the dead:
I cannot think, whate'er they say, 175
They had to do with Martha Ray.

---

155 *No more I know, I wish I did* The disclaimer is typical of the narrator.
172–4 *Some . . . dead* The balance of the syntax suggests that the 'living voices' and the 'voices of the dead' are equally real, even though the former are evidently ('plainly') audible and the latter are merely reported; the effect is characteristic of a poem fascinated by the link and gap between reality and supposition.

XVII

But that she goes to this old thorn,
The thorn which I've described to you,
And there sits in a scarlet cloak,
I will be sworn is true.
For one day with my telescope,
To view the ocean wide and bright,
When to this country first I came,
Ere I had heard of Martha's name,
I climbed the mountain's height: 185
A storm came on, and I could see
No object higher than my knee.

XVIII

'Twas mist and rain, and storm and rain,
No screen, no fence could I discover,
And then the wind! in faith, it was 190
A wind full ten times over.
I looked around, I thought I saw
A jutting crag, and off I ran,
Head-foremost, through the driving rain,
The shelter of the crag to gain, 195
And, as I am a man,
Instead of jutting crag, I found
A woman seated on the ground.

XIX

I did not speak – I saw her face,
Her face it was enough for me; 200
I turned about and heard her cry,
'O misery! O misery!'
And there she sits, until the moon
Through half the clear blue sky will go,
And when the little breezes make 205
The waters of the pond to shake,
As all the country know,
She shudders and you hear her cry,
'Oh misery! oh misery!'

XX

'But what's the thorn? and what's the pond? 210
'And what's the hill of moss to her?
'And what's the creeping breeze that comes
'The little pond to stir?'
I cannot tell; but some will say
She hanged her baby on the tree, 215
Some say she drowned it in the pond,
Which is a little step beyond,
But all and each agree,

192–5 *I looked . . . gain* Wordsworth uses enjambment to mimic the speaker's rush towards the shelter which he mistakenly thinks he has found.

>   The little babe was buried there,
>   Beneath that hill of moss so fair.   220
>
>   XXI
>
>   I've heard the scarlet moss is red
>   With drops of that poor infant's blood;
>   But kill a new-born infant thus!
>   I do not think she could.
>   Some say, if to the pond you go,   225
>   And fix on it a steady view,
>   The shadow of a babe you trace,
>   A baby and a baby's face,
>   And that it looks at you;
>   Whene'er you look on it, 'tis plain   230
>   The baby looks at you again.
>
>   XXII
>
>   And some had sworn an oath that she
>   Should be to public justice brought;
>   And for the little infant's bones
>   With spades they would have sought.   235
>   But then the beauteous hill of moss
>   Before their eyes begun to stir;
>   And for full fifty yards around,
>   The grass it shook upon the ground;
>   But all do still aver   240
>   The little babe is buried there,
>   Beneath that hill of moss so fair.
>
>   XXIII
>
>   I cannot tell how this may be,
>   But plain it is, the thorn is hound
>   With heavy tufts of moss, that strive   245
>   To drag it to the ground.
>   And this I know, full many a time,
>   When she was on the mountain high,
>   By day, and in the silent night,
>   When all the stars shone clear and bright,   250
>   That I have heard her cry,
>   'Oh misery! oh misery!
>   'O woe is me! oh misery!'

240 *all do still aver* As occurs elsewhere in the poem, the phrasing evokes a close-knit community in which report, gossip and hearsay are powerful forces.

247 *And this I know* What the narrator does 'know' is the fact of Martha's 'misery', a fact which may involve projection on his part.

The Last of the Flock

Composed between March and May 1798, the poem illustrates Wordsworth's assertion that in the *Lyrical Ballads* the feeling will be found to give importance to the action and situation. A poem of encounter, it studies the impact of hardship on a man forced to sell his flock of sheep to provide for his family since he is not poor enough (because of his flock) to qualify for parish relief under the so-called 'Speenhamland system' whereby wage levels could be raised by the parish. The poem uses its 10-line stanzas (octosyllabic lines, with a shorter six-syllable eighth line, rhymed *aabbcdedff*, a scheme that leaves the fifth and seventh lines unrhymed) to articulate the man's sorrow at losing his flock, a sorrow that is marked by two features: an obsession with the arithmetic of loss (as in the final stanza where he counts down from 50 sheep to one, the last of his flock) and the gradual loss of concern for the fate of his family: 'I prayed,' he says in the poem's most compelling lines, 'yet every day I thought / I loved my children less' (ll. 87–8). The poem may again engage with Godwin and his arguments against property; the farmer in the poem is attached to his flock in ways that seem not be allowed for by Godwin. The poem's intensity has a quasi-Shakespearean resonance when one recalls the Lear who railed against calculations concerning 'need' in response to Goneril's taunting question 'What need one?' (*King Lear*, 2. 4. 259, 258).

Text from *Lyrical Ballads 1798*.

In distant countries I have been,
And yet I have not often seen
A healthy man, a man full grown,
Weep in the public roads alone.
But such a one, on English ground, 5
And in the broad high-way, I met;
Along the broad high-way he came,
His cheeks with tears were wet.
Sturdy he seemed, though he was sad;
And in his arms a lamb he had. 10

He saw me, and he turned aside,
As if he wished himself to hide:
Then with his coat he made essay
To wipe those briny tears away.
I follow'd him, and said, 'My friend 15
'What ails you? wherefore weep you so?'
—'Shame on me, Sir! this lusty lamb,
He makes my tears to flow.
To-day I fetched him from the rock;
He is the last of all my flock. 20

When I was young, a single man,
And after youthful follies ran,
Though little given to care and thought,
Yet, so it was, a ewe I bought;
And other sheep from her I raised, 25
As healthy sheep as you might see,
And then I married, and was rich
As I could wish to be;
Of sheep I numbered a full score,
And every year increas'd my store. 30

Year after year my stock it grew,
And from this one, this single ewe,
Full fifty comely sheep I raised,
As sweet a flock as ever grazed!
Upon the mountain did they feed; 35
They throve, and we at home did thrive.
—This lusty lamb of all my store

---

4 *Weep in . . . alone* The strong stress on 'Weep' (at odds with the iambic pulse) conveys the shock of seeing a full-grown, healthy man in tears.
11 *He saw . . . aside* The gesture conveys feeling, as often in Wordsworth's poems.

13 *made essay* This slightly pompous locution for 'tried' is, in context, affecting; its cumbersome nature seems right for the man's failed attempt to disguise his tears.

Is all that is alive;
And now I care not if we die,
And perish all of poverty. 40

Six children, Sir! had I to feed,
Hard labour in a time of need!
My pride was tamed, and in our grief,
I of the parish ask'd relief.
They said I was a wealthy man; 45
My sheep upon the mountain fed,
And it was fit that thence I took
Whereof to buy us bread:
"Do this; how can we give to you,"
They cried, "what to the poor is due?" 50

I sold a sheep as they had said,
And bought my little children bread,
And they were healthy with their food;
For me it never did me good.
A woeful time it was for me, 55
To see the end of all my gains,
The pretty flock which I had reared
With all my care and pains,
To see it melt like snow away!
For me it was a woeful day. 60

Another still! and still another!
A little lamb, and then its mother!
It was a vein that never stopp'd,
Like blood-drops from my heart they dropp'd.
Till thirty were not left alive 65
They dwindled, dwindled, one by one,
And I may say that many a time
I wished they all were gone:
They dwindled one by one away;
For me it was a woeful day. 70

To wicked deeds I was inclined,
And wicked fancies cross'd my mind,
And every man I chanc'd to see,
I thought he knew some ill of me.
No peace, no comfort could I find, 75
No ease, within doors or without,
And crazily, and wearily
I went my work about.
Oft-times I thought to run away;
For me it was a woeful day. 80

Sir! 'twas a precious flock to me,
As dear as my own children be;
For daily with my growing store

39–42 *And now . . . in a time of need!* The ordering of these assertions implies the speaker's conflicted feelings of carelessness about and responsibility for his family. If the former seem to have supplanted the latter, it is the case that, in the telling, the latter follow the former.

60, 70, 80 *For . . . woeful day* The refrain-like line which concludes these three stanzas reinforces the speaker's absorption in grief; the couplet which concludes the next stanza includes the same rhyme word (see l. 89), sustaining the effect.

> I loved my children more and more.
> Alas! it was an evil time; 85
> God cursed me in my sore distress,
> I prayed, yet every day I thought
> I loved my children less;
> And every week, and every day,
> My flock, it seemed to melt away. 90
>
> They dwindled, Sir, sad sight to see!
> From ten to five, from five to three,
> A lamb, a weather, and a ewe;
> And then at last, from three to two;
> And of my fifty, yesterday 95
> I had but only one,
> And here it lies upon my arm,
> Alas! and I have none;
> To-day I fetched it from the rock;
> It is the last of all my flock.' 100

93 *weather* Wether, a castrated ram.
96 *I had but only one* The shorter line is terse with loss; in all previous stanzas the sixth line has eight syllables.

The Idiot Boy

In the Preface, Wordsworth speaks of 'tracing the maternal passion through many of its more subtle windings' in this poem and in 'The Mad Mother' (Preface to *Lyrical Ballads*, vol. 1, p. xv). The 'maternal passion' displayed by Betty Foy has as its object her seemingly mentally disabled son, 'Him whom she loves, her idiot Boy', as Wordsworth phrases it in a touching and, with variations, repeated line (ll. 11, 16, 51, and, later, at ll. 376 and 381). In a letter of June 1802 to John Wilson, who admired Wordsworth's poetry but took issue with his choice of subject-matter, Wordsworth points both to the 'pleasure' with which he wrote (and reads) the poem, and to the fact that he has 'often looked upon the conduct of fathers and mothers of the lower classes of society towards Idiots as the great triumph of the human heart'. The poem is a comic and affecting triumph that rejoices not only in Johnny's essential humanity, but also in his access to a condition of visionary wonder in which the ordinary things of everyday life are seen in a new light (one of the suggestions of ll. 460–1, the only words spoken by Johnny in the poem). Johnny is, literally, an embodiment of the 1790s Wordsworthian ideal of 'joy' (see ll. 84–6), an at-one-ness with, and pleasure in the energies of, nature; at the same time, he has not full motor co-ordination, and yet any laughter at him is full of tenderness. For we see Johnny from Betty's perspective, as well as from that of the good-natured narrator, full of impish delight in not giving us a ballad of horror such as Gottfried Bürger's *Lenore*. And for Betty nothing in the world is as precious as Johnny, as is shown by her last-minute reluctance that he should fetch a doctor for the ailing Susan Gale. That stanza, starting at line 77, shows the dexterity with which in this poem Wordsworth uses a five-line stanza form, the first line unrhymed, the next four rhymed *abba*: the first line, 'And now that Johnny is just going', wanders off on its own, rather as Betty's much-loved son is about to, while the circling *abba* rhyme-scheme brings us back to Betty's inner feelings while 'She gently pats the pony's side . . . And seems no longer in a hurry' (ll. 79, 81), those inner feelings underscored by a feminine rhyme that subdues the earlier 'mighty flurry' (l. 78). The strong sense that Betty's maternal feelings are a natural and, therefore, good power is brought to a head by the simile at line 384 describing the nature of her 'joy' (l. 383): 'She darts as with a torrent's force'. The poet derives much amusement from teasing us about Johnny's adventures, adventures contrasted with the melodramatic events of ghostly ballads, but hinted at by stanzas such as those starting at lines 292 and 297. The poem's sharpness, evident in its metrical movement as well as its lively characterization of the grumpy doctor's speech, wards off sentimentalism. So Susan Gale's recovery at the end, after she has begun to worry about others ('her messenger and nurse', l. 424), seems less a fairy-tale miracle than a deft insight into the nature of psychosomatic illness. Again, the sequence of stanzas describing Betty's mounting anxiety and search for Johnny combines quiet amusement with considerable sympathy and perceptiveness about parental worry.

Text from *Lyrical Ballads 1798*.

'Tis eight o'clock, – a clear March night,
The moon is up – the sky is blue,
The owlet in the moonlight air,
He shouts from nobody knows where;
He lengthens out his lonely shout, 5
Halloo! halloo! a long halloo!

– Why bustle thus about your door,
What means this bustle, Betty Foy?
Why are you in this mighty fret?
And why on horseback have you set 10
Him whom you love, your idiot boy?

Beneath the moon that shines so bright,
Till she is tired, let Betty Foy
With girt and stirrup fiddle-faddle;
But wherefore set upon a saddle 15
Him whom she loves, her idiot boy?

There's scarce a soul that's out of bed;
Good Betty! put him down again;
His lips with joy they burr at you,
But, Betty! what has he to do 20
With stirrup, saddle, or with rein?

The world will say 'tis very idle,
Bethink you of the time of night;
There's not a mother, no not one,
But when she hears what you have done, 25
Oh! Betty she'll be in a fright.

But Betty's bent on her intent,
For her good neighbour, Susan Gale,
Old Susan, she who dwells alone,
Is sick, and makes a piteous moan, 30
As if her very life would fail.

There's not a house within a mile,
No hand to help them in distress:
Old Susan lies a bed in pain,
And sorely puzzled are the twain, 35
For what she ails they cannot guess.

And Betty's husband's at the wood,
Where by the week he doth abide,
A woodman in the distant vale;
There's none to help poor Susan Gale, 40
What must be done? what will betide?

3 *owlet* Young owl.
4 *shouts from nobody knows where* The owlet's untraceable shout suggests the presence in nature of unknowable mysteries, with which Johnny is in contact.
7–8 *Why bustle thus . . .?* The narrator's initial question helps to establish the tone of his relationship with the characters; one that is good-humoured, teasingly in the know (so, here, he knows only too well why Betty bustles), and celebratory.

12 *Beneath the moon* The moon plays a benign, quasi-parental role in the poem, as though watching over Johnny, even if Betty's appeal to it at line 161 seems initially to be unanswered.
22 *very idle* 'idle' here seems initially to mean 'ineffective, worthless, vain', but, as elsewhere in *Lyrical Ballads* 'idleness' in this poem has a positive sense, as when at line 86 Johnny is 'idle all for very joy'.
36 *what she ails* The phrase means, 'what ails her'.

And Betty from the lane has fetched
Her pony, that is mild and good,
Whether he be in joy or pain,
Feeding at will along the lane, 45
Or bringing faggots from the wood.

And he is all in travelling trim,
And by the moonlight, Betty Foy
Has up upon the saddle set,
The like was never heard of yet, 50
Him whom she loves, her idiot boy.

And he must post without delay
Across the bridge that's in the dale,
And by the church, and o'er the down,
To bring a doctor from the town, 55
Or she will die, old Susan Gale.

There is no need of boot or spur,
There is no need of whip or wand,
For Johnny has his holly-bough,
And with a hurly-burly now 60
He shakes the green bough in his hand.

And Betty o'er and o'er has told
The boy who is her best delight,
Both what to follow, what to shun,
What do, and what to leave undone, 65
How turn to left, and how to right.

And Betty's most especial charge,
Was, 'Johnny! Johnny! mind that you
'Come home again, nor stop at all,
'Come home again, whate'er befal, 70
'My Johnny do, I pray you do.'

To this did Johnny answer make,
Both with his head, and with his hand,
And proudly shook the bridle too,
And then! his words were not a few, 75
Which Betty well could understand.

And now that Johnny is just going,
Though Betty's in a mighty flurry,
She gently pats the pony's side,
On which her idiot boy must ride, 80
And seems no longer in a hurry.

---

50 *The like was . . . yet* The phrase mocks the gossipy tone of neighbours as well as the melodramatic assertions of Bürger-like ballads, and also asks to be read straight; for 'The Idiot Boy' makes genuinely new claims on its reader.
59 *holly-bough* Johnny's comic symbol of equestrian command brings out his kinship with the natural world; he is, at such a moment, a descendant of the ancient folkloric figure of the 'Green Man', as in the medieval poem, *Sir Gawain and the Green Knight*.

62–6 *o'er and o'er has told . . . right* The stanza captures Betty's motherly concern, mimicking her anxious instructions.
75–6 *his words . . . understand* Amusingly and yet affectingly, these lines suggest the bond between son and mother; Betty is attuned to the specifically individual meanings of Johnny's babble, the 'burr, burr, burr' (l. 115) which Coleridge in *Biographia Literaria* disliked for bringing to mind 'disgusting images of ordinary morbid idiocy'.

But when the pony moved his legs,
Oh! then for the poor idiot boy!
For joy he cannot hold the bridle,
For joy his head and heels are idle, 85
He's idle all for very joy.

And while the pony moves his legs,
In Johnny's left-hand you may see,
The green bough's motionless and dead;
The moon that shines above his head 90
Is not more still and mute than he.

His heart it was so full of glee,
That till full fifty yards were gone,
He quite forgot his holly whip,
And all his skill in horsemanship, 95
Oh! happy, happy, happy John.

And Betty's standing at the door,
And Betty's face with joy o'erflows,
Proud of herself, and proud of him,
She sees him in his travelling trim; 100
How quietly her Johnny goes.

The silence of her idiot boy,
What hopes it sends to Betty's heart!
He's at the guide-post – he turns right,
She watches till he's out of sight, 105
And Betty will not then depart.

Burr, burr – now Johnny's lips they burr,
As loud as any mill, or near it,
Meek as a lamb the pony moves,
And Johnny makes the noise he loves, 110
And Betty listens, glad to hear it.

Away she hies to Susan Gale:
And Johnny's in a merry tune,
The owlets hoot, the owlets curr,
And Johnny's lips they burr, burr, burr, 115
And on he goes beneath the moon.

His steed and he right well agree,
For of this pony there's a rumour,
That should he lose his eyes and ears,
And should he live a thousand years, 120
He never will be out of humour.

But then he is a horse that thinks!
And when he thinks his pace is slack;
Now, though he knows poor Johnny well,
Yet for his life he cannot tell 125
What he has got upon his back.

86 *idle . . . very joy* 'idle' here is complex in its working: it means being unable to carry out a physical task because of the 'joy' created by simply living in a world where such a task is to be performed.
98 *with joy o'erflows* Sustains the reference to 'joy' and prepares for the climactic simile at line 383.

102 *The silence . . . boy* Betty is impressed by Johnny's 'silence', but the narrator alerts us to the loud sounds made by Johnny as he rides.
114 *curr* Coo.

So through the moonlight lanes they go,
And far into the moonlight dale,
And by the church, and o'er the down,
To bring a doctor from the town, 130
To comfort poor old Susan Gale.

And Betty, now at Susan's side,
Is in the middle of her story,
What comfort Johnny soon will bring,
With many a most diverting thing, 135
Of Johnny's wit and Johnny's glory.

And Betty's still at Susan's side:
By this time she's not quite so flurried;
Demure with porringer and plate
She sits, as if in Susan's fate 140
Her life and soul were buried.

But Betty, poor good woman! she,
You plainly in her face may read it,
Could lend out of that moment's store
Five years of happiness or more, 145
To any that might need it.

But yet I guess that now and then
With Betty all was not so well,
And to the road she turns her ears,
And thence full many a sound she hears, 150
Which she to Susan will not tell.

Poor Susan moans, poor Susan groans,
'As sure as there's a moon in heaven,'
Cries Betty, "he'll be back again;
'They'll both be here, 'tis almost ten, 155
'They'll both be here before eleven.'

Poor Susan moans, poor Susan groans,
The clock gives warning for eleven;
'Tis on the stroke – 'If Johnny's near,"
Quoth Betty "he will soon be here, 160
'As sure as there's a moon in heaven.'

The clock is on the stroke of twelve,
And Johnny is not yet in sight,
The moon's in heaven, as Betty sees,
But Betty is not quite at ease; 165
And Susan has a dreadful night.

And Betty, half an hour ago,
On Johnny vile reflections cast;
'A little idle sauntering thing!'
With other names, an endless string, 170
But now that time is gone and past.

---

136 *Johnny's wit . . . glory* The effect is almost or initially mock-heroic, and yet the poem will suggest that Johnny has his own form of 'wit' and attains a kind of 'glory'.

171 *But now . . . past* Betty's anxiety about Johnny has reached a point where she no longer upbraids him.

And Betty's drooping at the heart,
That happy time all past and gone,
'How can it be he is so late?
'The doctor he has made him wait, 175
'Susan! they'll both be here anon.'

And Susan's growing worse and worse,
And Betty's in a sad quandary;
And then there's nobody to say
If she must go or she must stay: 180
– She's in a sad quandary.

The clock is on the stroke of one;
But neither Doctor nor his guide
Appear along the moonlight road,
There's neither horse nor man abroad, 185
And Betty's still at Susan's side.

And Susan she begins to fear
Of sad mischances not a few,
That Johnny may perhaps be drown'd,
Or lost perhaps, and never found; 190
Which they must both for ever rue.

She prefaced half a hint of this
With, 'God forbid it should be true!'
At the first word that Susan said
Cried Betty, rising from the bed, 195
'Susan, I'd gladly stay with you.

'I must be gone, I must away,
'Consider, Johnny's but half-wise;
'Susan, we must take care of him,
'If he is hurt in life or limb'– 200
'Oh God forbid!" poor Susan cries.

'What can I do?" says Betty, going,
'What can I do to ease your pain?
'Good Susan tell me, and I'll stay;
'I fear you're in a dreadful way, 205
'But I shall soon be back again.'

'Good Betty go, good Betty go,
'There's nothing that can ease my pain.'
Then off she hies, but with a prayer
That God poor Susan's life would spare, 210
Till she comes back again.

So, through the moonlight lane she goes,
And far into the moonlight dale;
And how she ran, and how she walked,
And all that to herself she talked, 215
Would surely be a tedious tale.

---

173 *past and gone* The echo of line 171 uses a balladic technique to convey Betty's state of worry.

181 *quandary* Rhymes with itself to suggest Betty's dilemma.

In high and low, above, below,
In great and small, in round and square,
In tree and tower was Johnny seen,
In bush and brake, in black and green,   220
'Twas Johnny, Johnny, every where.

She's past the bridge that's in the dale,
And now the thought torments her sore,
Johnny perhaps his horse forsook,
To hunt the moon that's in the brook,   225
And never will be heard of more.

And now she's high upon the down,
Alone amid a prospect wide;
There's neither Johnny nor his horse,
Among the fern or in the gorse;   230
There's neither doctor nor his guide.

'Oh saints! what is become of him?
'Perhaps he's climbed into an oak,
'Where he will stay till he is dead;
'Or sadly he has been misled,   235
'And joined the wandering gypsey-folk.

'Or him that wicked pony's carried
'To the dark cave, the goblins' hall,
'Or in the castle he's pursuing,
'Among the ghosts, his own undoing;   240
'Or playing with the waterfall.'

At poor old Susan then she railed,
While to the town she posts away;
'If Susan had not been so ill,
'Alas! I should have had him still,   245
'My Johnny, till my dying day.'

Poor Betty! in this sad distemper,
The doctor's self would hardly spare,
Unworthy things she talked and wild,
Even he, of cattle the most mild,   250
The pony had his share.

And now she's got into the town,
And to the doctor's door she hies;
'Tis silence all on every side;
The town so long, the town so wide,   255
Is silent as the skies.

And now she's at the doctor's door,
She lifts the knocker, rap, rap, rap,
The doctor at the casement shews,
His glimmering eyes that peep and doze;   260
And one hand rubs his old night-cap.

---

221 *'Twas Johnny, Johnny, every where* Because the searching mother thinks she sees him wherever she looks.
237–41 *Or him . . . waterfall* Betty's fears recall the spectral plots of Gothic ballads.
251 *The pony . . . share* True to the poem's tonal balance, Betty's railings against the pony are at once comically unfair and emotionally understandable.
254 *silence* Silence will prove sympathetic to human beings in the poem, but at this point Wordsworth conveys vividly the unwelcoming silence of a town at night.

'Oh Doctor! Doctor! where's my Johnny?'
'I'm here, what is't you want with me?'
'Oh Sir! you know I'm Betty Foy,
'And I have lost my poor dear boy, 265
'You know him – him you often see;

'He's not so wise as some folks be.'
'The devil take his wisdom!' said
The Doctor, looking somewhat grim,
'What, woman! should I know of him?' 270
And, grumbling, he went back to bed.

'O woe is me! O woe is me!
'Here will I die; here will I die;
'I thought to find my Johnny here,
'But he is neither far nor near, 275
'Oh! what a wretched mother I!'

She stops, she stands, she looks about,
Which way to turn she cannot tell.
Poor Betty! it would ease her pain
If she had heart to knock again; 280
– The clock strikes three – a dismal knell!

Then up along the town she hies,
No wonder if her senses fail,
This piteous news so much it shock'd her,
She quite forgot to send the Doctor, 285
To comfort poor old Susan Gale.

And now she's high upon the down,
And she can see a mile of road,
'Oh cruel! I'm almost three-score;
'Such night as this was ne'er before, 290
'There's not a single soul abroad.'

She listens, but she cannot hear
The foot of horse, the voice of man;
The streams with softest sound are flowing,
The grass you almost hear it growing, 295
You hear it now if e'er you can.

The owlets through the long blue night
Are shouting to each other still:
Fond lovers, yet not quite hob nob,
They lengthen out the tremulous sob, 300
That echoes far from hill to hill.

Poor Betty now has lost all hope,
Her thoughts are bent on deadly sin;
A green-grown pond she just has pass'd,
And from the brink she hurries fast, 305
Lest she should drown herself therein.

267–71 *He's not . . . bed* Betty's faltering attempt to explain Johnny's condition is met by the Doctor's brusque dismissal. The humour lies in the relish with which Wordsworth 'does' the different voices.

295–6 *The grass . . . can* The lines have the effect of an aside that reminds us of the poem's central trust in nature.

And now she sits her down and weeps;
Such tears she never shed before;
'Oh dear, dear pony! my sweet joy!
'Oh carry back my idiot boy!   310
'And we will ne'er o'erload thee more.'

A thought is come into her head;
'The pony he is mild and good,
'And we have always used him well;
'Perhaps he's gone along the dell,   315
'And carried Johnny to the wood.'

Then up she springs as if on wings;
She thinks no more of deadly sin;
If Betty fifty ponds should see,
The last of all her thoughts would be,   320
To drown herself therein.

Oh reader! now that I might tell
What Johnny and his horse are doing
What they've been doing all this time,
Oh could I put it into rhyme,   325
A most delightful tale pursuing!

Perhaps, and no unlikely thought!
He with his pony now doth roam
The cliffs and peaks so high that are,
To lay his hands upon a star,   330
And in his pocket bring it home.

Perhaps he's turned himself about,
His face unto his horse's tail,
And still and mute, in wonder lost,
All like a silent horseman-ghost,   335
He travels on along the vale.

And now, perhaps, he's hunting sheep,
A fierce and dreadful hunter he!
Yon valley, that's so trim and green,
In five months' time, should he be seen,   340
A desert wilderness will be.

Perhaps, with head and heels on fire,
And like the very soul of evil,
He's galloping away, away,
And so he'll gallop on for aye,   345
The bane of all that dread the devil.

I to the muses have been bound,
These fourteen years, by strong indentures;
Oh gentle muses! let me tell
But half of what to him befel,   350
For sure he met with strange adventures.

322–51 *Oh reader . . . strange adventures* The stanzas recall the teasing of the 'gentle reader' in 'Simon Lee' (l. 69), mock the imaginings of other ballads, and serve as an intimation that Johnny did meet with 'strange adventures': possibly the adventure of communing with nature.

Oh gentle muses! is this kind?
Why will ye thus my suit repel?
Why of your further aid bereave me?
And can ye thus unfriended leave me? 355
Ye muses! whom I love so well.

Who's yon, that, near the waterfall,
Which thunders down with headlong force,
Beneath the moon, yet shining fair,
As careless as if nothing were, 360
Sits upright on a feeding horse?

Unto his horse, that's feeding free,
He seems, I think, the rein to give;
Of moon or stars he takes no heed;
Of such we in romances read, 365
– 'Tis Johnny! Johnny! as I live.

And that's the very pony too.
Where is she, where is Betty Foy?
She hardly can sustain her fears;
The roaring water-fall she hears, 370
And cannot find her idiot boy.

Your pony's worth his weight in gold,
Then calm your terrors, Betty Foy!
She's coming from among the trees,
And now, all full in view, she sees 375
Him whom she loves, her idiot boy.

And Betty sees the pony too:
Why stand you thus Good Betty Foy?
It is no goblin, 'tis no ghost,
'Tis he whom you so long have lost, 380
He whom you love, your idiot boy.

She looks again – her arms are up –
She screams – she cannot move for joy;
She darts as with a torrent's force,
She almost has o'erturned the horse, 385
And fast she holds her idiot boy.

And Johnny burrs and laughs aloud,
Whether in cunning or in joy,
I cannot tell; but while he laughs,
Betty a drunken pleasure quaffs, 390
To hear again her idiot boy.

And now she's at the pony's tail,
And now she's at the pony's head,
On that side now, and now on this,
And almost stifled with her bliss, 395
A few sad tears does Betty shed.

She kisses o'er and o'er again,
Him whom she loves, her idiot boy,
She's happy here, she's happy there,

---

379 *It is . . . ghost* Again, Wordsworth brings into play, only to deny, the possibility of some superstitious or spectral occurrence.

380 *'Tis he . . . lost* The pathos is largely but not solely comic.

She is uneasy every where; 400
Her limbs are all alive with joy.

She pats the pony, where or when
She knows not, happy Betty Foy!
The little pony glad may be,
But he is milder far than she, 405
You hardly can perceive his joy.

'Oh! Johnny, never mind the Doctor;
'You've done your best, and that is all.'
She took the reins, when this was said,
And gently turned the pony's head 410
From the loud water-fall.

By this the stars were almost gone,
The moon was setting on the hill,
So pale you scarcely looked at her:
The little birds began to stir, 415
Though yet their tongues were still.

The pony, Betty, and her boy,
Wind slowly through the woody dale:
And who is she, be-times abroad.
That hobbles up the steep rough road? 420
Who is it, but old Susan Gale?

Long Susan lay deep lost in thought,
And many dreadful fears beset her,
Both for her messenger and nurse;
And as her mind grew worse and worse, 425
Her body it grew better.

She turned, she toss'd herself in bed,
On all sides doubts and terrors met her;
Point after point did she discuss;
And while her mind was fighting thus, 430
Her body still grew better.

'Alas! what is become of them?
'These fears can never be endured,
'I'll to the wood.' – The word scarce said,
Did Susan rise up from her bed, 435
As if by magic cured.

Away she posts up hill and down,
And to the wood at length is come,
She spies her friends, she shouts a greeting;
Oh me! it is a merry meeting, 440
As ever was in Christendom.

The owls have hardly sung their last,
While our four travellers homeward wend;
The owls have hooted all night long,
And with the owls began my song, 445
And with the owls must end.

---

401 *Her limbs . . . joy* Recalls line 86, but 'all alive' brings to the surface the poem's animism, the sense that the same life-force flows through human beings as through nature.

> For while they all were travelling home,
> Cried Betty, 'Tell us Johnny, do,
> 'Where all this long night you have been,
> 'What you have heard, what you have seen, 450
> 'And Johnny, mind you tell us true.'
>
> Now Johnny all night long had heard
> The owls in tuneful concert strive;
> No doubt too he the moon had seen;
> For in the moonlight he had been 455
> From eight o'clock till five.
>
> And thus to Betty's question, he
> Made answer, like a traveller bold,
> (His very words I give to you,)
> 'The cocks did crow to-whoo, to-whoo, 460
> 'And the sun did shine so cold.'
> – Thus answered Johnny in his glory,
> And that was all his travel's story.

459 *(His . . . you)* Wordsworth mimics the claims for veracity made by travellers' tales.

Expostulation and Reply

According to the Advertisement to the 1798 edition of *Lyrical Ballads*, the poem, like 'The Tables Turned', 'arose out of conversation with a friend who was somewhat unreasonably attached to modern books of moral philosophy'. This friend is likely to have been William Hazlitt, who in 'My First Acquaintance with Poets' recalls getting 'into a metaphysical argument with Wordsworth. . . , in which we neither of us succeeded in making ourselves perfectly clear and intelligible' (Wu, *Romanticism: An Anthology*, 3rd edn, p. 781). Wordsworth transposes their conversation from Alfoxden to the Lake District and gives his interlocutor the name of 'Matthew', the name he gives his former schoolmaster, William Taylor. The poem's ballad form, with a shorter final line (and sometimes shorter second line) in its quatrains, serves as the vehicle for sharp if affectionate exchange. The affection shows in the use of the author's first name in lines 1 and 3, and the opening tone is one of well-intentioned reproach. Matthew is described as 'my good friend' (l. 15). Stanza 4, sketching a state of mind in which 'life was sweet, I knew not why' (l. 14), before the poet begins his reply, does much to support his subsequent preference for a 'wise passiveness' (l. 24) rather than the book-centred learning recommended by Matthew. The poem suggests that the senses and physical experience are the source of wisdom. Wordsworth is less a supporter of empirical philosophy, however, according to which the senses make possible the formation of ideas, than a believer in the process of 'Conversing' (l. 30) with the natural world.

Text from *Lyrical Ballads 1798*.

> 'Why William, on that old grey stone,
> 'Thus for the length of half a day,
> 'Why William, sit you thus alone,
> 'And dream your time away?
>
> 'Where are your books? that light bequeath'd 5
> 'To beings else forlorn and blind!
> 'Up! Up! and drink the spirit breath'd
> 'From dead men to their kind.

7–8 *Up, up . . . kind!* Matthew might have been reading Edmund Burke's *Reflections on the Revolution in France*, in which the idea of a bond between living and dead is powerfully stated. At the same time, 'the spirit breath'd / From dead men to their kind' has an ironic inflection, given the poet's fascination with the spirit breathed by and to the living.

'You look round on your mother earth,
'As if she for no purpose bore you;   10
'As if you were her first-born birth,
'And none had lived before you!'

One morning thus, by Esthwaite lake,
When life was sweet I knew not why,
To me my good friend Matthew spake,   15
And thus I made reply.

'The eye it cannot chuse but see,
'We cannot bid the ear be still;
'Our bodies feel, where'er they be,
'Against, or with our will.   20

'Nor less I deem that there are powers,
'Which of themselves our minds impress,
'That we can feed this mind of ours,
'In a wise passiveness.

'Think you, mid all this mighty sum   25
'Of things for ever speaking,
'That nothing of itself will come,
'But we must still be seeking?

'— Then ask not wherefore, here, alone,
'Conversing as I may,   30
'I sit upon this old grey stone,
'And dream my time away.'

11–12 *As if none ... you!* The poet is represented as a kind of revolutionary, prepared to ignore the cumulative sum of human wisdom.
13 *Esthwaite Lake* Close to Hawkshead in the Lake District.
19 *feel, where'er they be* The poet advances the claims of bodily experience, which is not harnessed solely by the 'will' (l. 20).
21 *powers* Wordsworth presents the belief in 'powers' as an intuition.
22 *our minds impress* 'impress' conveys a strong sense of the quasi-physical 'impression' made on our 'minds' by 'powers' (l. 21).

23 *we can ... ours* The words imply that we can actively bring our minds into harmony with the surrounding 'powers' through 'a wise passiveness', a word that – true to its meaning – deliberately refuses to assert its status as a rhyme-word (see Brennan O'Donnell, 1995, p. 143).
26 *things for ever speaking* Things 'speak' in a way that books do not, though Wordsworth conveys this thought in a poem that ends up in a book.
27 *nothing ... will come* Wordsworth plays against and with the idea that 'Nothing will come of nothing'. On his account, it is the process of 'seeking' which will prevent us from finding.

The Tables Turned; An Evening Scene, on the same subject

In this poem, the tables are turned on the expostulating friend, as is shown by the first line where the friend's upbraiding formula, 'Up! up!', is used against him (l. 1); now it is the turn of the poet to urge his friend to leave his books and 'Let Nature be your teacher' (l. 16). The poem is less of a dialogue in itself than is the poem to which it is a companion-piece. The stanza form is the same as in 'Expostulation and Reply', but in this poem the second line is constantly shorter, giving rise to a greater sense of achieved clarity and definition, as befits a turning of the tables. The skill with which Wordsworth adapts the stanza form to his expressive purposes is considerable: so, in the second stanza, the run-on lines support the sense of a 'spreading' and 'freshening lustre' (l. 6), while in the penultimate stanza the misshaping work of the intellect is mocked by the way the syntactical arrangement plays against the natural tendency of the stanza to fall into two units of two lines (see O'Donnell, 1995, p. 147). Feminine rhymes occur in the second and fourth lines of the first four stanzas, kick-starting the poem's mood of buoyant confidence. The last four stanzas have a deepened seriousness as they seek to articulate the 'wisdom' (l. 19) accessible through nature.

Text from *Lyrical Ballads 1798*.

Up! up! my friend, and clear your looks,
Why all this toil and trouble?
Up! up! my friend, and quit your books,
Or surely you'll grow double.

The sun above the mountain's head, 5
A freshening lustre mellow,
Through all the long green fields has spread,
His first sweet evening yellow.

Books! 'tis a dull and endless strife,
Come, hear the woodland linnet, 10
How sweet his music; on my life
There's more of wisdom in it.

And hark! how blithe the throstle sings!
And he is no mean preacher;
Come forth into the light of things, 15
Let Nature be your teacher.

She has a world of ready wealth,
Our minds and hearts to bless –
Spontaneous wisdom breathed by health,
Truth breathed by chearfulness. 20

One impulse from a vernal wood
May teach you more of man;
Of moral evil and of good,
Than all the sages can.

Sweet is the lore which nature brings; 25
Our meddling intellect
Misshapes the beauteous forms of things;
– We murder to dissect.

Enough of science and of art;
Close up these barren leaves; 30
Come forth, and bring with you a heart
That watches and receives.

---

2 *toil and trouble* Echoes the witches in *Macbeth* ('Double, double, toil and trouble', 4. 1. 10). The echo is teasing, but it suggests, albeit lightly, the dangers of book-learning.
7 *Through ... spread* The monosyllables and extra stress (on 'green') slow down the line, making the reader dwell on the showing forth of the 'lustre' (l. 6).
9–12 *Books ... in it* The short phrases suggest the speaker is responding to something happening as he speaks.
15 *Come ... light of things* Has the air of a heterodox scriptural precept. Again, 'things' are the object of Wordsworth's praise.
19, 20 *breathed* The use of the verb is Wordsworth's retaliation against its use in 'Expostulation and Reply', line 7.
21 *One impulse* Conveys a sense of a power in nature that communicates through impulsions. Newton's universe, based on his three laws of motion, has become animate.
22 *May teach* 'May' avoids the stridency involved in 'will'; at the same time, the word hints that the ability to be taught depends on the receptivity of the student.
23 *moral evil* The speaker's 'chearfulness' (l. 20) does not lead to a rejection of the idea of 'evil'.
28 *We murder to dissect* That is, through 'dissecting' (over-analysing) we 'murder' (destroy the object of analysis). Force is given by a means of expression that places the effect ('murder') before the cause ('dissect').
29 *science ... art* Knowledge; skill.
30 *barren leaves* Pages of the book that the friend is reading; but possibly, too, the very pages in which escape from books is being recommended.

Lines Written a few miles above Tintern Abbey, on revisiting the banks of the Wye during a Tour, July 13, 1798

The poem concludes the 1798 edition of *Lyrical Ballads*. Written in blank verse, it is markedly more elevated in tone and diction than many of the balladic poems in the same collection. The poem shows the impress of ideas and style from Coleridge's conversational poems; so, Coleridge writes in 'This Lime-Tree Bower' that 'Henceforth I shall know / That Nature ne'er deserts the wise and pure' (ll. 59–60), anticipating Wordsworth's sense of 'Knowing that Nature never did betray / The heart that loved her' (ll. 123–4). But, as the fear warded off by 'betray' suggests, 'Tintern Abbey' achieves an 'impassioned' music and complexity all its own. 'Impassioned' was the word which Wordsworth himself applied to the poem (in a note to the poem in 1800) when suggesting that it had something in common with an ode. The poem incorporates within its turns and transitions something of the changes of direction typical of the ode; in 'Tintern Abbey', however, these turns and transitions are adapted to Wordsworth's solemn but conversational manner. The poem's blank verse, full of enjambments and differently placed caesural pauses, is the perfect vehicle for the toing and froing of changing feeling and thought. The poem's reflections on the passage of time result in a balancing of 'loss' (l. 88) and 'Abundant recompence' (l. 89). The poem's plot is one of return, memory, reflection. After five years' absence, Wordsworth returns to Tintern Abbey, or, rather, to the surrounding countryside. The poem is built round two scalings of imaginative heights, followed by a long coda addressed by the poet to his sister. The first of these heights is reached when the poet affirms the value of memory which has enshrined 'These forms of beauty' (l. 24) in his mind, allowing him access to a quasi-mystical 'blessed mood' (l. 38) in which 'We see into the life of things' (l. 50). This assertion passes quickly into the fear that it may only name a 'vain belief' (l. 51), before the poet returns to the passage of time between his last visit and this visit; his language is unspecific but powerful as he describes his past self as 'more like a man / Flying from something that he dreads, than one / Who sought the thing he loved' (ll. 71–3), possibly hinting at a state of 'dread' deriving from a time of political and personal trauma to do with France. It is at this moment that the central balancing act of the poem occurs: the acceptance that 'That time is past' (l. 84), and the weighing up of lost joys and raptures against new gifts. Chief among the new gifts is the 'sense sublime / Of something far more deeply interfused' (ll. 96–7), a grandly indefinable 'something' felt to be present in nature and 'in the mind of man' (l. 100). This passage, the second of the poem's climaxes, may owe a debt to Virgil's depiction in the *Aeneid* (vi, 724–7) of 'an inner spirit' which sustains all creation. As close to pantheism as Wordsworth will get, it, too, is followed by a hint of anxiety (see ll. 112–14), but, securing himself against self-doubt, the poet turns to his sister, at once an embodiment of his former self, ally in his faith in nature, and a much-loved other person, and addresses her with an eloquent tenderness. Again, Wordsworth engages with forces that oppose 'Our cheerful faith that all which we behold / Is full of blessings' (ll. 134–5) as he confronts the possibility that, in the future, Dorothy may experience 'solitude, or fear, or pain, or grief' (l. 144). The poem ends quietly and touchingly, asserting, in the event of future separation, how Dorothy, will not 'forget' (l. 150) that the features of the landscape celebrated in the poem 'were to me / More dear, both for themselves, and for thy sake' (ll. 159–60). Critics who feel that Wordsworth is in some way using Dorothy, or denying her otherness, neglect the implications of a phrase like 'to me', in which Wordsworth recognizes the irreducible fact of individuality.

Text from *Lyrical Ballads 1798*.

    Five years have passed; five summers, with the length
Of five long winters! and again I hear
These waters, rolling from their mountain-springs
With a sweet inland murmur. – Once again
Do I behold these steep and lofty cliffs,   5
Which on a wild secluded scene impress
Thoughts of more deep seclusion; and connect

Title The poem is set 'a few miles above Tintern Abbey', and does not take as its subject the condition of the vagrants who lived in and around the Abbey, a detail relevant in the debate initiated by recent historicist criticism, which has reproved Wordsworth for not dealing directly with the condition of the vagrants who lived in and around the Abbey. 'July 13' is the day before Bastille Day.

4 *inland murmur* 'The river is not affected by the tides a few miles above Tintern' (Wordsworth's note).
6–7 *impress . . . seclusion* The wording mingles nature and mind; the 'cliffs' (l. 5) are the agents by which 'thoughts' are 'impressed'.

The landscape with the quiet of the sky.
The day is come when I again repose
Here, under this dark sycamore, and view   10
These plots of cottage-ground, these orchard-tufts,
Which, at this season, with their unripe fruits,
Among the woods and copses lose themselves,
Nor, with their green and simple hue, disturb
The wild green landscape. Once again I see   15
These hedge-rows, hardly hedge-rows, little lines
Of sportive wood run wild; these pastoral farms
Green to the very door; and wreathes of smoke
Sent up, in silence, from among the trees,
With some uncertain notice, as might seem,   20
Of vagrant dwellers in the houseless woods,
Or of some hermit's cave, where by his fire
The hermit sits alone.

                        Though absent long,
These forms of beauty have not been to me,
As is a landscape to a blind man's eye: 25
But oft, in lonely rooms, and mid the din
Of towns and cities, I have owed to them,
In hours of weariness, sensations sweet,
Felt in the blood, and felt along the heart,
And passing even into my purer mind   30
With tranquil restoration: – feelings too
Of unremembered pleasure; such, perhaps,
As may have had no trivial influence
On that best portion of a good man's life;
His little, nameless, unremembered acts   35
Of kindness and of love. Nor less, I trust,
To them I may have owed another gift,
Of aspect more sublime; that blessed mood,
In which the burthen of the mystery,
In which the heavy and the weary weight   40
Of all this unintelligible world
Is lighten'd: – that serene and blessed mood,
In which the affections gently lead us on,
Until, the breath of this corporeal frame,
And even the motion of our human blood   45

9, 10 *again . . . Here* Wordsworth uses 'again' four times in the opening paragraph to convey the fact of his return; 'Here' insists on the particularity of place and is picked up, affectingly, in line 115. Later in the paragraph 'these' and 'this' also identify the landscape as made up of highly particularized features.

17 *pastoral farms* Farms where sheep pasture.

23 *The hermit sits alone* The hermit seems 'connected' to the poet (to use Wordsworth's verb in l. 7), who is about to tell of 'lonely rooms' (l. 26).

29 *Felt . . . heart* The prepositions, as often in Wordsworth's poetry, are worthy of note; as Christopher Ricks has pointed out, one might expect 'in' and 'along' to be in reverse order (*The Force of Poetry*, Oxford University Press, 1984, p. 121). The effect of 'along the heart' is to make the 'heart' a pervasive presence in the body.

39 *the burthen of the mystery* Keats makes the phrase central to his comments on the poem in his letter of 3 May 1818 as being 'explorative of . . . dark passages' (see Wu, *Romanticism: An Anthology*, 3rd edn (Oxford: Blackwell, 2006), p. 1353); Wordsworth sees 'the burthen' as persistent, only occasionally 'lighten'd' by 'that blessed mood' (l. 42).

43 *gently lead us on* The switch from 'I' to 'us' helps to make Wordsworth's experience of more general import; a similar tactic is at work in the movement from 'I have felt' (l. 94) to 'the mind of man' (l. 100).

> Almost suspended, we are laid asleep
> In body, and become a living soul:
> While with an eye made quiet by the power
> Of harmony, and the deep power of joy,
> We see into the life of things.   50
>   If this
> Be but a vain belief, yet, oh! how oft,
> In darkness, and amid the many shapes
> Of joyless day-light; when the fretful stir
> Unprofitable, and the fever of the world,
> Have hung upon the beatings of my heart,   55
> How oft, in spirit, have I turned to thee
> O sylvan Wye! Thou wanderer through the woods,
> How often has my spirit turned to thee!
>
> And now, with gleams of half-extinguish'd thought,
> With many recognitions dim and faint,   60
> And somewhat of a sad perplexity,
> The picture of the mind revives again:
> While here I stand, not only with the sense
> Of present pleasure, but with pleasing thoughts
> That in this moment there is life and food   65
> For future years. And so I dare to hope
> Though changed, no doubt, from what I was, when first
> I came among these hills; when like a roe
> I bounded o'er the mountains, by the sides
> Of the deep rivers, and the lonely streams,   70
> Wherever nature led; more like a man
> Flying from something that he dreads, than one
> Who sought the thing he loved. For nature then
> (The coarser pleasures of my boyish days,
> And their glad animal movements all gone by,)   75
> To me was all in all. – I cannot paint
> What then I was. The sounding cataract
> Haunted me like a passion: the tall rock,

47 *become a living soul* Compare Genesis 2:7, describing the creation of Adam: 'and man became a living soul'. The allusion suggests that in this 'blessed mood' (l. 42) we are created anew.

48 *an eye made quiet* Picks up and develops the earlier description of 'the quiet of the sky' (l. 8), and indicates the need to escape the state described in *The Prelude* when 'the eye was master of the heart' (*1805*, XI. 171).

49 *deep power of joy* 'joy', for Wordsworth and Coleridge in this period, connotes a state of delight arising from awareness of affinities between human beings and the natural world.

50 *We see . . . things* This marks Wordsworth's break from a picturesque poetry; it is less the outward landscape that he values than the capacity to see beyond its features and 'into' a life-force at work.

50–1 *If . . . belief* The moment of unsureness is typical of the poem's overall ebbs and flows of confidence in its 'belief' in nature. The tangled mood of the next few lines is also noteworthy, finally ironing itself out in line 58, where 'How oft' (ll. 51, 56) becomes 'How often' and there are no caesural interruptions.

61 *somewhat . . . perplexity* The present experience is 'perplexed' by memories which are 'dim and faint' (l. 60).

66 *And so . . . hope* The formulation is typically hedged-in.

68–73 *when . . . loved* Lines that depict Wordsworth's sense of 'what I was' (l. 67) when he first visited the Wye Valley. The simile at lines 71–3 suggests a condition of severe pressure; in 1793 Wordsworth, one might surmise, was caught up in a state of turmoil caused by his involvement with the French Revolution and relationship with Annette Vallon, by whom he had a child, Caroline, in December 1792, and to whom he was prevented from returning by the outbreak of war between Britain and France.

76–8 *I cannot . . . passion* Wordsworth vividly conjures up his former 'passionate' relationship with nature; 'Haunted' gives the lie to the assertion, 'I cannot paint', with the last word of which it correctively half-chimes.

The mountain, and the deep and gloomy wood,
Their colours and their forms, were then to me   80
An appetite: a feeling and a love,
That had no need of a remoter charm,
By thought supplied, or any interest
Unborrowed from the eye. – That time is past,
And all its aching joys are now no more,   85
And all its dizzy raptures. Not for this
Faint I, nor mourn nor murmur: other gifts
Have followed, for such loss, I would believe,
Abundant recompence. For I have learned
To look on nature, not as in the hour   90
Of thoughtless youth, but hearing oftentimes
The still, sad music of humanity,
Not harsh nor grating, though of ample power
To chasten and subdue. And I have felt
A presence that disturbs me with the joy   95
Of elevated thoughts; a sense sublime
Of something far more deeply interfused,
Whose dwelling is the light of setting suns,
And the round ocean, and the living air,
And the blue sky, and in the mind of man,   100
A motion and a spirit, that impels
All thinking things, all objects of all thought,
And rolls through all things. Therefore am I still
A lover of the meadows and the woods,
And mountains; and of all that we behold   105
From this green earth; of all the mighty world
Of eye and ear, both what they half-create,
And what perceive; well pleased to recognize
In nature and the language of the sense,
The anchor of my purest thoughts, the nurse,   110
The guide, the guardian of my heart, and soul
Of all my moral being.

                      Nor, perchance,
If I were not thus taught, should I the more
Suffer my genial spirits to decay:

84–6 *That time . . . raptures* Because these lines conclude with the 'dizzy raptures' which are 'no more', their continued hold over the poet is apparent.

88 *I would believe* The choice of 'would' rather than 'do' brings out the element of hope that underlies the poet's belief.

91–2 *hearing . . . humanity* Wordsworth has 'learned / To look on nature' (ll. 89–90) by way of the 'music of humanity'; hearing proves to be a superior form of looking than sight.

95 *disturbs . . . joy* That 'joy' should 'disturb' is typical of the poem's bringing together of differing feelings.

96–7 *a sense . . . interfused* The wording allows for latitude of interpretation. The poet's 'sense' is derived from sense-impressions yet it is also a supra-rational intuition; the object of apprehension cannot be defined (it is 'something'); and 'more deeply interfused' raises the question, 'more deeply interfused than what?', which is difficult to answer.

101 *A motion and a spirit* The nouns couple the material and the spiritual.

107 *half-create* Wordsworth's note reads: 'This line has a close resemblance to an admirable line of Young, the exact expression of which I cannot recollect'; the echo is of Edward Young, *Night Thoughts*, vi, 427: 'And half create the wondrous world they see'.

109 *the language of the sense* The information given the poet by his senses. The poet implies a continuity between this 'language' and the earlier and loftier 'sense sublime' (l. 96), and the later 'language of my former heart' (l. 118).

114 *genial spirits* Echoes Milton's *Samson Agonistes*, 594: 'So much I feel my genial spirits droop'.

For thou art with me, here, upon the banks 115
Of this fair river; thou, my dearest Friend,
My dear, dear Friend, and in thy voice I catch
The language of my former heart, and read
My former pleasures in the shooting lights
Of thy wild eyes. Oh! yet a little while 120
May I behold in thee what I was once,
My dear, dear Sister! And this prayer I make,
Knowing that Nature never did betray
The heart that loved her; 'tis her privilege,
Through all the years of this our life, to lead 125
From joy to joy: for she can so inform
The mind that is within us, so impress
With quietness and beauty, and so feed
With lofty thoughts, that neither evil tongues,
Rash judgments, nor the sneers of selfish men, 130
Nor greetings where no kindness is, nor all
The dreary intercourse of daily life,
Shall e'er prevail against us, or disturb
Our chearful faith that all which we behold
Is full of blessings. Therefore let the moon 135
Shine on thee in thy solitary walk;
And let the misty mountain winds be free
To blow against thee: and in after years,
When these wild ecstasies shall be matured
Into a sober pleasure, when thy mind 140
Shall be a mansion for all lovely forms,
Thy memory be as a dwelling-place
For all sweet sounds and harmonies; Oh! then,
If solitude, or fear, or pain, or grief,
Should be thy portion, with what healing thoughts 145
Of tender joy wilt thou remember me,
And these my exhortations! Nor, perchance,
If I should be, where I no more can hear
Thy voice, nor catch from thy wild eyes these gleams
Of past existence, wilt thou then forget 150
That on the banks of this delightful stream
We stood together; and that I, so long
A worshipper of Nature, hither came,
Unwearied in that service: rather say
With warmer love, oh! with far deeper zeal 155

---

115 *thou art with me* Echoes Psalm 23:4: 'though I walk through the valley of the shadow of death, I will fear no evil; for thou art with me; thy rod and thy staff, they comfort me'. The allusion points up Wordsworth's need for 'comfort'.
117–20 *and in thy voice . . . wild eyes* Positioned at the end of the lines, the active verbs 'catch' and 'read' highlight Wordsworth's turn to his sister. Indeed, throughout this paragraph, the verbs are often placed at the end of the lines, as though to underscore the importance of the benevolence which Wordsworth ascribes to the activity of nature and memory.

128 *quietness* The word's resonance derives from previous uses of 'quiet' in the poem (ll. 8, 48). Something comparable occurs in the next line where 'lofty thoughts' recall the 'lofty cliffs' (l. 5) of the opening.
139–40 *When . . . pleasure* Wordsworth imagines for Dorothy a 'maturing' parallel to his own as described in the poem.
149–50 *gleams . . . existence* Recalls the earlier 'gleams of half-extinguish'd thought' (l. 59). The echo may suggest Wordsworth regrets that his own knowledge of 'past existence' is 'half-extinguish'd'.

Of holier love. Nor wilt thou then forget,
That after many wanderings, many years
Of absence, these steep woods and lofty cliffs,
And this green pastoral landscape, were to me
More dear, both for themselves, and for thy sake. 160

The Ruined Cottage

The textual status of 'The Ruined Cottage', never published as a separate poem in Wordsworth's lifetime, is complex. A version of the poem was read to Coleridge in June 1797; it was expanded the following year, Wordsworth adding a long section about the upbringing and beliefs of the figure who tells the story of Margaret to the unnamed narrator. By 1799 this section was hived off as a separate poem, 'The Pedlar', a poem which has affinities with 'Tintern Abbey' and *The Prelude*. The version of 'The Ruined Cottage' printed here is from a 1799 manuscript (MS D). Along with 'The Pedlar', 'The Ruined Cottage' appeared in revised form in the first book of *The Excursion* (1814), and would have been known to poets such as Byron, Shelley, Hemans and Keats in that revised form. The poem is written in blank verse, and divided in the version printed here into two parts. In the first part, the narrative structure is established, involving the telling of Margaret's story by the Pedlar to the narrator, whose own inner state is the subject of the reticent but troubled opening passage. The Pedlar begins his story, not as a consecutive narrative but as a controlled emotional meditation on the 'bond / Of brotherhood' (ll. 84–5) between nature and humans that has been broken by Margaret's death. The question of appropriate feeling about Margaret's plight, after economic hardship has led to her desertion by her husband, Robert, who enlists as a soldier, is intermittently to the fore throughout the poem. This question concludes the first part and begins the second part, where the Pedlar warns against 'vain dalliance with the misery / Even of the dead' (ll. 223–4). At the poem's close, after we have learned of Margaret's 'sore heart-wasting' (l. 449), to which the increasing desolation of her cottage bears witness, consolation of a kind is offered by the Pedlar (ll. 508–25). Whether this consolation, the product of a particular 'image of tranquillity' (l. 517), can erase or compensate for Margaret's tragic sufferings is the subject of considerable critical debate. The poem is remarkable for the restraint and sureness of touch with which it conveys feeling, especially Margaret's changing feelings, which include the never-quelled hope that her husband will return to her.

First Part

'Twas summer and the sun was mounted high;
Along the south the uplands feebly glared
Through a pale steam, and all the northern downs,
In clearer air ascending, shewed far off
Their surfaces with shadows dappled o'er 5
Of deep embattled clouds: far as the sight
Could reach those many shadows lay in spots
Determined and unmoved, with steady beams
Of clear and pleasant sunshine interposed –
Pleasant to him who on the soft cool moss 10
Extends his careless limbs beside the root
Of some huge oak whose aged branches make
A twilight of their own, a dewy shade
Where the wren warbles while the dreaming man,

1–18 '*Twas . . . mine* The poem's opening evokes a landscape of variegated light and shade, unmovable shadows and 'clear and pleasant sunshine interposed' (l. 9); after this tacit suggestion of the varied nature of experience, the writing depicts, in its second half, a pastoral retreat, from which the narrator ('Other lot was mine', l. 18) is cut off.

6 *deep embattled clouds* As Wu notes (*Romanticism: An Anthology*, 3rd edn, p. 422), the phrase echoes Charlotte Smith's sonnet LIX, ll. 3–4: 'Sudden, from many a deep embattled cloud / Terrific thunders burst'. Wordsworth turns away from 'Terrific thunders' to 'A tale of silent suffering, hardly clothed / In bodily form' (ll. 233–4).

14 *the dreaming man* Note the Pedlar's wish not be 'a dreamer among men' (l. 230).

Half-conscious of that soothing melody, 15
With sidelong eye looks out upon the scene,
By those impending branches made more soft,
More soft and distant. Other lot was mine.
Across a bare wide Common I had toiled
With languid feet which by the slipp'ry ground 20
Were baffled still, and when I stretched myself
On the brown earth my limbs from very heat
Could find no rest, nor my weak arm disperse
The insect host which gathered round my face
And joined their murmurs to the tedious noise 25
Of seeds of bursting gorse that crackled round.
I rose and turned towards a group of trees
Which midway in that level stood alone,
And thither come at length, beneath a shade
Of clustering elms that sprang from the same root 30
I found a ruined house, four naked walls
That stared upon each other. I looked round,
And near the door I saw an aged Man
Alone, and stretched upon the cottage bench;
An iron-pointed staff lay at his side. 35
With instantaneous joy I recognized
That pride of nature and of lowly life,
The venerable Armytage, a friend
As dear to me as is the setting sun.
                    Two days before 40
We had been fellow-travellers. I knew
That he was in this neighbourhood, and now
Delighted found him here in the cool shade.
He lay, his pack of rustic merchandise
Pillowing his head – I guess he had no thought 45
Of his way-wandering life. His eyes were shut;
The shadows of the breezy elms above
Dappled his face. With thirsty heat oppressed
At length I hailed him, glad to see his hat
Bedewed with water-drops, as if the brim 50
Had newly scooped a running stream. He rose
And pointing to a sun-flower, bade me climb
The [ ] wall where that same gaudy flower
Looked out upon the road. It was a plot
Of garden-ground now wild, its matted weeds 55
Marked with the steps of those whom as they pass'd,
The goose-berry trees that shot in long lank slips,
Or currants hanging from their leafless stems
In scanty strings, had tempted to o'erleap
The broken wall. Within that cheerless spot, 60
Where two tall hedgerows of thick willow boughs
Joined in a damp cold nook, I found a well
Half-cover'd up with willow-flowers and grass.

---

27 *I rose* One of a number of active verbs in this verse paragraph; the narrator's actions and responses are crucial in the poem.
32 *stared ... other* The metaphor bestows human characteristics on the walls, making them contemplators of their ruin.
53 *The [ ] wall* There is a gap in the manuscript.

I slaked my thirst and to the shady bench
Returned, and while I stood unbonneted 65
To catch the motion of the cooler air
The old Man said, 'I see around me here
Things which you cannot see. We die, my Friend,
Nor we alone, but that which each man loved
And prized in his peculiar nook of earth 70
Dies with him, or is changed, and very soon
Even of the good is no memorial left.
The Poets, in their elegies and songs
Lamenting the departed call the groves,
They call upon the hills and streams to mourn, 75
And senseless rocks, nor idly; for they speak
In these their invocations with a voice
Obedient to the strong creative power
Of human passion. Sympathies there are
More tranquil, yet perhaps of kindred birth, 80
That steal upon the meditative mind
And grow with thought. Beside yon spring I stood,
And eyed its waters till we seemed to feel
One sadness, they and I. For them a bond
Of brotherhood is broken: time has been 85
When every day the touch of human hand
Disturbed their stillness, and they ministered
To human comfort. When I stooped to drink
A spider's web hung to the water's edge,
And on the wet and slimy foot-stone lay 90
The useless fragment of a wooden bowl;
It moved my very heart. The day has been
When I could never pass this road but she
Who lived within these walls, when I appeared,
A daughter's welcome gave me, and I loved her 95
As my own child. Oh Sir! The good die first,
And they whose hearts are dry as summer dust
Burn to the socket. Many a passenger
Has blessed poor Margaret for her gentle looks
When she upheld the cool refreshment drawn 100
From that forsaken spring, and no one came
But he was welcome, no one went away
But that it seemed she loved him. She is dead,
The worm is on her cheek, and this poor hut,
Stripp'd of its outward garb of household flowers, 105
Of rose and sweet-briar, offers to the wind
A cold bare wall whose earthy top is tricked

67–8 *I see . . . see* The more forceful because of the emphasis in previous lines on what the narrator had been doing.

71 *changed* The first use of a word that will be charged with feeling later in the poem.

91 *The useless . . . bowl* Wordsworth's homely version of the broken golden bowl and pitcher in Ecclesiastes 12: 6: 'Or ever the silver cord be loosed, or the golden bowl be broken, or the pitcher be broken at the fountain, or the wheel broken at the cistern'.

93–4 *she . . . walls* This use of a pronoun followed by a relative clause that unfolds across a line-break is a characteristic form of expression in the poem; arguably, it helps to draw attention to character at its most elemental: not character in action, the traditional formulation, so much as character in a state of 'suffering'; compare lines 374–5: 'when he shall come again / For whom she suffered'.

96–8 *The good . . . socket* An outburst of dismay that deepens the pathos of the earlier line, 'Even of the good is no memorial left' (l. 72).

With weeds and the rank spear-grass. She is dead,
And nettles rot and adders sun themselves
Where we have sate together while she nurs'd   110
Her infant at her breast. The unshod Colt,
The wandering heifer and the Potter's ass,
Find shelter now within the chimney-wall
Were I have seen her evening hearth-stone blaze
And through the window spread upon the road   115
Its chearful light. – You will forgive me, Sir,
But often on this cottage do I muse
As on a picture, till my wiser mind
Sinks, yielding to the foolishness of grief.
    She had a husband, an industrious man,   120
Sober and steady. I have heard her say
That he was up and busy at his loom
In summer ere the mower's scythe had swept
The dewy grass, and in the early spring
Ere the last star had vanished. They who passed   125
At evening, from behind the garden-fence
Might hear his busy spade, which he would ply
After his daily work till the day-light
Was gone, and every leaf and flower were lost
In the dark hedges. So they pass'd their days   130
In peace and comfort, and two pretty babes
Were their best hope next to the God in Heaven.
– You may remember, now some ten years gone,
Two blighting seasons when the fields were left
With half a harvest. It pleased heaven to add   135
A worse affliction in the plague of war;
A happy land was stricken to the heart –
'Twas a sad time of sorrow and distress.
A wanderer among the cottages,
I with my pack of winter raiment saw   140
The hardships of that season. Many rich
Sunk down as in a dream among the poor,
And of the poor did many cease to be,
And their place knew them not. Meanwhile abridg'd
Of daily comforts, gladly reconciled   145
To numerous self-denials, Margaret
Went struggling on through those calamitous years
With chearful hope. But ere the second autumn
A fever seized her husband. In disease
He lingered long, and when his strength returned   150
He found the little he had stored to meet
The hour of accident or crippling age,
Was all consumed. As I have said, 'twas now
A time of trouble: shoals of artisans
Were from their daily labour turned away   155
To hang for bread on parish charity,

---

119 *yielding . . . grief* The Pedlar, for all his sense that 'grief' is 'foolish', 'yields' to it.
128 *daily work* Suggests the consolations of 'work'. Compare the depiction of Robert when work dries up (ll. 161–85).

136 *plague of war* Wordsworth has in mind the aftermath of the American War of Independence which finished in 1783.
144 *And . . . not* See Job 7: 10: He shall return no more to his house, neither shall his place know him any more'.

They and their wives and children – happier far
Could they have lived as do the little birds
That peck along the hedges, or the kite
That makes her dwelling in the mountain rocks. 160
Ill fared it now with Robert, he who dwelt
In this poor cottage. At his door he stood
And whistled many a snatch of merry tunes
That had no mirth in them, or with his knife
Carved uncouth figures on the heads of sticks, 165
Then idly sought about through every nook
Of house or garden any casual task
Of use or ornament, and with a strange,
Amusing but uneasy novelty
He blended where he might the various tasks 170
Of summer, autumn, winter, and of spring.
But this endured not; his good humour soon
Became a weight in which no pleasure was,
And poverty brought on a petted mood
And a sore temper. Day by day he drooped, 175
And he would leave his home, and to the town
Without an errand would he turn his steps,
Or wander here and there among the fields.
One while he would speak lightly of his babes
And with a cruel tongue; at other times 180
He played with them wild freaks of merriment,
And 'twas a piteous thing to see the looks
Of the poor innocent children. "Every smile",
Said Margaret to me here beneath these trees,
"Made my heart bleed."' At this the old Man paus'd 185
And looking up to those enormous elms
He said, ''Tis now the hour of deepest noon.
At this still season of repose and peace,
This hour when all things which are not at rest
Are chearful, while this multitude of flies 190
Fills all the air with happy melody,
Why should a tear be in an old man's eye?
Why should we thus with an untoward mind
And in the weakness of humanity
From natural wisdom turn our hearts away, 195
To natural comfort shut our eyes and ears,
And feeding on disquiet, thus disturb
The calm of Nature with our restless thoughts?'

Second Part

He spake with somewhat of a solemn tone,
But when he ended there was in his face 200
Such easy chearfulness, a look so mild,
That for a little time it stole away
All recollection, and that simple tale
Passed from my mind like a forgotten sound.

---

178 *wander . . . fields* Compare Margaret after Robert has left: 'and many days / About the fields I wander' (ll. 349–50).
183–5 *Every smile . . . bleed* Margaret's speech has a powerfully intensifying effect, especially when set against the Pedlar's ensuing words warning against (and thus testifying to the impact of) 'our restless thoughts' (l. 198).

A while on trivial things we held discourse, 205
To me soon tasteless. In my own despite
I thought of that poor woman as of one
Whom I had known and loved. He had rehearsed
Her homely tale with such familiar power,
With such an active countenance, an eye 210
So busy, that the things of which he spake
Seemed present, and, attention now relaxed,
There was a heartfelt chillness in my veins.
I rose, and turning from that breezy shade
Went out into the open air and stood 215
To drink the comfort of the warmer sun.
Long time I had not stayed ere, looking round
Upon that tranquil ruin, I returned
And begged of the old man that for my sake
He would resume his story. He replied, 220
'It were a wantonness, and would demand
Severe reproof, if we were men whose hearts
Could hold vain dalliance with the misery
Even of the dead, contented thence to draw
A momentary pleasure, never marked 225
By reason, barren of all future good.
But we have known that there is often found
In mournful thoughts, and always might be found,
A power to virtue friendly; were't not so
I am a dreamer among men, indeed 230
An idle dreamer. 'Tis a common tale
By moving accidents uncharactered,
A tale of silent suffering, hardly clothed
In bodily form, and to the grosser sense
But ill adapted, scarcely palpable 235
To him who does not think. But at your bidding
I will proceed.
       While thus it fared with them
To whom this cottage till that hapless year
Had been a blessed home, it was my chance
To travel in a country far remote; 240
And glad I was when, halting by yon gate
That leads from the green lane, again I saw
These lofty elm-trees. Long I did not rest –
With many pleasant thoughts I chear'd my way
O'er the flat common. At the door arrived, 245
I knocked, and when I entered with the hope
Of usual greeting, Margaret looked at me
A little while, then turned her head away
Speechless, and sitting down upon a chair
Wept bitterly. I wist not what to do 250
Or how to speak to her. Poor wretch! At last
She rose from off her seat – and then, oh Sir!
I cannot tell how she pronounced my name:

207–8 *I thought . . . loved* Brings out how the narrator has internalized the tale.

232 *moving accidents uncharactered* Does not possess the excitement typified by Othello's tales in which he spoke 'Of moving accidents by flood and field' (see 1. iii. 134). Compare Wordsworth's 'Hart-leap Well': 'The moving accident is not my trade' (l. 97).

248 *turned . . . away* As elsewhere in the poem, Wordsworth conveys strong feeling through gesture.

With fervent love, and with a face of grief
Unutterably helpless, and a look 255
That seem'd to cling upon me, she enquir'd
If I had seen her husband. As she spake
A strange surprise and fear came to my heart,
Nor had I power to answer ere she told
That he had disappeared – just two months gone. 260
He left his house: two wretched days had passed,
And on the third by the first break of light,
Within her casement full in view she saw
A purse of gold. 'I trembled at the sight',
Said Margaret, 'for I knew it was his hand 265
That placed it there, and on that very day
By one, a stranger, from my husband sent,
The tidings came that he had joined a troop
Of soldiers going to a distant land.
He left me thus – Poor Man, he had not heart 270
To take a farewell of me, and he feared
That I should follow with my babes, and sink
Beneath the misery of a soldier's life.'
   This tale did Margaret tell with many tears,
And when she ended I had little power 275
To give her comfort, and was glad to take
Such words of hope from her own mouth as serv'd
To chear us both. But long we had not talked
Ere we built up a pile of better thoughts,
And with a brighter eye she looked around 280
As if she had been shedding tears of joy.
We parted. It was then the early spring;
I left her busy with her garden tools,
And well remember, o'er that fence she looked,
And, while I paced along the foot-way path, 285
Called out and sent a blessing after me,
With tender chearfulness, and with a voice
That seemed the very sound of happy thoughts.
   I roved o'er many a hill and many a dale
With this my weary load, in heat and cold, 290
Through many a wood, and many an open ground,
In sunshine or in shade, in wet or fair,
Now blithe, now drooping, as it might befall,
My best companions now the driving winds
And now the 'trotting brooks' and whispering trees, 295
And now the music of my own sad steps,
With many a short-lived thought that pass'd between
And disappeared. I came this way again
Towards the wane of summer, when the wheat
Was yellow, and the soft and bladed grass 300
Sprang up afresh and o'er the hay-field spread
Its tender green. When I had reached the door

---

292 *sunshine . . . shade* Recalls the blend of sunshine and shadow in the poem's opening description.
295 *'trotting brooks'* Alludes to Robert Burns's poem 'To William Simpson': 'The Muse, nae poet ever fand her, / Till by himself he learned to wander / Adown some trottin burn's meander' (85–7). The allusion suggests that the Pedlar is a poet-figure.

I found that she was absent. In the shade
Where we now sit I waited her return.
Her cottage in its outward look appeared 305
As chearful as before; in any shew
Of neatness little changed, but that I thought
The honeysuckle crowded round the door
And from the wall hung down in heavier wreaths,
And knots of worthless stone-crop started out 310
Along the window's edge, and grew like weeds
Against the lower panes. I turned aside
And stroll'd into her garden – It was changed.
The unprofitable bindweed spread his bells
From side to side and with unwieldy wreaths 315
Had dragg'd the rose from its sustaining wall
And bent it down to earth. The border tufts,
Daisy and thrift and lowly camomile,
And thyme had straggled out into the paths
Which they were used to deck. Ere this an hour 320
Was wasted. Back I turned my restless steps,
And as I walked before the door it chanced
A stranger passed, and guessing whom I sought
He said that she was used to ramble far.
The sun was sinking in the west, and now 325
I sate with sad impatience. From within
Her solitary infant cried aloud.
The spot though fair seemed very desolate,
The longer I remained more desolate;
And, looking round, I saw the corner-stones, 330
Till then unmark'd, on either side the door
With dull red stains discoloured and stuck o'er
With tufts and hairs of wool, as if the sheep
That feed upon the commons thither came
Familiarly and found a couching-place 335
Even at her threshold – The house-clock struck eight:
I turned and saw her distant a few steps.
Her face was pale and thin, her figure too
Was chang'd. As she unlocked the door she said,
'It grieves me you have waited here so long, 340
But in good truth I've wandered much of late,
And sometimes – to my shame I speak – have need
Of my best prayers to bring me back again.'
While on the board she spread our evening meal
She told me she had lost her elder child, 345
That he for months had been a serving-boy,
Apprenticed by the parish. 'I perceive
You look at me, and you have cause. Today
I have been travelling far, and many days
About the fields I wander, knowing this 350
Only, that what I seek I cannot find.
And so I waste my time: for I am changed,
And to myself', said she, 'have done much wrong,

---

313 *It was changed* Prepares the reader for the later revelation of Margaret's 'change': 'her figure too / Was changed' (ll. 338–9) and 'I am changed' (l. 352).

And to this helpless infant. I have slept
Weeping, and weeping I have waked. My tears 355
Have flow'd as if my body were not such
As others are, and I could never die.
But I am now in mind and in my heart
More easy, and I hope', said she, 'that heaven
Will give me patience to endure the things 360
Which I behold at home.' It would have grieved
Your very soul to see her. Sir, I feel
The story linger in my heart. I fear
'Tis long and tedious, but my spirit clings
To that poor woman. So familiarly 365
Do I perceive her manner and her look
And presence, and so deeply do I feel
Her goodness, that not seldom in my walks
A momentary trance comes over me
And to myself I seem to muse on one 370
By sorrow laid asleep or borne away,
A human being destined to awake
To human life, or something very near
To human life, when he shall come again
For whom she suffered. Sir, it would have griev'd 375
Your very soul to see her: evermore
Her eye-lids drooped, her eyes were downward cast,
And when she at her table gave me food
She did not look at me. Her voice was low,
Her body was subdued, In every act 380
Pertaining to her house-affairs appeared
The careless stillness which a thinking mind
Gives to an idle matter – still she sighed,
But yet no motion of the breast was seen,
No heaving of the heart. While by the fire 385
We sate together, sighs came on my ear –
I knew not how, and hardly whence they came.
I took my staff, and when I kissed her babe
The tears stood in her eyes. I left her then
With the best hope and comfort I could give; 390
She thanked me for my will, but for my hope
It seemed she did not thank me.
                               I returned
And took my rounds along this road again
Ere on its sunny bank the primrose flower
Had chronicled the earliest day of spring. 395
I found her sad and drooping; she had learn'd
No tidings of her husband; if he lived,
She knew not that he lived; if he were dead
She knew not he was dead. She seemed the same
In person or appearance, but her house 400
Bespoke a sleepy hand of negligence.

365–75 *So familiarly ... suffered* The Pedlar's reverie does much to deepen our understanding of his engagement with Margaret; at the same time, his 'momentary trance' (l. 369) can only briefly hold at bay the everyday facts of suffering to which the following lines return.

391–2 *She ... me* It 'seemed' (l. 392) that Margaret did not wish to be given 'hope' (l. 391), but the next visit makes clear that she clings to hope.

401 *sleepy ... negligence* By this stage, the cottage's disrepair chimes with Margaret's 'change'.

The floor was neither dry nor neat, the hearth
Was comfortless,
The windows too were dim, and her few books,
Which one upon the other heretofore   405
Had been piled up against the corner-panes
In seemly order, now with straggling leaves
Lay scattered here and there, open or shut
As they had chanced to fall. Her infant babe
Had from its mother caught the trick of grief,   410
And sighed among its playthings. Once again
I turned towards the garden-gate, and saw
More plainly still that poverty and grief
Were now come nearer to her. The earth was hard,
With weeds defaced and knots of withered grass;   415
No ridges there appeared of clear black mould,
No winter greenness. Of her herbs and flowers
It seemed the better part were gnawed away
Or trampled on the earth. A chain of straw
Which had been twisted round the tender stem   420
Of a young apple-tree lay at its root;
The bark was nibbled round by truant sheep.
Margaret stood near, her infant in her arms,
And, seeing that my eye was on the tree,
She said, 'I fear it will be dead and gone   425
Ere Robert come again.' Towards the house
Together we returned, and she inquired
If I had any hope. But for her babe
And for her little friendless Boy, she said,
She had no wish to live, that she must die,   430
Of sorrow. Yet I saw the idle loom
Still in its place. His Sunday garments hung
Upon the self-same nail, his very staff
Stood undisturbed behind the door. And when
I passed this way beaten by Autumn winds,   435
She told me that her little babe was dead
And she was left alone. That very time,
I yet remember, through the miry lane
She walked with me a mile, when the bare trees
Trickled with foggy damps, and in such sort   440
That any heart had ached to hear her begg'd
That wheresoe'er I went I still would ask
For him whom she had lost. We parted then,
Our final parting, for from that time forth
Did many seasons pass ere I returned   445
Into this tract again.
                    Five tedious years
She lingered in unquiet widowhood,
A wife and widow. Needs must it have been

425–6 *She said . . . again* Again, as at lines 183–5, a paragraph concludes with Margaret's speech; here the effect is surprising: one expects her, at the end of the catalogue of decay just described, to say something depressed, but, in fact, her words indicate the survival in her of hope that Robert will 'come again', a phrase which repeats the Pedlar's earlier words and recalls, in the most subdued way, the biblical idea that Christ will come again, as in John 14: 3, a verse with affecting relevance to the poem: 'And if I go and prepare a place for you, I will come again, and receive you unto myself; that where I am, *there* ye may be also'.

A sore heart-wasting. I have heard, my friend,
That in that broken arbour she would sit   450
The idle length of half a sabbath day –
There, where you see the toadstool's lazy head –
And when a dog passed by she still would quit
The shade and look abroad. On this old Bench
For hours she sate, and evermore her eye   455
Was busy in the distance, shaping things
Which made her heart beat quick. Seest thou that path? –
The greensward now has broken its grey line –
There to and fro she paced through many a day
Of the warm summer, from a belt of flax   460
That girt her waist, spinning the long-drawn thread
With backward steps. – Yet ever as there passed
A man whose garments shewed the Soldier's red,
Or crippled Mendicant in Sailor's garb,
The little child who sate to turn the wheel   465
Ceased from his toil, and she with faltering voice,
Expecting still to learn her husband's fate,
Made many a fond enquiry; and when they
Whose presence gave no comfort were gone by,
Her heart was still more sad. And by yon gate   470
Which bars the traveller's road she often stood
And when a stranger came, the latch
Would lift, and in his face look wistfully,
Most happy if from aught discovered there
Of tender feeling she might dare repeat   475
The same sad question. Meanwhile her poor hut
Sunk to decay; for he was gone whose hand
At the first nippings of October frost
Closed up each chink and with fresh bands of straw
Chequered the green-grown thatch. And so she lived   480
Through the long winter, reckless and alone,
Till this reft house by frost, and thaw, and rain
Was sapped; and when she slept the nightly damps
Did chill her breast, and in the stormy day
Her tattered clothes were ruffled by the wind   485
Even at the side of her own fire. Yet still
She loved this wretched spot, nor would for worlds
Have parted hence; and still that length of road
And this rude bench one torturing hope endeared,
Fast rooted at her heart, and here, my friend,   490
In sickness she remained, and here she died,
Last human tenant of these ruined walls.'
   The old Man ceased; he saw that I was mov'd.
From that low Bench, rising instinctively,
I turned aside in weakness, nor had power   495
To thank him for the tale which he had told.
I stood, and leaning o'er the garden gate
Reviewed that Woman's suff'rings, and it seemed
To comfort me while with a brother's love
I blessed her in the impotence of grief.   500

481 *reckless* Taking no care.
500 *impotence of grief* Again, the poem suggests the insufficiency of 'grief' as a response to suffering.

At length towards the cottage I returned
Fondly, and traced with milder interest
That secret spirit of humanity
Which, 'mid the calm oblivious tendencies
Of nature, 'mid her plants, her weeds, and flowers,   505
And silent overgrowings, still survived.
The old man, seeing this, resumed, and said,
'My Friend, enough to sorrow have you given,
The purposes of wisdom ask no more:
Be wise and chearful, and no longer read   510
The forms of things with an unworthy eye:
She sleeps in the calm earth, and peace is here.
I well remember that those very plumes,
Those weeds, and the high spear-grass on that wall,
By mist and silent rain-drops silvered o'er,   515
As once I passed did to my mind convey
So still an image of tranquillity,
So calm and still, and looked so beautiful
Amid the uneasy thoughts which filled my mind,
That what we feel of sorrow and despair   520
From ruin and from change, and all the grief
The passing shews of being leave behind,
Appeared an idle dream that could not live
Where meditation was. I turned away
And walked along my road in happiness.'   525
  He ceased. By this the sun declining shot
A slant and mellow radiance which began
To fall upon us where beneath the trees
We sate on that low bench, and now we felt,
Admonished thus, the sweet hour coming on.   530
A linnet warbled from those lofty elms,
A thrush sang loud, and other melodies
At distance heard peopled the milder air.
The old man rose and hoisted up his load.
Together casting then a farewell look   535
Upon those silent walls, we left the shade
And ere the stars were visible attained
A rustic inn, our evening resting-place.

---

512 *She sleeps . . . here* The line conveys consolation, but only through a metaphor (of death as sleep) that recalls sleep's use in an earlier comforting fiction (see l. 371).

513–25 *I well remember . . . happiness* This consolation derives from a momentary if beautifully eloquent intuition.

Strange fits of passion I have known

This poem, plus the two that follow, are among the so-called Lucy poems. Lucy's identity has been much debated. Coleridge surmised of one poem ('A slumber did my spirit seal') that it arose from 'some gloomier moment' when Wordsworth 'had fancied the moment in which his sister might die' (letter of April 1799). The repetition by Coleridge of 'moment' is relevant to poems that pivot on and capture a lyric intensity of feeling. In 'Strange fits of passion', written in late 1798, Wordsworth uses a straightforward ballad form to convey what is far from straightforward, an uncanny sense of connection between the declining moon and Lucy's possible death. The poem brackets its evocation of the uncanny by half-apologizing in the first stanza for 'Strange fits of passion' and in the last stanza for 'fond and wayward thoughts' (l. 25).

The word 'fits' hovers between meaning 'sudden transitory state' and 'capricious impulse', while 'fond' implies 'foolishness', but the poem will not easily allow the reader to shake off the strong impression created by the brief narrative of the ride to Lucy's cottage. Feeling gives overpowering interest to the situation.

Text from *Lyrical Ballads 1800*.

    Strange fits of passion I have known,
    And I will dare to tell,
    But in the lover's ear alone,
    What once to me befel.

    When she I lov'd, was strong and gay   5
    And like a rose in June,
    I to her cottage bent my way,
    Beneath the evening moon.

    Upon the moon I fix'd my eye,
    All over the wide lea;   10
    My horse trudg'd on, and we drew nigh
    Those paths so dear to me.

    And now we reach'd the orchard plot,
    And, as we climb'd the hill,
    Towards the roof of Lucy's cot   15
    The moon descended still.

    In one of those sweet dreams I slept,
    Kind Nature's gentlest boon!
    And, all the while, my eyes I kept
    On the descending moon.   20

    My horse mov'd on; hoof after hoof
    He rais'd and never stopp'd:
    When down behind the cottage roof
    At once the planet dropp'd.

    What fond and wayward thoughts will slide   25
    Into a Lover's head—
    'O mercy!' to myself I cried,
    'If Lucy should be dead!'

9–10 *Upon . . . lea* The lines imply that the speaker's eye is both 'fix'd' on the moon and wandering across the 'lea' (meadow); the subliminal sense created is one of obsession.
17–18 *In one . . . boon!* Although Wordsworth appeals to general experience in these lines, his poem stresses the highly individual nature of the speaker's 'fits of passion' (l. 1).
21–22 *My horse . . . stopp'd* Suggests the speaker's tranced state, as though he were watching his horse moving unstoppably even as he rides on.
24 *planet* The choice of word is apt since planets were the name given to heavenly bodies with a supposed influence on human affairs.

Song: 'She dwelt among th' untrodden ways'

This poem, among Wordsworth's most affecting lyrics, shows his fascination with the irreducible fact of singleness and individuality: the subject of the second stanza's two images. Those images yield contrasting implications – of shy beauty (the half-hidden violet) and sublime splendour (the solitary star). The poem as a whole brings different feelings together, including those conveyed by the speaker's reticence and his final exclamation, an exclamation ('Oh!', l. 11) which rhymes with 'know' (l. 9), as if to put knowledge in its place when set against deep, barely communicable feeling.

Text from *Lyrical Ballads 1800*.

She dwelt among th' untrodden ways
    Beside the springs of Dove,
A Maid whom there were none to praise
    And very few to love.

A Violet by a mossy stone   5
    Half-hidden from the Eye!
—Fair, as a star when only one
    Is shining in the sky!

She *liv'd* unknown, and few could know
    When Lucy ceas'd to be;   10
But she is in her Grave, and Oh!
    The difference to me.

1 *dwelt* The verb gives a strong sense of Lucy abiding in a particular place.
2 *Dove* A river, probably in Derbyshire.
3–4 *A Maid . . . love* The contrast between there being 'none to praise' and 'very few to love' delicately suggests a gap between the unsaid and the felt.
5–8 *A Violet . . . sky!* There is no main verb in this stanza, which gives it a suspended air, as the poet allows himself to 'praise' (l. 3) Lucy. While (as the Headnote argues) there is a difference between the images that corresponds to differing aspects of the impression made by Lucy, the fact that they represent the same person is conveyed, in part, through the assonance linking 'Violet' with 'shining'.
9 *liv'd* By contrast with 'dwelt', the word has a starker existential sense, implying that her life is over.
10–11 *ceas'd to be . . . is in her Grave* The lines illustrate how much work the verb 'to be' does in Wordsworth's poetry. 'But she *is* in her Grave' (emphasis added) allows Lucy a kind of life beyond death, possibly in the speaker's memory.

A slumber did my spirit seal

The shortest and most enigmatic of the Lucy poems, 'A slumber did my spirit seal' was composed, like the previous two poems, in the last part of 1798. The poem 'seals' itself off from interpretation by refusing to comment on, or spell out, the speaker's feelings. The two-stanza structure implies a movement between states: one in which the poet had 'no human fears' (l. 2), the other in which his lack of fear is rebuked (a human being is now dead) or proved right (it would have been wrong to have human fear since Lucy is now part of the natural cycle, reabsorbed into 'earth's diurnal course', l. 7). On this latter reading, the person who 'seem'd a thing' (l. 3) has turned out to be precisely that, as much a thing as 'rocks and stones and trees' (l. 8). It is possible to hear a more sardonic inflection: the person who seemed beyond 'The touch of earthly years' (l. 4) is now in daily contact with the earthly. If the poem is an elegy or 'sublime Epitaph' (Coleridge's description in a letter of April 1799), it refuses to grieve in any evident way, and offers an inscrutable consolation. It may be a pantheist celebration, or it may be a far more disturbing poem about misunderstanding in life and loss of spiritual dignity in death.

Text from *Lyrical Ballads 1800*.

A slumber did my spirit seal,
    I had no human fears:
She seem'd a thing that could not feel
    The touch of earthly years.

No motion has she now, no force;   5
    She neither hears nor sees;
Roll'd round in earth's diurnal course
    With rocks and stones and trees!

1 *my spirit* Brings into play the idea of something not merely 'earthly' (l. 4).
2 *no human fears* 'human' is a key word: did the speaker experience 'fears' that were in some way not 'human'?
5 *motion . . . force* Words associated with Newtonian understanding of the workings of the universe. There may be an underlying bleakness in the description of Lucy as deprived of 'motion' and 'force'; no immortality seems to be accorded to her 'spirit' (l. 1).
6 *She . . . sees* The line feels like an ironic fulfilment of line 3.
7 *diurnal* Daily. Wordsworth uses the word in *The Prelude* (1805), 1, l. 487; it conveys the august, possibly chilling regularity of the earth's 'course'.

The Two April Mornings

Composed in 1798–9, this poem structures itself round memory and loss, pleasure and grief, the present and the past, youth and age. There may even be a pun on 'morning' ('mourning') in the title. It shows Wordsworth's interest in associations, Matthew being reminded by a beautiful April morning of a previous April morning, years back, when he 'stopp'd short / Beside my Daughter's grave' (ll. 31–2). The poem also shows Wordsworth's fascination with the 'subtle windings' of emotion: moving from a sense of loss to one of 'pure delight' (l. 48), Matthew describes how he saw a 'blooming Girl, whose hair was wet / With points of morning dew' (ll. 43–4), and yet, for all his 'sigh of pain' (l. 53), presumably caused by recollection of his daughter, he 'look'd at her and look'd again; / – And did not wish her mine' (55–6). 'And', there, rather than 'But' makes clear that the 'pain' felt for the loss of the dead daughter is inseparable from a sense that she cannot be replaced. The poem concludes with a twist when we discover that Matthew is now dead; the poem's past tense turns out to be more significant than the reader initially supposed. Much as he remembered his daughter, Matthew is remembered by the speaker. Memory emerges as the source of value and of pain in this poem, another poem that uses a simple ballad stanza to depict troubled feeling.

Text from *Lyrical Ballads 1800*.

We walk'd along, while bright and red
Uprose the morning sun,
And Matthew stopp'd, he look'd, and said,
'The will of God be done!'

A village Schoolmaster was he,   5
With hair of glittering grey;
As blithe a man as you could see
On a spring holiday.

And on that morning, through the grass,
And by the steaming rills,   10
We travell'd merrily to pass
A day among the hills.

'Our work,' said I, 'was well begun;
Then, from thy breast what thought,
Beneath so beautiful a sun,   15
So sad a sigh has brought?

A second time did Matthew stop,
And fixing still his eye
Upon the eastern mountain-top
To me he made reply.   20

'You cloud with that long purple cleft
Brings fresh into my mind
A day like this which I have left
Full thirty years behind.

1–2 *bright . . . sun* Echoes Coleridge's 'The Rime of the Ancyent Marinere', lines 93–4: 'Nor dim ne red, like God's own head / The glorious Sun uprist' (spellings from 1798 version). Coleridge's 'glorious sun' turns 'bloody' (l. 108); Wordsworth's sun presides over a scene of mingled feelings.

21–4 *Yon cloud . . . behind* The stanza is the first in the poem without any caesura: the two earlier moments of 'stopping' by Matthew (ll. 3, 17) served as preludes and give way to a complex flow of involuntary memory – involuntary, because Matthew thought he had 'left / Full thirty years behind' the day with which the present day chimes.

'And on that slope of springing corn
The self-same crimson hue
Fell from the sky that April morn,
The same which now I view!

'With rod and line my silent sport
I plied by Derwent's wave,
And, coming to the church, stopp'd short
Beside my Daughter's grave.

'Nine summers had she scarcely seen
The pride of all the vale;
And then she sang! – she would have been
A very nightingale.

'Six feet in earth my Emma lay,
And yet I lov'd her more,
For so it seem'd, than till that day
I e'er had lov'd before.

'And, turning from her grave, I met
Beside the church-yard Yew
A blooming Girl, whose hair was wet
With points of morning dew.

'A basket on her head she bare,
Her brow was smooth and white,
To see a Child so very fair,
It was a pure delight!

'No fountain from its rocky cave
E'er tripp'd with foot so free,
She seem'd as happy as a wave
That dances on the sea.

'There came from me a sigh of pain
Which I could ill confine;
I look'd at her and look'd again;
—And did not wish her mine.'

Matthew is in his grave, yet now
Methinks I see him stand,
As at that moment, with his bough
Of wilding in his hand.

---

29 *silent sport* Mason (p. 291) notes the poignancy of 'silent': both because it means that the speaker is on his own and because of the contrast with the memories of Emma's singing.
35 *And . . . been* The line records a catch in the speaker's voice after 'sang'.
40 *I . . . before* Matthew's statement is unconditional; he feels he loves Emma more than he had ever loved (anyone).
51–2 *She . . . sea* Echoes Florizel's words to Perdita in *The Winter's Tale* 4. 4. 140–1: 'When you do dance, I wish you / A wave o' the sea'. The context is relevant since Perdita is another lost daughter.
57 *Matthew . . . grave* Possibly echoes *Macbeth*, 3. 2. 24,

'Duncan is in his grave'; 'After life's fitful fever he sleeps well', Macbeth says in the next line. Matthew is in his grave, but 'life' was not necessarily for him a 'fitful fever' because of his capacity to accept.
57–60 *yet now . . . hand* The poem enters the present tense and provides an image of Matthew that is as haunting as his memories of his daughter. 'Methinks' in line 58 is another moment when the subjectivity of feeling is brought home: compare 'For so it seem'd' (l. 39). 'As at that moment' presumably refers to the moment when Matthew stopped in their walk; he was, we assume, carrying a staff, or 'bough / Of wilding'; 'wilding' means a 'plant sown by natural agency, especially wild crab-apple'.

The Fountain, A Conversation

This poem, probably written in 1798–9, serves as a companion-piece to 'The Two April Mornings'. Its subtitle, 'A Conversation', is misleading if it suggests the give-and-take of talk. In fact, Wordsworth's emphasis is on the gap between the speaker and Matthew. Matthew's response to the younger man's request for some merriment is a meditation on the painful gifts reserved for old age: the pangs of memory, the awareness of a mismatch between the face presented to others and the inner self, the bitter fact that 'many love me, but by none / Am I enough belov'd' (ll. 55–6). The speaker's attempt to lift Matthew's spirits ('I'll be a son to thee!', l. 62) results in a saddened rebuff: 'At this he grasped his hands, and said / "Alas! that cannot be"' (ll. 63–4). As commentators have noted, 'his hands' is not 'my hands' (though in 1815 Wordsworth did change the reading to 'my hand'). And yet Matthew, at the end, does comply with the speaker's earlier request that he sing 'those witty rhymes / About the crazy old church clock / And the bewilder'd chimes' (ll. 70–2). The final phrase, 'bewilder'd chimes', takes on a larger resonance in the poem, suggesting the bewilderment caused by memory and attempted connection.

Text from *Lyrical Ballads 1800*.

We talk'd with open heart, and tongue
Affectionate and true,
A pair of Friends, though I was young,
And Matthew seventy-two.

We lay beneath a spreading oak, 5
Beside a mossy seat,
And from the turf a fountain broke,
And gurgled at our feet.

Now, Matthew, let us try to match
This water's pleasant tune 10
With some old Border-song, or catch
That suits a summer's noon.

Or of the Church-clock and the chimes
Sing here beneath the shade,
That half-mad thing of witty rhymes 15
Which you last April made!

In silence Matthew lay, and eyed
The spring beneath the tree;
And thus the dear old Man replied,
The grey-hair'd Man of glee. 20

'Down to the vale this water steers,
How merrily it goes!
T'will murmur on a thousand years,
And flow as now it flows.

And here, on this delightful day, 25
I cannot chuse but think
How oft, a vigorous Man, I lay
Beside this Fountain's brink.

---

20 *grey-hair'd . . . glee* The alliteration points up the co-presence of apparent opposites.

26 *cannot . . . think* Thought in the form of human self-consciousness is not a question of choice.

My eyes are dim with childish tears.
My heart is idly stirr'd,   30
For the same sound is in my ears,
Which in those days I heard.

Thus fares it still in our decay:
And yet the wiser mind
Mourns less for what age takes away   35
Than what it leaves behind.

The blackbird in the summer trees,
The lark upon the hill,
Let loose their carols when they please,
Are quiet when they will.   40

With Nature never do *they* wage
A foolish strife; they see
A happy youth, and their old age
Is beautiful and free:

But we are press'd by heavy laws,   45
And often, glad no more,
We wear a face of joy, because
We have been glad of yore.

If there is one who need bemoan
His kindred laid in earth,   50
The household hearts that were his own,
It is the man of mirth.

My days, my Friend, are almost gone,
My life has been approv'd,
And many love me, but by none   55
Am I enough belov'd.'

'Now both himself and me he wrongs,
The man who thus complains!
I live and sing my idle songs
Upon these happy plains,   60

And, Matthew, for thy Children dead
I'll be a son to thee!'
At this he grasp'd his hands, and said,
'Alas! that cannot be.'

We rose up from the fountain-side,   65
And down the smooth descent
Of the green sheep-track did we glide,
And through the wood we went,

And, ere we came to Leonard's Rock,
He sang those witty rhymes   70
About the crazy old church-clock
And the bewilder'd chimes.

34–6 *And yet . . . behind* The twisting syntax results in a characteristically unexpected insight: that age is painful less for what it erases than for what it permits to remain.
46–8 *And often . . . yore* Again, the writing shows a blend of simple diction and complex syntax, and exhibits the psychological penetration typical of Wordsworth's poems in *Lyrical Ballads*.
69 *Leonard's Rock* Alludes to 'The Brothers', another poem in *Lyrical Ballads* 1800.

Nutting

'Nutting' was probably written in late 1798. The blank verse in which it is written allows for a fluid and disconcerting movement between autobiographical recall of innocent boyish nut-gathering and recollection of something more invasive and destructive in the boy's relationship with nature. The play of metaphor and comparison is crucial to endowing the memory with various significances. Proto-erotic conquest is to the fore in the lines describing the boy's response to the 'virgin scene' (l. 19), a response which is sexualized. The 'merciless ravage' (l. 43) of 'the shady nook / Of hazels' (ll. 43–4) is akin to a figurative rape of the natural. The poem registers a strong sense of unspoken shame as it describes the 'Deform'd and sullied' (l. 45) natural scene that 'patiently gave up / [Its] quiet being' (ll. 45–6), and invites comparison with other transgressive boyhood experiences depicted in *The Prelude*. In the Fenwick Note on the poem Wordsworth says that it 'was intended as part of a poem on my own life, but struck out as not being wanted there'. Though 'Nutting' closes with an exhortation to respect the natural, the poem's force derives from its entwining of feelings: exultation as the boy's power over nature is recreated and the accompanying 'sense of pain' (l. 50).

Text from *Lyrical Ballads 1800*.

          It seems a day,
One of those heavenly days which cannot die,
When forth I sallied from our cottage-door,
And with a wallet o'er my shoulder slung,
A nutting crook in hand, I turn'd my steps   5
Towards the distant woods, a Figure quaint,
Trick'd out in proud disguise of Beggar's weeds
Put on for the occasion, by advice
And exhortation of my frugal Dame.
Motley accoutrements! of power to smile   10
At thorns, and brakes, and brambles, and, in truth,
More ragged than need was. Among the woods,
And o'er the pathless rocks, I forc'd my way
Until, at length, I came to one dear nook
Unvisited, where not a broken bough   15
Droop'd with its wither'd leaves, ungracious sign
Of devastation, but the hazels rose
Tall and erect, with milk-white clusters hung,
A virgin scene!—A little while I stood,
Breathing with such suppression of the heart   20
As joy delights in; and with wise restraint
Voluptuous, fearless of a rival, eyed
The banquet, or beneath the trees I sate
Among the flowers, and with the flowers I play'd;

2 *one . . . cannot die* Again, Wordsworth is concerned with the singular, even as he claims that it is representative.
3 *our cottage-door* 'The house at which I was boarded during the time I was at School' (Wordsworth's note). The note implies that the poem is directly autobiographical; certainly, it dispenses with the narrative complexities apparent in many other poems by Wordsworth in *Lyrical Ballads*.
7 *weeds* Clothes.
9 *frugal Dame* Ann Tyson, Wordsworth's landlady while he went to Hawkshead School. Along with the concluding 'Maiden' (l. 52), the word 'Dame' gives rise to associations of a femaleness regarded as protecting and in need of protection, associations that contrast with the more erotically destructive 'merciless ravage' (l. 43) at the poem's centre.
13 *forc'd my way* Anticipates the violent relationship with nature which is about to be depicted.
21 *joy* A less evidently benign emotion here than elsewhere in poems of the same period.
21–2 *wise restraint / Voluptuous* A Miltonic turn, that allows 'restraint' to be both 'wise' and, unexpectedly, 'Voluptuous'.

A temper known to those, who, after long 25
And weary expectation, have been bless'd
With sudden happiness beyond all hope.—
—Perhaps it was a bower beneath whose leaves
The violets of five seasons re-appear
And fade, unseen by any human eye, 30
Where fairy water-breaks do murmur on
For ever, and I saw the sparkling foam,
And with my cheek on one of those green stones
That, fleec'd with moss, beneath the shady trees,
Lay round me scatter'd like a flock of sheep, 35
I heard the murmur and the murmuring sound,
In that sweet mood when pleasure loves to pay
Tribute to ease, and, of its joy secure
The heart luxuriates with indifferent things,
Wasting its kindliness on stocks and stones, 40
And on the vacant air. Then up I rose,
And dragg'd to earth both branch and bough, with crash
And merciless ravage; and the shady nook
Of hazels, and the green and mossy bower
Deform'd and sullied, patiently gave up 45
Their quiet being: and unless I now
Confound my present feelings with the past,
Even then, when from the bower I turn'd away,
Exulting, rich beyond the wealth of kings
I felt a sense of pain when I beheld 50
The silent trees and the intruding sky.—

    Then, dearest Maiden! move along these shades
In gentleness of heart with gentle hand
Touch,—for there is a Spirit in the woods.

25–7 *A temper . . . hope* By means of comparison Wordsworth links his subjective, particular response to a familiar human emotion. The technique is one of the means by which the poem is made more unsettling in its impact. See also line 37 ('that sweet mood').

41–2 *Then up . . . crash* The stressed monosyllables give disturbing vigour to the writing.

46–7 *unless . . . past* Wordsworth's alertness to this possibility adds a further complication to the poem.

Michael, A Pastoral Poem

Composed in 1800, 'Michael' was the last poem in *Lyrical Ballads* 1800. The poem draws on Wordsworth's admiration for 'statesmen' or 'independent *proprietors* of land . . . , men of respectable education who daily labour on their own little properties', as he describes them in a letter of 1801 to Charles James Fox. Wordsworth goes on to remark, in terms relevant to 'Michael': 'Their little tract of land serves as a kind of permanent rallying point for their domestic feelings, as a tablet upon which they are written which makes them objects of memory in a thousand instances when they would otherwise be forgotten'. The poem is deeply concerned with the relationship between 'land', 'domestic feelings', 'memory', and the fear of being 'forgotten'. The blank verse of 'Michael' is quite unlike that of 'Tintern Abbey': whereas 'Tintern Abbey' aims for an impassioned eloquence, 'Michael' has an austere bareness, especially at the climax when, after Luke's desertion, Michael is thought by the villagers to have gone alone to the sheepfold, symbol of the 'covenant' (l. 424) between father and son, 'And never lifted up a single stone' (l. 475). Matthew Arnold chose the line as a touchstone of Wordsworth's poetic genius, revealing 'expression of the highest and most truly expressive kind' (Preface to *Poems of Wordsworth*, chosen and edited by Matthew Arnold. London: Macmillan, 1879, p. xxiii); what it expresses is Michael's tragic dignity in the face of total loss, though Michael's privacy is also respected by the line, which only tells what was 'believ'd by all' (l. 473). The verse is an appropriate vehicle for a story of quasi-biblical power and resonance. Much of the finest poetry in 'Michael' concerns deep feelings of attachment – to land, to children and to unconditional love – and expresses itself through echoes and anticipations. Wordsworth, declaring his concern for 'youthful Poets' (l. 38), brings into play the theme of heirs and legacy central to the poem. The climax of the poem, recounting Michael's continued labour after the terrible news about Luke's going to the bad, implies both links and gaps between the past and the present, about which fine commentary can be found in Jonathan Wordsworth's *The Music of Humanity*. Wordsworth subtitles the poem 'A Pastoral', and yet its pastoral mode is in close kinship with the tragic.

Text from *Lyrical Ballads 1800*.

    If from the public way you turn your steps
Up the tumultuous brook of Green-head Gill,
You will suppose that with an upright path
Your feet must struggle; in such bold ascent
The pastoral Mountains front you, face to face.   5
But, courage! for beside that boisterous Brook
The mountains have all open'd out themselves,
And made a hidden valley of their own.
No habitation there is seen; but such
As journey thither find themselves alone   10
With a few sheep, with rocks and stones, and kites
That overhead are sailing in the sky.
It is in truth an utter solitude,
Nor should I have made mention of this Dell
But for one object which you might pass by,   15
Might see and notice not. Beside the brook
There is a straggling heap of unhewn stones!
And to that place a story appertains,
Which, though it be ungarnish'd with events,
Is not unfit, I deem, for the fire-side,   20
Or for the summer shade. It was the first,
The earliest of those tales that spake to me
Of Shepherds, dwellers in the vallies, men
Whom I already lov'd, not verily
For their own sakes, but for the fields and hills   25
Where was their occupation and abode.
And hence this Tale, while I was yet a boy
Careless of books, yet having felt the power
Of Nature, by the gentle agency
Of natural objects led me on to feel   30
For passions that were not my own, and think
At random and imperfectly indeed
On man; the heart of man and human life.
Therefore, although it be a history
Homely and rude, I will relate the same   35
For the delight of a few natural hearts,

---

2 *Green-head Gill* A stream in the Lake District, in the Vale of Grasmere.

10 *find themselves alone* The phrase introduces the theme of 'aloneness', which is central to the effect of the story; see line 477, Michael 'Sitting alone'.

11 *kites* The kite is a 'large bird of prey, of hawk family, with long wings, usually forked tail, and no tooth in the bill'.

31 *passions . . . own* Central to Wordsworth's achievement in *Lyrical Ballads*, this concern can be overlooked by those who stress what Keats calls the 'wordsworthian or egotistical sublime' (*The Major Works*, Oxford University Press, ed. Elizabeth Cook, p. 418).

33 *man; the heart of man* The 'heart' is a crucial term in the poem.

  And with yet fonder feeling, for the sake
  Of youthful Poets, who among these Hills
  Will be my second self when I am gone.

  UPON the Forest-side in Grasmere Vale   40
  There dwelt a Shepherd, Michael was his name,
  An old man, stout of heart, and strong of limb.
  His bodily frame had been from youth to age
  Of an unusual strength: his mind was keen
  Intense and frugal, apt for all affairs,   45
  And in his Shepherd's calling he was prompt
  And watchful more than ordinary men.
  Hence he had learn'd the meaning of all winds,
  Of blasts of every tone, and often-times
  When others heeded not, He heard the South   50
  Make subterraneous music, like the noise
  Of Bagpipers on distant Highland hills;
  The Shepherd, at such warning, of his flock
  Bethought him, and he to himself would say
  The winds are now devising work for me!   55
  And truly at all times the storm, that drives
  The Traveller to a shelter, summon'd him
  Up to the mountains: he had been alone
  Amid the heart of many thousand mists
  That came to him and left him on the heights.   60
  So liv'd he till his eightieth year was pass'd.

  And grossly that man errs, who should suppose
  That the green Valleys, and the Streams and Rocks
  Were things indifferent to the Shepherd's thoughts.
  Fields, where with chearful spirits he had breath'd   65
  The common air; the hills, which he so oft
  Had climb'd with vigorous steps; which had impress'd
  So many incidents upon his mind
  Of hardship, skill or courage, joy or fear;
  Which like a book preserv'd the memory   70
  Of the dumb animals, whom he had sav'd,
  Had fed or shelter'd, linking to such acts,
  So grateful in themselves, the certainty
  Of honorable gains; these fields, these hills
  Which were his living Being, even more   75
  Than his own Blood – what could they less? had laid
  Strong hold on his affections, were to him
  A pleasurable feeling of blind love,
  The pleasure which there is in life itself.

  He had not passed his days in singleness.   80
  He had a Wife, a comely Matron, old

---

60 *came . . . heights* In the light of the overall tragedy, there is a suggestive bringing together here of visitation and abandonment.
65–79 *Fields . . . itself* The long sentence mimes the process of 'linking' which binds Michael to his land.
80 *singleness* The poem plays many variations on themes of 'singleness', pairing and multiplicity. Luke is an 'only Child' (l. 89); Isabel has two spinning wheels; Michael and Isabel have 'two brave sheep dogs' (l. 93), of whom 'one' was 'of inestimable worth' (l. 94); the lamp in the cottage is the 'Surviving Comrade of uncounted Hours' (l. 120); when Luke was born he slept for 'Two days' (l. 352); Luke is asked by his father to 'lay one Stone' (l. 396) of the sheepfold; and, climactically, Michael's inability 'many and many a day' (l. 474) to lift 'a single stone' (l. 475) was 'believ'd by all' (l. 473).

Though younger than himself full twenty years.
She was a woman of a stirring life
Whose heart was in her house: two wheels she had
Of antique form, this large for spining wool, 85
That small for flax, and if one wheel had rest,
It was because the other was at work.
The Pair had but one Inmate in their house,
An only Child, who had been born to them
When Michael telling o'er his years began 90
To deem that he was old, in Shepherd's phrase,
With one foot in the grave. This only son,
With two brave sheep dogs tried in many a storm,
The one of an inestimable worth,
Made all their Household. I may truly say, 95
That they were as a proverb in the vale
For endless industry. When day was gone,
And from their occupations out of doors
The Son and Father were come home, even then
Their labour did not cease, unless when all 100
Turn'd to their cleanly supper-board, and there
Each with a mess of pottage and skimm'd milk,
Sate round their basket pil'd with oaten cakes,
And their plain home-made cheese. Yet when their meal
Was ended, Luke (for so the Son was nam'd) 105
And his old Father, both betook themselves
To such convenient work, as might employ
Their hands by the fire-side; perhaps to card
Wool for the House-wife's spindle, or repair
Some injury done to sickle, flail, or scythe, 110
Or other implement of house or field.

Down from the ceiling by the chimney's edge,
Which in our ancient uncouth country style
Did with a huge projection overbrow
Large space beneath, as duly as the light 115
Of day grew dim, the House-wife hung a lamp;
An aged utensil, which had perform'd
Service beyond all others of its kind.
Early at evening did it burn and late,
Surviving Comrade of uncounted Hours 120
Which going by from year to year had found
And left the Couple neither gay perhaps
Nor chearful, yet with objects and with hopes
Living a life of eager industry.
And now, when Luke was in his eighteenth year, 125
There by the light of this old lamp they sate,
Father and Son, while late into the night
The House-wife plied her own peculiar work,
Making the cottage through the silent hours
Murmur as with the sound of summer flies. 130
Not with a waste of words, but for the sake
Of pleasure, which I know that I shall give
To many living now, I of this Lamp

---

114 *overbrow* Overhang.   120 *uncounted* Countless.

Speak thus minutely: for there are no few
Whose memories will bear witness to my tale, 135
The Light was famous in its neighbourhood,
And was a public Symbol of the life,
The thrifty Pair had liv'd. For, as it chane'd,
Their Cottage on a plot of rising ground
Stood single, with large prospect North and South, 140
High into Easedale, up to Dunmal-Raise,
And Westward to the village near the Lake.
And from this constant light so regular
And so far seen, the House itself by all
Who dwelt within the limits of the vale, 145
Both old and young, was nam'd The Evening Star.

Thus living on through such a length of years,
The Shepherd, if he lov'd himself, must needs
Have lov'd his Help-mate; but to Michael's heart
This Son of his old age was yet more dear – 150
Effect which might perhaps have been produc'd
By that instinctive tenderness, the same
Blind Spirit, which is in the blood of all,
Or that a child, more than all other gifts,
Brings hope with it, and forward-looking thoughts, 155
And stirrings of inquietude, when they
By tendency of nature needs must fail.
From such, and other causes, to the thoughts
Of the old Man his only Son was now
The dearest object that he knew on earth. 160
Exceeding was the love he bare to him,
His Heart and his Heart's joy! For oftentimes
Old Michael, while he was a babe in arms,
Had done him female service, not alone
For dalliance and delight, as is the use 165
Of Fathers, but with patient mind enforc'd
To acts of tenderness; and he had rock'd
His cradle with a woman's gentle hand.

And in a later time, ere yet the Boy
Had put on Boy's attire, did Michael love, 170
Albeit of a stern unbending mind,
To have the young one in his sight, when he
Had work by his own door, or when he sate
With sheep before him on his Shepherd's stool,
Beneath that large old Oak, which near their door 175
Stood, and from its enormous breadth of shade
Chosen for the Shearer's covert from the sun,
Thence in our rustic dialect was call'd
The Clipping Tree, a name which yet it bears.
There, while they two were sitting in the shade, 180

---

137 *public Symbol* Implies the connection at this stage between Michael and his family, and the larger community. The poem shows how Michael is taken by suffering from this sense of communal ties into a private arena of feeling.
149 *Help-mate* Isabel.
156 *inquietude* 'Uneasiness of mind or body'.

170 *Boy's attire* At that time boys and girls were both dressed in frocks in their early years.
179 *a name . . . bears* Relates to the overall concern with survivals and legacies. Wordsworth's note to this line reads: 'Clipping is the word used in the North of England for shearing'.

With others round them, earnest all and blithe,
Would Michael exercise his heart with looks
Of fond correction and reproof bestow'd
Upon the child, if he disturb'd the sheep
By catching at their legs, or with his shouts   185
Scar'd them, while they lay still beneath the shears.

And when by Heaven's good grace the Boy grew up
A healthy Lad, and carried in his cheek
Two steady roses that were five years old,
Then Michael from a winter coppice cut   190
With his own hand a sapling, which he hoop'd
With iron, making it throughout in all
Due requisites a perfect Shepherd's Staff,
And gave it to the Boy; wherewith equipp'd
He as a Watchman oftentimes was plac'd   195
At gate or gap, to stem or turn the flock,
And to his office prematurely call'd
There stood the urchin, as you will divine,
Something between a hindrance and a help,
And for this cause not always, I believe,   200
Receiving from his Father hire of praise.
Though nought was left undone which staff or voice,
Or looks, or threatening gestures could perform.
But soon as Luke, full ten years old, could stand
Against the mountain blasts, and to the heights,   205
Not fearing toil, nor length of weary ways,
He with his Father daily went, and they
Were as companions, why should I relate
That objects which the Shepherd loved before
Were dearer now? that from the Boy there came   210
Feelings and emanations, things which were
Light to the sun and music to the wind;
And that the Old Man's heart seemed born again.
Thus in his Father's sight the Boy grew up:
And now when he had reached his eighteenth year,   215
He was his comfort and his daily hope.

While this good household thus were living on
From day to day, to Michael's ear there came
Distressful tidings. Long before the time
Of which I speak, the Shepherd had been bound   220
In surety for his Brother's Son, a man
Of an industrious life, and ample means,
But unforeseen misfortunes suddenly
Had press'd upon him, and old Michael now
Was summon'd to discharge the forfeiture,   225
A grievous penalty, but little less
Than half his substance. This un-look'd for claim
At the first hearing, for a moment took

---

208 *why . . . relate* This formula disguises the fact that the following lines are among the most emotionally explicit and affecting in the poem.

221 *In surety* Michael has taken responsibility for his nephew's payment of debt.
226 *but little less* Only slightly less.

More hope out of his life than he supposed
That any old man ever could have lost. 230
As soon as he had gather'd so much strength
That he could look his trouble in the face,
It seem'd that his sole refuge was to sell
A portion of his patrimonial fields.
Such was his first resolve; he thought again, 235
And his heart fail'd him. 'Isabel,' said he,
Two evenings after he had heard the news,
'I have been toiling more than seventy years,
And in the open sun-shine of God's love
Have we all liv'd, yet if these fields of ours 240
Should pass into a Stranger's hand, I think
That I could not lie quiet in my grave.
Our lot is a hard lot; the Sun itself
Has scarcely been more diligent than I,
And I have liv'd to be a fool at last 245
To my own family. An evil Man
That was, and made an evil choice, if he
Were false to us; and if he were not false,
There are ten thousand to whom loss like this
Had been no sorrow. I forgive him – but 250
'Twere better to be dumb than to talk thus.
When I began, my purpose was to speak
Of remedies and of a chearful hope.
Our Luke shall leave us, Isabel; the land
Shall not go from us, and it shall be free, 255
He shall possess it, free as is the wind
That passes over it. We have, thou knowest,
Another Kinsman, he will be our friend
In this distress. He is a prosperous man,
Thriving in trade, and Luke to him shall go, 260
And with his Kinsman's help and his own thrift,
He quickly will repair this loss, and then
May come again to us. If here he stay,
What can be done? Where every one is poor
What can be gain'd?' At this, the old man paus'd, 265
And Isabel sate silent, for her mind
Was busy, looking back into past times.
There's Richard Bateman, thought she to herself,
He was a parish-boy – at the church-door
They made a gathering for him, shillings, pence, 270
And halfpennies, wherewith the Neighbours bought
A Basket, which they fill'd with Pedlar's wares,
And with this Basket on his arm, the Lad
Went up to London, found a Master there,
Who out of many chose the trusty Boy 275

---

229 *than he supposed* Takes us inside Michael's mind, recording not just his shock, but his shock at his shock.
234 *patrimonial fields* Lands inherited from his forefathers.
255 *free* Michael does not wish Luke to labour under the same burden as he did in his youth, of paying off a mortgage (see ll. 384–8).

268 *Richard Bateman* 'The story alluded to here is well known in the country. The chapel is called Ings Chapel; and is on the right hand side of the road leading from Kendal to Ambleside' (Wordsworth's later note).
269 *parish-boy* Maintained by the parish.

To go and overlook his merchandise
Beyond the seas, where he grew wond'rous rich,
And left estates and monies to the poor,
And at his birth-place built a Chapel, floor'd
With Marble, which he sent from foreign lands. 280
These thoughts, and many others of like sort,
Pass'd quickly through the mind of Isabel,
And her face brighten'd. The Old Man was glad,
And thus resum'd. 'Well! Isabel, this scheme
These two days has been meat and drink to me. 285
Far more than we have lost is left us yet.
– We have enough – I wish indeed that I
Were younger, but this hope is a good hope.
– Make ready Luke's best garments, of the best
Buy for him more, and let us send him forth 290
To-morrow, or the next day, or to-night:
– If he could go, the Boy should go to-night.'

Here Michael ceas'd, and to the fields went forth
With a light heart. The House-wife for five days
Was restless morn and night, and all day long 295
Wrought on with her best fingers to prepare
Things needful for the journey of her Son.
But Isabel was glad when Sunday came
To stop her in her work; for, when she lay
By Michael's side, she for the two last nights 300
Heard him, how he was troubled in his sleep:
And when they rose at morning she could see
That all his hopes were gone. That day at noon
She said to Luke, while they two by themselves
Were sitting at the door, 'Thou must not go, 305
We have no other Child but thee to lose,
None to remember – do not go away,
For if thou leave thy Father he will die.'
The Lad made answer with a jocund voice,
And Isabel, when she had told her fears, 310
Recover'd heart. That evening her best fare
Did she bring forth, and all together sate
Like happy people round a Christmas fire.

Next morning Isabel resum'd her work,
And all the ensuing week the house appear'd 315
As cheerful as a grove in Spring: at length
The expected letter from their Kinsman came,
With kind assurances that he would do
His utmost for the welfare of the Boy,
To which requests were added that forthwith 320
He might be sent to him. Ten times or more
The letter was read over; Isabel
Went forth to shew it to the neighbours round:
Nor was there at that time on English Land
A prouder heart than Luke's. When Isabel 325

279–80 *built . . . Marble* Contrasts with other buildings in the poem, notably the cottage and the sheepfold.

Had to her house return'd, the Old Man said,
'He shall depart to-morrow.' To this word
The House-wife answered, talking much of things
Which, if at such short notice he should go,
Would surely be forgotten. But at length   330
She gave consent, and Michael was at ease.

Near the tumultuous brook of Green-head Gill,
In that deep Valley, Michael had design'd
To build a Sheep-fold, and, before he heard
The tidings of his melancholy loss,   335
For this same purpose he had gathered up
A heap of stones, which close to the brook side
Lay thrown together, ready for the work.
With Luke that evening thitherward he walk'd;
And soon as they had reach'd the place he stopp'd,   340
And thus the Old Man spake to him. 'My Son,
To-morrow thou wilt leave me; with full heart
I look upon thee, for thou art the same
That wert a promise to me ere thy birth,
And all thy life hast been my daily joy.   345
I will relate to thee some little part
Of our two histories; 'twill do thee good
When thou art from me, even if I should speak
Of things thou canst not know of. – After thou
First cam'st into the world, as it befalls   350
To new-born infants, thou didst sleep away
Two days, and blessings from thy Father's tongue
Then fell upon thee. Day by day pass'd on,
And still I lov'd thee with encreasing love.
Never to living ear came sweeter sounds   355
Than when I heard thee by our own fire-side
First uttering without words a natural tune,
When thou, a feeding babe, didst in thy joy
Sing at thy Mother's breast. Month follow'd month,
And in the open fields my life was pass'd   360
And in the mountains, else I think that thou
Hadst been brought up upon thy father's knees.
– But we were playmates, Luke; among these hills,
As well thou know'st, in us the old and young
Have play'd together, nor with me didst thou   365
Lack any pleasure which a boy can know.'

Luke had a manly heart; but at these words
He sobb'd aloud; the Old Man grasp'd his hand,
And said, 'Nay do not take it so – I see
That these are things of which I need not speak.   370
– Even to the utmost I have been to thee
A kind and a good Father: and herein

---

334 *Sheep-fold* 'It may be proper to inform some readers, that a sheep-fold in these mountains in an unroofed building of stone walls, with different divisions. It is generally placed by the side of a brook, for the convenience of washing the sheep; but it is also useful as a shelter for them, and as a place to drive them into, to enable the shepherds conveniently to single out one or more for any particular purpose' (Wordsworth's later note). Again, 'singling out' is in Wordsworth's mind.

I but repay a gift which I myself
Receiv'd at others hands, for, though now old
Beyond the common life of man, I still 375
Remember them who lov'd me in my youth.
Both of them sleep together: here they liv'd
As all their Forefathers had done, and when
At length their time was come, they were not loth
To give their bodies to the family mold. 380
I wish'd that thou should'st live the life they liv'd.
But 'tis a long time to look back, my Son,
And see so little gain from sixty years.
These fields were burthen'd when they came to me;
'Till I was forty years of age, not more 385
Than half of my inheritance was mine.
I toil'd and toil'd; God bless'd me in my work,
And 'till these three weeks past the land was free.
– It looks as if it never could endure
Another Master. Heaven forgive me, Luke, 390
If I judge ill for thee, but it seems good
That thou should'st go.' At this the Old Man paus'd,
Then, pointing to the Stones near which they stood,
Thus, after a short silence, he resum'd:
'This was a work for us, and now, my Son, 395
It is a work for me. But, lay one Stone –
Here, lay it for me, Luke, with thine own hands.
I for the purpose brought thee to this place.
Nay, Boy, be of good hope: – we both may live
To see a better day. At eighty-four 400
I still am strong and stout; – do thou thy part,
I will do mine. – I will begin again
With many tasks that were resign'd to thee;
Up to the heights, and in among the storms,
Will I without thee go again, and do 405
All works which I was wont to do alone,
Before I knew thy face. – Heaven bless thee, Boy!
Thy heart these two weeks has been beating fast
With many hopes – it should be so – yes – yes –
I knew that thou could'st never have a wish 410
To leave me, Luke, thou hast been bound to me
Only by links of love, when thou art gone
What will be left to us! – But, I forget
My purposes. Lay now the corner-stone,
As I requested, and hereafter, Luke, 415
When thou art gone away, should evil men
Be thy companions, let this Sheep-fold be
Thy anchor and thy shield; amid all fear
And all temptation, let it be to thee
An emblem of the life thy Fathers liv'd, 420
Who, being innocent, did for that cause
Bestir them in good deeds. Now, fare thee well –

375–6 *I still / Remember* One of the poem's major concerns is memory.
380 *family mold* Earth, but also possibly pattern.
384 *These fields . . . me* Michael's lands came to him burdened by a mortgage.

415 *Luke* The fourth time in the paragraph Michael calls his son by name, stressing the closeness of their bond.

When thou return'st, thou in this place wilt see
A work which is not here, a covenant
'Twill be between us – but whatever fate 425
Befall thee, I shall love thee to the last,
And bear thy memory with me to the grave.'

The Shepherd ended here; and Luke stoop'd down,
And as his Father had requested, laid
The first stone of the Sheep-fold; at the sight 430
The Old Man's grief broke from him, to his heart
He press'd his Son, he kissed him and wept;
And to the House together they return'd.

Next morning, as had been resolv'd, the Boy
Began his journey, and when he had reach'd 435
The public Way, he put on a bold face;
And all the Neighbours as he pass'd their doors
Came forth, with wishes and with farewell pray'rs,
That follow'd him 'till he was out of sight.

A good report did from their Kinsman come, 440
Of Luke and his well-doing; and the Boy
Wrote loving letters, full of wond'rous news,
Which, as the House-wife phrased it, were throughout
The prettiest letters that were ever seen.
Both parents read them with rejoicing hearts. 445
So, many months pass'd on: and once again
The Shepherd went about his daily work
With confident and cheerful thoughts; and now
Sometimes when he could find a leisure hour
He to that valley took his way, and there 450
Wrought at the Sheep-fold. Meantime Luke began
To slacken in his duty, and at length
He in the dissolute city gave himself
To evil courses: ignominy and shame
Fell on him, so that he was driven at last 455
To seek a hiding-place beyond the seas.

There is a comfort in the strength of love;
'Twill make a thing endurable, which else
Would break the heart: – Old Michael found it so.
I have convers'd with more than one who well 460
Remember the Old Man, and what he was
Years after he had heard this heavy news.
His bodily frame had been from youth to age
Of an unusual strength. Among the rocks
He went, and still look'd up upon the sun, 465
And listen'd to the wind; and as before

---

424 *covenant* Recalls the biblical covenant made by God with Abraham (Genesis 17: 2).
451–5 *Meantime Luke . . . on him* Wordsworth may have drawn here on the story of the Prodigal Son, a parable appropriately told only in Luke's Gospel (ch. 15). However, the poem has no happy ending to match that of the parable.

463–4 *His bodily . . . strength* Repeats lines 43–4.
465–6 *still . . . wind* Takes the reader back to lines 210–12, when, working with Luke, Michael received 'Feelings and emanations' (l. 211) which were 'Light to the sun and music to the wind' (l. 212). Lines 465–6 assert continuity but, movingly, imply difference between then and now.

Perform'd all kinds of labour for his Sheep,
And for the land his small inheritance.
And to that hollow Dell from time to time
Did he repair, to build the Fold of which 470
His flock had need. 'Tis not forgotten yet
The pity which was then in every heart
For the Old Man – and 'tis believ'd by all
That many and many a day he thither went,
And never lifted up a single stone. 475

There, by the Sheep-fold, sometimes was he seen
Sitting alone, with that his faithful Dog,
Then old, beside him, lying at his feet.
The length of full seven years from time to time
He at the building of this Sheep-fold wrought, 480
And left the work unfinished when he died.

Three years, or little more, did Isabel,
Survive her Husband: at her death the estate
Was sold, and went into a Stranger's hand.
The Cottage which was nam'd The Evening Star 485
Is gone, the ploughshare has been through the ground
On which it stood; great changes have been wrought
In all the neighbourhood, yet the Oak is left
That grew beside their Door; and the remains
Of the unfinished Sheep-fold may be seen 490
Beside the boisterous brook of Green-head Gill.

491 *boisterous* Wordsworth chooses this adjective for the brook rather than 'tumultuous' (used at ll. 2 and 332). 'Boisterous' (already used at l. 6) means 'noisily cheerful' and accentuates the gap between human suffering and nature.

The Prelude, 1805, Book 1

The Prelude exists in a number of different forms: the most important are the Two-Part version of 1799, which contains many of the most famous 'spots of time' in the poem, that is, moments of intense imaginative experience which confirm Wordsworth in his belief that he was meant to be a poet; the greatly expanded 1805 version in 13 books; and the considerably revised 14-book version issued by Wordsworth's executors in 1850 after his death. It is worth remembering that *The Prelude* was not published in Wordsworth's life. Only a few passages were printed. Thus a poem at the very heart of Romanticism was scarcely known by the poet's contemporaries. The text chosen here is the 1805 version, from which we print the first book. The book begins with the so-called 'Glad Preamble' (ll. 1–54) in which Wordsworth celebrates a mood of unfettered liberty and anticipates creative labour on 'chosen tasks' (l. 34). Another response to Milton's epic vision in *Paradise Lost*, *The Prelude* starts where Milton's poem leaves off; if, for Adam and Eve at the close of *Paradise Lost*, 'The world was all before them' (12. 646), for Wordsworth at his poem's opening, 'The earth is all before me' (l. 15). However, whereas Milton seeks to 'justify the ways of God to men' (*Paradise Lost*, 1. 26), Wordsworth depicts the growth of his mind as a poet. The Romantic poet's daring lies in the suggestion that his theme is equal in significance to Milton's. The 'Glad Preamble' evokes the kindling of the poet's inspiration in response to nature, but Wordsworth's 'corresponding mild creative breeze' (l. 43) is, to begin with, without a subject other than itself. At some level, the poem always retains a quality of self-celebration: the very fact of the poem's existence is proof of the poet's right to assert that he is a poet. But the reader is quickly involved in the poet's anxiety about his vocation as he rehearses his attempt to find a subject. It is only when he asks the guilt-ridden question, 'Was it for this . . . ?' (l. 272), that he stumbles on his subject: the formative influences that fostered his imagination and led to his becoming a poet. Once launched, much of the rest of Book 1 consists in the interplay between evocation of and commentary on 'spots of time' concerned with significant childhood experiences. Wordsworth shows the importance for his development of experiences that combine 'beauty' and 'fear' (l. 307); he speaks of the central role played by nature; and he outlines an account of imaginative growth that lays stress on the associations roused in him by the 'scenes which were a witness of [his] joy' (l. 628). The poem is written in a blank verse remarkable for its flexibility: Wordsworth can be conversational; he can also be sublime. Above all, he can find rhythms and images appropriate to the enactment of experience: in one passage, he writes, 'on the perilous ridge I hung alone' (l. 348), where 'hung alone', suspended at the end of the line, mimics the boy's 'perilous' position; in another, he depicts his mind invaded by 'huge and mighty forms that do not live / Like living men' (ll. 426–7), leaving in haunting doubt the question of the forms' mode of existence. The title was given to the poem after Wordsworth's death; he thought of it as the 'Poem, Title not yet Fixed upon . . . Addressed to S. T. Coleridge' (quoted from *The Thirteen-Book 'Prelude'*, ed. Mark L. Reed, 2 vols [Ithaca: Cornell University Press, 1991], vol. 1, p. 105).

Text based on manuscript.

Introduction, Childhood and School time

Oh there is blessing in this gentle breeze
That blows from the green fields and from the clouds
And from the sky: it beats against my cheek,
And seems half-conscious of the joy it gives.
O welcome Messenger! O welcome Friend!   5
A Captive greets thee, coming from a house
Of bondage, from yon City's walls set free,
A prison where he hath been long immured.
Now I am free, enfranchis'd and at large,
May fix my habitation where I will.   10
What dwelling shall receive me? In what Vale
Shall be my harbour? Underneath what grove
Shall I take up my home, and what sweet stream
Shall with its murmurs lull me to my rest?
The earth is all before me: with a heart   15
Joyous, nor scar'd at its own liberty,
I look about, and should the guide I chuse
Be nothing better than a wandering cloud,
I cannot miss my way. I breathe again;
Trances of thought and mountings of the mind   20
Come fast upon me. It is shaken off,
As by miraculous gift 'tis shaken off,
That burthen of my own unnatural self,
The heavy weight of many a weary day
Not mine, and such as were not made for me.   25
Long months of peace (if such bold word accord,
With any promises of human life),
Long months of ease and undisturb'd delight

1 *gentle breeze* A common Romantic image for inspiration.
19 *cannot miss my way* The overt sense is joyful, but the phrasing betrays a fear of not knowing where to go, which is picked up in the passage from ll. 95–271.
20 *Trances . . . mind* These 'trances' and 'mountings' are the more potent for their contentless state; it is the fact of mental and imaginative energy to which Wordsworth draws attention.

21–5 *It is shaken off . . . not made for me* The language captures the poet's relief at a shaking off that is less the result of will than a 'miraculous gift' (l. 22). What is 'shaken off' is the 'burden of my own unnatural self'. Like other Romantics, Wordsworth is most alarmed by the fear of self-betrayal.

Are mine in prospect: whither shall I turn?
By road or pathway, or through open field, 30
Or shall a twig or any floating thing
Upon the river, point me out my course?
  Enough that I am free, for months to come
May dedicate myself to chosen tasks;
May quit the tiresome sea and dwell on shore, 35
If not a settler on the soil, at least
To drink wild water, and to pluck green herbs,
And gather fruits fresh from their native tree.
Nay more, if I may trust myself, this hour
Hath brought a gift that consecrates my joy; 40
For I, methought, while the sweet breath of Heaven
Was blowing on my body, felt within
A corresponding mild creative breeze,
A vital breeze which travell'd gently on
O'er things which it had made, and is become 45
A tempest, a redundant energy
Vexing its own creation. 'Tis a power
That does not come unrecognis'd, a storm
Which, breaking up a long-continued frost
Brings with it vernal promises, the hope 50
Of active days, of dignity and thought,
Of prowess in an honorable field,
Pure passions, virtue, knowledge, and delight,
The holy life of music and of verse.
  Thus far, O Friend! did I, not used to make 55
A present joy the matter of my Song,
Pour out that day, my soul in measur'd strains,
Even in the very words which I have here
Recorded: to the open fields I told
A prophecy; poetic numbers came 60
Spontaneously, and cloth'd in priestly robe
My spirit, thus singled out, as it might seem,
For holy services: great hopes were mine;
My own voice chear'd me, and, far more, the mind's
Internal echo of the imperfect sound: 65
To both I listen'd, drawing from them both
A chearful confidence in things to come.
  Whereat, being not unwilling now to give
A respite to this passion, I paced on
Gently, with careless steps, and came erelong 70
To a green shady place where down I sate
Beneath a tree, slackening my thoughts by choice
And settling into gentler happiness.
'Twas Autumn, and a calm and placid day

46–7 *A tempest . . . creation* The 'mild creative breeze' (l. 43) transforms itself into an imaginative storm that in some sense disturbs itself. Wordsworth writes as much about internal imaginative processes as about transactions between the mind and nature.

60–1 *poetic . . . Spontaneously* Compare Wordsworth in his Preface to *Lyrical Ballads* (1800): 'For all good poetry is the spontaneous overflow of powerful feelings' (p. xiv). In both cases 'spontaneous' means 'voluntary'. The position of the adverb (at the start of l. 61) mimics the meaning.

64–5 *My own . . . sound* Wordsworth is cheered by his 'voice' and, more deeply, by his 'mind's' interiorizing of his voice: a characteristically self-reflexive effect.

With warmth as much as needed from a sun 75
Two hours declin'd towards the west, a day
With silver clouds and sunshine on the grass
And, in the sheltered grove where I was couch'd,
A perfect stillness. On the ground I lay
Passing through many thoughts, yet mainly such 80
As to myself pertain'd. I made a choice
Of one sweet Vale whither my steps should turn,
And saw, methought, the very house and fields
Present before my eyes: nor did I fail
To add, meanwhile, assurance of some work 85
Of glory, there forthwith to be begun –
Perhaps, too, there performed. Thus long I lay
Chear'd by the genial pillow of the earth
Beneath my head, sooth'd by a sense of touch
From the warm ground, that balanced me, else lost 90
Entirely, seeing nought, nought hearing, save
When here and there, about the grove of Oaks
Where was my bed, an acorn from the trees
Fell audibly, and with a startling sound.
   Thus occupied in mind, I linger'd here 95
Contented, nor rose up until the sun
Had almost touch'd the horizon; bidding then
A farewell to the City left behind,
Even on the strong temptation of that hour
And with its chance equipment, I resolved 100
To journey towards the Vale which I had chosen.
It was a splendid evening: and my soul
Did once again make trial of her strength
Restored to her afresh; nor did she want
Eolian visitations; but the harp 105
Was soon defrauded, and the banded host
Of harmony dispers'd in straggling sounds
And lastly, utter silence. 'Be it so,
It is an injury,' said I, 'to this day
To think of any thing but present joy.' 110
So like a Peasant I pursued my road
Beneath the evening sun; nor had one wish
Again to bend the sabbath of that time
To a servile yoke. What need of many words?
A pleasant loitering journey, through two days 115
Continued, brought me to my hermitage.
   I spare to speak, my Friend, of what ensued,
The admiration and the love, the life
In common things; the endless store of things
Rare, or at least so seeming, every day 120
Found all about me in one neighbourhood,
The self-congratulation, the complete
Composure, and the happiness entire.
But speedily a longing in me rose

---

105 *Eolian visitations* Aeolus, Greek god of wind, is often associated with poetic inspiration in poetry of the period: see Coleridge's 'The Eolian Harp'.

108 *utter silence* The pause after 'silence' suggests the petering out of inspiration.

122 *self-congratulation* Rejoicing.

              To brace myself to some determin'd aim, 125
              Reading or thinking, either to lay up
              New stores, or rescue from decay the old
              By timely interference. I had hopes
              Still higher, that with a frame of outward life
              I might endue, might fix in a visible home 130
              Some portion of those phantoms of conceit
              That had been floating loose about so long,
              And to such Beings temperately deal forth
              The many feelings that oppress'd my heart.
              But I have been discouraged: gleams of light 135
              Flash often from the East, then disappear
              And mock me with a sky that ripens not
              Into a steady morning: if my mind,
              Remembering the sweet promise of the past,
              Would gladly grapple with some noble theme, 140
              Vain is her wish; where'er she turns she finds
              Impediments from day to day renew'd.
                 And now it would content me to yield up
              Those lofty hopes awhile for present gifts
              Of humbler industry. But, O dear Friend! 145
              The Poet, gentle creature as he is,
              Hath, like the Lover, his unruly times;
              His fits when he is neither sick nor well,
              Though no distress be near him but his own
              Unmanageable thoughts. The mind itself, 150
              The meditative mind, best pleased, perhaps,
              While she, as duteous as the Mother Dove,
              Sits brooding, lives not always to that end,
              But hath less quiet instincts, goadings-on
              That drive her as in trouble through the groves. 155
              With me is now such passion, which I blame
              No otherwise than as it lasts too long.
                 When, as becomes a man who would prepare
              For such a glorious work, I through myself
              Make rigorous inquisition, the report 160
              Is often chearing, for I neither seem
              To lack, that first great gift! the vital soul,
              Nor general truths which are themselves a sort
              Of Elements and Agents, Under-Powers,
              Subordinate helpers of the living mind. 165
              Nor am I naked in external things,
              Forms, images; nor numerous other aids
              Of less regard, though won perhaps with toil
              And needful to build up a Poet's praise.

125 *determin'd aim* Defined purpose. See also the assertion that the poem's 'theme' is 'Single, and of determin'd bounds' (669–70). And yet the poem's originality has much to do with the fact that Wordsworth's concern is often with 'a dim and undetermin'd sense / Of unknown modes of being' (ll. 420–1).
128–32 *I had hopes ... long* As Jonathan Wordsworth observes, Wordsworth is rephrasing Theseus' account in Shakespeare's *A Midsummer Night's Dream* of poetic creativity: 'as imagination bodies forth / The forms of things unknown, the poet's pen / Turns them to shapes, and gives to airy nothing / A local habitation and a name' (5. i. 14–17). Wordsworth's passage is more tentative than Theseus', more haunted by the way 'phantoms of conceit' refuse to submit to words.
153 *Sits brooding* Compare Milton, *Paradise Lost*, I. 21: 'Dove-like sat'st brooding'.

                    Time, place, and manners; these I seek, and these   170
                    I find in plenteous store; but nowhere such
                    As may be singled out with steady choice;
                    No little Band of yet remember'd names
                    Whom I, in perfect confidence, might hope
                    To summon back from lonesome banishment   175
                    And make them inmates in the hearts of men
                    Now living, or to live in times to come.
                    Sometimes, mistaking vainly, as I fear,
                    Proud spring-tide swellings for a regular sea
                    I settle on some British theme, some old   180
                    Romantic tale, by Milton left unsung:
                    More often, resting at some gentle place
                    Within the groves of Chivalry, I pipe
                    Among the Shepherds, with reposing Knights
                    Sit by a Fountain-side and hear their tales.   185
                    Sometimes, more sternly mov'd, I would relate
                    How vanquish'd Mithridates northward pass'd,
                    And, hidden in the cloud of years, became
                    That Odin, Father of a Race by whom
                    Perish'd the Roman Empire; how the Friends   190
                    And Followers of Sertorius, out of Spain
                    Flying, found shelter in the Fortunate Isles;
                    And left their usages, their arts and laws
                    To disappear by a slow gradual death;
                    To dwindle and to perish one by one   195
                    Starved in those narrow bounds: but not the Soul
                    Of Liberty, which fifteen hundred years
                    Surviv'd, and when the European came
                    With skill and power that could not be withstood,
                    Did like a pestilence maintain its hold   200
                    And wasted down by glorious death that Race
                    Of natural Heroes: or I would record
                    How in tyrannic times some unknown Man,
                    Unheard of in the Chronicles of Kings,
                    Suffer'd in silence for the love of truth: 205
                    How that one Frenchman, through continued force
                    Of meditation on the inhuman deeds
                    Of the first Conquerors of the Indian Isles,
                    Went single in his ministry across
                    The Ocean, not to comfort the Oppress'd,   210
                    But, like a thirsty wind, to roam about,
                    Withering the Oppressor: how Gustavus found
                    Help at his need in Dalecarlia's Mines;
                    How Wallace fought for Scotland, left the name
                    Of Wallace to be found like a wild flower   215

187 *vanquish'd Mithridates* King of Pontus (131–63 BCE); referred to, with Odin (see l. 188), in Edward Gibbons, *Decline and Fall of the Roman Empire*, ch. 10.
191 *Sertorius* Roman general (c. 112–72 BCE); subject of one of Plutarch's *Lives*.
206 *that one Frenchman* A note to the first edition (1850), drawn from Hakluyt's *Navigation*, reads: 'Dominique de Gourges, a French gentleman who went in 1566 to Florida to avenge the massacre of the French by the Spaniards there'.
212 *Gustavus* Gustavus I of Sweden (1496–1560), who freed the country from Danish rule, with support from the miners of Dalecarlia.
214 *Wallace* William Wallace (c. 1272–1305), Scottish leader, captured and executed by Edward I.

All over his dear country, left the deeds
Of Wallace, like a Family of Ghosts,
To people the steep rocks and river banks,
Her natural sanctuaries, with a local soul
Of independence and stern liberty. 220
Sometimes it suits me better to shape out
Some Tale from my own heart, more near akin
To my own passions and habitual thoughts,
Some variegated story, in the main
Lofty, with interchange of gentler things; 225
But deadening admonitions will succeed,
And the whole beauteous Fabric seems to lack
Foundation, and withal appears throughout
Shadowy and unsubstantial. Then, last wish,
My last and favourite aspiration! then 230
I yearn towards some philosophic Song
Of Truth that cherishes our daily life;
With meditations passionate from deep
Recesses in man's heart, immortal verse
Thoughtfully fitted to the Orphean lyre; 235
But from this awful burthen I full soon
Take refuge, and beguile myself with trust
That mellower years will bring a riper mind
And clearer insight. Thus from day to day
I live, a mockery of the brotherhood 240
Of vice and virtue, with no skill to part
Vague longing that is bred by want of power
From paramount impulse not to be withstood,
A timorous capacity from prudence;
From circumspection, infinite delay. 245
Humility and modest awe themselves
Betray me, serving often for a cloak
To a more subtle selfishness, that now
Doth lock my functions up in blank reserve,
Now dupes me by an over anxious eye 250
That with a false activity beats off
Simplicity and self-presented truth.
– Ah! better far than this, to stray about
Voluptuously through fields and rural walks,
And ask no record of the hours, given up 255

220 *stern liberty* The passage on possible themes to do with struggle and liberty begins with the poet being 'more sternly mov'd' (l. 186) and ends with further 'sternness' as Wordsworth imagines a series of uncompromising heroes and acts of heroism.
222 *Some tale . . . heart* Wordsworth approaches here what will become the subject of his poem.
227–9 *whole beauteous . . . unsubstantial* Wordsworth recalls Prospero's speech in *The Tempest* 4. 1. 148–63. Wordsworth bids farewell to the 'unsubstantial' at his poem's outset; Prospero discovers, towards the close of the play, that reality is an 'insubstantial pageant' (4. 1. 155).
234–5 *immortal verse . . . Orphean lyre* Echoes Milton's *L'Allegro*, ll. 136–7, 'soft Lydian airs / Married to immortal verse', and *Paradise Lost* 3. 17, 'Orphean lyre'. Orpheus was thought of as an archetypal poet with access to esoteric mysteries.
241–3 *with no skill . . . withstood* The very precision of the distinction belies Wordsworth's opening disclaimer, creating in the reader a subliminal confidence in his ability to find an appropriate subject.
249 *Doth . . . up* Compare Pope, *Imitations of Horace*, Epistle I: 'So slow the unprofitable moments roll, / That lock up all the functions of my soul', ll. 39–40. Unconfined by the demands of the heroic couplet, Wordsworth allows the idea of unprofitability fuller expression than Pope does, the Romantic poet's syntax mimicking his sense of 'Unprofitably travelling towards the grave' (l. 270).

To vacant musing, unreprov'd neglect
Of all things, and deliberate holiday:
Far better never to have heard the name
Of zeal and just ambition, than to live
Thus baffled by a mind that every hour   260
Turns recreant to her task, takes heart again
Then feels immediately some hollow thought
Hang like an interdict upon her hopes.
This is my lot; for either still I find
Some imperfection in the chosen theme;   265
Or see of absolute accomplishment
Much wanting, so much wanting in myself,
That I recoil and droop, and seek repose
In indolence from vain perplexity,
Unprofitably travelling towards the grave,   270
Like a false Steward who hath much receiv'd
And renders nothing back. – Was it for this
That one, the fairest of all Rivers, lov'd
To blend his murmurs with my Nurse's song,
And from his alder shades and rocky falls,   275
And from his fords and shallows sent a voice
That flow'd along my dreams? For this didst Thou,
O Derwent! travelling over the green Plains
Near my sweet birth-place, didst thou, beauteous Stream,
Make ceaseless music through the night and day 280
Which with its steady cadence tempering
Our human waywardness, composed my thoughts
To more than infant softness, giving me
Among the fretful dwellings of mankind
A knowledge, a dim earnest of the calm   285
Which Nature breathes among the hills and groves.
    When, having left his Mountains, to the Towers
Of Cockermouth that beauteous River came,
Behind my Father's House he pass'd, close by,
Along the margin of our Terrace Walk –   290
He was a Playmate whom we dearly lov'd.
Oh! many a time have I, a five years' Child,
A naked Boy, in one delightful Rill,
A little Mill-race sever'd from his stream,
Made one long bathing of a summer's day,   295
Bask'd in the sun, and plunged, and bask'd again
Alternate all a summer's day, or cours'd
Over the sandy fields, leaping through groves
Of yellow grunsel, or, when crag and hill,
The woods, and distant Skiddaw's lofty height, 300

271 *false steward* Compare Matthew 25: 14–30, the parable of the talents, in which the 'good and faithful servant' (14: 21) succeeds in adding to his initial quota, while 'the unprofitable servant' (14: 30) does not.
272 *Was it for this* These lines appear to be the first lines of *The Prelude* written by Wordsworth. They begin in a state of anxiety about his failure to fulfil his gifts as a talent, yet quickly make clear that childhood experiences are at the heart of his poetic identity. Jonathan Wordsworth adduces a number of parallels to the question, including this strikingly relevant passage from *Samson Agonistes*, ll. 361–2: 'For this did the angel twice descend? for this / Ordained thy nurture holy, as of a plant'. Wordsworth, the echo suggests, has spurned until now the quasi-angelic interventions made on his behalf by natural influences.
279 *sweet birthplace* Alludes to Coleridge's 'Frost at Midnight': 'already had I dreamt / Of my sweet birthplace', ll. 32–3.

Were bronz'd with a deep radiance, stood alone
Beneath the sky, as if I had been born
On Indian Plains and from my Mother's hut
Had run abroad in wantonness, to sport,
A naked Savage, in the thunder shower. 305
    Fair seed-time had my soul, and I grew up
Foster'd alike by beauty and by fear;
Much favor'd in my birth-place, and no less
In that beloved Vale to which, erelong,
I was transplanted. Well I call to mind 310
('Twas at an early age, ere I had seen
Nine summers) when upon the mountain slope
The frost and breath of frosty wind had snapp'd
The last autumnal crocus, 'twas my joy
To wander half the night among the Cliffs 315
And the smooth Hollows where the woodcocks ran
Along the open turf. In thought and wish
That time, my shoulder all with springes hung,
I was a fell destroyer. On the heights,
Scudding away from snare to snare, I plied 320
My anxious visitation, hurrying on,
Still hurrying, hurrying onward: moon and stars
Were shining o'er my head; I was alone,
And seem'd to be a trouble to the peace
That was among them. Sometimes it befel 325
In these night-wanderings, that a strong desire
O'erpower'd my better reason, and the bird
Which was the captive of another's toils
Became my prey; and, when the deed was done,
I heard among the solitary hills 330
Low breathings coming after me, and sounds
Of undistinguishable motion, steps
Almost as silent as the turf they trod.
    Nor less in spring-time when on southern banks
The shining sun had from his knot of leaves 335
Decoy'd the primrose flower, and when the Vales
And woods were warm, was I a plunderer then
In the high places, on the lonesome peaks
Where'er, among the mountains and the winds,
The Mother Bird had built her lodge. Though mean 340
My object, and inglorious, yet the end
Was not ignoble. Oh! when I have hung

---

303 *Indian* American Indian. Wordsworth's self-description, 'A naked savage' (l. 305), suggests the influence of Rousseau's idea and ideal of the 'noble savage'.
307 *Foster'd ... fear* 'beauty' and 'fear' correspond to the Burkean terms, 'the beautiful' and 'the sublime'.
317–19 *In thought ... destroyer* The language is mock-heroic, capturing the boy's self-dramatizing as he lays 'springes' or snares for the woodcocks, which would be sold for eating and sent by carriage to London.
323–5 *I was alone ... among them* Though 'Foster'd' by nature, the child is 'a trouble' to natural peace;
Wordsworth's sense of the interaction between consciousness and nature is, as in many of the spots of time, a complicated one; events of psychological significance take place in, and are catalysed (and recalled) by natural scenes.
329 *when ... done* A Macbeth-like guilt caused by the stealing of another person's trapped bird.
330–3 *I heard ... they trod* The child's guilty conscience makes it appear that he is pursued. The rhythms capture the stealthy presence of these uncanny (and unreal) pursuers.

       Above the raven's nest, by knots of grass,
And half-inch fissures in the slippery rock
But ill sustain'd, and almost, as it seem'd,   345
Suspended by the blast which blew amain,
Shouldering the naked crag; Oh! at that time,
While on the perilous ridge I hung alone,
With what strange utterance did the loud dry wind
Blow through my ears! the sky seem'd not a sky   350
Of earth, and with what motion mov'd the clouds!
    The mind of man is framed even like the breath
And harmony of music. There is a dark
Invisible workmanship that reconciles
Discordant elements, and makes them move   355
In one society. Ah me! that all
The terrors, all the early miseries,
Regrets, vexations, lassitudes, that all
The thoughts and feelings which have been infus'd
Into my mind should ever have made up   360
The calm existence that is mine when I
Am worthy of myself. Praise to the end!
Thanks likewise for the means! But I believe
That Nature, oftentimes, when she would frame
A favor'd Being, from his earliest dawn   365
Of infancy doth open out the clouds
As at the touch of lightning, seeking him
With gentlest visitation: not the less,
Though haply aiming at the self-same end,
Does it delight her sometimes to employ   370
Severer interventions, ministry
More palpable, and so she dealt with me.
    One evening (surely I was led by her)
I went alone into a Shepherd's Boat,
A Skiff that to a Willow tree was tied   375
Within a rocky Cave, its usual home.
'Twas by the Shores of Patterdale, a vale
Wherein I was a Stranger, thither come
A School-Boy Traveller, at the Holidays.
Forth rambled from the Village Inn alone   380
No sooner had I sight of this small Skiff,
Discover'd thus by unexpected chance,
Than I unloos'd her tether and embark'd.

343 *the raven's nest* Wordsworth, probably let down the crag on a rope held by his fellows, was destroying the raven's nest for a reward offered by the parish – since ravens were a danger to lambs (see *Prelude: The Four Texts*, pp. 559–60).

348 *I hung alone* Again, in this spot of time Wordsworth stresses his solitariness.

350–1 *the sky . . . clouds!* The line-ending ('a sky / Of earth') posits briefly that the 'sky' was some other kind of 'sky', as though usual boundaries had been abolished; a similar uncertainty governs the final words, where the exclamation might easily be a question (see Christopher Ricks for a slightly different emphasis in *The Force of Poetry*, pp. 110–11).

352–6 *The mind of man . . . one society* Wordsworth emphasizes a reconciling harmony, but gives a full sense, too, of the mind's seemingly 'Discordant elements'.

373–428 *One evening . . . of my dreams* The stolen boat episode, one of the major 'spots of time' in *The Prelude*, and one which illustrates the poet's narrative control at its greatest; the episode moves from initial ordinariness (a fine evocation of rowing in the stolen boat) to the terror that descends on the boy when he seems to be pursued by a 'huge Cliff' (l. 410), a terror that is also a recognition of august sublimity, through to the account of the incident's aftermath, in which the boy experiences a kind of sensory blackout.

            The moon was up, the Lake was shining clear
            Among the hoary mountains: from the Shore 385
            I push'd, and struck the oars and struck again
            In cadence, and my little Boat mov'd on
            Even like a Man who walks with stately step
            Though bent on speed. It was an act of stealth
            And troubled pleasure: nor without the voice 390
            Of mountain-echoes did my Boat move on,
            Leaving behind her still on either side
            Small circles glittering idly in the moon
            Until they melted all into one track
            Of sparkling light. A rocky steep uprose 395
            Above the Cavern of the Willow tree,
            And now, as suited one who proudly row'd
            With his best skill, I fix'd a steady view
            Upon the top of that same craggy ridge,
            The bound of the horizon, for behind 400
            Was nothing but the stars and the grey sky.
            She was an elfin Pinnace; lustily
            I dipped my oars into the silent Lake,
            And, as I rose upon the stroke, my Boat
            Went heaving through the water like a Swan, 405
            When from behind that craggy Steep, till then
            The bound of the horizon, a huge Cliff,
            As if with voluntary power instinct,
            Uprear'd its head: I struck, and struck again,
            And, growing still in stature, the huge Cliff 410
            Rose up between me and the stars, and still,
            With measur'd motion, like a living thing
            Strode after me. With trembling hands I turn'd,
            And through the silent water stole my way
            Back to the Cavern of the Willow tree. 415
            There in her mooring-place, I left my Bark
            And through the meadows homeward went with grave
            And serious thoughts: and after I had seen
            That spectacle, for many days my brain
            Work'd with a dim and undetermin'd sense 420
            Of unknown modes of being: in my thoughts
            There was a darkness, call it solitude,
            Or blank desertion, no familiar shapes
            Of hourly objects, images of trees,
            Of sea, or sky, no colours of green fields, 425

388–9 *Even like a man . . . bent on speed* Compare *Paradise Lost*, Bk. 12, lines 1–2: 'As one who in his journey bates at noon, / Though bent on speed, so here the archangel paused . . .'.

390 *troubled pleasure* In *The Prelude* 'troubled' or 'trouble' often refer to a state of disturbance that is imaginatively productive. See, for example, the close of this episode, line 428, 'the trouble of my dreams'.

402 *elfin Pinnace* The boy views the adventure in quasi-Spenserian terms.

408 *As if . . . instinct* As though imbued with a will of its own.

410 *growing . . . stature* The more the boy tries to row away from the cliff, the larger it grows.

412 *measur'd motion* Recalls Coleridge's 'Kubla Khan', with its 'mazy motion' (l. 25) and 'mingled measure' (l. 33).

420–1 *dim . . . being* The lineation and wording enact the boy's new awareness of something which defeats definition.

But huge and mighty Forms that do not live
Like living men mov'd slowly through my mind
By day and were the trouble of my dreams.
    Wisdom and Spirit of the Universe!
Thou Soul that art the Eternity of Thought,   430
That giv'st to forms and images a breath
And everlasting motion! not in vain,
By day or starlight thus from my first dawn
Of Childhood didst Thou intertwine for me
The passions that build up our human Soul,   435
Not with the mean and vulgar works of Man,
But with high objects, with enduring things,
With life and nature, purifying thus
The elements of feeling and of thought,
And sanctifying by such discipline   440
Both pain and fear until we recognise
A grandeur in the beatings of the heart.
    Nor was this fellowship vouchsaf'd to me
With stinted kindness. In November days
When vapours, rolling down the valleys, made   445
A lonely scene more lonesome; among woods
At noon, and 'mid the calm of summer nights,
When by the margin of the trembling Lake
Beneath the gloomy hills I homeward went
In solitude, such intercourse was mine;   450
'Twas mine among the fields both day and night,
And by the waters all the summer long.
– And in the frosty season, when the sun
Was set, and, visible for many a mile,
The cottage windows through the twilight blaz'd,   455
I heeded not the summons: – happy time
It was indeed for all of us; to me
It was a time of rapture: clear and loud
The village clock toll'd six; I wheel'd about,
Proud and exulting, like an untir'd horse,   460
That cares not for its home. All shod with steel
We hiss'd along the polish'd ice, in games
Confederate, imitative of the chace,
And woodland pleasures, the resounding horn,
The Pack, loud bellowing, and the hunted hare.   465
So through the darkness and the cold we flew,

426–8 *But huge . . . dreams* Again, Wordsworth's blank verse proves to be a supple medium, able to suggest that the 'Forms' do not live the way that 'living men' live and that, though they do not live, they moved like living men; 'living', a key word, with its intimation of an animated natural world, picks up the account of the cliff as being 'like a living thing' (l. 412).

434 *intertwine* At the heart of this apostrophe is the idea that the 'Wisdom and Spirit of the Universe' (l. 429) linked together central 'passions' (l. 435) with 'high objects' (l. 437): feelings were associated with worthy natural scenes in such a way as to give those feelings dignity, 'grandeur' (l. 442).

453–90 *And in the frosty season . . . summer sea* Another major set-piece from Book 1, the skating episode embodies a sense of reciprocal give-and-take between Wordsworth and nature; it is after the boys have surrendered to nature ('given our bodies to the wind', l. 480) that nature appears to make 'visible . . . her diurnal round' (l. 487). The writing is superbly mimetic of the physical act of skating and of the atmosphere in which it takes place: one mingling 'rapture' (l. 458) with awareness of 'an alien sound / Of melancholy' (ll. 471–2).

And not a voice was idle: with the din,
Meanwhile, the precipices rang aloud,
The leafless trees, and every icy crag
Tinkled like iron, while the distant hills 470
Into the tumult sent an alien sound
Of melancholy, not unnoticed, while the stars
Eastward, were sparkling clear, and in the west
The orange sky of evening died away.
    Not seldom from the uproar I retired 475
Into a silent bay, or sportively
Glanced sideway, leaving the tumultuous throng,
To cut across the image of a star
That gleam'd upon the ice: and oftentimes,
When we had given our bodies to the wind, 480
And all the shadowy banks, on either side,
Came sweeping through the darkness, spinning still
The rapid line of motion; then at once
Have I, reclining back upon my heels,
Stopp'd short, yet still the solitary Cliffs 485
Wheel'd by me, even as if the earth had roll'd
With visible motion her diurnal round;
Behind me did they stretch in solemn train
Feebler and feebler, and I stood and watch'd
Till all was tranquil as a summer sea. 490
    Ye Presences of Nature, in the sky
Or on the earth! Ye Visions of the hills
And Souls of lonely places! can I think
A vulgar hope was yours when Ye employ'd
Such ministry, when Ye through many a year 495
Haunting me thus among my boyish sports,
On caves and trees, upon the woods and hills,
Impress'd upon all forms the characters
Of danger or desire, and thus did make
The surface of the universal earth 500
With triumph, and delight, and hope, and fear
Work like a sea?
              Not uselessly employ'd,
I might pursue this theme through every change
Of exercise and play, to which the year
Did summon us in its delightful round. 505
– We were a noisy crew; the sun in heaven
Beheld not vales more beautiful than ours
Nor saw a race, in happiness and joy
More worthy of the fields where they were sown.
I would record with no reluctant voice 510

475 *I retired* Wordsworth emphasizes his individual experience in this paragraph; see also line 484.
490 *a summer sea* The space taken up by this phrase was left blank when the 1805 fair copies were being made; in 1809, when this excerpt was printed in *The Friend*, the reading was 'a summer sea'. Later, Wordsworth revised to 'a dreamless sleep'.
498 *Impress'd* Stamped. The argument in this paragraph is circular. Throughout the natural world traces are to be found of human emotions ('danger or desire', l. 499) associated with the natural world.
502 *Not uselessly employ'd* Wordsworth's double negatives can be a stylistic tic; here they indicate a latent fear that writing about his formative experiences might be regarded as 'useless'. See also 'no reluctant voice' (l. 510).

The woods of autumn and their hazel bowers
With milk-white clusters hung; the rod and line,
True symbol of the foolishness of hope
Which with its strong enchantment led us on
By rocks and pools, shut out from every star 515
All the green summer, to forlorn cascades
Among the windings of the mountain-brooks.
– Unfading recollections! at this hour
The heart is almost mine with which I felt
From some hill-top, on sunny afternoons, 520
The Kite high up among the fleecy clouds
Pull at its rein, like an impatient Courser,
Or, from the meadows sent on gusty days
Beheld her breast the wind, then suddenly
Dash'd headlong; and rejected by the storm. 525
   Ye lowly Cottages in which we dwelt,
A ministration of your own was yours,
A sanctity, a safeguard, and a love!
Can I forget you, being as ye were
So beautiful among the pleasant fields 530
In which ye stood? Or can I here forget
The plain and seemly countenance with which
Ye dealt out your plain comforts? Yet had ye
Delights and exultations of your own.
Eager and never weary we pursued 535
Our home amusements by the warm peat-fire
At evening; when with pencil and with slate,
In square divisions parcell'd out, and all
With crosses and with cyphers scribbl'd o'er,
We schemed and puzzled, head opposed to head, 540
In strife too humble to be named in Verse;
Or round the naked Table, snow-white deal,
Cherry, or maple, sate in close array,
And to the combat, Lu or Whist, led on
A thick-ribb'd Army, not as in the world 545
Neglected and ungratefully thrown by
Even for the very service they had wrought,
But husbanded through many a long campaign.
Uncouth assemblage was it, where no few
Had changed their functions, some, plebean cards 550
Which Fate beyond the promise of their birth
Had glorified, and call'd to represent
The persons of departed Potentates.
Oh! with what echoes on the Board they fell!
Ironic Diamonds; Clubs, Hearts, Diamonds, Spades, 555
A congregation piteously akin;
Cheap matter did they give to boyish wit,

---

519 *almost mine* 'Almost' concedes the gap between child and adult; see also line 662.
539 *With crosses... scribbl'd o'er* Compare *Paradise Lost*, 8. 83, 'With centric and eccentric scribbled o'er', where Raphael mocks human efforts to understand the heavens. Wordsworth's passage is among the moments when his epic has dealings with mock-heroic.
542–63 *Or round... visages* Modelled on Pope's mock-heroic card-game in *The Rape of the Lock*.

Those sooty Knaves, precipitated down
With scoffs and taunts, like Vulcan out of Heaven;
The paramount Ace, a moon in her eclipse; 560
Queens, gleaming through their splendour's last decay,
And Monarchs, surly at the wrongs sustain'd
By royal visages. Meanwhile, abroad
The heavy rain was falling, or the frost
Raged bitterly, with keen and silent tooth, 565
And, interrupting the impassion'd game,
From Esthwaite's neighbouring Lake the splitting ice,
While it sank down towards the water, sent
Among the meadows and the hills, its long
And dismal yellings, like the noise of wolves 570
When they are howling round the Bothnic Main.
    Nor, sedulous as I have been to trace
How Nature by extrinsic passion first
Peopled my mind with beauteous forms or grand,
And made me love them, may I well forget 575
How other pleasures have been mine, and joys
Of subtler origin; how I have felt,
Not seldom, even in that tempestuous time,
Those hallow'd and pure motions of the sense
Which seem, in their simplicity, to own 580
An intellectual charm, that calm delight
Which, if I err not, surely must belong
To those first-born affinities that fit
Our new existence to existing things
And, in our dawn of being, constitute 585
The bond of union betwixt life and joy.
    Yes, I remember when the changeful earth,
And twice five seasons on my mind had stamp'd
The faces of the moving year, even then,
A Child, I held unconscious intercourse 590
With the eternal Beauty, drinking in
A pure organic preasure from the lines
Of curling mist, or from the level plain
Of waters colour'd by the steady clouds.

563–4 *Meanwhile . . . silent tooth* Recalls Cowper's *The Task*, 4, ll. 308–10: 'how the frost / Raging abroad, and rough wind, endear / The silence and the warmth enjoyed within'. Jonathan Wordsworth, who points out this echo, also draws attention to a reference to Amiens' song in Shakespeare's *As You Like It*, 2. 7. 174–7: 'Blow, blow, thou winter wind, / Thou art not so unkind / As man's ingratitude. / Thy tooth is not so keen' (*The Four Texts*, p. 545). Wordsworth again suggests the subliminal impression made on the child's mind; the child is enjoying his card-game, but associates it (in some corner of his mind) with natural processes that have their own grandeur and bracing severity.
571 *the Bothnic Main* The northern Baltic.
572–86 *Nor . . . joy* Wordsworth moves away from episodes through which nature brought him to love 'beauteous forms or grand' (l. 574) by means of 'extrinsic passion' (l. 573), passion, that is, not directly involving love of nature, to 'joys / Of subtler origin' (576–7), which spring more straightforwardly from the affinity between the human and the natural, an affinity present in our 'dawn of being' (l. 585).
572 *sedulous* Anxious.
579 *hallow'd . . . sense* Compare and contrast with Shakespeare, *Measure for Measure*, 1. 4. 59: 'The wanton stings and motions of the sense'.
581 *intellectual* Spiritual.
591–4 *drinking . . . clouds* Absorbing a purely sensuous ('organic', l. 592) pleasure from natural sights. Wordsworth's use of 'lines' at the end of line 592 momentarily identifies the lines of mist with the poetic lines he is constructing; see Ricks, *The Force of Poetry*, pp. 95–6.

William Wordsworth (1770–1850) 155

        The Sands of Westmoreland, the Creeks and Bays   595
Of Cumbria's rocky limits, they can tell
How when the Sea threw off his evening shade
And to the Shepherd's hut beneath the crags
Did send sweet notice of the rising moon,
How I have stood to fancies such as these,   600
Engrafted in the tenderness of thought,
A stranger, linking with the spectacle
No conscious memory of a kindred sight,
And bringing with me no peculiar sense
Of quietness or peace, yet I have stood,   605
Even while mine eye has mov'd o'er three long leagues
Of shining water, gathering, as it seem'd,
Through every hair-breadth of that field of light,
New pleasure, like a bee among the flowers.
    Thus, often in those fits of vulgar joy   610
Which through all seasons, on a child's pursuits
Are prompt attendants, 'mid that giddy bliss
Which, like a tempest, works along the blood
And is forgotten; even then I felt
Gleams like the flashing of a shield: the earth   615
And common face of Nature spake to me
Rememberable things: sometimes, 'tis true,
By chance collisions, and quaint accidents
Like those ill-sorted unions, work suppos'd
Of evil-minded fairies, yet not vain,   620
Nor profitless, if haply they impress'd
Collateral objects and appearances,
Albeit lifeless then, and doom'd to sleep
Until maturer seasons call'd them forth
To impregnate and to elevate the mind.   625
– And if the vulgar joy by its own weight
Wearied itself out of the memory
The scenes which were a witness of that joy
Remained, in their substantial lineaments
Depicted on the brain, and to the eye   630
Were visible, a daily sight: and thus,
By the impressive discipline of fear,
By pleasure, and repeated happiness
So frequently repeated, and by force
Of obscure feelings representative   635
Of joys that were forgotten, these same scenes
So beauteous and majestic in themselves,
Though yet the day was distant, did at length
Become habitually dear; and all
Their hues and forms were by invisible links   640
Allied to the affections.

595–609 *The sands . . . flowers* The long sentence mimics the cumulative process of 'gathering' (l. 607) experience of which Wordsworth writes.

622 *Collateral . . . appearances* 'Collateral' means 'Connected but aside from the main subject'; Wordsworth describes here and throughout the paragraph processes of association that endow objects with deepened meaning in later life.

632–3 *impressive . . . happiness* The boy's feelings were nurtured by the impressions made on him by both 'fear' and 'happiness' experienced in the presence of nature.

                    I began
My Story early, feeling as I fear,
The weakness of a human love, for days
Disown'd by memory, ere the birth of spring
Planting my snow-drops among winter snows. 645
Nor will it seem to thee, my Friend! so prompt
In sympathy, that I have lengthen'd out
With fond and feeble tongue, a tedious tale.
Meanwhile, my hope has been that I might fetch
Invigorating thoughts from former years, 650
Might fix the wavering balance of my mind,
And haply meet reproaches, too, whose power
May spur me on, in manhood now mature,
To honorable toil. Yet should these hopes
Be vain, and thus should neither I be taught 655
To understand myself, nor thou to know
With better knowledge how the heart was fram'd
Of him thou lovest, need I dread from thee
Harsh judgments, if I am so loth to quit
Those recollected hours that have the charm 660
Of visionary things, and lovely forms
And sweet sensations that throw back our life
And almost make our Infancy itself
A visible scene on which the sun is shining?
    One end hereby at least hath been attain'd – 665
My mind hath been reviv'd, and if this mood
Desert me not, I will forthwith bring down
Through later years, the story of my life.
The road lies plain before me; 'tis a theme
Single, and of determin'd bounds; and hence 670
I chuse it rather, at this time, than work
Of ampler or more varied argument.

646 *my Friend!* Coleridge.
654 *honorable toil* Wordsworth does not mean the poem he is now writing, for which he half-apologizes in surrounding lines, but the philosophical poem *The Recluse* which, urged by Coleridge, he planned to write but never did.

664 *is shining* The tense makes the past present.
665–72 *One end . . . varied argument* Wordsworth embarks on *The Prelude*, probably the finest long poem written by the Romantics, with a sense of it being a more manageable task than others he might undertake.

Resolution and Independence

Composed in May–July 1802, the poem's first version was entitled 'The Leech-gatherer'; the poem, which is often read as responding to Coleridge's 'Dejection: An Ode', is written in the same stanzaic form as Thomas Chatterton uses in 'An Excelente Balade of Charitie' (published 1777), in which there is 'A hapless pilgrim' (l. 17) 'Longe bretful of [filled with] the miseries of neede' (l. 19) (quoted from *Eighteenth-Century Poetry: An Annotated Poetry*, ed. David Fairer and Christine Gerrard [Oxford: Blackwell, 2nd edn, 2004]). Wordsworth's comments on the poem in his 1815 Preface focus on the workings of the imagination, as shown in line 5 and lines 64–84, and the poem is concerned with being a poet, with the restoration of imaginative confidence, after the imagining of Coleridge-like 'dejection' (l. 25), through the encounter with the aged leech-gatherer who manages to survive 'with God's good help' (l. 111). As often in Wordsworth's poems of encounter, the near-sublime joins hands with the almost-banal, and the poem's switches of register have been the subject of much critical comment. The poem begins with a present-tense delight in nature that shifts into the past tense at line 15, which ushers in the poet's changed mood, especially his anxieties about the future and fear that 'gladness' (l. 48) may give way to 'despondency and madness' (l. 49). It is at this point that Wordsworth meets the leech-gatherer, who offers, so the poet feels, 'human strength, and strong admonishment' (l. 119). In addition to the example he sets of self-reliance and persistence, the leech-gatherer also provides solace by triggering the poet's imagination. As in *The Prelude*, Wordsworth is 'troubled' (l. 135) imaginatively, but this imaginative 'troubling' serves to reaffirm his poetic vocation.

Text from *Poems, in Two Volumes 1807*.

    There was a roaring in the wind all night;
    The rain came heavily and fell in floods;
    But now the sun is rising calm and bright;
    The birds are singing in the distant woods;
    Over his own sweet voice the Stock-dove broods;   5
    The Jay makes answer as the Magpie chatters;
    And all the air is fill'd with pleasant noise of waters.

    All things that love the sun are out of doors;
    The sky rejoices in the morning's birth;
    The grass is bright with rain-drops; on the moors   10
    The Hare is running races in her mirth;
    And with her feet she from the plashy earth
    Raises a mist; which, glittering in the sun,
    Runs with her all the way, wherever she doth run.

    I was a Traveller then upon the moor;   15
    I saw the Hare that rac'd about with joy;
    I heard the woods, and distant waters, roar;
    Or heard them not, as happy as a Boy:
    The pleasant season did my heart employ:
    My old remembrances went from me wholly;   20
    And all the ways of men, so vain and melancholy.

    But, as it sometimes chanceth, from the might
    Of joy in minds that can no farther go,
    As high as we have mounted in delight
    In our dejection do we sink as low,   25
    To me that morning did it happen so;
    And fears, and fancies, thick upon me came;
    Dim sadness, and blind thoughts I knew not nor could name.

    I heard the Sky-lark singing in the sky;
    And I bethought me of the playful Hare: 30
    Even such a happy Child of earth am I;
    Even as these blissful Creatures do I fare;
    Far from the world I walk, and from all care;
    But there may come another day to me,
    Solitude, pain of heart, distress, and poverty.   35

    My whole life I have liv'd in pleasant thought,
    As if life's business were a summer mood;

---

5 *Over . . . broods* In the 1815 Preface Wordsworth explains how 'by the intervention of the metaphor *broods*, the affections are called in by the imagination to assist in marking the manner in which the Bird reiterates and prolongs her soft note, as if herself delighting to listen to it' (*1815*, p. xxiii).
6 *makes answer* Blends yet contrasts with the previous line, in which the stockdove is depicted as self-communing.

11–14 *The Hare .. run* The image of the hare surrounded by a glittering halo of mist comes close to finding a natural equivalent for what in 'Ode: Intimations of Immortality' Wordsworth calls 'a glory' (l. 18). As an image of oneness in nature, it anticipates the cloud at line 82 that 'moveth altogether, if it move at all' (l. 84).
28 *Dim sadness . . . name* Wordsworth's feelings resist easy labelling.

As if all needful things would come unsought
To genial faith, still rich in genial good;
But how can He expect that others should 40
Build for him, sow for him, and at his call
Love him, who for himself will take no heed at all?

I thought of Chatterton, the marvellous Boy,
The sleepless Soul that perish'd in its pride;
Of Him who walk'd in glory and in joy 45
Behind his plough, upon the mountain-side:
By our own spirits are we deified;
We Poets in our youth begin in gladness;
But thereof comes in the end despondency and madness.

Now, whether it were by peculiar grace, 50
A leading from above, a something given,
Yet it befel, that, in this lonely place,
When up and down my fancy thus was driven,
And I with these untoward thoughts had striven,
I saw a Man before me unawares: 55
The oldest Man he seem'd that ever wore grey hairs.

My course I stopped as soon as I espied
The Old Man in that naked wilderness:
Close by a Pond, upon the further side,
He stood alone: a minute's space I guess 60
I watch'd him, he continuing motionless:
To the Pool's further margin then I drew;
He being all the while before me full in view.

As a huge Stone is sometimes seen to lie
Couch'd on the bald top of an eminence; 65
Wonder to all who do the same espy
By what means it could thither come, and whence;
So that it seems a thing endued with sense:
Like a Sea-beast crawl'd forth, which on a shelf
Of rock or sand reposeth, there to sun itself. 70

Such seem'd this Man, not all alive nor dead,
Nor all asleep; in his extreme old age:
His body was bent double, feet and head
Coming together in their pilgrimage;

---

40 *He* The change from 'I' (l. 36) to 'He' allows Wordsworth to widen the focus of his attention, while still permitting the lines to have a personal applicability.
43 *Chatterton ... Boy* Thomas Chatterton (1752–70), thought to have killed himself, became for the Romantic poets the type of the tragically doomed poet.
45 *Him* Robert Burns.
48–9 *We Poets ... madness* The feminine rhyme and the long final line (as in each stanza an alexandrine) create an effect close to doleful wryness.
50–1 *whether ... given* All three possibilities stress the fact that the leech-gatherer's appearance is 'given' to Wordsworth.
53–4 *When up and down ... striven* Revised from 1820 onwards to 'When I with these untoward thoughts had striven, / Beside a Pool bare to the eye of Heaven'.

55 *unawares* Unexpectedly.
60 *He stood alone* The caesura here ensures that the old man's 'aloneness' is emphasized.
64–84 *As a huge Stone ... move at all* Wordsworth, in the 1815 Preface, quotes these lines to exhibit the conjunction of 'the conferring, the abstracting, and the modifying powers of the Imagination, immediately and mediately acting' (*1815*, p. xxvi). The imagery, that is, confers life on the stone, thus bringing it into connection with the sea-beast; the sea-beast, in turn, is 'stripped of some of its vital qualities to assimilate it to the stone', and this 'intermediate image' is then applied to the old man. A similar process, Wordsworth implies in the Preface, is at work in the image of the cloud (ll. 82–4) (see *1815*, pp. xxvi, xxvii).
74 *their* From 1820 revised to 'life's'.

> As if some dire constraint of pain, or rage
> Of sickness felt by him in times long past,
> A more than human weight upon his frame had cast.

> Himself he propp'd, his body, limbs, and face,
> Upon a long grey Staff of shaven wood:
> And, still as I drew near with gentle pace,
> Beside the little pond or moorish flood
> Motionless as a Cloud the Old Man stood;
> That heareth not the loud winds when they call;
> And moveth altogether, if it move at all.

> At length, himself unsettling, he the Pond
> Stirred with his Staff, and fixedly did look
> Upon the muddy water, which he conn'd,
> As if he had been reading in a book:
> And now such freedom as I could I took;
> And, drawing to his side, to him did say,
> 'This morning gives us promise of a glorious day.'

> A gentle answer did the Old Man make,
> In courteous speech which forth he slowly drew:
> And him with further words I thus bespake,
> 'What kind of work is that which you pursue?
> This is a lonesome place for one like you.'
> He answer'd me with pleasure and surprize;
> And there was, while he spake, a fire about his eyes.

> His words came feebly, from a feeble chest,
> Yet each in solemn order follow'd each,
> With something of a lofty utterance drest;
> Choice word, and measured phrase; above the reach
> Of ordinary men; a stately speech!
> Such as grave Livers do in Scotland use,
> Religious men, who give to God and Man their dues.

> He told me that he to this Pond had come
> To gather Leeches, being old and poor:
> Employment hazardous and wearisome!
> And he had many hardships to endure:
> From Pond to Pond he roam'd, from moor to moor,
> Housing, with God's good help, by choice or chance:
> And in this way he gain'd an honest maintenance.

> The Old Man still stood talking by my side;
> But now his voice to me was like a stream
> Scarce heard; nor word from word could I divide;
> And the whole Body of the man did seem
> Like one whom I had met with in a dream;
> Or like a Man from some far region sent,
> To give me human strength, and strong admonishment.

113–19 *The Old Man ... admonishment* The stanza conveys the near-trance that envelops Wordsworth as the old man talks to him. The shifts between the ordinary and the deeply imaginative and inward are carefully calculated here and in succeeding stanzas.

My former thoughts return'd: the fear that kills; 120
The hope that is unwilling to be fed;
Cold, pain, and labour, and all fleshly ills;
And mighty Poets in their misery dead.
And now, not knowing what the Old Man had said,
My question eagerly did I renew, 125
'How is it that you live, and what is it you do?'

He with a smile did then his words repeat;
And said, that, gathering Leeches, far and wide
He travelled; stirring thus about his feet
The waters of the Ponds where they abide. 130
'Once I could meet with them on every side;
But they have dwindled long by slow decay;
Yet still I persevere, and find them where I may.'

While he was talking thus, the lonely place,
The Old Man's shape, and speech, all troubled me: 135
In my mind's eye I seem'd to see him pace
About the weary moors continually,
Wandering about alone and silently.
While I these thoughts within myself pursued,
He, having made a pause, the same discourse renewed. 140

And soon with this he other matter blended,
Chearfully uttered, with demeanour kind,
But stately in the main; and, when he ended,
I could have laugh'd myself to scorn, to find
In that decrepit Man so firm a mind. 145
'God,' said I, 'be my help and stay secure;
I'll think of the Leech-gatherer on the lonely moor.'

120 *My . . . return'd* The leech-gatherer does not offer a straightforward solution; the poet re-experiences his former anxieties.
124 *And . . . said* Revised from 1820 to 'Perplexed, and longing to be comforted,'.

136 *In my mind's eye* Again, the leech-gatherer has been transformed by Wordsworth's imagination.
146 *God* A significant figure in the poem, which fuses religious consolation and rediscovery of imaginative power.

The world is too much with us

One of a number of sonnets written in 1802 and included in *Poems* (1807), 'The world is too much with us' revises the Petrarchan or Italian form (two rhymes in the octave, three in the sestet) by employing only two rhymes in the sestet. Skilfully combining formal restraint and the inflections of passionate speech (the opening movement overrides the octave division), it expresses discontent with a culture that ignores nature and imagination in favour of 'Getting and spending' (l. 2). The sonnet was influential for Shelley, who echoes pointedly line 4 in 'An Exhortation', a poem written with Wordsworth in mind, and Keats, who picks up Wordsworth's use of 'forlorn' (l. 12) in his 'Ode to a Nightingale'.

Text from *Poems, in Two Volumes 1807*.

The world is too much with us; late and soon,
Getting and spending, we lay waste our powers:
Little we see in nature that is ours;
We have given our hearts away, a sordid boon!

2 *we lay waste* The strong active verb makes us the agents of our own undoing.

3 *Little* This stress-shift, straight after a similar opening to line 2, helps to establish the poem's forceful tone.

This Sea that bares her bosom to the moon; 5
The Winds that will be howling at all hours
And are up-gathered now like sleeping flowers;
For this, for every thing, we are out of tune;
It moves us not—Great God! I'd rather be
A Pagan suckled in a creed outworn; 10
So might I, standing on this pleasant lea,
Have glimpses that would make me less forlorn;
Have sight of Proteus coming from the sea;
Or hear old Triton blow his wreathed horn.

9   *Great God!* Placed suggestively before Wordsworth's preference for a 'creed outworn' (l. 10) over contemporary utilitarian concerns.
11   *lea* Meadow.
13–14   *Have sight . . . horn* Compare Edmund Spenser, 'Colin Clouts Come Home Againe', lines 245–8: 'Triton blowing loud his wreathed horne . . . And Proteus eke with him does drive his heard'. As he does elsewhere, Wordsworth combines sight and hearing in his evocation of a visionary experience; compare: 'Ode: Intimations of Immortality', lines 169–70.

Composed upon Westminster Bridge, Sept. 3, 1803

Also included in *Poem, in Two Volumes* (1807), and also an example of an Italian sonnet modified to include only two rhymes in the sestet, this poem responds to the spectacle of an early summer morning in London 1802 (to which year the poem's title-date is often revised) as Wordsworth and Dorothy were on their way to France to meet Annette Vallon and Caroline, her daughter by Wordsworth. Dorothy describes the 'beautiful morning' in her Journal: 'The City, St Paul's, with the river and a multitude of little boats, made a most beautiful sight as we crossed Westminster Bridge. The houses were not overhung by their cloud of smoke and they were spread out endlessly, yet the sun shone so brightly, with such a pure sight, that there was even something like the purity of one of Nature's own great spectacles'. As this entry suggests, the poem depends upon contrasts and commingling – between the civic scene at dawn, caught at an uncharacteristic moment of 'calm' (l. 11), and the beauty associated with the natural world bathed in the sun's 'first splendor' (l. 10). The poem does not just describe; its final exclamations record the impact of the sight on the poet's imagination, which conceives of the houses as 'asleep' (l. 13) and brings the dead metaphor of London as the heart of the country to startling life.

Text (including '1803' date) from *Poems, in Two Volumes 1807*.

Earth has not any thing to shew more fair:
Dull would he be of soul who could pass by
A sight so touching in its majesty:
This City now doth like a garment wear
The beauty of the morning; silent, bare, 5
Ships, towers, domes, theatres, and temples lie
Open unto the fields, and to the sky;
All bright and glittering in the smokeless air.
Never did sun more beautifully steep
In his first splendor valley, rock, or hill; 10
Ne'er saw I, never felt, a calm so deep!
The river glideth at his own sweet will:
Dear God! the very houses seem asleep;
And all that mighty heart is lying still!

8   *smokeless air* 'smokeless' because, as Dorothy puts it in her journal (31 July 1802), 'The houses were not overhung by their cloud of smoke'.
9   *steep* Bathe.
13   *Dear God!* Compare 'Great God!' in 'The world is too much with us', line 9.

Ode (from 1815 entitled 'Ode: Intimations of Immortality from Recollections of Early Childhood')

Often regarded as Wordsworth's finest shorter poem, 'Ode: Intimations of Immortality' was composed between March 1802 and March 1804. In the Fenwick Note to the poem, Wordsworth relates it to his childhood inability to 'admit the notion of death as a state applicable to my own being' and to his experience as a boy of an 'abyss of idealism' from which he would 'recall' himself by grasping at 'a wall or a tree'. In the same Note he observes that this early sense became in later life a matter for rejoicing, and he refers the reader to the lines about 'obstinate questionings' (l. 144). Wordsworth also alludes in the Note to the use he makes of the Platonic notion of 'a prior state of existence', remarking that he does not claim for it the status of truth, while pointing out that 'though the idea is not advanced in revelation, there is nothing there to contradict it, and the fall of man presents an analogy in its favour'. Essentially, he made the 'best use of [the idea] as I could as a poet'. The poem, true to its epigraph from Virgil, aims at a loftier tone than is attempted by most of the *Poems, in Two Volumes* and *Lyrical Ballads*, though it has evident affinities with 'Tintern Abbey' in its fascination with the interplay in life of 'loss' (l. 88) and 'recompence' (l. 89). Generically, the poem is a recognizable descendant of the Pindaric ode, associated with exalted flights of imagination and irregularity of stanzaic design, and it can be read as falling loosely into three parts corresponding to the traditional divisions of the ode (strophe, antistrophe, and epode). In the first part (ll. 1–57), the poet articulates his sense of loss for 'the glory and the dream' (l. 57), despite attempts not to grieve; in the second part (ll. 58–131), his personal sense of loss is placed in a larger context and explained as an experience that occurs in every life as we all move further away from our origins in pre-existent splendour; in the final section (ll. 132–206), Wordsworth accepts the fact of loss, argues that, because of memory, it is not absolute, and claims that time does not only erase, since it also makes us wiser as we reflect on suffering. Each section is itself made up of conflicts, qualifications, hesitations, and subtilizings, caught in the delicate web of Wordsworth's responsive syntax and poetic art. As in 'Tintern Abbey', the poem lives in and through its skilful and often affecting transitions that give the sense of a poet refusing ever to simplify his deepest feelings into any design. The poem mixes passages of great eloquence and complex metaphorical patterns with an affecting bareness of utterance. A particular stylistic feature to which our notes draw attention is the nuanced reworking of key words and their cognate forms, words such as 'birth', 'grief', 'sleep', 'thought', 'forgetting', 'take', 'glory', 'dream', 'thanks', 'strong', 'day', 'common', 'be'. So, 'The sunshine is a glorious birth' (l. 16), but this 'gloriousness' cannot refute the conviction, stated just two lines later, 'That there hath pass'd away a glory from the earth' (l. 18). The result is to make us aware of two ways of understanding what 'glory' might mean: one attentive to the beauty of the here and now, the other alert to a visionary 'glory' no longer apprehensible. We are reminded that while Wordsworth praises childhood, he must do so from an adult perspective; if the child communes with 'the eternal Silence' (l. 158), rather as, in 'The Idiot Boy', Johnny exists in a state which is the other side of language, the poet must convey his visionary intimations through words. See Helen Vendler's chapter 'Lionel Trilling and Wordsworth's Immortality Ode', in *The Music of What Happens: Poems, Poets, Critics* (Cambridge, MA: Harvard University Press, 1988), pp. 93–114, for acute analysis of what she calls the poem's 'powerfully plotted succession ... of "wounds" and "cures"' (p. 107). Vendler observes that the only passage in the poem which does not engage in its 'consciously self-echoing' (p. 110) procedures is that beginning 'But for those obstinate questionings' (ll. 144–50).

Text from *Poems, in Two Volumes 1807*.

Paulò majora canamus.

There was a time when meadow, grove, and stream,
The earth, and every common sight,
  To me did seem
  Apparell'd in celestial light,
The glory and the freshness of a dream. 5

Epigraph Paulo majora canamus 'Let us sing of somewhat higher things', Virgil, *Eclogue* 4. 1. From 1815, Wordsworth substituted the following lines (composed the day before he began work on the 'Ode') as the epigraph:

'The Child is Father to the Man; / And I could wish my days to be / Bound each to each by natural piety'.

1–9 *There was ... no more* The diction illustrates the 'bareness' mentioned in the Headnote, a bareness only

>   It is not now as it has been of yore;—
>   Turn wheresoe'er I may,
>   By night or day,
>   The things which I have seen I now can see no more.
>
>   The Rainbow comes and goes,   10
>   And lovely is the Rose,
>   The Moon doth with delight
>   Look round her when the heavens are bare;
>   Waters on a starry night
>   Are beautiful and fair;   15
>   The sunshine is a glorious birth;
>   But yet I know, where'er I go,
>   That there hath pass'd away a glory from the earth.
>
>   Now, while the Birds thus sing a joyous song,
>   And while the young Lambs bound   20
>   As to the tabor's sound,
>   To me alone there came a thought of grief:
>   A timely utterance gave that thought relief,
>   And I again am strong.
>   The Cataracts blow their trumpets from the steep,   25
>   No more shall grief of mine the season wrong;
>   I hear the Echoes through the mountains throng,
>   The Winds come to me from the fields of sleep,
>   And all the earth is gay,
>   Land and sea   30

broken by the fittingly lofty language of the fourth line. The movement and wording of these lines calls to mind lines 9 to 16 from Coleridge's 'The Mad Monk', a passage which begins, 'There was a time when earth, and sea, and skies, / The bright green vale and forest's dark recess, / When all things lay before mine eyes / In steady loveliness (ll. 9–12), and concludes, 'Then wherefore must I know that such a time has been!' (l. 16). More generally, the 'Ode' participates in a dialogue with Coleridge conducted in poems of 1802 concerning the nature of poetic inspiration and the workings of the imagination: if the 'Ode' replies to 'the Mad Monk', Coleridge's 'Dejection: An Ode' replies to the 'Ode', while Wordsworth's 'Resolution and Independence', in turn, responds to 'Dejection'.

2 *common* Always a complex word in Wordsworth: it can mean something shared by all; it can mean something merely ordinary, as in the 'light of common day' (l. 76).

3 *To me* Compare line 22, line 28, the variation in line 136, and the return to the phrase at the start of the penultimate line of the poem (l. 205). 'To me' reminds us that, while Wordsworth describes a 'common' predicament, it is one that has, for him, a virtually incommunicable uniqueness.

9 *The things . . . more* 'Things' claims that what the poet saw were realities; at the same time, it allows for the colloquial sense that he was 'seeing things' (that is, perceiving what from one perspective was only imaginary).

10–11 *The Rainbow . . . Rose* Wording and movement here seem purposefully numb.

12–13 *The Moon . . . bare* Only seems to recapture the earlier sense of all nature as alive and connected to the poet's feelings. Wordsworth catches himself attributing feeling to the natural world.

19 *Now, while* Moves into an immediate present in an effort to relegate the opening sadness to the past. Yet in line 22 Wordsworth slips back into the past tense ('To me alone there came a thought of grief'), as though recapturing his inability wholly to live and delight in the beauty and joy of the present.

21 *tabor's sound* The sound of a small drum.

22 *a thought of grief* Wordsworth does not quite say he experienced 'grief': more, that he experienced a 'thought of grief'. Though he seeks to banish such a thought, it is arguable that faintly adumbrated here are the final complexly consoling 'Thoughts' of the poem's last line.

23 *A timely utterance* Has been interpreted as 'Resolution and Independence' but the composition dates will not support this reading ('Resolution and Independence' was written two months after the opening stanzas of the 'Ode'); the 'timely utterance' is better thought of as the 'Ode' itself.

28 *The Winds . . . sleep* An enigmatic, haunting line: perhaps associates 'Winds' with 'inspiration' and 'sleep' with the sources of 'dream' (see l. 5). It anticipates the assertion at line 58, 'Our birth is but a sleep and a forgetting'. Indeed, the fact that the winds 'come' to the poet foreshadows the claim that the 'Soul' (l. 59) 'Cometh from afar' (l. 61).

        Give themselves up to jollity,
           And with the heart of May
      Doth every Beast keep holiday,
           Thou Child of Joy,
Shout round me, let me hear thy shouts, thou happy Shepherd Boy!   35

Ye blessed Creatures, I have heard the call
    Ye to each other make; I see
The heavens laugh with you in your jubilee;
    My heart is at your festival,
      My head hath its coronal,   40
The fullness of your bliss, I feel—I feel it all.
    Oh evil day! if I were sullen
      While the Earth herself is adorning,
        This sweet May-morning,
      And the Children are pulling,   45
        On every side,
In a thousand vallies far and wide,
  Fresh flowers; while the sun shines warm,
And the Babe leaps up on his mother's arm:—
    I hear, I hear, with joy I hear!   50
  —But there's a Tree, of many one,
A single Field which I have look'd upon,
Both of them speak of something that is gone:
    The Pansy at my feet
    Doth the same tale repeat: 55
Whither is fled the visionary gleam?
Where is it now, the glory and the dream?

Our birth is but a sleep and a forgetting:
The Soul that rises with us, our life's Star,
    Hath had elsewhere its setting,   60
      And cometh from afar:
  Not in entire forgetfulness,
  And not in utter nakedness,
But trailing clouds of glory do we come
    From God, who is our home: 65

---

35 *Shout . . . Shepherd Boy!* The imperative suggests the poet's need for proof of 'happiness'. Again, in this and ensuing lines Wordsworth writes dramatically, bringing out the poet's attempt to silence his unspoken thoughts.

50 *I hear . . . with joy I hear!* The triple repetition conveys Wordsworth's desperation to assert that he does still experience 'joy'. The verb 'hear' becomes central to the poem's development; as Wordsworth posits for the child a deeper experience than the merely sensory he depicts him 'as deaf and silent' (l. 112), as though indifferent to the sounds of this world. When he imagines an adult condition briefly vouchsafed a vision of what had seemed to be lost he says that we can 'hear the mighty waters rolling evermore' (l. 170).

51–3 *But . . . gone* The triple rhyme points up the sudden turn from attempted joy to a renewed sense of loss. Wordsworth's emphasis is on singleness, the irreducible fact of particular loss.

54 *The Pansy* Plays with the French word 'pensée' from which the 'pansy' derives its name; the French word means 'thought', thus connecting with the poem's several uses of the word 'thought'.

56–7 *Whither . . . dream?* The two questions do not merely repeat one another; the second by means of the crucial word 'now' (repeated from l. 9 but minimally more hopeful here), allows for a small amount of hope, that 'the glory and the dream' may exist elsewhere, thus supplying the germ of the following passage.

58 *Our birth . . . forgetting* The answer to the questions just preceding this line begins here; 'but' meaning 'only' or 'merely' advises us that there is more to the origins of our existence than physical 'birth'.

59–61 *our life's Star . . . afar* This image makes the soul a rising star which sets elsewhere (in a pre-existent life), and which will fade 'into the light of common day' (l. 76) as life goes on.

64 *clouds of glory* Links with and helps to explain by giving an enriched meaning to the previous mentions of 'glory' (ll. 5, 18, 57).

Heaven lies about us in our infancy!
Shades of the prison-house begin to close
      Upon the growing Boy,
But He beholds the light, and whence it flows,
      He sees it in his joy;   70
The Youth, who daily farther from the East
    Must travel, still is Nature's Priest,
        And by the vision splendid
        Is on his way attended;
At length the Man perceives it die away,   75
And fade into the light of common day.

Earth fills her lap with pleasures of her own;
Yearnings she hath in her own natural kind,
And, even with something of a Mother's mind,
      And no unworthy aim,   80
The homely Nurse doth all she can
To make her Foster-child, her Inmate Man,
      Forget the glories he hath known,
And that imperial palace whence he came.

Behold the Child among his new-born blisses,   85
A four year's Darling of a pigmy size!
See, where mid work of his own hand he lies,
Fretted by sallies of his Mother's kisses,
With light upon him from his Father's eyes!
See, at his feet, some little plan or chart,   90
Some fragment from his dream of human life,
Shap'd by himself with newly-learned art;
      A wedding or a festival,
      A mourning or a funeral;
        And this hath now his heart,   95
And unto this he frames his song:
        Then will he fit his tongue
To dialogues of business, love, or strife;
        But it will not be long
        Ere this be thrown aside,   100
        And with new joy and pride
The little Actor cons another part,
Filling from time to time his 'humorous stage'
With all the Persons, down to palsied Age,
That Life brings with her in her Equipage;   105

69–70 *But He . . . joy* The verbs 'beholds' and 'sees' suggest a contemplative capacity for wonder, and the persistence of visionary seeing in childhood. By contrast, there is an implied deadening of vision and emergence of analytical awareness in the later verb 'perceives' (l. 75).

77 *Earth* It is noteworthy that Wordsworth does not speak of 'Nature' here; it is as though he is reluctant to concede that nature may have betrayed the heart that loved her.

80 *no unworthy aim* The double negative is expressive here: Earth does her best for man, but cannot match the 'glories he hath known' (l. 83).

85–107 *Behold . . . imitation* The tone is affectionate but ironic, even tragic, as the writing charts the process of acculturation that takes place in childhood. The child is a 'little Actor' (l. 102) preparing for life by rehearsing its various stages.

86 *four year's* From 1815 this reads 'six year's'.

87 *See* What is seen is the growing loss of visionary sight, a loss unknowingly condoned and perhaps accelerated by the 'light' (l. 89) of paternal love that loses sight of the 'clouds of glory' (l. 64) that, mediated by 'obstinate questionings' (l. 144), should be the 'master light of all our seeing' (l. 155).

103 *'humorous stage'* Wordsworth quotes from Samuel Daniel's dedicatory sonnet to his sequence *Musophilus*, 'To the Right Worthy and Judicious Favourer of Virtue, Mr Fulke Grevill', ll. 1–2: 'I do not here upon this hum'rous stage / Bring my transformed verse'.

> As if his whole vocation
> Were endless imitation.
>
> Thou, whose exterior semblance doth belie
>   Thy Soul's immensity;
> Thou best Philosopher, who yet dost keep   110
> Thy heritage, thou Eye among the blind,
> That, deaf and silent, read'st the eternal deep,
> Haunted for ever by the eternal mind,—
>   Mighty Prophet! Seer blest!
>   On whom those truths do rest,   115
> Which we are toiling all our lives to find;
> Thou, over whom thy Immortality
> Broods like the Day, a Master o'er a Slave,
> A Presence which is not to be put by;
>   To whom the grave   120
> Is but a lonely bed without the sense or sight
>   Of day or the warm light,
> A place of thought where we in waiting lie;
> Thou little Child, yet glorious in the might
> Of untam'd pleasures, on thy Being's height,   125
> Why with such earnest pains dost thou provoke
> The Years to bring the inevitable yoke,
> Thus blindly with thy blessedness at strife?
> Full soon thy Soul shall have her earthly freight,
> And custom lie upon thee with a weight,   130
> Heavy as frost, and deep almost as life!
>
>   O joy! that in our embers
>   Is something that doth live,
>   That nature yet remembers
>   What was so fugitive!   135
> The thought of our past years in me doth breed
> Perpetual benedictions: not indeed
> For that which is most worthy to be blest;
> Delight and liberty, the simple creed
> Of Childhood, whether fluttering or at rest,   140
> With new-born hope for ever in his breast:—

108 *Thou* Wordsworth now addresses the child directly, drawing attention to the mysterious potential of childhood (because the child is closer to 'the eternal mind', l. 113) and lamenting its impulse to subject itself to 'the inevitable yoke' (l. 127).

112 *eternal deep* Brings in the image of eternity as a sea, which will be developed later in the poem at lines 164–70.

118 *Broods . . . Day* This 'Day' is distinguished from the 'common day' (l. 76).

120–3 *To whom . . . lie* Deleted after 1815 in response to Coleridge's criticism in *Biographia Literaria* (1817), ch. XXII, of the lines as a 'frightful notion'.

127 *the inevitable yoke* Compare Gray, 'Elegy Written in a Country Churchyard', line 35: 'the inevitable hour' (quoted from *the Poems of Gray, Collins, and Goldsmith*, ed. Roger Lonsdale (London: Longmans, 1969). Gray refers to death, Wordsworth to the 'yoke' of custom and habit.

132–3 *O joy . . . live* This affecting transition, singled out for praise by Gerard Manley Hopkins, marks the start of the poem's movement towards resolution. Yet the 'joy' is located in a deliberately minimal source, the fact that in our 'embers' (a word that implies the dying of a fire) is '*something* that doth live' (emphasis added).

134 *nature yet remembers* The word 'nature' must mean primarily our 'human nature', but it almost seems to suggest that the physical world itself to which, for Wordsworth, we have such strong ties, retains residues of memory. 'Yet' is a small word that does a great deal of work in the poem (see ll. 154, 192 and 198 for later repetitions); it implies that something is 'still' operative.

139–40 *the simple . . . Childhood* Wordsworth makes clear that the value of childhood lies in something other than its simplicity.

        Not for these I raise
      The song of thanks and praise;
    But for those obstinate questionings
      Of sense and outward things,   145
      Fallings from us, vanishings;
      Blank misgivings of a Creature
Moving about in worlds not realiz'd,
High instincts, before which our mortal Nature
Did tremble like a guilty Thing surpriz'd: 150
      But for those first affections,
      Those shadowy recollections,
        Which, be they what they may,
Are yet the fountain light of all our day,
Are yet a master light of all our seeing;   155
      Uphold us, cherish us, and make
Our noisy years seem moments in the being
Of the eternal Silence: truths that wake,
      To perish never;
Which neither listlessness, nor mad endeavour,   160
    Nor Man nor Boy,
Nor all that is at enmity with joy,
Can utterly abolish or destroy!
Hence, in a season of calm weather,
      Though inland far we be,   165
Our Souls have sight of that immortal sea
      Which brought us hither,
      Can in a moment travel thither,
And see the Children sport upon the shore,
And hear the mighty waters rolling evermore.   170

Then, sing ye Birds, sing, sing a joyous song!
      And let the young Lambs bound
      As to the tabor's sound!
We in thought will join your throng,
      Ye that pipe and ye that play,   175
      Ye that through your hearts to day
      Feel the gladness of the May!
What though the radiance which was once so bright
Be now for ever taken from my sight,

144–5 *obstinate . . . things* Questionings that refused to accept the view that the evidence of the senses was final, or that external reality was solid and sure. The rhyme of 'questionings' and 'things' points up a troubled relationship.

146–53 *Fallings . . . may* The appositional phrasing recaptures the child's sense of 'Blank misgivings', while 'be they what they may' concedes the impossibility of defining the poet's early experiences.

150 *like . . . surpriz'd* The phrase recalls Horatio's account of the ghost in *Hamlet*, I. i. 129–30: 'And then it started like a guilty thing / Upon a fearful summons'.

158 *eternal Silence* Recalls the 'eternal deep' (l. 112) and 'eternal mind' (l. 113).

163 *utterly* The word, again, implies a minimal consolation. It suggests that forces inimical to joy come very close to abolishing and destroying it.

169–70 *see . . . hear* The two verbs unite the senses of sight and hearing, each lent a visionary dimension by Wordsworth's metaphor of the 'immortal sea' (l. 166).

178–83 *What though . . . behind* The language balances between awareness of loss and determination to find value in what 'remains behind'. As elsewhere in the poem, Wordsworth's syntax is delicately attuned to complicated feelings. 'What though . . .', which governs the subordinate clause appears to expect the answer 'it does not finally matter', but when the 'What' drops out as the 'though' is repeated, the verse is suddenly if momentarily given over to complete awareness of loss (in ll. 180–1).

>   Though nothing can bring back the hour   180
>   Of splendour in the grass, of glory in the flower;
>   We will grieve not, rather find
>   Strength in what remains behind,
>   In the primal sympathy
>   Which having been must ever be,   185
>   In the soothing thoughts that spring
>   Out of human suffering,
>   In the faith that looks through death,
>   In years that bring the philosophic mind.
>
>   And oh ye Fountains, Meadows, Hills, and Groves,   190
>   Think not of any severing of our loves!
>   Yet in my heart of hearts I feel your might;
>   I only have relinquish'd one delight
>   To live beneath your more habitual sway.
>   I love the Brooks which down their channels fret,   195
>   Even more than when I tripp'd lightly as they;
>   The innocent brightness of a new-born Day
>   Is lovely yet;
>   The Clouds that gather round the setting sun
>   Do take a sober colouring from an eye   200
>   That hath kept watch o'er man's mortality;
>   Another race hath been, and other palms are won.
>   Thanks to the human heart by which we live,
>   Thanks to its tenderness, its joys, and fears,
>   To me the meanest flower that blows can give   205
>   Thoughts that do often lie too deep for tears.

182 *We will grieve not* The 'will', there, is a form of the verb 'to will'; it is not merely a form of the future tense; the line is steeling itself against the impulse to 'grieve'.

183 *Strength* Revises and deepens the earlier assertion, 'And I again am strong' (l. 24); the poem itself has made us conscious of what it is to be 'strong'.

185 *ever* Wordsworth's assertion of the enduring nature of the 'primal sympathy' (l. 184) is set against his admission that 'radiance' (l. 178) is 'now for ever taken from my sight' (l. 179). The two uses of 'ever' map the poles of loss and recovery between which the poem moves.

190-1 *And oh ... loves!* Despite his sense that meaning is given to life by a power beyond it, Wordsworth seeks to reassure the natural world of his continued love for it.

198 *Is lovely yet* The shortened line-length gives the statement a quiet pathos.

200 *take* Another example of how Wordsworth proceeds in this poem by investing individual words with a weight of strong feeling. At line 179 he speaks of radiance having been for ever 'taken from my sight'. Here that very awareness of loss allows 'The Clouds' (l. 199) to 'take a sober colouring' (l. 200). What is 'taken away' is thus 'taken back', in accord with the poem's movement towards recompense for loss.

201 *kept watch* The two stressed syllables support the meaning.

202 *Another ... won* Wordsworth has left behind delight in nature for a hard-won victory that has involved reflection on 'man's mortality' (l. 201). There is probably an allusion to I Corinthians 9: 24: 'Know ye not that they which run in a race run all, but one receiveth the prize? So run, that ye may obtain'.

203-6 *Thanks ... tears* At the close Wordsworth reveals that the deepest note in his often sorrowing 'song of thanks and praise' (l. 143) is less his belief in 'the faith that looks through death' (l. 188), than his commitment to 'the human heart by which we live'. The writing moves between the general ('the human heart by which we live') and the highly subjective ('To me'); 'often' in the final line prevents the wording from seeming glib or sentimental. In line 205, 'the meanest flower' recalls Gray's uncompleted 'Ode on the Pleasure Arising from Vicissitude', 'The meanest flowret of the vale' (l. 45). Gray's poem is highly relevant to Wordsworth's; its theme of 'pleasure' derived from 'vicissitude' provides a point of comparison with Wordsworth's 'joy' over the fact 'that in our embers / Is something that doth live' (ll. 132-3). It might be said that Wordsworth's conclusion reworks this consolatory couplet in Gray's poem: 'Behind the steps that Misery treads, / Approaching Comfort view' (ll. 35-6).

206 *too deep for tears* This depth opposes the oppressive heaviness of 'custom' (l. 130) that lies 'deep almost as life' (l. 131).

The Solitary Reaper

The poem, published in *Poems in Two Volumes* (1807), was, according to Wordsworth's note, 'suggested by a beautiful sentence in a MS tour of Scotland written by a Friend, the last line being taken from it *verbatim*' (*1807*, p. 162). The sentence in question was printed in Thomas Wilkinson's *Tours to the British Mountains* (1824): 'Passed a female who was reaping alone: she sung in Erse as she bended over her sickle; the sweetest human voice I ever heard: her strains were tenderly melancholy, and felt delicious, long after they were heard no more' (p. 24). 'Erse' means 'Highland Gaelic'. As Geoffrey Hartman suggested (in *Wordsworth's Poetry, 1787–1814* (Cambridge, MA: Harvard University Press, 1971), the poem owes something to the tradition of the epitaph in which the traveller is told to 'Stop here', though in 'The Solitary Reaper' the command passes into a less abrupt alternative, 'or gently pass' (l. 4). The poem's response to the reaper's singing allows Wordsworth to meditate implicitly on the power of lyric song, a power that resides in something beyond 'theme' (l. 25). At the end, with its unexpected movement into the past tense ('the Maiden sang', l. 25), it turns out, too, to be a poem about the role played by memory in preserving and internalizing experience. The stanza form permits a lyrical musical flow, but allows, too, for surprise; the fourth line is shorter by a foot than the surrounding octosyllabic lines; the rhymes resolve into two couplets in the second half of the stanza after an *abcb* scheme in the first four lines of stanzas one and four, and an *abab* scheme in the first four lines of stanzas two and three. The reaper, 'single in the field' (l. 1), is another of Wordsworth's solitary figures. This solitary, however, is associated with connections, harmony and doubling (evident in verbal patterns such as 'Reaping and singing' (l. 3) or 'cuts, and binds' (l. 5), and in the fact that the solitary reaper is celebrated by the solitary poet.

Text from *Poems, in Two Volumes 1807*.

Behold her, single in the field,
Yon solitary Highland Lass!
Reaping and singing by herself;
Stop here, or gently pass!
Alone she cuts, and binds the grain,   5
And sings a melancholy strain;
O listen! for the Vale profound
Is overflowing with the sound.

No Nightingale did ever chaunt
So sweetly to reposing bands   10
Of Travellers in some shady haunt,
Among Arabian Sands:
No sweeter voice was ever heard
In spring-time from the Cuckoo-bird,
Breaking the silence of the seas   15
Among the farthest Hebrides.

Will no one tell me what she sings?
Perhaps the plaintive numbers flow
For old, unhappy, far-off things,
And battles long ago: 20
Or is it some more humble lay,
Familiar matter of today?
Some natural sorrow, loss, or pain,
That has been, and may be again!

1–3 *Behold . . . herself* The lines stress the utter aloneness of the reaper.
7–8 *Oh listen! . . . sound* The enjambment helps to mimic the 'overflowing' of the sound.
13–16 *No sweeter . . . Hebrides* The run-on lines tug the reader with them as they move from the familiar (the cuckoo) to the mysterious and strange ('the farthest Hebrides').
17 *Will . . . sings?* The poet does not know the subject of the reaper's song, and speculates about it for the remainder of the stanza.

Whate'er the theme, the Maiden sang 25
As if her song could have no ending;
I saw her singing at her work,
And o'er the sickle bending;
I listen'd till I had my fill:
And, as I mounted up the hill, 30
The music in my heart I bore,
Long after it was heard no more.

26, 28 *ending . . . bending* The feminine rhymes (along with 'singing', l. 27) create an effect of ongoing song.

29 *till . . . fill* Revised from 1820 to 'motionless and still'.

Elegiac Stanzas, Suggested by a Picture of Peele Castle in a Storm, Painted by Sir George Beaumont

'Elegaic Stanzas', first published in *Poems in Two Volumes* (1807), is among the Romantic poems that take as their subject ideas and feelings 'suggested' by a work of art in another medium (Keats's 'Ode on a Grecian Urn' [p. 458] is another example): this time, a picture of Peele Castle in a storm (now hanging in the Wordsworth Museum, Grasmere), by Sir George Beaumont (1753–1827), a friend and patron of Wordsworth and Coleridge. Peele (or Piel) Castle is in northern Lancashire, opposite Rampside, where Wordsworth spent a summer in 1794. Beaumont's painting was shown at the Royal Academy, 2 May 1806, when Wordsworth may have seen it. The poem responds to the death of the poet's brother John (1773–1805), who died in the sinking on 25 February 1805 of the *Earl of Abergavenny*, of which he was Captain. Central to this response is Wordsworth's new feelings about the role of poetry and his own poetic imagination. If he grieves for John, he grieves as well for a loss of 'power' (see l. 35). Wordsworth approaches his subject indirectly, describing the apparent tranquillity of the natural scene surrounding Peele Castle when he visited it in 1794, and the kind of calm, contemplative picture he would have then produced, 'if mine had been the Painter's hand' (l. 13). This picture would have depicted a scene 'of lasting ease, / Elysian quiet, without toil or strife' (ll. 25–6). It is a testimony to the hold such a picture has over Wordsworth's imagination that his evocation of it takes up a considerable part of the poem; the poem requires us to reinhabit what in 1807 Wordsworth calls 'the fond delusion of my heart' (l. 29). Now, as result of the 'deep distress' (l. 36) resulting from John's death he views nature in a changed light, and welcomes a painting such as Beaumont's which shows nature at its most unruly; such 'sights of what is to be borne' (l. 58) bring out in the spectator a corresponding 'fortitude' (l. 57). Echoing the Book of Common Prayer's 'Order for the Burial of the Dead' which says that we should 'not be sorry, as men without hope, for them that sleep in him [that is, God]', Wordsworth finishes with a consoling line that brings out how easy it would be to live 'without hope'. The poem is written in quatrains made up of iambic pentameters rhyming *abab*. Wordsworth's art shows in his manipulation of pace as he enters fully though always conditionally into the description of his 'fond delusion', then switches, regretfully but decisively, into speaking of the 'new controul' to which he has 'submitted' (l. 34); the pentameters serve as a perfect medium for Wordsworth's dallying with illusion and his subsequent rejection of 'the Heart that lives alone' (l. 53). The poem has been read as bidding farewell to the unmediated faith in nature so often proclaimed in Wordsworth's previous poetry. The poem's verbal qualifyings and doublings (e.g. 'A faith, a trust', l. 32, or 'Farewell, farewell', l. 53) suggest a continual process of vacillation and self-steeling.

Text from *Poems, in Two Volumes 1807*.

I was thy Neighbour once, thou rugged Pile!
Four summer weeks I dwelt in sight of thee:
I saw thee every day; and all the while
Thy Form was sleeping on a glassy sea.

1 *rugged Pile* Piel Castle; 'pile' is a 'lofty mass of buildings; large building'.

So pure the sky, so quiet was the air!
So like, so very like, was day to day!
Whene'er I look'd, thy Image still was there;
It trembled, but it never pass'd away.

How perfect was the calm! it seem'd no sleep;
No mood, which season takes away, or brings:
I could have fancied that the mighty Deep
Was even the gentlest of all gentle Things.

Ah! then, if mine had been the Painter's hand,
To express what then I saw; and add the gleam,
The light that never was, on sea or land,
The consecration, and the Poet's dream;

I would have planted thee, thou hoary Pile!
Amid a world how different from this!
Beside a sea that could not cease to smile;
On tranquil land, beneath a sky of bliss:

Thou shouldst have seem'd a treasure-house, a mine
Of peaceful years; a chronicle of heaven:—
Of all the sunbeams that did ever shine
The very sweetest had to thee been given.

A Picture had it been of lasting ease,
Elysian quiet, without toil or strife;
No motion but the moving tide, a breeze,
Or merely silent Nature's breathing life.

Such, in the fond delusion of my heart,
Such Picture would I at that time have made:
And seen the soul of truth in every part;
A faith, a trust, that could not be betray'd.

So once it would have been,—'tis so no more;
I have submitted to a new controul:
A power is gone, which nothing can restore;
A deep distress hath humaniz'd my Soul.

Not for a moment could I now behold
A smiling sea and be what I have been:
The feeling of my loss will ne'er be old;
This, which I know, I speak with mind serene.

5–8 *So pure ... passed away* Wordsworth's syntax (two exclamations, each containing incremental phrases, followed by a qualified sentence) holds up the communication of sense in an eloquent way; the reader is drawn into the tranquillity of the scene.
9 *seem'd* An important word that suggests the potentially deceptive nature of the scene; repeated at line 21.
15–16 *The light ... the Poet's dream* Among the most memorable accounts in Romantic poetry of the poetic imagination, the wording here swings between suggesting the imagination's creativity and its illusoriness.
17 *hoary* Venerable.

28 *Or ... life* In the context of the poem, even this possibility, dear to Wordsworth's heart, of nature enjoying a 'breathing life' may be a 'delusion' (l. 29).
29 *delusion* Altered to 'illusion' in Wordsworth's 1815 *Poems* and later.
32 *A faith ... betray'd* Compare and contrast with 'Tintern Abbey', ll. 123–4: 'Knowing that Nature never did betray / The heart that loved her'.
35 *A power ... restore* Wordsworth's phrasing is unspecific; but context suggests an imaginative 'power' dependent on the conviction that nature is benign.
36 *A deep distress* 'distress' might mean John's death or Wordsworth's response to it, or both; 'humaniz'd' means 'made human' or 'given human character to'.

Then, Beaumont, Friend! who would have been the Friend,
If he had lived, of Him whom I deplore,
This Work of thine I blame not, but commend;
This sea in anger, and that dismal shore.

Oh 'tis a passionate Work!—yet wise and well; 45
Well chosen is the spirit that is here;
That Hulk which labours in the deadly swell,
This rueful sky, this pageantry of fear!

And this huge Castle, standing here sublime,
I love to see the look with which it braves, 50
Cased in the unfeeling armour of old time,
The light'ning, the fierce wind, and trampling waves.

Farewell, farewell the Heart that lives alone,
Hous'd in a dream, at distance from the Kind!
Such happiness, wherever it be known, 55
Is to be pitied; for 'tis surely blind.

But welcome fortitude, and patient chear,
And frequent sights of what is to be borne!
Such sights, or worse, as are before me here.—
Not without hope we suffer and we mourn. 60

---

41 *would have been* Even after Wordsworth has abandoned one form of conditionality (the picture he would have painted), he imagines another.

49 *sublime* The castle is depicted as withstanding the wrath of nature, and is thus 'sublime'.

51 *Cased . . . time* Sandwiched between the verb 'braves,' (l. 50) and its objects (l. 52), the line stresses the Castle's 'bravery' and the elemental forces with which it has to contend. The Castle serves as an emblem of stoical courage, yet 'unfeeling' brings out its difference from human beings whose 'fortitude' (l. 57) shows in the way they deal with 'feeling'.

54 *the Kind* Humanity.

Samuel Taylor Coleridge (1772–1834)

Among the voluminous mass of Coleridge's various writings, ranging from polemical essays to abstruse theological and philosophical meditations, his poems comprise, in quantitative terms, only a small body of work. In qualitative terms, however, they are among the great achievements of first-generation Romantic poetry. It would over-simplify to regard them as examples of what Leigh Hunt calls 'pure poetry'.[1] But you can see what Hunt means when you examine lines like these from 'Kubla Khan':

> A damsel with a dulcimer
> In a vision once I saw:
> It was an Abyssinian maid,
> And on her dulcimer she played,
> Singing of Mount Abora.
>
> (ll. 37–41)

Hunt was struck by the poem's 'music', 'so varied . . . , and yet leaving on the ear so unbroken and single an effect'.[2] The compliment is justified; but the musicality of the lines serves structural purposes. That 'damsel' emerges as a counterpoint to the more evidently sexual 'woman wailing for her demon lover' in previous lines. Her song of Mount Abora takes the poem into poignant territory: the longing for some prelapsarian innocence associated with Eden, a longing that is clearer in the poem's manuscript, where Coleridge wrote 'Amara' for 'Abora'; 'Amara' appears in Milton's *Paradise Lost* as 'by some supposed / True Paradise under the Ethiop line' (4. 281–2), and, as Duncan Wu notes, it also appears in *Purchas his Pilgrimage* 'as the navel of the Ethiopian body, and centre of their empire'.[3] It is clear, then, that there is a relationship between Coleridge's religious and philosophical thinking, here specifically ideas to do with the Fall, and his poetic imaginings. To read and think about any of his poems is to enter an interpretative labyrinth.

Coleridge was born at Ottery St Mary in Devon, the last child in a family of 10. His father died in 1781 when he was only eight. Soon after, he was admitted to the school Christ's Hospital in London, where he met Charles Lamb and was taught by James Boyer, of whom he has left a vivid account in the first chapter of *Biographia Literaria*. More intimate details of his childhood are given in a series of remarkable autobiographical letters to his friend Thomas Poole. In one of these he speaks of his very early reading of such works as 'the Arabian Nights' entertainments', and says that 'before I was eight years old, I was a character'.[4] A 'character', in the sense of a deeply and richly idiosyncratic person, he was to remain throughout his life. In 1791, just two years after the Fall of the Bastille, he entered Jesus College, Cambridge. Two years later, worried about debts, he enlisted in a company of dragoons as Silas Tomkyn Comberbache. In 1794 he returned to Cambridge, though he would leave without taking a degree after meeting Robert Southey, with whom he planned to establish a Utopian or 'Pantisocratic' community in America. The scheme fell through, though not before Coleridge had contracted what would be an unhappy marriage with Sara Fricker (Southey married her sister, Edith). Throughout the 1790s Coleridge's radical sympathies are evident in his various prose writings and lectures. Much controversy has raged over the question of whether Coleridge, in later life, renounced his youthful siding with causes of reform, but two consistent strains throughout his career are his longing to unite heart and head, and his conviction of the need for a religious solution to the contradictions of existence.

Certainly when Coleridge met Wordsworth he described him as a 'semi-atheist', and he quickly seems to have transmitted to Wordsworth his own quasi-pantheist belief in the 'One Life'. Most famously celebrated in lines added to 'The Eolian Harp' in an errata slip for his collection of poems *Sibylline Leaves* (1817), this belief is more intuition than conviction and is felt by Coleridge to be at odds with orthodox Christian dogma. The major product of the relationship with Wordsworth, which began in 1795 and was at its memorable height in 1797–8, was their shared collection *Lyrical Ballads*. In *Biographia Literaria*'s

---

1 'What Is Poetry?', *Imagination and Fancy* (London: Smith, Elder & Co, 1891), p. 250.
2 Ibid., p. 251.
3 Duncan Wu (ed.), *Romanticism: An Anthology* (3rd edn., Oxford: Blackwell, 2006), p. 622.
4 *Selected Letters*, ed. H. J. Jackson (Oxford: Oxford University Press, 1988), p. 59.

retrospective account, Coleridge saw his 'endeavours' as 'directed to persons and characters supernatural, or at least romantic; yet so as to transfer from our inward nature a human interest and a semblance of truth sufficient to procure for these shadows of imagination that willing suspension of disbelief for the moment, which constitutes poetic faith'.[5] The description fits 'The Rime of the Ancient Mariner', which remains, through its various incarnations, a poem that displays Coleridge's metrical ingenuity; capacity to create haunting images; knowledge of guilt, aloneness, and existential terror; and strong desire for community. The Mariner's slaying of the albatross permits Coleridge to explore all that opposed his optimistic hopes. In the two other 'supernatural poems' – 'Christabel' and 'Kubla Khan' – Coleridge created enigmatic masterpieces that resist yet prompt the interpretative intelligence. Neither poem was published until 1816, when both appeared with 'The Pains of Sleep'. All three poems are concerned with evil and suffering. It would over-simplify to say that Coleridge's career as a great poet ends with 'Dejection: An Ode' – much important work, including, and perhaps especially, revision remained to be done – but 'Dejection' gives us Coleridge at his most affecting: the elegist of his own lost inspiration. 'Dejection', which began life as a 'Letter' to Sara Hutchinson, is the last and pos-sibly greatest of the conversation poems written by Coleridge, a form which he can be said, following the example of Cowper, to have patented. Marked, above all, by its preoccupation with relationship (and, therefore, isolation), the conversation poem, in Coleridge's hands, is a form of great tonal and emotional sensitivity, able to modulate from the low-key to the epiphanic, to capture the workings of consciousness while remaining alert to external reality. The major examples produced by Coleridge are 'The Eolian Harp', 'This Lime-Tree Bower My Prison', and, above all, 'Frost at Midnight'.

Coleridge's career was dogged by personal difficulties. His marriage effectively broke down after he fell in love with Sara Hutchinson, Wordsworth's sister-in-law, a relationship that was dogged by unhappiness and distress. His opium habit caused him endless problems, and he began to doubt his ability to write poetry. His close but difficult relationship with Wordsworth underwent a major crisis in 1810, when adverse remarks supposedly made about him by Wordsworth were passed on by a mutual friend, Basil Montagu. Despite Wordsworth's dignified refutations and a patched-up reconciliation, the relationship between the two authors of *Lyrical Ballads* would never recover its former closeness. Coleridge, anyway, had for a while been critical of, or had wished to subtilize, the assumptions underpinning Wordsworth's commitment in the Preface to *Lyrical Ballads* to the 'language really spoken by men'. By contrast, Coleridge emerges in his poetry and criticism (especially *Biographia Literaria*) as a champion of the Imagination, conceived of as the creative power to bestow life and meaning on a universe that would otherwise be dead and spiritless. So, too, he claimed, was Wordsworth at his most quintessential. Coleridge is wryly aware, however, that what may look like creative triumph may, from a different perspective, seem to be projective delusion, a concern of 'Constancy to an Ideal Object'. It is ironic that a poet who longed to synthesize and harmonize, who persuaded himself and Wordsworth that the latter's true vocation was that of the first philosopher-poet (hence the tragic-comic failure by Wordsworth to write *The Recluse*), should be one whom we value not only for his visions of unity, but also for his readiness to articulate obstacles in the way of harmony and synthesis.

Texts are based on those in the 1834 edition of Coleridge's *Poetical Works*.

Further Reading

Primary Texts

Lyrical Ballads (1798); see the facsimile, intro. Jonathan Wordsworth (Oxford: Woodstock, 1990).

Sibylline Leaves (1817); see the facsimile, intro. Jonathan Wordsworth (Oxford: Woodstock, 1990).

Poetical Works (1834).

Coleridge: Poetical Works, ed. Ernest Hartley Coleridge (London: Oxford University Press, 1969).

Poems, ed. John Beer, new edn (London: Dent, 1993).

The Complete Poems, ed. William Keach (London: Penguin, 1997).

The Collected Works of Samuel Taylor Coleridge (Princeton, NJ: Princeton University Press/London: Routledge).

Collected Letters of Samuel Taylor Coleridge, ed. Earl Leslie Griggs, 6 vols (Oxford: Clarendon Press, 1956–1971). [hereafter *CL*]

Coleridge's Notebooks: A Selection, ed. Seamus Perry (Oxford: Oxford University Press, 2002).

Biographia Literaria, ed. W. Jackson Bate and James Engell (Princeton, NJ: Princeton University Press, 1983) [hereafter *BL*]

---

5 *Biographia Literaria*, vol. 2, p. 6.

Secondary Texts

John Beer, *Coleridge the Visionary* (London: Chatto and Windus, 1959).
John Beer, *Coleridge's Poetic Intelligence* (London: Macmillan, 1977).
Paul Hamilton, *Coleridge's Poetics* (Oxford: Blackwell, 1983).
Anthony John Harding, *Coleridge and the Idea of Love* (Cambridge, UK: Cambridge University Press, 1974).
Richard Holmes, *Coleridge: Early Visions* (London: Hodder and Stoughton, 1982).
Richard Holmes, *Coleridge: Darker Reflections* (London: Harper Collins, 1998).
Lucy Newlyn (ed.), *The Cambridge Companion to Coleridge* (Cambridge, UK: Cambridge University Press, 2002).
Seamus Perry, *Coleridge and the Uses of Division* (Oxford: Clarendon, 1999).
Nicholas Roe (ed.), *Samuel Taylor Coleridge and the Sciences of Life* (Oxford: Clarendon, 2001).
Kathleen Wheeler, *The Creative Mind in Coleridge's Poetry* (London: Heinemann, 1981).

The Eolian Harp. Composed at Clevedon, Somersetshire

'The Eolian Harp' was first published in 1796 as 'Effusion XXXV', with a subtitle informing us that the poem was composed on 'August 20th 1795' (before, that is, Coleridge married Sara Fricker on 4 October 1795). Subsequently the poem went through a series of revisions, the implications of which are discussed by Jack Stillinger in *Coleridge and Textual Instability* (Oxford University Press, 1994). The text used here is based on the final form it reached in Coleridge's lifetime (1834). In 'The Eolian Harp' Coleridge devised a new kind of poem, usually referred to as 'the conversation poem', in which the poet, drawing on the example of Cowper's 'divine chit-chat' in *The Task*, employs an easy, familiar style that is capable of modulating into passages of emotional and philosophical intensity. Coleridge's conversation poems seek to establish a relationship with an addressee and affirm the possibility of connection with a force beyond the self. Ultimately, they strive towards a vision of existence as a related, harmonious or unified whole, a desired wholeness mirrored formally by the circularity of the poetry's movement. The poetry often ends where it started, yet with a new sense of possibilities and meanings. The poems have been mined in recent years for their deconstructive impulses, but, as with many of the Romantics, Coleridge is highly conscious of threats to poetic dreams of unity. The conversation poems are continually in touch with process in the natural world, and they are responsive to the stage-by-stage process of their own poetic development. The theory of the association of ideas, which Coleridge derived from David Hartley, has left its mark on 'The Eolian Harp', but the poem seeks to bring the streamy flow of association under imaginative control. 'The Eolian Harp' reflects Coleridge's early happiness with Sara Fricker, and its central image – of an Eolian harp – serves ultimately to represent the poet's fascination with the mind at work, despite the fact that the harp, wakened into sound by the action of external breezes, appears to be an image that denies the mind's agency. The poem blends lightness of touch with considerable philosophical agility. It concludes with a vehement rejection of where fanciful intimations may lead, and brings out how Coleridge made poetry out of a tension-ridden vision.

'The Eolian Harp' is written in blank verse paragraphs, and, as in the other conversational poems, its transitions repay study. The poem is fascinated by relationship. One kind of relationship is that between the poet and his 'pensive Sara' (l. 1). To begin with, there is a quietly erotic dimension to this relationship, yet such a dimension is soon made subservient to notions of 'Innocence and Love' (l. 5). The second relationship explored by the poem, between the mind and the external world, shows itself with subtle implicitness in the opening paragraph, when the poet describes how 'the distant Sea' (l. 11) intimates 'silence' (l. 12). This relationship emerges, in the next three paragraphs, as the subject of playful and bold speculation. In the second paragraph the poem focuses on the Eolian harp ('that simplest Lute', l. 12), which is associated, at first, with the opening eroticism (it is compared to 'some coy maid half yielding to her lover', l. 15). The poem stays with pleasure, now of an aesthetic kind. The notes produced by the harp, as the breeze plays upon it, compose 'a soft floating witchery of sound' (l. 20), a phrase that captures one of Coleridge's poetic strengths and goals, the desire and ability to create a poetry that is imaginatively bewitching through its 'sounds'. The 'one Life within us and abroad' (l. 26) glides into the poem at this point, a fluent and musical distillation of Coleridge's ideal of unity, and the final lines of the paragraph show how far Coleridge has travelled in the poem: from a private 'world *so* hush'd' (l. 10) to a quasi-pantheist 'world so fill'd' (l. 31); from a solitary consciousness to 'Rhythm in all thought, and joyance every where' (29).

It is at this point that an 'And thus' (l. 34) links Coleridge's own mental processes with the sense of 'one Life'. There is a noticeable drop in seriousness in the phrasing, and it is possible that one of the joins caused by revision shows at this point. And yet the poetry derives life from its movement between the idly 'flitting' (l. 40) and the serious. The next transition, into a speculation that all of 'animated nature' (l. 44) consists of 'organic Harps' (l. 45) breathed over by 'one intellectual breeze' (l. 47), contrives to be both a dazzlingly far-reaching pantheist speculation and an almost nonchalant piece of play with a metaphor. In the concluding paragraph, Coleridge backs off from his pantheist surmise, warned by a look of 'mild reproof' (l. 49) in Sara's eye; the writing is seemingly full of a sense of stricken religious guilt, as Coleridge, now 'A sinful and most miserable man' (l. 62), rejects what has gone before as 'shapings of the unregenerate mind' (l. 55). Critics sometimes lament this change of heart in the poem; but it is more profitable, in our view, to value the poem for its fidelity to the twists and turns of Coleridge's thoughts and emotions.

My pensive Sara! thy soft cheek reclined
Thus on mine arm, most soothing sweet it is
To sit beside our Cot, our Cot o'ergrown
With white-flower'd Jasmin, and the broad-leav'd Myrtle,
(Meet emblems they of Innocence and Love!) 5
And watch the clouds, that late were rich with light,
Slow saddening round, and mark the star of eve
Serenely brilliant (such should Wisdom be)
Shine opposite! How exquisite the scents
Snatch'd from yon bean-field! and the world *so* hush'd! 10
The stilly murmur of the distant Sea
Tells us of silence.
    And that simplest Lute,
Placed length-ways in the clasping casement, hark!
How by the desultory breeze caress'd,
Like some coy maid half yielding to her lover, 15
It pours such sweet upbraiding, as must needs
Tempt to repeat the wrong! And now, its strings
Boldlier swept, the long sequacious notes
Over delicious surges sink and rise,
Such a soft floating witchery of sound 20
As twilight Elfins make, when they at eve
Voyage on gentle gales from Fairy-Land,
Where Melodies round honey-dropping flowers,
Footless and wild, like birds of Paradise,
Nor pause, nor perch, hovering on untam'd wing! 25
O! the one Life within us and abroad,
Which meets all motion and becomes its soul,
A light in sound, a sound-like power in light,
Rhythm in all thought, and joyance every where—
Methinks, it should have been impossible 30
Not to love all things in a world so fill'd;

1–12 *My pensive . . . silence* The sharpened or heightened attention to sense-impressions in lines 9–12 is underscored by the use of two brief exclamations and one brief sentence after the opening sentence that curves its sinuous way for nine lines.
2 *Thus* The word takes an unexpected emphasis (usually the first syllable of an iambic foot is left unstressed) and creates an effect of immediacy.
12 *silence* A low-key version of the absolutes that emerge later in the poem.
12 *that simplest Lute* An Eolian harp is a stringed instrument placed in an open window to catch the breeze.

21 *As twilight Elfins make* The simile does not disguise its figurative nature; it makes us aware of the poet casting about for comparisons. Not that it is forced, since it picks up the concern with sound and silence of the opening, and works towards the major declaration in line 28.
26–9 *O! . . . where* The lines enact their meanings through the fluent rhythm and through the chiastic phrasing of line 28, which enfolds two reference to 'sound' within the two outriding references to 'light'.
31 *a world so fill'd* The phrase echoes and moves beyond 'the world *so* hush'd' (l. 10).

Where the breeze warbles, and the mute still air
Is Music slumbering on her instrument.

And thus, my Love! as on the midway slope
Of yonder hill I stretch my limbs at noon, 35
Whilst through my half-clos'd eye-lids I behold
The sunbeams dance, like diamonds, on the main,
And tranquil muse upon tranquillity;
Full many a thought uncall'd and undetain'd,
And many idle flitting phantasies, 40
Traverse my indolent and passive brain,
As wild and various as the random gales
That swell and flutter on this subject Lute!

And what if all of animated nature
Be but organic Harps diversely fram'd, 45
That tremble into thought, as o'er them sweeps
Plastic and vast, one intellectual breeze,
At once the Soul of each, and God of all?

But thy more serious eye a mild reproof
Darts, O beloved Woman! nor such thoughts 50
Dim and unhallow'd dost thou not reject,
And biddest me walk humbly with my God.
Meek Daughter in the family of Christ!
Well hast thou said and holily disprais'd
These shapings of the unregenerate mind; 55
Bubbles that glitter as they rise and break
On vain Philosophy's aye-babbling spring.
For never guiltless may I speak of him,
The Incomprehensible! save when with awe
I praise him, and with Faith that inly *feels*; 60
Who with his saving mercies healed me,
A sinful and most miserable man,
Wilder'd and dark, and gave me to possess
Peace, and this Cot, and thee, heart-honour'd Maid!

41 *indolent and passive brain* One consequence of this representation of the 'brain' as 'passive' is that Coleridge can avoid full responsibility for the surmise of lines 44ff.
47 *Plastic* Shaping. Compare Coleridge's sonnet 'To the Rev. W. L. Bowles', which speaks of 'that great Spirit, who with plastic sweep / Mov'd on the darkness of the formless Deep!' (ll. 13–14).
47 *intellectual* A breeze that is not merely physical, but is metaphysical (and metaphorical).
50–1 *nor . . . reject* The tangle of Coleridge's now guilt-ridden thoughts is suggested by the double negatives. Interestingly, Charles Lamb and his sister responded to the depiction of 'Mrs C checking your wild wanderings' with pleasure; 'your own self-reproof that follows delighted us' (E. Marrs, ed., *The Letters of Charles and Mary Anne Lamb* (Ithaca, NY: Cornell University Press, 1975–8), vol. 1, p. 12). It is possible that contemporary criticism (which has usually criticized the paragraph adversely) is not wholly attuned to an element of self-mockery in the writing.
64 *Peace . . . Maid!* The poem returns to its starting point; 'this Cot' now seems a place of escape from as well as point of origin for Coleridge's 'idle flitting phantasies' (l. 40).

Reflections on Having Left a Place of Retirement

First published in a periodical, the *Monthly Magazine*, in October 1796, 'Reflections' signals its affinity with 'The Eolian Harp' through its epigraph (first added in 1797) which quotes a phrase of Horace meaning 'more akin to prose', thus pointing up the poem's deployment of a familiar style. Its initial title was significantly different: 'Reflections on Entering into Active Life. A Poem Which Affects Not to Be Poetry'. The subtitle advertises Coleridge's awareness of writing a poetry that broke in its manner with anything too stilted or formal in diction and rhythm. The original title commits itself robustly to the 'Active

Life'; the revised title lays the emphasis on the fact of 'Having Left a Place of Retirement'. Coleridge was active as a lecturer and journalist in Bristol in 1796, hostile to the war with France waged by the English government under Pitt, but deploring revolutionary violence and radical atheism, and preaching universal benevolence. It was a heady mix; what we hear in 'Reflections' is the poet in meditative mood, enjoying domestic love and a rest from ideological controversy before taking arms once again in 'the bloodless fight / Of Science, Freedom, and the Truth in Christ' (ll. 61–2). Still, it would over-simplify the poem to see it as representing the time away from the 'bloodless fight' as evasive escapism. Coleridge thought that love of one person was the source of the love of many. In a letter to Southey in 1794, he writes 'I love my Friend – such as he is, all mankind are or might be! . . . Some home-born Feeling is the center of the Ball, that rolling on thro' Life collects and assimilates every congenial Affection' (*CL*, vol. 1, p. 86). A shade moralistically, his 'Valley of Seclusion' (l. 9) induces feelings other than the 'thirst of idle gold' (l. 13) in Bristol's 'wealthy son of Commerce' (l. 11) who takes time out from making money to stroll by Coleridge's cottage on a Sunday. But the major way in which 'Reflections' justifies retirement is through its discovery (or seeming discovery) of 'Omnipresence' (l. 38) in nature. The revelation that comes to Coleridge at the top of the 'stony Mount' (l. 27), though stated barely and without afflatus, foreshadows the affirmations of other Romantics, chiefly Wordsworth. Coleridge's vision is of the sheer goodness of being, and its power helps to explain the note of regret in the line and a half, 'Ah! quiet Dell! dear Cot, and Mount sublime! / I was constrain'd to quit you' (ll. 43–4). The self-recrimination in what follows cannot disguise the fact that Coleridge is reluctant to leave a place that combines the 'quiet', the 'dear', and the 'sublime', and the final paragraph imagines, in an anticipation of Wordsworth's 'Tintern Abbey', how the poet's 'spirit shall revisit' (l. 65) the scenes depicted in the poem.

As in 'The Eolian Harp', Coleridge is able, in 'Reflections', to convey shifting moods and mental processes economically and expressively. His blank verse ranges down and up the scales. It is at home with the at-home, *sotto voce* understatement of the opening, 'Low was our pretty Cot; our tallest Rose / Peep'd at the chamber-window' (ll. 1–2), where the initial stresses tauten the rhythm. It is at ease, too, with the more prolonged work asked of the syntax in lines 18–26, when the poem describes the skylark. There, the moral drawn by the poet for the benefit of his young wife, the value of spiritual attentiveness, emerges in an unforced way from the account of their 'Long-listening to the viewless sky-lark's note / (Viewless, or haply for a moment seen / Gleaming on sunny wings)' (19–21). The bracketed words, while valuing the 'viewless', indicate how patience will be rewarded with a glimpse of the skylark, and illustrate the expert control Coleridge has developed over rhythm; the poem's sense is echoed by its movement. 'Reflections' modulates persuasively, too, from a descriptive language that manages to be bare yet evocative (ll. 29–42) to a language of polemical exhortation (ll. 43–62). Persuasively, and yet not without a certain sense of strain that is appropriate to a poem that wants to believe that the retired and active lives support one another, but entertains, at some level, a sense that this may be wishful thinking.

Sermoni propriora.—HOR.

Low was our pretty Cot: our tallest Rose
Peep'd at the chamber-window. We could hear
At silent noon, and eve, and early morn,
The Sea's faint murmur. In the open air
Our Myrtles blossom'd; and across the porch　　　　　　　　　5
Thick Jasmins twined: the little landscape round
Was green and woody, and refresh'd the eye.
It was a spot which you might aptly call
The Valley of Seclusion! Once I saw
(Hallowing his Sabbath-day by quietness)　　　　　　　　　　10
A wealthy son of Commerce saunter by,
Bristowa's citizen: methought, it calm'd

1–2 *Low . . . window* The opening may share the same scenic props as 'The Eolian Harp', but its syntax differs markedly, made up as it is of a series of short sentences. The effect is to prepare us for a more considered rhetorical performance than we get in 'The Eolian Harp', which stresses its improvisatory, catching-thoughts-on-the-wing nature.

12 *Bristowa's citizen* Citizen of Bristol.

His thirst of idle gold, and made him muse
With wiser feelings: for he paus'd, and look'd
With a pleas'd sadness, and gaz'd all around, 15
Then eyed our Cottage, and gaz'd round again,
And sigh'd, and said, it was a Blessed Place.
And we *were* bless'd. Oft with patient ear
Long-listening to the viewless sky-lark's note
(Viewless, or haply for a moment seen 20
Gleaming on sunny wings) in whisper'd tones
I've said to my Beloved, 'Such, sweet Girl!
The inobtrusive song of Happiness,
Unearthly minstrelsy! then only heard
When the Soul seeks to hear; when all is hush'd, 25
And the Heart listens!'

               But the time, when first
From that low Dell, steep up the stony Mount
I climb'd with perilous toil and reach'd the top,
Oh! what a goodly scene! *Here* the bleak mount,
The bare bleak mountain speckled thin with sheep; 30
Grey clouds, that shadowing spot the sunny fields;
And river, now with bushy rocks o'er-brow'd,
Now winding bright and full, with naked banks;
And seats, and lawns, the Abbey and the wood,
And cots, and hamlets, and faint city-spire; 35
The Channel *there*, the Islands and white sails,
Dim coasts, and cloud-like hills, and shoreless Ocean—
It seem'd like Omnipresence! God, methought,
Had built him there a Temple: the whole World
Seem'd *imag'd* in its vast circumference: 40
No *wish* profan'd my overwhelmed heart.
Blest hour! It was a luxury,—to be!

   Ah! quiet Dell! dear Cot, and Mount sublime!
I was constrain'd to quit you. Was it right,
While my unnumber'd brethren toil'd and bled, 45
That I should dream away the entrusted hours
On rose-leaf beds, pampering the coward heart
With feelings all too delicate for use?
Sweet is the tear that from some Howard's eye
Drops on the cheek of one he lifts from earth: 50
And he that works me good with unmov'd face.
Does it but half: he chills me while he aids,
My benefactor, not my brother man!
Yet even this, this cold beneficence
Praise, praise it, O my Soul! oft as thou scann'st 55

29–30 *the bleak ... sheep* The repetition of 'bleak' shows Coleridge feeling his way towards an association of bleakness with what is 'goodly'.
38 *seem'd like Omnipresence* The use of 'seem'd' here and in line 40 (which on first publication read 'Was imag'd') signals a retreat from over-sure assertion. In poetic terms, 'seem'd' is more in keeping with the attempt to capture the workings of consciousness, as Coleridge moves from his picturesque description into intimations of sublimity.
45 *While ... bled* Refers to the war between Britain and France that had been going on since 1793.
49 *Howard's* John Howard (1726–90), prison reformer and philanthropist.

The sluggard Pity's vision-weaving tribe!
Who sigh for Wretchedness, yet shun the Wretched,
Nursing in some delicious solitude
Their slothful loves and dainty sympathies!
I therefore go, and join head, heart, and hand, 60
Active and firm, to fight the bloodless fight
Of Science, Freedom, and the Truth in Christ.

Yet oft when after honourable toil
Rests the tir'd mind, and waking loves to dream,
My spirit shall revisit thee, dear Cot! 65
Thy Jasmin and thy window-peeping Rose,
And Myrtles fearless of the mild sea-air.
And I shall sigh fond wishes—sweet Abode!
Ah!—had none greater! And that all had such!
It might be so—but the time is not yet. 70
Speed it, O Father! Let thy Kingdom come!

69–70 *Ah!—had none . . . yet* The wistfully fragmented syntax is used to support Coleridge's representation of his domestic idyll as a type of what all shall enjoy, come the millennium.

This Lime-Tree Bower My Prison

First published in the *Annual Anthology* (1800) and revised over the years (the text here is from 1834), 'This Lime-Tree Bower My Prison' was sent in a letter to Robert Southey in July 1797. Coleridge had returned from a visit to Wordsworth in Racedown with Wordsworth and Dorothy, settling them at Alfoxden, a few miles from Nether Stowey where Coleridge lived. Charles Lamb was staying with Coleridge. Coleridge was unable to accompany his friends on the walk he describes because 'dear Sara accidentally emptied a skillet of boiling milk on my foot'; he wrote the poem 'sitting in the arbour of T. Poole's garden' (*CL*, vol. 1, pp. 334–6).

'This Lime-Tree Bower My Prison' works through acts of sympathetic imagination. Coleridge summons up memories of the landscapes he knows will greet his friends on their walk, and weaves them into a subtle plot of loss and recompense. Though he has 'lost / Beauties and feelings' (ll. 2–3), he quickly leaves self-pity behind and transfers his and our attention onto the natural details of the scene. These details are relished in ways that imply the poet's valuation of the seemingly insignificant aspects of nature. Coleridge's mind may have 'ached to behold and know something great, something one and indivisible', as he put it in a letter of 1797; but in 'This Lime-Tree Bower', such an ache, though present, does not stop him from looking at and listening to the particulars of nature with great care. His delight in the 'creeking' (l. 74) sound of the rook's wings, which he was pleased to find substantiated in a passage from the travel writer William Bartram, is a case in point. At the end of the first paragraph he singles out the 'dark green file of long lank weeds' (l. 17), for instance, using monosyllables to create an impression of attending carefully to the particular. Attention is its own reward and yet restores the poet's sense of emotional equipoise.

A subtle transition and judiciously placed line-ending allow friends, poet and poem to 'emerge / Beneath the wide wide Heaven' (ll. 20–1). Coleridge 'emerges' more openly as contriver of his poem and as imaginer of the experience of others. A surmising 'perhaps' (l. 24) leads into a capping 'Yes!' (l. 26) as though Coleridge were choreographing the movements of his friends. Later, the climactic vision is preceded by a series of exclamatory imperatives ('richlier burn, ye clouds!', l. 35). These imperatives have a double impact; Coleridge urges the natural elements to do what he at the same time implies they would be doing anyway. This doubleness corresponds to the interplay promoted by the poem. Coleridge, in particular, projects on to 'gentle-hearted Charles' experiences he had had, or can imagine himself having. Just as Coleridge has been deprived of first-hand sensuous experience, with its attendant 'Beauties and feelings', so Lamb has 'hunger'd after Nature' (l. 29) and experienced 'strange calamity' (l. 32) (his sister Mary when deranged had killed their mother with a kitchen knife). At the poem's climax, the gaze 'till all doth seem / Less gross than bodily' (ll. 40–1), it is Lamb who stands in for Coleridge. Coleridge treats Lamb with tact ('So my friend, / Struck with deep joy may stand' (ll. 37–8)), even if Lamb objected to the epithet 'gentle-hearted' (l. 28): 'For God's sake', he wrote to Coleridge, 'don't make me ridiculous any more by terming me gentle-hearted in print' (Marrs, vol. 1, pp. 217–18). The central experience is one in which a kind of spiritualization of matter is imagined taking place; Coleridge even suggests that intimations of godhead can be felt at such a moment. But the emphasis falls squarely on imagined and imaginative experience.

Coleridge switches tenses to eloquent effect in the poem, placing us in the present tense at the start of the final paragraph ('A delight / Comes sudden on my heart', ll. 43–4). It is as if the possibility of 'deep joy' for Lamb coalesces with his own recollection of such joy to persuade him of the value of the present moment. Having done this, however, his next move is to go over the immediate past, as he recounts what he has seen; the poet's role as the discoverer of significances emerges from the poetry's accurate notations and stippled light–dark symbolism. These significances include the sense that everything that lives is holy and extend to the suggestion that seeming evil and imperfection are part of some subsuming goodness; this suggestion is carried by the image of the rook, ominous in *Macbeth*, but here the object of blessing, as its wing crosses 'the mighty Orb's dilated glory' (l. 72). The result is to make credible the subsequent assertion 'That Nature ne'er deserts the wise and pure' (l. 60), and the poem concludes with a folding together of different concerns: hard-earned, though joyous, trust in 'Life' (l. 76), affection for another ('gentle-hearted Charles') and attention to nature (the 'creeking' wings of the rook) all coalesce.

In the June of 1797 some long-expected friends paid a visit to the author's cottage; and on the morning of their arrival, he met with an accident, which disabled him from walking during the whole time of their stay. One evening, when they had left him for a few hours, he composed the following lines in the garden-bower.

> WELL, they are gone, and here must I remain,
> This lime-tree bower my prison! I have lost
> Beauties and feelings, such as would have been
> Most sweet to my remembrance even when age
> Had dimm'd mine eyes to blindness! They, meanwhile,   5
> Friends, whom I never more may meet again,
> On springy heath, along the hill-top edge,
> Wander in gladness, and wind down, perchance,
> To that still roaring dell, of which I told;
> The roaring dell, o'erwooded, narrow, deep,   10
> And only speckled by the mid-day sun;
> Where its slim trunk the ash from rock to rock
> Flings arching like a bridge;—that branchless ash,
> Unsunn'd and damp, whose few poor yellow leaves
> Ne'er tremble in the gale, yet tremble still,   15
> Fann'd by the water-fall! and there my friends
> Behold the dark green file of long lank weeds,
> That all at once (a most fantastic sight!)
> Still nod and drip beneath the dripping edge
> Of the blue clay-stone.
>   Now, my friends emerge   20
> Beneath the wide wide Heaven—and view again
> The many-steepled tract magnificent
> Of hilly fields and meadows, and the sea,
> With some fair bark, perhaps, whose sails light up
> The slip of smooth clear blue betwixt two Isles   25
> Of purple shadow! Yes! they wander on
> In gladness all; but thou, methinks, most glad,

7 *springy* 'Elastic, I mean' (Coleridge's note to Southey).
9 *that . . . dell* Coleridge's description of the dell is at once coloured by his own initial low spirits and absorbed in the details of the natural world.

27 *gladness* Repeated from line 8, the word takes on a different tone here; it is as though Coleridge were now saying it with meditative seriousness rather than half-stifled envy.

My gentle-hearted Charles! for thou hast pined
And hunger'd after Nature, many a year,
In the great City pent, winning thy way 30
With sad yet patient soul, through evil and pain
And strange calamity! Ah! slowly sink
Behind the western ridge, thou glorious Sun!
Shine in the slant beams of the sinking orb,
Ye purple heath-flowers! richlier burn, ye clouds! 35
Live in the yellow light, ye distant groves!
And kindle, thou blue Ocean! So my friend
Struck with deep joy may stand, as I have stood,
Silent with swimming sense; yea, gazing round
On the wide landscape, gaze till all doth seem 40
Less gross than bodily; and of such hues
As veil the Almighty Spirit, when yet he makes
Spirits perceive his presence.

      A delight
Comes sudden on my heart, and I am glad
As I myself were there! Nor in this bower, 45
This little lime-tree bower, have I not mark'd
Much that has sooth'd me. Pale beneath the blaze
Hung the transparent foliage; and I watch'd
Some broad and sunny leaf, and lov'd to see
The shadow of the leaf and stem above 50
Dappling its sunshine! And that walnut-tree
Was richly ting'd, and a deep radiance lay
Full on the ancient ivy, which usurps
Those fronting elms, and now, with blackest mass
Makes their dark branches gleam a lighter hue 55
Through the late twilight: and though now the bat
Wheels silent by, and not a swallow twitters,
Yet still the solitary humble-bee
Sings in the bean-flower! Henceforth I shall know
That Nature ne'er deserts the wise and pure; 60
No plot so narrow, be but Nature there,
No waste so vacant, but may well employ
Each faculty of sense, and keep the heart
Awake to Love and Beauty! and sometimes
'Tis well to be bereft of promis'd good, 65
That we may lift the soul, and contemplate
With lively joy the joys we cannot share.

---

30 *In the great City pent* Alludes to the account of Satan in *Paradise Lost*, 9. 445: 'As one who long in populous city pent'.
30 *winning* The meaning is emphasized by the stress reversal: the poem celebrates Lamb's 'sad yet patient soul' (l. 31) as well as Coleridge's experience of sudden 'delight' (l. 43).
38–9 *Struck . . . sense* Both lines begin with stressed syllables, a metrical effect that, in keeping with the mood, does much to slow down and solemnize.
40 *On the wide landscape* When he sent the poem to Southey (in a version which read 'view' for 'landscape'), Coleridge commented: 'You remember, I am a Berkeleian'. George Berkeley, Bishop of Cloyne (1685–1753), asserted that reality, essentially the product of consciousness, was ultimately sustained by the mind of God.
41 *Less gross than bodily* Coleridge's spiritualizing of the landscape takes the form, it should be noted, of distinguishing between two material states: the one (left behind) is 'gross', the other is 'bodily' (like the sight of the risen Christ). On initial publication, the phrase was followed by 'a living thing / Which acts upon the mind', which reinforces an intermingling of thing and mind.
44–5 *and . . . there* The word 'glad' is now reclaimed by the poet for his own rather than his projected experience.

My gentle-hearted Charles! when the last rook
Beat its straight path along the dusky air
Homewards, I blest it! deeming its black wing   70
(Now a dim speck, now vanishing in light)
Had cross'd the mighty Orb's dilated glory,
While thou stood'st gazing; or, when all was still,
Flew creeking o'er thy head, and had a charm
For thee, my gentle-hearted Charles, to whom   75
No sound is dissonant which tells of Life.

74 *Flew creeking* Coleridge added the following note: 'Some months after I had written this line, it gave me pleasure to find that Bartram had observed the same circumstances of the Savanna Crane. "When these Birds move their wings in flight, their strokes are slow, moderate and regular; and even when at a considerable distance or high above us, we plainly hear the quill-feathers; their shafts and webs upon one another creek as the joints or working of a vessel in a tempestuous sea."' Coleridge refers to William Bartram's *Travels through North and South Carolina* (1794).

Kubla Khan: Or, A Vision in a Dream. A Fragment

A version of 'Kubla Khan' composed in November 1797 exists in manuscript (the so-called Crewe manuscript). The poem was not published until 1816, when it appeared with 'Christabel' and 'The Pains of Sleep'; as modified in 1834, it is this version, with its accompanying Preface, which is used as copy-text. The manuscript version has a brief note, asserting 'This fragment with a good deal more, not recoverable, composed in a sort of reverie brought on by two grains of opium taken to check a dysentery, at a farm-house between Porlock and Lynton, a quarter of a mile from Culbone Church, in the fall of the year 1797'.

The poem has always mesmerized and intrigued readers. John Livingston Lowes devotes chapters to it in *The Road to Xanadu* (first published 1927; London: Pan, 1978), his fascinating study of influence and the 'hooked atoms' of creative association in this poem and 'The Rime of the Ancient Mariner'. Whatever the circumstances of composition – the help provided by opium, the reality or otherwise of the 'person on business from Porlock' – the poem has mythic status as an enactment as well as description of genius, creative aspiration and the longing to recover Edenic harmony. And yet, if Kubla Khan presides over an Eden, it is an Eden which, for all its 'sacred river' (l. 3), contains traces of post-lapsarian sexuality, figured by the 'woman wailing for her demon-lover' (l. 16), and anticipations of conflict, provided by the 'Ancestral voices prophesying war' (l. 30).

Unlike the conversation poems which sought to sustain dialogue with an addressee, 'Kubla Khan' appears to talk, or rather chant, only to itself. But heard and imagined auditors are crucial to the poem's development. The poem begins with a 'decree' (l. 2); the second paragraph stages a scene of erotic longing in the image of the 'woman wailing for her demon-lover'; Kubla Khan hears 'Ancestral voices'; a passive construction tells us that the 'mingled measure' 'was heard' (l. 33), though it does not tell us by whom; at the close, the poet conceives of himself as listener (to the damsel) rather than as listened to (by a bewildered and awe-stricken audience). The sense of a sealed-off purity of lyric voice conflicts with a poignant desire for the relay of knowledge, pleasure and inspiration. The poem's air of self-communion is created, in part, by the interlacing vowel music rippling through the opening five lines. The chiastic sound-pattern (*abba* – 'Xan' (*a*), 'du' (*b*), 'Ku' (*b*), 'Khan' (*a*)) of the first line mimics a self-enclosed world presided over by Kubla Khan. Indeed, order emerges as a central concern in the initial paragraph, with its repeated demonstrations of quasi-divine fiat – 'And there' (l. 8), 'And here' (l. 10) – and its use of precise measurement ('So twice five miles', l. 6). Yet chiasmus, a figure that implies a circular completeness, gives way to the awareness of chasms, with the mention of 'caverns measureless to man' (l. 4). Xanadu may be a *hortus conclusus*, a pleasure park, an enclosed garden that is 'girdled round' (l. 7) and furnished with exotica, but through it runs 'Alph, the sacred river' (l. 3), a river that recalls Alpha and, by extension, Omega; it is, in other words, a place astir with cosmic, 'sacred' forces. Is Kubla Khan's decree shown up as a piece of tyrannical folly, the autocratic attempt to tame the wildness of what is ungovernable by human beings? If the poem's hypnotic mode makes it peculiarly hard to be sure that such an interpretation is justified, there is built in to 'Kubla Khan' a distinction between modes of creativity. Kubla's is that of a man of power and authority, seeking control. The poet's at the close is more a matter of wish and aspiration. It is relevant here to cite Coleridge's distinction in *Biographia Literaria* between 'men of commanding genius' and 'men of absolute Genius' (*BL*, vol. 1, pp. 32, 31), even if it may, finally, be the lack of exact fit between these terms and the categories suggested by the poem that is of greatest interest. To be sure, Coleridge's wording echoes his great lyric triumph: of 'men of commanding genius' he writes that 'in tranquil times' they 'are formed to exhibit a perfect poem in palace or temple or landscape-garden' (Kubla's decree comes to mind), while 'in times of tumult they are the men destined to come forth as the shaping spirit of Ruin' (*BL*, vol. 1, pp. 32, 33), which may hint at what will result from Kubla's hearing amidst 'tumult' (l. 29) 'Ancestral voices prophesying war'. 'Men of absolute genius', by contrast, are marked by God-like 'self-sufficing power' (*BL*, vol. 1, p. 31): God-like, or poet-like, 'Kubla Khan' might say, and the close of the poem offers a glimpse of what such 'absolute power' might be like in its depiction of the inspired poet, even if Coleridge only presents such a state of 'absolute genius' as a conditional imagining.

The order decreed by Kubla Khan has underestimated energies that come into prominence in the second paragraph. If the poem communes with itself, it engages in highly intense dialogue between different perspectives. The 'But' of line 12 introduces a passage that is antithesis to the opening thesis. The syntax becomes excited and exclamatory, as Coleridge offers two sentences without main verbs, suggesting the excitement and awe with which he views 'the deep romantic chasm' (l. 12) that is 'savage' yet 'enchanted' (l. 14). Profanely sexual and 'holy' (l. 14), the chasm is associated with 'ceaseless turmoil' (l. 17) and serves as a passage for 'the sacred river' that will, in due course, move into 'a lifeless ocean' (l. 28). If the 'chasm' is a portal through which the river passes to an almost post-coital lifelessness, it is at the same time the centre and symbol of 'ceaseless' life and energy. The controlled tempo of the opening paragraph, with its masculine rhythms and its use of curb-like shorter lines, yields to a section full of feminine rhymes, exclamations and a dynamic syntax suggestive of 'turmoil'. Masculine will meets female sexuality. When a simile brings the savage, holy and enchanted world of the chasm into connection with 'rebounding hail' (l. 21) and 'chaffy grain' (l. 22), earthier associations replace the exotic scenery of the opening. The paragraph closes with an ominous hint of how the energies depicted have the potential to presage, perhaps turn into, human conflict when Kubla hears 'Ancestral voices prophesying war'. Those 'ancestral voices' indicate that Kubla's Eden is fallen. Deep within its psyche are 'voices' that confirm the ruler's fear of or inclination towards 'war'. We remember, too, the hint in 'sinuous rills' (l. 8) of the possible presence in Xanadu of 'sin'.

It is at this point of maximum strain between order and tumult that the poem achieves a brief but stunning reconciliation, a momentary aesthetic truce. The truce is conducted, appropriately enough, through images that centre on water; it is 'on the waves' (l. 32) that the 'shadow' of the 'dome of pleasure' (l. 31) 'Floated' (l. 32). To this sight is added the sounds, the 'mingled measure' synthesizing sounds from both ends of the river: fountain and caves. Coleridge's passive construction – 'Where was heard' (l. 33) – helps to convey a dream-like escape from will or striving in the scene; 'a miracle of rare device' (l. 35) it may have been, but the deviser has withdrawn, fashioning, through suspension of will, a synthesis out of images. In a flash of self-delighted paradox, the scene shapes itself as an embodiment of harmonized opposites, almost half-mocking its ghostly success in the line, 'A sunny pleasure-dome with caves of ice!' (l. 36).

'Kubla Khan' could have stopped there, but Coleridge, giving the lie to his own representation of the poem as an unfinished fragment, moves into what is, in effect, a fourth phase. For so untranslatable a poem, 'Kubla Khan' is almost rigid in construction. We have had the thesis of the Khan's decree, followed by the antithesis of the 'romantic chasm' and the synthesis of the 'mingled measure'. Now the poet brings out more explicitly his ambitions as a poet, staging a scene of creation – or recreation, since he begins by imagining a muse-like 'damsel with a dulcimer' (l. 37) whose song of 'Mount Abora' (l. 41) (or in the Crewe manuscript 'Amara') brings to mind intimations of paradise. These intimations are the more poignantly post-lapsarian in the 1816 version because of the way we are thrown off the Edenic track by the replacement of Amara with Abora. The metrical change that ushers in the 'damsel with a dulcimer' has an electrifying effect; we move from the delighted resolution of the iambic couplet of lines 35–6 into a passage that cunningly mixes up stresses in lines of mainly four feet and speaks of implicit loss and desired recovery. 'In a vision once I saw' (l. 38) offers a mingling of enchantment and disenchantment: on the one hand, we have the sweetly vivid, Botticelli-like 'damsel' and her alliterating 'dulcimer', herself generated, it would seem, by the poet's desire for sublimation of the wild power of the 'woman wailing'; on the other, the poet speaks of a 'vision' that 'once' tells us is firmly in the past. The concluding chant sustains this duality: the rhythmic effect is of mounting certainty, yet the imagined rebuilding in imagination is heavily conditional. 'Could I revive within me' (l. 42); ''twould win me' (l. 44); 'I would build' (l. 46); 'should see' (l. 48); 'should cry' (l. 49): Coleridge's phrasing insists that we hear an unbroken chain of maybes; its ecstatic hopes found themselves knowingly on shifting sands. Fulfilled, they would lead to the creation of a 'dome in air' (l. 46), a formulation that is too close for comfort to 'castles in the air' and that phrase's suggestion of spurious fantasy. And yet too strong an emphasis on the passage's undermining of itself would be wrong. Coleridge breaks through here to one of Romantic poetry's archetypal versions of the poet, a fantasy figure of absolute power, to be approached only with 'holy dread' (l. 52), possessed by visions of 'Paradise' (l. 54).

The Preface in the 1816 edition makes a huge difference to the way the poem has been understood. Coleridge presents his poem as a 'fragment'. Offering it 'rather as a psychological curiosity, than on the ground of any supposed *poetic* merits', he constructs an account of the process of inspiration, in which he purports to have 'composed... from two to three hundred lines' while in a 'profound sleep, at least of the external senses,' to have had a 'distinct recollection of the whole', to have written down the lines that survive, but to have been then interrupted 'by a person on business from Porlock', and to have found on returning to his room that the rest had vanished from memory. To illustrate this process Coleridge quotes lines from his poem 'The Picture', which end with an image of recomposed wholeness, an 'after restoration' that the poet explicitly says has never happened in the case of 'Kubla Khan'. Coleridge goes on to say that he had 'frequently purposed to finish for himself what had been originally, as it were, given to him', but 'the to-morrow is yet to come'. The Preface is best read as a powerful, mystifying and evocative performance that counterpoints the poem proper. Preface and poem share a desire to 'revive' a 'vision', in the poem's words. Yet, for all its use of a conditional mood, the poem's closing emphasis is less on failure and fragmentation than on an imagining of creative triumph, albeit triumph achieved at the cost of bardic isolation. The Preface's prose poem evokes the experience of vanishing inspiration and tempts us to see the poem as typifying the work of Romantic genius, its broken arc suggestive of a perfect round that at once haunts and eludes its maker.

THE following fragment is here published at the request of a poet of great and deserved celebrity [Lord Byron], and, as far as the Author's own opinions are concerned, rather as a psychological curiosity, than on the ground of any supposed *poetic* merits.

In the summer of the year 1797, the Author, then in ill health, had retired to a lonely farm-house between Porlock and Linton, on the Exmoor confines of Somerset and Devonshire. In consequence of a slight indisposition, an anodyne had been prescribed, from the effects of which he fell asleep in his chair at the moment that he was reading the following sentence, or words of the same substance, in 'Purchas's Pilgrimage': 'Here the Khan Kubla commanded a palace to be built, and a stately garden thereunto. And thus ten miles of fertile ground were inclosed with a wall.' The Author continued for about three hours in a profound sleep, at least of the external senses, during which time he has the most vivid confidence, that he could not have composed less than from two to three hundred lines; if that indeed can be called composition in which all the images rose up before him as *things*, with a parallel production of the correspondent expressions, without any sensation or consciousness of effort. On awaking he appeared to himself to have a distinct recollection of the whole, and taking his pen, ink, and paper, instantly and eagerly wrote down the lines that are here preserved. At this moment he was unfortunately called out by a person on business from Porlock, and detained by him above an hour, and on his return to his room, found, to his no small surprise and mortification, that though he still retained some vague and dim recollection of the general purport of the vision, yet, with the exception of some eight or ten scattered lines and images, all the rest had passed away like the images on the surface of a stream into which a stone has been cast, but, alas! without the after restoration of the latter!

              Then all the charm
Is broken—all that phantom-world so fair
Vanishes, and a thousand circlets spread,
And each mis-shape['s] the other. Stay awhile,
Poor youth! who scarcely dar'st lift up thine eyes—
The stream will soon renew its smoothness, soon
The visions will return! And lo, he stays,
And soon the fragments dim of lovely forms
Come trembling back, unite, and now once more
The pool becomes a mirror.
                    [From *The Picture; or,
the Lover's Resolution*, ll. 91–100.]

Preface
poet of great and deserved celebrity Byron, who had heard the poem recited and described it as 'a fine wild poem' (Leslie Marchand, ed., *Byron's Letters and Journals*, 12 vols, Cambridge, MA: Harvard University Press/London: John Murray, 1973–82), vol. 5, p. 108).
Purchas's Pilgrimage Samuel Purchas, *Purchas His Pilgrimage*. In the 1626 edition of the work, the relevant passage reads: 'In Xamdu did Cublai Can build a stately Palace, encompassing sixteene Miles of plaine ground with a wall, wherein are fertile Meddowes, pleasant Springs, delightfull Streames, and all sorts of beasts of chase and game, and in the middest thereof a sumptuous house of pleasure'.
Then all the charm... mirror Lines 91–100 from Coleridge's poem 'The Picture; or, the Lover's Resolution'.
Σαμερον... ἄσω 'I shall sing a sweeter song tomorrow'; reworked by Coleridge from Theocritus, *Idyll* I. 145.

Yet from the still surviving recollections in his mind, the Author has frequently purposed to finish for himself what had been originally, as it were, given to him. Σαμερον αδιον ασω [Αὔριον ἄδιον ἄσω *1834*]: but the to-morrow is yet to come.

As a contrast to this vision, I have annexed a fragment of a very different character, describing with equal fidelity the dream of pain and disease.

<blockquote>
IN Xanadu did Kubla Khan
A stately pleasure-dome decree:
Where Alph, the sacred river, ran
Through caverns measureless to man
    Down to a sunless sea.   5
So twice five miles of fertile ground
With walls and towers were girdled round:
And there were gardens bright with sinuous rills,
Where blossomed many an incense-bearing tree;
And here were forests ancient as the hills,   10
Enfolding sunny spots of greenery.

But oh! that deep romantic chasm which slanted
Down the green hill athwart a cedarn cover!
A savage place! as holy and enchanted
As e'er beneath a waning moon was haunted   15
By woman wailing for her demon-lover!
And from this chasm, with ceaseless turmoil seething,
As if this earth in fast thick pants were breathing,
A mighty fountain momently was forced:
Amid whose swift half-intermitted burst   20
Huge fragments vaulted like rebounding hail,
Or chaffy grain beneath the thresher's flail:
And 'mid these dancing rocks at once and ever
It flung up momently the sacred river.
Five miles meandering with a mazy motion   25
Through wood and dale the sacred river ran,
Then reached the caverns measureless to man,
And sank in tumult to a lifeless ocean:
And 'mid this tumult Kubla heard from far
</blockquote>

Poem

1 *Khan* Rhymes with 'ran' and 'man', and appears to have been pronounced as 'can': a possible pun that points up the Khan's capacity to make things happen. The word may also have struck Coleridge as associated with Cain, the subject of an unfinished prose-poem, 'The Wanderings of Cain' (composed 1797–8; first published 1828).

3 *Alph* May suggest 'Alpha'; may also suggest the river Alpheus, supposed to flow beneath the earth and sea, and arise in a fountain; see J. Livingston Lowes, *The Road to Xanadu*, pp. 359–62.

8–10 *And there were . . . And here were* There is no mention of any effort; 'gardens' and 'forests' appear as immediately as 'light' at God's fiat in Genesis; see Seamus Perry, *Coleridge and the Uses of Division* (Oxford: Clarendon Press, 1999), p. 201.

12–18 *But . . . breathing* The rhyme scheme of these seven lines repeats exactly that in the poem's opening seven lines.

14 *holy and enchanted* Livingston Lowes compares William Collins, 'The Passions. An Ode for Music', which speaks in successive lines of 'some haunted Stream' and 'an holy Calm' (ll. 65–6), and in the previous line (l. 64) refers to 'the mingled Measure' (compare 'Kubla Khan', l. 33).

Ancestral voices prophesying war! 30
  The shadow of the dome of pleasure
  Floated midway on the waves;
  Where was heard the mingled measure
  From the fountain and the caves.
It was a miracle of rare device, 35
A sunny pleasure-dome with caves of ice!

  A damsel with a dulcimer
  In a vision once I saw:
  It was an Abyssinian maid,
  And on her dulcimer she played, 40
  Singing of Mount Abora.
  Could I revive within me
  Her symphony and song,
  To such a deep delight 'twould win me,
That with music loud and long, 45
I would build that dome in air,
That sunny dome! those caves of ice!
And all who heard should see them there,
And all should cry, Beware! Beware!
His flashing eyes, his floating hair! 50
Weave a circle round him thrice,
And close your eyes with holy dread,
For he on honey-dew hath fed,
And drunk the milk of Paradise.

30 *Ancestral . . . war* In Samuel Purchas, *Purchas His Pilgrimage*, close to the passage quoted in Coleridge's Preface, occurs an account of the 'Priests' of the Tartars: 'No warres are begunne or made without their word': see Lowes, pp. 362–3.
33 *measure* Both a musical term for harmony and an indication of a drawing into a state of order of the 'measureless' caverns (an ordering that, in its miraculous freedom from the willed, differs from the Khan's imposition of 'walls and towers', l. 7).
46–50 *air . . . hair!* The incantatory momentum of the close has much to do with the fact that four of these five lines end with the same rhyme sound.
50 *His . . . hair!* This vision of the inspired poet has analogues in Plato's *Ion*, where he writes that 'the lyric poets are not in their senses when they make their lovely lyric poems' and compares such poets to 'the bacchants who, when possessed, draw milk and honey from the rivers, but not when in their senses'. It may also be an answer to Collins's question in his 'Ode on the Poetical Character' (much admired by Coleridge): 'Where is the Bard, whose Soul can now / Its high presuming Hopes avow?' (ll. 51–2).

The Rime of the Ancient Mariner. In Seven Parts

The poem was initially published in *Lyrical Ballads* (1798) where it opened the volume and, in keeping with a work 'professedly written in imitation of the style as well as of the spirit of the elder poets' (Advertisement to *Lyrical Ballads*, 1798), was entitled, 'The Rime of the Ancyent Marinere'. In 1800 it appeared in revised form with the subtitle, 'A Poet's Reverie', to which Charles Lamb took eloquent exception: 'it is as bad as Bottom the Weaver's declaration that he is not a Lion but only the scenical representation of a Lion. What new idea is gained by this Title, but one subversive of all credit, which the tale should force upon us, of its truth?' (Marrs, vol. 1, p. 266). Much later, in *Biographia Literaria* (1817) Coleridge himself, in describing the rationale of his contributions to *Lyrical Ballads*, spoke of seeking to 'procure for these shadows of imagination that willing suspension of disbelief for the moment, which constitutes poetic faith. . . . With this view I wrote the "Ancient Mariner".' The poem generates such a 'suspension of disbelief', and yet Coleridge decided to add a gloss in the 1817 text, where the poem appears shorn of many of its calculated archaisms, which had been heavily criticized when it was first published. In a review for *The Critical Review* (24), October 1798, Southey thought the poem a 'Dutch attempt at German sublimity', intending to be hostile, though the description can be twisted into a compliment, since the poem combines 'sublimity' of overall design with precision in the handling of local details and episodes.

Wordsworth recalled that the poem 'was founded on a strange dream, which a friend of Coleridge [John Cruikshank] had, who fancied he saw a skeleton ship, with figures in it'. The poem was among those composed to 'defray the expenses of a little excursion we were to make together'. Wordsworth assisted, but soon dropped out, though he says that he contributed a number of lines to the poem. In 1843 Wordsworth also claimed to have suggested 'certain parts' of the poem: including the idea of the committing of a crime which should bring upon the mariner 'spectral persecution' and, via George Shelvocke's *Voyage round the World, by the Way of the Great South Sea* (1726), the nature of that crime, as well as 'the navigation of the ship by the dead men'. In Shelvocke a melancholy second captain shoots a 'disconsolate black Albitross', hoping that the sailors 'would have a fair wind' following the shooting (quoted from *Lyrical Ballads*, ed. Michael Mason [London: Longman, 1992], pp. 367, 368, 383 [hereafter Mason]). Certainly the poem draws on a range of travel writings, as Livingston Lowes has shown. Though Coleridge eschews dates and names, the imagined date of the poem's events is likely to be, as Michael Mason puts it, 'between the voyages of Columbus (1492) and Magellan (1519)' (Mason, p. 177). In preparing the 1800 edition of *Lyrical Ballads*, Wordsworth took a critical view of the poem, which he held responsible for poor sales. He provided an apologetic note about it in 1800, in which he listed four main 'defects': the mariner 'has no distinct character'; the mariner 'does not act, but is continually acted upon'; 'the events having no necessary connection do not produce each other'; and the 'imagery is somewhat too laboriously accumulated'. To be fair to Wordsworth, who appears at his most obtuse in the note, he also acknowledged that the poem 'contains many delicate touches of passion, and indeed the passion is every where true to nature' (Mason, pp. 39–40).

Interpretative rather than evaluative controversy has always attended the poem. Some read the poem as portraying a clear moral vision: the mariner's killing of the albatross violates the sanctity of bonds linking humanity to the natural world; he is punished; repents when he blesses the water-snakes; returns to land, and offers a moral (somewhat wryly rephrased by William Empson as 'don't pull poor pussy's tail'). If the gloss is accorded authority in reading the poem, it reinforces this moral reading since at several moments it articulates a religious understanding of the poem's events; the tersely recounted killing – 'With my cross-bow / I shot the ALBATROSS' (ll. 81–2) – is the point of departure for a more embroidered comment: 'The ancient Mariner inhospitably killeth the pious bird of good omen'. Against this reading is the view that the poem portrays a world that is absurd, effectively godless and without meaning, in which the consequences of killing the albatross go way beyond any notion of retributive justice (all the mariner's fellow-sailors die) and in which chance, symbolized in the dice-playing of Death and Life-in-Death and arguably at work in the mariner's blessing of the water-snakes, governs events. In such a world, what is offered is a ghastly parody of unity, everything being tugged into the vortex of the mariner's suffering. The poem's very lack of sense of purpose provokes, on this reading, the maker of the gloss (written in a style distinctly not of Coleridge's age) to impose a moral pattern on events that will not be so explained. Coleridge sides ambiguously with both perspectives in his famous retort to Anna Barbauld, when she complained that the poem's only faults were that 'it was improbable, and had no moral': Coleridge remarked that the poem's 'only, or chief fault' 'was that it had too much' (Mason, p. 367).

Throughout, the poem fuses clarity and enigma. Stanza after stanza charts the mariner's experience through unforgettable, sharply etched images. Physical description is given an unnatural beauty and clarity that makes it seem revelatory of a mind. In lines 51–4, for instance, the series of 'ands' locate us in a state of chilled, wide-eyed wonder as 'ice, mast-high, came floating by / As green as emerald' (ll. 53–4). The hugeness, the movement and the jewel-like colour pass before us with a dream-like blend of unstoppability and slow motion. Again, in the stanza after Death and Life-in-Death have 'diced', as the gloss puts it, 'for the ship's crew', imagery conveys a nightmare serenity; the whole of creation is alive, and the language tautens in response, as active verbs animate their nouns with a stealthy power: 'The Sun's rim dips; the stars rush out: / At one stride comes the dark' (ll. 199–200). The striding entrance of 'the dark', conveyed through the succession of quick but strongly stressed monosyllables, is more than literal, and presages the death of the sailors and the living death of the mariner. As the ballad progresses, we realize how subtly the poetry suggests the internal nature of the mariner's suffering. In the stanza just quoted, we are told, for example, that 'With far-heard whisper, o'er the sea, / Off shot the spectre-bark' (ll. 201–2): 'far-heard' does much to turn the entire scene into a gigantic ear, intently attuned to the strains of evil discord produced by the spectre-bark. It is with that already hallucinatory whisper in our thoughts that we read of the failure of the mariner's attempt to pray: 'A wicked whisper came, and made / My heart as dry as dust' (ll. 246–7). That whisper, now openly 'wicked', shows how the spectre-bark has, so to speak, internalized itself within the mariner's psyche; 'came' makes the 'whisper' an event both within consciousness and beyond conscious control. Much, indeed, of the poem coheres if we grant the mariner the 'distinct character' denied him by Wordsworth, and make his states of consciousness the poem's central concern.

And yet Wordsworth was, at least descriptively, right about some major elements: the connection between events is often harder to grasp than the sheer momentum of the narrative allows us to think. Why does the mariner kill the albatross? Coleridge is laconic to the point of silence on this score. Just as in Macbeth we do not see the killing of Duncan, but rather its impact on the suffering murderer, so in 'The Ancient Mariner' we see the killer's suffering before we know he carried out a killing, the wedding guest intuiting that the mariner is plagued by 'fiends' (l. 80); indeed, the 'fiends' may be those that drove him to commit the original deed as well as those that subsequently torment him, as if, in retelling the tale, he were reliving it. If the killing is unexplained, the blessing of the water-snakes by the light of the moon takes place 'unaware' (ll. 285, 287). Why does the mariner bless the water-snakes 'unaware'? Why does his punishment continue after this repentance, if repentance it is? Why do the other sailors die? Why does the poem continue for so long after the albatross has fallen from the mariner's neck? Why does Coleridge set the poem in a distinctly medieval, Catholic framework?

All these 'whys' can be reconciled with either of the main interpretative models outlined above. For the first such model, according to which the poem is about the consequences of a crime against the 'One Life', these 'whys' merely show the inscrutability of providence and the unendingness and arbitrariness of evil once it has been brought into existence, views that are perfectly orthodox in theological terms. On this model, too, the choice of a Catholic framework, as when 'Heaven's Mother' is invoked at line 178, suggests the transcultural nature of the sacrilege committed by the mariner; it also gives Coleridge scope to explore questions of evil and atonement at odds with the brand of Unitarianism which he professed in the 1790s. On the second model, according to which the poem's events expose a universe that is godless and absurd, the 'whys?' earn their keep by refusing to be answered coherently. Ingeniously finding a third interpretative way, Seamus Perry has suggested that the poem is engaged in a characteristically Coleridgean 'hovering in between': the forces of guilt and evil are allowed to dominate the poem, while 'being notionally contained by their dramatic attribution to a fallible narrator' (Seamus Perry, 'Coleridge, *Kubla Khan*, *The Ancient Mariner* and *Christabel*', in *A Companion to Romanticism*, ed. Duncan Wu [Oxford: Blackwell, 1998], p. 139).

What is certain is that we see the mariner as someone by whose experiences we are imaginatively compelled. The final meanings of these experiences may be in doubt (they may, among other things, disclose just what has to be undergone if someone is to be a poet); their immediate and lasting impact is indubitable. This distinction between impact and meaning can be seen at work in the scene of the blessing of the water-snakes. The poetry refuses to articulate why this blessing takes place beyond or below the level of the will; yet the sense of release is like a drenching downpour after rainless months. It may be divine grace; it may be repentance at the very depths of the mariner's being; it may be psychological luck (the mariner has been taken out of himself): what we can be sure of is that the moment offers an escape from the sterility of the earlier, futile attempt to pray. Again, the poem's use of sun and moon lends itself less to the exposition of themes through symbols than to the revelation of the mariner's feelings as he looks out onto a universe that bodies forth his fears and longings.

Compellingly the poem blends power and indeterminacy. If the 1817 text obliges us to respond to the voice of the gloss, the gloss, as suggested already, has a sureness at odds with the openness to possibility exhibited by the epigraph from Burnet, which asserts that there are 'more invisible than visible Natures in the universe of things', but says in virtually the same breath that 'The human intellect has always sought the knowledge of these things, but never attained it'. Moreover, the gloss often exhibits a will to rationalize and moralize events which in the poem proper affect us as hard to explain, even arbitrary. The poem's narrative method also warrants comment in this context. The narrator is a withdrawn figure, heard most memorably at the very start, 'It is an ancient Mariner' (l. 1), a line which, on rereading, seems suggestive of the mariner's Wandering Jew-like existence in an eternal present, and at the very end when he tersely depicts the impact of the story on the wedding guest: 'A sadder and a wiser man, / He rose the morrow morn' (ll. 624–5). The narrator is noticeably unforthcoming about the nature either of the 'sadness' (whose principal meaning is 'seriousness') or the 'wisdom'. The most prominent voice we hear is that of the mariner, buttonholing the unfortunate wedding guest. If the former has something of the power claimed by the Romantics for the poet, the latter is in the position of the reader, bewildered and haunted by the 'glittering eye' (l. 13) and 'strange power of speech' (l. 587) of the mariner. The criss-crossing between the two provides the poem with much of its strength. Coleridge refuses to allow an easy reconciliation between the mariner, who has known appalling loneliness out at sea, and the wedding-guest who wishes to attend 'the merry din' (l. 8) of the marriage-feast. Indeed, at the close the mariner remains still partly alienated from human society and he alienates the wedding guest, drawing him from the marriage he wishes to attend. The mariner's 'ghastly tale' (l. 584) has no evidently beneficial effect on his listener; he comes to those on shore, not as the bearer of insight, but as a crazed figure, who induces terror, compelled to speak at intervals of an 'agony' which returns in the telling and is only allayed when the tale is told. 'The Rime of the Ancient Mariner' opens itself to the strange, the uncanny and the inexplicable; it is, in Coleridge's words, 'a work of pure imagination', and yet it does not renounce the will to comprehend what may resist comprehension.

The copy-text for this edition is provided by the latest text arrived at in Coleridge's lifetime. Some of the major changes made to the 1798 version are commented on in the notes.

Facile credo, plures esse Naturas invisibiles quam visibiles in rerum universitate. Sed horum omnium familiam quis nobis enarrabit? et gradus et cognationes et discrimina et singulorum munera? Quid agunt? quae loca habitant? Harum rerum notitiam semper ambivit ingenium humanum, nunquam attigit. Juvat, interea, non diffiteor, quandoque in animo, tanquam in tabula, majoris et melioris mundi imaginem contemplari: ne mens assuefacta hodiernae vitae minutiis se contrahat nimis, et tota subsidat in pusillas cogitationes. Sed veritati interea invigilandum est, modusque servandus, ut certa ab incertis, diem a nocte, distinguamus.—T. BURNET, *Archaeol. Phil.* p. 68.

PART I

An ancient Mariner meeteth three Gallants bidden to a wedding-feast, and detaineth one.

IT is an ancient Mariner
And he stoppeth one of three.
'By thy long grey beard and glittering eye,
Now wherefore stopp'st thou me?

The Bridegroom's doors are opened wide, 5
And I am next of kin;
The guests are met, the feast is set:
May'st hear the merry din.'

He holds him with his skinny hand,
'There was a ship,' quoth he. 10
'Hold off! unhand me, grey-beard loon!'
Eftsoons his hand dropt he.

The Wedding-Guest is spellbound by the eye of the old seafaring man, and constrained to hear his tale.

He holds him with his glittering eye—
The Wedding-Guest stood still,
And listens like a three years' child: 15
The Mariner hath his will.

Tha Wedding-Guest sat on a stone:
He cannot choose but hear;
And thus spake on that ancient man,
The bright-eyed Mariner. 20

Epigraph This epigraph from Burnet translates:

I can easily believe there to be more invisible than visible Natures in the universe of things. But who will describe in detail for us the family of all of these beings? And the ranks and relations and distinguishing features and duties of each? What do they do? What places do they inhabit? The human intellect has always sought the knowledge of these things, but never attained it. It is helpful, meanwhile, I do not deny, sometimes to contemplate in the mind, as on a tablet, the image of a greater and better world; lest the mind, grown used to the minutiae of daily life, contract itself too much, and subside wholly into trivial thought. But, meanwhile, we need to be vigilant about the truth and keep proportion, so that we may distinguish the certain from the uncertain, day from night.

In the 1798 version the poem was preceded by the following 'Argument': 'How a Ship having passed the Line was driven by storms to the cold Country towards the South Pole; and how from thence she made her course to the tropical Latitude of the Great Pacific Ocean; and of the strange things that befell; and in what manner the Ancyent Marinere came back to his own Country.'

7 *The guests . . . set* This use of internal rhyme in the unrhymed first or, as here, third line of quatrains occurs frequently in the poem, serving to change tempo and heighten emphasis.

12 *Eftsoons* Immediately.

16 *The Mariner . . . will* The first appearance of the poem's concern with compulsion: the wedding guest is 'constrained' to hear, the mariner 'forced' (l. 580) to tell.

The Mariner tells how the ship sailed southward with a good wind and fair weather, till it reached the line.	'The ship was cheered, the harbour cleared, Merrily did we drop Below the kirk, below the hill, Below the lighthouse top.	
	The Sun came up upon the left, Out of the sea came he! And he shone bright, and on the right Went down into the sea.	25
	Higher and higher every day, Till over the mast at noon—' The Wedding-Guest here beat his breast, For he heard the loud bassoon.	30
The Wedding-Guest heareth the bridal music; but the Mariner continueth his tale.	The bride hath paced into the hall, Red as a rose is she; Nodding their heads before her goes The merry minstrelsy.	35
	The Wedding-Guest he beat his breast, Yet he cannot choose but hear; And thus spake on that ancient man, The bright-eyed Mariner.	40
The ship driven by a storm toward the south pole.	'And now the STORM-BLAST came, and he Was tyrannous and strong: He struck with his o'ertaking wings, And chased us south along.	
	With sloping masts and dipping prow, As who pursued with yell and blow Still treads the shadow of his foe, And forward bends his head, The ship drove fast, loud roared the blast, And southward aye we fled.	45 50
	And now there came both mist and snow, And it grew wondrous cold: And ice, mast-high, came floating by As green as emerald.	
The land of ice, and of fearful sounds where no living thing was to be seen.	And through the drifts the snowy clifts Did send a dismal sheen: Nor shapes of men nor beasts we ken— The ice was all between.	55
	The ice was here, the ice was there, The ice was all around:	60

22–4 *Merrily . . . top* This 'dropping' 'below' church ('kirk'), land and 'lighthouse top' (with its signals intended to ensure safety) symbolically launches the perilous voyage.
25 *The Sun* With the moon, the sun has been freighted with symbolic meanings by critics. Many changes in the way both bodies are viewed, however, can be read psychologically as telling us about the mariner's state of mind.

41, 51 *And now* In 1798, the stanzas began, 'Listen, Stranger!' and 'Listen Stranger!'
45–50 *With sloping . . . fled* Not in 1798. This lengthening of the usual quatrain (with alternating four-stress unrhymed and three-stress rhymed lines) for variation and expressive effect is used at crucial moments in the poem.
55 *clifts* A 'by-form' of 'cliffs'.

It cracked and growled, and roared and howled,
Like noises in a swound!

Till a great sea-bird,
called the Albatross,
came through the
snow-fog, and was
received with great
joy and hospitality.

At length did cross an Albatross,
Thorough the fog it came;
As if it had been a Christian soul,
We hailed it in God's name.   65

It ate the food it ne'er had eat,
And round and round it flew.
The ice did split with a thunder-fit;
The helmsman steered us through!   70

And lo! the
Albatross proveth a
bird of good omen,
and followeth the
ship as it returned
northward through
fog and floating ice.

And a good south wind sprung up behind;
The Albatross did follow,
And every day, for food or play,
Came to the mariner's hollo!

In mist or cloud, on mast or shroud,   75
It perched for vespers nine;
While all the night, through fog-smoke white,
Glimmered the white Moon-shine.'

The ancient
Mariner,
inhospitably killeth
the pious bird of
good omen.

'God save thee, ancient Mariner!
From the fiends, that plague thee thus!—   80
Why look'st thou so?'—With my cross-bow
I shot the ALBATROSS.

PART II

The Sun now rose upon the right:
Out of the sea came he,
Still hid in mist, and on the left   85
Went down into the sea.

And the good south wind still blew behind,
But no sweet bird did follow,
Nor any day for food or play
Came to the mariners' hollo!   90

His shipmates cry
out against the
ancient Mariner, for
killing the bird of
good luck.

And I had done a hellish thing,
And it would work 'em woe:
For all averred, I had killed the bird
That made the breeze to blow.
Ah wretch! said they, the bird to slay,   95
That made the breeze to blow!

But when the fog
cleared off, they
justify the same,
and thus make

Nor dim nor red, like God's own head,
The glorious Sun uprist:
Then all averred, I had killed the bird
That brought the fog and mist.   100

61–2 *It . . . swound* The ice's animal-like sounds are conveyed, first, as very loud through the verbs, then as 'noises in a swound' (swoon). The transition from outer to inner made by the simile contributes to the effect of something happening in a dream or trance.
76 *vespers* Literally evenings, but the word's liturgical overtones are also relevant.

97–8 *Nor dim . . . uprist* The phrasing is ambiguous: the primary sense is that the sun, neither dim nor red, uprose like God's head; but there is also an opposite sense, caused by the syntax, that the sun uprose, but not in the dim or red way associated with God's head. This unsettling second possibility looks ahead to the 'bloody Sun' (l. 112) and the sun's nightmare 'broad and burning face' (l. 180).

themselves accomplices in the crime.	'Twas right, said they, such birds to slay, That bring the fog and mist.	
The fair breeze continues; the ship enters the Pacific Ocean, and sails north-ward, even till it reaches the Line.	The fair breeze blew, the white foam flew, The furrow followed free; We were the first that ever burst Into that silent sea.	105
The ship hath been suddenly becalmed.	Down dropt the breeze, the sails dropt down, 'Twas sad as sad could be; And we did speak only to break The silence of the sea!	110
	All in a hot and copper sky, The bloody Sun, at noon, Right up above the mast did stand, No bigger than the Moon.	
	Day after day, day after day, We stuck, nor breath nor motion; As idle as a painted ship Upon a painted ocean.	115
And the Albatross begins to be avenged.	Water, water, every where, And all the boards did shrink; Water, water, every where, Nor any drop to drink.	120
	The very deep did rot: O Christ! That ever this should be! Yea, slimy things did crawl with legs Upon the slimy sea.	125
A Spirit had followed them; one of the invisible inhabitants of this planet, neither departed souls nor angels; concerning whom the learned Jew, Josephus, and the Platonic Constantinopolitan, Michael Psellus, may be consulted. They are very numerous, and there is no climate or element without one or more.	About, about, in reel and rout The death-fires danced at night; The water, like a witch's oils, Burnt green, and blue and white. And some in dreams assured were Of the Spirit that plagued us so; Nine fathom deep he had followed us From the land of mist and snow. And every tongue, through utter drought, Was withered at the root; We could not speak, no more than if We had been choked with soot.	130 135

109–10 *We . . . sea* Even as the mariner's sufferings are about to start, there is an exhilarated sense here of exploration.
128 *death-fires* St Elmo's fire.
Gloss to 131–4 *neither departed souls nor angels* Daemons (not demons); in the 'Platonic sense of a being intermediary between gods and men' (Lowes, p. 213). The mariner's universe is simultaneously populated with invisible beings and a place of total aloneness.
Josephus Flavius Josephus (c.37–c.100 CE), author of *Antiquitates Judaicae* and *De Bello Judaico*.
The Platonic . . . Psellus Michael Constantine Psellus (c.1018–c.1105), author of a commentary on the Chaldaean Oracles.

The shipmates, in their sore distress, would fain throw the whole guilt on the ancient Mariner: in sign whereof they hang the dead sea-bird round his neck.	Ah! well a-day! what evil looks Had I from old and young! Instead of the cross, the Albatross About my neck was hung.	140

PART III

	There passed a weary time. Each throat Was parched, and glazed each eye. A weary time! a weary time! How glazed each weary eye,	145
The ancient Mariner beholdeth a sign in the element afar off.	When looking westward, I beheld A something in the sky.	
	At first it seemed a little speck, And then it seemed a mist; It moved and moved, and took at last A certain shape, I wist.	150
	A speck, a mist, a shape, I wist! And still it neared and neared: As if it dodged a water-sprite, It plunged and tacked and veered.	155
At its nearer approach, it seemeth him to be a ship; and at a dear ransom he freeth his speech from the bonds of thirst.	With throats unslaked, with black lips baked, We could nor laugh nor wail; Through utter drought all dumb we stood! I bit my arm, I sucked the blood, And cried, A sail! a sail!	160
A flash of joy;	With throats unslaked, with black lips baked, Agape they heard me call: Gramercy! they for joy did grin, And all at once their breath drew in, As they were drinking all.	165
And horror follows. For can it be a ship that comes onward without wind or tide?	See! see! (I cried) she tacks no more! Hither to work us weal; Without a breeze, without a tide, She steadies with upright keel!	170
	The western wave was all a-flame. The day was well nigh done! Almost upon the western wave Rested the broad bright Sun; When that strange shape drove suddenly Betwixt us and the Sun.	175
It seemeth him but the skeleton of a ship.	And straight the Sun was flecked with bars, (Heaven's Mother send us grace!) As if through a dungeon-grate he peered With broad and burning face.	180

161 *And cried* The mariner's speech, however brief, breaks the inability to 'speak' of line 137, and may foreshadow his ultimate tale-telling fate.

168 *Hither ... weal* The mariner's first thought is that the ship comes to help.

	Alas! (thought I, and my heart beat loud)	
And its ribs are seen as bars on the face of the setting Sun.	How fast she nears and nears! Are those *her* sails that glance in the Sun, Like restless gossameres?	
The Spectre-Woman and her Death-mate, and no other on board the skeleton ship.	Are those *her* ribs through which the Sun Did peer, as through a grate? And is that Woman all her crew? Is that a DEATH? and are there two? Is DEATH that woman's mate?	185
Like vessel, like crew! Death and Life-in-Death have diced for the ship's crew, and she (the latter) winneth the ancient Mariner.	*Her* lips were red, *her* looks were free, Her locks were yellow as gold: Her skin was as white as leprosy, The Night-mare LIFE-IN-DEATH was she, Who thicks man's blood with cold. The naked hulk alongside came, And the twain were casting dice; 'The game is done! I've won! I've won!' Quoth she, and whistles thrice.	190 195
No twilight within the courts of the Sun.	The Sun's rim dips; the stars rush out: At one stride comes the dark; With far-heard whisper, o'er the sea, Off shot the spectre-bark.	200
At the rising of the Moon,	We listened and looked sideways up! Fear at my heart, as at a cup, My life-blood seemed to sip! The stars were dim, and thick the night, The steersman's face by his lamp gleamed white; From the sails the dew did drip— Till clomb above the eastern bar The horned Moon, with one bright star Within the nether tip.	205 210
One after another,	One after one, by the star-dogged Moon, Too quick for groan or sigh, Each turned his face with a ghastly pang, And cursed me with his eye.	215
His shipmates drop down dead.	Four times fifty living men, (And I heard nor sigh nor groan) With heavy thump, a lifeless lump, They dropped down one by one.	

184 *gossameres* Cobwebs.
188 *a DEATH?* A skeleton. Between 1798 and 1817 there was a considerable amount of rewriting round this part of the poem that reduces Gothic charnel-house horror and increases the sense of 'Night-mare' (l. 193); only in 1817 were the woman and her mate identified as Life-in-Death and Death respectively.
199–211 *The Sun's rim ... nether tip* The passage is mainly new in 1817.

203–5 *We listened ... sip!* Lines that contain some of the most eloquent metrical variations in the poem: line 203 pauses unexpectedly on 'looked', stressing the fear-bound 'sideways up' stare of the sailors; 'Fear' in line 204 dominates the line after the initial stress, and the agonizing slowness of the experience of 'Fear' – represented as a kind of diabolical communion – is brought out by the stressed monosyllables of line 205.
209 *clomb* Climbed.

But Life-in-Death begins her work on the ancient Mariner.	The souls did from their bodies fly,— They fled to bliss or woe! And every soul, it passed me by, Like the whizz of my cross-bow!	220

PART IV

The Wedding-Guest feareth that a Spirit is talking to him;	'I fear thee, ancient Mariner! I fear thy skinny hand! And thou art long, and lank, and brown, As is the ribbed sea-sand!	225
But the ancient Mariner assureth him of his bodily life, and proceedeth to relate his horrible penance.	I fear thee and thy glittering eye, And thy skinny hand, so brown.'— Fear not, fear not, thou Wedding-Guest! This body dropt not down. Alone, alone, all, all alone, Alone on a wide wide sea! And never a saint took pity on My soul in agony.	230 235
He despiseth the creatures of the calm,	The many men, so beautiful! And they all dead did lie: And a thousand thousand slimy things Lived on; and so did I.	
And envieth that *they* should live, and so many lie dead.	I looked upon the rotting sea, And drew my eyes away; I looked upon the rotting deck, And there the dead men lay.	240
	I looked to heaven, and tried to pray; But or ever a prayer had gusht, A wicked whisper came, and made My heart as dry as dust.	245
	I closed my lids, and kept them close, And the balls like pulses beat; For the sky and the sea, and the sea and the sky Lay like a load on my weary eye, And the dead were at my feet.	250
But the curse liveth for him in the eye of the dead men.	The cold sweat melted from their limbs, Nor rot nor reek did they: The look with which they looked on me Had never passed away.	255
	An orphan's curse would drag to hell A spirit from on high; But oh! more horrible than that	

232–5 *Alone ... agony* This central stanza, repeated with significant variation of phrasing and syntax at lines 597–600, dispenses with a main verb to give immediacy to the mariner's sense of being marooned in an unprotected universe.
236 *The ... beautiful!* At this stage the mariner is struck by the beauty of his dead comrades, a beauty contrasted with the 'thousand thousand slimy things' (l. 238) allowed to live on, along with himself. His later admiration of the 'beauty' of the 'happy living things' (ll. 283, 282) gains in force when this earlier passage is borne in mind.
250 *For ... sky* The longer line and repetitions convey the mariner's sense of weariness.

	Is the curse in a dead man's eye!	260
	Seven days, seven nights, I saw that curse,	
	And yet I could not die.	

In his loneliness and fixedness he yearneth towards the journeying Moon, and the stars that still sojourn, yet still move onward; and every where the blue sky belongs to them, and is their	The moving Moon went up the sky, And no where did abide: Softly she was going up, And a star or two beside—	265
	Her beams bemocked the sultry main, Like April hoar-frost spread But where the ship's huge shadow lay, The charmed water burnt alway A still and awful red.	270

appointed rest, and their native country and their own natural homes, which they enter unannounced, as lords that are certainly expected and yet there is a silent joy at their arrival.

By the light of the Moon he beholdeth God's creatures of the great calm.	Beyond the shadow of the ship, I watched the water-snakes: They moved in tracks of shining white, And when they reared, the elfish light Fell off in hoary flakes.	275
	Within the shadow of the ship I watched their rich attire: Blue, glossy green, and velvet black, They coiled and swam; and every track Was a flash of golden fire.	280
Their beauty and their happiness. He blesseth them in his heart.	O happy living things! no tongue Their beauty might declare: A spring of love gushed from my heart, And I blessed them unaware: Sure my kind saint took pity on me, And I blessed them unaware.	285
The spell begins to break.	The self-same moment I could pray; And from my neck so free The Albatross fell off, and sank Like lead into the sea.	290

PART V

Oh sleep! it is a gentle thing,	
Beloved from pole to pole!	
To Mary Queen the praise be given!	
She sent the gentle sleep from Heaven,	295
That slid into my soul.	

263–6 *The moving . . . beside* In this stanza, and its graceful gloss, the mariner's 'yearning' towards 'the journeying Moon' shows a movement out of self that anticipates the blessing of the water-snakes (and is marked off from the previous stanza that closes with two uses of 'I' in successive lines, 261, 262).
267–81 *Her beams . . . golden fire* Colours are vital here:

the mariner is first able to see beyond the apparently permanent 'still and awful red' (l. 271) to 'the tracks of shining white' (l. 274) when the water-snakes are 'Beyond the shadow of the ship' (l. 272); then, as though empowered by this seeing, he sees, even 'Within the shadow of the ship' (l. 277), the snakes' 'rich attire' (l. 278) and its various colours.

By grace of the holy Mother, the ancient Mariner is refreshed with rain.	The silly buckets on the deck, That had so long remained, I dreamt that they were filled with dew; And when I awoke, it rained.	300
	My lips were wet, my throat was cold, My garments all were dank; Sure I had drunken in my dreams, And still my body drank.	
	I moved, and could not feel my limbs: I was so light—almost I thought that I had died in sleep, And was a blessed ghost.	305
He heareth sounds and seeth strange sights and commotions in the sky and the element.	And soon I heard a roaring wind: It did not come anear; But with its sound it shook the sails, That were so thin and sere.	310
	The upper air burst into life! And a hundred fire-flags sheen, To and fro they were hurried about! And to and fro, and in and out, The wan stars danced between.	315
	And the coming wind did roar more loud, And the sails did sigh like sedge; And the rain poured down from one black cloud; The Moon was at its edge.	320
	The thick black cloud was cleft, and still The Moon was at its side: Like waters shot from some high crag, The lightning fell with never a jag, A river steep and wide.	325
The bodies of the ship's crew are inspired and the ship moves on;	The loud wind never reached the ship, Yet now the ship moved on! Beneath the lightning and the Moon The dead men gave a groan.	330
	They groaned, they stirred, they all uprose, Nor spake, nor moved their eyes; It had been strange, even in a dream, To have seen those dead men rise.	
	The helmsman steered, the ship moved on; Yet never a breeze up-blew; The mariners all 'gan work the ropes, Where they were wont to do; They raised their limbs like lifeless tools— We were a ghastly crew.	335 340

Gloss to 297–300 *By grace of the holy Mother* The sentiment is profoundly pre-Reformation, at odds with the usual critical view that the gloss is written in the manner of a seventeenth-century scholar.
297 *silly* Plain, simple; might also mean 'holy'.

327–8 *The loud . . . moved on* Reverses the meaning of 1798, in which 'The strong wind reach'd the ship: it roar'd / And dropp'd down, like a stone!'. The later version (an 1800 revision) stresses the ship's mysterious movement.

Samuel Taylor Coleridge (1772–1834) 199

                The body of my brother's son
                Stood by me, knee to knee:
                The body and I pulled at one rope,
                But he said nought to me.

But not by the souls   'I fear thee, ancient Mariner!'   345
of the men, nor by   Be calm, thou Wedding-Guest!
dæmons of earth or   'Twas not those souls that fled in pain,
middle air, but by a   Which to their corses came again,
blessed troop of
angelic spirits, sent   For when it dawned—they dropped their arms,   350
down by the   And clustered round the mast;
invocation of the   Sweet sounds rose slowly through their mouths,
guardian saint.   And from their bodies passed.

                Around, around, flew each sweet sound,
                Then darted to the Sun;   355
                Slowly the sounds came back again,
                Now mixed, now one by one.

                Sometimes a-dropping from the sky
                I heard the sky-lark sing;
                Sometimes all little birds that are,   360
                How they seemed to fill the sea and air
                With their sweet jargoning!

                And now 'twas like all instruments,
                Now like a lonely flute;
                And now it is an angel's song,   365
                That makes the heavens be mute.

                It ceased; yet still the sails made on
                A pleasant noise till noon,
                A noise like of a hidden brook
                In the leafy month of June,   370
                That to the sleeping woods all night
                Singeth a quiet tune.

                Till noon we quietly sailed on,
                Yet never a breeze did breathe:
                Slowly and smoothly went the ship,   375
                Moved onward from beneath.

The lonesome Spirit   Under the keel nine fathom deep,
from the south-pole   From the land of mist and snow,
carries on the ship   The spirit slid: and it was he
as far as the Line, in   That made the ship to go.   380
obedience to the   The sails at noon left off their tune,
angelic troop, but   And the ship stood still also.
still requireth
vengeance.   The Sun, right up above the mast,
                Had fixed her to the ocean:

---

344 *nought to me* Followed in 1798 by the lines, 'And I quak'd to think of my own voice / How frightful it would be!'.
345–9 *'I fear ... blest* Not in 1798.
350–72 *For when ... tune* Contrast this beautiful if eerie evocation of 'sweet sounds' with the mariner's inability to speak earlier in the poem; it has the effect of a paradisal interlude between the poem's versions of the *Inferno* and the *Purgatorio*. In 1798 there are four stanzas following line 372 omitted in the later version.

But in a minute she 'gan stir, 385
With a short uneasy motion—
Backwards and forwards half her length
With a short uneasy motion.

Then like a pawing horse let go,
She made a sudden bound; 390
It flung the blood into my head,
And I fell down in a swound.

<small>The Polar Spirit's fellow-dæmons, the invisible inhabitants of the element, take part in his wrong; and two of them relate, one to the other, that penance long and heavy for the ancient Mariner hath been accorded to the Polar Spirit, who returneth southward.</small>

How long in that same fit I lay,
I have not to declare;
But ere my living life returned, 395
I heard and in my soul discerned
Two voices in the air.

'Is it he?' quoth one, 'Is this the man?
By him who died on cross,
With his cruel bow he laid full low 400
The harmless Albatross.

The spirit who bideth by himself
In the land of mist and snow,
He loved the bird that loved the man
Who shot him with his bow.' 405

The other was a softer voice,
As soft as honey-dew:
Quoth he, 'The man hath penance done,
And penance more will do.'

PART VI

FIRST VOICE

'But tell me, tell me! speak again, 410
Thy soft response renewing—
What makes that ship drive on so fast?
What is the ocean doing?'

SECOND VOICE

'Still as a slave before his lord,
The ocean hath no blast; 415
His great bright eye most silently
Up to the Moon is cast—

If he may know which way to go;
For she guides him smooth or grim.
See, brother, see! how graciously 420
She looketh down on him.'

FIRST VOICE

<small>The Mariner hath been cast into a</small>

'But why drives on that ship so fast,
Without or wave or wind?'

---

396 *in my soul discerned* The inwardness of the phrasing is striking.
402–9 *The spirit . . . will do.'* The two voices articulate different views of the mariner's suffering; the first implies that it is the penance owed to and exacted by 'the spirit who bideth by himself'; the second, less causal in his approach, asserts merely that the mariner has done and will continue to do penance.

trance; for the angelic power causeth the vessel to drive northward faster than human life could endure.

SECOND VOICE

'The air is cut away before,
And closes from behind.   425

Fly, brother, fly! more high, more high!
Or we shall be belated:
For slow and slow that ship will go,
When the Mariner's trance is abated.'

The super-natural motion is retarded; the Mariner awakes, and his penance begins anew.

I woke, and we were sailing on   430
As in a gentle weather:
'Twas night, calm night, the moon was high;
The dead men stood together.

All stood together on the deck,
For a charnel-dungeon fitter: 435
All fixed on me their stony eyes,
That in the Moon did glitter.

The pang, the curse, with which they died,
Had never passed away:
I could not draw my eyes from theirs,   440
Nor turn them up to pray.

The curse is finally expiated.

And now this spell was snapt: once more
I viewed the ocean green,
And looked far forth, yet little saw
Of what had else been seen—   445

Like one, that on a lonesome road
Doth walk in fear and dread,
And having once turned round walks on,
And turns no more his head;
Because he knows, a frightful fiend   450
Doth close behind him tread.

But soon there breathed a wind on me,
Nor sound nor motion made:
Its path was not upon the sea,
In ripple or in shade.   455

It raised my hair, it fanned my cheek
Like a meadow-gale of spring—
It mingled strangely with my fears,
Yet it felt like a welcoming.

Swiftly, swiftly flew the ship,   460
Yet she sailed softly too:
Sweetly, sweetly blew the breeze—
On me alone it blew.

And the ancient Mariner beholdeth his native country.

Oh! dream of joy! is this indeed
The light-house top I see?   465
Is this the hill? is this the kirk?
Is this mine own countree?

446–51 *Like one . . . tread* The triple *b* rhyme in this stanza reinforces the terror of the simile.
458 *It mingled . . . fears* A line that captures the double mood of the mariner's voyage at this stage: though the gloss at line 442 asserts that 'The curse is finally expiated' there is an immediate movement into 'fear and dread' (l. 447), and an equally abrupt switch into the 'welcoming' (l. 459) of the unearthly wind of line 452.

We drifted o'er the harbour-bar,
And I with sobs did pray—
O let me be awake, my God! 470
Or let me sleep alway.

The harbour-bay was clear as glass,
So smoothly it was strewn!
And on the bay the moonlight lay,
And the shadow of the Moon. 475

The rock shone bright, the kirk no less,
That stands above the rock:
The moonlight steeped in silentness
The steady weathercock.

The angelic spirits leave the dead bodies,

And the bay was white with silent light, 480
Till rising from the same,
Full many shapes, that shadows were,
In crimson colours came.

And appear in their own forms of light.

A little distance from the prow
Those crimson shadows were: 485
I turned my eyes upon the deck—
Oh, Christ! what saw I there!

Each corse lay flat, lifeless and flat,
And, by the holy rood!
A man all light, a seraph-man, 490
On every corse there stood.

This seraph-band, each waved his hand:
It was a heavenly sight!
They stood as signals to the land,
Each one a lovely light; 495

This seraph-band, each waved his hand,
No voice did they impart—
No voice; but oh! the silence sank
Like music on my heart.

But soon I heard the dash of oars, 500
I heard the Pilot's cheer;
My head was turned perforce away
And I saw a boat appear.

The Pilot and the Pilot's boy,
I heard them coming fast: 505
Dear Lord in Heaven! it was a joy
The dead men could not blast.

I saw a third—I heard his voice:
It is the Hermit good!
He singeth loud his godly hymns 510
That he makes in the wood.
He'll shrieve my soul, he'll wash away
The Albatross's blood.

498–9 *No voice . . . heart* Another moment of counterpoint: voiceless silence that is like music; joy that speaks volumes about preceding pain.

PART VII

The Hermit of the Wood,

This Hermit good lives in that wood
Which slopes down to the sea.   515
How loudly his sweet voice he rears!
He loves to talk with marineres
That come from a far countree.

He kneels at morn, and noon, and eve—
He hath a cushion plump: 520
It is the moss that wholly hides
The rotted old oak-stump.

The skiff-boat neared: I heard them talk,
'Why, this is strange, I trow!
Where are those lights so many and fair,   525
That signal made but now?'

Approacheth the ship with wonder.

'Strange, by my faith!' the Hermit said—
'And they answered not our cheer!
The planks looked warped! and see those sails,
How thin they are and sere!   530
I never saw aught like to them,
Unless perchance it were

Brown skeletons of leaves that lag
My forest-brook along;
When the ivy-tod is heavy with snow,   535
And the owlet whoops to the wolf below,
That eats the she-wolf's young.'

'Dear Lord! it hath a fiendish look—
(The Pilot made reply)
I am a-feared'—'Push on, push on!'   540
Said the Hermit cheerily.

The boat came closer to the ship,
But I nor spake nor stirred;
The boat came close beneath the ship,
And straight a sound was heard.   545

The ship suddenly sinketh.

Under the water it rumbled on,
Still louder and more dread:
It reached the ship, it split the bay;
The ship went down like lead.

The ancient Mariner is saved in the Pilot's boat.

Stunned by that loud and dreadful sound,   550
Which sky and ocean smote,
Like one that hath been seven days drowned
My body lay afloat;
But swift as dreams, myself I found
Within the Pilot's boat.   555

Upon the whirl, where sank the ship,
The boat spun round and round;

519–22 *He kneels ... oak-stump* The Hermit has an attachment to nature that seems not fully to accommodate the terrors experienced by the mariner. It may be telling that his 'cushion' is 'the moss that wholly hides / The rotted old oak-stump', as though disguising less appealing aspects of the natural world.

And all was still, save that the hill
Was telling of the sound.

I moved my lips—the Pilot shrieked 560
And fell down in a fit;
The holy Hermit raised his eyes,
And prayed where he did sit.

I took the oars: the Pilot's boy,
Who now doth crazy go, 565
Laughed loud and long, and all the while
His eyes went to and fro.
'Ha! ha!' quoth he, 'full plain I see,
The Devil knows how to row.'

And now, all in my own countree, 570
I stood on the firm land!
The Hermit stepped forth from the boat,
And scarcely he could stand.

<small>The ancient Mariner earnestly entreateth the Hermit to shrieve him; and the penance of life falls on him.</small>

'O shrieve me, shrieve me, holy man!'
The Hermit crossed his brow. 575
'Say quick,' quoth he, 'I bid thee say—
What manner of man art thou?'

Forthwith this frame of mine was wrenched
With a woful agony,
Which forced me to begin my tale; 580
And then it left me free.

<small>And ever and anon through out his future life an agony constraineth him to travel from land to land.</small>

Since then, at an uncertain hour,
That agony returns:
And till my ghastly tale is told,
This heart within me burns. 585

I pass, like night, from land to land;
I have strange power of speech;
That moment that his face I see,
I know the man that must hear me:
To him my tale I teach. 590

What loud uproar bursts from that door!
The wedding-guests are there:
But in the garden-bower the bride
And bride-maids singing are:
And hark the little vesper bell, 595
Which biddeth me to prayer!

O Wedding-Guest! this soul hath been
Alone on a wide wide sea:
So lonely 'twas, that God himself
Scarce seemed there to be. 600

O sweeter than the marriage-feast,
'Tis sweeter far to me,
To walk together to the kirk
With a goodly company!—

---

579 *woful agony* The mariner's compulsion to tell his story is more 'agony' than expiation, even though telling it leaves him 'free' (l. 581), for a while.

590 *teach* The mariner views his 'tale' as having a capacity to instruct.

> To walk together to the kirk, 605
> And all together pray,
> While each to his great Father bends,
> Old men, and babes, and loving friends
> And youths and maidens gay!

And to teach, by his own example, love and reverence to all things that God made and loveth.

> Farewell, farewell! but this I tell 610
> To thee, thou Wedding-Guest!
> He prayeth well, who loveth well
> Both man and bird and beast.
>
> He prayeth best, who loveth best
> All things both great and small; 615
> For the dear God who loveth us,
> He made and loveth all.
>
> The Mariner, whose eye is bright,
> Whose beard with age is hoar,
> Is gone: and now the Wedding-Guest 620
> Turned from the bridegroom's door.
>
> He went like one that hath been stunned,
> And is of sense forlorn:
> A sadder and a wiser man,
> He rose the morrow morn. 625

Christabel

The poem, first published with 'Kubla Khan' and 'The Pains of Sleep' in 1816, was originally meant for the second edition of *Lyrical Ballads* (1800), but was omitted from that volume as a result of a feeling that it 'was in direct opposition to the very purpose for which the Lyrical Ballads were published' (*CL*, vol. 1, p. 631). These are Coleridge's words in a letter, but they appear to describe Wordsworth's views, since in another letter Coleridge writes that Wordsworth 'rejected it from his volume as disproportionate both in size & merit, & as discordant in it's character' (*CL*, 1, p. 643). Coleridge seems in due course to have interpreted the omission of the poem as rejection, one that strengthened his growing feeling of poetic inadequacy. The poem was circulated in manuscript and heard at recitals: Scott heard it recited in 1802, while Byron heard Scott quote from the poem in 1815, and urged his publisher John Murray to publish it.

Coleridge represents the poem as unfinished and gave several accounts of how or in what spirit he might have completed it. Yet it may be that the poem is as completed as it could have been. Like 'The Ancient Mariner' in its concern with evil, 'Christabel' is unlike the earlier poem in that it avoids, in Richard Holmes's words, 'the traditional form of a ballad tale, with its rapid sequence of unfolding action' (*Coleridge: Early Visions*, p. 287). The poem depends less on plot than on mood, and, especially in Part 1, deploys great metrical and narrative cunning to explore the scarcely expressible feelings induced by the sinister, glamorous Geraldine's obscurely hypnotic and sexual seduction of the innocent Christabel, a name that mingles the associations of 'Christ' and 'Abel', the first victim of murder. Part 1 is a night-piece, in which Christabel, praying out 'in the midnight wood' (l. 29) for her 'own betrothed knight' (l. 28), befriends the apparently distressed Geraldine, a 'damsel bright' (l. 58) who tells a story of abduction by 'Five warriors' (l. 81). Geraldine is carried over the castle threshold by Christabel, who misses various warning signs (Geraldine's inability to pray; the mastiff bitch's moan; the lighting up of the extinguished torches) and goes to sleep with the stranger. There are strong lesbian and vampiric suggestions in the writing. There are also hints that Geraldine is sinned against as well as sinning, compelled to exercise power over Christabel: 'Deep from within' (l. 257), we are told before she lies down with Christabel, 'she seems half-way / To lift some weight with sick assay, / And eyes the maid and seeks delay' (ll. 257–9), the triple rhyme enforcing the 'delay' she seeks. The Conclusion to Part 1 concedes that Geraldine has gained power over Christabel, but seeks to limit the damage: 'O Geraldine! one hour was thine — / Thou'st had thy will!' (ll. 305–6). The voice Coleridge contrives here approaches and shies away from the meaning of the experiences that it glosses, and it finishes with the piously groundless hope 'That saints will aid if men will call! / For the blue sky bends over all!' (ll. 330–1). That 'For' is deliberately inconsequential.

The narrator is clutching at straws; Part 1 has touched delicately and disquietingly on the idea of one person's violation of another, and, more disturbingly even, of the victim's possible complicity: support for this is given by the mixture in Christabel of latent sexuality and overt piety, as when the poetry moves from her 'dreams all yesternight / Of her own betrothed knight' (ll. 27–8) to her act of praying for him. When she sees Geraldine, she is first afraid, then fascinated: 'Mary mother, save me now! / (Said Christabel,) And who art thou?' (ll. 69–70). Her vulnerability comes across in that imploring of the great Catholic mother-figure, Mary, and Christabel's innocence and goodness are overtly affirmed at several moments. Still, it is she who, albeit unintentionally, carries the evil represented by Geraldine into the castle and who, albeit without conscious sexual intention, beseeches Geraldine 'This night, to share your couch with me' (l. 122). We later learn that Christabel's mother 'died the hour that I was born' (l. 197), and there is, in part, an eerie sense in which Geraldine performs the role of stepmother; so, in the Conclusion, the narrator, distressed by the 'harms' done to Christabel, speaks wonderingly of how 'the worker of these harms, / That holds the maiden in her arms, / Seems to slumber still and mild, / As a mother with her child' (ll. 298–301).

Coleridge's own phrase – 'witchery by daylight' (see *The Collected Works of Samuel Taylor Coleridge: Table Talk*, 2 vols, ed. Carl Woodring (Princeton, NJ: Princeton University Press, 1990), vol. 1, p. 410) – describes the atmosphere of the second Part. Here Geraldine's control over Christabel extends to her manipulation of Christabel's father, Sir Leoline, friend in his youth of his visitor's supposed father, Lord Roland, from whom he was estranged. The description of this estrangement shows a fascination with perversities of feeling which echoes the perversion of goodness at the poem's centre: 'to be wroth with one we love, / Doth work like madness in the brain' (ll. 412–13), the narrator comments. His 'we' draws the reader into recognizing an only too familiar form of 'madness' and brings a seemingly Gothic tale into connection with quotidian human experience; so, too, does the Conclusion to Part 2. Apparently unrelated to the story, it serves as a psychological spin-off from Sir Leoline's anger with his daughter for pleading that he send Geraldine away, and describes a frightening process of over-compensation by which 'love's excess' (l. 664) can find expression only through 'words of unmeant bitterness' (l. 665). Geraldine's conquest seems total when Christabel is effectively hypnotized, passively imitating her conqueror's 'look of dull and treacherous hate' (l. 606) through 'forced unconscious sympathy' (l. 609). Bard Bracy's dream of a dove strangled by a serpent allegorizes Christabel's peril. But Bracy reveals, too, through his dream and subsequent resolution 'To wander through the forest bare' (l. 562), the poem's fascination with transgression and the forbidden.

Preface

THE first part of the following poem was written in the year 1797, at Stowey, in the county of Somerset. The Second part, after my return from Germany, in the year 1800, at Keswick, Cumberland. It is probable that if the poem had been finished at either of the former periods, or if even the first and second part had been published in the year 1800, the impression of its originality would have been much greater than I dare at present expect. But for this I have only my own indolence to blame. The dates are mentioned for the exclusive purpose of precluding charges of plagiarism or servile imitation from myself. For there is amongst us a set of critics, who seem to hold, that every possible thought and image is traditional; who have no notion that there are such things as fountains in the world, small as well as great; and who would therefore charitably derive every rill they behold flowing, from a perforation made in some other man's tank. I am confident, however, that as far as the present poem is concerned, the celebrated poets whose writings I might be suspected of having imitated, either in particular passages, or in the tone and the spirit of the whole, would be among the first to vindicate me from the charge, and who, on any striking coincidence, would permit me to address them in this doggerel version of two monkish Latin hexameters.

'Tis mine and it is likewise yours;
But an if this will not do;
Let it be mine, good friend!
for I Am the poorer of the two.

I have only to add that the metre of Christabel is not, properly speaking, irregular, though it may seem so from its being founded on a new principle: namely, that of counting in each line the accents, not the syllables. Though the latter may vary from seven to twelve, yet in each line the accents will be found to be only four. Nevertheless, this occasional variation in number of syllables is not introduced wantonly, or for the mere ends of convenience, but in correspondence with some transition in the nature of the imagery or passion.

PART I

'TIS the middle of night by the castle clock,
And the owls have awakened the crowing cock;
Tu—whit!—Tu—whoo!
And hark, again! the crowing cock,
How drowsily it crew.   5

Sir Leoline, the Baron rich,
Hath a toothless mastiff bitch;
From her kennel beneath the rock
She maketh answer to the clock,
Four for the quarters, and twelve for the hour;   10
Ever and aye, by shine and shower,
Sixteen short howls, not over loud;
Some say, she sees my lady's shroud.

Is the night chilly and dark?
The night is chilly, but not dark.   15
The thin gray cloud is spread on high,
It covers but not hides the sky.
The moon is behind, and at the full;
And yet she looks both small and dull.
The night is chill, the cloud is gray: 20
'Tis a month before the month of May,
And the Spring comes slowly up this way.

The lovely lady, Christabel,
Whom her father loves so well,
What makes her in the wood so late,   25
A furlong from the castle gate?
She had dreams all yesternight
Of her own betrothed knight;
And she in the midnight wood will pray
For the weal of her lover that's far away.   30

She stole along, she nothing spoke,
The sighs she heaved were soft and low,
And naught was green upon the oak
But moss and rarest misletoe:
She kneels beneath the huge oak tree,   35

Preface
I have only . . . passion This account of the poem's 'metre' shows Coleridge's sense that 'variation' – in this poem not of 'accents', but of 'number of syllables' – bears vitally on the meaning, occurring, as it does, 'in correspondence with some transition in the nature of the imagery or passion'. So, in the opening lines, the longer second line, 'And the owls have awakened the crowing cock' (l. 2), creates, for all its apparent air of jubilation, an effect of something inverted and hollow; an effect reinforced by the shorter fifth line, 'How drowsily it crew', where the awoken cock succumbs to drowsiness in a faintly sinister way.

Throughout the poem, each line seems like a stealthy event.
13 *Some say . . . shroud* Christabel's dead mother is introduced here with the narrative obliquity ('Some say') favoured by the poem. This dead mother is here not merely for melodramatic purposes, but to reinforce Christabel's vulnerability to the hypnotizing force of another woman's will.
27–30 *She had dreams . . . away* Coleridge implies that Christabel's feelings are a mixture of the sacred ('she . . . will pray') and unconsciously erotic ('dreams all yesternight').
30 *weal* Welfare.

And in silence prayeth she.

The lady sprang up suddenly,
The lovely lady, Christabel!
It moaned as near, as near can be,
But what it is she cannot tell.— 40
On the other side it seems to be,
Of the huge, broad-breasted, old oak tree.

The night is chill; the forest bare;
Is it the wind that moaneth bleak?
There is not wind enough in the air 45
To move away the ringlet curl
From the lovely lady's cheek—
There is not wind enough to twirl
The one red leaf, the last of its clan,
That dances as often as dance it can, 50
Hanging so light, and hanging so high,
On the topmost twig that looks up at the sky.

Hush, beating heart of Christabel!
Jesu, Maria, shield her well!
She folded her arms beneath her cloak, 55
And stole to the other side of the oak.
            What sees she there?

There she sees a damsel bright,
Drest in a silken robe of white,
That shadowy in the moonlight shone: 60
The neck that made that white robe wan,
Her stately neck, and arms were bare;
Her blue-veined feet unsandal'd were,
And wildly glittered here and there
The gems entangled in her hair. 65

I guess, 'twas frightful there to see
A lady so richly clad as she—
Beautiful exceedingly!

Mary mother, save me now!
(Said Christabel,) And who art thou? 70

The lady strange made answer meet,
And her voice was faint and sweet:—
Have pity on my sore distress,
I scarce can speak for weariness:
Stretch forth thy hand, and have no fear! 75
Said Christabel, How camest thou here?
And the lady, whose voice was faint and sweet,
Did thus pursue her answer meet:—

My sire is of a noble line,
And my name is Geraldine: 80

44–5 *Is it the wind . . . air* As earlier (ll. 14–15) and later (149–50), Coleridge uses the question-and-answer format to generate unease.

78 *Did thus pursue . . . meet* A suggestion hovers in the wording here that Geraldine has got her 'answer' off pat.

Five warriors seized me yestermorn,
Me, even me, a maid forlorn:
They choked my cries with force and fright,
And tied me on a palfrey white.
The palfrey was as fleet as wind,   85
And they rode furiously behind.

They spurred amain, their steeds were white:
And once we crossed the shade of night.
As sure as Heaven shall rescue me,
I have no thought what men they be;   90
Nor do I know how long it is
(For I have lain entranced I wis)
Since one, the tallest of the five,
Took me from the palfrey's back,
A weary woman, scarce alive.   95
Some muttered words his comrades spoke:
He placed me underneath this oak;
He swore they would return with haste;
Whither they went I cannot tell—
I thought I heard, some minutes past,   100
Sounds as of a castle bell.
Stretch forth thy hand (thus ended she),
And help a wretched maid to flee.

Then Christabel stretched forth her hand,
And comforted fair Geraldine: 105
O well, bright dame! may you command
The service of Sir Leoline;
And gladly our stout chivalry
Will he send forth and friends withal
To guide and guard you safe and free   110
Home to your noble father's hall.

She rose: and forth with steps they passed
That strove to be, and were not, fast.
Her gracious stars the lady blest,
And thus spake on sweet Christabel: 115
All our household are at rest,
The hall as silent as the cell;
Sir Leoline is weak in health,
And may not well awakened be,
But we will move as if in stealth,   120
And I beseech your courtesy,
This night, to share your couch with me.

They crossed the moat, and Christabel
Took the key that fitted well;
A little door she opened straight,   125
All in the middle of the gate;
The gate that was ironed within and without,

---

88 *And once . . . night* This line is made the more uncanny by the repeated rhyme-sound in lines 83–4, 87–8.
113 *That . . . fast* The use of 'and' where one might expect 'but' emphasizes Christabel's domination by Geraldine. In an earlier version Coleridge wrote, 'yet were not fast'.

121–2 *And . . . me* It is Christabel who (in all innocence) invites Geraldine to sleep with her, just as in lines 130–2 it is Christabel who lifts Geraldine 'Over the threshold of the gate'.

Where an army in battle array had marched out.
The lady sank, belike through pain,
And Christabel with might and main 130
Lifted her up, a weary weight,
Over the threshold of the gate:
Then the lady rose again,
And moved, as she were not in pain.

So free from danger, free from fear, 135
They crossed the court: right glad they were.
And Christabel devoutly cried
To the lady by her side,
Praise we the Virgin all divine
Who hath rescued thee from thy distress! 140
Alas, alas! said Geraldine,
I cannot speak for weariness.
So free from danger, free from fear,
They crossed the court: right glad they were.

Outside her kennel, the mastiff old 145
Lay fast asleep, in moonshine cold.
The mastiff old did not awake,
Yet she an angry moan did make!
And what can ail the mastiff bitch?
Never till now she uttered yell 150
Beneath the eye of Christabel.
Perhaps it is the owlet's scritch:
For what can ail the mastiff bitch?

They passed the hall, that echoes still,
Pass as lightly as you will! 155
The brands were flat, the brands were dying,
Amid their own white ashes lying;
But when the lady passed, there came
A tongue of light, a fit of flame;
And Christabel saw the lady's eye, 160
And nothing else saw she thereby,
Save the boss of the shield of Sir Leoline tall,
Which hung in a murky old niche in the wall.
O softly tread, said Christabel,
My father seldom sleepeth well. 165

Sweet Christabel her feet doth bare,
And jealous of the listening air
They steal their way from stair to stair,
Now in glimmer, and now in gloom,
And now they pass the Baron's room, 170
As still as death, with stifled breath!
And now have reached her chamber door;
And now doth Geraldine press down
The rushes of the chamber floor.

The moon shines dim in the open air, 175
And not a moonbeam enters here.

134 *as she were not in pain* This links with the equally uncertain 'belike through pain' (l. 129).
160–1 *And . . . thereby* The first explicit mention of a motif – the power exercised by a gaze – that is central to the poem.

But they without its light can see
The chamber carved so curiously,
Carved with figures strange and sweet,
All made out of the carver's brain, 180
For a lady's chamber meet:
The lamp with twofold silver chain
Is fastened to an angel's feet.

The silver lamp burns dead and dim;
But Christabel the lamp will trim. 185
She trimmed the lamp, and made it bright,
And left it swinging to and fro,
While Geraldine, in wretched plight,
Sank down upon the floor below.

O weary lady, Geraldine, 190
I pray you, drink this cordial wine!
It is a wine of virtuous powers;
My mother made it of wild flowers.

And will your mother pity me,
Who am a maiden most forlorn? 195
Christabel answered—Woe is me!
She died the hour that I was born.
I have heard the grey-haired friar tell
How on her death-bed she did say,
That she should hear the castle-bell 200
Strike twelve upon my wedding-day.
O mother dear! that thou wert here!
I would, said Geraldine, she were!

But soon with altered voice, said she—
'Off, wandering mother! Peak and pine! 205
I have power to bid thee flee.'
Alas! what ails poor Geraldine?
Why stares she with unsettled eye?
Can she the bodiless dead espy?
And why with hollow voice cries she, 210
'Off, woman, off! this hour is mine—
Though thou her guardian spirit be,
Off, woman, off! 'tis given to me.'

Then Christabel knelt by the lady's side,
And raised to heaven her eyes so blue— 215
Alas! said she, this ghastly ride—
Dear lady! it hath wildered you!
The lady wiped her moist cold brow,
And faintly said, ''tis over now!'

Again the wild-flower wine she drank: 220
Her fair large eyes 'gan glitter bright,
And from the floor whereon she sank,

---

180 *All made . . . brain* A suggestive line, implying the subjective meaning-making of both Christabel (see l. 239) and, possibly, Coleridge, too.
203–4 *I would . . . she* It is possible to read the 'altered voice' of line 204 both ways: as proof that either Geraldine was genuine or that she was insincere in wishing that Christabel's mother were present.
207 *Alas! . . . Geraldine?* The question's wording picks up on lines 149 and 153. It is noteworthy that the narrator drops any pretence here of attempting to provide an answer.

The lofty lady stood upright:
She was most beautiful to see,
Like a lady of a far countree. 225

And thus the lofty lady spake—
'All they who live in the upper sky,
Do love you, holy Christabel!
And you love them, and for their sake
And for the good which me befel, 230
Even I in my degree will try,
Fair maiden, to requite you well.
But now unrobe yourself; for I
Must pray, ere yet in bed I lie.'

Quoth Christabel, So let it be! 235
And as the lady bade, did she.
Her gentle limbs did she undress,
And lay down in her loveliness.

But through her brain of weal and woe
So many thoughts moved to and fro, 240
That vain it were her lids to close;
So half-way from the bed she rose,
And on her elbow did recline
To look at the lady Geraldine.

Beneath the lamp the lady bowed, 245
And slowly rolled her eyes around;
Then drawing in her breath aloud,
Like one that shuddered, she unbound
The cincture from beneath her breast:
Her silken robe, and inner vest, 250
Dropt to her feet, and full in view,
Behold! her bosom and half her side—
A sight to dream of, not to tell!
O shield her! shield sweet Christabel!

Yet Geraldine nor speaks nor stirs; 255
Ah! what a stricken look was hers!
Deep from within she seems half-way
To lift some weight with sick assay,
And eyes the maid and seeks delay;
Then suddenly, as one defied, 260
Collects herself in scorn and pride,
And lay down by the Maiden's side!—
And in her arms the maid she took,
    Ah wel-a-day!
And with low voice and doleful look 265
These words did say:
'In the touch of this bosom there worketh a spell,
Which is lord of thy utterance, Christabel!

---

248 *Like one that shuddered* The simile carefully stops short of saying that Geraldine did shudder.
252 *Behold . . . side* In the manuscript, Coleridge wrote:

    Behold! her bosom and half her side
    Are lean and old and foul of hue –
    A sight to dream of, not to tell,
    And she is to sleep with Christabel.

255–9 *Yet . . . delay* A key passage (first published in 1828) so far as Geraldine's presentation is concerned, since it indicates her reluctance to go through with her sorcery.
267–8 *'In . . . utterance* Christabel's 'lord' is no longer 'her lover that's far away' (l. 30), but Geraldine's 'spell'.

Thou knowest to-night, and wilt know to-morrow,
This mark of my shame, this seal of my sorrow; 270
    But vainly thou warrest,
      For this is alone in
    Thy power to declare,
      That in the dim forest
    Thou heard'st a low moaning, 275
And found'st a bright lady, surpassingly fair;
And didst bring her home with thee in love and in charity,
To shield her and shelter her from the damp air.'

THE CONCLUSION TO PART I

It was a lovely sight to see
The lady Christabel, when she 280
Was praying at the old oak tree.
    Amid the jagged shadows
    Of mossy leafless boughs,
    Kneeling in the moonlight,
    To make her gentle vows; 285
Her slender palms together prest,
Heaving sometimes on her breast;
Her face resigned to bliss or bale—
Her face, oh call it fair not pale,
And both blue eyes more bright than clear, 290
Each about to have a tear.

With open eyes (ah woe is me!)
Asleep, and dreaming fearfully,
Fearfully dreaming, yet, I wis,
Dreaming that alone, which is— 295
O sorrow and shame! Can this be she,
The lady, who knelt at the old oak tree?
And lo! the worker of these harms,
That holds the maiden in her arms,
Seems to slumber still and mild, 300
As a mother with her child.

A star hath set, a star hath risen,
O Geraldine! since arms of thine
Have been the lovely lady's prison.
O Geraldine! one hour was thine— 305
Thou'st had thy will! By tairn and rill,
The night-birds all that hour were still.
But now they are jubilant anew,
From cliff and tower, tu—whoo! tu—whoo!
Tu—whoo! tu—whoo! from wood and fell! 310

And see! the lady Christabel
Gathers herself from out her trance;
Her limbs relax, her countenance
Grows sad and soft; the smooth thin lids
Close o'er her eyes; and tears she sheds— 315

---

295 *Dreaming that alone, which is* An ironic convergence of dream and reality: Christabel's fearful dreams are grounded in what has happened to her.

Large tears that leave the lashes bright!
And oft the while she seems to smile
As infants at a sudden light!

Yea, she doth smile, and she doth weep,
Like a youthful hermitess, 320
Beauteous in a wilderness,
Who, praying always, prays in sleep.
And, if she move unquietly,
Perchance, 'tis but the blood so free
Comes back and tingles in her feet. 325
No doubt, she hath a vision sweet.
What if her guardian spirit 'twere,
What if she knew her mother near?
But this she knows, in joys and woes,
That saints will aid if men will call: 330
For the blue sky bends over all!

Part II

Each matin bell, the Baron saith,
Knells us back to a world of death.
These words Sir Leoline first said,
When he rose and found his lady dead: 335
These words Sir Leoline will say
Many a morn to his dying day!

And hence the custom and law began
That still at dawn the sacristan,
Who duly pulls the heavy bell, 340
Five and forty beads must tell
Between each stroke—a warning knell,
Which not a soul can choose but hear
From Bratha Head to Wyndermere.

Saith Bracy the bard, So let it knell! 345
And let the drowsy sacristan
Still count as slowly as he can!
There is no lack of such, I ween,
As well fill up the space between.
In Langdale Pike and Witch's Lair, 350
And Dungeon-ghyll so foully rent,
With ropes of rock and bells of air
Three sinful sextons' ghosts are pent,
Who all give back, one after t'other,
The death-note to their living brother; 355
And oft too, by the knell offended,
Just as their one! two! three! is ended,
The devil mocks the doleful tale
With a merry peal from Borodale.

The air is still! through mist and cloud 360
That merry peal comes ringing loud;
And Geraldine shakes off her dread,

323–4 *And, if . . . free* The narrator behaves now like someone anxious not to think the worst.

362 *And Geraldine . . . dread* A further suggestion of Geraldine's inner conflict.

And rises lightly from the bed;
Puts on her silken vestments white,
And tricks her hair in lovely plight, 365
And nothing doubting of her spell
Awakens the lady Christabel.
'Sleep you, sweet lady Christabel?
I trust that you have rested well.'

And Christabel awoke and spied 370
The same who lay down by her side—
O rather say, the same whom she
Raised up beneath the old oak tree!
Nay, fairer yet! and yet more fair!
For she belike hath drunken deep 375
Of all the blessedness of sleep!
And while she spake, her looks, her air
Such gentle thankfulness declare,
That (so it seemed) her girded vests
Grew tight beneath her heaving breasts. 380
'Sure I have sinn'd!' said Christabel,
'Now heaven be praised if all be well!'
And in low faltering tones, yet sweet,
Did she the lofty lady greet
With such perplexity of mind 385
As dreams too lively leave behind.

So quickly she rose, and quickly arrayed
Her maiden limbs, and having prayed
That He, who on the cross did groan,
Might wash away her sins unknown, 390
She forthwith led fair Geraldine
To meet her sire, Sir Leoline.

The lovely maid and the lady tall
Are pacing both into the hall,
And pacing on through page and groom, 395
Enter the Baron's presence-room.

The Baron rose, and while he prest
His gentle daughter to his breast,
With cheerful wonder in his eyes
The lady Geraldine espies, 400
And gave such welcome to the same,
As might beseem so bright a dame!

But when he heard the lady's tale,
And when she told her father's name,
Why waxed Sir Leoline so pale, 405
Murmuring o'er the name again,
Lord Roland de Vaux of Tryermaine?

Alas! they had been friends in youth;
But whispering tongues can poison truth;
And constancy lives in realms above; 410
And life is thorny; and youth is vain;
And to be wroth with one we love
Doth work like madness in the brain.
And thus it chanced, as I divine,
With Roland and Sir Leoline. 415

Each spake words of high disdain
And insult to his heart's best brother:
They parted—ne'er to meet again!
But never either found another
To free the hollow heart from paining— 420
They stood aloof, the scars remaining,
Like cliffs which had been rent asunder;
A dreary sea now flows between;—
But neither heat, nor frost, nor thunder,
Shall wholly do away, I ween, 425
The marks of that which once hath been.

Sir Leoline, a moment's space,
Stood gazing on the damsel's face:
And the youthful Lord of Tryermaine
Came back upon his heart again. 430

O then the Baron forgot his age,
His noble heart swelled high with rage;
He swore by the wounds in Jesu's side
He would proclaim it far and wide,
With trump and solemn heraldry, 435
That they, who thus had wronged the dame,
Were base as spotted infamy!
'And if they dare deny the same,
My herald shall appoint a week,
And let the recreant traitors seek 440
My tourney court—that there and then
I may dislodge their reptile souls
From the bodies and forms of men!'
He spake: his eye in lightning rolls!
For the lady was ruthlessly seized; and he kenned 445
In the beautiful lady the child of his friend!
And now the tears were on his face,
And fondly in his arms he took
Fair Geraldine, who met the embrace,
Prolonging it with joyous look. 450
Which when she viewed, a vision fell
Upon the soul of Christabel,
The vision of fear, the touch and pain!
She shrunk and shuddered, and saw again—
(Ah, woe is me! Was it for thee, 455
Thou gentle maid! such sights to see?)

Again she saw that bosom old,
Again she felt that bosom cold,
And drew in her breath with a hissing sound:
Whereat the Knight turned wildly round, 460
And nothing saw, but his own sweet maid
With eyes upraised, as one that prayed.

The touch, the sight, had passed away,
And in its stead that vision blest,

445–6 *For the lady . . . friend!* In the longer lines Coleridge captures how Sir Leoline warms to his theme, a good example of extra syllables being introduced for emotionally mimetic effect.

Which comforted her after-rest 465
While in the lady's arms she lay,
Had put a rapture in her breast,
And on her lips and o'er her eyes
Spread smiles like light!
                    With new surprise,
'What ails then my beloved child?' 470
The Baron said—His daughter mild
Made answer, 'All will yet be well!'
I ween, she had no power to tell
Aught else: so mighty was the spell.

Yet he, who saw this Geraldine, 475
Had deemed her sure a thing divine:
Such sorrow with such grace she blended,
As if she feared she had offended
Sweet Christabel, that gentle maid!
And with such lowly tones she prayed 480
She might be sent without delay
Home to her father's mansion.
                            'Nay!
Nay, by my soul!' said Leoline.
'Ho! Bracy the bard, the charge be thine!
Go thou, with music sweet and loud, 485
And take two steeds with trappings proud,
And take the youth whom thou lov'st best
To bear thy harp, and learn thy song,
And clothe you both in solemn vest,
And over the mountains haste along, 490
Lest wandering folk, that are abroad,
Detain you on the valley road.

'And when he has crossed the Irthing flood,
My merry bard! he hastes, he hastes
Up Knorren Moor, through Halegarth Wood, 495
And reaches soon that castle good
Which stands and threatens Scotland's wastes.

'Bard Bracy! bard Bracy! your horses are fleet,
Ye must ride up the hall, your music so sweet,
More loud than your horses' echoing feet! 500
And loud and loud to Lord Roland call,
Thy daughter is safe in Langdale hall!
Thy beautiful daughter is safe and free—
Sir Leoline greets thee thus through me!
He bids thee come without delay 505
With all thy numerous array
And take thy lovely daughter home:
And he will meet thee on the way
With all his numerous array
White with their panting palfreys' foam: 510
And, by mine honour! I will say,
That I repent me of the day
When I spake words of fierce disdain
To Roland de Vaux of Tryermaine!—
—For since that evil hour hath flown, 515

Many a summer's sun hath shone;
Yet ne'er found I a friend again
Like Roland de Vaux of Tryermaine.

The lady fell, and clasped his knees,
Her face upraised, her eyes o'erflowing; 520
And Bracy replied, with faltering voice,
His gracious Hail on all bestowing!—
'Thy words, thou sire of Christabel,
Are sweeter than my harp can tell;
Yet might I gain a boon of thee, 525
This day my journey should not be,
So strange a dream hath come to me,
That I had vowed with music loud
To clear yon wood from thing unblest,
Warned by a vision in my rest! 530
For in my sleep I saw that dove,
That gentle bird, whom thou dost love,
And call'st by thy own daughter's name—
Sir Leoline! I saw the same
Fluttering, and uttering fearful moan, 535
Among the green herbs in the forest alone.
Which when I saw and when I heard,
I wonder'd what might ail the bird;
For nothing near it could I see,
Save the grass and green herbs underneath the old tree.

'And in my dream methought I went 541
To search out what might there be found;
And what the sweet bird's trouble meant,
That thus lay fluttering on the ground.
I went and peered, and could descry 545
No cause for her distressful cry;
But yet for her dear lady's sake
I stooped, methought, the dove to take,
When lo! I saw a bright green snake
Coiled around its wings and neck. 550
Green as the herbs on which it couched,
Close by the dove's its head it crouched;
And with the dove it heaves and stirs,
Swelling its neck as she swelled hers!
I woke; it was the midnight hour, 555
The clock was echoing in the tower;
But though my slumber was gone by,
This dream it would not pass away—
It seems to live upon my eye!
And thence I vowed this self-same day 560
With music strong and saintly song
To wander through the forest bare,
Lest aught unholy loiter there.'
Thus Bracy said: the Baron, the while,

541–63 *'And in my dream . . . there.'* Bracy's dream, suggestive of the crushing of innocence by evil, focuses on seeing: in line 549, 'I saw a bright green snake', the verb recalls the earlier uses of 'I saw' at lines 531, 534 and 537; seeing passes into compelled vision in line 559 when he says that the dream 'seems to live upon my eye'.

Half-listening heard him with a smile; 565
Then turned to Lady Geraldine,
His eyes made up of wonder and love;
And said in courtly accents fine,
'Sweet maid, Lord Roland's beauteous dove,
With arms more strong than harp or song, 570
Thy sire and I will crush the snake!'
He kissed her forehead as he spake,
And Geraldine in maiden wise
Casting down her large bright eyes,
With blushing cheek and courtesy fine 575
She turned her from Sir Leoline;
Softly gathering up her train,
That o'er her right arm fell again;
And folded her arms across her chest,
And couched her head upon her breast, 580
And looked askance at Christabel—
Jesu, Maria, shield her well!

A snake's small eye blinks dull and shy;
And the lady's eyes they shrunk in her head,
Each shrunk up to a serpent's eye, 585
And with somewhat of malice, and more of dread,
At Christabel she looked askance!—
One moment—and the sight was fled!
But Christabel in dizzy trance
Stumbling on the unsteady ground 590
Shuddered aloud, with a hissing sound;
And Geraldine again turned round,
And like a thing, that sought relief,
Full of wonder and full of grief,
She rolled her large bright eyes divine 595
Wildly on Sir Leoline.

The maid, alas! her thoughts are gone,
She nothing sees—no sight but one!
The maid, devoid of guile and sin,
I know not how, in fearful wise, 600
So deeply had she drunken in
That look, those shrunken serpent eyes,
That all her features were resigned
To this sole image in her mind:
And passively did imitate 605
That look of full and treacherous hate!
And thus she stood, in dizzy trance,
Still picturing that look askance
With forced unconscious sympathy
Full before her father's view— 610
As far as such a look could be
In eyes so innocent and blue!

---

583 *A snake's . . . and shy* Compare the earlier description of the moon as 'both small and dull' (l. 19).
603–6 *That all . . . hate!* Coleridge describes here a process of passive imitation, an opposite yet eerie parody of the unifying imaginative activity he often recommended.

And when the trance was o'er, the maid
Paused awhile, and inly prayed:
Then falling at the Baron's feet, 615
'By my mother's soul do I entreat
That thou this woman send away!'
She said: and more she could not say:
For what she knew she could not tell,
O'er-mastered by the mighty spell. 620

Why is thy cheek so wan and wild,
Sir Leoline? Thy only child
Lies at thy feet, thy joy, thy pride,
So fair, so innocent, so mild;
The same, for whom thy lady died! 625
O by the pangs of her dear mother
Think thou no evil of thy child!
For her, and thee, and for no other,
She prayed the moment ere she died:
Prayed that the babe for whom she died, 630
Might prove her dear lord's joy and pride!
   That prayer her deadly pangs beguiled,
      Sir Leoline!
And wouldst thou wrong thy only child,
      Her child and thine? 635

Within the Baron's heart and brain
If thoughts, like these, had any share,
They only swelled his rage and pain,
And did but work confusion there.
His heart was cleft with pain and rage, 640
His cheeks they quivered, his eyes were wild,
Dishonoured thus in his old age;
Dishonoured by his only child,
And all his hospitality
To the wronged daughter of his friend 645
By more than woman's jealousy
Brought thus to a disgraceful end—
He rolled his eye with stern regard
Upon the gentle minstrel bard,
And said in tones abrupt, austere— 650
'Why, Bracy! dost thou loiter here?
I bade thee hence!' The bard obeyed;
And turning from his own sweet maid,
The aged knight, Sir Leoline,
Led forth the lady Geraldine! 655

The Conclusion to Part II

A little child, a limber elf,
Singing, dancing to itself,
A fairy thing with red round cheeks,
That always finds, and never seeks,
Makes such a vision to the sight 660
As fills a father's eyes with light;
And pleasures flow in so thick and fast
Upon his heart, that he at last

Must needs express his love's excess
With words of unmeant bitterness. 665
Perhaps 'tis pretty to force together
Thoughts so all unlike each other;
To mutter and mock a broken charm,
To dally with wrong that does no harm.
Perhaps 'tis tender too and pretty 670
At each wild word to feel within
A sweet recoil of love and pity.
And what, if in a world of sin
(O sorrow and shame should this be true!)
Such giddiness of heart and brain 675
Comes seldom save from rage and pain,
So talks as it's most used to do.

673–4 *And what ... true!)* The mention of 'sin', 'sorrow and shame' provide a clear link with the poem proper.

Frost at Midnight

'Frost at Midnight', for many critics the finest of Coleridge's conversation poems, was first published in 1798 in a quarto pamphlet with 'France An Ode' and 'Fears in Solitude'. The poem's literary point of departure is Book IV of William Cowper's *The Task*, 'The Winter Evening', lines 267–310. Cowper describes the pleasures of watching a fire in 'parlour twilight' (l. 278); he mentions 'The sooty films that play upon the bars' (l. 292) and presage 'some stranger's near approach' (l. 295); and he speaks of himself as 'creating what I saw' (l. 290). Coleridge reworks key words from Cowper – 'gaz'd' (l. 290), for instance, or fancy's 'toys' (l. 307) – in a poem that greatly subtilizes the passage from *The Task*. To achieve this subtlety, 'Frost at Midnight' underwent many revisions before ending up in the form by which it is best known (the 1834 text). The revisions perform a number of functions. Two worthy of comment are the following: the revisions turn self-consciousness from something advertised, as when, in 1798, Coleridge talks about the 'self-watching subtilizing mind', into something less explicit, more subliminal and fluid; and, through the deletion at the close of six lines in 1798 that describe Coleridge's 'babe' imagined in its 'mother's arms', they allow the poem to shape itself into a satisfying circle. The poem that begins with the frost's 'secret ministry' (l. 1) now closes with 'the secret ministry of frost' (l. 72). But whereas the opening secrecy was tense and withheld, 'Unhelped by any wind' (l. 2), by the end the frost's ministry is at the service of benign purposes, shaping 'silent icicles' (l. 73) that shine 'to the quiet Moon' (l. 74). The preposition speaks volumes about the giving (and taking) going on in the natural world, and the final image is more than an emblem of the mind's own relationship with external reality; it is indicative of a vision that relates God to humanity, father to son, humans to nature, and nature to itself.

'Frost at Midnight' is deeply concerned with creativity. At the start the absence of any helping wind suggests an inability to perceive creatively. We move, then, to the solitary, experiencing self of the poet, who comments, a shade ruefully, on the way 'the idling Spirit' (l. 20) interprets the fluttering film on the grate. At this stage, the poem seems to confirm that at best the external is 'a companionable form' (l. 19) to the mind's insatiable need to find itself mirrored in all that it contemplates. But subtler effects of language have already suggested that the mind's tyrannical control can be challenged; when, for instance, the poet notes how 'the thin blue flame / Lies on my low-burnt fire, and quivers not!' (ll. 13–14), the phrasing carries us back to the quivering flame.

Language can make presences out of absences, and 'Frost at Midnight' as a whole does just that, riding currents of association that take Coleridge back from his late-night vigil with his 'cradled infant' (l. 7) by his side to other occasions marked by watching the film. At school, he would see the film as a 'fluttering *stranger*' (l. 26) that, as a footnote to 'film' in line 15 by Coleridge tells us, was 'supposed to portend the arrival of some absent friend'. By a series of beautifully managed transitions, Coleridge comes back to the baby by his side, and from looking back to his own childhood he now looks forward to his son's growing up, which he hopes will be nourished by nature and thus differ from his own 'pent' schooling 'In the great city' (l. 52). Coleridge's Nature is more immediately theologized than Wordsworth's, presented as synonymous with 'that eternal language, which thy God /

Utters, who from eternity doth teach / Himself in all, and all things in himself' (ll. 60–2). This formulation is full of toings and froings, circular and chiastic returns, harmonious duplications, and builds on the preceding description of mountain scenery imaged in a lake. In the final paragraph, the tone is quieter, full of attractive description, and yet the passage pivots on a resonant 'Therefore' (l. 65) (which Wordsworth will borrow in 'Tintern Abbey'); it is because of the faith in a God whose 'eternal language' is nature that Coleridge can be confident of a goodness and harmony in life.

In recent years, there has been debate about whether the poem represents a retreat from political commitment. Paul Magnuson passes on a point made by Jack Stillinger: 'that when the printer set up copy for *Sibylline Leaves* (1817), "Frost at Midnight" was included among "Poems Connected with Political Events"'.

Coleridge insisted that the poem be moved 'among my domestic & meditative Poems', but the poem has been read as either a quietist retreat from political radicalism or, more interestingly, by Magnuson as a poem that shows Coleridge portraying himself as both 'a loyal patriot, who loves his country, and as a devoutly religious man, on the one hand, and on the other, as one who continues to support the Jacobin ideals of liberty that he has always held' (*Reading Public Romanticism* [Princeton, NJ: Princeton University Press, 1998], pp. 85, 78). Huge questions of how one reads poetry are explicitly raised by Magnuson with his unabashed insistence on context as determining meaning. To the degree, though, that the poem formulates images of freedom and happiness, it participates in the elusive but real political impact of many poems celebrating 'joy' produced by Wordsworth and Coleridge between 1797 and 1802.

THE Frost performs its secret ministry,
Unhelped by any wind. The owlet's cry
Came loud—and hark, again! loud as before.
The inmates of my cottage, all at rest,
Have left me to that solitude, which suits   5
Abstruser musings: save that at my side
My cradled infant slumbers peacefully.
'Tis calm indeed! so calm, that it disturbs
And vexes meditation with its strange
And extreme silentness. Sea, hill, and wood,   10
This populous village! Sea, and hill, and wood,
With all the numberless goings-on of life,
Inaudible as dreams! the thin blue flame
Lies on my low-burnt fire, and quivers not;
Only that film, which fluttered on the grate,   15
Still flutters there, the sole unquiet thing.
Methinks, its motion in this hush of nature
Gives it dim sympathies with me who live,
Making it a companionable form,
Whose puny flaps and freaks the idling Spirit   20
By its own moods interprets, every where
Echo or mirror seeking of itself,
And makes a toy of Thought.

6 *Abstruser musings* Because this phrase is followed by a caesura, the reader is made to slow down over it; the phrase is of importance for the poem in that, throughout, we sense as a possibility the emergence of 'musings' 'Abstruser' than those about which we have yet heard.

8–10 *so calm ... silentness* The paradoxical nature of a 'calm' that 'vexes' is suited to this phase of the poem, in which there is an uncertainty about the significance of 'silentness' that will be resolved later on.

10–11 *Sea ... wood* The repetition shows Coleridge fascinated by the conversion of external reality into a stuff 'Inaudible as dreams' (l. 13).

20–3 *Whose ... Thought* In 1798 these lines read:

With which I can hold commune. Idle thought!
But still the living spirit in our frame,
That loves not to behold a lifeless thing,
Transfuses into all its own delights,
Its own volition, sometimes with deep faith
And sometimes with fantastic playfulness.

23 *But* In 1798 the opening of the second paragraph reads:

Ah me! amus'd by no such curious toys
Of the self-watching subtilizing mind,
How often in my early school-boy days
With most believing superstitious wish ...

                        But O! how oft,
How oft, at school, with most believing mind,
Presageful, have I gazed upon the bars,   25
To watch that fluttering *stranger*! and as oft
With unclosed lids, already had I dreamt
Of my sweet birth-place, and the old church-tower,
Whose bells, the poor man's only music, rang
From morn to evening, all the hot Fair-day,   30
So sweetly, that they stirred and haunted me
With a wild pleasure, falling on mine ear
Most like articulate sounds of things to come!
So gazed I, till the soothing things, I dreamt,
Lulled me to sleep, and sleep prolonged my dreams!   35
And so I brooded all the following morn,
Awed by the stern preceptor's face, mine eye
Fixed with mock study on my swimming book:
Save if the door half opened, and I snatched
A hasty glance, and still my heart leaped up,   40
For still I hoped to see the *stranger's* face,
Townsman, or aunt, or sister more beloved,
My play-mate when we both were clothed alike!

    Dear Babe, that sleepest cradled by my side,
Whose gentle breathings, heard in this deep calm,   45
Fill up the interspersed vacancies
And momentary pauses of the thought!
My babe so beautiful! it thrills my heart
With tender gladness, thus to look at thee,
And think that thou shalt learn far other lore,   50
And in far other scenes! For I was reared
In the great city, pent 'mid cloisters dim,
And saw nought lovely but the sky and stars.
But *thou*, my babe! shalt wander like a breeze
By lakes and sandy shores, beneath the crags   55
Of ancient mountain, and beneath the clouds,
Which image in their bulk both lakes and shores
And mountain crags: so shalt thou see and hear
The lovely shapes and sounds intelligible
Of that eternal language, which thy God   60
Utters, who from eternity doth teach
Himself in all, and all things in himself.
Great universal Teacher! he shall mould
Thy spirit, and by giving make it ask.

24 *with . . . mind* The contrast pointed up by 'But O!' (l. 23) is between adult playfulness and boyish credulity: the poem suggests that such credulity was of value.
33 *Most . . . come!* It is typical of the supple movements of mind in the poem that Coleridge revisits his childhood to remember his boyish anticipations of the future.
37 *stern preceptor's face* The Rev. James Boyer, headmaster of Christ's Hospital; Boyer is treated with not unaffectionate irony in the first chapter of *Biographia Literaria* as 'a very sensible, though at the same time, a very severe master' (*BL*, p. 8).
43 *My play-mate . . . alike!* Gracefully takes us right back to the poet's infancy and prepares for the return to the present in the next line.
51–3 *For . . . stars* Coleridge's sense of being 'pent' and suffering sensory deprivation during his childhood is reinforced by the extra stresses on the third syllables of lines 52 and 53.
60 *thy God* The use of 'thy' may suggest that Coleridge sees his baby as having a special closeness to God.
63 *Great universal Teacher!* The wording may owe a debt to Cowper's reference to 'the face / Of universal nature' (*The Task*, IV, ll. 324–5).

> Therefore all seasons shall be sweet to thee, 65
> Whether the summer clothe the general earth
> With greenness, or the redbreast sit and sing
> Betwixt the tufts of snow on the bare branch
> Of mossy apple-tree, while the nigh thatch
> Smokes in the sun-thaw; whether the eave-drops fall 70
> Heard only in the trances of the blast,
> Or if the secret ministry of frost
> Shall hang them up in silent icicles,
> Quietly shining to the quiet Moon.

65–74 *Therefore ... Moon* The stresses on the first syllables of a number of the lines in this passage contribute to its effect of understated but crisp resolution.
72 *Or if* Coleridge changes from the generalizing 'whether' (66 and 70) to alight on a more specific, present-tense imagining.
74 *Moon* After this word, 1798 (with a comma at the end of line 74) went on as follows:

> Like those, my babe! which ere tomorrow's warmth
> Have capp'd their sharp keen points with pendulous drops,
> Will catch thine eye, and with their novelty
> Suspend thy little soul; then make thee shout,
> And stretch and flutter from thy mother's arms
> As thou wouldst fly for very eagerness.

France: An Ode

'France: An Ode' was published with 'Fears in Solitude' and 'Frost at Midnight' in the quarto pamphlet of 1798, after it had appeared in the *Morning Post*, 16 April that year, with the title 'The Recantation: An Ode'. It was written in response to the French invasion of Switzerland, an event that shocked many supporters of the French Revolution. A note, written by the paper's editor, Daniel Stuart, prefaced its appearance in the *Morning Post*:

> The following excellent Ode will be in unison with the feelings of every friend to Liberty and foe to Oppression; of all who, admiring the French Revolution, detest and deplore the conduct of France towards Switzerland. It is very satisfactory to find so zealous and steady an advocate for Freedom as Mr. COLERIDGE concur with us in condemning the conduct of France towards the Swiss Cantons. Indeed his concurrence is not singular; we know of no Friend to Liberty who is not of his opinion. What we most admire is the *avowal* of his sentiments, and public censure of the unprincipled and atrocious conduct of France. The Poem itself is written with great energy. The second, third, and fourth stanzas contain some of the most vigorous lines we have ever read. The lines in the fourth stanza: –
>
> 'To scatter rage and trait'rous guilt
> Where Peace her jealous home had built,'
>
> to the end of the stanza are particularly expressive and beautiful.

The note suggests how Coleridge was viewed in the 1790s, as a supporter of the French Revolution and an 'advocate for Freedom'. 'France: An Ode' articulates the political experience of a generation that passed from radical enthusiasm to disillusionment. The various stages of the poet's journey from former support for France to a love of 'Liberty' as a force that can never be 'gratified or realised, under any form of human government' are well caught in the 'Argument' added to the corrected copy of the poem printed in the *Morning Post* in 1802:

> ARGUMENT. *First Stanza*. An invocation to those objects in Nature the contemplation of which had inspired the Poet with a devotional love of Liberty. *Second Stanza*. The exultation of the Poet at the commencement of the French Revolution, and his unqualified abhorrence of the Alliance against the Republic. *Third Stanza*. The blasphemies and horrors during the domination of the Terrorists regarded by the Poet as a transient storm, and as the natural consequence of the former despotism and of the foul superstition of Popery. Reason, indeed, began to suggest many apprehensions; yet still the Poet struggled to retain the hope that France would make conquests of no other

means than by presenting to the observation of Europe a people more happy and better instructed than under other forms of Government. *Fourth Stanza.* Switzerland, and the Poet's recantation. *Fifth Stanza.* An address to Liberty, in which the Poet expresses his conviction that those feelings and that grand *ideal* of Freedom which the mind attains by its contemplation of its individual nature, and of the sublime surrounding objects (see Stanza the First) do not belong to men, as a society, nor can possibly be either gratified or realised, under any form of human government; but belong to the individual man, so far as he is pure, and inflamed with the love and adoration of God in Nature.

As this 'ARGUMENT' shows, the poem seeks to trace the different political postures adopted by Coleridge in the 1790s and to suggest that the common factor in his various attitudes has been his adoration of 'The spirit of divinest Liberty' (l. 21). Stuart was right to praise the 'vigorous' writing. Coleridge shows a rhetorical mastery throughout: in, for instance, the way infinitives (ll. 72, 74, 77, 81, 83, 84) in stanza 4 build to a crescendo of indignation against France, the bogus 'Champion of human kind' (l. 80). The control of complex syntax and rhyming accompanies an impressive drive and momentum, conveyed, in part, by forceful verbs that enact the burningly onward-going nature of the quest for freedom: so France is said to have 'Stamped her strong foot and said she would be free' (l. 24), a line which, opening with a trochee and a spondee, is itself marked by usage of 'strong' feet; while at the close, the poet's experience of liberty emerging from his response to nature occurs when he 'shot my being through earth, sea, and air' (l. 103). Coleridge uses an intricate stanza form (21 lines, rhyming *abbacdcdeefgfghihjjij*, basically iambic pentameter, but changing to iambic tetrameter in lines 9, 11, and 13 in each stanza) that exists in tense counterpoint with the insistence on nature's and liberty's refusal to submit to human control. In a sense, the formal regularity and order pay homage to and are emblematic of the 'eternal laws' referred to in line 4.

The poem is a public apology: 'Forgive me, Freedom!' (l. 64) Coleridge writes of his earlier excuses for the Reign of Terror. It also serves as an apologia, an explanation just as much as an expression of contrition. In stanza 2 Coleridge not only restates but implicitly justifies his opposition to Britain's siding in February 1793 with Austria and Prussia against the French Republic (Wordsworth expresses a similar opposition in *The Prelude*, 1805, X, 227–89). Despite his susceptibility to 'patriot emotion' (l. 34), Coleridge recalls, 'still my voice, unaltered, sang defeat / To all that braved the tyrant-quelling lance' (ll. 36–7). Coleridge thus presents himself as fundamentally 'unaltered' in a turbulent political period, dedicated, throughout that time, to liberty. In stanza 3 Coleridge uses the device of direct speech in the third stanza to communicate his past refusal to give up political hope, despite his 'fears that would not flee' (l. 58). Coleridge may concede that he misread the significance of the Reign of Terror. But he claims that any such misreading issued from idealistic motives. The poem also provides an analysis of why the Revolution has turned tyrannical when Coleridge writes, 'The Sensual and the Dark rebel in vain, / Slaves by their own compulsion!' (ll. 85–6), an analysis that would influence Shelley, an admirer of Coleridge's Ode. In stanza 3 Coleridge recalls how he assured himself that France would 'compel the nations to be free' (l. 62). The hint, there, in 'compel' that such a belief was awry blossoms into explicit statement in the use of 'compulsion' in line 86, which brings to the fore an awareness that 'liberty' can only exist when human beings free themselves from compelling, or being compelled by, others.

The poem combines Coleridge's love of nature with his commitment to freedom. But 'freedom' is now effectively depoliticized, or seen as operative only when cut off from 'forms of human power' (l. 92). Imaginatively Coleridge is able to resolve the tension between retirement and commitment evident in earlier poems. Yet the price is high. 'France: An Ode' preserves the ideal of liberty at the expense of locating it only within the natural world and presenting it as available only to inspired individuals.

I

Ye Clouds! that far above me float and pause,
   Whose pathless march no mortal may controul!
Ye Ocean-Waves! that, wheresoe'er ye roll,
Yield homage only to eternal laws!
Ye Woods! that listen to the night-birds singing, 5
   Midway the smooth and perilous slope reclined,
Save when your own imperious branches swinging,
   Have made a solemn music of the wind!
Where, like a man beloved of God,
Through glooms, which never woodman trod, 10

How oft, pursuing fancies holy,
My moonlight way o'er flowering weeds I wound,
    Inspired, beyond the guess of folly,
By each rude shape and wild unconquerable sound!
O ye loud Waves! and O ye Forests high!   15
    And O ye Clouds that far above me soared!
Thou rising Sun! thou blue rejoicing Sky!
    Yea, every thing that is and will be free!
    Bear witness for me, wheresoe'er ye be,
With what deep worship I have still adored   20
    The spirit of divinest Liberty.

II

When France in wrath her giant-limbs upreared,
    And with that oath, which smote air, earth, and sea,
    Stamped her strong foot and said she would be free,
Bear witness for me, how I hoped and feared!   25
With what a joy my lofty gratulation
    Unawed I sang, amid a slavish band:
And when to whelm the disenchanted nation,
    Like fiends embattled by a wizard's wand,
        The Monarchs marched in evil day,   30
        And Britain joined the dire array;
Though dear her shores and circling ocean,
Though many friendships, many youthful loves
    Had swoln the patriot emotion
And flung a magic light o'er all her hills and groves;   35
Yet still my voice, unaltered, sang defeat
    To all that braved the tyrant-quelling lance,
And shame too long delayed and vain retreat!
For ne'er, O Liberty! with partial aim
I dimmed thy light or damped thy holy flame;   40
    But blessed the paeans of delivered France,
And hung my head and wept at Britain's name.

III

'And what,' I said, 'though Blasphemy's loud scream
    With that sweet music of deliverance strove!
    Though all the fierce and drunken passions wove   45
A dance more wild than e'er was maniac's dream!
    Ye storms, that round the dawning East assembled,
The Sun was rising, though ye hid his light!'
    And when, to soothe my soul, that hoped and trembled,
The dissonance ceased, and all seemed calm and bright;   50

---

13 *Inspired . . . folly* Compare and contrast with the depiction of inspiration at the close of 'Kubla Khan'.
22 *When France . . .* The onset of the French Revolution.
28 *disenchanted* Freed from enchantment.
39 *with partial aim* Coleridge's opposition to Britain's war with France is cited to show that his support of liberty has never served a 'partial' (self-interested) goal.
43–6 *'And . . . dream* Refers specifically to the attack on the clergy and more generally to the violence that characterized the Reign of Terror.

When France her front deep-scarr'd and gory
Concealed with clustering wreaths of glory;
   When, insupportably advancing,
Her arm made mockery of the warrior's ramp;
   While timid looks of fury glancing, 55
   Domestic treason, crushed beneath her fatal stamp,
Writhed like a wounded dragon in his gore;
   Then I reproached my fears that would not flee;
'And soon,' I said, 'shall Wisdom teach her lore
In the low huts of them that toil and groan! 60
And, conquering by her happiness alone,
   Shall France compel the nations to be free,
Till Love and Joy look round, and call the Earth their own.'

IV

Forgive me, Freedom! O forgive those dreams!
   I hear thy voice, I hear thy loud lament, 65
   From bleak Helvetia's icy caverns sent—
I hear thy groans upon her blood-stained streams!
   Heroes, that for your peaceful country perished,
And ye that, fleeing, spot your mountain-snows
   With bleeding wounds; forgive me, that I cherished 70
One thought that ever blessed your cruel foes!
   To scatter rage, and traitorous guilt,
   Where Peace her jealous home had built;
     A patriot-race to disinherit
Of all that made their stormy wilds so dear; 75
   And with inexpiable spirit
To taint the bloodless freedom of the mountaineer—
O France, that mockest Heaven, adulterous, blind,
   And patriot only in pernicious toils!
Are these thy boasts, Champion of human kind? 80
   To mix with Kings in the low lust of sway,
Yell in the hunt, and share the murderous prey;
To insult the shrine of Liberty with spoils
   From freemen torn; to tempt and to betray?

V

   The Sensual and the Dark rebel in vain, 85
Slaves by their own compulsion! In mad game
They burst their manacles and wear the name
   Of Freedom, graven on a heavier chain!
O Liberty! with profitless endeavour

---

53 *insupportably* Without support.
66 *Helvetia's* Switzerland's.
69 *And ye* 'Ye' here are defenders of Swiss freedom; the pronouns throughout the poem show Coleridge's impulse to establish a direct relationship with different 'addressees': nature (l. 19), France (l. 80), and liberty (l. 90).

77 *bloodless freedom* 'Bloodless' points up the horror of 'blood-stained streams' (l. 67) and 'bleeding wounds' (l. 70).
81 *To mix . . . sway* To prove no better than kings in the desire for power.

>   Have I pursued thee, many a weary hour;   90
>   But thou nor swell'st the victor's strain, nor ever
>   Didst breathe thy soul in forms of human power.
>   Alike from all, howe'er they praise thee,
>   (Nor prayer, nor boastful name delays thee)
>   Alike from Priestcraft's harpy minions,   95
>   And factious Blasphemy's obscener slaves,
>   Thou speedest on thy subtle pinions,
>   The guide of homeless winds, and playmate of the waves!
>   And there I felt thee!—on that sea-cliff's verge,
>   Whose pines, scarce travelled by the breeze above,   100
>   Had made one murmur with the distant surge!
>   Yes, while I stood and gazed, my temples bare,
>   And shot my being through earth, sea, and air,
>   Possessing all things with intensest love,
>   O Liberty! my spirit felt thee there.   105

89 *profitless endeavour* Coleridge's pursuit of liberty (in forms of political government) has proved unavailing.
98 *homeless winds* The winds are 'homeless' because free, not governed by national boundaries. In this sense, liberty is marked by its participation in the 'sublime', one of whose traits for writers since Burke was its connection with infinity. At a darker level, 'homeless' may subliminally suggest that liberty has no 'home'.

The Nightingale: A Conversation Poem, April, 1798

'The Nightingale' was initially published in *Lyrical Ballads* (1798). Subtitled in 1798 'A Conversational Poem, Written in April 1798', it first received its subtitle 'A Conversation Poem' in 1817, a description now widely used to cover a group of blank verse, meditative poems written in the 1790s. The poem, addressed to William and Dorothy Wordsworth, begins with description of absence (negatives cluster in the first three lines), but the absence of an eye-catching sunset motivates Coleridge to concentrate on the natural beauty at hand. The passage from disappointment to enjoyment communicates through the syntax and rhythms of lines 7 to 10, which begins 'though the stars be dim' (l. 8) and ends with the poet recommending that he and his friends 'find / A pleasure in the dimness of the stars' (ll. 10–11). That last line's gracefully relaxed pentameter is expressive of the newfound 'pleasure'. The opening paragraph is concerned with the most appropriate way of responding to nature and opposes itself to subjective projection of feeling on to the natural world. In line 13 Coleridge quotes from Milton's 'Il Penseroso', in which the nightingale is called 'Most musical, most melancholy' and argues that such a reading of nature merely represents the understandable but flawed egotism of human beings (a footnote to the line, in effect, claims that Milton anticipated him by giving the phrase to 'the character of a melancholy Man'). 'In Nature there is nothing melancholy' (l. 15), he asserts. The nightingale's song has been thought melancholy, Coleridge suggests, only because 'some night-wandering man' (l. 16) who has experienced emotional distress has 'filled all things with himself' (l. 19). It is an exuberant indictment of a pervasive tendency in Romantic poetry, and it raises the question whether projection of human feeling on to nature is easier to condemn than avoid. The paragraph offers as a better model for response to nature a wise passiveness: poets should surrender their spirits to 'the influxes' (l. 27) of nature rather than spend their time 'building up the rhyme' (l. 24). And yet the very existence of the poem indicates a trust in the active power of the mind.

The second paragraph celebrates the 'different lore' (l. 41) shared by the poet with William and Dorothy Wordsworth, their triangular closeness shown by the fact that Coleridge refers to 'our Sister' (l. 40).

Coleridge asserts that they do 'not thus profane / Nature's sweet voices' (ll. 41–2), where 'thus' refers back to the mode of response castigated in the first paragraph. When he describes the song of the nightingale, however, he implicitly concedes that understanding of the natural depends on the mind's best surmises in the very formulation beginning 'As he were fearful ...' (l. 46). Here Coleridge makes the nightingale into a kind of poet who would 'utter forth / His love-chant' (ll. 47–8). But he accurately identifies the song as that of male courtship and jettisons the sentimental myth of female lament, 'Philomela's pity-pleading strains' (l. 39). The tightrope on which the poem balances is that it would not 'profane' the natural, yet it allows its imaginings full scope, seeking to practise what it preaches: the entrance into an uncoercive relationship with nature. The third paragraph presents us with a mixture of the observed and the imagined, as Coleridge describes with great virtuosity nightingales singing in 'a grove / Of large extent' (ll. 49–50). He keeps his eye steadily on the object, but the poetry flirts with the symbolic (the nightingales 'answer and provoke each other's song', l. 58, like friendly poets) and the complicating (the song of the nightingales – emblematic of the natural – might make the listener 'almost / Forget it was not day', ll. 63–4).

But the poetry stays on its tightrope. Imagination can, it suggests, help us form a right relationship with the real. In the fourth paragraph the 'most gentle Maid' (l. 69) brings into the poem a fleeting but suggestive sense of 'something more than Nature in the grove' (l. 73); her reported experience of hearing the birds 'in choral minstrelsy' (l. 80) responding to the moon's emergence is twinned with the awakening throughout nature of 'one sensation' (l. 79), a low-key replaying of the pantheist surmise found in 'The Eolian Harp'. Indeed, Coleridge uses the central image of the harp stirred into sound by wind in lines 81–2. However, in 'The Nightingale' the final paragraph does not seek to repudiate what has gone before. Instead, the poet turns to his son, and to the hope that he will become 'Nature's play-mate' (l. 97) and, moreover, as he grows up, be able to 'associate joy' (l. 109) with the night. Though the jokey couplets sent by Coleridge to Wordsworth in a letter containing 'The Nightingale' suggest with comic coarseness that 'There's something falls off at his bottom' (see Mason, p. 33), the poem's ending satisfyingly fuses the literary man (able to quote *Twelfth Night* in l. 90), the loving father, the good friend, and the sensitive appreciator of nature.

>No cloud, no relique of the sunken day
>Distinguishes the West, no long thin slip
>Of sullen light, no obscure trembling hues.
>Come, we will rest on this old mossy bridge!
>You see the glimmer of the stream beneath,   5
>But hear no murmuring: it flows silently,
>O'er its soft bed of verdure. All is still,
>A balmy night! and though the stars be dim,
>Yet let us think upon the vernal showers
>That gladden the green earth, and we shall find   10
>A pleasure in the dimness of the stars.
>And hark! the Nightingale begins its song,
>'Most musical, most melancholy' bird!
>A melancholy bird? Oh! idle thought!
>In Nature there is nothing melancholy.   15
>But some night-wandering man whose heart was pierced
>With the remembrance of a grievous wrong,
>Or slow distemper, or neglected love,
>(And so, poor wretch! filled all things with himself,

4 *Come, we will rest* The tone is that of a tactful guide, ensuring that he and his friends respond to the night in a fashion appropriate to the 'different lore' about which we hear later.
13 *'Most musical, most melancholy' bird!* The phrase is quoted from Milton's 'Il Penseroso', line 62. Coleridge added the following footnote to the line:

This passage in Milton possesses an excellence far superior to that of mere description; it is spoken in the character of the melancholy Man, and has therefore a *dramatic* propriety. The Author makes this remark, to rescue himself from the charge of having alluded with levity to a line in Milton; a charge than which none could be more painful to him, except perhaps that of having ridiculed his Bible.

And made all gentle sounds tell back the tale 20
Of his own sorrow) he, and such as he,
First named these notes a melancholy strain.
And many a poet echoes the conceit;
Poet who hath been building up the rhyme
When he had better far have stretched his limbs 25
Beside a brook in mossy forest-dell,
By sun or moon-light, to the influxes
Of shapes and sounds and shifting elements
Surrendering his whole spirit, of his song
And of his fame forgetful! so his fame 30
Should share in Nature's immortality,
A venerable thing! and so his song
Should make all Nature lovelier, and itself
Be loved like Nature! But 'twill not be so;
And youths and maidens most poetical, 35
Who lose the deepening twilights of the spring
In ball-rooms and hot theatres, they still
Full of meek sympathy must heave their sighs
O'er Philomela's pity-pleading strains.

My Friend, and thou, our Sister! we have learnt 40
A different lore: we may not thus profane
Nature's sweet voices, always full of love
And joyance! 'Tis the merry Nightingale
That crowds, and hurries, and precipitates
With fast thick warble his delicious notes, 45
As he were fearful that an April night
Would be too short for him to utter forth
His love-chant, and disburthen his full soul
Of all its music!
               And I know a grove
Of large extent, hard by a castle huge, 50
Which the great lord inhabits not; and so
This grove is wild with tangling underwood,
And the trim walks are broken up, and grass,
Thin grass and king-cups grow within the paths.
But never elsewhere in one place I knew 55
So many nightingales; and far and near,
In wood and thicket, over the wide grove,
They answer and provoke each other's song,
With skirmish and capricious passagings,
And murmurs musical and swift jug jug, 60
And one low piping sound more sweet than all—
Stirring the air with such a harmony,
That should you close your eyes, you might almost

24–30 *Poet . . . forgetful!* The leisurely syntax and rhythm are expressive of the surrender to nature advocated by Coleridge.
24 *building up the rhyme* Compare Milton, 'Lycidas', lines 10–11: 'he knew / Himself to sing, and build the lofty rhyme'.
39 *Philomela's . . . strains* Philomela was turned into a nightingale after being raped by Tereus, who cut out her tongue to prevent her from speaking; she was able to tell her sister Procne what had happened through a piece of needlework.
60 *jug jug* Traditionally used to represent the nightingale's song.

Forget it was not day! On moonlight bushes,
Whose dewy leaflets are but half-disclosed, 65
You may perchance behold them on the twigs,
Their bright, bright eyes, their eyes both bright and full,
Glistening, while many a glow-worm in the shade
Lights up her love-torch.
                A most gentle Maid,
Who dwelleth in her hospitable home 70
Hard by the castle, and at latest eve
(Even like a Lady vowed and dedicate
To something more than Nature in the grove)
Glides through the pathways; she knows all their notes,
That gentle Maid! and oft, a moment's space, 75
What time the moon was lost behind a cloud,
Hath heard a pause of silence; till the moon
Emerging, hath awakened earth and sky
With one sensation, and those wakeful birds
Have all burst forth in choral minstrelsy, 80
As if some sudden gale had swept at once
A hundred airy harps! And she hath watched
Many a nightingale perch giddily
On blossomy twig still swinging from the breeze,
And to that motion tune his wanton song 85
Like tipsy Joy that reels with tossing head.

Farewell, O Warbler! till to-morrow eve,
And you, my friends! farewell, a short farewell!
We have been loitering long and pleasantly,
And now for our dear homes.—That strain again! 90
Full fain it would delay me! My dear babe,
Who, capable of no articulate sound,
Mars all things with his imitative lisp,
How he would place his hand beside his ear,
His little hand, the small forefinger up, 95
And bid us listen! And I deem it wise
To make him Nature's play-mate. He knows well
The evening-star; and once, when he awoke
In most distressful mood (some inward pain
Had made up that strange thing, an infant's dream—) 100
I hurried with him to our orchard-plot,
And he beheld the moon, and, hushed at once,
Suspends his sobs, and laughs most silently,
While his fair eyes, that swam with undropped tears,
Did glitter in the yellow moon-beam! Well!— 105
It is a father's tale: But if that Heaven
Should give me life, his childhood shall grow up
Familiar with these songs, that with the night
He may associate joy.—Once more, farewell,
Sweet Nightingale! once more, my friends! farewell. 110

---

90 *That strain again!* Quotes Shakespeare, *Twelfth Night*, I. i. 4. It is part of the poem's playful ease that Coleridge, while recommending a view of nature that sheds human self-regard, should quote the extremely self-regarding Orsino.

109 *associate joy* Both verb (with its reference to the theory of associationism) and noun (with its suggestion of a state of union between human and natural) are key words in Coleridge's poetry.

The Pains of Sleep

The poem was first published in the same 1816 volume as 'Christabel' and 'Kubla Khan'. Coleridge sent a draft of the poem to Southey in a letter of 10 September 1803 (*CL*, 2, pp. 982–4) and an extract from the poem to Thomas Poole in a letter of 3 October 1803 (*CL*, 2, 1009–10). As the letter to Southey implies, the poem springs from and addresses the nightmares experienced by Coleridge as he struggled with his addiction to opium. The text used is based on the published version, a toned-down, though highly confessional, account of the poet's sufferings. The manuscript version is more explicit about the degradation experienced by Coleridge in his dreams: 'whom I scorned, those only strong!' (l. 20) is the published version's truncation of several lines in the manuscript on 'men whom I despis'd'; the manuscript's reference to 'Rage, sensual passion, mad'ning Brawl' gives way in the published version to the more decorous 'Fantastic passions! maddening brawl!' (l. 25); and the manuscript's 'For all was Horror, Guilt, and Woe' is replaced by the published version's 'For all seemed guilt, remorse or woe' (l. 30), which dispenses with 'horror' and substitutes 'seemed' for the more certain 'was'. Crucially, the manuscript accepts moral responsibility for evil more openly than the published version, even as it describes the experience of evil as a kind of diabolical possession. In both versions Coleridge cannot understand why he should be experiencing 'punishments . . . due / To natures deepliest stained with sin' (ll. 43–4). But as he describes the 'hell' (l. 46) such natures endure (and which he also, however unfairly, experiences), he shifts his emphasis. The manuscript speaks of 'The self-created Hell within'; the published version refers to 'The unfathomable hell within' (l. 46).

In deliberate and effectively shocking counterpoint to its content, the poem is written in rhyming tetrameters, which normally fall into couplets, though there are some notable variations to this rhyming pattern, variations that help to quicken the pace or change key. So in the second stanza the onset of 'anguish' and 'agony' (l. 15) is substantiated by a forceful triple rhyme (ll. 18–20). The tone, at the opening, is that of a child's prayer. Indeed, the first line of the published version is the same as the first line of Coleridge's 'A Child's Evening Prayer'. In the first stanza, Coleridge establishes a picture of himself as confessedly 'weak, yet not unblest' (l. 11) since cared for by 'Eternal Strength and Wisdom' (l. 13). As in 'The Ancient Mariner', the terrifying possibility that this may not be the case erupts into the poem. The second stanza opens with 'But' (l. 14), denying the reassurance of the first stanza, and falls headlong into a superbly paced, appositional list of the terrors to which the poet has been subject. The rhythms, varied, agitated, and yet under control, do much to bring alive the abstractions with which the stanza is full. So in lines 21–2, the shifting position of the caesurae – after the fourth syllable in line 21, then after the third syllable in line 22 – suggest how the poet's 'powerless will' (l. 21) is thwarted, 'baffled, and yet burning still' (l. 22). In the heavily stressed last line of the stanza, the double use of 'stifled' in different adjectival compounds indicates how Coleridge is suffocated by 'fear' and 'shame' (l. 32). There is some reprieve for the poet in the final stanza when he is awakened from 'the fiendish dream' (l. 38) by the sound of his 'own loud scream' (l. 37), and returns to a child-like state, 'I wept as I had been a child' (l. 40). The attempted return to childhood is an attempt to collapse difference. Other wordings seek to stress the difference between the speaker and 'natures deepliest stained with sin' (l. 44), and there is a noticeable tension in the language between affinity and dissimilitude: the four rhymes on the same rhyme sound (ll. 43, 45, 47 and 48) suggest how Coleridge is being made to 'do', or imagine 'doing', what he loathes. In lines 49 and 50, the attempt to distinguish the poet from 'such men' shows in the repetition of 'such' and his sense of the unfairness of what he has suffered manifests itself in the repetition of 'wherefore' in line 50's plangent question. Finally the poem concludes with further repetition, this time of the word 'love', where again the language poignantly makes us aware of Coleridge's capacity to 'love', and his 'need' 'To be beloved' (ll. 51–2). This last couplet's switch of direction from feelings of moral inadequacy is marked; it ends with a suggestion that, at the back of all the poet's anguish, lies an overwhelming feeling of affective starvation and opens the poem up to a psychoanalytical reading.

> ERE on my bed my limbs I lay,
> It hath not been my use to pray
> With moving lips or bended knees;
> But silently, by slow degrees,
> My spirit I to Love compose,   5

---

1 *Ere* 'When' (letter to Southey).
5 *Love* Predominantly a theological idea here, God as 'Love', by contrast with the human 'love' Coleridge speaks of at the poem's close.

In humble trust mine eye-lids close,
With reverential resignation,
No wish conceived, no thought exprest,
Only a sense of supplication;
A sense o'er all my soul imprest   10
That I am weak, yet not unblest,
Since in me, round me, every where
Eternal Strength and Wisdom are.

But yester-night I prayed aloud
In anguish and in agony,   15
Up-starting from the fiendish crowd
Of shapes and thoughts that tortured me:
A lurid light, a trampling throng,
Sense of intolerable wrong,
And whom I scorned, those only strong!   20
Thirst of revenge, the powerless will
Still baffled, and yet burning still!
Desire with loathing strangely mixed
On wild or hateful objects fixed.
Fantastic passions! maddening brawl!   25
And shame and terror over all!
Deeds to be hid which were not hid,
Which all confused I could not know
Whether I suffered, or I did:
For all seemed guilt, remorse or woe,   30
My own or others still the same
Life-stifling fear, soul-stifling shame.

So two nights passed: the night's dismay
Saddened and stunned the coming day.
Sleep, the wide blessing, seemed to me   35
Distemper's worst calamity.
The third night, when my own loud scream
Had waked me from the fiendish dream,
O'ercome with sufferings strange and wild,
I wept as I had been a child;   40
And having thus by tears subdued
My anguish to a milder mood,
Such punishments, I said, were due
To natures deepliest stained with sin,—
For aye entempesting anew   45
The unfathomable hell within,
The horror of their deeds to view,
To know and loathe, yet wish and do!
Such griefs with such men well agree,
But wherefore, wherefore fall on me?   50
To be beloved is all I need,
And whom I love, I love indeed.

---

13 *Wisdom* 'Goodness' (letter to Southey).
16 *Up-starting* 'Awaking' (letter to Southey); a particularly effective revision, capturing the physical 'start' of the poet's body and not quite saying that he did awake, even if this is implied by 'prayed aloud' (l. 14).
33 *So* 'Thus' (letter to Southey).

Dejection: An Ode

This poem is a shortened, shaped and far less rawly personal version of the 'Letter to Sara Hutchinson'. The 'Letter' began life, in part, as a response to the first four stanzas of Wordsworth's 'Ode: Intimations of Immortality'. It expresses Coleridge's domestic unhappiness: 'my own peculiar lot, my house-hold Life / It is, & will remain, Indifference or Strife' (ll. 163–4). It also speaks of his love for Sara Hutchinson, Wordsworth's sister-in-law, evoking domestic scenes that are the more affecting for falling just the right side of the fence between tenderness and mawkishness. In the 'Letter', Coleridge embeds his fear of lost poetic inspiration in a biographical context of marital discord and emotional unfulfilment. Revising the poem into 'Dejection: An Ode', first published in the *Morning Post* on 4 October 1802, Coleridge censors the confessional material concerning Sara Hutchinson and his unhappy marriage, allowing a state of 'dejection' to pervade the poem; the reader has to surmise its cause. The failed marriage between imagination and nature is now to the fore, not that between Coleridge and his wife Sara. Wedding imagery is at the poem's heart, and indeed, it was published on the day of Wordsworth's marriage in a version that made Wordsworth (as 'Edmund') the addressee. In the version printed below, based on the 1834 text, Coleridge defines 'Joy' as the consequence of a marriage between the mind and nature: 'Joy, Lady! is the spirit and the power, / Which wedding Nature to us gives in dower / A new Earth and new Heaven' (ll. 67–9). The dowry brought to us by 'wedding Nature' is a version of millennial transformation, an ability to experience life with that creativity and imaginative interchange which Coleridge calls 'joy'.

'Joy' is a conspicuous absence for much of the poem. Consisting and making full use of three long sentences, with their ability to modulate from phrase to phrase, the opening stanza slides expertly from mimicry of a casual conversational tone to exposure of inner distress, the 'dull pain' (l. 20) which afflicts the poet. This pain does not affect the poet's capacity for keen observation, as in his description of the 'New-moon winter-bright' (l. 9), and in the second stanza, after converting 'dull pain' into a more inward 'grief without a pang' (l. 21), Coleridge defines his 'wan and heartless mood' (l. 25) by enacting what it is like, in the presence of nature's vivid objects, to 'see, not feel, how beautiful they are' (l. 38). The poetry captures the yearning with which he reaches out to objects that, for all their lustre, remain resolutely objects. As if recognizing this, the short but central third stanza obeys the typically contrapuntal movement associated with the ode form and moves from 'outward forms' (l. 45) to recognize that the source of failure lies 'within'. The fourth section movingly generalizes from the poet's experience, asserting that 'we receive but what we give, / And in our life alone does Nature live' (ll. 47–8). The fact that the poem is addressed to a 'Lady' (l. 47) allows hints to suggest themselves, almost sub-textually, of possible parallels between a personal relationship and the relationship between the mind and nature. The stanza's paradox is that in the midst of gloom it evokes the beauty of self-generated spiritual value, the melody and fluency of the verse permitting us to overhear 'A sweet and potent voice' (l. 57).

In the fifth stanza Coleridge sustains his evocation of such a 'voice', now imagining it fully as a 'strong music in the soul' (l. 60) and as a 'beautiful and beauty-making power' (l. 63). The very word 'power' rhymes with itself later in the same stanza (l. 67) and triggers a series of chimes in the rhyme position (ll. 65, 66, 68), as Coleridge defines with great virtuosity the 'Joy' (l. 64) which he lacks as both 'Life, and Life's effluence' (l. 66). Both source and product of our capacity to 'rejoice', there is an elegant circularity about Coleridge's wording; 'Joy' shows itself in the fact that 'We in ourselves rejoice' (l. 72). A triple use of 'all' in the stanza's last three lines ensures that joy defines 'all that charms or ear or sight' (l. 73).

The stanza marks an affecting high-point in the poet's attempt to recover as luminous a sense as possible of what it is that he has lost. In stanza 6 the opening phrase, 'There was a time' (l. 76), recalling the start of Wordsworth's 'Immortality Ode', initiates a regretful awareness of his present incapacity to sustain 'joy'. If once, 'This joy within me dallied with distress' (l. 77), that is now no longer the case; 'now afflictions bow me to down to earth' (l. 82), confesses Coleridge, anticipating Shelley's own distressed cry in 'Ode to the West Wind', 'I fall upon the thorns of life! I bleed' (l. 55). It is at this point that the poet bemoans the suspension of 'My shaping spirit of Imagination' (l. 86), a line which itself covertly refutes the suspension of which it speaks, as it caps 'each visitation' (l. 84) of affliction. The last seven lines of the stanza define with painful vividness the self-destructive nature of the means by which Coleridge has sought 'not to think of what I needs must feel' (l. 87); he has engaged in 'abstruse research' (l. 89), probably philosophical thought, as a distraction from his growing dejection, but in doing so has further alienated himself from the sources of creativity that constitute 'joy' for the poet. Or at least paraphrase might suggest something of this kind. What impresses poetically is the presence not only of precision, as though dejection beautifully sharpened the poet's gift for memorably distilled expression, but also of suggestiveness; the rhythms move with a slowness that implies an underlying personal distress, without spelling out the nature of that distress, as he does in the original 'Letter to Sara Hutchinson'. The seeming clumsiness of referring to 'the habit of my soul' (l. 93) just two lines after referring to 'abstruse research' as 'my sole resource' (l. 91) is, in fact, a means of speaking wryly of the way 'habit' operates to the poet's spiritual detriment.

The seventh stanza seeks to banish such 'viper thoughts, that coil around my mind, / Reality's dark dream!' (ll. 94–5). At the equivalent point in the 'Letter' the 'dark distressful dream' (l. 185) alluded to the thought of being absent from Sara Hutchinson while she was ill. In the 'Ode' Coleridge identifies 'viper thoughts' with 'Reality's dark dream', a dream at odds with creativity, joy, and the Imagination's shaping spirit. The lines function as a clarification and brilliant elaboration of what has gone before, as though the poet were himself, in the poem's working-out, newly aware of what was at stake in allowing himself to be dictated to by 'Reality's dark dream'. Instead, he turns back to the wind, and apostrophizes it as a 'Mad Lutanist' (l. 104), 'Actor, perfect in all tragic sounds' (l. 108), and 'mighty Poet' (l. 109). In so describing the wind, Coleridge projects on to it his own longing for inspiration, whether to tell of epic struggle or 'A tale of less affright' (l. 118), such as Thomas Otway (or, indeed, in the *Morning Post* version, Wordsworth or 'Edmund') might have written. The writing self-consciously offers itself as writing, parading the poet's wish to write. Affectingly it catches fire as the imagined 'tender lay' (l. 120) comes close to home with the account of the lost child, that 'now screams loud, and hopes to make her mother hear' (l. 125). Regardless of the child's gender, the reader hears the line as describing the poet's own traumatized sense of being lost.

And yet all is mimed, all is controlled. The poem is always that, a poem, never merely a cry of pain. Great formal control and skill are apparent throughout. The final stanza begins with a single line, one that reticently speaks of the poet's unhappiness, 'small thoughts have I of sleep' (l. 126). It attends, then, to the poem's addressee, ' my friend' (l. 127), continuing the self-escaping movement out of 'viper thoughts' practised in the previous stanza, but now able to find an authentic focus for such a movement in the thought of another person. The poem concludes with a prayer that, 'guided from above' (l. 137), the friend, the 'Dear Lady' (l. 138), should enjoy contented sleep and be able to live in a state of harmony with 'all things' (l. 135). There is a strong echo of the conclusion to 'Frost at Midnight', but whereas, in the earlier poem, the poet was part of imagined harmony, in 'Dejection: An Ode' his heartfelt wish that Sara should 'ever, evermore rejoice' (l. 139) tells us that he is exiled, possibly 'evermore', from joy.

> Late, late yestreen I saw the new Moon,
> With the old Moon in her arms;
> And I fear, I fear, my Master dear!
> We shall have a deadly storm.
>   *Ballad of Sir Patrick Spence.*

I

WELL! If the Bard was weather-wise, who made
   The grand old ballad of Sir Patrick Spence,
   This night, so tranquil now, will not go hence
Unroused by winds, that ply a busier trade
Than those which mould yon cloud in lazy flakes,   5
Or the dull sobbing draft, that moans and rakes
Upon the strings of this Æolian lute,
     Which better far were mute.
   For lo! the New-moon winter-bright!

Epigraph 'The Ballad of Sir Patrick Spens' was printed in Thomas Percy's influential *Reliques of Ancient English Poetry* (1765). The image of the 'new Moon / With the old Moon in her arms' influenced Shelley in *The Triumph of Life* (1822), lines 79–84, possibly as a result of reading Coleridge's poem.

1 *Well* Compare the opening of 'This Lime-Tree Bower My Prison', which also starts with a conversational 'Well'. In this case, Coleridge contrives a deliberately fake calm.

6 *dull sobbing draft* The 'draft' is a 'draught' of wind; at once 'dull' and 'sobbing', it offers a clue to the speaker's state of mind.

8 *Which . . . mute* The short line brings the sentence to an eloquently abrupt halt.

        And overspread with phantom light,   10
        (With swimming phantom light o'erspread
        But rimmed and circled by a silver thread)
I see the old Moon in her lap, foretelling
        The coming-on of rain and squally blast.
And oh! that even now the gust were swelling,   15
        And the slant night-shower driving loud and fast!
Those sounds which oft have raised me, whilst they awed,
        And sent my soul abroad,
Might now perhaps their wonted impulse give,
Might startle this dull pain, and make it move and live!   20

II

A grief without a pang, void, dark, and drear,
    A stifled, drowsy, unimpassioned grief,
    Which finds no natural outlet, no relief,
        In word, or sigh, or tear—
O Lady! in this wan and heartless mood,   25
To other thoughts by yonder throstle woo'd,
    All this long eve, so balmy and serene,
Have I been gazing on the western sky,
    And its peculiar tint of yellow green:
And still I gaze—and with how blank an eye!   30
And those thin clouds above, in flakes and bars,
That give away their motion to the stars;
Those stars, that glide behind them or between,
Now sparkling, now bedimmed, but always seen:
Yon crescent Moon, as fixed as if it grew   35
In its own cloudless, starless lake of blue;
I see them all so excellently fair,
I see, not feel, how beautiful they are!

III

    My genial spirits fail;
    And what can these avail   40
To lift the smothering weight from off my breast?
    It were a vain endeavour,
    Though I should gaze for ever
On that green light that lingers in the west:

10–12 *And . . . thread* The repetition in line 11 and the refinement of perception in line 12 enacts Coleridge's ability to see how beautiful objects are, even if he can no longer feel the truth of their beauty.

13–20 *I see . . . live!* The writing generates a sense of momentum, as Coleridge imagines how he 'Might' be inspired by the storm, but the energy is virtual rather than actual.

21–4 *A grief . . . tear—* Coleridge relies heavily on negation to create a sense of the difficult-to-define quality of his 'dull pain' (l. 20).

25 *O Lady!* Breaks out of stagnant self-concern, an effect sustained by the flowing rhyme scheme, which directs us to the 'serene' (l. 27) evening and 'its peculiar tint of yellow green' (l. 28), a phrase which does much to authenticate our feeling that the poem is taking place at a very particular time.

25 *heartless* Dispirited.

30 *And* 'And' rather than 'But' does much to create the effect here: longing is one with disappointment.

31–2 *And those . . . stars* The couplet evokes the world of reciprocal natural harmony from which the speaker is debarred by his dejection.

39 *My . . . fail* Compare Milton, *Samson Agonistes*, 594: 'my genial spirits droop'.

42–4 *It . . . west* The rhyme of 'vain endeavour' with 'for ever' brings out the futility of the poet's search for hope through gazing 'On that green light'.

I may not hope from outward forms to win 45
The passion and the life, whose fountains are within.

IV

O Lady! we receive but what we give,
And in our life alone does Nature live:
Ours is her wedding garment, ours her shroud!
    And would we aught behold, of higher worth, 50
Than that inanimate cold world allowed
To the poor loveless ever-anxious crowd,
    Ah! from the soul itself must issue forth
A light, a glory, a fair luminous cloud
        Enveloping the Earth— 55
And from the soul itself must there be sent
    A sweet and potent voice, of its own birth,
Of all sweet sounds the life and element!

V

O pure of heart! thou need'st not ask of me
What this strong music in the soul may be! 60
What, and wherein it doth exist,
This light, this glory, this fair luminous mist,
This beautiful and beauty-making power.
    Joy, virtuous Lady! Joy that ne'er was given,
Save to the pure, and in their purest hour, 65
Life, and Life's effluence, cloud at once and shower,
Joy, Lady! is the spirit and the power,
Which wedding Nature to us gives in dower
    A new Earth and new Heaven,
Undreamt of by the sensual and the proud— 70
Joy is the sweet voice, Joy the luminous cloud—
    We in ourselves rejoice!
And thence flows all that charms or ear or sight,
    All melodies the echoes of that voice,
All colours a suffusion from that light. 75

VI

There was a time when, though my path was rough,
    This joy within me dallied with distress,
And all misfortunes were but as the stuff
    Whence Fancy made me dreams of happiness:

45–6 *I ... within* The lines have a succinct memorableness typical of the poem; unhappiness provokes Coleridge to a series of Romantic aphorisms, which are more than isolated perceptions; the poem achieves a fluent eloquence.

47–8 *O ... live* The couplet allows, in its second line, for 'Nature' living 'in our life', which makes such a life more than merely our own preoccupations projected on to the external world.

51–2 *allowed ... crowd* The rhyme accentuates the cramped absence of joy experienced by most people.

53, 56 *must* In both cases, Coleridge describes what has to happen; such is the writing's evocative force it is easy to overlook the fact that, for him, the conditions necessary for joy do not obtain. And yet we are conscious that the poem does assume, in its own way, 'A sweet and potent voice' (l. 57).

66 *Life and Life's effluence* Life and what flows forth from life; Coleridge's suggestion of reciprocal harmony finds expression in the suggestive rhyming here and elsewhere; the 'power' (l. 63) can be conceived of as a 'shower' (l. 66) that 'gives in dower' (l. 68) a transformed world.

70 *the sensual ... proud* Compare 'France: An Ode', line 85: 'The Sensual and the Dark rebel in vain'.

79 *Fancy* Possibly compared as an inferior mode of creative activity, dealing in 'fixities and definites' (as in *BL*, ch. 13, vol. 1, p. 305), with 'Imagination' (l. 86).

For hope grew round me, like the twining vine, 80
And fruits, and foliage, not my own, seemed mine.
But now afflictions bow me down to earth:
Nor care I that they rob me of my mirth;
    But oh! each visitation
Suspends what nature gave me at my birth, 85
   My shaping spirit of Imagination.
For not to think of what I needs must feel,
   But to be still and patient, all I can;
And haply by abstruse research to steal
   From my own nature all the natural man— 90
This was my sole resource, my only plan:
Till that which suits a part infects the whole,
And now is almost grown the habit of my soul.

VII

Hence, viper thoughts, that coil around my mind,
   Reality's dark dream! 95
I turn from you, and listen to the wind,
   Which long has raved unnoticed. What a scream
Of agony by torture lengthened out
That lute sent forth! Thou Wind, that rav'st without,
   Bare crag, or mountain-tairn, or blasted tree, 100
Or pine-grove whither woodman never clomb,
Or lonely house, long held the witches' home,
   Methinks were fitter instruments for thee,
Mad Lutanist! who in this month of showers,
Of dark-brown gardens, and of peeping flowers, 105
Mak'st Devils' yule, with worse than wintry song,
The blossoms, buds, and timorous leaves among.
   Thou Actor, perfect in all tragic sounds!
Thou mighty Poet, e'en to frenzy bold!
    What tell'st thou now about? 110
   'Tis of the rushing of an host in rout,
With groans, of trampled men, with smarting wounds—
At once they groan with pain, and shudder with the cold!
But hush! there is a pause of deepest silence!
   And all that noise, as of a rushing crowd, 115
With groans, and tremulous shudderings—all is over—
   It tells another tale, with sounds less deep and loud!
    A tale of less affright,
    And tempered with delight,
As Otway's self had framed the tender lay,— 120

87–93 *For ... soul* The broken syntax and halting rhythms enact the poet's distaste for the self-destructive escape-mechanism he has developed.
96 *I turn from you* Articulates in expressive form the 'turn' which is central to the formal workings of most Odes. The wind, carefully introduced at the start, now returns after being 'unnoticed' (l. 97) for several stanzas. Now the poet seeks to create the impression of imaginative activity by consciously hyping-up the poem's emotions; the result is affecting precisely because Coleridge's handling of language tells us that he knows he is doing this.
111–12 *'Tis' ... wounds—* The scenario would be familiar from the recent wars with France.
120 *Otway's self* Thomas Otway (1652–85), author associated with pathos. See note 9 on p. 15.

'Tis of a little child
Upon a lonesome wild,
Not far from home, but she hath lost her way:
And now moans low in bitter grief and fear,
And now screams loud, and hopes to make her mother hear.   125

VIII

'Tis midnight, but small thoughts have I of sleep:
Full seldom may my friend such vigils keep!
Visit her, gentle Sleep! with wings of healing,
   And may this storm be but a mountain-birth,
May all the stars hang bright above her dwelling,   130
    Silent as though they watched the sleeping Earth!
      With light heart may she rise,
      Gay fancy, cheerful eyes,
    Joy lift her spirit, joy attune her voice;
To her may all things live, from pole to pole,   135
Their life the eddying of her living soul!
   O simple spirit, guided from above,
Dear Lady! friend devoutest of my choice,
Thus mayest thou ever, evermore rejoice.

121–5 *'Tis . . . hear* Recalls Wordsworth's poem 'Lucy Grey', about a lost child, but adds to it a sharp sense of childish terror.

126 *'Tis . . . sleep* Another example of a transition; after the emotional intensity of the preceding lines, this line is marked by its affecting restraint.

130–1 *May . . . Earth!* The prayer is touching, partly because it supposes that Nature is concerned for humans in ways that have, in effect, been ruled out or redefined earlier in the poem.

George Gordon, Lord Byron (1788–1824)

'Mad, bad and dangerous to know', George Gordon, 6th Baron Byron, was born in 1788 to Captain John Byron, 'Mad Jack', and his second wife, Catherine Gordon. Doomed to become both one of the most lionized, and eventually ostracized, figures in Regency London, Byron was born with a club foot (a liability which motivated him to excel at numerous sports, including swimming, fencing, boxing and riding) and was initially brought up in impoverished conditions. He was raised as a child in Aberdeen by his Scottish mother (his father died in 1791) until, at the age of 10, he succeeded to the title following the death of the previous Lord Byron (his great-uncle), and moved with his mother to Newstead Abbey, the family seat outside Nottingham. Before this move, he had fallen in love with his cousin Mary Duff when he was barely seven, then was apparently sexually abused by his nurse, May Gray, from the age of nine to eleven. His sexual and emotional precocity continued to manifest itself after he became a student at Harrow in 1801, when he fell in love in successive years with two first cousins, Margaret Parker and Mary Chaworth. As he later wrote in *Detached Thoughts*, 'My passions were developed very early – so early – that few would believe me – if I were to state the period – and the facts that accompanied it. – Perhaps this was one of the reasons which caused the anticipated melancholy of my thoughts – having anticipated life' (*Byron's Letters and Journals*, ed. Leslie Marchand [hereafter *BLJ*], vol. 9, p. 40). Passion is, of course, one of the words most immediately and comprehensively identified with Byron – whether the tempestuous love affairs, first in Regency London then later in Venice; the outspoken political liberalism on display in England and Greece; or the various personae of the 'Byronic Hero' – and it is integral to his legacy, however inflected.

After Harrow, Byron went up to Cambridge in 1805, and it was during his time there that he published his first two volumes of poetry, including *Hours of Idleness* (1807). A hostile notice in the *Edinburgh Review* prompted Byron in turn to write his first mature poem, *English Bards and Scotch Reviewers* (1809), a scathing (and impolitic) satire on contemporary literary mores written in heroic couplets. It is telling that, at the age of 21, Byron should have been writing in both a form and a mode so prominently identified not with contemporary literary fashions but with those of the Augustan writers (notably Pope, Swift and Prior) whom he revered far more than he did most of his contemporaries. Though he came to admire Shelley's poetry late in his life, Byron was profoundly unimpressed by the work of those poets whom we now view as the most canonical of the Romantic writers. In their stead, he valorized Walter Scott, Samuel Rogers, Thomas Moore and Thomas Campbell (see *BLJ*, vol. 3, pp. 219–20). Ten years later, in *Don Juan* (most prominently in the 'Dedication'), the same impatience with 'revolutionary' poetical programmes was on display in his ridicule of Wordsworth's 'new system', Coleridge's metaphysics and Southey's apostasy – all this in a comic verse form (*ottava rima*) which has become virtually synonymous with Byron in light of his renovation of it for his masterpiece.

Upon attaining his majority in 1809, Byron took his place in the House of Lords (he would later speak eloquently in defence of the Nottingham frame-breakers, the Luddites), but soon thereafter left England with his Cambridge friend John Cam Hobhouse for an exotic two-year tour of Portugal, Spain, Malta, Albania and Greece. Among other exploits, he swam the Hellespont and met the Ali Pasha; more importantly, he saw the condition of Greece under Turkish rule (a memory which would eventually motivate him to return and fight for Greek independence) and amassed the materials for the first two cantos of *Childe Harold's Pilgrimage*. When the poem was published in March 1812, Byron was suddenly the most sought-after celebrity in London – as he famously remarked, 'I awoke one morning and found myself famous'. Integral to this fame was the public's fascination with the figure of Childe Harold – indeed, its identification of Byron with his own hero – described by Francis Jeffrey (in the *Edinburgh Review*) as a tormented, world-weary misanthrope:

Childe Harold is a sated epicure – sickened with the very fullness of prosperity – oppressed with ennui, and stung with occasional remorse; – his heart hardened by a long course of sensual indulgence, and his opinion of mankind degraded by his acquaintance with the baser part of them. In this state he wanders over the fairest and most interesting parts of Europe, in the vain hope of stimulating his palsied sensibility by novelty, or at least of occasionally forgetting his mental anguish in the toils and perils of his journey. Like Milton's fiend, however, he 'sees undelighted all delight', and passes on through the great wilderness of the world with a heart shut to all human sympathy – sullenly despising the stir both of its business and its pleasures – but hating and despising himself most of all, for beholding it with so little emotion.[1]

With remarkable discernment, Jeffrey here articulates many of the terms that would come to define the Byronic hero, not only over the course of Byron's career but also after his death: 'stung' with remorse, alienated, wandering, passionate, moody, satanic (in the Miltonic sense), doomed, and unable to forget something mysterious. In Byron's own words, Harold 'through Sin's long labyrinth had run':

> And now Childe Harold was sore sick at heart,
> And from his fellow bacchanals would flee;
> 'Tis said, at times the sullen tear would start,
> But Pride congeal'd the drop within his ee:
> Apart he stalk'd in joyless reverie,
> And from his native land resolv'd to go,
> And visit scorching climes beyond the sea;
> With pleasure drugg'd he almost longed for woe,
> And e'en for change of scene would seek the
>   shades below.
>   (I. ll. 46–54)

In the wake of *Childe Harold*, the gloomy, misanthropic Byronic hero reappeared in a series of verse romances set in the Levant – *The Bride of Abydos* (1813), *The Giaour* (1813), *The Corsair* (1814) and *Lara* (1814) – all of which sold well (indeed, *The Corsair* sold 25,000 copies in the first month) and served to cement his reputation as the leading literary figure of the day.

Shortly after the publication of *Childe Harold*, Byron began a tempestuous affair with Lady Caroline Lamb, who purportedly fell in love with him while reading an advance copy of the poem. Though Byron broke with her before the end of the year, Lady Caroline was unable to let him go and continued to pursue him, waiting for him at night in the street and attempting to gain entry wherever he was. (In 1816, she published *Glenarvon*, a *roman-à-clef* based on their affair.) Also in the spring of 1813, Byron met Annabella Milbanke (a cousin of Caroline's husband William Lamb, later Lord Melbourne), whom he would wed, disastrously, two years later. Whereas Lady Caroline was outspoken and flamboyant (dressing up publicly as a page-boy), Annabella Milbanke was quiet and reclusive (preferring mathematics and the classics to contemporary poetry and society). His most important relationship at this time, however, was with his half-sister, Augusta Leigh (his father's daughter by his first wife), with whom he was unacquainted as a child, had met briefly at about the time he went off to Harrow, and only came to know after his return from his travels. From the summer of 1813, the two of them were nearly inseparable, in London as well as the country, and the daughter to whom she gave birth in 1814 may well have been his.[2] Though he felt closer to Augusta than to any other woman he had known, the intimacy of their relationship was not tenable in the long run, and Byron was urged by his friends (including Annabella's aunt, Lady Melbourne) to distance himself from her by marrying another. Augusta concurred and in January 1815 Byron married Annabella Milbanke. Their daughter, Augusta Ada, was born in December of the same year. By early 1816, however, the marriage had come undone amidst the turmoil of financial distress (Byron made no money from his poetry at this time, having given the copyrights to his publisher, John Murray, who made a fortune) and allegations against Byron of emotional cruelty, infidelity and, finally, of insanity. They separated in February 1816 (as Byron later remarked to Madame de Staël, 'The separation may have been *my fault* – but it was *her* choice . . .', *BLJ*, vol. 5, p. 88), and when rumours of his incestuous relations with Augusta became public, the once-fêted Byron was ostracized by London society. He left England for the continent on 25 April and never returned.

Travelling once again with Hobhouse, Byron went via Belgium (for the express purpose of visiting the field at Waterloo) to Geneva, where he soon met Shelley, along with Mary Godwin and her half-sister Claire Clairmont (with whom Byron had been briefly involved in London, and who would later give birth to his daughter, Allegra, in 1817). Staying at the Villa Diodati (where Milton had stopped on his return from Italy to England in 1639), Byron had a remarkably productive summer – as did Shelley and Mary Godwin. Mary began work on *Frankenstein* and Shelley wrote two of his most important lyrics ('Hymn to Intellectual Beauty' and 'Mont Blanc'), while Byron wrote the intimate lyrics to Augusta ('Stanzas to [Augusta]' and '[Epistle to Augusta]'; see below, p. 243), 'The Prisoner of Chillon', 'Prometheus', and 'Darkness', at the same time as completing the third canto of *Childe Harold* and beginning *Manfred*. All of the poetry of 1816 marks significant changes in voice and form for Byron, as if in leaving England he was also discarding his earlier personae in favour of something altogether less narrative, less easily assimilated

---

[1] *The Edinburgh Review*, February 1812; cited in *Byron: The Critical Heritage*, ed. Andrew Rutherford (London and New York: Barnes & Noble, 1970), pp. 38–9.
[2] See Leslie A. Marchand, *Byron: A Biography*, 3 vols (New York: Knopf, 1957/ London: John Murray, 1958), p. 446 and note.

into the literary fashions of the day (for which he was himself of course largely responsible).

He left Switzerland for Italy in the autumn of 1816, establishing himself in Venice, where he completed *Manfred* (and compiled an Armenian dictionary). His travels from Venice to Rome in the spring of 1817 provided the material for the fourth and final canto of *Childe Harold*, but the most important writing he undertook that year was 'Beppo', a serio-comic tale of adultery in *ottava rima* told by a gossipy, ironic narrator. This was Byron's first sustained experiment with the form he would deploy to great effect in his masterpiece, *Don Juan* (see headnote below, p. 254), and it allowed him to end his use of the Spenserian stanzas in which *Childe Harold* was written. Unlike the musical, highly modulated and interlocking rhymes of the longer English stanza with the closing Alexandrine (*ababbcbcc*), the comic Italian tradition of the *ottava rima* (*abababcc*) lent itself both to metrical momentum (two rhymes over six lines) and to bathos (the anticlimax offered by the clinching couplet, often in a double-rhyme). As handled by Byron, it allows for both narrative and digression, both the adventures of Juan and the voice of the glib narrator who increasingly takes over the poem for his own ends. When Byron embarked upon the first two cantos of *Don Juan*, he did not have any plans for a poem of such scope but proceeded as though he were writing another poem in the same style as 'Beppo'; it was both the poem's initial success and the public's increasing outrage over it that motivated him to continue. In fact, the poem's ribaldry and freedom go hand-in-hand with a decidedly Juvenalian sense of satiric purpose. As Byron wrote to Murray in 1822:

> D[on] Juan will be known by and bye for what it is intended a *satire* on *abuses* of the present *states* of Society – and not an eulogy of vice; – it may be now and then voluptuous – I can't help that – Ariosto is worse – Smollett . . . ten times worse – and Fielding no better. – No girl will ever be seduced by reading D[on] J[uan] – no – no . . . not the Don – who laughs at that – and – and most other things.
> (*BLJ*, vol. 10, p. 68)

Simultaneously outraged and irreverent, Byron's masterpiece continues to exert its influence not least because it is, as he initially claimed, 'a little quietly facetious about everything' (*BLJ*, vol. 6, p. 67).

At the same time as he was arranging for the publication of *Don Juan* in the spring of 1819, Byron met and fell in love with Teresa Guiccioli, the last significant love of his life and, at the time, the 20-year-old wife of the 60-year-old Count Guiccioli (see below, p. 251). He soon became her *cavaliere servente* (the publicly acknowledged lover of a married woman), and eventually followed her first to Ravenna, then to Pisa in 1821 (at which point she had left her husband). This latter move was occasioned by the nationalist politics of Teresa's family, the Gambas, which were at odds with Austrian control over northern Italy, but it also allowed Byron to rejoin Shelley, who was living there with Mary (now his wife). At Shelley's urging (and with the assistance of Leigh Hunt), they established a journal devoted to contemporary literature and politics, *The Liberal*. Though the plans foundered, when Shelley drowned in July 1822 and Byron found himself unable to work with Hunt, *The Liberal* did publish Byron's important satire, 'The Vision of Judgment' as well as his verse drama *Heaven and Earth*. In addition to continuing work on *Don Juan* (Cantos III–V were published together in 1821, followed by Cantos VI–XVI in four separate volumes in 1823–4), Byron embarked during this period upon a series of closet dramas, including *Cain*, *Sardanapalus*, and *The Two Foscari*. By 1823, however, he had grown impatient with poetry, with Italy, and with Teresa, and in July sailed for Greece, to participate in the fight for independence from the Turks. He financed and organized a corps of Greek soldiers at Missolonghi but before he saw military action contracted a fever whilst riding in a heavy rain in April 1824. He died later the same month, shortly after his 36th birthday. When his body eventually arrived in England in July, it was denied burial at both Westminster Abbey and St Paul's, before eventually being interred in the family vault near Newstead Abbey. As the funeral procession left London, there were only three carriages of mourners, followed by nearly 50 empty carriages sent by those who wished, however obliquely, to pay their respects. As Hobhouse noted, 'On the whole as much honour was done to the deceased as circumstances would admit of – He was buried like a nobleman, since we could not bury him as a poet'.[3]

Further Reading

Primary Texts

The Prisoner of Chillon and Other Poems (London: John Murray, 1816).
Don Juan. Cantos I and II (London: John Murray, 1819). [hereafter *1819*]
Letters and Journals of Lord Byron, with notices of his life, 2 vols, ed. Thomas Moore (London: John Murray, 1830). [hereafter *Moore*]
The Works of Lord Byron: With His Letters and Journals, and His Life, 17 vols (London: John Murray, 1832–4). [hereafter *1832*]

---

3 Cited in Marchand, *Byron: A Biography*, p. 1260.

Byron's *Don Juan: A Variorum Edition*, 4 vols, ed. T. G. Steffan and W. W. Pratt (Austin: University of Texas Press, 1957, 2nd edn 1971). [hereafter *DJV*]

Byron's *Letters and Journals*, 12 vols, ed. Leslie Marchand (Cambridge, MA: Harvard University Press/London: John Murray, 1973–82). [*BLJ*]

Lord Byron: The Complete Poetical Works, 7 vols, ed. Jerome J. McGann (Oxford: Clarendon Press, 1980–93). [hereafter *CPW*]

Lord Byron: The Complete Miscellaneous Prose, ed. Andrew Nicholson (Oxford: Clarendon Press, 1991).

Lord Byron: Selected Poems, ed. Susan J. Wolfson and Peter Manning (London and New York: Penguin Books, 1996).

Secondary Texts

Jerome Christensen, *Lord Byron's Strength: Romantic Writing and Commercial Society* (Baltimore: Johns Hopkins University Press, 1993.

Michael Foot, *The Politics of Paradise* (London: Collins, 1988).

Robert Gleckner, *Byron and the Ruins of Paradise* (Baltimore: Johns Hopkins University Press, 1967).

Leslie Marchand, *Byron: A Biography*, 3 vols (New York: Knopf, 1957/London: John Murray, 1958).

Leslie Marchand, *Byron: A Portrait* (New York: Knopf, 1970/London: John Murray, 1971).

Jerome J. McGann, *Don Juan in Context* (London and Chicago: Chicago University Press, 1976).

Jerome J. McGann, *Fiery Dust: Byron's Poetic Development* (London and Chicago: Chicago University Press, 1968).

Hadley J. Mozer, '"I WANT a Hero": Advertising for an Epic Hero in *Don Juan*', *Studies in Romanticism* 44.2 (2005), pp. 239–60.

Jane Stabler, *Byron, Poetics, and History* (Cambridge, UK: Cambridge University Press, 2002).

Susan Wolfson, '"Their she condition": Cross-Dressing and the Politics of Gender in *Don Juan*'. *ELH* 54.3 (1987), pp. 585–617.

Stanzas to [Augusta]

Written in July 1816, the poem was first published in *The Prisoner of Chillon and Other Poems* (1816) as 'Stanzas to * * * *' (in light of Augusta's reservations regarding the appearance of her name in a volume of Byron's poetry). Lady Byron had left Byron in January 1816, and in February undertook proceedings against him for a legal separation. At the centre of Lady Byron's complaint were allegations of acts of adultery and cruelty, including her suspicions of Byron's incestuous relations with his half-sister, Augusta Leigh. (For a fuller account of Byron's relationship with his half-sister, see the biographical headnote above.) Though these suspicions were never confirmed or pursued by legal means, rumours of Byron's intimacy with Augusta were rampant in London until his departure for the continent in April 1816 (after which he never saw Augusta again). In his letters from the same summer, Byron did not hesitate to express his love for Augusta nor his regret that 'circumstances' forbad their being together; as he wrote from Switzerland in August, '. . . do not be uneasy – and do not "hate yourself" . . . if you hate either let it be *me* – but do not – it would kill me; we are the last persons in the world – who ought – or could cease to love one another' (*BLJ*, vol. 5, p. 89). (For one of many later, entirely uninhibited expressions of his love for Augusta, see Byron's letter of 17 May 1819, in which he declares that 'I can never be other than I have been – and whenever I love anything it is because it reminds me in some way or other of yourself'; *BLJ*, vol. 6, p. 129.)

In a February 1816 letter to Thomas Moore, Byron bluntly depicted his predicament with a pride and sense of isolation that can be heard as well in his poetry from the same period:

> . . . I am at war 'with all the world and his wife'; or rather, 'all the world and *my* wife' are at war with me, and have not yet crushed me, – whatever they *may* do. I don't know that in the course of a hair-breadth existence I was ever, at home or abroad, in a situation so completely uprooting of present pleasure, or rational hope for the future, as this same. I say this, because I think so, and feel it. But I shall not sink under it the more for that mode of considering the question – I have made up my mind.
>
> By the way, however, you must not believe all you hear on the subject; and don't attempt to defend me.
>
> (*BLJ*, vol. 5, p. 35)

Resolved not to sink and determined to defend himself alone, Byron's isolated, embattled position very much corresponds to that of his various personae throughout the poetry of 1816, from 'The Prisoner of Chillon' to 'Prometheus' to *Manfred* – and including the lyrics addressed to Augusta. Of the three poems of 1816 most explicitly connected with Augusta – 'Stanzas to Augusta' ('When all around grew drear and dark'), 'Stanzas to [Augusta]', and '[Epistle to Augusta]' – only the second poem (under consideration here) was published during Byron's lifetime. Central to each is a tension between the tyranny of fate and the ennobling power of romantic love. As Edgar Allen Poe later remarked of 'Stanzas to [Augusta]' (in 'The Poetic Principle'):

> Among the minor poems of Lord Byron is one which has never received from the critics the praise which it undoubtedly deserves, ['Stanzas to [Augusta]' then follows in full] ... Although the rhythm here is one of the most difficult, the versification could scarcely be improved. No nobler theme ever engaged the pen of poet. It is the soul-elevating idea that no man can consider himself entitled to complain of Fate while in his adversity he still retains the unwavering love of woman.
>
> (Edgar Allan Poe, *Essays and Reviews*, ed. G. R. Thompson [New York: The Library of America, 1984], pp. 90–1.)

Poe's remarks are notable furthermore for their attention to Byron's metre and versification here. The rhythm takes its bearings from an irregular mixture of iambs and anapests in trimeter lines that vary between eight and eleven syllables, in eightline stanzas rhyming *ababcdcd*. The varying lengths of the feet, and consequently the lengths of the lines (depending on the relation of iambs to anapests, as well as the heavy reliance on double rhymes) creates an undulating rhythm that is ultimately held in place and regulated only by the grid of the rhyme scheme. (For a more regular deployment of anapests, see Byron's 'The Destruction of Sennacherib'.)

Text follows *The Prisoner of Chillon and Other Poems* (1816).

1

Though the day of my destiny's over,
    And the star of my fate hath declined,
Thy soft heart refused to discover
    The faults which so many could find;
Though thy soul with my grief was acquainted,   5
    It shrunk not to share it with me,
And the love which my spirit hath painted
    It never hath found but in *thee*.

2

Then when nature around me is smiling
    The last smile which answers to mine,   10
I do not believe it beguiling
    Because it reminds me of thine;
And when winds are at war with the ocean,
    As the breasts I believed in with me,
If their billows excite an emotion   15
    It is that they bear me from *thee*.

3 *discover* Here to be understood both as 'to come to the knowledge of' and 'to reveal' (and thus to betray).

7 *painted* Depicted or described; imagined.

3

Though the rock of my last hope is shiver'd,
    And its fragments are sunk in the wave,
Though I feel that my soul is deliver'd
    To pain—it shall not be its slave. 20
There is many a pang to pursue me:
    They may crush, but they shall not contemn—
They may torture, but shall not subdue me—
    'Tis of *thee* that I think—not of them.

4

Though human, thou didst not deceive me, 25
    Though woman, thou didst not forsake,
Though loved, thou forborest to grieve me,
    Though slander'd, thou never could'st shake,—
Though trusted, thou didst not betray me,
    Though parted, it was not to fly, 30
Though watchful, 'twas not to defame me,
    Nor, mute, that the world might belie.

---

17 *rock of my last hope* Compare Psalm 62, in which David says of God, 'He only *is* my rock and my salvation; *he* is my defence' (2, 6) and 'In God *is* my salvation and my glory; the rock of my strength, *and* my refuge' (7).

17 *shiver'd* 'broken or split into small fragments; shattered'.

21–3 *There is many a pang . . . shall not subdue me* The speaker's emphasis here on his proud, isolated resistance to the pain of his existence recalls Byron's representations of Prometheus' manifold gift to 'Man' in 'Prometheus' (also written in 1816):

> But baffled as thou wert from high,
> Still in thy patient energy,
> In the endurance, and repulse
> Of thine impenetrable Spirit,
> Which Earth and Heaven could not convulse,
> A mighty lesson we inherit:
> Thou art a symbol and a sign
> To Mortals of their fate and force;
> Like thee, Man is in part divine,
> A troubled stream from a pure source;
> And man in portions can foresee
> His own funeral destiny;
> His wretchedness, and his resistance,
> And his sad unallied existence.
>   (ll. 39–52)

In equal parts wretched and resistant, 'Man' (and the persona of 'Stanzas to [Augusta]') emulates Prometheus' own defiance of the sentence that was passed on him by Zeus.

22 *They may crush* Compare Byron's letter to Moore (29 February 1816), cited in the headnote above.

25–32 *Though human . . . the world might belie* This stanza's emphasis on Augusta's steadfast fidelity is characteristic of Byron's numerous representations of her in his occasional poetry; compare 'Stanzas to Augusta' ('When all around grew drear and dark'):

> When fortune changed – and love fled far,
>   And hatred's shafts flew thick and fast,
> Thou wert the solitary star
>   Which rose and set not to the last.
>   (ll. 9–12)

27 *forborest* From 'forebear', here in the sense of having refrained or withheld from saying or doing something.

29 *betray* Previously 'disclaim', until McGann's *CPW* (vol. 4, pp. 457–8), which suggests that Byron's publisher, John Murray, modified 'betray' (in Byron's manuscript) in order to secure a perfect rhyme with 'defame me' (l. 31).

32 *belie* 'to give a false representation or account of, to misrepresent'.

5

Yet I blame not the world, nor despise it,
    Nor the war of the many with one—
If my soul was not fitted to prize it   35
    'Twas folly not sooner to shun:
And if dearly that error hath cost me,
    And more than I once could foresee,
I have found that, whatever it lost me,
    It could not deprive me of *thee*.   40

6

From the wreck of the past, which hath perish'd,
    Thus much I at least may recall,
It hath taught me that what I most cherish'd
    Deserved to be dearest of all:
In the desert a fountain is springing,   45
    In the wide waste there still is a tree,
And a bird in the solitude singing,
    Which speaks to my spirit of *thee*.

---

34 *war of the many with one* Compare Byron's letter to Moore (29 February 1816), cited in the headnote above.

36 *'Twas folly not sooner to shun* Compare '[Epistle to Augusta]', 'Had I but sooner known the crowd to shun / I had been better than I now can be' (ll. 93–4).

38 *foresee* Closely allied with Prometheus and promethean forethought; compare 'Prometheus', 'And man in portions can foresee / His own funereal destiny' (ll. 49–50).

45 *In the desert a fountain is springing* Compare 'Stanzas to Augusta' ('when all around grew drear and dark'):

    And these, when all was lost beside,
        Were found and still are fix'd in thee; –
    And bearing still a breast so tried,
        Earth is no desert – ev'n to me.
                              (ll. 41–4)

Compare also Milton, *Samson Agonistes*, 'But God who caus'd a fountain at thy prayer / From the dry ground to spring' (ll. 581–2) and Judges 15: 18–19.

46 *wide waste* Compare Shelley, 'Alastor', 'Many a wide waste and tangled wilderness / Has lured his fearless steps' (ll. 78–9).

46 *there still is a tree*, Compare 'Stanzas to Augusta' ('When all around grew drear and dark'), 'Thou stood'st, as stands a lovely tree, / That still unbroke, though gently bent, / Still waves with fond fidelity' (ll. 25–7).

[Epistle to Augusta]

Written in August 1816, it was first published in *Moore* (1830), due to Augusta's objections (see *BLJ*, vol. 5, pp. 90–1 and note). One of three poems addressed to Byron's sister Augusta from 1816 (for further details see headnote to 'Stanzas to [Augusta]', p. 243), this last written is, in both form and theme, arguably the most intimate of the three. The epistolary conventions allow the speaker to apostrophize Augusta from the outset ('My Sister – my sweet Sister', as opposed to the immediate emphasis on 'my destiny' and 'my fate' with which the 'Stanzas to [Augusta]' commence), and catalyse in turn a more open revelation of his feelings – their shared history, his present prospects and his defiantly passionate feelings for her, 'a loved regret which I would not resign' (l. 6 below). As he wrote to her from Switzerland shortly after composing the '[Epistle to Augusta]':

> What a fool I was to marry – and *you* not very wise – my dear – we might have lived so single and so happy – as old maids and bachelors; I shall never find anyone like you – nor you (vain as it may seem) like me. We are just formed to pass our lives together, and therefore – we – at least – I – am by a crowd of circumstances removed from the only being who could ever have loved me, or whom I can unmixedly feel attached to.
>
>   (*BLJ*, vol. 5, p. 96)

George Gordon Byron (1788–1824) 247

In addition to the intimacy of the reflections here, the '[Epistle to Augusta]' is furthermore noteworthy as Byron's first sustained composition in *ottava rima* (an octave in iambic pentameter rhyming *abababcc*), the stanzaic form which he would later use to such great effect in 'Beppo', *Don Juan*, and 'The Vision of Judgment'. (For further details on this important form, see headnote to *Don Juan*, p. 254.)

Text follows *1832*.

1

My Sister—my sweet Sister—if a name
    Dearer and purer were—it should be thine.
Mountains and Seas divide us—but I claim
    No tears—but tenderness to answer mine:
Go where I will, to me thou art the same—   5
    A loved regret which I would not resign—
There yet are two things in my destiny
A world to roam through—and a home with thee.

2

The first were nothing—had I still the last
    It were the haven of my happiness—   10
But other claims and other ties thou hast—
    And mine is not the wish to make them less.
A strange doom was thy father's son's and past
    Recalling—as it lies beyond redress—   15
Reversed for him our grandsire's fate of yore
He had no rest at sea—nor I on shore.

3

If my inheritance of storms hath been
    In other elements—and on the rocks
Of perils overlooked or unforeseen
    I have sustained my share of worldly shocks   20
The fault was mine—nor do I seek to screen
    My errors with defensive paradox—

---

3 *Mountains and Seas divide us* At the time of the poem's composition (August 1816), Byron was residing outside Geneva, Switzerland, on the shore of Lake Geneva (otherwise Lac Léman; see l. 75).

8 *a home with thee* Compare Byron's letter to Augusta (17 September 1816), cited in the headnote above.

11 *But other claims and other ties* See Byron's letter to Augusta (17 September 1816), where he writes, 'The great obstacle would be that you are so admirably yoked – and necessary as a housekeeper – and a letter writer – and a place-hunter to that very helpless gentleman your Cousin [Augusta's husband, their cousin George Leigh]' (*BLJ*, vol. 5, p. 96).

13 *A strange doom* Fate; compare l. 28, 'a fate or will that walked astray'.

13 *thy father's son's* Byron; Byron and Augusta had the same father, Captain John (Mad Jack) Byron.

15 *our grandsire's fate of yore* Byron's manuscript note reads:

> Admiral Byron [1723–86] was remarkable for never making a voyage without a tempest. He was known to the sailors by the facetious name of 'Foul-weather Jack'.
>
> > But, though it were tempest-tost,
> > Still his bark could not be lost.
>
> He returned safely from the wreck of the Wager (in Anson's Voyage), and subsequently circumnavigated the world, many years after, as commander of a similar expedition.

Compare Shakespeare, *Macbeth*, 'Though his bark cannot be lost, / Yet it shall be tempest-tost' (I. iii. 24–5).

I have been cunning in mine overthrow
The careful pilot of my proper woe.

4

Mine were my faults—and mine be their reward—
   My whole life was a contest—since the day
That gave me being gave me that which marred
   The gift—a fate or will that walked astray—
And I at times have found the struggle hard
   And thought of shaking off my bonds of clay—
But now I fain would for a time survive
If but to see what next can well arrive.

5

Kingdoms and empires in my little day
   I have outlived and yet I am not old—
And when I look on this, the petty spray
   Of my own years of trouble, which have rolled
Like a wild bay of breakers, melts away:—
   Something—I know no what—does still uphold
A spirit of slight patience;—not in vain
Even for its own sake do we purchase pain.

6

Perhaps—the workings of defiance stir
   Within me,—or perhaps a cold despair—
Brought on when ills habitually recur,—
   Perhaps a harder clime—or purer air—
For to all such may change of soul refer—
   And with light armour we may learn to bear—
Have taught me a strange quiet—which was not
The chief companion of a calmer lot.

7

I feel almost at times as I have felt
   In happy childhood—trees and flowers and brooks
Which do remember me of where I dwelt
   Ere my young mind was sacrificed to books—
Come as of yore upon me—and can melt
   My heart with recognition of their looks—
And even at moments I could think I see
Some living things to love—but none like thee.

---

24 *proper woe* Both appropriate (proportionally) and belonging strictly to himself.
30 *shaking off my bonds of clay* Compare Shakespeare, *Hamlet*, 'When we have shuffled off this mortal coil' (III. i. 67), and *Childe Harold*, 'Spurning the clay-cold bonds which round our being cling' (III. 73. 9). See also *Manfred*, 'The mind, the spirit, the Promethean spark, / / ... shall not yield to yours, though coop'd in clay!' (I. i. 154–7).
31 *fain* 'gladly, willingly, with pleasure'.

41–8 *Perhaps ... a calmer lot* Compare the resignation expressed by the speaker of 'The Prisoner of Chillon' when finally released:

> At last men came to set me free,
>   I ask'd not why, and reck'd not where,
> It was at length the same to me,
> Fetter'd or fetterless to be,
>   I learn'd to love despair.
>
> (ll. 370–74)

8

Here are the Alpine landscapes—which create
　　A fund for contemplation—to admire
Is a brief feeling of a trivial date—
　　But something worthier do such scenes inspire:　　　　60
Here to be lonely is not desolate—
　　For much I view which I could most desire—
And above all a lake I can behold—
Lovelier—not dearer—than our own of old.

9

Oh that thou wert but with me!—but I grow　　　　65
　　The fool of my own wishes—and forget
The solitude which I have vaunted so
　　Has lost its praise in this but one regret—
There may be others which I less may show—
　　I am not of the plaintive mood—and yet　　　　70
I feel an ebb in my philosophy
And the tide rising in my altered eye.

10

I did remind thee of our own dear lake
　　By the old Hall which may be mine no more—
Leman's is fair—but think not I forsake　　　　75
　　The sweet remembrance of a dearer shore—
Sad havoc Time must with my memory make
　　Ere *that* or *thou* can fade these eyes before—
Though like all things which I have loved—they are
Resigned for ever—or divided far.　　　　80

11

The world is all before me—I but ask
　　Of Nature that with which she will comply—

---

57 *Here are the Alpine landscapes* Compare *Childe Harold,* III. 72. See also the 'Alpine Journal' Byron kept for Augusta during his September 1816 tour of the Berne Alps, especially his concluding entry:

> ... I am a lover of Nature – and an Admirer of Beauty – I can bear fatigue – & welcome privation – and have seen some of the noblest views in the world. – But in all this – the recollections of bitterness – & more especially of recent & more home desolation – which must accompany me through life – have preyed upon me here – and neither the music of the Shepherd – the crashing of the Avalanche – nor the torrent – the mountain – the Glacier – the Forest – nor the Cloud – have for one moment – lightened the weight upon my heart – nor enabled me to lose my own wretched identity in the majesty & the power and the Glory – around – above – & beneath me.
> 　　　　　　　　　　　　　(*BLJ*, vol. 5, pp. 104–5)

60–1 *But something worthier ... not desolate* Compare *Childe Harold* III. 68–72, especially 'But soon in me shall loneliness renew / Thoughts hid, but not less cherished than of old' (III. 68.7–8) and III. 88–91, especially 'Then stirs the feeling infinite, so felt / In solitude, when we are *least* alone' (III. 90. 1–2).

63–4 *a lake ... our own of old.* The lake at Newstead Abbey (Nottinghamshire), the ancestral Byron home.

73 *our own dear lake* See note to lines 63–4 above.

74 *the old Hall which may be mine no more* Byron was eventually obliged to sell Newstead Abbey (in 1817) to settle his debts.

75 *Leman's* Lac Léman, otherwise known as Lake Geneva.

81 *The world is all before me* Compare Milton, *Paradise Lost,* 'The world was all before them, where to choose / Their place of rest, and Providence their guide' (12. 646–7). While Byron's speaker may have the world before him ('A world to roam through', l. 8), he is irrevocably separated from the one companion (the Eve to his Adam) who would make a difference in his pilgrimage.

> It is but in her Summer's sun to bask—
>   To mingle in the quiet of her sky—
> To see her gentle face without a mask
>   And never gaze on it with apathy—
> She was my early friend—and now shall be
> My Sister—till I look again on thee.

12

> I can reduce all feelings but this one
>   And that I would not—for at length I see
> Such scenes as those wherein my life begun
>   The earliest—were the only paths for me.
> Had I but sooner known the crowd to shun
>   I had been better than I now can be
> The passions which have torn me would have slept—
> *I* had not suffered—and *thou* hadst not wept.

13

> With false Ambition what had I to do?
>   Little with love, and least of all with fame!
> And yet they came unsought and with me grew,
>   And made me all which they can make—a Name
> Yet this was not the end I did pursue—
>   Surely I once beheld a nobler aim.
> But all is over—I am one the more
> To baffled millions which have gone before.

14

> And for the future—this world's future may
>   From me demand but little from my care;
> I have outlived myself by many a day,
>   Having survived so many things that were—
> My years have been no slumber—but the prey
>   Of ceaseless vigils;—for I had the share
> Of life which might have filled a century
> Before its fourth in time had passed me by.

---

84 *the quiet of her sky* Compare Wordsworth, 'Lines Written a Few Miles Above Tintern Abbey', 'and connect / The landscape with the quiet of the sky' (ll. 7–8), an influence perhaps attributable to the time Byron and Shelley spent together in the summer of 1816: 'Shelley, when I was in Switzerland [1816], used to dose me with Wordsworth physic even to nausea; and I do remember then reading some things of his with pleasure. He had once a feeling of Nature, which he carried almost to a deification of it' (*Medwin's Conversations of Lord Byron*, ed. Ernest J. Lovell, Jr. [Princeton: Princeton University Press, 1966], p. 194). For Byron's attitude toward the older Wordsworth, see the 'Dedication' to *Don Juan*, ll. 25–48.
93 *Had I but sooner known the crowd to shun* Compare 'Stanzas to [Augusta]', 'If my soul was not fitted to prize it / 'Twas folly not sooner to shun' (ll. 36–7). See also *Childe Harold*, III, 'in the crowd / They could not deem me one of such; I stood / Among them, but not of them' (III. 113. 5–7).
100 *a Name* Regarding the stupendous success of *Childe Harold*, I–II, Byron later remarked that 'I awoke one morning and found myself famous' (*Moore*, vol. 1, p. 346).
110 *ceaseless vigils* Compare *Manfred*:

> My slumbers (if I slumber) are not sleep
> But a continuance of enduring thought,
> Which then I can resist not. In my heart
> There is a vigil, and these eyes but close
> To look within. . . .
>   (I. i. 3–7)

15

And for the remnants which may be to come
  I am content—and for the past I feel
Not thankless—for within the crowded sum 115
  Of struggles—happiness at times would steal—
And for the present—I would not benumb
  My feelings farther—nor shall I conceal
That with all this I still can look around
And worship Nature with a thought profound. 120

16

For thee—my own sweet Sister—in thy heart
  I know myself secure—as thou in mine
We were and are—I am—even as though art—
  Beings—who ne'er each other can resign
It is the same together or apart— 125
  From life's commencement to its slow decline—
We are entwined—let death come slow or fast—
The tie which bound the first endures the last.

118–20 *nor shall I conceal . . . a thought profound* Compare Wordsworth, 'Lines Written a Few Miles Above Tintern Abbey', lines 103–8 and 152–4. See also *Childe Harold*, III. 13.
123–5 *We were and are . . . together or apart* Compare Byron's letter to Augusta (17 September 1816), cited in the headnote above.
128 *The tie* Byron's blood tie to his sister Augusta, as opposed to his legal tie to his wife Annabella.

Stanzas to the Po

Written 2 June 1819, 'Stanzas to the Po' was first published in Thomas Medwin's *Journal of the Conversations of Lord Byron* (1824). Occasioned by Byron's separation from the Countess Teresa Guiccioli in the spring of 1819, the poem may also be read as a lyric meditation on precisely the sort of *l'amour passion* which Byron had shunned after leaving England and Augusta in 1816 (see especially ll. 45 ff). In April, 1819, Byron began an affair with the young Contessa Teresa Guiccioli (*née* Gamba), whom he had met at a Venetian *conversazione* in April (and who would prove to be the last great love of his life; for more details, see biographical headnote p. 242). As he wrote to Douglas Kinnaird later that month:

I have fallen in love within the last month with a Romagnuola Countess from Ravenna – the Spouse of a year of Count Guiccioli – who is sixty – the Girl twenty . . . She is fair as Sunrise – and warm as Noon – we had but ten days – to manage all our little matters in beginning middle and end. & we managed them; – and I have done my duty – with the proper consummation.

(*BLJ*, vol. 6, p. 114; see also p. 107)

When, shortly thereafter, the Count abruptly took his young wife away from Venice to an estate of his on the Po, Byron and Teresa began making plans to meet in Ravenna, which they eventually did later that summer. In the interim, Byron found himself in the throes of a more passionate love than any he had known since Augusta, to whom he wrote anew of his abiding love for her. Thus, at the same time as he was writing to Teresa that 'I kiss you with all my soul – a thousand and a thousand times – and am eternally your lover' (*BLJ*, vol. 6, p. 122), he professed to Augusta that

252   George Gordon Byron (1788–1824)

... I have never ceased nor can cease to feel for a moment that perfect & boundless attachment which bound & binds me to you – which renders me utterly incapable of *real* love for any other human being – what could they be to me after *you*? ... I can never be other than I have been – and whenever I love anything it is because it reminds me in some way or other of yourself. ...

(*BLJ*, vol. 6, p. 129)

Byron left Venice on 1 June, and located his lyric address to the Po upriver from where he imagined Teresa to be residing at the moment (the Count's estate Ca' Zen, near the river's mouth on the Adriatic), at the time of his 'passing the Po' (*BLJ*, vol. 7, p. 76) en route to Bologna. He eventually sent the verses to Kinnaird and considered publishing them, before deciding against it on the grounds that 'they are mere verses of Society – & written upon private feelings and passions' (*BLJ*, vol. 7, p. 97).

'Stanzas to the Po' was printed by Medwin (and often thereafter) as a series of heroic quatrains (an iambic pentameter quatrain rhyming *abab*), a decision which formally underscores the elevated tone of the speaker's sentiments for 'the Lady of my Love' as he compares the strength of his passion with the depth and power of the river's course.

Text follows *1832*. (For an alternative text and a detailed textual history, see *CPW*, vol. 4, pp. 210–12, 496–9.)

I

River, that rollest by the ancient walls,
    Where dwells the lady of my love, when she
Walks by thy brink, and there perchance recalls
    A faint and fleeting memory of me;

II

What if thy deep and ample stream should be   5
    A mirror of my heart, where she may read
The thousand thoughts I now betray to thee,
    Wild as thy wave, and headlong as thy speed!

III

What do I say – a mirror of my heart?
    Are not thy waters sweeping, dark, and strong?   10
Such as my feelings were and are, thou art;
    And such as thou art were my passions long.

IV

Time may have somewhat tamed them, – not for ever;
    Thou overflow'st thy banks, and not for aye
Thy bosom overboils, congenial river!   15
    Thy floods subside, and mine have sunk away.

1–2 *River!* ... *the Lady of my Love* Byron's poem may be understood as a sustained apostrophe to the Po (the initial trochee and immediate caesura here in the first line serve to underscore the force of this apostrophe), metaphorically capable of carrying the poet's voice downstream to Teresa Guiccioli, 'the Lady of my Love', who is imagined as living and walking on its banks, from which she may 'read' the state of the poet's heart in the waters of the river (ll. 6–7).
7 *betray* To disclose or reveal (that which ought to be kept secret).

11 *were and are, thou art* In both this line and the next, Byron aligns the river's present strength (its waters 'sweeping, dark, and strong') with the past and continuing status of his own emotions.
15 *congenial river* The Po is congenial to the speaker because it seems both to mirror his heart (ll. 6 and 9) and to share his spirit (*genius*) and disposition: as the speaker's untamed passions have caused his heart to 'overboil', so has the river overflowed its own banks.

V

But left long wrecks behind, and now again,
    Borne in our old unchanged career, we move;
Thou tendest wildly onwards to the main,
    And I – to loving *one* I should not love.   20

VI

The current I behold will sweep beneath
    Her native walls and murmur at her feet;
Her eyes will look on thee, when she shall breathe
    The twilight air, unharm'd by summer's heat.

VII

She will look on thee, – I have look'd on thee,   25
    Full of that thought; and, from that moment, ne'er
Thy waters could I dream of, name, or see,
    Without the inseparable sigh for her!

VIII

Her bright eyes will be imaged in thy stream, –
    Yes! they will meet the wave I gaze on now: 30
Mine cannot witness, even in a dream,
    That happy wave repass me in its flow!

IX

The wave that bears my tears returns no more:
    Will she return by whom that wave shall sweep?–
Both tread thy banks, both wander on thy shore,   35
    I by thy source, she by the dark-blue deep.

X

But that which keepeth us apart is not
    Distance, nor depth of wave, nor space of earth,
But the distraction of a various lot,
    As various as the climates of our birth.   40

---

18 *career* Figuratively, 'a person's course or progress through life'.
19 *the main* The high sea (in this case the Adriatic), into which the Po will empty.
20 *loving one I should not love* Byron's friends, especially Hobhouse, were against his liaison with Teresa. Byron also had reservations during this period about his relations with Teresa: describing her somewhat equivocally as 'a sort of an Italian Caroline Lamb' (*BLJ*, vol. 6, p. 115; see biographical headnote p. 241), he worried that 'if She should plant [*piantare*, abandon] me – and I should make a "fiasco" never could I show my face on the Piazza' (*BLJ*, vol. 6, p. 107) and that he 'should not like to be frittered down into a regular Cicisbeo [publicly acknowledged lover of a married woman]' (*BLJ*, vol. 6, p. 108).
36 *I by thy source . . . dark-blue deep* Byron crossed the Po in Piedmont, near its headwaters, and imagined that Teresa was at the Guiccioli estate Ca' Zen, near its mouth on the Adriatic.
37–9 *But that which keepeth . . . distractions of a various lot* Among other worldly 'distractions', the complications of communicating with Teresa whilst she remained sequestered with the Count.

XI

A stranger loves the lady of the land,
   Born far beyond the mountains, but his blood
Is all meridian, as if never fann'd
   By the black wind that chills the polar flood.

XII

My blood is all meridian; were it not,
   I had not left my clime, nor should I be,
In spite of tortures, ne'er to be forgot,
   A slave again of love, – at least of thee.

XIII

'Tis vain to struggle – let me perish young –
   Live as I lived, and love as I have loved;
To dust if I return, from dust sprung,
   And then, at least, my heart can ne'er be moved.

---

43 *meridian* 'of or belonging to the south'; here, the 'passion' of the Mediterranean (as opposed to the cold north 'beyond the Mountains').

45 *my blood is all meridian* All passion; see Byron's recollection of the composition of the verses to the Po, 'they were written in *red-hot Earnest* – & that makes them good' (*BLJ*, vol. 7, p. 115).

48 *slave* A slave again of love; see Byron's letter to Teresa of 22 April 1819, 'You sometimes tell me that I have been your *first* real love – and I assure you that you shall be my last Passion (*BLJ*, vol. 6, p. 112) and his complaint later that month that 'I am damnably in love' (*BLJ*, vol. 6, p. 115). 'Slave' here also resonates with *cavalier servente*, a publicly acknowledged lover of a married woman who attends to her every need. See Byron's letter to Augusta of 19 December 1816: 'I told my fair one – at setting out – that as to the love and the Cavaliership – I was quite of accord – *but as to the servitude* – it would not suit me at all – so I begged to hear no more about it' (*BLJ*, vol. 5, p. 145).

48–50 *of Love! . . . as I have loved* See Byron's letter to Teresa of 25 April 1819:

> For some years I have been trying systematically to avoid strong passions, having suffered too much from the tyranny of Love. *Never to feel admiration* – and to enjoy myself without giving too much importance to the enjoyment in itself – to feel indifference toward human affairs – contempt for many, but hatred for none, – this was the basis of my philosophy. I did not mean to love any more, nor did I hope to receive Love. You have put to flight all my resolutions – now I am all yours. . . .
>
>   (*BLJ*, vol. 6, p. 118)

Don Juan

Begun in the summer of 1818 and left incomplete at the time of Byron's death in 1824, *Don Juan* not only marks a radical break in voice and form from *Childe Harold's Pilgrimage*, the Eastern Tales, and *Manfred*, but is recognized now as his masterpiece – arguably the most significant long poem in English published between *Paradise Lost* (1667) and *The Prelude* (1850). After first experimenting with *ottava rima* in the '[Epistle to Augusta]' (see p. 246), Byron undertook a longer, more light-hearted work in the same form when he wrote 'Beppo' in 1817. Indebted both to the Italian serio-comic use of *ottava rima* (as handled by Casti, Berni, Boiardo, and Pulci) and to John Hookham Frere's *Whistlecraft* (1817), 'Beppo' tells a rambling Venetian story of marital infidelity in a gossipy, facetious voice. It was with this comic narrative that Byron discovered the suitability of the form (an eight-line stanza in decasyllabic lines rhyming *abababcc*) for both narrative (the interlocking rhymes of the first six lines) and digression (the ease with which the clinching couplet lends itself to bathos and anticlimax), especially when handled in an irreverent, ironic narrative voice. Indeed, when Byron embarked upon *Don Juan* (to be pronounced *Ju*-an with a hard 'J'; see below, Canto I, l. 6 and note), he did not have a 'plan' *per se*, but thought of it as simply another poem 'in the style and manner of *Beppo*. . . . It is called *Don Juan*, and is meant to be a little quietly facetious about everything' (*BLJ*, vol. 6, p. 67).

As conversational as it is improvisational, *Don Juan* defies categorization. Epic in length if not in ambition ('if one's years can't be better spent than in sweating poesy – a man had better be a ditcher', *BLJ*, vol. 6, p. 105), confessional in voice if not in content, and satirical at the expense of what Byron repeatedly denounces as 'the damned Cant and Toryism of the day' (*BLJ*, vol. 6, pp. 76–7), *Don Juan* in fact often resembles what Byron (however disingenuously) later suggested: 'a poetical T[ristram] Shandy – or Montaigne's *Essays* with a story for a hinge' (*BLJ*, vol. 10, p. 150). Byron's letters provide valuable insight into the protean evolution of the poem, and many suggest, if not his 'plans' for the poem, then at least how his readers might approach it in a fashion simultaneously 'quietly facetious' and quietly serious. For example: in a letter to his publisher, John Murray, of August 1819, Byron writes:

> You ask me for the plan of Donny Johnny – I *have* no plan – I *had* no plan – but I had or have materials – though if like Tony Lumpkin – I am 'to be snubbed so when I am in spirits' [Goldsmith, *She Stoops to Conquer*] the poem will be naught – and the poet turn serious again. – If it don't take I will leave it off where it is with all due respect to the Public – but if continued it must be in my own way – you might as well make Hamlet (or Diggory [another character from *She Stoops to Conquer*]) 'act mad' in a strait waistcoat – as trammel my buffoonery – if I am to be a buffoon – their gestures and my thoughts would only be pitiably absurd – and ludicrously constrained. – Why Man the Soul of such writing is it's license? – at least the *liberty* of that *license* if one likes – *not* that one should abuse it – it is like trial by Jury and Peerage – and the Habeas Corpus – a very fine thing – but chiefly in the *reversion* – because no one wishes to be tried for the mere pleasure of proving his possession of the privilege. – But a truce with these reflections; – you are too earnest and eager about a work never intended to be serious; – do you suppose that I could have any intention but to giggle and make giggle? – a playful satire with as little poetry as could be helped – was what I meant. . . .
>
> (*BLJ*, vol. 6, pp. 207–8)

Sandwiched between Byron's light-hearted comments here – acting mad at the outset and giggling in conclusion – is a pointed and principled commentary on the licence of the poet, whether or not actively exercised. Here and elsewhere (see *BLJ*, vol. 6, pp. 76–7, 232), Byron inflects this licence as one both of poetic situation (the freedom of the satiric poet in choosing his situations and topics) and of voice (the freedom of discarding previous personae, of raising and lowering one's voice at will), thus revealing a pronounced commitment to poetic and political liberty behind the veil of giggling and acting mad. Similarly, a letter from later in 1819 to his friend and literary executor, Douglas Kinnaird, reveals Byron both boasting over the poem's ability to capture and articulate '*the thing*', and the dangers of doing so at the present time:

> As to *Don Juan* – confess – confess – you dog – and be candid – that it is the sublime of *that there* sort of writing – it may be bawdy – but is it not good English? – it may be profligate – but is it not *life*, is it not *the thing*? – Could any man have written it – who has not lived in the world? – and tooled in a post-chaise? in a hackney coach? in a Gondola? against a wall? in a court carriage? in a vis-à-vis? – on a table? – and under it? – I have written about a hundred stanzas of a third Canto – but it is damned modest – the outcry has frightened me. – I had such projects for the Don – but the *Cant* is so much stronger than *Cunt* – now a days, – that the benefit of experience in a man who had well weighed the worth of both monosyllables – must be lost to despairing posterity. . . .
>
> (*BLJ*, vol. 6, p. 232)

Whereas Byron previously declared that he had no plans for 'Donny Johnny' and that he was not going to be beholden to anything other than his own antic as well as political sense of licence, here he admits that he does in fact have 'projects', projects which he may be hesitant to execute in light of the public's response to the first two cantos. Critically, these plans are held in place (or in check) by two powerful monosyllables, 'cant' and 'cunt' – whining hypocrisy and brazen sexuality, broadly speaking – both of which are integral to an understanding of Byron's poem (the first rhyme of *Canto I*, after all, is built around 'cant'). What is at stake in Byron's letter, as throughout his poem, is not only the 'weight' of these arbitrarily linked monosyllables but, consequently, the equally weighty poetic licence to speak freely, regardless of persona.

The nuances of Byronic dissimulation are also succinctly on display in a stanza never incorporated in the body of the poem (though written for inclusion in Canto I):

I would to Heaven that I were so much clay –
  As I am blood – bone – marrow, passion – feeling –
Because at least the past were past away –
  And for the future – (but I write this reeling
Having got drunk exceedingly to day
  So that I seem to stand upon the ceiling)
I say – the future is a serious matter –
And so – for Godsake – Hock and Soda water.
  (*DJV*, vol. 2, p. 156)

Here, in a voice initially reminiscent of Manfred (the moribund 'clay' of humanity), the speaker laments the pains of his heavy mortal existence, only to interrupt himself with a parenthetical digression on drunkenness just at the moment when, looking ahead to the future, he would appear to have gained some forward momentum. Then, after turning this voice and its goals upside down in the parenthetical aside, the 'I' resumes its position in the couplet – to no avail, however, for any seriousness of tone or purpose has been lost. 'And so . . . ,' he calls for a drink. The style is conversational (the aside, with its conspiratorial confidentiality, keeps the reader engaged yet off-balance), while the wit is both pointed and ridiculous: the double rhymes, which reinflect 'feeling' not so much as 'passion' but as nausea, followed by the bathos of the couplet, with its own slightly off-key double-rhyme swiftly undoing anything 'serious' about the 'matter'. Such rhetorical and vocal strategies abound throughout *Don Juan*, as the narrator whimsically turns aside and, in so turning, continually deflects the course of the poem's narrative toward whatever catches his attention – every bit as arbitrarily and accidentally as, say, Don Alfonso suddenly catches sight of Juan's shoes in his wife's bedroom.

Partially because of *Don Juan*'s poetic licences (and seeming licentiousness), Byron was repeatedly urged against publishing the first cantos by his friends, who anticipated a backlash against, among other things, the bawdiness of language, the apparent satire of Lady Byron in the figure of Donna Inez and the blasphemous 'poetical commandments' at the end of Canto I. Amongst his friends, only Shelley was unequivocal in his support, declaring upon reading Cantos III–V that 'This poem carries with it at once the stamp of originality and a defiance of imitation. Nothing has ever been written like it in English' (*The Letters of Percy Bysshe Shelley*, ed. Frederick L. Jones [Oxford University Press, 1964], vol. 2, p. 357). Though he eventually suppressed the 'Dedication' (see headnote below) when the decision was made to publish anonymously, Byron was adamant that there should be neither mutilation nor omission of the text as he had prepared it (*BLJ*, vol. 6, p. 104). And although Byron acknowledged that 'the outcry has frightened me' (*BLJ*, vol. 6, p. 232), he proceeded in increasing defiance of the tastes of the English reading public, eventually changing publishers from the conservative John Murray (Cantos I–V) to the radical John Hunt (Cantos VI–XVI). As he wrote to Murray after the publication of Cantos III–V,

The 5th. is so far from being the last of D. J. that it is hardly the beginning. – I meant to take him the tour of Europe – with a proper mixture of siege – battle – and adventure – and to make him finish an *Anacharsis Cloots* – in the French Revolution. – To how many cantos this may extend – I know not – nor whether (even if I live) I shall complete it – but this was my notion. – I meant to have made him a Cavalier Servente in Italy and a cause for a divorce in England – and a Sentimental 'Werther-faced man' in Germany – so as to show the different ridicules of the society in each of those countries—and to have displayed him gradually gaté and blasé as he grew older – as is natural. – But I had not quite fixed whether to make him end in Hell – or in an unhappy marriage, – not knowing which would be the severest. – The Spanish tradition says Hell – but it is probably only an Allegory of the other state. . . .
  (*BLJ*, vol. 8, p. 78)

Dedication

The Dedication to *Don Juan* was written in July–September 1818 and first published in *1832*. Though suppressed when Cantos I–II were published in 1819, the dedicatory verses to Robert Southey (contemporary of Wordsworth and Coleridge and Poet Laureate from 1813–43) are integral to understanding the conception and execution of *Don Juan*, not least its remorseless exposure of what Byron repeatedly called 'the damned Cant and Toryism of the day' (*BLJ*, vol. 6, pp. 76–7). Shortly after completing the Dedication and Cantos I–II (September 1818), Byron explained to Thomas Moore that *Don Juan* was 'dedicated to S[outhey] in good, simple, savage verse, upon the [Laureate's] politics, and the way he got them' (*BLJ*, vol. 6, p. 68). Elsewhere, in a prose Preface to *Don Juan* (unpublished until 1901), Byron offered several suppositions for the 'tenor of the dedication' of the poem to Southey, the last of which reads thus:

... the dedication may be further supposed to be produced by someone who may have a cause of aversion from the said Southey – for some personal reason – perhaps a gross calumny invented or circulated by this Pantisocratic apostle of apostasy – who is sometimes as unguarded in his assertions – as atrocious in his conjectures and feeds the cravings of his wretched Vanity disappointed in it's nobler hopes – & reduced to prey upon such Snatches of fame as his contributions to the *Quarterly Review* – and the consequent praise with which a powerful Journal repays it's assistants can afford him – by the abuse of whosoever may be more consistent – or more successful than himself; – and the provincial gang of scribblers gathered round him

(*DJV*, vol. 2, pp. 6–7)

In addition to his contempt for Southey's apostasy – his renunciation of the radical politics of his youth for the servility required of the Poet Laureate (see below, note to l. 1) – Byron was convinced that Southey ('a burning liar . . . a dirty, lying rascal', *BLJ*, vol. 6, pp. 82–3) had spread scandalous, unfounded rumours about his having formed, with Shelley, a 'League of Incest' in Switzerland in the summer of 1816 (*BLJ*, vol. 6, pp. 76, 82). Consequently, 'I have given it to Master Southey, and he shall have more before I have done with him' (*BLJ*, vol. 6, p. 82). When Byron eventually decided to publish the first cantos without his name, he suppressed this attack, on the grounds that since 'the Poem is to be published anonymously *omit* the dedication – I won't attack the dog in the dark – such things are for Scoundrels and renegadoes like himself' (cited by McGann, *CPW*, vol. 5, pp. 670–1; see also *BLJ*, vol. 6, pp. 123, 127). After Byron read the Dedication to him, Shelley remarked in a letter to Thomas Love Peacock that it was 'more like a mixture of wormwood & verdigrease than satire. The poor wretch will writhe under the lash' (*Letters of Percy Bysshe Shelley*, vol. 2, p. 42).

Though reserving most of his contempt here for Southey and the callowness of his apostasy, Byron also takes aim at two other focal points of his derision: the poetry of the Lake poets (Wordsworth, Coleridge and Southey), and the politics of the Foreign Secretary, Viscount Castlereagh (see below, note to l. 88). For Byron, the Lake poets represented all that was misguided about the 'wrong revolutionary poetical system' (*BLJ*, vol. 5, p. 265) governing English literature, while Castlereagh embodied the most tyrannical components of English foreign policy during and after the Napoleonic wars.

Text from *1832*.

Difficile est proprie communia dicere.
Hor[ace], *Epist*[*ola*] *ad Pison*[*es*].

1

Bob Southey! You're a poet—poet Laureate,
 And representative of all the race;
Although 'tis true you turn'd out a Tory at
 Last,—yours has lately been a common case:—

Epigraph Horace, 'The Art of Poetry', l. 128: 'It is difficult to speak of common things in an appropriate manner'. See *BLJ*, vol. 6, p. 96n and *Hints from Horace*, ll. 181–4 and note, where there are two variations on this precept: 'Of common things tis difficult to write' and 'Tis no slight task to write on common things'. Though the Dedication was suppressed in 1819, Byron's epigraph appeared on the title pages of Cantos I–II when they were published together in 1819, then with Cantos III–V when they appeared in 1821.

1 *Bob Southey!* Robert Southey was appointed Poet Laureate in 1813 (which post he held until 1843), following the death of Henry Pye (see note to l. 8) and Walter Scott's refusal of the position. Byron condemns Southey as a renegade (see note to l. 5) because acceptance of the post entailed the composition of occasional poetry according to the dictates of the Crown – further evidence that Southey had renounced the independent, 'Jacobinical' principles and poetry of his youth (e.g. *Wat Tyler* and the 'Botany Bay Eclogues') in favour of 'legitimate' politics and sycophantic poetry. For additional satires at the expense of Southey's 'renegado-ism', see the Preface to Cantos I and II of *Don Juan* (*DJV*, vol. 2, pp. 3–7) and 'The Vision of Judgment'.

1 *Laureate* It is representative of Byron's voice throughout *Don Juan* that he should begin the poem with a triple-rhyme (*Laur*-e-ate / *To*-ry-at / *are*-ye-at), at once colloquial (the slangy 'are-ye-at') and pointed in its wit (the alignment of Laureate verses with Tory politics).

4 *a common case* By the mid-1810s, all three of the Lake poets (see note to l. 6) had 'turned' from the populist revolutionary politics of their youths in the 1790s to endorse the reactionary politics of the Regency: Southey wrote poetry in praise of the King and Regent; Wordsworth was Distributor of Stamps for Westmoreland; and Coleridge was lecturing on philosophy as well as writing for Tory newspapers. See also line 134.

                    And now, my epic renegade! what are ye at,　　　　　　　　　　　5
                        With all the Lakers in and out of place?
                    A nest of tuneful persons, to my eye
                    Like four and twenty blackbirds in a pie;

                                            2

                    'Which pie being open'd, they began to sing'—
                        (This old song and new simile holds good)　　　　　　　　10
                    'A dainty dish to set before the King,'
                        Or Regent, who admires such kind of food.
                    And Coleridge, too, has lately taken wing,
                        But, like a hawk encumber'd with his hood,
                    Explaining metaphysics to the nation—　　　　　　　　　　　15
                    I wish he would explain his Explanation.

                                            3

                    You, Bob! are rather insolent, you know,
                        At being disappointed in your wish
                    To supersede all warblers here below,
                        And be the only Blackbird in the dish;　　　　　　　　　　20
                    And then you overstrain yourself, or so,
                        And tumble downward like the flying fish
                    Gasping on deck, because you soar too high, Bob,
                    And fall, for lack of moisture, quite adry, Bob!

                                            4

                    And Wordsworth, in a rather long 'Excursion',　　　　　　　　25
                        (I think the quarto holds five hundred pages)

5 *renegade* 'One who has reneged on or renounced a previous commitment; a deserter of a political party or religious faith; an apostate'. In March, 1817 (following the publication of *Wat Tyler*), Southey had been denounced in the House of Commons by William Smith as a '*renegado*', a castigation which Coleridge sought to redress later that month in the pages of the *Courier*.
6 *the Lakers* Wordsworth, Coleridge and Southey, so denominated by Francis Jeffrey, editor of the *Edinburgh Review*.
8 *pie* Henry James Pye, Poet Laureate from 1790 until his death in 1813. Byron elsewhere mocks Pye (and aligns him with Southey) in *Hints from Horace* (notes to ll. 189, 617) and in 'The Vision of Judgment' (ll. 735–6).
12 *Regent* George, Prince of Wales, later George IV. Due to the mental instability of George III, a Regency was declared in 1811 (lasting until 1820), during which the Prince of Wales governed in his father's stead as Prince Regent.
13 *Coleridge* Byron had made arrangements to publish Coleridge's 'Christabel', 'Kubla Khan' and 'The Pains of Sleep' with his own publisher, John Murray, in 1816. When he read Coleridge's *Biographia Literaria* the following year, he found in it (ch. 23) an attack on his part in the administration of Drury Lane (Byron was on the committee of management), for not having accepted a play of Coleridge's, at which point he wrote to Murray, 'Mr. Coleridge may console himself with the "fervour – the almost religious fervour" of his and Wordsworth's disciples as he calls it . . . He is a shabby fellow – and I wash my hands of, and after him' (*BLJ*, vol. 5, p. 267).
15–16 *Explaining metaphysics . . . his Explanation* Coleridge's prose, most particularly *Biographia Literaria* (1817) but also *The Statesman's Manual* (1816) and *A Lay Sermon* (1817).
24 *adry, Bob!* Contemporary slang for sexual intercourse without ejaculation; also to be understood here as a commentary on the sterility of Southey's poetry. Had the Dedication been published in 1819, this rhyme was to have been suppressed, thus leaving Southey 'high' and 'dry'; see *BLJ*, vol. 6, p. 94.
25 *And Wordsworth . . . 'Excursion'* Wordsworth's *Excursion* (1814) was singled out for its inordinate length by its first reviewers (e.g. Jeffrey and Hazlitt); Wordsworth himself remarks in the Preface that it is 'only a portion of a poem . . . belong[ing] to the second part of a long and laborious Work'.

> Has given a sample from the vasty version
>   Of his new system to perplex the sages:
> 'Tis poetry—at least by his assertion,
>   And may appear so when the dogstar rages;
> And he who understands it would be able
> To add a story to the Tower of Babel.
>
> 5
>
> You, Gentlemen! by dint of long seclusion
>   From better company have kept your own
> At Keswick, and through still continued fusion
>   Of one another's minds at last have grown
> To deem as a most logical conclusion
>   That Poesy has wreaths for you alone;
> There is a narrowness in such a notion
> Which makes me wish you'd change your lakes for ocean.
>
> 6
>
> I would not imitate the petty thought,
>   Nor coin my self-love to so base a vice,
> For all the glory your conversion brought,
>   Since gold alone should not have been its price.
> You have your salary—was't for that you wrought?
>   And Wordsworth has his place in the Excise.
> You're shabby fellows—true—but poets still,
> And duly seated on the immortal hill.

28 *his new system* See Wordsworth, Preface to *The Excursion*: 'It is not the Author's intention formally to announce a system . . . the Reader will have no difficulty in extracting the system for himself'.
30 *when the dogstar rages* 'The star Sirius, in the constellation of the Greater Dog, the brightest of the fixed stars'. See Pope, *Epistle to Dr. Arbuthnot*:

> The dog-star rages! nay 'tis past a doubt,
> All Bedlam, or Parnassus, is let out:
> Fire in each eye, and papers in each hand,
> They rave, recite, and madden round the land.
>   (ll. 3–6)

32 *Tower of Babel* Tower built by humans, in defiance of God, to reach heaven; in response, God confounded their language and scattered them, so they no longer understood each other's speech. See Genesis 11:1–9.
33 *You, Gentlemen* See *Don Juan* III. 93–5 (stanza 95 was originally written for insertion between ll. 32–3).
35 *Keswick* Small market town in the Lake District where Southey lived (and, briefly, Coleridge); here, metonymy for the Lake District.
38 *wreaths* Poetic laurels and laureateships.
42–3 *Nor coin . . . your conversion brought* Here, 'to make money out of'; to transform or convert (gold into coinage) – hence a pun on 'conversion' as apostasy.
45 *for that you wrought* That which Southey shaped or fashioned (his poetry), but also that which he prepared for commerce (the sacrificing of his poetry for the annual salary provided to the Laureate).
46 *place in the Excise* 'Wordsworth's place may be in the Customs: it is, I think, in that of the Excise; besides another at Lord Lonsdale's table, where this poetical charlatan and political parasite picks up the crum[b]s with a hardened alacrity, the converted Jacobin having long subsided into the clownish sycophant of the worst prejudices of aristocracy' (Byron's note). See also the Preface to Cantos I and II, 'Amongst these last in self-degradation, this Thraso of poetry – has long been a Gnatho in Politics [see Terence, *Eunuchus*] – and may be met in print at some booksellers and several trunkmakers, and in person at dinner at Lord Lonsdale's' (*DJV*, vol. 2, p. 4). Lord Lonsdale was instrumental in arranging Wordsworth's sinecure as Distributor of Stamps in 1813; Wordsworth dedicated *The Excursion* to him the following year.
48 *the immortal hill* Mount Parnassus, Greek mountain located to the north of Delphi; sacred to Apollo and the muses, and thus to poetry.

7

Your bays may hide the baldness of your brows,
    Perhaps some virtuous blushes—let them go,   50
To you I envy neither fruit nor boughs—
    And for the fame you would engross below
The field is universal, and allows
    Scope to all such as feel the inherent glow—
Scott, Rogers, Campbell, Moore, and Crabbe, will try   55
'Gainst you the question with posterity.

8

For me who, wandering with pedestrian Muses,
    Contend not with you on the winged steed,
I wish your fate may yield ye, when she chooses,
    The fame you envy, and the skill you need;   60
And recollect a poet nothing loses
    In giving to his brethren their full meed
Of merit, and complaint of present days
Is not the *certain* path to future praise.

9

He that reserves his laurels for posterity   65
    (Who does not often claim the bright reversion?)
Has generally no great crop to spare it, he
    Being only injured by his own assertion;
And although here and there some glorious rarity
    Arise, like Titan from the sea's immersion,   70
The major part of such appellants go
To—God knows where—for no one else can know.

10

If, fallen in evil days on evil tongues,
    Milton appeal'd to the Avenger, Time,

---

49 *Your bays* The iconic laurels signifying the Laureateship.

55 *Scott, Rogers, Campbell, Moore, and Crabbe* Walter Scott, Samuel Rogers, Thomas Campbell, Thomas Moore and George Crabbe: all five were popular and well-respected poets during the 1810s, and all were esteemed by Byron. See Byron's journal entry for 24 November 1813: '[Scott] is undoubtedly the Monarch of Parnassus, and the most *English* of bards. I should place Rogers next in the living list . . . Moore and Campbell both *third* – Southey and Wordsworth and Coleridge below' (*BLJ*, vol. 3, pp. 219–20).

57–8 *pedestrian Muses . . . winged steed* Byron distinguishes his digressive, meandering earth-bound muse from Pegasus, the 'winged steed' of Parnassus.

60 *The fame you envy* See Southey, *Carmen Nuptiale. The Lay of the Laureate*, 'There was a time when all my youthful thought / Was of the muse; and of the poet's fame' (ll. 1–2).

66 *bright reversion* See the Preface to Cantos I and II, where Byron mocks Southey for the 'Postobits he has granted upon Posterity & usurious self-applause, in which he has anticipated with some profusion perhaps the opinion of future ages who are always more enlightened than Contemporaries – more especially in the eyes of those whose figure in their own times has been disproportioned to their deserts' (*DJV*, vol. 2, p. 6).

70 *Arise, like Titan* Helios, son of Hyperion and Thea; the Sun.

71 *appellants* Legal term for those who appeal an unsatisfactory decision to a higher tribunal.

73 *If, fallen in evil days on evil tongues* See Milton, *Paradise Lost*, 'More Safe I sing with mortal voice, unchanged / To hoarse or mute, though fallen on evil days, / On evil days though fallen' (7. 24–6).

74 *the Avenger, Time* In lines following those cited above, Milton exhorts his muse, Urania, 'still govern thou my song, / Urania, and fit audience find, though few' (7. 30–1).

If, Time, the Avenger, execrates his wrongs, 75
    And makes the word *'Miltonic'* mean *'sublime'*,
He deign'd not to belie his soul in songs,
    Nor turn his very talent to a crime—
He did not loathe the sire to laud the son,
But closed the tyrant-hater he begun. 80

11

Think'st thou, could he, the blind Old Man, arise
    Like Samuel from the grave, to freeze once more
The blood of monarchs with his prophecies,
    Or be alive again—again all hoar
With time and trials, and those helpless eyes 85
    And heartless daughters, worn, and pale, and poor,
Would *he* adore a sultan? *he* obey
The intellectual eunuch Castlereagh?

12

Cold-blooded, smooth-faced, placid miscreant!
    Dabbling its sleek young hands in Erin's gore, 90
And thus for wider carnage taught to pant,
    Transferr'd to gorge upon a sister-shore;
The vulgarest tool that tyranny could want,
    With just enough of talent, and no more,
To lengthen fetters by another fix'd, 95
And offer poison long already mix'd.

13

An orator of such set trash of phrase
    Ineffably, legitimately vile,
That even its grossest flatterers dare not praise,
    Nor foes—all nations—condescend to smile: 100
Not even a *sprightly* blunder's spark can blaze
    From that Ixion grindstone's ceaseless toil,

77–80 *He deign'd not . . . tyrant-hater he begun* Unlike Southey, who turned from writing regicidal plays (*Wat Tyler*) to composing birthday odes for kings, Milton stands here for the ideal of a poet whose political convictions did not become vitiated with age and the possibility of preferment. Milton criticized both Charles I and Charles II; Southey criticized George III and praised the future George IV.
81 *the blind Old Man* Milton.
82 *Like Samuel from the grave* See I Samuel 28: 11–14.
84 *all hoar* 'Grey-haired with age; venerable'.
86 *And heartless daughters* '"Pale, but not cadaverous [Johnson, *Lives of the English Poets*]". Milton's two elder daughters are said to have robbed him of his books, besides cheating and plaguing him in the economy of his house, etc. Hayley compares him to Lear' (Byron's note).
88 *Castlereagh* Robert Stewart, Viscount Castlereagh (1769–1822), British Foreign Secretary (1812–22). As Foreign Secretary, Castlereagh organized the Grand Alliance against Napoleon (1814) and was a principal designer of the policies ratified at the Congress of Vienna (1815). He committed suicide in 1822.
89 *miscreant!* 'misbeliever'; more generally, villain.
90 *Erin's gore* Ireland's. As Chief Secretary for Ireland (1797–1801), Castlereagh arrested the leaders of the United Irish rebellion, and subsequently replaced the Irish militia with English troops.
95 *To lengthen fetters by another fix'd* From 1814 to 1821, Castlereagh supported Austrian control of Italy; see lines 122–4.
102 *Ixion grindstone's* After murdering his father-in-law, Ixion, King of Thessaly, was exonerated by Zeus. He then attempted to seduce Zeus' wife, Hera; consequently, Zeus had him bound to a fiery wheel, constantly revolving, in Hades.

That turns and turns, to give the world a notion
Of endless torments, and perpetual motion.

14

A bungler even in its disgusting trade, 105
   And botching, patching, leaving still behind
Something of which its masters are afraid,
   States to be curb'd, and thoughts to be confined,
Conspiracy or Congress to be made—
   Cobbling at manacles for all mankind— 110
A tinkering slavemaker, who mends old chains,
With God and man's abhorrence for its gains.

15

If we may judge of matter by the mind,
   Emasculated to the marrow, *It*
Hath but two objects—how to serve, and bind, 115
   Deeming the chain it wears even men may fit;
Eutropius of its many masters—blind
   To worth as freedom, wisdom as to wit—
Fearless, because *no* feeling dwells in ice,
Its very courage stagnates to a vice. 120

16

Where shall I turn me not to *view* its bonds?
   For I will never *feel* them—Italy!
Thy late reviving Roman soul desponds
   Beneath the lie this state-thing breathed o'er thee;
Thy clanking chain, and Erin's yet green wounds, 125
   Have voices—tongues to cry aloud for me.
Europe has slaves, allies, kings, armies still,
And Southey lives to sing them very ill.

17

Meantime, Sir Laureate, I proceed to dedicate
   In honest, simple verse, this song to you; 130
And if in flattering strains I do not predicate,
   'Tis that I still retain my 'buff and blue'.

108–9 *States to be curb'd . . . to be made* Byron refers here to the policies of the Grand Alliance (designed to 'curb' Napoleonic France) and the Congress of Vienna (which repartitioned Europe after the Napoleonic Wars).
117 *Eutropius* Roman eunuch raised to ministerial office under the Roman Emperor Arcadius (378–408 CE), he pretentiously assumed the character of a Roman general; see Gibbon, *The History of the Decline and Fall of the Roman Empire*, ch. 32.
123 *Thy late reviving Roman soul* Byron refers here to the growing dissatisfaction of Italian liberals with the subjugation of the Italian states to Austrian rule; see the note to line 95 above.

128 *sing them very ill* See, for example, Southey's 'The Poet's Pilgrimage to Waterloo'.
129 *Sir Laureate* Southey; see line 1 above and note.
131 *predicate* 'to affirm . . . extol, commend' (from 'proclaim'). Another triple rhyme (*ded*-i-cate / *pred*-i-cate / *ed*-u-cate), which here underscores the satiric nature of a dedication which does not praise (predicate) but seeks (however obliquely) to educate.
132 *'buff and blue'* Colours of the Whig Club, first adopted by Charles James Fox. As a Tory, Southey has renounced the Whig allegiances and commitments of his youth.

My politics, as yet, are all to educate,
    Apostasy's so fashionable too,
To keep *one* creed's a task grown quite Herculean, 135
Is it not so, my Tory ultra-Julian?

136 *my Tory ultra-Julian* 'I allude not to our friend [Walter Savage] Landor's hero, the traitor Count Julian, but to Gibbon's hero [*The History of the Decline and Fall of the Roman Empire*], vulgarly yclept "The Apostate"' (Byron's note). Roman Emperor from 360–3 CE, Julian was denominated 'the Apostate' because he renounced Christianity and attempted to restore worship of the pagan gods; see Gibbon, *The History of the Decline and Fall of the Roman Empire*, ch. 23.

Canto I

Canto I was written in July–September 1818, and published anonymously in 1819 as *Don Juan, Cantos I and II*. See general headnote above to *Don Juan*.

Text follows *1819* (with suppressed lines and stanzas restored).

I.

I want a hero: an uncommon want,
    When every year and month sends forth a new one,
Till, after cloying the gazettes with cant,
    The age discovers he is not the true one;
Of such as these I should not care to vaunt, 5
    I'll therefore take our ancient friend Don Juan,
We all have seen him in the Pantomime
Sent to the devil, somewhat ere his time.

II.

Vernon, the butcher Cumberland, Wolfe, Hawke,
    Prince Ferdinand, Granby, Burgoyne, Keppel, Howe, 10
Evil and good, have had their tithe of talk,
    And fill'd their sign-posts then, like Wellesley now;

1 *I want a hero* 'Want' is to be understood here as both 'lack' and 'desire'.
6 *Juan* Here and throughout, to be pronounced *Ju-an* (with a hard 'J'), an inflection in keeping with Byron's exploitation of double-rhymes (here comically suggesting that, as a hero, *Ju*-an is both the *new*-one and the *true*-one). See lines 39–40.
7 *pantomime* 'dramatic performance consisting of action without speech'; here, possibly a popular adaptation of Thomas Shadwell's *The Libertine* (1675). McGann suggests that Byron took Don Juan as his model due to Coleridge's consideration of his dramatic character in *Biographia Literaria* (ch. 23); see *CPW*, vol. 5, pp. 668, 673.
9–10 *Vernon . . . Howe* eighteenth-century military heroes.
12 *sign-posts then, like Wellesley now* Wellington Street and Waterloo Bridge were dedicated on 18 June 1817, the second anniversary of the battle of Waterloo.

> Each in their turn like Banquo's monarchs stalk,
>   Followers of fame, "nine farrow" of that sow;
> France, too, had Buonaparté and Dumourier,
> Recorded in the Moniteur and Courier.

III.

> Barnave, Brissot, Condorcet, Mirabeau,
>   Petion, Clootz, Danton, Marat, La Fayette,
> Were French, and famous people, as we know;
>   And there were others, scarce forgotten yet,
> Joubert, Hoche, Marceau, Lannes, Dessaix, Moreau,
>   With many of the military set,
> Exceedingly remarkable at times,
> But not at all adapted to my rhymes.

IV.

> Nelson was once Britannia's god of war,
>   And still should be so, but the tide is turn'd;
> There's no more to be said of Trafalgar,
>   'Tis with our hero quietly inurn'd;
> Because the army's grown more popular,
>   At which the naval people are concern'd:
> Besides, the Prince is all for the land-service,
> Forgetting Duncan, Nelson, Howe, and Jervis.

V.

> Brave men were living before Agamemnon
>   And since, exceeding valorous and sage,
> A good deal like him too, though quite the same none;
>   But then they shone not on the poet's page,
> And so have been forgotten:—I condemn none,
>   But can't find any in the present age
> Fit for my poem (that is, for my new one);
> So, as I said, I'll take my friend Don Juan.

---

13 *like Banquo's monarchs stalk* See *Macbeth* IV. i. 112–24, where the witches conjure for Macbeth a vision of the dead Banquo in a procession with eight kings.
14 *'nine farrow'* Compare *Macbeth*, 'Pour in sow's blood, that hath eaten / Her nine farrow [litter]' (IV. i. 64–5).
15 *Dumourier* Charles Dumourier, French military commander who defeated the Austrians in 1792 at Jemappes.
16 *Moniteur and Courier* French newspapers founded respectively in 1789 and 1796, associated with the Revolution.
17–21 *Barnave . . . Moreau* French military and political figures from the French Revolution.
23–4 *Exceedingly remarkable . . . adapted to my rhymes* Exemplary use of a bathetic couplet to clinch the stanza, as a (mock-epic) list of military heroes gives way to a figure from the pantomime, one whose 'fitness' for the poem is first and foremost a matter of rhyme.
25 *Nelson* Lord Nelson (1758–1805), distinguished British admiral, killed at the Battle of Trafalgar, October 1805.
27 *Trafalgar* Formerly pronounced *Tra*-fal-*gar*.
29 *the army's grown more popular* Byron suggests here that after Wellington's victory over Napoleon at Waterloo in June 1815, the army (visibly supported by the Prince Regent) received the public admiration previously reserved for the navy. Byron reserved his admiration for Nelson: 'Nelson was a hero – the other is a mere corporal' (*BLJ*, vol. 9, p. 48).
32 *Duncan, Nelson, Howe, and Jervis* British naval heroes.
33 *Brave men . . . Agamemnon* Agamemnon was commander-in-chief of the Greek expedition against Troy. See Horace, *Odes*, 4.9.25.

VI.

Most epic poets plunge in 'medias res,'
   (Horace makes this the heroic turnpike road)
And then your hero tells, whene'er you please,
   What went before—by way of episode,
While seated after dinner at his ease,   45
   Beside his mistress in some soft abode,
Palace, or garden, paradise, or cavern,
Which serves the happy couple for a tavern.

VII.

That is the usual method, but not mine—
   My way is to begin with the beginning;   50
The regularity of my design
   Forbids all wandering as the worst of sinning,
And therefore I shall open with a line
   (Although it cost me half an hour in spinning)
Narrating somewhat of Don Juan's father,   55
And also of his mother, if you'd rather.

VIII.

In Seville was he born, a pleasant city,
   Famous for oranges and women—he
Who has not seen it will be much to pity,
   So says the proverb—and I quite agree;   60
Of all the Spanish towns is none more pretty,
   Cadiz perhaps—but that you soon may see:—
Don Juan's parents lived beside the river,
A noble stream, and call'd the Guadalquivir.

IX.

His father's name was Jóse—*Don*, of course,   65
   A true Hidalgo, free from every stain
Of Moor or Hebrew blood, he traced his source
   Through the most Gothic gentlemen of Spain;
A better cavalier ne'er mounted horse,
   Or, being mounted, e'er got down again,   70
Than Jóse, who begot our hero, who
Begot—but that's to come—Well, to renew:

X.

His mother was a learned lady, famed
   For every branch of every science known—
In every christian language ever named,   75
   With virtues equall'd by her wit alone,

---

41 *'medias res'* 'in the middle of things'; see Horace, *Ars Poetica*, l. 148.

57 *a pleasant city* The digression, or 'wandering' just denounced (l. 52), begins here; it is characteristic of the poem that the persona should distract attention from Juan to himself and to the composition of the poem.

60 *so says the proverb* '*Quien no ha visto Sevilla / No ha visto maravilla*' (Whoever has not seen Seville has not seen a marvel).

66 *A true Hidalgo* One of the lower nobility.

73 *His mother was a learned lady* Commonly thought to be a satirical representation of Lady Byron, though Byron denied as much (see *BLJ*, vol. 6, p. 257 and note).

She made the cleverest people quite ashamed,
    And even the good with inward envy groan,
Finding themselves so very much exceeded
    In their own way by all the things that she did   80

XI.

Her memory was a mine: she knew by heart
    All Calderon and greater part of Lopé,
So that if any actor miss'd his part
    She could have served him for the prompter's copy;
For her Feinagle's were an useless art,   85
    And he himself obliged to shut up shop—he
Could never make a memory so fine as
That which adorn'd the brain of Donna Inez.

XII.

Her favourite science was the mathematical,
    Her noblest virtue was her magnanimity,   90
Her wit (she sometimes tried at wit) was Attic all,
    Her serious sayings darken'd to sublimity;
In short, in all things she was fairly what I call
    A prodigy—her morning dress was dimity,
Her evening silk, or, in the summer, muslin,   95
And other stuffs, with which I won't stay puzzling.

XIII.

She knew the Latin—that is, "the Lord's prayer,"
    And Greek—the alphabet—I'm nearly sure;
She read some French romances here and there,
    Although her mode of speaking was not pure;   100
For native Spanish she had no great care,
    At least her conversation was obscure;
Her thoughts were theorems, her words a problem,
As if she deem'd that mystery would ennoble 'em.

XIV.

She liked the English and the Hebrew tongue,   105
    And said there was analogy between 'em;
She proved it somehow out of sacred song,
    But I must leave the proofs to those who've seen 'em,
But this I heard her say, and can't be wrong,
    And all may think which way their judgments lean 'em,   110

---

82   *Calderon . . . Lopé* Pedro Calderón de la Barca (1600–81) and Lopé de la Vega (1562–1635), Spanish dramatists.
85   *Feinagle's* Gregor von Feinagle (1765–1819), inventor of a system of mnemonics.
88   *Donna Inez* As with Jóse and Juan, Byron puts the stress on the first syllable.
89   *the mathematical* Byron quipped that Lady Byron was 'the Princess of Parallelograms' (*BLJ*, vol. 4, p. 48). See also *Don Juan* II. 18–19 and 'Beppo', line 624.

91   *Attic* 'of or pertaining to Attica, or its capitol Athens' (i.e. of or pertaining to classical Greece); hence, 'marked by simple and refined elegance, pure, classical'.
94   *dimity* 'A stout cotton fabric . . . , usually employed undyed for beds and bedroom hangings, and sometimes for garments'.

"Tis strange—the Hebrew noun which means "I am,"
  The English always use to govern d—n.'

XV.

Some women use their tongues—she look'd a lecture,
  Each eye a sermon, and her brow a homily,
An all-in-all-sufficient self-director,   115
  Like the lamented late Sir Samuel Romilly,
The Law's expounder, and the State's corrector,
  Whose suicide was almost an anomaly—
One sad example more, that 'All is vanity',—
  (The jury brought their verdict in 'Insanity').   120

XVI.

In short, she was a walking calculation,
  Miss Edgeworth's novels stepping from their covers,
Or Mrs. Trimmer's books on education,
  Or 'Coelebs' Wife' set out in quest of lovers,
Morality's prim personification,   125
  In which not Envy's self a flaw discovers,
To others' share let 'female errors fall,'
For she had not even one—the worst of all.

XVII.

Oh! she was perfect past all parallel—
  Of any modern female saint's comparison;   130
So far above the cunning powers of hell,
  Her guardian angel had given up his garrison;
Even her minutest motions went as well
  As those of the best time-piece made by Harrison:
In virtues nothing earthly could surpass her,   135
Save thine 'incomparable oil,' Macassar!

XVIII.

Perfect she was, but as perfection is
  Insipid in this naughty world of ours,

111–12 *"I am"... d—n.'* The Hebrew 'Yahweh', distilled from a verb for 'to be'. See Exodus 3: 13–14: 'And Moses said unto God ... What *is* his name? what shall I say unto them? And God said unto Moses, I AM THAT I AM'.
116 *Sir Samuel Romilly* Sir Samuel Romilly (1757–1818) was retained by Byron in 1816 as part of his separation proceedings from Lady Byron. Romilly then took Lady Byron's part in the proceedings, thus securing Byron's abiding hated. He committed suicide following the death of his own wife. See *BLJ*, vol. 6, p. 84, 150. (This stanza was suppressed in *1819*.)
119 *'All is vanity'* See Ecclesiastes 1: 2: 'Vanity of vanities, saith the Preacher, vanity of vanities; all *is* vanity'.
122 *Miss Edgeworth's novels* Maria Edgeworth (1767–1849), author (with her father) of a treatise on education, *Practical Education* (1798), as well as numerous influential novels, including *Castle Rackrent* (1800) and *Belinda* (1801).
123 *Mrs Trimmer's books* Sarah Trimmer (1741–1810), author of numerous books on education, including *An Easy Introduction to the Knowledge of Nature* (1790), and publisher of the *Guardian to Education* (1802–6).
124 *'Coelebs' Wife'* Popular novel by Hannah More (1745–1833), *Coelebs in Search of a Wife* (1809).
127 *let 'female errors fall'* Pope, *The Rape of the Lock*, 'If to her share some female errors fall, / Look on her face, and you'll forget 'em all' (II. 17–18).
134 *Harrison* John Harrison (1693–1776), prominent eighteenth-century horologist.
136 *'incomparable oil', Macassar!* 'Description des *vertus incomparables* de l'huile de Macassar. See the Advertisement' (Byron's note). Popular hair oil of the nineteenth century, ostensibly extracted from trees from Macassar in Indonesia.

Where our first parents never learn'd to kiss
    Till they were exiled from their earlier bowers,
Where all was peace, and innocence, and bliss,
    (I wonder how they got through the twelve hours)
Don Jóse, like a lineal son of Eve,
Went plucking various fruit without her leave.

XIX.

He was a mortal of the careless kind,
    With no great love for learning, or the learn'd,
Who chose to go where'er he had a mind,
    And never dream'd his lady was concern'd:
The world, as usual, wickedly inclined
    To see a kingdom or a house o'erturn'd,
Whisper'd he had a mistress, some said *two*,
But for domestic quarrels *one* will do.

XX.

Now Donna Inez had, with all her merit,
    A great opinion of her own good qualities;
Neglect, indeed, requires a saint to bear it,
    And such, indeed, she was in her moralities;
But then she had a devil of a spirit,
    And sometimes mix'd up fancies with realities,
And let few opportunities escape
Of getting her liege lord into a scrape.

XXI.

This was an easy matter with a man
    Oft in the wrong, and never on his guard;
And even the wisest, do the best they can,
    Have moments, hours, and days, so unprepared,
That you might 'brain them with their lady's fan;'
    And sometimes ladies hit exceeding hard,
And fans turn into falchions in fair hands,
And why and wherefore no one understands.

XXII.

'Tis pity learned virgins ever wed
    With persons of no sort of education,
Or gentlemen, who, though well-born and bred,
    Grow tired of scientific conversation:
I don't choose to say much upon this head,
    I'm a plain man, and in a single station,
But—Oh! ye lords of ladies intellectual,
Inform us truly, have they not hen-peck'd you all?

---

165 *'brain them with their lady's fan'* Shakespeare, *Henry IV, Part I* (spoken by Hotspur), 'Zounds, and I were now by this rascal I could brain him with his lady's fan' (II. iii. 22–3).
167 *falchions* Broad swords (curved, with the edge on the convex side).
175 *ladies intellectual* A reference to London 'bluestockings', groups of women who gathered for intellectual conversation on literary subjects.
175–6 *intellectual . . . hen-peck'd you all?* According to Leigh Hunt, the 'happiest triple rhyme, perhaps, that ever was written' (*The Selected Writings of Leigh Hunt* [London: Pickering and Chatto, 2003], vol. 4, p. 37).

XXIII.

Don Jóse and his lady quarrell'd—*why*,
   Not any of the many could divine,
Though several thousand people chose to try,
   'Twas surely no concern of theirs nor mine;
I loathe that low vice curiosity,
   But if there's any thing in which I shine
'Tis in arranging all my friends' affairs,
Not having, of my own, domestic cares.

XXIV.

And so I interfered, and with the best
   Intentions, but their treatment was not kind;
I think the foolish people were possess'd,
   For neither of them could I ever find,
Although their porter afterwards confess'd—
   But that's no matter, and the worst's behind,
For little Juan o'er me threw, down stairs,
A pail of housemaid's water unawares.

XXV.

A little curly-headed, good-for-nothing,
   And mischief-making monkey from his birth;
His parents ne'er agreed except in doting
   Upon the most unquiet imp on earth;
Instead of quarrelling, had they been but both in
   Their senses, they'd have sent young master forth
To school, or had him soundly whipp'd at home,
To teach him manners for the time to come.

XXVI.

Don Jóse and the Donna Inez led
   For some time an unhappy sort of life,
Wishing each other, not divorced, but dead;
   They lived respectably as man and wife,
Their conduct was exceedingly well-bred,
   And gave no outward signs of inward strife,
Until at length the smother'd fire broke out,
And put the business past all kind of doubt.

XXVII.

For Inez call'd some druggists and physicians,
   And tried to prove her loving lord was *mad*,
But as he had some lucid intermissions,
   She next decided he was only *bad*;
Yet when they ask'd her for her depositions,
   No sort of explanation could be had,

---

210 *her loving lord was* mad Byron maintained that Lady Byron had attempted to obtain proof of his insanity during their separation in 1816.

213 *depositions* Formal legal testimony (that Byron was 'bad' and 'mad') retained as evidence.

Save that her duty both to man and God 215
Required this conduct—which seem'd very odd.

XXVIII.

She kept a journal, where his faults were noted,
    And open'd certain trunks of books and letters,
All which might, if occasion served, be quoted:
    And then she had all Seville for abettors, 220
Besides her good old grandmother (who doted);
    The hearers of her case became repeaters,
Then advocates, inquisitors, and judges,
Some for amusement, others for old grudges.

XXIX.

And then this best and meekest woman bore 225
    With such serenity her husband's woes,
Just as the Spartan ladies did of yore,
    Who saw their spouses kill'd, and nobly chose
Never to say a word about them more—
    Calmly she heard each calumny that rose, 230
And saw *his* agonies with such sublimity,
That all the world exclaim'd, 'What magnanimity!'

XXX.

No doubt, this patience, when the world is damning us,
    Is philosophic in our former friends;
'Tis also pleasant to be deem'd magnanimous,
    The more so in obtaining our own ends; 235
And what the lawyers call a '*malus animus*,'
    Conduct like this by no means comprehends:
Revenge in person's certainly no virtue,
But then 'tis not *my* fault, if *others* hurt you. 240

XXXI.

And if our quarrels should rip up old stories,
    And help them with a lie or two additional,
I'm not to blame, as you well know, no more is
    Any one else—they were become traditional;
Besides, their resurrection aids our glories 245
    By contrast, which is what we just were wishing all:
And science profits by this resurrection—
Dead scandals form good subjects for dissection.

---

218 *trunks of books and letters,* See Byron's letter to Augusta of 14 September 1816, 'You know I supposed that Lady B[yro]n *secretly opened my letter trunks before she left Town* . . .' (*BLJ*, vol. 5, p. 93).
220 *abettors* An abettor is 'One who encourages, countenances, or supports another in any proceeding'.
230 *calumny* 'False and malicious misrepresentation of the words and actions of others, calculated to injure their reputation'.
237 '*malus animus*' Evil heart.

XXXII.

Their friends had tried at reconciliation,
    Then their relations, who made matters worse;
('Twere hard to tell upon a like occasion
    To whom it may be best to have recourse—
I can't say much for friend or yet relation):
    The lawyers did their utmost for divorce,
But scarce a fee was paid on either side
Before, unluckily, Don Jóse died.

XXXIII.

He died: and most unluckily, because,
    According to all hints I could collect
From counsel learned in those kinds of laws,
    (Although their talk's obscure and circumspect)
His death contrived to spoil a charming cause;
    A thousand pities also with respect
To public feeling, which on this occasion
Was manifested in a great sensation.

XXXIV.

But ah! he died; and buried with him lay
    The public feeling and the lawyers' fees:
His house was sold, his servants sent away,
    A Jew took one of his two mistresses,
A priest the other—at least so they say:
    I ask'd the doctors after his disease,
He died of the slow fever call'd the tertian,
And left his widow to her own aversion.

XXXV.

Yet Jóse was an honourable man,
    That I must say, who knew him very well;
Therefore his frailties I'll no further scan,
    Indeed there were not many more to tell;
And if his passions now and then outran
    Discretion, and were not so peaceable
As Numa's (who was also named Pompilius),
He had been ill brought up, and was born bilious.

XXXVI.

Whate'er might be his worthlessness or worth,
    Poor fellow! he had many things to wound him,

249–50 *Their friends ... Then their relations* Byron's friends John Cam Hobhouse, Thomas Moore and (in Switzerland) Madame de Staël, and his sister Augusta and his cousin George Anson Byron (who eventually went over to Lady Byron's side).

271 *the tertian* 'An intermittent fever which returns every other day'.

273 *Jóse was an honourable man* Compare Shakespeare, *Julius Caesar*, in which Antony repeatedly denounces Brutus via the phrase 'And Brutus is an honourable man' (III. ii. 84, 88, 96).

279 *Numa's* Numa, second king of Rome, remembered for the peacefulness of his reign; see *Childe Harold*, IV. 1026.

Let's own, since it can do no good on earth;
   It was a trying moment that which found him
Standing alone beside his desolate hearth,   285
   Where all his household gods lay shiver'd round him;
No choice was left his feelings or his pride
Save death or Doctors' Commons—so he died.

XXXVII.

Dying intestate, Juan was sole heir
   To a chancery suit, and messuages, and lands,   290
Which, with a long minority and care,
   Promised to turn out well in proper hands:
Inez became sole guardian, which was fair,
   And answer'd but to nature's just demands;
An only son left with an only mother   295
Is brought up much more wisely than another.

XXXVIII.

Sagest of women, even of widows, she
   Resolved that Juan should be quite a paragon,
And worthy of the noblest pedigree:
   (His sire was of Castile, his dam from Arragon).   300
Then for accomplishments of chivalry,
   In case out lord the king should go to war again,
He learn'd the arts of riding, fencing, gunnery,
And how to scale a fortress—or a nunnery.

XXXIX.

But that which Donna Inez most desired,   305
   And saw into herself each day before all
The learned tutors whom for him she hired,
   Was, that his breeding should be strictly moral;
Much into all his studies she inquired,
   And so they were submitted first to her, all,   310
Arts, sciences, no branch was made a mystery
To Juan's eyes, excepting natural history.

XL.

The languages, especially the dead,
   The sciences, and most of all the abstruse,
The arts, at least all such as could be said   315
   To be the most remote from common use,

---

286 *lay shiver'd round him* Broken or split into small fragments, shattered; compare 'Stanzas to [Augusta]', 'Though the rock of my last hope is shiver'd' (l. 17). See also Byron's resentment (in a letter to Thomas Moore, 19 September 1818) over the way in which he was treated by Lady Byron during their separation: 'I could have forgiven the dagger or the bowl, any thing, but the deliberate desolation piled upon me, when I stood alone upon my hearth, with my household gods shivered around me' (*BLJ*, vol. 6, p. 69).

288 *Doctors' Commons* A London society of civil lawyers, which administered several courts, including a divorce court.

290 *and messuages* Messuage, 'a dwelling-house with its outbuildings and curtilage and the adjacent land assigned to its use'.

303–4 *gunnery . . . nunnery* Another exemplary triple rhyme, in which the seemingly laudable progression from 'pedigree' to 'chivalry' is bathetically undone by linking 'gunnery' with 'nunnery'.

> In all these he was much and deeply read;
>> But not a page of any thing that's loose,
> Or hints continuation of the species,
>> Was ever suffer'd, lest he should grow vicious.

XLI.

> His classic studies made a little puzzle,
>> Because of filthy loves of gods and goddesses,
> Who in the earlier ages raised a bustle,
>> But never put on pantaloons or boddices;
> His reverend tutors had at times a tussle,
>> And for their Æneids, Iliads, and Odysseys,
> Were forced to make an odd sort of apology,
> For Donna Inez dreaded the mythology.

XLII.

> Ovid's a rake, as half his verses show him,
>> Anacreon's morals are a still worse sample,
> Catullus scarcely has a decent poem,
>> I don't think Sappho's Ode a good example,
> Although Longinus tells us there is no hymn
>> Where the sublime soars forth on wings more ample;
> But Virgil's songs are pure, except that horrid one
> Beginning with '*Formosum Pastor Corydon.*'

XLIII.

> Lucretius' irreligion is too strong
>> For early stomachs, to prove wholesome food;
> I can't help thinking Juvenal was wrong,
>> Although no doubt his real intent was good,
> For speaking out so plainly in his song,
>> So much indeed as to be downright rude;
> And then what proper person can be partial
> To all those nauseous epigrams of Martial?

XLIV.

> Juan was taught from out the best edition,
>> Expurgated by learned men, who place,
> Judiciously, from out the schoolboy's vision,
>> The grosser parts; but fearful to deface

---

320 *vicious* 'Addicted to vice or immorality; of depraved habits'. Positioned as the second rhyme of the couplet, 'vicious' retrospectively makes 'species' appear to rhyme with 'specious'.

329–44 *Ovid's a rake . . . Martial?* As McGann notes, 'The stanzas amount to an ironic defence of *Don Juan*, which was attacked for its supposed indecency and coarseness, as well as its candid social and political satire. The passage is deeply autobiographical, since these authors are all among Byron's favourites' (*CPW*, vol. 5, p. 676). For Ovid, see the *Amores* and the *Ars Amatoria*; Anacreon and Catullus wrote passionate love lyrics; Sappho's *Ode to Aphrodite* is celebrated by Longinus in *On the Sublime* (section 10); for Virgil, see *Eclogues* 2, which tells of the homoerotic love of Corydon for Alexis; Lucretius' *De rerum natura* attempts to explain the history of the world without divine intervention playing any role; Juvenal's satires expose the depravities of Roman society; and Martial was the author of over 1,000 witty, often obscene epigrams (see note to l. 351).

346 *Expurgated* 'Purified by the removal of anything objectionable'.

Too much their modest bard by this omission,
  And pitying sore his mutilated case,
They only add them all in an appendix,
Which saves, in fact, the trouble of an index;

XLV.

For there we have them all at one fell swoop,
  Instead of being scatter'd through the pages;
They stand forth marshall'd in a handsome troop,
  To meet the ingenuous youth of future ages,
Till some less rigid editor shall stoop
  To call them back into their separate cages,
Instead of standing staring altogether,
Like garden gods—and not so decent either.

XLVI.

The Missal too (it was the family Missal)
  Was ornamented in a sort of way
Which ancient mass-books often are, and this all
  Kinds of grotesques illumined; and how they,
Who saw those figures on the margin kiss all,
  Could turn their optics to the text and pray
Is more than I know—but Don Juan's mother
Kept this herself, and gave her son another.

XLVII.

Sermons he read, and lectures he endured,
  And homilies, and lives of all the saints;
To Jerome and to Chrysostom inured,
  He did not take such studies for restraints;
But how faith is acquired, and then insured,
  So well not one of the aforesaid paints
As Saint Augustine in his fine Confessions,
Which make the reader envy his transgressions.

XLVIII.

This, too, was a seal'd book to little Juan—
  I can't but say that his mamma was right,
If such an education was the true one.
  She scarcely trusted him from out her sight;
Her maids were old, and if she took a new one
  You might be sure she was a perfect fright,
She did this during even her husband's life—
I recommend as much to every wife.

---

352 *trouble of an index* 'Fact. There is, or was, such an edition, with all the obnoxious epigrams of Martial placed by themselves at the end' (Byron's note).
361 *Missal* Roman Catholic book containing both prayers and masses for the liturgical year; often illuminated (i.e. illustrated).
364 *grotesques* 'A kind of decorative painting or sculpture, consisting of representations of portions of human and animal forms, fantastically combined and interwoven with foliage and flowers'.
371 *To Jerome and to Chrysostom* Late fourth-century ascetic Christian theologians.
375–6 *As Saint Augustine . . . his transgressions* The *Confessions* of Saint Augustine, which underscore the sensuousness of his life before his conversion to Catholicism.

XLIX.

Young Juan wax'd in goodliness and grace;
    At six a charming child, and at eleven
With all the promise of as fine a face
    As e'er to man's maturer growth was given:
He studied steadily, and grew apace,
    And seem'd, at least, in the right road to heaven,
For half his days were pass'd at church, the other
Between his tutors, confessor, and mother.

L.

At six, I said, he was a charming child,
    At twelve he was a fine, but quiet boy;
Although in infancy a little wild,
    They tamed him down amongst them; to destroy
His natural spirit not in vain they toil'd,
    At least it seem'd so; and his mother's joy
Was to declare how sage, and still, and steady,
Her young philosopher was grown already.

LI.

I had my doubts, perhaps I have them still,
    But what I say is neither here nor there:
I knew his father well, and have some skill
    In character—but it would not be fair
From sire to son to augur good or ill:
    He and his wife were an ill-sorted pair—
But scandal's my aversion—I protest
Against all evil speaking, even in jest.

LII.

For my part I say nothing—nothing—but
    This I will say—my reasons are my own—
That if I had an only son to put
    To school (as God be praised that I have none)
'Tis not with Donna Inez I would shut
    Him up to learn his catechism alone,
No—no—I'd send him out betimes to college,
For there it was I pick'd up my own knowledge.

LIII.

For there one learns—'tis not for me to boast,
    Though I acquired—but I pass over *that*,
As well as all the Greek I since have lost:
    I say that there's the place—but '*Verbum sat*,'
I think, I pick'd up too, as well as most,
    Knowledge of matters—but no matter *what*—
I never married—but, I think, I know
That sons should not be educated so.

---

405 *augur* 'To divine, forbode, anticipate'.
414 *catechism* Elementary instruction in the principles of Christian religion.
420 'Verbum sat' 'A word [to the wise] will suffice'.

LIV.

Young Juan now was sixteen years of age,
    Tall, handsome, slender, but well knit; he seem'd
Active, though not so sprightly, as a page;
    And every body but his mother deem'd
Him almost man; but she flew in a rage,
    And bit her lips (for else she might have scream'd),
If any said so, for to be precocious
Was in her eyes a thing the most atrocious.

LV.

Amongst her numerous acquaintance, all
    Selected for discretion and devotion,
There was the Donna Julia, whom to call
    Pretty were but to give a feeble notion
Of many charms in her as natural
    As sweetness to the flower, or salt to ocean,
Her zone to Venus, or his bow to Cupid,
(But this last simile is trite and stupid.)

LVI.

The darkness of her oriental eye
    Accorded with her Moorish origin;
(Her blood was not all Spanish, by the by;
    In Spain, you know, this is a sort of sin.)
When proud Grenada fell, and, forced to fly,
    Boabdil wept, of Donna Julia's kin
Some went to Africa, some staid in Spain,
Her great great grandmamma chose to remain.

LVII.

She married (I forget the pedigree)
    With an Hidalgo, who transmitted down
His blood less noble than such blood should be;
    At such alliances his sires would frown,
In that point so precise in each degree
    That they bred *in and in*, as might be shown,
Marrying their cousins—nay, their aunts and nieces,
Which always spoils the breed, if it increases.

LVIII.

This heathenish cross restored the breed again,
    Ruin'd its blood, but much improved its flesh;
For, from a root the ugliest in Old Spain
    Sprung up a branch as beautiful as fresh;

---

439 *zone to Venus* The magical girdle of Venus (Aphrodite), which would make its wearer irresistible to others.
446 *Boabdil* Boabdil (Mohammed XI), the last Moorish king of Granada, allegedly wept when the city was besieged and surrendered in 1492 (hence the phrase 'the last sigh of the Moor').
450 *Hidalgo* See note to line 66.

The sons no more were short, the daughters plain:
   But there's a rumour which I fain would hush,
'Tis said that Donna Julia's grandmamma
Produced her Don more heirs at love than law.

LIX.

However this might be, the race went on
   Improving still through every generation,
Until it center'd in an only son,
   Who left an only daughter; my narration
May have suggested that this single one
   Could be but Julia (whom on this occasion
I shall have much to speak about), and she
Was married, charming, chaste, and twenty-three.

LX.

Her eye (I'm very fond of handsome eyes)
   Was large and dark, suppressing half its fire
Until she spoke, then through its soft disguise
   Flash'd an expression more of pride than ire,
And love than either; and there would arise
   A something in them which was not desire,
But would have been, perhaps, but for the soul
Which struggled through and chasten'd down the whole.

LXI.

Her glossy hair was cluster'd o'er a brow
   Bright with intelligence, and fair and smooth;
Her eyebrow's shape was like the aerial bow,
   Her cheek all purple with the beam of youth,
Mounting, at times, to a transparent glow,
   As if her veins ran lightning; she, in sooth,
Possess'd an air and grace by no means common:
Her stature tall—I hate a dumpy woman.

LXII.

Wedded she was some years, and to a man
   Of fifty, and such husbands are in plenty;
And yet, I think, instead of such a ONE
   'Twere better to have TWO of five and twenty,
Especially in countries near the sun;
   And now I think on't, 'mi vien in mente,'
Ladies even of the most uneasy virtue
Prefer a spouse whose age is short of thirty.

LXIII.

'Tis a sad thing, I cannot choose but say,
   And all the fault of that indecent sun,

---

464 *more heirs at love than law.* She bore her husband more children when they were unmarried than when they were married.

486 *in sooth* 'in truth, truly'.

494 *'mi vien in mente'* 'it occurs to me' (here nearly tautological, in relation to the first half of the line).

    Who cannot leave alone our helpless clay,
        But will keep baking, broiling, burning on,
    That howsoever people fast and pray
        The flesh is frail, and so the soul undone:
    What men call gallantry, and gods adultery,
    Is much more common where the climate's sultry.

LXIV.

    Happy the nations of the moral north!
        Where all is virtue, and the winter season
    Sends sin, without a rag on, shivering forth;
        ('Twas snow that brought St. Anthony to reason);
    Where juries cast up what a wife is worth
        By laying whate'er sum, in mulct, they please on
    The lover, who must pay a handsome price,
    Because it is a marketable vice.

LXV.

    Alfonso was the name of Julia's lord,
        A man well looking for his years, and who
    Was neither much beloved, nor yet abhorr'd;
        They lived together as most people do,
    Suffering each other's foibles by accord,
        And not exactly either *one* or *two*;
    Yet he was jealous, though he did not show it,
    For jealousy dislikes the world to know it.

LXVI.

    Julia was—yet I never could see why—
        With Donna Inez quite a favourite friend;
    Between their tastes there was small sympathy,
        For not a line had Julia ever penn'd:
    Some people whisper (but, no doubt, they lie,
        For malice still imputes some private end)
    That Inez had, ere Don Alfonso's marriage,
    Forgot with him her very prudent carriage;

LXVII.

    And that still keeping up the old connexion,
        Which time had lately render'd much more chaste,
    She took his lady also in affection,
        And certainly this course was much the best:

---

499 *clay* Common Byronic usage for 'flesh'; compare, for example, 'His slender frame and pallid aspect lay, / As fair a thing as e'er was form'd of clay' (*Don Juan*, II. 879–80).
502 *The flesh is frail* See Matthew 26: 41: '. . . the spirit indeed *is* willing, but the flesh *is* weak'.
508 *'Twas snow . . . Anthony to reason* It was not St Anthony but St Francis who, when he felt besieged by temptations, hurled himself naked into ditches full of snow; see the *Life of St Francis* in Jacobus de Voragine's *Golden Legend*.
510 *mulct* 'A fine . . . a compulsory payment (usually implying unfair or arbitrary exaction)'.
517 *foibles* Failings or weaknesses of character (Fr. *faiblesse*).
528 *carriage* 'Habitual conduct or behaviour' (here suggesting also that Donna Inez may have been 'carried' out of herself in so 'carrying on' with Don Alfonso).

She flatter'd Julia with her sage protection,
　　And complimented Don Alfonso's taste;
And if she could not (who can?) silence scandal, 535
At least she left it a more slender handle.

LXVIII.

I can't tell whether Julia saw the affair
　　With other people's eyes, or if her own
Discoveries made, but none could be aware
　　Of this, at least no symptom e'er was shown; 540
Perhaps she did not know, or did not care,
　　Indifferent from the first, or callous grown:
I'm really puzzled what to think or say,
She kept her counsel in so close a way.

LXIX.

Juan she saw, and, as a pretty child, 545
　　Caress'd him often, such a thing might be
Quite innocently done, and harmless styled,
　　When she had twenty years, and thirteen he;
But I am not so sure I should have smiled
　　When he was sixteen, Julia twenty-three, 550
These few short years make wondrous alterations,
Particularly amongst sun-burnt nations.

LXX.

Whate'er the cause might be, they had become
　　Changed; for the dame grew distant, the youth shy,
Their looks cast down, their greetings almost dumb, 555
　　And much embarrassment in either eye;
There surely will be little doubt with some
　　That Donna Julia knew the reason why,
But as for Juan, he had no more notion
Than he who never saw the sea of ocean. 560

LXXI.

Yet Julia's very coldness still was kind,
　　And tremulously gentle her small hand
Withdrew itself from his, but left behind
　　A little pressure, thrilling, and so bland
And slight, so very slight, that to the mind 565
　　'Twas but a doubt; but ne'er magician's wand
Wrought change with all Armida's fairy art
Like what this light touch left on Juan's heart.

---

555 *dumb* Silent; a sly reminder that Byron's Juan is, after all, a figure from the pantomime.
567 *Armida's fairy art* Armida is the sorceress in Torquato Tasso's epic, *Jerusalem Delivered*, who is responsible for Rinaldo forgetting his vows as a crusader.

LXXII.

And if she met him, thought she smiled no more,
    She look'd a sadness sweeter than her smile,
As if her heart had deeper thoughts in store
    She must not own, but cherish'd more the while,
For that compression in its burning core;
    Even innocence itself has many a wile,
And will not dare to trust itself with truth,
And love is taught hypocrisy from youth.

LXXIII.

But passion most dissembles yet betrays
    Even by its darkness; as the blackest sky
Foretells the heaviest tempest, it displays
    Its workings through the vainly guarded eye,
And in whatever aspect it arrays
    Itself, 'tis still the same hypocrisy;
Coldness or anger, even disdain or hate,
Are masks it often wears, and still too late.

LXXIV.

Then there were sighs, the deeper for suppression,
    And stolen glances, sweeter for the theft,
And burning blushes, though for no transgression,
    Tremblings when met, and restlessness when left;
All these are little preludes to possession,
    Of which young Passion cannot be bereft,
And merely tend to show how greatly Love is
Embarrass'd at first starting with a novice.

LXXV.

Poor Julia's heart was in an awkward state;
    She felt it going, and resolved to make
The noblest efforts for herself and mate,
    For honour's, pride's, religion's, virtue's sake;
Her resolutions were most truly great,
    And almost might have made a Tarquin quake;
She pray'd the Virgin Mary for her grace,
As being the best judge of a lady's case.

LXXVI.

She vow'd she never would see Juan more,
    And next day paid a visit to his mother,
And look'd extremely at the opening door,
    Which, by the Virgin's grace, let in another;
Grateful she was, and yet a little sore—

---

598 *a Tarquin quake* The Tarquins were a Roman family legendary for their arrogance and cruelty.

Again it opens, it can be no other,
  'Tis surely Juan now—No! I'm afraid
That night the Virgin was no further pray'd.

LXXVII.

She now determined that a virtuous woman
  Should rather face and overcome temptation,
That flight was base and dastardly, and no man
  Should ever give her heart the least sensation;
That is to say, a thought beyond the common
  Preference, that we must feel upon occasion,
For people who are pleasanter than others,
But then they only seem so many brothers.

LXXVIII.

And even if by chance—and who can tell?
  The devil's so very sly—she should discover
That all within was not so very well,
  And, if still free, that such or such a lover
Might please perhaps, a virtuous wife can quell
  Such thoughts, and be the better when they're over;
And if the man should ask, 'tis but denial:
I recommend young ladies to make trial.

LXXIX.

And then there are such things as love divine,
  Bright and immaculate, unmix'd and pure,
Such as the angels think so very fine,
  And matrons, who would be no less secure,
Platonic, perfect, 'just such love as mine':
  Thus Julia said—and thought so, to be sure,
And so I'd have her think, were I the man
On whom her reveries celestial ran.

LXXX.

Such love is innocent, and may exist
  Between young persons without any danger,
A hand may first, and then a lip be kist;
  For my part, to such doings I'm a stranger,
But *hear* these freedoms form the utmost list
  Of all o'er which such love may be a ranger:
If people go beyond, 'tis quite a crime,
But not my fault—I tell them all in time.

---

608 *That night . . . no further pray'd* An allusion to the story of Dante's doomed lovers, Paolo and Francesca, who 'no further read' after finally acknowledging their passion for one another; see Dante, *Inferno*, V. 133–8. See also Byron's own translation, 'Francesca of Rimini', 'Accursed was the book and he who wrote! / That day no further leaf did we uncover' (ll. 41–2).

629 *'just such love as mine'* Julia continues here to rationalize her love for Juan as not passionate (characterized by dissembling and hypocrisy; see ll. 576–82) but Platonic – 'divine, / Bright and immaculate, unmix'd and pure' (ll. 625–6).

637 *list* Here, both catalogue and boundary.

LXXXI.

Love, then, but love within its proper limits,
    Was Julia's innocent determination
In young Don Juan's favour, and to him its
    Exertion might be useful on occasion;
And, lighted at too pure a shrine to dim its
    Etherial lustre, with what sweet persuasion
He might be taught, by love and her together—
I really don't know what, nor Julia either.

LXXXII.

Fraught with this fine intention, and well fenced
    In mail of proof—her purity of soul,
She, for the future of her strength convinced,
    And that her honour was a rock, or mole,
Exceeding sagely from that hour dispensed
    With any kind of troublesome control;
But whether Julia to the task was equal
Is that which must be mention'd in the sequel.

LXXXIII.

Her plan she deem'd both innocent and feasible,
    And, surely, with a stripling of sixteen
Not scandal's fangs could fix on much that's seizable,
    Or if they did so, satisfied to mean
Nothing but what was good, her breast was peaceable—
    A quiet conscience makes one so serene!
Christians have burnt each other, quite persuaded
That all the Apostles would have done as they did.

LXXXIV.

And if in the mean time her husband died,
    But heaven forbid that such a thought should cross
Her brain, though in a dream! (and then she sigh'd)
    Never could she survive that common loss;
But just suppose that moment should betide,
    I only say suppose it—*inter nos*,
(This should be *entre nous*, for Julia thought
In French, but then the rhyme would go for nought.)

LXXXV.

I only say suppose this supposition:
    Juan being then grown up to man's estate
Would fully suit a widow of condition,
    Even seven years hence it would not be too late;
And in the interim (to pursue this vision)

---

650 *mail of proof* Finely wrought chain-mail, here to be understood metaphorically as the 'strength' of Julia's 'purity of soul'.
652 *mole* 'The collective mass of any object'; alternatively, a massive structure made from stone (here, in both instances, the 'rock' of Julia's honour).
670 inter nos between us.
671–2 *This should be . . . go for nought* Another bathetic couplet in which the narrator reminds the reader that his first responsibility is not to the poem's characters or narrative but to the 'fitness' of the rhymes.

  The mischief, after all, could not be great,
  For he would learn the rudiments of love,
  I mean the seraph way of those above.   680

LXXXVI.

So much for Julia. Now we'll turn to Juan,
 Poor little fellow! he had no idea
Of his own case, and never hit the true one;
 In feelings quick as Ovid's Miss Medea,
He puzzled over what he found a new one,   685
 But not as yet imagined it could be a
Thing quite in course, and not at all alarming,
Which, with a little patience, might grow charming.

LXXXVII.

Silent and pensive, idle, restless, slow,
 His home deserted for the lonely wood,   690
Tormented with a wound he could not know,
 His, like all deep grief, plunged in solitude:
I'm fond myself of solitude or so,
 But then, I beg it may be understood,
By solitude I mean a sultan's, not   695
A hermit's, with a haram for a grot.

LXXXVIII.

'Oh Love! in such a wilderness as this,
 'Where transport and security entwine,
'Here is the empire of thy perfect bliss,
 'And here thou art a god indeed divine.'   700
The bard I quote from does not sing amiss,
 With the exception of the second line,
For that same twining 'transport and security'
Are twisted to a phrase of some obscurity.

LXXXIX.

The poet meant, no doubt, and thus appeals   705
 To the good sense and senses of mankind,
The very thing which every body feels,
 As all have found on trial, or may find,
That no one likes to be disturb'd at meals
 Or love.—I won't say more about 'entwined'   710
Or 'transport,' as we knew all that before,
But beg 'Security' will bolt the door.

---

680 *the seraph way* The seraphim are the highest class of angels, distinguished by the fervour of their love (as opposed to the cherubim, distinguished by their knowledge).

681–5 *Juan ... new one* Compare the opening stanza of Canto I, where Byron uses the same set of rhymes to distinguish Juan as a new and true 'hero'.

684 *Ovid's Miss Medea* See Ovid, *Metamorphoses*, VII. 9–12, where Medea is suddenly overwhelmed by her love for Jason.

693–96 *I'm fond myself ... a haram for a grot* In substituting his own predilections for those of Juan's, the narrator again suspends the narrative of Juan and Julia's love (which he has been doing on a regular basis, usually in the couplet, since at least stanza 80) in favour of his own conversational asides.

697–700 *'Oh Love! ... indeed divine.'* 'Campbell's *Gertrude of Wyoming* (I think) the opening of Canto II; but quote from memory' (Byron's note). In fact, Canto III, 1–4. See also 'Dedication', line 55 and note.

XC.

Young Juan wander'd by the glassy brooks
    Thinking unutterable things; he threw
Himself at length within the leafy nooks
    Where the wild branch of the cork forest grew;
There poets find materials for their books,
    And every now and then we read them through,
So that their plan and prosody are eligible,
Unless, like Wordsworth, they prove unintelligible.

XCI.

He, Juan (and not Wordsworth) so pursued
    His self-communion with his own high soul,
Until his mighty heart, in its great mood,
    Had mitigated part, though not the whole
Of its disease; he did the best he could
    With things not very subject to control,
And turn'd, without perceiving his condition,
Like Coleridge, into a metaphysician.

XCII.

He thought about himself, and the whole earth,
    Of man the wonderful, and of the stars,
And how the deuce they ever could have birth;
    And then he thought of earthquakes, and of wars,
How many miles the moon might have in girth,
    Of air-balloons, and of the many bars
To perfect knowledge of the boundless skies;
And then he thought of Donna Julia's eyes.

XCIII.

In thoughts like these true wisdom may discern
    Longings sublime, and aspirations high,
Which some are born with, but the most part learn
    To plague themselves withal, they know not why:
'Twas strange that one so young should thus concern
    His brain about the action of the sky;
If *you* think 'twas philosophy that this did,
I can't help thinking puberty assisted.

XCIV.

He pored upon the leaves, and on the flowers,
    And heard a voice in all the winds; and then
He thought of wood nymphs and immortal bowers,
    And how the goddesses came down to men:

---

720 *like Wordsworth* See 'Dedication', lines 25–32 and notes, where Byron castigates *The Excursion* for being 'unintelligible'.
721 *(and not Wordsworth)* In fact, both Juan and Wordsworth are on display here for their (Wordsworthian) 'self-communion'.
723 *his mighty heart* Compare Wordsworth, 'Composed Upon Westminster Bridge', 'And all that mighty heart is lying still' (l. 14).
728 *Like Coleridge* See 'Dedication', lines 13–16 and notes, where Byron satirizes Coleridgean metaphysical obscurity.
734 *Of air-balloons* The first air-balloon was invented and launched by Joseph Michel Montgolfier in 1783.

He miss'd the pathway, he forgot the hours,
    And when he look'd upon his watch again,
He found how much old Time had been a winner—
He also found that he had lost his dinner.

XCV.

Sometimes he turn'd to gaze upon his book,
    Boscan, or Garcilasso;—by the wind
Even as the page is rustled while we look,
    So by the poesy of his own mind
Over the mystic leaf his soul was shook,
    As if 'twere one whereon magicians bind
Their spells, and give them to the passing gale,
According to some good old woman's tale.

XCVI.

Thus would he while his lonely hours away
    Dissatisfied, nor knowing what he wanted;
Nor glowing reverie, nor poet's lay,
    Could yield his spirit that for which it panted,
A bosom whereon he his head might lay,
    And hear the heart beat with the love it granted,
With—several other things, which I forget,
Or which, at least, I need not mention yet.

XCVII.

Those lonely walks, and lengthening reveries,
    Could not escape the gentle Julia's eyes;
She saw that Juan was not at his ease;
    But that which chiefly may, and must surprise,
Is, that the Donna Inez did not tease
    Her only son with question or surmise;
Whether it was she did not see, or would not,
Or, like all very clever people, could not.

XCVIII.

This may seem strange, but yet 'tis very common;
    For instance—gentlemen, whose ladies take
Leave to o'erstep the written rights of woman,
    And break the—Which commandment is't they break?
(I have forgot the number, and think no man
    Should rashly quote, for fear of a mistake.)
I say, when these same gentlemen are jealous,
They make some blunder, which their ladies tell us,

---

754 *Boscan, or Garcilasso* Juan Boscán Almogáver and Garcilaso de la Vega, two sixteenth-century Spanish poets who, through their imitations of Petrarch, were responsible for introducing Italian styles into Castilian poetry.

763 *poet's lay* A short lyric poem intended to be sung.

774 *surmise* Conjecture; an idea that something may be true, but without certainty and on very slight evidence.

780 *Which commandment is't they break?* The seventh commandment, 'Thou shalt not commit adultery'; Exodus 20: 14.

XCIX.

A real husband always is suspicious,   785
    But still no less suspects in the wrong place,
Jealous of some one who had no such wishes,
    Or pandering blindly to his own disgrace
By harbouring some dear friend extremely vicious;
    The last indeed's infallibly the case: 790
And when the spouse and friend are gone off wholly,
He wonders at their vice, and not his folly.

C.

Thus parents also are at times short-sighted;
    Though watchful as the lynx, they ne'er discover,
The while the wicked world beholds delighted,   795
    Young Hopeful's mistress, or Miss Fanny's lover,
Till some confounded escapade has blighted
    The plan of twenty years, and all is over;
And then the mother cries, the father swears,
And wonders why the devil he got heirs.   800

CI.

But Inez was so anxious, and so clear
    Of sight, that I must think, on this occasion,
She had some other motive much more near
    For leaving Juan to this new temptation;
But what that motive was, I sha'n't say here;   805
    Perhaps to finish Juan's education,
Perhaps to open Don Alfonso's eyes,
In case he thought his wife too great a prize.

CII.

It was upon a day, a summer's day;—
    Summer's indeed a very dangerous season,   810
And so is spring about the end of May;
    The sun, no doubt, is the prevailing reason;
But whatsoe'er the cause is, one may say,
    And stand convicted of more truth than treason,
That there are months which nature grows more merry in,   815
March has its hares, and May must have its heroine.

CIII.

'Twas on a summer's day—the sixth of June:—
    I like to be particular in dates,
Not only of the age, and year, but moon;
    They are a sort of post-house, where the Fates   820

---

788 *pandering* A 'pander' is a go-between in a clandestine affair; hence to pander, 'to subserve or minister to base passions, tendencies, or designs'.
789 *vicious* see note to line 320.
791 *gone off wholly* When his wife has deserted him in favour of his 'vicious' friend.

796 *Young Hopeful's . . . Miss Fanny's* Stock characters from eighteenth-century novels and comedies.
812 *The sun* See lines 498–504, regarding the deleterious effects of 'that indecent sun'.
820 *post-house* An inn where horses are kept for the use of travellers.

Change horses, making history change its tune,
    Then spur away o'er empires and o'er states,
Leaving at last not much besides chronology,
Excepting the post-obits of theology.

CIV.

'Twas on the sixth of June, about the hour
    Of half-past six—perhaps still nearer seven,
When Julia sate within as pretty a bower
    As e'er held houri in that heathenish heaven
Described by Mahomet, and Anacreon Moore,
    To whom the lyre and laurels have been given,
With all the trophies of triumphant song—
He won them well, and may he wear them long!

CV.

She sate, but not alone; I know not well
    How this same interview had taken place,
And even if I knew, I should not tell—
    People should hold their tongues in any case;
No matter how or why the thing befel,
    But there were she and Juan, face to face—
When two such faces are so, 'twould be wise,
But very difficult, to shut their eyes.

CVI.

How beautiful she look'd! her conscious heart
    Glow'd in her cheek, and yet she felt no wrong.
Oh Love! how perfect is thy mystic art,
    Strengthening the weak, and trampling on the strong,
How self-deceitful is the sagest part
    Of mortals whom thy lure hath led along—
The precipice she stood on was immense,
So was her creed in her own innocence.

CVII.

She thought of her own strength, and Juan's youth,
    And of the folly of all prudish fears,
Victorious virtue, and domestic truth,
    And then of Don Alfonso's fifty years:
I wish these last had not occurr'd, in sooth,

---

824 *post-obits* A bond which secures a loan with a promise to pay after death; here, the 'debt' a Christian owes God for the life granted to him. In the Preface to *Don Juan*, Byron ridicules Southey for 'the Postobits he has granted upon Posterity & usurious self-applause in which he has anticipated with some profusion perhaps the opinion of future ages' (*DJV*, vol. 2, p. 6). See also below, line 1000 and note.
829 *houri* Nymph of the Muslim Paradise; figuratively applied to any voluptuously beautiful woman.
829–30 *heathenish heaven ... Anacreon Moore* Byron's friend Thomas Moore (see 'Dedication', l. 54 and note) was popularly known as 'Anacreon Moore' in light of his translations of Anacreon (pub. 1800); 'heathenish heaven' derives from Moore's *Lalla Rookh* (1817).
848 *creed* belief in, conviction of.
852 *Don Alfonso's fifty years* Soon after he began his liaison with Teresa Guiccioli (see headnote to 'Stanzas to the Po') Byron repeatedly made a similar point about the age of her husband, Count Guiccioli, '... but he is sixty ... but he is sixty' (*BLJ*, vol. 6, p. 114).

    Because that number rarely much endears,
    And through all climes, the snowy and the sunny,   855
    Sounds ill in love, whate'er it may in money.

CVIII.

    When people say, 'I've told you *fifty* times,'
        They mean to scold, and very often do;
    When poets say, 'I've written *fifty* rhymes,'
        They make you dread that they'll recite them too;   860
    In gangs of *fifty* thieves commit their crimes;
        At *fifty* love for love is rare, 'tis true,
    But then, no doubt, it equally as true is,
    A good deal may he bought for fifty Louis.

CIX.

    Julia had honour, virtue, truth, and love,   865
        For Don Alfonso; and she inly swore,
    By all the vows below to powers above,
        She never would disgrace the ring she wore,
    Nor leave a wish which wisdom might reprove;
        And while she ponder'd this, besides much more,   870
    One hand on Juan's carelessly was thrown,
    Quite by mistake—she thought it was her own;

CX.

    Unconsciously she lean'd upon the other,
        Which play'd within the tangles of her hair;
    And to contend with thoughts she could not smother,   875
        She seem'd by the distraction of her air.
    'Twas surely very wrong in Juan's mother
        To leave together this imprudent pair,
    She who for many years had watch'd her son so—
    I'm very certain *mine* would not have done so.   880

CXI.

    The hand which still held Juan's, by degrees
        Gently, but palpably confirm'd its grasp,
    As if it said 'detain me, if you please;'
        Yet there's no doubt she only meant to clasp
    His fingers with a pure Platonic squeeze;   885
        She would have shrunk as from a toad, or asp,
    Had she imagined such a thing could rouse
    A feeling dangerous to a prudent spouse.

---

864   *Louis* Gold coin.

874   *tangles of her hair* Compare Milton, 'Lycidas', 'Were it not better done as others use, / To sport with Amaryllis in the shade, / Or with the tangles of Naera's hair?' (ll. 67–9). See also line 1354 below.

885   *a pure Platonic squeeze* See above, line 629, when Julia muses on her love for Juan as 'Platonic, perfect'; see also lines 921–8.

886   *asp* Small, venomous, hooded serpent; poetically, any venomous serpent. Cleopatra applied an asp to her breast in order to take her own life. See Byron, *Childe Harold's Pilgrimage*, '. . . the enormous asp / Enforces pang on pang, and stifles gasp on gasp' (IV. 1440).

CXII.

I cannot know what Juan thought of this,
   But what he did, is much what you would do;
His young lip thank'd it with a grateful kiss,
   And then, abash'd at its own joy, withdrew
In deep despair, lest he had done amiss,
   Love is so very timid when 'tis new:
She blush'd, and frown'd not, but she strove to speak,
And held her tongue, her voice was grown so weak.

CXIII.

The sun set, and up rose the yellow moon:
   The devil's in the moon for mischief; they
Who call'd her CHASTE, methinks, began too soon
   Their nomenclature; there is not a day,
The longest, not the twenty-first of June,
   Sees half the business in a wicked way
On which three single hours of moonshine smile—
And then she looks so modest all the while.

CXIV.

There is a dangerous silence in that hour,
   A stillness, which leaves room for the full soul
To open all itself, without the power
   Of calling wholly back its self-control;
The silver light which, hallowing tree and tower,
   Sheds beauty and deep softness o'er the whole,
Breathes also to the heart, and o'er it throws
A loving languor, which is not repose.

CXV.

And Julia sate with Juan, half embraced
   And half retiring from the glowing arm.
Which trembled like the bosom where 'twas placed;
   Yet still she must have thought there was no harm,
Or else 'twere easy to withdraw her waist;
   But then the situation had its charm,
And then—God knows what next—I can't go on;
I'm almost sorry that I e'er begun.

CXVI.

Oh Plato! Plato! you have paved the way,
   With your confounded fantasies, to more
Immoral conduct by the fancied sway
   Your system feigns o'er the controlless core
Of human hearts, than all the long array

898–9 *the moon . . . CHASTE* Variously affiliated with Artemis, Diana, and Cynthia, the moon was classically identified with female chastity.
900 *nomenclature* 'The system or set of names for things'.
921 *Oh Plato! Plato!* As elsewhere, the narrator's apostrophe here serves not to intensify but to dilute and defer, as it turns us away (*apo*-away; *strophe*-turn) from the scene of Juan and Julia's assignation towards a digression on Plato.
923 *sway* 'Prevailing, overpowering, or controlling influence'.

Of poets and romancers:—You're a bore,
A charlatan, a coxcomb—and have been,
At best, no better than a go-between.

CXVII.

And Julia's voice was lost, except in sighs,
    Until too late for useful conversation;
The tears were gushing from her gentle eyes,
    I wish, indeed, they had not had occasion,
But who, alas! can love, and then be wise?
    Not that remorse did not oppose temptation,
A little still she strove, and much repented,
And whispering 'I will ne'er consent'—consented.

CXVIII.

'Tis said that Xerxes offer'd a reward
    To those who could invent him a new pleasure;
Methinks, the requisition's rather hard,
    And must have cost his majesty a treasure:
For my part, I'm a moderate-minded bard,
    Fond of a little love (which I call leisure);
I care not for new pleasures, as the old
Are quite enough for me, so they but hold.

CXIX.

Oh Pleasure! you're indeed a pleasant thing,
    Although one must be damn'd for you, no doubt;
I make a resolution every spring
    Of reformation, ere the year run out,
But, somehow, this my vestal vow takes wing,
    Yet still, I trust, it may be kept throughout:
I'm very sorry, very much ashamed,
And mean, next winter, to be quite reclaim'd.

CXX.

Here my chaste Muse a liberty must take—
    Start not! still chaster reader—she'll be nice hence-
Forward, and there is no great cause to quake;
    This liberty is a poetic licence,
Which some irregularity may make
    In the design, and as I have a high sense
Of Aristotle and the Rules, 'tis fit
To beg his pardon when I err a bit.

---

928 *a go-between* That is, a pander; see above, line 788 and note.

937 *Xerxes offer'd a reward* In *Of Experience*, Montaigne remarks of the Persian general Xerxes that, surrounded as he was by pleasures of all sorts, he offered a reward to anyone who could discover a new one for him. See also *Don Juan*, 'Ring for your valet – bid him quickly bring / Some hock and soda-water, then you'll know / A pleasure worthy Xerxes the great king' (II. 1433–5).

949 *vestal vow* Pertaining to chastity or purity; the vow made by a vestal virgin.

953 *chaste Muse* See other indulgences with the muse in *Don Juan* (e.g. 'Hard words, which stick in the soft Muses' gullets', VII. 624).

957–8 *Which some irregularity . . . In the design* The only thing regular about Byron's design throughout *Don Juan* is of course its irregularity.

959 *Aristotle and the Rules* Aristotle's 'rules' (in the *Poetics*) call for, among other things, the unity of time and place, which Byron violates here by interrupting the scene in June to fast-forward to one in November.

CXXI.

This licence is to hope the reader will
    Suppose from June the sixth (the fatal day,
Without whose epoch my poetic skill
    For want of facts would all be thrown away),
But keeping Julia and Don Juan still 965
    In sight, that several months have pass'd; we'll say
'Twas in November, but I'm not so sure
About the day—the era's more obscure.

CXXII.

We'll talk of that anon.—'Tis sweet to hear
    At midnight on the blue and moonlit deep 970
The song and oar of Adria's gondolier,
    By distance mellow'd, o'er the waters sweep;
'Tis sweet to see the evening star appear;
    'Tis sweet to listen as the nightwinds creep
From leaf to leaf; 'tis sweet to view on high 975
The rainbow, based on ocean, span the sky.

CXXIII.

'Tis sweet to hear the watchdog's honest bark
    Bay deep-mouth'd welcome as we draw near home;
'Tis sweet to know there is an eye will mark
    Our coming, and look brighter when we come; 980
'Tis sweet to be awaken'd by the lark,
    Or lull'd by falling waters; sweet the hum
Of bees, the voice of girls, the song of birds,
The lisp of children, and their earliest words.

CXXIV.

Sweet is the vintage, when the showering grapes 985
    In Bacchanal profusion reel to earth
Purple and gushing: sweet are our escapes
    From civic revelry to rural mirth;
Sweet to the miser are his glittering heaps,
    Sweet to the father is his first-born's birth, 990
Sweet is revenge—especially to women,
Pillage to soldiers, prize-money to seamen.

CXXV.

Sweet is a legacy, and passing sweet
    The unexpected death of some old lady
Or gentleman of seventy years complete, 995
    Who've made 'us youth' wait too—too long already
For an estate, or cash, or country-seat,
    Still breaking, but with stamina so steady,

---

971 *Adria's* Belonging to Venice (on the Adriatic); see *Childe Harold's Pilgrimage*, IV. 19–27.
973 *the evening star* Hesperus.
986 *Bacchanal profusion* Bacchus, Roman god of wine; here, the grapes themselves are depicted as Bacchanalian revellers, 'reeling' to earth as they fall from the vine.

992 *prize-money to seamen* Money realized from the sale of a prize (e.g. a ship captured during war at sea) and distributed among the captors; compare *Don Juan*, II. 1565, 'A sailor when the prize has struck in fight'.
996 *'us youth'* As spoken by Falstaff, Shakespeare, *Henry IV, Part I*, 'They hate us youth' (II. ii. 93).

That all the Israelites are fit to mob its
Next owner for their double-damn'd post-obits.

CXXVI.

'Tis sweet to win, no matter how, one's laurels
   By blood or ink; 'tis sweet to put an end
To strife; 'tis sometimes sweet to have our quarrels,
   Particularly with a tiresome friend;
Sweet is old wine in bottles, ale in barrels;
   Dear is the helpless creature we defend
Against the world; and dear the schoolboy spot
We ne'er forget, though there we are forgot.

CXXVII.

But sweeter still than this, than these, than all,
   Is first and passionate love—it stands alone,
Like Adam's recollection of his fall;
   The tree of knowledge has been pluck'd—all's known—
And life yields nothing further to recall
   Worthy of this ambrosial sin, so shown,
No doubt in fable, as the unforgiven
Fire which Prometheus filch'd for us from heaven.

CXXVIII.

Man's a strange animal, and makes strange use
   Of his own nature, and the various arts,
And likes particularly to produce
   Some new experiment to show his parts;
This is the age of oddities let loose,
   Where different talents find their different marts;
You'd best begin with truth, and when you've lost your
Labour, there's a sure market for imposture.

CXXIX.

What opposite discoveries we have seen!
   (Signs of true genius, and of empty pockets.)
One makes new noses, one a guillotine,
   One breaks your bones, one sets them in their sockets;
But vaccination certainly has been
   A kind antithesis to Congreve's rockets,

---

999 *Israelites* That is, money-lenders.
1000 *double-damn'd post-obits.* Inheritances or legacies, here 'damned' because of the high interest rates at which they were borrowed against. See also line 824 and note.
1012–13 *the tree of knowledge . . . And life* Compare *Manfred*, 'The Tree of Knowledge is not that of Life' (I. i. 12).
1016 *Fire which Prometheus filch'd* Amongst various gifts to humankind, Prometheus stole the fire which Zeus had hidden, for which he was punished. See Byron, 'Prometheus'.

1025–31 *What opposite discoveries . . . paid off an old pox* Recent, controversial scientific innovations: Benjamin Charles Perkins, an American quack doctor, 'made' new noses; the guillotine was refined by the French doctor (and member of the National Assembly) Joseph-Ignace Guillotin; Sir William Congreve invented the 'Congreve Rocket', used against the French at the Battle of Leipzig (1813); and the Englishman Edward Jenner first vaccinated against smallpox in 1796.

With which the doctor paid off an old pox
By borrowing a new one from an ox.

CXXX.

Bread has been made (indifferent) from potatoes;
   And galvanism has set some corpses grinning,
But has not answer'd like the apparatus
   Of the Humane Society's beginning,
By which men are unsuffocated gratis:
   What wondrous new machines have late been spinning!
I said the small-pox has gone out of late,
Perhaps it may be followed by the great.

CXXXI.

'Tis said the great came from America,
   Perhaps it may set out on its return;
The population there so spreads, they say,
   'Tis grown high time to thin it in its turn,
With war, or plague, or famine, any way,
   So that civilization they may learn,
And which in ravage the more loathsome evil is,
Their real lues, or our pseudo-syphilis.

CXXXII.

This is the patent age of new inventions
   For killing bodies, and for saving souls,
All propagated with the best intentions;
   Sir Humphrey Davy's lantern, by which coals
Are safely mined for in the mode he mentions,
   Tombuctoo travels, voyages to the Poles,
Are ways to benefit mankind, as true,
Perhaps, as shooting them at Waterloo.

CXXXIII.

Man's a phenomenon, one knows not what,
   And wonderful beyond all wondrous measure;
'Tis pity though, in this sublime world, that
   Pleasure's a sin, and sometimes sin's a pleasure;

1031–2 *With which ... from an ox* Murray suppressed this couplet, as well as lines 1039–40 and all of the following stanza (ll. 1041–8), due to its outspoken commentary on venereal disease. John Cam Hobhouse similarly counselled Byron to suppress these lines, 'Mon Cher ne touchez pas à la petite vérole [My dear friend, do not touch on the topic of small pox]' (cited by McGann, *CPW*, vol. 5, p. 678).

1033–8 *Bread has been made ... have late been spinning* A second catalogue of recent innovations: the Italian Luigi Galvani used galvanism (the contraction of a muscle due to the application of an electrical current) for therapeutic purposes in the late eighteenth century; the Royal Humane Society (founded 1774) attempted to recover drowned persons with a resuscitator; and the 'spinning-jenny' (patented by James Hargreaves in 1770) and other inventions in the textiles industry, led to frame-breaking riots in the 1810s.

1040 *the great* Syphilis.

1048 *lues* Syphilis.

1052 *Sir Humphry Davy's lantern* Sir Humphry Davy (1778–1829), friend of Wordsworth and Coleridge and whom Byron had met in London, developed the first miner's safety lantern in 1815.

1060 *Pleasure's a sin ... sin's a pleasure;* The narrator's chiasmus here underscores his own primary commitment to pleasure.

Few mortals know what end they would be at,
　　But whether glory, power, or love, or treasure,
The path is through perplexing ways, and when
The goal is gain'd, we die, you know—and then—

CXXXIV.

What then?—I do not know, no more do you—
　　And so good night.—Return we to our story:
'Twas, in November, when fine days are few,
　　And the far mountains wax a little hoary,
And clap a white cape on their mantles blue;
　　And the sea dashes round the promontory,
And the loud breaker boils against the rock;
And sober suns must set at five o'clock.

CXXXV.

'Twas, as the watchmen say, a cloudy night;
　　No moon, no stars, the wind was low or loud
By gusts, and many a sparkling hearth was bright
　　With the piled wood, round which the family crowd;
There's something cheerful in that sort of light,
　　Even as a summer sky's without a cloud:
I'm fond of fire, and crickets, and all that,
A lobster salad, and champaigne, and chat.

CXXXVI.

'Twas midnight—Donna Julia was in bed,
　　Sleeping, most probably,—when at her door
Arose a clatter might awake the dead,
　　If they had never been awoke before,
And that they have been so we all have read,
　　And are to be so, at the least, once more—
The door was fasten'd, but with voice and fist
First knocks were heard, then 'Madam—Madam—hist!

CXXXVII.

'For God's sake, Madam—Madam—here's my master,
　　With more than half the city at his back—
Was ever heard of such a curst disaster!
　　'Tis not my fault—I kept good watch—Alack!
Do, pray undo the bolt a little faster—
　　They're on the stair just now, and in a crack
Will all be here; perhaps he yet may fly—
Surely the window's not so *very* high!'

1082–6 *when at her door . . . once more* Compare I Corinthians 15: 51–2, 'Behold, I shew you a mystery; We shall not all sleep, but we shall all be changed. In a moment, in the twinkling of an eye, at the last trump; for the trumpet shall sound, and the dead shall be raised incorruptible, and we shall be changed'. The irony of Byron's allusion here consists in the fact that all (Julia, Alfonso and Juan) shall be changed before the night is over, but none shall prove incorruptible.
1094 *in a crack* 'immediately'.

CXXXVIII.

By this time Don Alfonso was arrived,
   With torches, friends, and servants in great number;
The major part of them had long been wived,
   And therefore paused not to disturb the slumber
Of any wicked woman, who contrived
   By stealth her husband's temples to encumber:
Examples of this kind are so contagious,
Were *one* not punish'd, *all* would be outrageous.

CXXXIX.

I can't tell how, or why, or what suspicion
   Could enter into Don Alfonso's head;
But for a cavalier of his condition
   It surely was exceedingly ill bred,
Without a word of previous admonition,
   To hold a levee round his lady's bed,
And summon lackeys, arm'd with fire and sword,
To prove himself the thing he most abhorr'd.

CXL.

Poor Donna Julia! starting as from sleep,
   (Mind——that I do not say—she had not slept)
Began at once to scream, and yawn, and weep;
   Her maid Antonia, who was an adept,
Contrived to fling the bed-clothes in a heap,
   As if she had just now from out them crept:
I can't tell why she should take all this trouble
To prove her mistress had been sleeping double.

CXLI.

But Julia mistress, and Antonia maid,
   Appear'd like two poor harmless women, who
Of goblins, but still more of men afraid,
   Had thought one man might be deterr'd by two,
And therefore side by side were gently laid,
   Until the hours of absence should run through,
And truant husband should return, and say,
'My dear, I was the first who came away.'

CXLII.

Now Julia found at length a voice, and cried,
   'In heaven's name, Don Alfonso, what d'ye mean?
Has madness seized you? would that I had died
   Ere such a monster's victim I had been!

1102 *temples to encumber* To impose horns, the traditional sign of the cuckold, on her husband.

1107–12 *But for a cavalier . . . most abhorr'd* It did not become a gentleman of Don Alfonso's social position either to enter his lady's bedroom unannounced or to publicly reveal to so many that he had been cuckolded ('To prove himself the thing he most abhorr'd').

1110 *levee* From the French, *lever*, to rise; a reception of visitors upon rising from bed.

1120 *To prove* The repetition of 'to prove' here underscores the irony that both Don Alfonso and Donna Julia are attempting to demonstrate precisely that which they would otherwise wish to deny – namely, that there had been another in Donna Julia's bed.

What may this midnight violence betide,
   A sudden fit of drunkenness or spleen?
Dare you suspect me, whom the thought would kill?
Search, then, the room!'—Alfonso said, 'I will.'

CXLIII.

He search'd, *they* search'd, and rummaged every where,
   Closet and clothes'-press, chest and window-seat,
And found much linen, lace, and several pair
   Of stockings, slippers, brushes, combs, complete,
With other articles of ladies fair,
   To keep them beautiful, or leave them neat:
Arras they prick'd and curtains with their swords,
And wounded several shutters, and some boards.

CXLIV.

Under the bed they search'd, and there they found—
   No matter what—it was not that they sought;
They open'd windows, gazing if the ground
   Had signs or footmarks, but the earth said nought;
And then they stared each others' faces round:
   'Tis odd, not one of all these seekers thought,
And seems to me almost a sort of blunder,
Of looking *in* the bed as well as under.

CXLV.

During this inquisition Julia's tongue
   Was not asleep—'Yes, search and search,' she cried,
'Insult on insult heap, and wrong on wrong!
   It was for this that I became a bride!
For this in silence I have suffer'd long
   A husband like Alfonso at my side;
But now I'll bear no more, nor here remain,
If there be law, or lawyers, in all Spain.

CXLVI.

'Yes, Don Alfonso! Husband now no more,
   If ever you indeed deserved the name,
Is't worthy of your years?—you have threescore,
   Fifty, or sixty—it is all the same—
Is't wise or fitting causeless to explore
   For facts against a virtuous woman's fame?
Ungrateful, perjured, barbarous Don Alfonso,
How dare you think your lady would go on so?

1134 *spleen* An illness characterized by melancholia, moodiness and irritability; see note to line 41 of Barbauld, 'To Mr. S. T. Coleridge'.
1138 *clothes'-press* 'A movable chest, in which clothes may be kept either folded or hanging'.
1143 *Arras they prick'd* It is through the arras (a hanging tapestry) in his mother's bedroom that Hamlet thrusts his rapier and kills Polonius; *Hamlet*, III. iv. 20–5.
1153–1256 *During this inquisition ... my pocket-handkerchief?* Compare Laura's upbraiding of her husband in 'Beppo', ll. 725–44. Whereas Don Alfonso arrives at Donna Julia's bed with a crowd of lackeys, Beppo and the Count resolve their situation privately, over a cup of coffee.
1167–8 *Alfonso ... go on so?* Given the context of the scene, the double-rhyme/repetition on Alfonso's name may be more accurately inflected here as a feminine rhyme, thus further emasculating the cuckolded husband.

CXLVII.

'Is it for this I have disdain'd to hold
    The common privileges of my sex?
That I have chosen a confessor so old
    And deaf, that any other it would vex,
And never once he has had cause to scold,
    But found my very innocence perplex
So much, he always doubted I was married—
How sorry you will be when I've miscarried!

CXLVIII.

'Was it for this that no Cortejo ere
    I yet have chosen from out the youth of Seville?
Is it for this I scarce went any where,
    Except to bull-fights, mass, play, rout, and revel?
Is it for this, whate'er my suitors were,
    I favour'd none—nay, was almost uncivil?
Is it for this that General Count O'Reilly,
Who took Algiers, declares I used him vilely?

CXLIX.

'Did not the Italian Musico Cazzani
    Sing at my heart six months at least in vain?
Did not his countryman, Count Corniani,
    Call me the only virtuous wife in Spain?
Were there not also Russians, English, many?
    The Count Strongstroganoff I put in pain,
And Lord Mount Coffeehouse, the Irish peer,
Who kill'd himself for love (with wine) last year.

1170 *common privileges of my sex?* To take a lover, a 'Cortejo' (see l. 1177 and note). See also Byron's letter to Hobhouse, 3 October 1819, 'here the *polygamy* is all on the female side' (*BLJ*, vol. 6, p. 226).
1176 *when I've miscarried* When I end up in the wrong hands.
1177 *Cortejo* Spanish variation on the Italian *cavalier servente*, a publicly acknowledged lover of a married woman (as Byron was to become cavalier servente to Teresa, Countess Guiccioli, in 1819). See *Don Juan*, III. 185–90:

> If single, probably his plighted fair
>   Has in his absence wedded some rich miser;
> But all the better, for the happy pair
>   May quarrel, and the lady growing wiser,
> He may resume his amatory care
>   As 'cavalier servente', or despise her.

See also *Don Juan*, IX. 401–8 and Byron's letter to Hobhouse of 3 October 1819: 'I'm not tired of Italy – but a man must be a Cicisbeo [cavalier servente] and a singer in duets and a Connoisseur of operas – or nothing here – I have made some progress in all of these accomplishments – but I can't say I don't feel the degradation' (*BLJ*, vol. 6, p. 226).
1180 *rout* 'A fashionable gathering or assembly, a large evening party or reception'.
1183 *General Count O'Reilly* 'Donna Julia here made a mistake. Count O'Reilly did not take Algiers – but Algiers very nearly took him: he and his army and fleet retreated with great loss, and not much credit, from before that city in the year 177[5]' (Byron's note). The Irish-born Spanish general Alexander O'Reilly was also the governor of Madrid and Cadiz.
1185 *Cazzani* Obscene pun on 'cazzo', both a 'penis' and a 'simpleton'; see Rochester, 'Signior Dildo'.
1187 *Corniani*, Obscene play on words, derived from 'cornuto', the 'horned' state of the cuckold.
1190 *Count Strongstroganoff* Possibly Count Alexander Stroganov, one of Byron's early friends and fellow revellers in Venice.
1191 *Lord Mount Coffeehouse, the Irish peer* Following the 1801 Act of Union between England and Ireland, a number of Irish peerages were created, which Byron here views with disdain. (Byron's bête noire Castlereagh held such a peerage; see note to 'Dedication', line 88.)

CL.

'Have I not had two bishops at my feet?
   The Duke of Ichar, and Don Fernan Nunez,
And is it thus a faithful wife you treat?
   I wonder in what quarter now the moon is:
I praise your vast forbearance not to beat
   Me also, since the time so opportune is—
Oh, valiant man! with sword drawn and cock'd trigger,
Now, tell me, don't you cut a pretty figure?

CLI.

'Was it for this you took your sudden journey,
   Under pretence of business indispensible
With that sublime of rascals your attorney,
   Whom I see standing there, and looking sensible
Of having play'd the fool? though both I spurn, he
   Deserves the worst, his conduct's less defensible,
Because, no doubt, 'twas for his dirty fee,
And not from any love to you nor me.

CLII.

'If he comes here to take a deposition,
   By all means let the gentleman proceed;
You've made the apartment in a fit condition:—
   There's pen and ink for you, sir, when you need—
Let every thing be noted with precision,
   I would not you for nothing should be feed—
But, as my maid's undrest, pray turn your spies out.'
Oh!' sobb'd Antonia, 'I could tear their eyes out.'

CLIII.

'There is the closet, there the toilet, there
   The anti-chamber—search them under, over;
There is the sofa, there the great arm-chair,
   The chimney—which would really hold a lover.
I wish to sleep, and beg you will take care
   And make no further noise, till you discover
The secret cavern of this lurking treasure—
And when 'tis found, let me, too, have that pleasure.

CLIV.

'And now, Hidalgo! now that you have thrown
   Doubt upon me, confusion over all,

1196 *what quarter now the moon is* That is, can the stage of the moon explain Don Alfonso's 'lunatic' behaviour.
1199 *sword drawn and cock'd trigger* Another obscene play on words.
1209 *deposition* Formal legal testimony; see note to line 213 and line 1506.
1214 *not you for nothing should be fee'd* Don Alfonso's lawyer should do some sort of work in light of the fees he is to receive.
1217 *toilet* Table on which articles for dressing are arranged.

Pray have the courtesy to make it known
    Who is the man you search for? how d'ye call
Him? what's his lineage? let him but be shown—
    I hope he's young and handsome—is he tall?
Tell me—and be assured, that since you stain
My honour thus, it shall not be in vain.

CLV.

'At least, perhaps, he has not sixty years,
    At that age he would be too old for slaughter,
Or for so young a husband's jealous fears—
    (Antonia! let me have a glass of water.)
I am ashamed of having shed these tears,
    They are unworthy of my father's daughter;
My mother dream'd not in my natal hour
That I should fall into a monster's power.

CLVI.

'Perhaps 'tis of Antonia you are jealous,
    You saw that she was sleeping by my side
When you broke in upon us with your fellows:
    Look where you please—we've nothing, sir, to hide;
Only another time, I trust, you'll tell us,
    Or for the sake of decency abide
A moment at the door, that we may be
Drest to receive so much good company.

CLVII.

'And now, sir, I have done, and say no more;
    The little I have said may serve to show
The guileless heart in silence may grieve o'er
    The wrongs to whose exposure it is slow:—
I leave you to your conscience as before,
    'Twill one day ask you *why* you used me so?
God grant you feel not then the bitterest grief!
Antonia! where's my pocket-handkerchief?'

CLVIII.

She ceased, and turn'd upon her pillow; pale
    She lay, her dark eyes flashing through their tears,
Like skies that rain and lighten; as a veil,
    Waved and o'ershading her wan cheek, appears
Her streaming hair; the black curls strive, but fail,
    To hide the glossy shoulder, which uprears
Its snow through all;—her soft lips lie apart,
And louder than her breathing beats her heart.

CLIX.

The Senhor Don Alfonso stood confused;
    Antonia bustled round the ransack'd room,
And, turning up her nose, with looks abused
    Her master, and his myrmidons, of whom
Not one, except the attorney, was amused;
    He, like Achates, faithful to the tomb,
So there were quarrels, cared not for the cause,
Knowing they must be settled by the laws.

CLX.

With prying snub-nose, and small eyes, he stood,
    Following Antonia's motions here and there,
With much suspicion in his attitude;
    For reputations he had little care;
So that a suit or action were made good,
    Small pity had he for the young and fair,
And ne'er believed in negatives, till these
Were proved by competent false witnesses.

CLXI.

But Don Alfonso stood with downcast looks,
    And, truth to say, he made a foolish figure;
When, after searching in five hundred nooks,
    And treating a young wife with so much rigour,
He gain'd no point, except some self-rebukes,
    Added to those his lady with such vigour
Had pour'd upon him for the last half-hour,
Quick, thick, and heavy—as a thunder-shower.

CLXII.

At first he tried to hammer an excuse,
    To which the sole reply were tears, and sobs,
And indications of hysterics, whose
    Prologue is always certain throes, and throbs,
Gasps, and whatever else the owners choose:—
    Alfonso saw his wife, and thought of Job's:
He saw too, in perspective, her relations,
And then he tried to muster all his patience.

CLXIII.

He stood in act to speak, or rather stammer,
    But sage Antonia cut him short before

1268 *myrmidons* 'Unscrupulously faithful followers or hired ruffians'.
1270 *Achates* Faithful companion of Aeneas.
1292 *certain throes* Violent spasms or convulsions; here 'certain' because they can be relied upon to indicate the onset of hysterics.
1294 *Job's* See Job 2: 9, 'Then said his wife unto him, Dost thou still retain thine integrity? curse God, and die'.

The anvil of his speech received the hammer,
   With 'Pray, sir, leave the room, and say no more,
Or madam dies.'—Alfonso mutter'd 'D—n her,'
   But nothing else, the time of words was o'er;
He cast a rueful look or two, and did,
He knew not wherefore, that which he was bid.

CLXIV.

With him retired his '*posse comitatus*,'
   The attorney last, who linger'd near the door,
Reluctantly, still tarrying there as late as
   Antonia let him—not a little sore
At this most strange and unexplain'd '*hiatus*'
   In Don Alfonso's facts, which just now wore
An awkward look; as he revolved the case
The door was fasten'd in his legal face.

CLXV.

No sooner was it bolted, than—Oh shame!
   Oh sin! Oh sorrow! and Oh womankind!
How can you do such things and keep your fame,
   Unless this world, and t'other too, be blind?
Nothing so dear as an unfilch'd good name!
   But to proceed—for there is more behind:
With much heart-felt reluctance be it said,
Young Juan slipp'd, half smother'd, from the bed.

CLXVI.

He had been hid—I don't pretend to say
   How, nor can I indeed describe the where—
Young, slender, and pack'd easily, he lay,
   No doubt, in little compass, round or square;
But pity him I neither must nor may
   His suffocation by that pretty pair;
'Twere better, sure, to die so, than be shut
With maudlin Clarence in his Malmsey butt.

CLXVII.

And, secondly, I pity not, because
   He had no business to commit a sin,
Forbid by heavenly, fined by human laws,
   At least 'twas rather early to begin;
But at sixteen the conscience rarely gnaws
   So much as when we call our old debts in

1305 'posse commitatus' 'power of the county'; an armed body with legal authority.

1309 'hiatus' 'A gap or lacuna in a series; a missing link in a chain of events'; here, the absence of a lover in Donna Julia's bedroom.

1317 *an unfilch'd good name!* An ironic allusion to *Othello*, when Iago comments that '. . . he that filches from me my good name / Robs me of that which not enriches him, / And makes me poor indeed' (III. iii. 163–5).

1328 *Clarence in his Malmsey butt* George, Duke of Clarence, brother of Richard III, was drowned in a cask of malmsey (a strong sweet wine made from the Malvasia grape); see *Richard III*, I. iv. 260.

At sixty years, and draw the accompts of evil,   1335
And find a deuced balance with the devil.

CLXVIII.

Of his position I can give no notion:
  'Tis written in the Hebrew Chronicle,
How the physicians, leaving pill and potion,
  Prescribed, by way of blister, a young belle,   1340
When old King David's blood grew dull in motion,
  And that the medicine answer'd very well;
Perhaps 'twas in a different way applied,
For David lived, but Juan nearly died.

CLXIX.

What's to be done? Alfonso will be back   1345
  The moment he has sent his fools away.
Antonia's skill was put upon the rack,
  But no device could be brought into play—
And how to parry the renew'd attack?
  Besides, it wanted but few hours of day: 1350
Antonia puzzled; Julia did not speak,
But press'd her bloodless lip to Juan's cheek.

CLXX.

He turn'd his lip to hers, and with his hand
  Call'd back the tangles of her wandering hair;
Even then their love they could not all command,   1355
  And half forgot their danger and despair:
Antonia's patience now was at a stand—
  'Come, come, 'tis no time now for fooling there,'
She whisper'd, in great wrath—'I must deposit
This pretty gentleman within the closet;   1360

CLXXI.

'Pray, keep your nonsense for some luckier night—
  Who can have put my master in this mood?
What will become on't?—I'm in such a fright,
  The devil's in the urchin, and no good—
Is this a time for giggling? this a plight?   1365
  Why, don't you know that it may end in blood?
You'll lose your life, and I shall lose my place,
My mistress all, for that half-girlish face.

1338–42   *'Tis written . . . answer'd very well* See I Kings 1: 1–4, 'Let there be sought for my lord the king a young virgin: and let her stand before the king, and let her cherish him . . . that my lord the king may get heat' (v. 2).

1340   *by way of blister* Here, an application designed to irritate, and hence to rejuvenate.

1348   *device* 'Contrivance or counsel'.

1354   *her wandering hair* See line 874 and note.

1367   *my place* Antonia's position as Donna Julia's maid.

CLXXII.

'Had it but been for a stout cavalier
　Of twenty-five or thirty—(Come, make haste)
But for a child, what piece of work is here!
　I really, madam, wonder at your taste—
(Come, sir, get in)—my master must be near.
　There, for the present, at the least he's fast,
And, if we can but till the morning keep
Our counsel—(Juan, mind, you must not sleep.)'

CLXXIII.

Now, Don Alfonso entering, but alone,
　Closed the oration of the trusty maid:
She loiter'd, and he told her to be gone,
　An order somewhat sullenly obey'd;
However, present remedy was none,
　And no great good seem'd answer'd if she staid:
Regarding both with slow and sidelong view,
She snuff'd the candle, curtsied, and withdrew.

CLXXIV.

Alfonso paused a minute—then begun
　Some strange excuses for his late proceeding;
He would not justify what he had done,
　To say the best, it was extreme ill-breeding;
But there were ample reasons for it, none
　Of which he specified in this his pleading:
His speech was a fine sample, on the whole,
Of rhetoric, which the learn'd call '*rigmarole*.'

CLXXV.

Julia said nought; though all the while there rose
　A ready answer, which at once enables
A matron, who her husband's foible knows,
　By a few timely words to turn the tables,
Which if it does not silence still must pose,
　Even if it should comprise a pack of fables;
'Tis to retort with firmness, and when he
Suspects with *one*, do you reproach with *three*.

CLXXVI.

Julia, in fact, had tolerable grounds,
　Alfonso's loves with Inez were well known;

1371 *what piece of work is here!* Compare Shakespeare, *Hamlet*, 'What a piece of work is man . . .' (II. ii. 303), here ironically reworked at the expense of Juan, a 'child' with a 'half-girlish face'.
1388 *extreme ill-breeding* See above, line 1108 and note.
1392 '*rigmarole*' 'A succession of incoherent statements; an unconnected or rambling discourse'.

1395 *foible* Weakness; see above, line 517 and note.
1397 *pose* Here in the sense of 'to perplex', to confuse or bewilder; compare 'But found my very innocence perplex / So much' (ll. 1174–5).
1402 *Alfonso's loves with Inez* See above, lines 525–44.

But whether 'twas that one's own guilt confounds,
   But that can't be, as has been often shown,
A lady with apologies abounds;
   It might be that her silence sprang alone
From delicacy to Don Juan's ear,
To whom she knew his mother's fame was dear.

CLXXVII.

There might be one more motive, which makes two,
   Alfonso ne'er to Juan had alluded,
Mention'd his jealousy, but never who
   Had been the happy lover, he concluded,
Conceal'd amongst his premises; 'tis true,
   His mind the more o'er this its mystery brooded;
To speak of lnez now were, one may say,
Like throwing Juan in Alfonso's way.

CLXXVIII.

A hint, in tender cases, is enough;
   Silence is best, besides there is a *tact*
(That modern phrase appears to me sad stuff,
   But it will serve to keep my verse compact)
Which keeps, when push'd by questions rather rough,
   A lady always distant from the fact—
The charming creatures lie with such a grace,
There's nothing so becoming to the face.

CLXXIX.

They blush, and we believe them; at least I
   Have always done so; 'tis of no great use,
In any case, attempting a reply,
   For then their eloquence grows quite profuse;
And when at length they're out of breath, they sigh,
   And cast their languid eyes down, and let loose
A tear or two, and then we make it up;
And then—and then—and then—sit down and sup.

CLXXX.

Alfonso closed his speech, and begg'd her pardon,
   Which Julia half withheld, and then half granted,
And laid conditions, he thought, very hard on,
   Denying several little things he wanted:

1403 *confounds* Here in the sense of to put to shame; Donna Julia's knowledge of her own guilt effectively silences her ability to reproach Don Alfonso.
1408 *dear* Here understood as something highly estimated or of great worth.
1418–22 tact ... *the fact* In the sense of a 'ready and delicate sense of what is fitting and proper in dealing with others', tact is a 'modern phrase' (the OED cites 1793 as the first instance of the usage above). Byron playfully deploys it here not merely to keep his verse (i.e. his rhyme) 'compact', but also in order to suggest that (at least in matrimonial relations) 'tact' may be said to consist in reaching a 'compact' without all the 'facts'.
1432 *sit down and sup.* Compare 'Beppo', when Beppo, his wife, and the Count sort out the matter of her supposed infidelity over coffee (l. 721).

He stood like Adam lingering near his garden,
    With useless penitence perplex'd and haunted,
Beseeching she no further would refuse,
When lo! he stumbled o'er a pair of shoes.

CLXXXI.

A pair of shoes!—what then? not much, if they
    Are such as fit with lady's feet, but these
(No one can tell how much I grieve to say)
    Were masculine; to see them, and to seize,
Was but a moment's act—Ah! Well-a-day!
    My teeth begin to chatter, my veins freeze—
Alfonso first examined well their fashion,
And then flew out into another passion.

CLXXXII.

He left the room for his relinquish'd sword,
    And Julia instant to the closet flew.
'Fly, Juan, fly! for heaven's sake—not a word—
    The door is open—you may yet slip through
The passage you so often have explored—
    Here is the garden-key—Fly—fly—Adieu!
Haste—haste!—I hear Alfonso's hurrying feet—,
Day has not broke—there's no one in the street.'

CLXXXIII.

None can say that this was not good advice,
    The only mischief was, it came too late;
Of all experience 'tis the usual price,
    A sort of income-tax laid on by fate:
Juan had reach'd the room-door in a trice,
    And might have done so by the garden gate,
But met Alfonso in his dressing-gown,
Who threaten'd death—so Juan knock'd him down.

CLXXXIV.

Dire was the scuffle, and out went the light,
    Antonia cried out 'Rape!' and Julia 'Fire!'
But not a servant stirr'd to aid the fight.
    Alfonso, pommell'd to his heart's desire,
Swore lustily he'd be revenged this night;
    And Juan, too, blasphemed an octave higher,
His blood was up; though young, he was a Tartar,
And not at all disposed to prove a martyr.

1437 *Adam lingering near his garden* Compare Milton, *Paradise Lost*, 'Whereat / In either hand the hast'ning angel caught / Our ling'ring parents and to the eastern gate / Led them direct . . .' (12. 636–9).

1449 *relinquish'd sword* Without his sword (previously 'drawn' and at the ready; see above, l. 1199), Don Alfonso is unmanned and lacks the ability (as a cavalier) either to 'prick' her (see above, l. 1143) or to defend her.

1460 *income-tax* The first such tax was introduced in Britain, as a war tax, in 1798.

1461 *in a trice* 'instantly, forthwith; without delay'.

1470 *blasphemed an octave higher,* Another reminder than Juan is not 'a stout cavalier / Of twenty-five or thirty', but a mere 'child' of 16 (see ll. 1369–71).

1471 *a Tartar* 'A rough and violent or irritable and intractable person'.

CLXXXV.

Alfonso's sword had dropp'd ere he could draw it,
   And they continued battling hand to hand,
For Juan very luckily ne'er saw it;
   His temper not being under great command,
If at that moment he had chanced to claw it,
   Alfonso's days had not been in the land
Much longer.—Think of husbands', lovers' lives!
And how ye may be doubly widows—wives!

CLXXXVI.

Alfonso grappled to detain the foe,
   And Juan throttled him to get away,
And blood ('twas from the nose) began to flow;
   At last, as they more faintly wrestling lay,
Juan contrived to give an awkward blow,
   And then his only garment quite gave way;
He fled, like Joseph, leaving it; but there,
I doubt, all likeness ends between the pair.

CLXXXVII.

Lights came at length, and men, and maids, who found
   An awkward spectacle their eyes before;
Antonia in hysterics, Julia swoon'd,
   Alfonso leaning, breathless, by the door;
Some half torn drapery scatter'd on the ground,
   Some blood, and several footsteps, but no more:
Juan the gate gain'd, turn'd the key about,
And liking not the inside, lock'd the out.

CLXXXVIII.

Here ends this canto.—Need I sing, or say,
   How Juan, naked, favour'd by the night,
Who favours what she should not, found his way,
   And reach'd his home in an unseemly plight?
The pleasant scandal which arose next day,
   The nine days' wonder which was brought to light,
And how Alfonso sued for a divorce,
Were in the English newspapers, of course.

1473 *Alfonso's sword had dropp'd* Another wry commentary on Alfonso's compromised masculinity; see l. 1449 and note.
1487–8 *He fled . . . between the pair* 'And she caught him by his garment, saying, Lie with me: and he left his garment in her hand, and fled, and got him out' (Genesis 39: 12). Byron refers here to the dilemma of Joseph (Genesis 39: 7–20), who refused to sleep with Potiphar's wife, who nonetheless accused him of attempted rape and had him imprisoned. The allusion here is particularly bathetic, for no sooner does it raise the expectation of some sort of revealing affinity between Juan and Joseph than it disappoints such a reading on two fronts: the only common denominator between the two is their lack of clothing, and Juan did after all enter into an adulterous liaison with a married woman.
1490 *spectacle* Here to be understood in a particularly theatrical sense as something set before the public gaze (the men and maids of l. 1489) as an object of curiosity (or contempt).
1504 *English newspapers* An allusion to the relentless, scandal-mongering newspaper coverage of Byron's separation from Lady Byron in early 1816.

CLXXXIX.

If you would like to see the whole proceedings, 1505
    The depositions, and the cause at full,
The names of all the witnesses, the pleadings
    Of counsel to nonsuit, or to annul,
There's more than one edition, and the readings
    Are various, but they none of them are dull, 1510
The best is that in short-hand ta'en by Gurney,
Who to Madrid on purpose made a journey.

CXC.

But Donna Inez, to divert the train
    Of one of the most circulating scandals
That had for centuries been known in Spain, 1515
    At least since the retirement of the Vandals,

1508 *to nonsuit, or to annul* To terminate a case due to the plaintiff's failure to provide evidence adequate to support the allegations.
1511 *Gurney* William Brodie Gurney (1777–1855), official shorthand clerk to the houses of Parliament who also produced transcripts of trials throughout England.
1512 *made a journey* Byron initially intended for seven stanzas on Henry Brougham (legal advisor to Lady Byron) to follow this stanza, before he suppressed them on the grounds that 'I will not at this distance publish *that* of a Man for which he has a claim upon another too remote to give him redress' (cited in *CPW*, vol. 5, p. 686; see also Byron's letter to Brougham of 6 May 1820, *BLJ*, vol. 7, pp. 95–6). Similar to the attacks on Southey and Castlereagh in the 'Dedication', Byron exposes Brougham's expedience and apostasy ('Tory by nurture, Whig by Circumstance'), all the while suggesting that, as a Bard, it is 'my duty to mankind' to warn them of such charlatans. The stanzas remained unpublished until 1957 in *DJV* (which text is followed here).

'Twas a fine cause for those in law delighting
    'Tis pity that they had no Brougham in Spain –
Famous for always talking, and ne'er fighting
    For calling names and taking them again,
For blustering, bungling, trimming, wrangling, writing,
    Groping all paths to power, and all in vain,
Losing elections, character, and temper,
A foolish clever fellow, 'Idem semper'!

Bully in Senates, Skulker in the field,
    The Adulterer's advocate when duly feed,
The libeller's gratis Counsel, dirty Shield
    Which Law affords to many a dirty deed,
A wondrous Warrior against those who yield,
    A Rod to weakness, to the brave a reed,
The People's Sycophant, the Prince's foe
And serving him the more by being so.

Tory by nurture, Whig by Circumstance,
    A Democrat some once or twice a year
Whene'er it suits his purpose to advance
    His vain ambition in its vague career,
A Sort of Orator by sufferance
    Less for the comprehension than the ear
With all the arrogance of endless power,
Without the Sense to keep it for an hour.

The House of Commons Damocles of words
    Above him hanging by a single hair
On each harangue depend some hostile Swords,
    And deems he that we *always* will forbear?
Although defiance oft declined affords
    A blotted shield no Shire's true knight would wear,
Thersites of the House, Parolles of Law,
The double Bobadil takes Scorn for awe.

How noble is his language, never pert,
    How grand his Sentiments which ne'er run riot,
As when he swore 'by G—d he'd sell his shirt
    To head the poll.' I wonder who would buy it?
The Skin has passed through such a deal of dirt
    In grovelling on to power, such stains now dye it,
So black the long worn Lion's hide in hue
You'd swear his very heart had sweated through.

Panting for power, as harts for cooling streams
    Yet half afraid to venture for the draught,
A Go-between, yet blundering in extremes,
    And tossed along the vessel fore and aft,
Now shrinking back, now midst the first he seems,
    Patriot by force, and Courtesan by craft,
Quick without wit, and violent without strength,
A disappointed Lawyer at full length.

A strange example of the force of law
    And hasty temper on a kindling mind,
Are these the dreams his young Ambition saw?
    Poor fellow! he had better far been blind,
I'm sorry thus to probe a wound so raw,
    But then as Bard my duty to mankind
For warning to the rest compels these raps
As Geographers lay down a shoal in Maps.

1513 *train* Here, the proper sequence or progression; development.

First vow'd (and never had she vow'd in vain)
    To Virgin Mary several pounds of candles;
And then, by the advice of some old ladies,
    She sent her son to be shipp'd off from Cadiz.

CXCI.

She had resolved that he should travel through
    All European climes, by land or sea,
To mend his former morals, and get new,
    Especially in France and Italy,
(At least this is the thing most people do.)
    Julia was sent into a convent; she
Grieved, but, perhaps, her feelings may be better
Shown in the following copy of her letter:

CXCII.

'They tell me 'tis decided; you depart:
    'Tis wise—'tis well, but not the less a pain;
I have no further claim on your young heart,
    Mine is the victim, and would be again;
To love too much has been the only art
    I used;—I write in haste, and if a stain
Be on this sheet, 'tis not what it appears,
My eyeballs burn and throb, but have no tears.

CXCIII.

'I loved, I love you, for this love have lost
    State, station, heaven, mankind's, my own esteem,
And yet can not regret what it hath cost,
    So dear is still the memory of that dream;
Yet, if I name my guilt, 'tis not to boast,
    None can deem harshlier of me than I deem:
I trace this scrawl because I cannot rest—
I've nothing to reproach, or to request.

CXCIV.

'Man's love is of man's life a thing apart,
    'Tis woman's whole existence; man may range
The court, camp, church, the vessel, and the mart,
    Sword, gown, gain, glory, offer in exchange
Pride, fame, ambition, to fill up his heart,
    And few there are whom these can not estrange;
Men have all these resources, we but one,
To love again, and be again undone.

CXCV.

'You will proceed in pleasure, and in pride,
    Beloved and loving many; all is o'er

1538 *station* Social position; having been divorced by Don Alfonso, Julia is now a disgraced woman.

'For me on earth, except some years to hide
    My shame and sorrow deep in my heart's core;
These I could bear, but cannot cast aside
    The passion which still rages as before,
And so farewell—forgive me, love me—No,
That word is idle now—but let it go.

CXCVI.

'My breast has been all weakness, is so yet;
    But still I think I can collect my mind;
My blood still rushes where my spirit's set,
    As roll the waves before the settled wind;
My heart is feminine, nor can forget—
    To all, except one image, madly blind;
So shakes the needle, and so stands the pole,
As vibrates my fond heart to my fix'd soul.

CXCVII.

'I have no more to say, but linger still,
    And dare not set my seal upon this sheet,
And yet I may as well the task fulfil,
    My misery can scarce be more complete:
I had not lived till now, could sorrow kill;
    Death shuns the wretch who fain the blow would meet,
And I must even survive this last adieu,
And bear with life, to love and pray for you!'

CXCVIII.

This note was written upon gilt-edged paper
    With a neat little crow-quill, slight and new;
Her small white hand could hardly reach the taper,
    It trembled as magnetic needles do,
And yet she did not let one tear escape her;
    The seal a sunflower; '*Elle vous suit partout,*'
The motto, cut upon a white cornelian;
The wax was superfine, its hue vermillion.

CXCIX.

This was Don Juan's earliest scrape; but whether
    I shall proceed with his adventures is
Dependant on the public altogether;
    We'll see, however, what they say to this,
Their favour in an author's cap's a feather,
    And no great mischief's done by their caprice;
And if their approbation we experience,
Perhaps they'll have some more about a year hence.

1582 'Elle vous suit partout' 'She follows you everywhere' – the motto of one of Byron's seals.
1583 *cornelian* Semi-transparent quartz (often of a deep, dull red or reddish white colouring) used for making seals; see Byron's early poem, 'The Cornelian'.
1590 *caprice* An arbitrary opinion or whim, here referring to the tastes of the English reading public.

CC.

My poem's epic, and is meant to be
  Divided in twelve books; each book containing,
With love, and war, a heavy gale at sea,
  A list of ships, and captains, and kings reigning,
New characters; the episodes are three:
  A panorama view of hell's in training,
After the style of Virgil and of Homer,
So that my name of Epic's no misnomer.

CCI.

All these things will be specified in time,
  With strict regard to Aristotle's rules,
The *vade mecum* of the true sublime,
  Which makes so many poets, and some fools;
Prose poets like blank-verse, I'm fond of rhyme,
  Good workmen never quarrel with their tools;
I've got new mythological machinery,
And very handsome supernatural scenery.

CCII.

There's only one slight difference between
  Me and my epic brethren gone before,
And here the advantage is my own, I ween;
  (Not that I have not several merits more,
But this will more peculiarly be seen)
  They so embellish, that 'tis quite a bore
Their labyrinth of fables to thread through,
Whereas this story's actually true.

CCIII.

If any person doubt it, I appeal
  To history, tradition, and to facts,
To newspapers, whose truth all know and feel,
  To plays in five, and operas in three acts;
All these confirm my statement a good deal,
  But that which more completely faith exacts
Is, that myself, and several now in Seville,
Saw Juan's last elopement with the devil.

1593 *My poem's epic* See Byron's comments to Thomas Medwin: 'If you must have an epic, there's *Don Juan* for you. I call that an epic: it is an epic as much in the spirit of our day as the Iliad was in Homer's. Love, religion, and politics form the argument, and are as much the cause of quarrels now as they were then' (*Medwin's Conversations of Lord Byron*, ed. Ernest J. Lovell, Jr. [Princeton University Press, 1964], p. 164).

1602 *Aristotle's rules* As set forth in Aristotle's *Poetics*; see line 959 and note.

1603 vade mecum 'go with me'; a reference volume or handbook. Byron provides a succinct *vade mecum* of the epic in the preceding stanza (and, more ironically, of his own poetic priorities in the 'poetical commandments' of ll. 1626–48).

1607 *machinery* 'supernatural personages and incidents introduced in narrative or dramatic poetry'; see Pope, 'The Machinery, Madam, is a Term invented by the Critics, to signify that Part which the Deities, Angels, or Daemons, are made to act in a Poem' (Dedicatory Letter, *The Rape of the Lock*).

1611 *ween* 'To think, surmise, suppose'.

1619 *To newspapers . . . know and feel* See line 1504 and note.

1624 *Juan's last elopement with the devil* When in Seville in July 1809, Byron may (or may not) have seen a performance of Tirso de Molina's seventeenth-century work *El Burlador de Sevilla y convidado di piedra* (*The Playboy of Seville, or Supper with a Statue*), an early play in the Don Juan tradition.

CCIV.

If ever I should condescend to prose,
    I'll write poetical commandments, which
Shall supersede beyond all doubt all those
    That went before; in these I shall enrich
My text with many things that no one knows,
    And carry precept to the highest pitch:
I'll call the work 'Longinus o'er a Bottle,
Or, Every Poet his *own* Aristotle.'

CCV.

Thou shalt believe in Milton, Dryden, Pope;
    Thou shalt not set up Wordsworth, Coleridge, Southey;
Because the first is crazed beyond all hope,
    The second drunk, the third so quaint and mouthey:
With Crabbe it may be difficult to cope,
    And Campbell's Hippocrene is somewhat drouthy:
Thou shalt not steal from Samuel Rogers, nor
Commit—flirtation with the muse of Moore.

CCVI.

Thou shalt not covet Mr. Sotheby's Muse,
    His Pegasus, nor any thing that's his;
Thou shalt not bear false witness like 'the Blues,'
    (There's one, at least, is very fond of this);
Thou shalt not write, in short, but what I choose:
    This is true criticism, and you may kiss—
Exactly as you please, or not, the rod,
But if you don't, I'll lay it on, by G—d!

CCVII.

If any person should presume to assert
    This story is not moral, first, I pray,
That they will not cry out before they're hurt,
    Then that they'll read it o'er again, and say,

1626 *poetical commandments* The light-hearted parody of the ten commandments in the following stanzas caused significant public outcry in England. See Byron's letter to Murray of 8 October 1820: 'Recollect that if you put my name to [Don] "Juan" in these canting days – any lawyer might oppose my Guardian right of my daughter in Chancery – on the plea of it's containing the *parody* – such are the perils of a foolish jest' (*BLJ*, vol. 7, p. 196).
1631–2 *'Longinus . . . Aristotle'* For Longinus, see lines 329–44 and note; for Aristotle, see line 959 and note.
1633–40 *Milton . . . Moore* Byron's 'first commandment' endorses three dead canonical poets (Milton, Dryden, Pope) at the expense of one cadre of contemporary poets, the Lake poets (Wordsworth, Coleridge, Southey), while elevating another poetic fraternity (Crabbe, Campbell, Rogers, Moore). Compare 'Dedication' line 55 and note.
1636 *drunk* 'Intoxicated or stupefied by opium'.
1636 *mouthey* As Byron earlier rhymed on 'Bob' at Southey's expense (see 'Dedication', line 24 and note), so he here rhymes 'Southey' with 'mouthey' and 'drouthy', suggesting that Southey is not merely bombastic but furthermore (once again) 'dry'. See also *The Blues*, 'On Wordsworths, for instance, I seldom alight, / Or on Mouthey, his friend, without taking to flight' (2. 97–8).
1638 *Hippocrene* fountain on Mount Helicon, sacred to Apollo and the Muses.
1641 *Mr. Sotheby's* William Sotheby (1757–1833), minor English poet praised by Byron in 'English Bards and Scotch Reviewers' before being satirized by him in 'Beppo' as 'Botherby', the 'sublime / Of mediocrity' (ll. 575, 581–2).
1642 *Pegasus* See 'Dedication', line 58 and note.
1643 *'the Blues'* London bluestockings; see line 175 and note.

  (But, doubtless, nobody will be so pert)
   That this is not a moral tale, though gay;
  Besides, in canto twelfth, I mean to show
   The very place where wicked people go.

CCVIII.

  If, after all, there should be some so blind
   To their own good this warning to despise,
  Led by some tortuosity of mind,
   Not to believe my verse and their own eyes,
  And cry that they 'the moral cannot find,'
   I tell him, if a clergyman, he lies;
  Should captains the remark or critics make,
  They also lie too—under a mistake.

CCIX.

  The public approbation I expect,
   And beg they'll take my word about the moral,
  Which I with their amusement will connect,
   (So children cutting teeth receive a coral);
  Meantime, they'll doubtless please to recollect
   My epical pretensions to the laurel:
  For fear some prudish readers should grow skittish,
  I've bribed my grandmother's review—the British.

CCX.

  I sent it in a letter to the editor,
   Who thank'd me duly by return of post—
  I'm for a handsome article his creditor;
   Yet if my gentle Muse he please to roast,
  And break a promise after having made it her,
   Denying the receipt of what it cost,
  And smear his page with gall instead of honey,
  All I can say is—that he had the money.

CCXI.

  I think that with this holy new alliance
   I may ensure the public, and defy
  All other magazines of art or science,
   Daily, or monthly, or three monthly; I
  Have not essay'd to multiply their clients,
   Because they tell me 'twere in vain to try,
  And that the Edinburgh Review and Quarterly
  Treat a dissenting author very martyrly.

1659 *tortuosity* 'Crookedness, with emphasis on mental or moral deviousness'.
1687 *Edinburgh Review and Quarterly* Leading quarterly periodicals of the day, with significant influence over literary and political tastes. The *Edinburgh Review* (founded 1802), edited by Francis Jeffrey until 1829, was decidedly Whiggish in its politics. The *Quarterly Review* (founded 1809 by John Murray, in large measure to counter the influence of the *Edinburgh*) and initially edited by William Gifford, advanced Tory positions.

CCXII.

'*Non ego hoc ferrem calida juventa*
   Consule Planco,' Horace said, and so   1690
Say I; by which quotation there is meant a
   Hint that some six or seven good years ago
(Long ere I dreamt of dating from the Brenta)
   I was most ready to return a blow,
And would not brook at all this sort of thing   1695
In my hot youth—when George the Third was King.

CCXIII.

But now at thirty years my hair is gray—
   (I wonder what it will be like at forty?
I thought of a peruke the other day)
   My heart is not much greener; and, in short, I   1700
Have squander'd my whole summer while 'twas May,
   And feel no more the spirit to retort; I
Have spent my life, both interest and principal,
And deem not, what I deem'd, my soul invincible.

CCXIV.

No more—no more—Oh! never more on me   1705
   The freshness of the heart can fall like dew,
Which out of all the lovely things we see
   Extracts emotions beautiful and new,
Hived in our bosoms like the bag o'the bee:
   Think'st thou the honey with those objects grew?   1710
Alas! 'twas not in them, but in thy power
To double even the sweetness of a flower.

CCXV.

No more—no more—Oh! never more, my heart,
   Canst thou be my sole world, my universe!
Once all in all, but now a thing apart,   1715
   Thou canst not be my blessing or my curse;
The illusion's gone for ever, and thou art
   Insensible, I trust, but none the worse,
And in thy stead I've got a deal of judgment,
Though heaven knows how it ever found a lodgement.   1720

CCXVI.

My days of love are over, me no more
   The charms of maid, wife, and still less of widow,
Can make the fool of which they made before,
   In short, I must not lead the life I did do;
The credulous hope of mutual minds is o'er,   1725
   The copious use of claret is forbid too,

1689–90 'Non ego hoc ... Consule Planco' 'I would not have borne such an insult in my youth when Plancus was consul' (Horace, *Odes*, III. 16. 27–8); see lines 1695–6 for Byron's more topical rendering of these lines.

1693 *Brenta* The Brenta flows into the Venetian lagoon. In the summer of 1817, Byron rented a villa on the Brenta.

1699 *peruke* Periwig, wig.

So for a good old-gentlemanly vice,
I think I must take up with avarice.

CCXVII.

Ambition was my idol, which was broken
    Before the shrines of Sorrow and of Pleasure;
And the two last have left me many a token
    O'er which reflection may be made at leisure:
Now, like Friar Bacon's brazen head, I've spoken,
    'Time is, Time was, Time's past,' a chymic treasure
Is glittering youth, which I have spent betimes—
My heart in passion, and my head on rhymes.

CCXVIII.

What is the end of fame? 'tis but to fill
    A certain portion of uncertain paper:
Some liken it to climbing up a hill,
    Whose summit, like all hills, is lost in vapour;
For this men write, speak, preach, and heroes kill,
    And bards burn what they call their 'midnight taper,'
To have, when the original is dust,
A name, a wretched picture, and worse bust.

CCXIX.

What are the hopes of man? old Egypt's King
    Cheops erected the first pyramid
And largest, thinking it was just the thing
    To keep his memory whole, and mummy hid;
But somebody or other rummaging,
    Burglariously broke his coffin's lid:
Let not a monument give you or me hopes,
Since not a pinch of dust remains of Cheops.

CCXX.

But I, being fond of true philosophy,
    Say very often to myself 'Alas!
All things that have been born were born to die,
    And flesh (which Death mows down to hay) is grass;
You've pass'd your youth not so unpleasantly,
    And if you had it o'er again—'twould pass—

1734 *'Time is, Time's past'* Spoken by the Brazen Head in Robert Greene, *Friar Bacon and Friar Bungay* (1594), xi, 59. According to popular legend, Roger Bacon fashioned a head from brass (complete with jaws, tongue, and teeth), which he then hoped to make speak with the aid of an herbal steam. When the head finally spoke – 'Time is; Time was; Time is past' – it immediately fell to the floor and shattered.

1734 *chymic* 'of or pertaining to alchemy'

1744 *worse bust* In Rome in the summer of 1817, Byron's friend Hobhouse commissioned a bust to be made of him by the Danish sculptor Thorwaldsen. Byron later remarked of it that '[t]he bust does not turn out a very good one – though it may be like for aught I know – as it exactly resembles a superannuated Jesuit' (*BLJ*, vol. 9, p. 213).

1746 *pyramid* See Byron's letter to Murray of 6 April 1819, in which he scornfully compares an epic poem to a pyramid: 'So you and Mr. Foscolo & c. want me to undertake what you call a "great work" an Epic poem I suppose or some such pyramid. – I'll try no such thing – I hate tasks . . .' (*BLJ*, vol. 6, p. 105).

1756 *And flesh . . . is grass* Compare Isaiah 40: 6, 'All flesh *is* grass, and all the goodliness thereof *is* as the flower of the field'.

So thank your stars that matters are no worse,
And read your Bible, sir, and mind your purse.' 1760

CCXXI.

But for the present, gentle reader! and
    Still gentler purchaser! the bard—that's I—
Must, with permission, shake you by the hand,
    And so your humble servant, and good bye!
We meet again, if we should understand 1765
    Each other; and if not, I shall not try
Your patience further than by this short sample—
'Twere well if others follow'd my example.

CCXXII.

'Go, little book, from this my solitude!
    I cast thee on the waters, go thy ways! 1770
And if, as I believe, thy vein be good,
    The world will find thee after many days.'
When Southey's read, and Wordsworth understood,
    I can't help putting in my claim to praise—
The four first rhymes are Southey's every line: 1775
For God's sake, reader! take them not for mine.

1768–9 *short sample . . . example* Another dig at the inordinate length of Wordsworth's *Excursion*; see 'Dedication', line 25 and note.

1769–72 *'Go . . . many days.'* The first four lines of the last stanza ('L'Envoy') of Southey's *Carmen Nuptiale – The Lay of the Laureate*.

1775–6 *line . . . mine.* The concluding rhyme of 'line' and 'mine' underscores that what is particularly Byron's in *Don Juan* is the brilliant exploitation of the form (in particular the manipulation of the narrative momentum of the *ottava rima* and its clinching couplet) to say whatever he likes about anything and everything. As he remarked to Moore after completing the first canto, *Don Juan* was 'meant to be a little quietly facetious upon every thing' (*BLJ*, vol. 6, p. 67) – here, again, on everything from Southey's rhymes to his own.

Percy Bysshe Shelley (1792–1822)

Percy Bysshe Shelley, born into the Sussex landed gentry, was expected, after education at Eton and Oxford, to follow his father into Parliament. In fact, he left Oxford in his first year, expelled for refusing to disavow co-authorship (with his friend, Thomas Jefferson Hogg) of *The Necessity of Atheism* (1811). The work, a short pamphlet, uses sceptical arguments from David Hume to repudiate belief in God, there being insufficient evidence, in the authors' view, for such belief. Finishing with a provocative 'Q. E. D' (*Quod Erat Demonstrandum* – 'which was to be demonstrated'), it was sent to heads of colleges and clerics. Indeed, pretending to be an elderly clergyman, 'Charles Meyton', Shelley sent a copy to one Rev. George S. Faber, a neighbour of the Hogg family, claiming to have been disturbed by the pamphlet's arguments.

The whole episode reveals both Shelley's capacity for mischievous irony and his passionate belief in the right to free speech. He had thrown down a gauntlet that challenged the entrenched interests of the Establishment of which he had been groomed by birth and education to be a member. For much of his subsequent life in England, which he finally left with Mary Shelley, his second wife, in 1818, Shelley wrote poetry and prose that showed his ardent hatred for war, tyranny and a Christian religion that, in his view, sanctioned social injustice and intellectual laziness. He quickly found support for his views in the writings of his second wife's father, William Godwin, author of *Enquiry Concerning Political Justice* (1793), whom Shelley met with his first wife, Harriet, in 1812. Shelley had married Harriet in 1811, supposedly liberating her from the tyranny of school and family; his attitude to women, at once idealizing and proto-feminist, contributes to the heady brew of ideas out of which his early work emerges. They include a Godwinian conviction that the untrammelled use of reason and enquiry would result in truth and right action, a trust in Necessity (virtually an optimistic belief that history would turn out as he desired it to), a fierce sense that the legacy of the French Revolution has been misunderstood by its erstwhile admirers who had grown fearful of its apparently violent consequences, dislike of a Christian God conceived (as Shelley saw the matter) in the image and likeness of a patriarchal earthly ruler, hatred of kings, adherence to vegetarianism and hostility to marriage as imposing shackles on freedom to love. In their most clear-cut form, most of these views can be found in *Queen Mab* (1813), a work which Shelley circulated privately but which, largely after his death, would become one of his best-known works, exercising huge and radicalizing influence. But they also recur in many later works.

However, central to Shelley's work is the idea of change, becoming and process. These forces, tracked by the emergent science of the day, were, for him, manifest in the physical world, as is shown by many passages of natural description in his poetry. The cloud which may 'change' but 'cannot die' ('The Cloud', l. 76) is virtually an image for Shelley's conviction in this respect. Yet transforming forces were at work, too, in the world of mind. Shelley himself undergoes much change in the course of his brief career, influenced greatly by his remarkable width and depth of reading. Possibly the major change is his view of art. In early works, there is a distinct whiff of propaganda. This has largely gone by the time of 'Alastor' (1816), the first of six poems we have included. 'Alastor', heavily influenced by and yet subtly responsive to Wordsworth, is among the first poems where Shelley's capacity for sustaining ambivalence in the midst of intense feeling is apparent. Its blank verse encourages sympathy for the figure of the Poet, even as there appear to be hints of criticism in the poem's Preface, especially its second paragraph. Wordsworth's view of nature as benign haunts the poem as an illusion that is pitilessly exposed. Human consciousness does not find an adequate fit for its conceptions in the natural world. In the two great shorter poems of 1816, 'Hymn to Intellectual Beauty' and 'Mont Blanc', Shelley returns to questions of nature's meaning and the role of 'the human mind's imaginings' ('Mont Blanc', l. 143). In the former poem, he posits a 'Power' (l. 1) which seems like a self-created deity, and addresses a hymn to it which freely appropriates and adapts to its own purposes the language of orthodox religious belief. 'God', it seems, was a question to which Shelley was continually drawn. His preference was for recognition of quasi-humanist 'visitations of the divinity in man' (p. 698), but the possibility of a transcendent 'Power' is present in the poem.[1] In 'Mont Blanc', also included in our selection, Shelley turns his attention to the relationship between the mind and the universe, and, particularly, to the dependence of an idea of ultimate purpose on the mind's capacity to imagine. Shelley's early scepticism had begun to unite with his idealistic hopes in ways that

---

1 Unless indicated otherwise, quotations from poems and prose not included in this work are taken from the Oxford Major Works, ed. Zachary Leader and Michael O'Neill (Oxford University Press, 2003).

proved to him the value of poetry. If reason was left, ultimately, with no answers, perhaps the imagination could provide them.

The 'Hymn' and 'Mont Blanc' were written in Switzerland, where Shelley had gone with Mary Godwin (having eloped with her in 1814, leaving Harriet, who killed herself in December 1816) and Mary's stepsister Claire Clairmont, who had had a brief affair with Byron, by whom she would have a child. Shelley met Byron in Geneva, a meeting of great significance for both men's future work. Byron imbibed some of Shelley's more Platonising and post-Wordsworthian ideas, as is evident from the third canto of *Childe Harold's Pilgrimage*. Shelley's poetry often engages in debate with Byronic irony and debunking. In *Julian and Maddalo* (completed in 1819), he dramatizes the difference between the two poets' views, and his capacity to enter into other minds is shown further in his tragic drama, *The Cenci* (published in 1819). Indeed, his great achievement, *Prometheus Unbound* (1820) manages to bear out his abhorrence of 'Didactic poetry' by relying on dramatic and imaginative means of communicating what in the work's Preface Shelley calls 'beautiful idealisms of moral excellence' (this edn., p. 352). It sustains a difficult optimism in the face of unyielding political realities: post-Waterloo arrangements seemed to Shelley and other liberals merely to restore or shore up corrupt and tyrannical governments. 'The Mask of Anarchy' demonstrates his outrage at the brutal response to a peaceful demonstration in favour of parliamentary reform in St Peter's Fields, Manchester; it also shows his capacity to use a great variety of forms, in this case a ballad imbued with Shelley's anger against the government which is memorably lampooned in the opening stanzas, but also infused with his desire to persuade the people to continue to protest peacefully, even as the poem warns those in government about the consequences of continued repression.

Many of Shelley's poems artfully use form to work on the imaginations of his audiences. Possibly his finest shorter poem, however, 'Ode to the West Wind' wishes that his words might be 'scattered ... among mankind' (ll. 66, 67), falling where they will. A full-blown poetics of the imagination is offered in *A Defence of Poetry*, in which Shelley argues that 'Poetry' differs fundamentally in its operation and effect from 'Ethical science'. 'Poetry', he contends, 'awakens and enlarges the mind itself by rendering it the receptacle of a thousand unapprehended combinations of thought' (p. 681). In much of his finest work, his poetry seeks to influence imaginatively 'the mind itself': 'Epipsychidion' (published in 1821) addresses the subject of love, a topic that finally outstrips the poem's 'winged words' (l. 588), by involving us in a proto-Symbolist poetic experience; *Adonais*, included here, his elegy for Keats, turns into a poem about the value of poetry itself, represented in images of fire and radiance; *Hellas* (published 1822), written in support of the Greeks in their War of Independence against Turkey, is much more than a piece of philhellenic propaganda since it views history from perspectives that question the reality of all but 'the One, / The unborn and the undying' (ll. 768–9), and ultimately confesses a weariness with 'the past' (l. 1100); and 'The Triumph of Life', unfinished at the poet's tragic death by drowning on 8 July 1822 as he returned across the Gulf of Spezia from meeting Leigh Hunt in Pisa, involves a radically imaginative exploration of poetic quest in relation to personal and historical disappointment. That Shelley should have written, among his last words, ' "what is Life?" I said' ('The Triumph of Life', l. 544), seems peculiarly appropriate for a poet who not only cherished high ideals but tested and questioned them in poetry of remarkable artistry and eloquence.

Further Reading

Primary Texts

Alastor ... and Other Poems (1816)
Prometheus Unbound ... with Other Poems (1820)
Adonais (1821)
The Complete Poetry of Percy Bysshe Shelley, ed. Donald H. Reiman and Neil Fraistat, 2 vols to date (Baltimore: Johns Hopkins University Press, 2000, 2004).
The Letters of Percy Bysshe Shelley, ed. Frederick L. Jones, 2 vols (Oxford: Oxford University Press, 1964); hereafter *SL*.
The Poems of Shelley, ed. Geoffrey Matthews and Kelvin Everest, 2 vols to date (London: Longman, 1989, 2000).
Shelley's Poetry and Prose, ed. Donald H. Reiman and Neil Fraistat (New York: Norton, 2002).
Percy Bysshe Shelley: The Major Works, ed. Zachary Leader and Michael O'Neill (Oxford: Oxford University Press, 2003).

Secondary Texts

Harold Bloom, *Shelley's Mythmaking* (New Haven, CT: Cornell University Press, 1959).
Timothy Clark, *Embodying Revolution: The Figure of the Poet in Shelley* (Oxford: Clarendon Press, 1989).
Richard Cronin, *Shelley's Poetic Thoughts* (Basingstoke, UK: Macmillan, 1981).
Stuart Curran, *Shelley's Annus Mirabilis: the Maturing of an Epic Vision* (San Marino, CA: Huntington Library, 1975).
William Keach, *Shelley's Style* (New York and London: Methuen, 1984).
Angela Leighton, *Shelley and the Sublime* (Cambridge, UK: Cambridge University Press, 1984).

Michael O'Neill, *The Human Mind's Imaginings: Conflict and Achievement in Shelley's Poetry* (Oxford: Clarendon Press, 1989).
Stuart M. Sperry, *Shelley's Major Verse* (Princeton, NJ: Princeton University Press, 1988).
Earl R. Wasserman, *Shelley: A Critical Reading* (Baltimore, MD: Johns Hopkins University Press, 1971).
Timothy Webb, *Shelley: A Voice Not Understood* (Manchester: Manchester University Press, 1977).
Susan J. Wolfson, *Formal Charges* (Stanford, CA: Stanford University Press, 1997).

Alastor; Or, The Spirit of Solitude

'Alastor', written in 1815 and published in 1816 as the title poem of a collection including 11 other shorter poems, makes a marked contrast with *Queen Mab*, Shelley's first significant longer poem. *Queen Mab* (1813), a poem in nine cantos, relies on direct and forceful rhetoric, and gives voice to Shelley's atheist and republican beliefs. Shelley's beliefs remained intransigently radical throughout his career; but his view of the function of poetry changes. Mary Shelley, in her 1839 Note on the poem, commented that '*Alastor* is written in a very different tone from *Queen Mab*', arguing that in the later poem Shelley was inclined 'rather to brood over the thoughts and emotions of his own soul than to glance abroad, and to make, as in *Queen Mab*, the whole universe the object and subject of his song' (*Shelley: Poetical Works*, ed. Thomas Hutchinson, revised G. M. Matthews [London: Oxford University Press, 1970], p. 30). The politics of the later poem are implicit and open to debate since in it Shelley turns his attention from the outward life of society to the inward life of the poet. Indeed, his later work often swings between works with their eye on social and public issues such as *Prometheus Unbound* and more personal poems such as *Adonais*, even though the two modes often interact.

'Alastor' is among the earliest and most important of Shelley's poems that transfer the burden of interpretation to the reader. The poem teems with interpretative riddles. These riddles begin with the title, which has left readers wondering whether 'Alastor' is the name of the main protagonist of the poem ('The Poet'), as many (including Yeats) have thought, or whether, as Shelley's friend Thomas Love Peacock, avers, it is a Greek-derived word for the 'evil spirit' of 'Solitude' (*The Works of Thomas Love Peacock*, ed. H. F. B. Brett-Smith and C. E. Jones, 10 vols [London: Constable, 1924–34], vol. 8. p. 100). They carry over into the Preface, the first paragraph of which seems sympathetic to the Poet, before the second paragraph appears to suggest that his 'self-centred seclusion' was justly 'avenged by the furies of an irresistible passion'. And they haunt the poem proper, which presents the Poet's fate from a vantage-point – the Narrator's – which is strongly in his favour, but which includes at least one moment (ll. 203–5) that reawakens the idea of just punishment. The Preface promises 'instruction', but the poem has prompted a range of opinions. Some see it as a critique of 'seclusion'; others, swayed by the evident admiration expressed for the Poet, regard Shelley as exploring an imaginative quest which he saw as dangerous, but also as essential to his creative being: a quest, possibly doomed, to find a female other who will correspond to the deepest desires of the male self. Influentially Earl R. Wasserman makes much of the poem's narrative structure, representing the Narrator as a Wordsworthian figure who laments the loss of a 'surpassing Spirit' (l. 714) and is brought to realize, by the events of the poem, the insufficiency of material nature in which, initially, he places his trust. On this reading, the Narrator is opposed to, yet has much in common with, the Poet or 'Visionary', as Wasserman calls him, who pursues 'a good beyond the limits of an inherently inadequate and negligible world'. The poem's contradictions are resolved by Wasserman through belief in *Alastor*'s use of 'purposeful ambiguity' (*Shelley: A Critical Reading*, pp. 39, 38). Arguably, Wasserman's reading is too 'purposeful', too intent on resolving all contradictions, but his emphasis on the poem's dialectical interplay is valuable.

As the quotation from *The Excursion* at the end of the Preface suggests, the poem works at close quarters with the example and words of Wordsworth. In its melodious blank verse 'Alastor' reflects Shelley's intent reading of Wordsworth, but its attitude to the older poet is far from uncritical homage. Indeed, Shelley's use of form and style often involves ideological sabotage; he employs a precursor's literary mode to bring to mind values and assumptions which his own poem will subvert. Shelley knew Wordsworth as the poet of *Lyrical Ballads*, *Poems, in Two Volumes* (1807), *Poems* (1815), and also *The Excursion* (1814), a poem whose conservatism troubled him, as is evident from his sonnet in the *Alastor* volume, 'To Wordsworth', which laments that the poet of *Lyrical Ballads* is effectively dead: 'thou leavest me to grieve', Shelley writes in that sonnet, 'Thus having been, that thou shouldst cease to be' (ll. 13–14). It is distinctly possible that, when he repeats Wordsworth's plangent words, 'The good die first, / And those whose hearts are dry as summer dust, / Burn to the socket' (Wordsworth has 'they' for 'those' and no comma after 'dust'), Shelley may be turning the older poet's lines against him. In Wordsworth's poem, the lines originally belonged to 'The Ruined Cottage', which was rewritten and incorporated in the first book of *The Excursion* (ll. 500–2); Shelley appears to have admired this book. But whereas 'The Ruined Cottage' concludes with an acceptance of the workings of nature, Shelley is, as Wasserman points out, of the opinion that 'Wordsworth has not set his sights high enough' (p. 20).

Wordsworth's conflicted but sympathetic rendering of the Solitary in *The Excursion* seems to have affected Shelley, to judge by a number of echoes in 'Alastor'. The Solitary is a dark double of Wordsworth. Like Wordsworth he welcomed the French Revolution; like Wordsworth he was disillusioned by its descent into bloodshed; but unlike Wordsworth he has found no 'Abundant recompence' (l. 89), as 'Tintern Abbey' has it, in love of nature. Shelley's poem reconsiders the question of 'solitude' raised by *The Excursion* (and by Wordsworth's earlier poem, 'Lines Left upon a Seat in a Yew-Tree', which presents a solitary's 'unfruitful life' (l. 29) with sympathy). That question connects in the poem to the younger poet's special fascination with quest. Certainly the poem derives much of its particular verbal colouring from its intertextual relations with Wordsworth, and from the driving momentum given to its blank verse by the theme of pursuit. The affinities between Narrator and Poet, too, imply a process of repetition as well as difference, as does the constant working and reworking of particular words (e.g. 'gaze', 'impulse', 'woven', 'suspended', 'vacant'). There may be a suggestion that the Narrator's idealizing view of the Poet is analogous with the Poet's idealizing view of the 'veiled maid' (l. 151). Long descriptive passages serve symbolic ends in ways that make the external a mirror of internal events and crises. The conclusion offers very little in the way of positive affirmation, which may explain the popularity of Marilyn Butler's reading of the poem as a 'rejection of the way of solitude for the poet' (*Romantics, Rebels and Reactionaries* [Oxford: Oxford University Press, 1981], p. 141) since this reading allows the poem to be squared with a robustly radical value-system. But whether the poem's experience is best interpreted in this manner is doubtful; much of its imaginative hold derives from its and our impulse to engage with the Poet's self-destroying desire.

'Alastor' relates to the events of Shelley's life in complex but discernible ways. It was written in 1815, the year after Shelley had left his first wife Harriet and eloped with Mary Godwin, whom he would eventually marry in 1816 following Harriet's suicide. Stuart Sperry suggests convincingly that the poem explores the question of 'idealization' central to Shelley's thinking about love and to his private life. In a letter written in August 1815, Shelley comes close to sketching what Sperry (*Shelley's Major Verse*, p. 25) calls 'the contradictory dialectics' of *Alastor*:

Yet who is there that will not pursue phantoms, spend his choicest hours in hunting after dreams, and wake only to perceive his error and regret that death is so near? One man there is, and he is a cold and calculating man, who knows better than to waste life, but who alas! cannot enjoy it.
(*SL*, vol. 1, pp. 429–30)

The alternatives suggested here resemble those offered by the second paragraph of the Preface, which distinguishes between 'luminaries of the world' (pursuers of phantoms) and 'Those . . . deluded by no generous error' (cold and calculating men).

The poem investigates the nature of what might be regarded as 'generous error'. Its imagery explores themes of narcissism, without passing adverse moral judgement; it is intrigued by the way the Poet pursues an ideal he has himself conceived, and it refers this pursuit to our uncertain hopes (for example) that 'death' may be a gateway to sleep's 'mysterious paradise' (l. 212). 'Alastor' uses questions at key moments, and it owes much of its power to its refusal to arrive at premature interpretative closure; it will not allow us, for instance, merely to dismiss the Poet's vision of the 'veiled maid' (l. 151) as auto-erotic, a glorified wet dream. Indeed, the poem, rather like the later essay 'On Love', may imply that narcissism is always involved in love, if one interprets narcissism as a falling in love with an idealized version of the self, or with an ideal based on the self's highest desires. In 'On Love', Shelley articulates the dynamics of love in this way: 'We dimly see within our intellectual nature a miniature as it were of our entire self, yet deprived of all that we condemn or despise, the ideal prototype of everything excellent or lovely that we are capable of conceiving as belonging to the nature of man' (p. 632). According to Shelley, we then seek for an 'antitype', a real person who corresponds to the 'ideal prototype' we have conceived. The search for this 'antitype', he adds with some pathos, is 'the invisible and unattainable point to which Love tends' (p. 632). This view of love as bound up with idealization haunts Shelley's work, though in *A Defence of Poetry* he tries to redefine love as a more other-centred process, 'a going out of our own nature, and an identification of ourselves with the beautiful which exists in thought, action or person, not our own' (p. 682).

PREFACE

The poem entitled 'ALASTOR,' may be considered as allegorical of one of the most interesting situations of the human mind. It represents a youth of uncorrupted feelings and adventurous genius led forth by an imagination inflamed and purified through familiarity with all that is excellent and majestic, to the contemplation of the universe. He drinks deep of the fountains of knowledge, and is still insatiate. The magnificence and beauty of the external world sinks profoundly into the frame of his conceptions, and affords to their modifications a variety not to be exhausted. So long as it is possible for his desires to point towards objects thus infinite and unmeasured, he is joyous, and tranquil, and self-possessed. But the period arrives when these objects cease to suffice. His mind is at length suddenly awakened and thirsts for intercourse with an intelligence similar to itself. He images to himself the Being whom he loves. Conversant with speculations of the sublimest and most perfect natures, the vision in which he embodies his own imaginations unites all of wonderful, or wise, or beautiful, which the poet, the philosopher, or the lover could depicture. The intellectual faculties, the imagination, the functions of sense, have their respective requisitions on the sympathy of corresponding powers in other human beings. The Poet is represented as uniting these requisitions, and attaching them to a single image. He seeks in vain for a prototype of his conception. Blasted by his disappointment, he descends to an untimely grave.

The picture is not barren of instruction to actual men. The Poet's self-centred seclusion was avenged by the furies of an irresistible passion pursuing him to speedy ruin. But that Power which strikes the luminaries of the world with sudden darkness and extinction, by awakening them to too exquisite a perception of its influences, dooms to a slow and poisonous decay those meaner spirits that dare to abjure its dominion. Their destiny is more abject and inglorious as their delinquency is more contemptible and pernicious. They who, deluded by no generous error, instigated by no sacred thirst of doubtful knowledge, duped by no illustrious superstition, loving nothing on this earth, and cherishing no hopes beyond, yet keep aloof from sympathies with their kind, rejoicing neither in human joy nor mourning with human grief; these, and such as they, have their apportioned curse. They languish, because none feel with them their common nature. They are morally dead. They are neither friends, nor lovers, nor fathers, nor citizens of the world, nor benefactors of their country. Among those who attempt to exist without human sympathy, the pure and tender-hearted perish through the intensity and passion of their search after its communities, when the vacancy of their spirit suddenly makes itself felt. All else, selfish, blind, and torpid, are those unfore seeing multitudes who constitute, together with their own, the lasting misery and loneliness of the world. Those who love not their fellow-beings, live unfruitful lives, and prepare for their old age a miserable grave.

> 'The good die first,
> And those whose hearts are dry as summer dust,
> Burn to the socket!'

December 14, 1815

Preface
allegorical That is, the poem's narrative serves as a means of giving external embodiment to 'one of the most interesting situations of the human mind'. 'Situations' may here have as part of its meaning, 'critical point or complication in drama'.
But . . . suffice This change is represented as inevitable.
Conversant . . . human beings The Poet seeks to find a single figure in whom his highest ideals of intellectual and imaginative achievement, and of physical beauty, will be discovered.
prototype 'An original . . . in relation to a copy'. Paradoxically, on this definition, the Poet's 'conception' is the 'copy'; he searches for the 'original', though whether he expects that 'original' to exist in this life is arguable.
actual men The phrase suggests Shelley's awareness of his poem's apparent remoteness from quotidian experience.
self-centred seclusion A key phrase that appears to involve moral criticism of the Poet. One notes, however, that in the next sentence he is surely among 'the luminaries of the world' (that is, among those who illuminate the world).
furies of an irresistible passion Recall the 'furies' of Classical tragedy, as in Aeschylus' *The Eumenides*.
But that Power . . . dominion This capitalized 'Power' gives a godlike status to a force which the reader may suppose is meant to be understood as working within human beings. Such a 'Power' can be aligned with Shelley's atheism, as stated in *The Necessity of Atheism* and elsewhere, but it may reveal his awareness of a 'God-shaped hole'; the word and the concept reappear in 'Hymn to Intellectual Beauty'.
They who . . . curse These figures do not appear in the poem, but they serve to define, by contrast, the value of the Poet's 'generous error'. There is a parallel between Shelley's paragraph and a famous passage in Burke's *Reflections on the Revolution in France* (1790) when, after lamenting that 'the age of chivalry is gone', Burke regrets sardonically that 'All the pleasing illusions, which made power gentle, and obedience liberal, . . . are to be dissolved by this new conquering empire of light and reason' (ed. Conor Cruise O'Brien, [Harmondsworth, UK: Penguin], 1969, pp. 170, 171). Shelley may be turning Burke's counter-revolutionary rhetoric to his own questing if enigmatic ends.
the vacancy of their spirit 'Vacancy' and 'vacant' are central terms in 'Alastor', 'Hymn to Intellectual Beauty' and 'Mont Blanc'; 'vacancy' is a state left by the vanishing of an ideal, a hope, possibly an error.

Nondum amabam, et amare amabam, quaerebam quid amarem, amans amare!
Confess. St. August.

Earth, ocean, air, beloved brotherhood!
If our great Mother has imbued my soul
With aught of natural piety to feel
Your love, and recompense the boon with mine;
If dewy morn, and odorous noon, and even, 5
With sunset and its gorgeous ministers,
And solemn midnight's tingling silentness;
If autumn's hollow sighs in the sere wood,
And winter robing with pure snow and crowns
Of starry ice the grey grass and bare boughs; 10
If spring's voluptuous pantings when she breathes
Her first sweet kisses, have been dear to me;
If no bright bird, insect, or gentle beast
I consciously have injured, but still loved
And cherished these my kindred; then forgive 15
This boast, beloved brethren, and withdraw
No portion of your wonted favour now!
  Mother of this unfathomabfe world!
Favour my solemn song, for I have loved
Thee ever, and thee only; I have watched 20
Thy shadow, and the darkness of thy steps,
And my heart ever gazes on the depth
Of thy deep mysteries. I have made my bed
In charnels and on coffins, where black death
Keeps record of the trophies won from thee, 25
Hoping to still these obstinate questionings
Of thee and thine, by forcing some lone ghost
Thy messenger, to render up the tale
Of what we are. In lone and silent hours,

Poem

Epigraph A favourite quotation of Shelley's, who had used it in an earlier unpublished collection, *The Esdaile Notebook*, and had written it in Claire Clairmont's 1814 journal, the epigraph comes from St Augustine's *Confessions* III. 1, and might be translated thus: 'I did not yet love, yet I was in love with loving; I sought what I might love, loving to love.' The bearing on the poem's quest for 'what I might love' is evident. At the same time, the epigraph points up the difference between Augustine, writing out of the knowledge that the appropriate object of love is God, and Shelley, exploring the proper object of love in what is effectively a post-Christian context.

1 *Earth ... brotherhood!* Appeals to three of the four elements; the missing element is fire. 'Fire' is associated (see l. 64) with the dead Poet.

3 *natural piety* One among a number of Wordsworthian echoes, the phrase recalls Wordsworth's 'My Heart Leaps Up' (published 1807), lines 8–9: 'And I could wish my days to be / Bound each to each by natural piety.'

13–15 *If ... kindred* The Narrator is a vegetarian, like the Poet (see l. 101) and like Shelley, who wrote *A Vindication of Natural Diet* (1813), in which he argues that 'On a natural system of diet [one that excluded all meat], old age would be our last and our only malady' (E. B. Murray, *The Prose Works of Percy Bysshe Shelley* [Oxford: Oxford University Press, 1993], p. 83; hereafter Murray).

18 *unfathomable world!* The phrase introduces a verse-paragraph that presents the Narrator as a quester after 'unfathomable' secrets and 'deep mysteries' (l. 23). His relationship with Nature is questioning, a point of affinity with the Poet.

23–9 *I have ... what we are* Shelley himself frequented churchyards as a youth in the hope of seeing a ghost.

26–7 *obstinate ... thine* Echoes Wordsworth's 'obstinate questionings / Of sense and outward things' in 'Ode: Intimations of Immortality', lines 141–2. But where Wordsworth retrospectively values these 'obstinate questionings' of childhood because they derive from a sense that 'The Soul that rises with us, our life's Star, / Hath had elsewhere its setting, / And cometh from afar' (ll. 59–61), Shelley's Narrator has no such ultimate assurance.

When night makes a weird sound of its own stillness, 30
Like an inspired and desperate alchymist
Staking his very life on some dark hope,
Have I mixed awful talk and asking looks
With my most innocent love, until strange tears
Uniting with those breathless kisses, made 35
Such magic as compels the charmed night
To render up thy charge: ... and, though ne'er yet
Thou hast unveil'd thy inmost sanctuary,
Enough from incommunicable dream,
And twilight phantasms, and deep noonday thought, 40
Has shone within me, that serenely now
And moveless, as a long-forgotten lyre
Suspended in the solitary dome
Of some mysterious and deserted fane,
I wait thy breath, Great Parent, that my strain 45
May modulate with murmurs of the air,
And motions of the forests and the sea,
And voice of living beings, and woven hymns
Of night and day, and the deep heart of man.

   There was a Poet whose untimely tomb 50
No human hands with pious reverence reared,
But the charmed eddies of autumnal winds
Built o'er his mouldering bones a pyramid
Of mouldering leaves in the waste wilderness:—
A lovely youth,—no mourning maiden decked 55
With weeping flowers, or votive cypress wreath,
The lone couch of his everlasting sleep:—
Gentle, and brave, and generous,—no lorn bard
Breathed o'er his dark fate one melodious sigh:
He lived, he died, he sung, in solitude. 60
Strangers have wept to hear his passionate notes,
And virgins, as unknown he passed, have pined
And wasted for fond love of his wild eyes.
The fire of those soft orbs has ceased to burn,
And Silence, too enamoured of that voice, 65
Locks its mute music in her rugged cell.
   By solemn vision, and bright silver dream,
His infancy was nurtured. Every sight
And sound from the vast earth and ambient air,
Sent to his heart its choicest impulses. 70
The fountains of divine philosophy
Fled not his thirsting lips, and all of great,
Or good, or lovely, which the sacred past

---

42 *long-forgotten lyre* In a manner that recalls Coleridge's 'The Eolian Harp', the Narrator compares himself to a 'lyre' or stringed musical instrument, awaiting Nature's 'breath' to inspire his 'strain' (l. 45). At the close of the poem, the image is recalled when the dead Poet is elegized as 'A fragile lute, on whose harmonious strings / The breath of heaven did wander' (ll. 667–8). It is possible to hear in the Narrator's plea for community a loneliness that anticipates that of the Poet.

44 *fane* Temple.

49 *the deep heart of man* Compare Wordsworth, 'Tintern Abbey', 'the mind of man' (l. 99).

67–8 *By ... nurtured* Compare the account of the Wanderer's upbringing in *The Excursion*, I, ll. 301–2: 'In dreams, in study, and in ardent thought, / Thus was he reared'.

71 *divine philosophy* Compare Milton, *Comus*, line 476: 'How charming is divine Philosophy!'

In truth or fable consecrates, he felt
And knew. When early youth had past, he left 75
His cold fireside and alienated home
To seek strange truths in undiscovered lands.
Many a wide waste and tangled wilderness
Has lured his fearless steps; and he has bought
With his sweet voice and eyes, from savage men, 80
His rest and food. Nature's most secret steps
He like her shadow has pursued, where'er
The red volcano overcanopies
Its fields of snow and pinnacles of ice
With burning smoke, or where bitumen lakes 85
On black bare pointed islets ever beat
With sluggish surge, or where the secret caves
Rugged and dark, winding among the springs
Of fire and poison, inaccessible
To avarice or pride, their starry domes 90
Of diamond and of gold expand above
Numberless and immeasurable halls,
Frequent with crystal column, and clear shrines
Of pearl, and thrones radiant with chrysolite.
Nor had that scene of ampler majesty 95
Than gems or gold, the varying roof of heaven
And the green earth lost in his heart its claims
To love and wonder; he would linger long
In lonesome vales, making the wild his home,
Until the doves and squirrels would partake 100
From his innocuous hand his bloodless food,
Lured by the gentle meaning of his looks,
And the wild antelope, that starts whene'er
The dry leaf rustles in the brake, suspend
Her timid steps to gaze upon a form 105
More graceful than her own.
                            His wandering step
Obedient to high thoughts, has visited
The awful ruins of the days of old:

76 *alienated home* One of the glancingly biographical suggestions that lend poignancy to the poem: Shelley quarrelled with his father after being expelled from Oxford and marrying Harriet Westbrook; he was thereafter (about January 1812) 'alienated' from his 'home'.
81–2 *Nature's . . . pursued* Recalls the Narrator's attempt to track Nature.
85 *bitumen lakes* Lakes of mineral pitch, associated with volcanic activity. There is probably an echo of Southey's epic poem *Thalaba* (much admired by Shelley) 'The black bitumen roll'd' (5. 22. 12).
89–90 *inaccessible . . . pride* Beyond the reach of those who are greedy for wealth ('avarice') or those who would use such stores 'Of diamond and of gold' (l. 91) for costly show ('the proud').
94 *chrysolite* A precious stone, a variety of olivine, a magnesium iron silicate mineral.
108 *awful . . . old* 'Awful' means 'awe-inspiring'; visiting ruins is, for Shelley, not merely a tourist occupation. In the wake of Volney's radical *Ruins of Empire* (1791), avidly read by Shelley (and a foundational text for the Creature in Mary Shelley's 1818 *Frankenstein*), ruins served to exemplify the time-bound, limited validity of all cultures and creeds. The Poet's 'high thoughts' (l. 107) would include reflections on the mutability of the ancient Greek and Persian empires, of which 'Athens, and Tyre, and Balbec' (l. 109) were, respectively, representative cities.

Athens, and Tyre, and Balbec, and the waste
Where stood Jerusalem, the fallen towers 110
Of Babylon, the eternal pyramids,
Memphis and Thebes, and whatsoe'er of strange
Sculptured on alabaster obelisk,
Or jasper tomb, or mutilated sphynx,
Dark Æthiopia in her desert hills 115
Conceals. Among the ruined temples there,
Stupendous columns, and wild images
Of more than man, where marble daemons watch
The Zodiac's brazen mystery, and dead men
Hang their mute thoughts on the mute walls around, 120
He lingered, poring on memorials
Of the world's youth, through the long burning day
Gazed on those speechless shapes, nor, when the moon
Filled the mysterious halls with floating shades
Suspended he that task, but ever gazed 125
And gazed, till meaning on his vacant mind
Flashed like strong inspiration, and he saw
The thrilling secrets of the birth of time.
    Meanwhile an Arab maiden brought his food,
Her daily portion, from her father's tent, 130
And spread her matting for his couch, and stole
From duties and repose to tend his steps:—
Enamoured, yet not daring for deep awe
To speak her love:—and watched his nightly sleep,
Sleepless herself, to gaze upon his lips 135
Parted in slumber, whence the regular breath
Of innocent dreams arose: then, when red morn
Made paler the pale moon, to her cold home
Wildered, and wan, and panting, she returned.

109–110 *the waste ... Jerusalem* Jerusalem was destroyed in 70 CE by the Roman Emperor Titus.
110–111 *the fallen ... Babylon* Babylon, in what is now southern Iraq, was one of the great cities of the ancient world, containing the hanging gardens, one of that world's seven wonders.
112 *Memphis and Thebes* Cities in Egypt.
112 *whatsoe'er of strange* This genitive usage is a stylistic feature of the poem: compare lines 72–3 and 480–3. It enacts the wish to gather up all that is available before the poetry finds that all which is so gathered up is wanting in some way.
115 *Dark Æthiopia* The ancient name Æthiopia was used either as a general name for Africa or for a specific territory south of Egypt.
118 *daemons* Spirits; in Plato daemons move between human beings and the gods. so in Shelley's translation of Plato's *Symposium* (1818), Diotima tells Socrates that 'Love' is 'A great Daemon ... and every thing daemoniacal hold[s] an intermediate place between what is divine and what is mortal' (James A. Notopoulos, *The Platonism of Shelley* [Durham, NC: Duke University Press, 1949], pp. 441–2).

119 *The Zodiac's brazen mystery* The Zodiac in the temple of Isis at Dendera in Egypt.
125 *gazed* A word that gathers in power (it has been used at ll. 22 and 105), implying here a deeply meditative act of attention.
126–7 *till ... Flashed* The Poet's mind is 'vacant' in the sense of being receptive; his experience of illumination recalls Wordsworth's in 'I wandered lonely as a cloud' (ll. 19–22): 'For oft, when on my couch I lie / In vacant or in pensive mood, / They flash upon that inward eye / Which is the bliss of solitude'. Shelley's poem goes on to explore the way 'the bliss of solitude' turns into its opposite.
128 *the birth of time* The Poet's voyage has involved a quest for cultural origins.
129 *an Arab maiden* A brief but crucial presence in the poem, the Arab maiden brings into the poem the theme of repressed love and sexuality. We are told nothing in this paragraph about the Poet's response (or non-response) to her.
136–9 *whence ... returned* Shelley's control of sounds (including repetitions in 'then, when red' and 'Made paler the pale', and the alliteration of 'w', especially in the stress-reversed 'Wildered') quickens our awareness of the Arab maiden's emotional state.

The Poet wandering on, through Arabie 140
And Persia, and the wild Carmanian waste,
And o'er the aerial mountains which pour down
Indus and Oxus from their icy caves,
In joy and exultation held his way;
Till in the vale of Cashmire, far within 145
Its loneliest dell, where odorous plants entwine
Beneath the hollow rocks a natural bower,
Beside a sparkling rivulet he stretched
His languid limbs. A vision on his sleep
There came, a dream of hopes that never yet 150
Had flushed his cheek. He dreamed a veiled maid
Sate near him, talking in low solemn tones.
Her voice was like the voice of his own soul
Heard in the calm of thought; its music long,
Like woven sounds of streams and breezes, held 155
His inmost sense suspended in its web
Of many-coloured woof and shifting hues.
Knowledge and truth and virtue were her theme,
And lofty hopes of divine liberty,
Thoughts the most dear to him, and poesy, 160
Herself a poet. Soon the solemn mood
Of her pure mind kindled through all her frame
A permeating fire: wild numbers then
She raised, with voice stifled in tremulous sobs
Subdued by its own pathos: her fair hands 165
Were bare alone, sweeping from some strange harp
Strange symphony, and in their branching veins
The eloquent blood told an ineffable tale.
The beating of her heart was heard to fill
The pauses of her music, and her breath 170
Tumultuously accorded with those fits
Of intermitted song. Sudden she rose,
As if her heart impatiently endured
Its bursting burthen: at the sound he turned,

140–45 *The Poet . . . Cashmire* A fascinating example of Romantic geography that involves an 'Orientalist' sense of the exotic appeal of the East. Yet the East is not just exotically different for Shelley; it is also a version of a fallen Paradise, the only snake in which is the Poet's own unfulfilled longings. The Poet travels eastwards through Arabia, Persia, the Desert of Karmin (now in the southeast of Iran); and then across 'aerial mountains' (the Hindu Kush mountains, the Indian Caucasus of *Prometheus Unbound*) from which the rivers Indus and Oxus begin, before he reaches the vale of Kashmir in northern India. His account of the vale of Kashmir owes debts to a novel by Sydney Owenson, *The Missionary: An Indian Tale* (1811).
149–91 *A vision . . . vacant brain* The Poet's dream of 'a veiled maid' is beyond his conscious agency ('A vision on his sleep / There came'), and even in the erotic climax he seems passive; it is the maid who 'Folded his frame in her dissolving arms' (l. 187). The phrase 'dissolving arms' illustrates Shelley's subtlety in the passage: the arms might be 'dissolving' the Poet; they might also themselves be vanishing. From one – especially a post-Freudian – perspective, the maid is the product of repression. From another perspective, she intimates the possibility that the poet's ideal exists – somewhere. Shelley frames these implicit alternatives with great skill in, say, line 153, 'Her voice was like the voice of his own soul', where 'like' brings together and holds apart Poet and maid. Again, in line 175 the writing is attuned to the Poet's belief that the maid's 'limbs' have their 'own life'.
155 *woven sounds* Compare the Narrator's 'woven hymns' at line 48. At lines 176–7 we encounter the maid's 'sinuous veil / Of woven wind'. Without the 'woven', there would be no medium for composing poetry or seeing visions, yet Poet and Narrator seek, in their different ways, to get beyond 'the woven'.
156 *His inmost sense suspended* 'Suspended' is a word whose sense ramifies. The poem 'Alastor' holds feelings 'suspended' in its own 'web' of sounds and suggestions. After the (imagined) love-making, sleep's 'flood', no longer 'suspended' (l. 190), flows back over the Poet's brain.

And saw by the warm light of their own life 175
Her glowing limbs beneath the sinuous veil
Of woven wind, her outspread arms now bare,
Her dark locks floating in the breath of night,
Her beamy bending eyes, her parted lips
Outstretched, and pale, and quivering eagerly. 180
His strong heart sunk and sickened with excess
Of love. He reared his shuddering limbs and quelled
His gasping breath, and spread his arms to meet
Her panting bosom: . . . she drew back a while,
Then, yielding to the irresistible joy, 185
With frantic gesture and short breathless cry
Folded his frame in her dissolving arms.
Now blackness veiled his dizzy eyes, and night
Involved and swallowed up the vision; sleep,
Like a dark flood suspended in its course, 190
Rolled back its impulse on his vacant brain.
    Roused by the shock he started from his trance—
The cold white light of morning, the blue moon
Low in the west, the clear and garish hills,
The distinct valley and the vacant woods, 195
Spread round him where he stood. Whither have fled
The hues of heaven that canopied his bower
Of yesternight? The sounds that soothed his sleep,
The mystery and the majesty of Earth,
The joy, the exultation? His wan eyes 200
Gaze on the empty scene as vacantly
As ocean's moon looks on the moon in heaven.
The spirit of sweet human love has sent
A vision to the sleep of him who spurned
Her choicest gifts. He eagerly pursues 205
Beyond the realms of dream that fleeting shade;
He overleaps the bounds. Alas! alas!
Were limbs, and breath, and being intertwined
Thus treacherously? Lost, lost, forever lost,
In the wide pathless desart of dim sleep, 210
That beautiful shape! Does the dark gate of death
Conduct to thy mysterious paradise,
O Sleep? Does the bright arch of rainbow clouds,
And pendent mountains seen in the calm lake,
Lead only to a black and watery depth, 215
While death's blue vault, with loathliest vapours hung,

---

185 *irresistible joy* Ironic in the wake of the Preface's reference to 'the furies of an irresistible passion'.
188 *veiled* This verb confirms the end of apparent revelation.
191 *vacant brain* This state of 'vacancy' differs from the state of joyous receptivity implied by 'vacant mind' at line 126; now, the Poet's brain is a site of absence.
195 *The . . . woods* The two adjectives establish a clarity that speaks eloquently about the post-vision state of loss.
196–8 *Whither . . . yesternight?* Compare Wordsworth, 'Ode: Intimations of Immortality', 'Whither is fled, the visionary gleam?' (l. 56).
200–2 *His wan . . . heaven* Lines that reveal how Shelley's poetry in 'Alastor' employs cunning images of reflection (in this case, the comparison has the Poet looking at the external world the way that the moon's reflection looks at the real moon, as though the Poet is now an emptied-out copy); again, the word 'Gaze' is used, this time to imply blank bewilderment.
203–5 *The spirit . . . gifts* The central lines for an interpretation that sees the Poet as punished for spurning 'human love'.
207 *He . . . bounds* Compare Satan in *Paradise Lost* (4.181–2), who 'At one slight bound high overleaped all bound / Of hill or highest wall'. The poetry, too, overleaps the bounds of the ostensible story and begins to ask ultimate existential questions.

Where every shade which the foul grave exhales
Hides its dead eye from the detested day,
Conduct, O Sleep, to thy delightful realms?
This doubt with sudden tide flowed on his heart,   220
The insatiate hope which it awakened, stung
His brain even like despair.
                  While day-light held
The sky, the Poet kept mute conference
With his still soul. At night the passion came,
Like the fierce fiend of a distempered dream,   225
And shook him from his rest, and led him forth
Into the darkness.—As an eagle grasped
In folds of the green serpent, feels her breast
Burn with the poison, and precipitates
Through night and day, tempest, and calm, and cloud,   230
Frantic with dizzying anguish, her blind flight
O'er the wide aëry wilderness: thus driven
By the bright shadow of that lovely dream,
Beneath the cold glare of the desolate night,
Through tangled swamps and deep precipitous dells,   235
Startling with careless step the moon-light snake,
He fled. Red morning dawned upon his flight,
Shedding the mockery of its vital hues
Upon his cheek of death. He wandered on
Till vast Aornos seen from Petra's steep   240
Hung o'er the low horizon like a cloud;
Through Balk, and where the desolated tombs
Of Parthian kings scatter to every wind
Their wasting dust, wildly he wandered on,
Day after day, a weary waste of hours,   245
Bearing within his life the brooding care
That ever fed on its decaying flame.
And now his limbs were lean; his scattered hair
Sered by the autumn of strange suffering
Sung dirges in the wind; his listless hand   250
Hung like dead bone within its withered skin;
Life, and the lustre that consumed it, shone
As in a furnace burning secretly
From his dark eyes alone. The cottagers,
Who ministered with human charity   255
His human wants, beheld with wondering awe
Their fleeting visitant. The mountaineer,
Encountering on some dizzy precipice
That spectral form, deemed that the Spirit of wind
With lightning eyes, and eager breath, and feet   260
Disturbing not the drifted snow, had paused

221–2 *The . . . despair* The nearness of 'hope' and 'despair' in the Poet's mind suggests the emotionally complex nature of the poem.

240 *vast . . . steep* Probably derives from Quintius Curtius's *History of Alexander*: 'Aornos' means 'birdless' and was a fortress stormed by Alexander; and was a fortress in India stormed by Alexander; there is no Petra known in the region, though Quintius Curtius refers to a 'petra', or rock. Following Alexander's footsteps, the Poet is at war only with himself.

242 *Balk* In Afghanistan.
243 *Parthian kings* Parthia lay east of Tehran in modern Iran.
245–54 *Day . . . alone* An emotional intensification occurs here, as the focus falls directly on the Poet's 'strange suffering'; the lines are marked by strong alliteration and repetition (see especially how 'waste' (l. 245) echoes 'wasting' (l. 244)), and earn their keep by emerging from and returning to the larger narrative.

In its career: the infant would conceal
His troubled visage in his mother's robe
In terror at the glare of those wild eyes,
To remember their strange light in many a dream 265
Of after-times; but youthful maidens, taught
By nature, would interpret half the woe
That wasted him, would call him with false names
Brother, and friend, would press his pallid hand
At parting, and watch, dim through tears, the path 270
Of his departure from their father's door.
    At length upon the lone Chorasmian shore
He paused, a wide and melancholy waste
Of putrid marshes. A strong impulse urged
His steps to the seashore. A swan was there, 275
Beside a sluggish stream among the reeds.
It rose as he approached, and with strong wings
Scaling the upward sky, bent its bright course
High over the immeasurable main.
His eyes pursued its flight.—'Thou hast a home, 280
Beautiful bird; thou voyagest to thine home,
Where thy sweet mate will twine her downy neck
With thine, and welcome thy return with eyes
Bright in the lustre of their own fond joy.
And what am I that I should linger here, 285
With voice far sweeter than thy dying notes,
Spirit more vast than thine, frame more attuned
To beauty, wasting these surpassing powers
In the deaf air, to the blind earth, and heaven
That echoes not my thoughts?' A gloomy smile 290
Of desperate hope wrinkled his quivering lips.
For sleep, he knew, kept most relentlessly
Its precious charge, and silent death exposed,
Faithless perhaps as sleep, a shadowy lure,
With doubtful smile mocking its own strange charms. 295
    Startled by his own thoughts he looked around.
There was no fair fiend near him, not a sight
Or sound of awe but in his own deep mind.
A little shallop floating near the shore
Caught the impatient wandering of his gaze. 300
It had been long abandoned, for its sides
Gaped wide with many a rift, and its frail joints
Swayed with the undulations of the tide.
A restless impulse urged him to embark
And meet lone Death on the drear ocean's waste; 305
For well he knew that mighty Shadow loves
The slimy caverns of the populous deep.
    The day was fair and sunny, sea and sky
Drank its inspiring radiance, and the wind

---

272 *Chorasmian shore* The eastern shore of the Caspian sea. The poet now diverges from Alexander's itinerary.
288 *wasting ... powers* Anticipates the Narrator's praise of the Poet as a 'surpassing Spirit' (l. 714), but the Poet is being less boastful about himself than using himself as a representative of human capacity. For all the Poet's love of nature, it is clear that he sees a disjunction between the human and the 'deaf air' (l. 289).
296 *Startled ... thoughts* Shelley internalizes the poem's action.
299 *shallop* Light open boat for shallow water.
304 *A restless impulse* Compare the 'strong impulse' at lines 274 and 415. The Poet is represented as driven, but as driven by internal impulses.

Swept strongly from the shore, blackening the waves. 310
Following his eager soul, the wanderer
Leaped in the boat, he spread his cloak aloft
On the bare mast, and took his lonely seat,
And felt the boat speed o'er the tranquil sea
Like a torn cloud before the hurricane. 315
    As one that in a silver vision floats
Obedient to the sweep of odorous winds
Upon resplendent clouds, so rapidly
Along the dark and ruffled waters fled
The straining boat.—A whirlwind swept it on, 320
With fierce gusts and precipitating force,
Through the white ridges of the chafed sea.
The waves arose. Higher and higher still
Their fierce necks writhed beneath the tempest's scourge
Like serpents struggling in a vulture's grasp. 325
Calm and rejoicing in the fearful war
Of wave ruining on wave, and blast on blast
Descending, and black flood on whirlpool driven
With dark obliterating course, he sate:
As if their genii were the ministers 330
Appointed to conduct him to the light
Of those beloved eyes, the Poet sate
Holding the steady helm. Evening came on,
The beams of sunset hung their rainbow hues
High mid the shifting domes of sheeted spray 335
That canopied his path o'er the waste deep;
Twilight, ascending slowly from the east,
Entwin'd in duskier wreaths her braided locks
O'er the fair front and radiant eyes of day;
Night followed, clad with stars. On every side 340
More horribly the multitudinous streams
Of ocean's mountainous waste to mutual war
Rushed in dark tumult thundering, as to mock
The calm and spangled sky. The little boat
Still fled before the storm; still fled, like foam 345
Down the steep cataract of a wintry river;
Now pausing on the edge of the riven wave;
Now leaving far behind the bursting mass
That fell, convulsing ocean. Safely fled—
As if that frail and wasted human form 350
Had been an elemental god.
                              At midnight

316–570 *As one . . . passing winds* The central section of the poem consists of the Poet's boat voyage. Voyages in boats are recurrent in Shelley's poetry, symbolic of spiritual quest. In this long section Shelley remodels the conventions of the loco-descriptive or picturesque poem. After the boat has been swept upriver into a cavern that is associated with natural beauty (it is 'Nature's dearest haunt', l. 429), a beauty the Poet finds insufficient, he seems to encounter 'A Spirit' (l. 479), possibly the 'veiled maid', possibly a projection of his mind. Then, following a speech in which he asserts that the stream 'imagest my life' (l. 505), he embarks on a journey downstream that mimics the passage from youth to age and hints at the 'immeasurable void' (l. 569) that lies in wait for life; descending, he takes refuge in a 'silent nook' (l. 572) where he dies, consoled by the nature that has failed to match his desires.

327 *ruining* A Miltonic Latinism, meaning 'falling in disorder'.

350–1 *As if . . . god* The lines bring the paragraph to a climax, effectively moving the Poet to centre-stage as they revise the Solitary's wish in *The Excursion* (4, ll. 509, 512–13), 'To have a body . . . / And to the elements surrender it / As if it were a spirit!' By this stage the poet's 'wasted . . . form' is proof of his self-destructive yet heroic pursuit of an ideal.

The moon arose: and lo! the etherial cliffs
Of Caucasus, whose icy summits shone
Among the stars like sunlight, and around
Whose cavern'd base the whirlpools and the waves   355
Bursting and eddying irresistibly
Rage and resound for ever.—Who shall save?—
The boat fled on,—the boiling torrent drove,—
The crags closed round with black and jagged arms,
The shattered mountain overhung the sea,   360
And faster still, beyond all human speed,
Suspended on the sweep of the smooth wave,
The little boat was driven. A cavern there
Yawned, and amid its slant and winding depths
Engulfed the rushing sea. The boat fled on   365
With unrelaxing speed.—'Vision and Love!'
The Poet cried aloud, 'I have beheld
The path of thy departure. Sleep and death
Shall not divide us long!'
                The boat pursued
The windings of the cavern. Day-light shone   370
At length upon that gloomy river's flow;
Now, where the fiercest war among the waves
Is calm, on the unfathomable stream
The boat moved slowly. Where the mountain, riven,
Exposed those black depths to the azure sky,   375
Ere yet the flood's enormous volume fell
Even to the base of Caucasus, with sound
That shook the everlasting rocks, the mass
Filled with one whirlpool all that ample chasm;
Stair above stair the eddying waters rose,   380
Circling immeasurably fast, and laved
With alternating dash the gnarled roots
Of mighty trees, that stretched their giant arms
In darkness over it. I' the midst was left,
Reflecting, yet distorting every cloud,   385
A pool of treacherous and tremendous calm.
Seized by the sway of the ascending stream,
With dizzy swiftness, round, and round, and round,
Ridge after ridge the straining boat arose,
Till on the verge of the extremest curve,   390
Where, through an opening of the rocky bank,
The waters overflow, and a smooth spot
Of glassy quiet mid those battling tides
Is left, the boat paused shuddering.—Shall it sink
Down the abyss? Shall the reverting stress   395
Of that resistless gulf embosom it?
Now shall it fall?—A wandering stream of wind,
Breathed from the west, has caught the expanded sail,
And, lo! with gentle motion, between banks
Of mossy slope, and on a placid stream,   400
Beneath a woven grove it sails, and, hark!

367–9 *The Poet . . . long!* Summarizes the Poet's understanding of his situation; for him, 'Vision and Love' (l. 366) lie the other side of 'Sleep and death'. (He is no longer concerned whether death leads to sleep.)

373 *the unfathomable stream* Compare the powerful close of *The Excursion*, book 3, where the Solitary imagines the 'stream' of 'human Life' heading towards 'The unfathomable gulf, where all is still!' (ll. 986, 987, 991).

The ghastly torrent mingles its far roar
With the breeze murmuring in the musical woods.
Where the embowering trees recede, and leave
A little space of green expanse, the cove 405
Is closed by meeting banks, whose yellow flowers
For ever gaze on their own drooping eyes,
Reflected in the crystal calm. The wave
Of the boat's motion marred their pensive task,
Which nought but vagrant bird, or wanton wind, 410
Or falling spear-grass, or their own decay
Had e'er disturbed before. The Poet longed
To deck with their bright hues his withered hair,
But on his heart its solitude returned,
And he forbore. Not the strong impulse hid 415
In those flushed cheeks, bent eyes, and shadowy frame,
Had yet performed its ministry: it hung
Upon his life, as lightning in a cloud
Gleams, hovering ere it vanish, ere the floods
Of night close over it. 420
            The noonday sun
Now shone upon the forest, one vast mass
Of mingling shade, whose brown magnificence
A narrow vale embosoms. There, huge caves,
Scooped in the dark base of their aery rocks
Mocking its moans, respond and roar forever. 425
The meeting boughs and implicated leaves
Wove twilight o'er the Poet's path, as led
By love, or dream, or god, or mightier Death,
He sought in Nature's dearest haunt, some bank,
Her cradle, and his sepulchre. More dark 430
And dark the shades accumulate. The oak,
Expanding its immense and knotty arms,
Embraces the light beech. The pyramids
Of the tall cedar overarching, frame
Most solemn domes within, and far below, 435
Like clouds suspended in an emerald sky,
The ash and the acacia floating hang
Tremulous and pale. Like restless serpents, clothed
In rainbow and in fire, the parasites,
Starred with ten thousand blossoms, flow around 440
The grey trunks, and, as gamesome infants' eyes,
With gentle meanings, and most innocent wiles,
Fold their beams round the hearts of those that love,
These twine their tendrils with the wedded boughs
Uniting their close union; the woven leaves 445
Make net-work of the dark blue light of day,
And the night's noontide clearness, mutable
As shapes in the weird clouds. Soft mossy lawns
Beneath these canopies extend their swells,

406 *yellow flowers* Narcissi. The Poet does not pick them (see l. 415) because, though they too are engaged in contemplating their reflection, they are at one with their surroundings as he is not.

417 *performed its ministry* Compare Coleridge, 'Frost at Midnight', line 1: 'The Frost performs its secret ministry'. Echo points up difference since, in Coleridge's poem, the Frost's 'ministry' will prove to be evidence of an ultimate harmony between God, human beings and nature.

430 *Her cradle, and his sepulchre* The cove is Nature's 'cradle' – hence the imagery of 'embosoming', l. 423) and of 'gamesome infants' eyes' (441) – but the Poet is cut off from the 'close union' (445) evident in the natural world.

Fragrant with perfumed herbs, and eyed with blooms 450
Minute yet beautiful. One darkest glen
Sends from its woods of musk-rose, twined with jasmine,
A soul-dissolving odour, to invite
To some more lovely mystery. Through the dell,
Silence and Twilight here, twin-sisters, keep 455
Their noonday watch, and sail among the shades,
Like vaporous shapes half seen; beyond, a well,
Dark, gleaming, and of most translucent wave,
Images all the woven boughs above,
And each depending leaf, and every speck 460
Of azure sky, darting between their chasms;
Nor aught else in the liquid mirror laves
Its portraiture, but some inconstant star
Between one foliaged lattice twinkling fair,
Or painted bird, sleeping beneath the moon, 465
Or gorgeous insect floating motionless,
Unconscious of the day, ere yet his wings
Have spread their glories to the gaze of noon.
    Hither the Poet came. His eyes beheld
Their own wan light through the reflected lines 470
Of his thin hair, distinct in the dark depth
Of that still fountain; as the human heart,
Gazing in dreams over the gloomy grave,
Sees its own treacherous likeness there. He heard
The motion of the leaves, the grass that sprung 475
Startled and glanced and trembled even to feel
An unaccustomed presence, and the sound
Of the sweet brook that from the secret springs
Of that dark fountain rose. A Spirit seemed
To stand beside him—clothed in no bright robes 480
Of shadowy silver or enshrining light,
Borrowed from aught the visible world affords
Of grace, or majesty, or mystery;—
But, undulating woods, and silent well,
And leaping rivulet, and evening gloom 485
Now deepening the dark shades, for speech assuming
Held commune with him, as if he and it
Were all that was,—only . . . when his regard
Was raised by intense pensiveness, . . . two eyes,
Two starry eyes, hung in the gloom of thought, 490
And seemed with their serene and azure smiles
To beckon him.
            Obedient to the light
That shone within his soul, he went, pursuing

469–92 *Hither . . . to beckon him* A reprise of earlier encounters and images of reflection. Like Narcissus, the Poet beholds himself as he stares into a well. He also senses a 'Spirit' who is not associated with 'aught the visible world affords' (l. 482). The verse is attuned to the Poet's processes of consciousness and surmise, as when the syntax breaks down in line 488 with the emergence of a new possibility.
486 *for speech assuming* Shelley's syntax is expressively tortuous; the Poet senses that the Spirit assumes 'for speech', that is, as a way of communicating with him, the 'undulating woods' (l. 484) and so on, even as it holds aloof from the natural scene.
489–90 *two . . . thought* The intense effort of communing with the Spirit results in the apparition of 'eyes', 'hung in the gloom of thought', where 'gloom of thought' is balanced ambiguously between outer and inner.
492–3 *Obedient . . . soul* The poet obeys his own will, at once driven and an agent.

The windings of the dell.—The rivulet
Wanton and wild, through many a green ravine 495
Beneath the forest flowed. Sometimes it fell
Among the moss with hollow harmony
Dark and profound. Now on the polished stones
It danced; like childhood laughing as it went:
Then, through the plain in tranquil wanderings crept, 500
Reflecting every herb and drooping bud
That overhung its quietness.—'O stream!
Whose source is inaccessibly profound,
Whither do thy mysterious waters tend?
Thou imagest my life. Thy darksome stillness, 505
Thy dazzling waves, thy loud and hollow gulphs,
Thy searchless fountain, and invisible course
Have each their type in me: and the wide sky,
And measureless ocean may declare as soon
What oozy cavern or what wandering cloud 510
Contains thy waters, as the universe
Tell where these living thoughts reside, when stretched
Upon thy flowers my bloodless limbs shall waste
I' the passing wind!'
                Beside the grassy shore
Of the small stream he went; he did impress 515
On the green moss his tremulous step, that caught
Strong shuddering from his burning limbs. As one
Roused by some joyous madness from the couch
Of fever, he did move; yet, not like him,
Forgetful of the grave, where, when the flame 520
Of his frail exultation shall be spent,
He must descend. With rapid steps he went
Beneath the shade of trees, beside the flow
Of the wild babbling rivulet, and now
The forest's solemn canopies were changed 525
For the uniform and lightsome evening sky.
Grey rocks did peep from the spare moss, and stemmed
The struggling brook: tall spires of windlestrae
Threw their thin shadows down the rugged slope,
And nought but gnarled roots of ancient pines 530
Branchless and blasted, clenched with grasping roots
The unwilling soil. A gradual change was here,
Yet ghastly. For, as fast years flow away,
The smooth brow gathers, and the hair grows thin
And white, and where irradiate dewy eyes 535
Had shone, gleam stony orbs:—so from his steps
Bright flowers departed, and the beautiful shade
Of the green groves, with all their odorous winds
And musical motions. Calm, he still pursued
The stream, that with a larger volume now 540
Rolled through the labyrinthine dell; and there
Fretted a path through its descending curves

503–4 *Whose . . . tend?* The idea of life as having an unknown source and destination pervades Shelley's poetry and helps to account for its quality of restless pursuit as it seeks answers to unanswerable questions.

528 *windlestrae* Scottish spelling of 'windlestraw', a dry grass-stalk.

With its wintry speed. On every side now rose
Rocks, which, in unimaginable forms,
Lifted their black and barren pinnacles 545
In the light of evening, and its precipice
Obscuring the ravine, disclosed above,
Mid toppling stones, black gulphs and yawning caves,
Whose windings gave ten thousand various tongues
To the loud stream. Lo! where the pass expands 550
Its stony jaws, the abrupt mountain breaks,
And seems, with its accumulated crags,
To overhang the world: for wide expand
Beneath the wan stars and descending moon
Islanded seas, blue mountains, mighty streams, 555
Dim tracts and vast, robed in the lustrous gloom
Of leaden-coloured even, and fiery hills
Mingling their flames with twilight, on the verge
Of the remote horizon. The near scene,
In naked and severe simplicity, 560
Made contrast with the universe. A pine,
Rock-rooted, stretched athwart the vacancy
Its swinging boughs, to each inconstant blast
Yielding one only response, at each pause
In most familiar cadence, with the howl 565
The thunder and the hiss of homeless streams
Mingling its solemn song, whilst the broad river,
Foaming and hurrying o'er its rugged path,
Fell into that immeasurable void
Scattering its waters to the passing winds. 570
    Yet the grey precipice and solemn pine
And torrent, were not all;—one silent nook
Was there. Even on the edge of that vast mountain,
Upheld by knotty roots and fallen rocks,
It overlooked in its serenity 575
The dark earth, and the bending vault of stars.
It was a tranquil spot, that seemed to smile
Even in the lap of horror. Ivy clasped
The fissured stones with its entwining arms,
And did embower with leaves forever green, 580
And berries dark, the smooth and even space
Of its inviolated floor, and here
The children of the autumnal whirlwind bore,
In wanton sport, those bright leaves, whose decay,
Red, yellow, or etherially pale, 585
Rivals the pride of summer. 'Tis the haunt
Of every gentle wind, whose breath can teach
The wilds to love tranquillity. One step,

---

546 *its precipice* That is, the ravine's in line 547.
561–4 *pine . . . response* Emblematic of the human condition at the approach of death; more specifically, it suggests the poet's state, amidst the 'vacancy' of nature, acting as a 'Rock-rooted' Aeolian harp played over by 'each inconstant blast' (l. 563).
566 *homeless streams* Emphasizes the lack of a 'home' for human life, here symbolized by the landscape.

567 *solemn song* Recalls the Narrator's 'solemn song' at line 19 and thus links the Poet's final kind of poetry (allegorized by the pine's sound) with the Narrator's opening poetic mode.
578 *lap of horror* A Gothic phrase, found, for example, in Ann Radclife's *The Mysteries of Udolpho* (1794).

One human step alone, has ever broken
The stillness of its solitude:—one voice 590
Alone inspired its echoes,—even that voice
Which hither came, floating among the winds,
And led the loveliest among human forms
To make their wild haunts the depository
Of all the grace and beauty that endued 595
Its motions, render up its majesty,
Scatter its music on the unfeeling storm,
And to the damp leaves and blue cavern mould,
Nurses of rainbow flowers and branching moss,
Commit the colours of that varying cheek, 600
That snowy breast, those dark and drooping eyes.
    The dim and horned moon hung low, and poured
A sea of lustre on the horizon's verge
That overflowed its mountains. Yellow mist
Filled the unbounded atmosphere, and drank 605
Wan moonlight even to fullness: not a star
Shone, not a sound was heard; the very winds,
Danger's grim playmates, on that precipice
Slept, clasped in his embrace.—O, storm of death!
Whose sightless speed divides this sullen night: 610
And thou, colossal Skeleton, that, still
Guiding its irresistible career
In thy devastating omnipotence,
Art king of this frail world, from the red field
Of slaughter, from the reeking hospital, 615
The patriot's sacred couch, the snowy bed
Of innocence, the scaffold and the throne,
A mighty voice invokes thee. Ruin calls
His brother Death. A rare and regal prey
He hath prepared, prowling around the world; 620
Glutted with which thou mayst repose, and men
Go to their graves like flowers or creeping worms,
Nor ever more offer at thy dark shrine
The unheeded tribute of a broken heart.
    When on the threshold of the green recess 625
The wanderer's footsteps fell, he knew that death
Was on him. Yet a little, ere it fled,
Did he resign his high and holy soul
To images of the majestic past,
That paused within his passive being now, 630
Like winds that bear sweet music, when they breathe
Through some dim latticed chamber. He did place
His pale lean hand upon the rugged trunk
Of the old pine. Upon an ivied stone
Reclined his languid head, his limbs did rest, 635
Diffused and motionless, on the smooth brink

589 *One human step alone* That of the Poet.
618–24 *Ruin . . . heart* Ruin has prepared for Death 'A rare and regal prey' (l. 619) (the Poet), in order to 'glut' Death and allow other men to die natural deaths (l. 622), so that no one will need, in the future, to offer at Death's 'dark shrine' (l. 623) the 'tribute of a broken heart' (l. 624) – since, one assumes, the broken-heartedness involved in the Poet's death is so great it exhausts all future disappointments. The 'broken heart' is both that of the Poet, broken-hearted by the failure of his quest, and the Narrator, broken-hearted by the Poet's death. In line 621 'thou' is Death.
631–2 *Like winds . . . chamber* The image is – once more – that of an Aeolian harp.

Of that obscurest chasm;—and thus he lay,
Surrendering to their final impulses
The hovering powers of life. Hope and despair,
The torturers, slept; no mortal pain or fear   640
Marred his repose, the influxes of sense,
And his own being unalloyed by pain,
Yet feebler and more feeble, calmly fed
The stream of thought, till he lay breathing there
At peace, and faintly smiling:—his last sight   645
Was the great moon, which o'er the western line
Of the wide world her mighty horn suspended,
With whose dun beams inwoven darkness seemed
To mingle. Now upon the jagged hills
It rests, and still as the divided frame   650
Of the vast meteor sunk, the Poet's blood,
That ever beat in mystic sympathy
With nature's ebb and flow, grew feebler still:
And when two lessening points of light alone
Gleamed through the darkness, the alternate gasp   655
Of his faint respiration scarce did stir
The stagnate night:—till the minutest ray
Was quenched, the pulse yet lingered in his heart.
It paused—it fluttered. But when heaven remained
Utterly black, the murky shades involved   660
An image, silent, cold, and motionless,
As their own voiceless earth and vacant air.
Even as a vapour fed with golden beams
That ministered on sunlight, ere the west
Eclipses it, was now that wondrous frame—   665
No sense, no motion, no divinity—
A fragile lute, on whose harmonious strings
The breath of heaven did wander— a bright stream
Once fed with many-voiced waves— a dream
Of youth, which night and time have quenched forever,   670
Still, dark, and dry, and unremembered now.
   O, for Medea's wondrous alchemy,
Which wheresoe'er it fell made the earth gleam
With bright flowers, and the wintry boughs exhale
From vernal blooms fresh fragrance! O, that God,   675
Profuse of poisons, would concede the chalice
Which but one living man has drained, who now,

645–71 *his last . . . unremembered now* The Poet's death prompts a reprise of much of what has gone before. The moon's horn is 'suspended' (l. 647), recalling other uses of 'suspended' in the poem, pauses before irretrievable choice, but also intimations of final uncertainty; with the description of 'inwoven darkness' (l. 648) Shelley reminds us of all the other occasions of 'woven' obstacles between the Poet and his quest, a weaving which might constitute as well what this world can offer, even if it is not enough for the Poet. The passage reminds us, too, of the Poet's 'mystic sympathy / With nature's ebb and flow' (ll. 652–3), for all his pursuit of an ideal other who lies beyond nature. The eyes of this ideal other are recalled in 'the two lessening points of light' (l. 654) (the tips of the crescent moon). The writing dwells on the final extinction of the Poet's being with nihilistic eloquence, as though the Narrator were turning bitterly against any trust that nature never betrayed the heart that loved her.

671 *Still . . . now* The adjectives apply, respectively, to the 'fragile lute' (l. 667), now 'Still'; the 'bright stream' (l. 668), now 'dark, and dry'; and the 'dream / Of youth' (ll. 669–70), now 'unremembered'.

672 *Medea's wondrous alchemy* Medea restored youth to Aeson, the old father of her lover Jason, with a magic potion.

677 *one living man* Ahasuerus, who appears in *Queen Mab* (and in *Hellas*), is a figure of medieval legend supposedly cursed by Jesus with the double-edged gift of eternal life; he is, accordingly, 'Lone as incarnate death' (l. 681).

Vessel of deathless wrath, a slave that feels
No proud exemption in the blighting curse
He bears, over the world wanders forever, 680
Lone as incarnate death! O, that the dream
Of dark magician in his visioned cave,
Raking the cinders of a crucible
For life and power, even when his feeble hand
Shakes in its last decay, were the true law 685
Of this so lovely world! But thou art fled
Like some frail exhalation; which the dawn
Robes in its golden beams,—ah! thou hast fled!
The brave, the gentle, and the beautiful,
The child of grace and genius. Heartless things 690
Are done and said i' the world, and many worms
And beasts and men live on, and mighty Earth
From sea and mountain, city and wilderness,
In vesper low or joyous orison,
Lifts still its solemn voice:—but thou art fled— 695
Thou canst no longer know or love the shapes
Of this phantasmal scene, who have to thee
Been purest ministers, who are, alas!
Now thou art not. Upon those pallid lips
So sweet even in their silence, on those eyes 700
That image sleep in death, upon that form
Yet safe from the worm's outrage, let no tear
Be shed—not even in thought. Nor, when those hues
Are gone, and those divinest lineaments,
Worn by the senseless wind, shall live alone 705
In the frail pauses of this simple strain,
Let not high verse, mourning the memory
Of that which is no more, or painting's woe
Or sculpture, speak in feeble imagery
Their own cold powers. Art and eloquence, 710
And all the shews o' the world are frail and vain
To weep a loss that turns their lights to shade.
It is a woe too 'deep for tears,' when all
Is reft at once, when some surpassing Spirit,
Whose light adorned the world around it, leaves 715
Those who remain behind, not sobs or groans,
The passionate tumult of a clinging hope;
But pale despair and cold tranquillity,
Nature's vast frame, the web of human things,
Birth and the grave, that are not as they were. 720

685–6 *the true ... world!* The Narrator is railing against his tale's evidence 'Of what we are' (l. 29).

686–720 *But ... as they were* Containing some of the most affectingly cadenced writing of a poem that is always rhythmically evocative, this final section consists of an elegy from the Narrator for the Poet, an elegy that spurns the consolations of elegy, rebukes the memorial pretensions of 'high verse' (l. 707), painting and sculpture, and denies the value of 'Art and eloquence' (l. 710). The verse makes powerful use of varying caesurae to ensure that a dying fall is often heard; for example, in line 699, the full stop after 'Now thou art not' obliges the reader to give full weight to the monosyllabic assertion of loss which precedes it.

694 *orison* Prayer.

697 *this phantasmal scene* Made up of illusions. Compare *Queen Mab*, 6. 192: 'the phantasmal scene', and 9. 74: 'life's phantasmal scene'. And yet 'phantasmal' reminds us of the Narrator's inclusion of 'twilight phantasms' (l. 40) in his catalogue of inspirational sources.

713 *too 'deep for tears'* Shelley quotes from the last line of Wordsworth, 'Ode: Intimations of Immortality', which speaks of 'Thoughts that do often lie too deep for tears'.

719–20 *Nature's ... were* Shelley returns to the image of life as a 'web', but though life continues, things 'are not as they were': the Narrator's knowledge of the Poet's desire and discontent, and their ultimate fate, has led to this altered perspective.

Hymn to Intellectual Beauty

The poem's composition began in 1816 while Shelley was in Switzerland. It was first published by Leigh Hunt in *The Examiner*, 19 January 1817; then in the *Rosalind and Helen* volume, 1819. Another finished version can be found in the Scrope Davies Notebook, which was discovered in 1976; some significant variations of phrasing are noted in the annotation (the Notebook is abbreviated to *SDN*). 'Hymn to Intellectual Beauty' reveals Shelley in the act of formulating an alternative to what in the poem he calls 'the name of God, and ghosts, and Heaven' (l. 27). That he feels the need for an alternative is itself suggestive of a quasi-religious impulse in his work. The alternative in which he places his trust is 'Intellectual Beauty', a concept addressed almost as though it were a deity, albeit one characterized by the enigmatic fugitiveness of its appearances. 'Intellectual' means 'immaterial', a beauty beyond the knowledge of the senses, and yet it is through the senses that some intimation of such beauty is found. Hence Shelley shapes a technique found elsewhere in his poetry, a use of similes and figures of speech to intimate a reality which cannot be defined or apprehended directly. In the opening stanza, for example, in which the poet does not speak directly of 'Intellectual Beauty' (the phrase, indeed, is not used throughout the poem), he describes the impact of the visitations made by 'The awful shadow of some unseen Power' (l. 1) through four similes (ll. 8–12); the last – 'Like aught . . .' – gives up the attempt to find a particular analogue for the impact of Intellectual Beauty.

This handling of similes may suggest a Platonic outlook, in which the material world is a copy or shadow of the 'real' immaterial world of ideas. And Platonism is certainly a strong impulse in Shelley's work. But it coexists with a scepticism about the capacity of the human mind to access true knowledge through the senses, even as the senses are the basis for knowledge. This scepticism, associated with David Hume, finds its way into the 'Hymn' in the fourth stanza. Again, a series of similes is offered, purporting to evoke the effect of Intellectual Beauty's 'light' (l. 32). But the images are elusive – the light is compared to 'mist o'er mountains driven' (l. 32), for instance – and there is a sense in which Shelley himself is embarking on his own version of the 'Frail spells' (l. 29) which he has rejected earlier in the stanza. He has, that is, betrayed or conceded that his own trust in 'Thy light alone' (l. 32) involves an act of faith, not dissimilar to that which underpins traditional religious quest. The result is to turn what might have been a poem setting out a series of heterodox beliefs into one that goes far more deeply into the nature of holding any beliefs. Shelley, it would seem, is determined not to allow his counter-belief to harden into an ideology that forgets that all human beliefs were created by human need. As a result, his choice of genre – a 'Hymn' – is not merely cocking a snook at traditional Christian hymns; it is in part conceding that his own 'hymn' is itself a 'Frail spell', if only because of the inadequacies of language (to which Shelley refers at the end of stanza 6).

The poem is written in 12-line stanzas, rhyming *abbaaccbddee*. The rhyme scheme, along with the alexandrine in the fifth line, tends to support a pattern of attempted forward movement checked by circling back for the first two-thirds of each stanza, before the final two couplets give a new impetus – of ongoing, accelerating energy in stanzas 1 and 5, of excited or composed vision in stanzas 3, 6 and 7, and of intensified reflection or anxiety in stanzas 2 and 4. The pattern of slowing and quickening is aided by the shorter lines in lines 6, 7, 10 and 11 of each stanza. The form adapts itself readily to quickenings and slowings of feeling, articulations of hope, crisis and resolution. The first stanza mingles confidence that the 'awful shadow' 'Floats though unseen amongst us' (l. 2) with a vivid awareness that this 'shadow', already at one remove from 'some unseen Power', is, like the original of which it is the copy, 'unseen' and 'inconstant' (l. 6). Stanza 2 develops the theme of Intellectual Beauty's inconstancy, asking it 'Why dost thou pass away' (l. 16), linking this fugitiveness to the transience inherent in life, and to the mysterious duality of human experience with its blend of 'love and hate, despondency and hope' (l. 24). Stanza 3 observes that traditional answers to the previous stanza's questions have been 'Frail spells', but in the transition already mentioned Shelley then articulates what is, in effect, his own knowingly frail spell as he invokes 'Thy light alone'. Stanza 4 remarks that human beings would be 'immortal, and omnipotent' (l. 39) were Intellectual Beauty not to vanish, and it concludes with a plea that it should 'Depart not' (ll. 46, 47), a plea that contains within it the fear that all human experience might be 'a dark reality' (l. 48). Throughout the poem, Intellectual Beauty is experienced within human beings, yet it is addressed as though it belonged to some other realm, and stanza 5 offers a humanist equivalent to ecstatic religious conversion as Shelley describes his first youthful encounter with Intellectual Beauty: 'I shrieked, and clasped my hands in extacy!' (l. 60). Stanza 7 continues the narrative of the poet's allegiance to Intellectual Beauty, his devotion to it involving an awareness of its potential to liberate human beings from political and religious oppression. The final stanza reminds us that one potent presence behind the poem is Wordsworth's 'Ode: Intimations of Immortality', with its account of maturation and the 'sober colouring' that attends its close. Shelley suggests, in the stanza, that autumn has a beauty denied to summer, and that in it things are 'heard or seen' (l. 76) which previously seemed beyond sense experience (as in stanza 5 when, praying to the traditional 'poisonous names', l. 53, the poet 'was not heard – I saw them not', l. 54). He ends with the prayer that Intellectual Beauty will serve as his future guide.

Wordsworth's 'Ode: Intimations of Immortality' is certainly one model for the poem's themes of fugitive visionary experience and emotional maturity. Shelley also owes a debt to Spenser's 'Hymn of Heavenly Beauty', and to Plato's dialogues, especially the *Symposium*, which he would translate two years later, rewriting what in Plato is 'the wide ocean of beauty' as 'the wide ocean of intellectual beauty'. His 1817 essay 'On Christianity' describes his sense of a 'power' ' by which we are surrounded, like the atmosphere in which some motionless lyre is suspended, which visits with its breath our silent chords, at will' (Murray, p. 251), and such a power, at once immanent and transcendent, haunts Shelley's avowedly atheist imaginings.

Text: 1817, with subsequent corrections in Shelley's hand.

1

The awful shadow of some unseen Power
   Floats though unseen amongst us,—visiting
   This various world with as inconstant wing
As summer winds that creep from flower to flower.—
Like moonbeams that behind some piny mountain shower,   5
      It visits with inconstant glance
      Each human heart and countenance;
Like hues and harmonies of evening,—
   Like clouds in starlight widely spread,—
   Like memory of music fled,—   10
   Like aught that for its grace may be
Dear, and yet dearer for its mystery.

2

Spirit of BEAUTY, that doth consecrate
   With thine own hues all thou dost shine upon
   Of human thought or form,—where art thou gone?   15
Why dost thou pass away and leave our state,
This dim vast vale of tears, vacant and desolate?

Title 'Intellectual Beauty' is a phrase that appears, among other places, in Mary Wollstonecraft's *Vindication of the Rights of Woman* (1792) and Godwin's *Memoirs of the Author of a Vindication of the Rights of Woman* (1798).
1 *The . . . Power* This reads 'The lovely shadow of some awful Power' in *SDN*.
2 *Floats* This reads 'Walks' in *SDN*.
2 *visiting* The use of the participle form in a subordinate clause for the shadow's visits is suggestive of its seemingly indifferent, even whimsical nature.
3 *various* This reads 'peopled' in *SDN*.
5 *shower* A verb, governed by 'moonbeams'.
7 *human . . . countenance* 'Human' is a key word (used again in l. 15); it locates the impact of Intellectual Beauty in the arena of human thought and feeling.
12 *Dear . . . mystery* The initial stress makes one pause over the 'dearness' of 'grace', before the line recovers momentum and a sense that 'mystery' is even 'dearer'.
13 *Spirit* This reads 'Shadow' in *SDN*.
13 *consecrate* A religious verb (meaning to 'set apart as sacred'), adapted to Shelley's humanist ends.
15 *where . . . gone?* Compare Wordsworth, 'Ode: Intimations of Immortality', lines 56–7 for the style of the question.
17 *vale of tears* A traditional Christian phrase for life on earth.
17 *vacant* A complex word in Shelley's work: it can imply an emptiness that makes life 'desolate'; it can suggest an emptiness, created by the sweeping away of outmoded ideas, that awaits the poet's own imaginings as a replacement.

> Ask why the sunlight not forever
> Weaves rainbows o'er yon mountain river,
> Why aught should fail and fade that once is shown, 20
> Why fear and dream and death and birth
> Cast on the daylight of this earth
> Such gloom,—why man has such a scope
> For love and hate, despondency and hope?
>
> 3
>
> No voice from some sublimer world hath ever 25
> To sage or poet these responses given—
> Therefore the name of God, and ghosts, and Heaven,
> Remain the records of their vain endeavour,
> Frail spells—whose uttered charm might not avail to sever,
> From all we hear and all we see 30
> Doubt, chance, and mutability.
> Thy light alone—like mist o'er mountains driven,
> Or music by the night wind sent
> Through strings of some still instrument,
> Or moonlight on a midnight stream, 35
> Gives grace and truth to life's unquiet dream.
>
> 4
>
> Love, Hope, and Self-esteem, like clouds depart
> And come, for some uncertain moments lent.
> Man were immortal, and omnipotent,
> Didst thou, unknown and awful as thou art, 40
> Keep with thy glorious train firm state within his heart.
> Thou messenger of sympathies,

18–24 *Ask . . . hope?* Though the sentence ends with a question mark, it begins less as a question than as a statement (i.e. 'You may as well ask why . . .'). As the sentence develops, Shelley's acceptance of perplexity passes into renewed questioning as the triple use of 'why' in lines 20, 21, 23 seems to forget the initial phrase, 'Ask why'.
24 *hate* This reads 'joy' in *SDN*.
25 *sublimer world* Reminds us that the poem is dealing with the subject-matter of the 'sublime', that which defeats or dwarfs human apprehension.
26 *sage or poet* This reads 'wisest poets' in *SDN*.
25–9 *ever . . . sever* The stanza opens with a cluster of feminine rhymes, suggestive in their quickening effect of urgent pursuit and a sense of 'vain endeavour'.
27 *the name . . . Heaven* Corrected by Shelley, in a handwritten emendation, from the *Examiner*'s printed reading, 'the names of Demon, Ghost, and Heaven', evidently a reading preferred because it avoids a direct attack on 'God'. On both readings, Shelley exposes the nominalist nature of traditional religious answers: that is, the names associated with these answers do not correspond to realities; they tell us only about the 'vain endeavour' (l. 28) of the questioners.
28 *vain endeavour* Compare Coleridge, 'Dejection: An Ode', line 42, 'It were a vain endeavour', one of many Coleridgean echoes in Shelley's poetry.

30 *From . . . see* The evidence of our senses confirms that life is subject to 'mutability' (l. 31). *SDN* reads 'feel' instead of 'hear'.
32–5 *Thy light . . . stream* As discussed in the Headnote, the comparisons suggest that the 'light' is far from a steady source of illumination; it is as transient as driven mist, as unexpected and beyond control as music awakened in an Aeolian harp (the 'still instrument' of l. 34), and as outside everyday experience as the sight of 'moonlight on a midnight stream'.
36 *Gives . . . dream* Compare John 1: 17: 'but grace and truth came by Jesus Christ'. Again, Shelley remodels traditional religious language for his own purposes.
37 *Love . . . Self-esteem* 'Self-esteem' replaces 'Faith' in the traditional Christian trinity of virtues. 'Faith' for Shelley was suspect because it propped up outmoded forms of belief. By 'Self-esteem' he means appropriate recognition of one's worth as a human being.
37–8 *depart / And come* The order of the verbs brings out how qualities associated with Intellectual Beauty, its 'glorious train' (l. 41), are fitful in their manifestations, and yet that they do return (they do not 'come and go'; they 'go and come').
40 *unknown and awful* Stresses again the sublime nature of Intellectual Beauty.

>   That wax and wane in lovers' eyes—
> Thou—that to human thought art nourishment,
>   Like darkness to a dying flame!
>   Depart not as thy shadow came,
>   Depart not—lest the grave should be,
> Like life and fear, a dark reality.

5

> While yet a boy I sought for ghosts, and sped
>   Through many a listening chamber, cave and ruin,
>   And starlight wood, with fearful steps pursuing
> Hopes of high talk with the departed dead.
> I called on poisonous names with which our youth is fed,
>   I was not heard—I saw them not—
>   When musing deeply on the lot
> Of life, at that sweet time when winds are wooing
>   All vital things that wake to bring
>   News of buds and blossoming,—
>   Sudden, thy shadow fell on me;
> I shrieked, and clasped my hands in extacy!

6

> I vowed that I would dedicate my powers
>   To thee and thine—have I not kept the vow?
>   With beating heart and streaming eyes, even now
> I call the phantoms of a thousand hours
> Each from his voiceless grave: they have in visioned bowers
>   Of studious zeal or love's delight
>   Outwatched with me the envious night—
> They know that never joy illumed my brow
>   Unlinked with hope that thou wouldst free
>   This world from its dark slavery,
>   That thou—O awful LOVELINESS,
> Wouldst give whate'er these words cannot express.

---

44 *SDN* reads 'the poets thought' for 'human thought'.
44–5 *Thou ... flame!* A complex simile that raises the question: how does darkness nourish a dying flame? One answer might be that it does not; it merely allows us better to see the flame. The comparison comes perilously close to suggesting that Intellectual Beauty is a non-existent 'darkness', though darkness is a traditional image for the 'unknown and awful' nature of deity.
52 *Hopes ... dead* Compare James Thomson, 'Winter', l. 432: 'And hold high converse with the mighty dead'. In *SDN* it reads 'Hopes of strange converse with the storied dead'.
53 *poisonous ... fed* This reads 'that false name with which our youth is fed' in *SDN*.
54 *I was ... not* The sight/hearing reference recalls line 30 and anticipates line 76.
58 *buds* Shelley corrected the *Examiner* text from 'birds'. *SDN* also has 'buds'.

59 *Sudden* The stress shift accentuates the 'suddenness' of the experience.
61 *vowed* Again, Shelley adapts the language of religious experience to his own ends.
66 *love's delight* Reads 'lore's delight' in *SDN*, as noted correctly in Reiman and Fraistat (eds), *Shelley's Poetry and Prose* (p. 95).
70 *dark slavery* Recalls the fear that all might be a 'dark reality' (l. 48), but here Shelley stresses the emancipatory powers of Intellectual Beauty.
72 *whate'er ... express* Declarations of language's inadequacy occur frequently in Shelley's poetry; often he works at the limits of words, though the rhyme between 'LOVELINESS' (l. 71) and 'express' suggests that, in the act of conceding the inadequacy of his words, he can convey an awareness of a reality beyond language.

7

>   The day becomes more solemn and serene
>   When noon is past—there is a harmony
>   In autumn, and a lustre in its sky, 75
>   Which through the summer is not heard or seen,
>   As if it could not be, as if it had not been!
>   Thus let thy power, which like the truth
>   Of nature on my passive youth
>   Descended, to my onward life supply 80
>   Its calm—to one who worships thee,
>   And every form containing thee,
>   Whom, SPIRIT fair, thy spells did bind
>   To fear himself, and love all human kind.

73–84 *The day . . . kind* The stanza recalls the close of Wordsworth's 'Ode: Intimations of Immortality'. But whereas Wordsworthian acceptance is full of loss, Shelley's prayer to Intellectual Beauty speaks of revelations hitherto concealed (see ll. 74–7).
77 *As if . . . been!* An excited sense of overcoming the limits of what seemed possible is reinforced by the *a* rhyme (three rhymes in five lines).
78 *Thus* That is, in the way depicted in the seasonal analogy just offered.

79 *passive youth* Passivity for Shelley is often the condition of receptivity to desirable influence.
81–2 *to one . . . thee* Shelley's reaching out to Intellectual Beauty shows in the repeated use of 'thee' to rhyme with itself.
83 SPIRIT *fair* This reads 'fleeting power' in *SDN*.
83 *spells* In contrast to the 'Frail spells' of line 29, these 'spells' have – the poet claims – proved effective.
84 *fear* Revere.

Mont Blanc. Lines written in the Vale of Chamouni

Shelley began composition of 'Mont Blanc' in Switzerland at the end of July 1816 when, with Mary Godwin and Claire Clairmont, he explored the Chamonix Valley, including the Mer de Glace, below Mont Blanc, Europe's highest mountain. There is a rough draft in *Bodleian Shelley Manuscripts*, vol. XI, ed. Michael Erkelenz (New York: Garland, 1992) and a finished alternative version in *SDN*, entitled 'Scene – Pont Pellisier in the vale of Servox'. Shelley appears to have lent *SDN* to Byron, who seems to have given it to his friend Scrope Davies to return to Shelley who had gone back to England while Byron stayed on in Europe; Scrope Davies fled from England, to escape his creditors, and did not return the Notebook to Shelley. In the case of 'Mont Blanc', Shelley must have rewritten the poem in the light of his rough draft. The poem was first published in *History of a Six Weeks' Tour* (1817), co-written with Mary Shelley (as by then she was), which supplies our copy-text.

'Mont Blanc' is among Shelley's most demanding poems. Written in irregularly rhyming paragraphs, it serves as a sceptical but not wholly unsympathetic answer to Coleridge's 'Hymn before Sun-rise, in the Vale of Chamouni' (1802). Coleridge sees God's creativity as manifested in the landscape; Shelley emphatically does not. Indeed, the mountain helps 'to repeal / Large codes of fraud and woe' (ll. 80–1) by being part of a material universe that calls into question the notion of divine agency. At the same time, both poets communicate the significance of the 'human mind's imaginings' (l. 143). The role of the mind in perception dominates the opening section of Shelley's poem. In that section, 'The everlasting universe of things' (l. 1) is said to flow 'through the mind' (l. 2), the mind being depicted as akin to mountain 'springs' (l. 4) that pour into a 'vast river' (l. 10), that is, the world available to the senses. Shelley's theory of how the mind works is rooted in eighteenth-century empiricism, with its emphasis on the importance of the role of sense-impressions. And yet a wildness and excitement about the writing are suggestive of an interaction between the 'mind' and the 'universe of things' that defies full understanding. It is this gap between excited experience and full understanding that gives momentum and impetus to the rest of the poem. In the second section, Shelley sees the scene before him as illustrative of his opening proposition, but the allegory becomes complicated when the Ravine, emblem of the mind, is said to be visited by 'Power in likeness of the Arve' (l. 16). The introduction of the concept of

'Power' brings into play notions of ultimate agency; able both to suggest the collective force of the material universe and to hint at an original force, Power comes close to serving as Shelley's substitute for 'God'. The section also introduces a hint of the imaginative experience which will prove crucial to its ending, when it refers to 'the strange sleep . . . when the voices of the desart fail' (ll. 27–8). At such a moment Shelley departs from a point-by-point illustration of the first section's assertions; when he does insist on the Ravine's emblematic function (ll. 34–48), he offers a bewildering yet fascinating account of the mind's 'self-experience' (to borrow Coleridge's phrase in *Biographia Literaria*, ch. 7) in the act of poetic creation, indeed, in the act of creating this poem. In looking at the Ravine, the lines say, Shelley seems to be looking at his mind as it engages with the outside world (which includes the Ravine, even though the Ravine emblematizes the mind), and as it pursues equivalents – presumably words and images – for what it beholds and what it feels as it beholds. Shelley's syntax here tends to blur easy distinctions, catching up mind, Ravine and poetry in one whirl of imaginative process.

In the third section, Shelley asks questions about the nature of reality, and asserts that the bleakness of the mountain scenery warrants a sceptical approach to the possibility of ultimate answers. But the 'mysterious tongue' (l. 76) of the wilderness prevents any belief in the mysteries beloved by Christianity. The product of reflection on the landscape is not Coleridgean theistic belief, but 'awful doubt' (l. 77), a kind of reverent scepticism. If there is any 'faith' it is one 'so mild' (l. 77) that human beings may 'In such a faith' (as *SDN* has it) be 'with nature reconciled' (l. 79). Reconciliation of this sort will involve recognition that nature is not the creation of a benign deity, and cannot be used by those in positions of power to bolster up their position through the promulgation of 'Large codes of fraud and woe' (l. 81). In sections 4 and 5, Shelley, in effect, takes his poem in two different directions. Section 4 is the most materialist in the poem. It places 'Power' at a remove from this material world, but it focuses on an amoral, dynamic cycle observable in the natural world below Mont Blanc, where the descending glaciers first destroy all in their path, then feed 'one majestic River (l. 123). This ecosystem is at once challenging to human beings, and supportive of them, but it obeys its own laws – laws which cannot be anthropomorphized.

In the final section, however, Shelley returns to the 'Power' which has been haunting the edges of the poem. Now it takes centre-stage as Shelley imagines it inhabiting the top of the mountain. The poetry involves us in a beautiful dance of presence and absence: Shelley asserts that no one can see the snows descending on the mountain's top, yet evokes that descent imaginatively. Imagination can get the better of scepticism, is, indeed, licensed by it. It is, therefore, possible to propose that there is a materialist counter-principle at the heart of creation, a 'secret strength of things' (l. 139), governing both 'thought' (l. 140) and the material world. And yet such a proposal is the product of the 'human mind's imaginings (l. 143), as the final, subtly phrased question brings out. Until that question, Shelley comes perilously close to repeating a Coleridgean solution in his proclamation of a 'secret strength of things'. With the question, he indicates his imaginative and conceptual originality, bringing to the fore the workings of his own 'imaginings', a subject always central to his poetry.

1

The everlasting universe of things
Flows through the mind, and rolls its rapid waves,
Now dark—now glittering—now reflecting gloom—
Now lending splendour, where from secret springs
The source of human thought its tribute brings   5
Of waters,—with a sound but half its own,

Subtitle 'Lines . . . Chamouni' Recalls Coleridge's 'Hymn before Sun-Rise, in the Vale of Chamouni'.
1–2 *The . . . mind* This feels like a reworking of the pantheist climax of 'Tintern Abbey', where Wordsworth speaks of a 'presence' (l. 97) whose 'dwelling' (l. 100) includes 'the mind of man' (l. 101). And yet Shelley might also be seen as merely if intensely describing an epistemological commonplace, that knowledge of things enters the mind by means of sensuous impressions.
3–4 *Now dark . . . splendour* The 'waves' take on the colouring of their surroundings (the mind), 'reflecting gloom'; they also bring their own colouring to the mind, 'lending splendour'.
4 *secret springs* The human mind, acting as a 'brook' (l. 7) that feeds 'a vast river' (l. 10), has its own sources of knowledge, distinct from those brought to it by impressions deriving from external reality. Words such as 'secret' and 'lone' (l. 8) help create a landscape that is also a mysterious mindscape.
6 *but half* In *SDN* this is 'not all'.

Such as a feeble brook will oft assume
In the wild woods, among the mountains lone,
Where waterfalls around it leap for ever,
Where woods and winds contend, and a vast river   10
Over its rocks ceaselessly bursts and raves.

2

Thus thou, Ravine of Arve—dark, deep Ravine—
Thou many-coloured, many-voiced vale,
Over whose pines, and crags, and caverns sail
Fast cloud shadows and sunbeams: awful scene,   15
Where Power in likeness of the Arve comes down
From the ice gulphs that gird his secret throne,
Bursting through these dark mountains like the flame
Of lightning through the tempest;—thou dost lie,
Thy giant brood of pines around thee clinging,   20
Children of elder time, in whose devotion
The chainless winds still come and ever came
To drink their odours, and their mighty swinging
To hear—an old and solemn harmony;
Thine earthly rainbows stretched across the sweep   25
Of the ethereal waterfall, whose veil
Robes some unsculptured image; the strange sleep
Which when the voices of the desart fail
Wraps all in its own deep eternity;—
Thy caverns echoing to the Arve's commotion,   30
A loud, lone sound no other sound can tame;

7–11 *Such as . . . raves* The brook, emblem of 'The source of human thought' (l. 5), 'will oft assume' a sound that does not wholly belong to it, since it derives, in large part, from the 'vast river' (l. 10) that serves as an image for 'The everlasting universe of things' (l. 1). The brook is brought in as a simile to describe the role played by the mind, but the simile, as it develops, give a powerful sense of the external world, even as we remember that the whole section is expounding an idea rather than describing a scene. The idea, of course, is to do with the overwhelming onslaught on the mind made by external reality.
12 *Thus thou . . . Ravine* The opening of section 2 suggests that the scene facing Shelley illustrates the pronouncements just made. 'Arve' neatly rearranges 'rave', as though Shelley were writing in anagrams. Yet there is no point-by-point exactness: if 'Power in likeness of the Arve' (l. 16) corresponds to 'The everlasting universe of things' (l. 1), 'Power' is at best implicit in the first section.
13 *many-coloured . . . vale* The 'vale' belongs to the phenomenal world as is suggested by the two adjectives, which may hint at an ultimately numinous whiteness and single voice, even as any such hint is rigorously held in check.
16 *Power in likeness of the Arve* The Arve river appears to correspond to the 'vast river' or 'everlasting universe of things' in section 1. But the idea of 'Power' may bring in quasi-Deist notions of a first cause. It is noteworthy, as Jonathan Wordsworth points out, that Shelley reverses the terms of what might have been a 'conventional smile', whereby the Arve would come down 'in the likeness of an abstract Power' ('The Secret Strength of Things', *The Wordsworth Circle* 18 (1987), p. 101).
22 *chainless* SDN reads 'charmed'.
23 *mighty swinging* Compare Coleridge, 'France: An Ode', 'imperious branches swinging' (l. 7), where 'swinging' is in the rhyme-position.
27 *Robes some unsculptured image* An image that has not been shaped by human beings. The phrase 'unsculptured image' may suggest, too, the search for an image that will be 'sculptured' by the 'human mind's imaginings'. 'Robes' typically applies a concrete word to an intangible, mental state.
27 *the strange sleep* Another phrase which departs from, or develops hints in, the opening section, 'the strange sleep' intimates an altered state of consciousness, one capable of swallowing up reality. This suggestion is heightened in SDN, which, after line 28, reads, 'And its hues wane, doth blend them all & steep / Their periods in its own eternity'.
31 *A loud, lone sound* The poem returns to 'sound' after its consideration of 'the strange sleep' (l. 27).

Thou art pervaded with that ceaseless motion,
Thou art the path of that unresting sound—
Dizzy Ravine! and when I gaze on thee
I seem as in a trance sublime and strange
To muse on my own separate phntasy,
My own, my human mind, which passively
Now renders and receives fast influencings,
Holding an unremitting interchange
With the clear universe of things around;
One legion of wild thoughts, whose wandering wings
Now float above thy darkness, and now rest
Where that or thou art no unbidden guest,
In the still cave of the witch Poesy,
Seeking among the shadows that pass by,
Ghosts of all things that are, some shade of thee,
Some phantom, some faint image; till the breast
From which they fled recalls them, thou art there!

3

Some say that gleams of a remoter world
Visit the soul in sleep,—that death is slumber,
And that its shapes the busy thoughts outnumber
Of those who wake and live.—I look on high;
Has some unknown omnipotence unfurled
The veil of life and death? or do I lie
In dream, and does the mightier world of sleep
Spread far around and inaccessibly
Its circles? For the very spirit fails,
Driven like a homeless cloud from steep to steep
That vanishes among the viewless gales!
Far, far above, piercing the infinite sky,
Mont Blanc appears,—still, snowy, and serene—
Its subject mountains their unearthly forms
Pile around it, ice and rock; broad vales between
Of frozen floods, unfathomable deeps,
Blue as the overhanging heaven, that spread
And wind among the accumulated steeps;
A desert peopled by the storms alone,

34–48 *Dizzy Ravine! . . . there!* Shelley, in a state of near-vertigo (an effect absent from *SDN* which reads 'Mighty Ravine'), sees in the ravine through which the Arve flows an objectification of his mind at work in the process of 'unremitting interchange' (l. 39) with 'the clear universe of things' (l. 40). As though in 'a trance sublime' (l. 35) ('vision deep' in *SDN*), he seems to behold the very process of poetic inspiration, during which the mind is 'Seeking' some approximation for its experience. During this process, and while such approximations are available to the mind, the Ravine – and by implication an objectified form of the mind itself – is present in the 'still cave of the witch Poesy' (l. 44); 'thou art there!' (l. 48) characteristically proclaims a presence even as it is on the verge of vanishing. The 'still cave' probably derives from Plato's *Republic*, where it serves as an image in a parable about the obscured nature of human perception. Shelley gives the image a more positive inflection.

49 *Some say that gleams* Shelley refuses wholly to endorse what 'some say'. But the pull of those 'gleams' is evident, and anticipates the use of 'gleam' (l. 121) and, as verb, 'gleams' (l. 127).

53–7 *Has some unknown . . . circles?* Has some unknown power dropped ('unfurled') a 'veil' before me? Or am I dreaming, surrounded by the world of sleep? The alternatives offered are an obscure vision of 'life and death' that recognizes that the access to final knowledge is impeded by a 'veil', and a condition of 'dream' surrounded by 'sleep' that seems to prevent any possibility of knowledge.

61 *Mont Blanc appears* Test-case for the poet's intuitions and theories, the mountain establishes itself, first of all, as a physical presence.

Save when the eagle brings some hunter's bone,
And the wolf tracks her there—how hideously
Its shapes are heaped around! rude, bare, and high, 70
Ghastly, and scarred, and riven.—Is this the scene
Where the old Earthquake-daemon taught her young
Ruin? Were these their toys? or did a sea
Of fire, envelope once this silent snow?
None can reply—all seems eternal now. 75
The wilderness has a mysterious tongue
Which teaches awful doubt, or faith so mild,
So solemn, so serene, that man may be
But for such faith with nature reconciled;
Thou hast a voice, great Mountain, to repeal 80
Large codes of fraud and woe; not understood
By all, but which the wise, and great, and good
Interpret, or make felt, or deeply feel.

4

The fields, the lakes, the forests, and the streams,
Ocean, and all the living things that dwell 85
Within the daedal earth; lightning, and rain,
Earthquake, and fiery flood, and hurricane,
The torpor of the year when feeble dreams
Visit the hidden buds, or dreamless sleep
Holds every future leaf and flower;—the bound 90
With which from that detested trance they leap;
The works and ways of man, their death and birth,
And that of him and all that his may be;
All things that move and breathe with toil and sound
Are born and die; revolve, subside and swell. 95
Power dwells apart in its tranquillity
Remote, serene, and inaccessible:
And *this*, the naked countenance of earth,

69 *tracks her there SDN* reads 'watches her'. Shelley may have changed to avoid repetition in line 101.
71–4 *Is this . . . snow?* Further questions, this time proposing alternative models for the Alpine scene, thought to be the creation of earthquake or fire.
75 *None can reply* By contrast with the 'many-voiced vale' (l. 13), the first impression given by the mountain is of speechlessness and silence.
76–83 *The wildernesss . . . feel* A voice is elicited from the scenery, but its function is to disabuse us of the beliefs promulgated (say) by Coleridge in his 'Hymn before Sunrise'. It teaches 'doubt' (l. 77) or possibly (but see note to l. 79) a Wordsworthian 'faith' (l. 77) in 'nature' (l. 79). Its 'voice' serves to 'repeal' (that is, revoke or annul) 'Large codes of fraud and woe' (ll. 80, 81): in other words, its refusal to serve as proof of God's existence frees human beings from the pious frauds of religion made use of by earthly rulers.
79 *But for such faith* A crux. In *SDN* Shelley has 'In such a faith'; in his manuscript, 'In such wise faith'. 'But for' may mean 'Only through', but it is interesting that Shelley did not recycle his manuscript reading when deprived of *SDN*. Shelley is likely to mean a faith that does not claim ultimate religious sanction or knowledge, merely a respect for the natural world.
81 *not understood* The antecedent is 'a voice'.
82–3 *the wise . . . feel* Again, the antecedent is 'a voice', which requires its own interpreters and disciples (among whom Shelley might include authors such as Godwin, Rousseau and himself) if its liberating counter-Christian message is to be heard.
84–97 *The fields . . . inaccessible* The contrast is (again) between the human and the phenomenal, on the one hand, and 'inaccessible' 'Power' (ll. 97, 96) on the other. The syntax is expressive: some 12 lines devoted to the former, only two to the latter, as though it could not be elaborated. At the same time, the fact that lines 96 and 97 rhyme, respectively, with line 93, and with lines 85 and 95 is a clue to the possible connection between 'Power' and 'All things that move and breathe' (l. 94).
86 *daedal* Intricate; the adjectives derives from Daedalus, the fashioner of the Cretan labyrinth in Greek mythology.
98 *this* The contrast just sketched, along with the inaccessibility of 'Power' (l. 96).

On which I gaze, even these primeval mountains
Teach the adverting mind. The glaciers creep
Like snakes that watch their prey, from their far fountains,
Slow rolling on; there, many a precipice,
Frost and the Sun in scorn of mortal power
Have piled: dome, pyramid, and pinnacle,
A city of death, distinct with many a tower
And wall impregnable of beaming ice.
Yet not a city, but a flood of ruin
Is there, that from the boundaries of the sky
Rolls its perpetual stream; vast pines are strewing
Its destined path, or in the mangled soil
Branchless and shattered stand; the rocks, drawn down
From yon remotest waste, have overthrown
The limits of the dead and living world,
Never to be reclaimed. The dwelling-place
Of insects, beasts, and birds, becomes its spoil;
Their food and their retreat for ever gone,
So much of life and joy is lost. The race
Of man flies far in dread; his work and dwelling
Vanish, like smoke before the tempest's stream,
And their place is not known. Below, vast caves
Shine in the rushing torrents' restless gleam,
Which from those secret chasms in tumult welling
Meet in the vale, and one majestic River,
The breath and blood of distant lands, for ever
Rolls its loud waters to the ocean waves,
Breathes its swift vapours to the circling air.

5

Mont Blanc yet gleams on high:—the power is there,
The still and solemn power of many sights,
And many sounds, and much of life and death.
In the calm darkness of the moonless nights,
In the lone glare of day, the snows descend
Upon that Mountain; none beholds them there,
Nor when the flakes burn in the sinking sun,
Or the star-beams dart through them:—Winds contend
Silently there, and heap the snow with breath
Rapid and strong, but silently! Its home

100–1 *The glaciers... prey* The glaciers are animated and given predatory purpose by the verb and simile.
103 *mortal SDN* reads 'human'.
107 *Yet not a city* Concedes that the earlier phrase 'A city of death' (l. 105) was fanciful; *SDN* reads 'A city's phantom'.
120 *their place is not known* Compare Job 7: 10: 'neither shall his place know him any more'.
120–2 *vast caves... welling* A cluster of echoes from Coleridge's 'Kubla Khan', published in 1816, gives the poem a more positive air; compare Shelley's 'vast caves' with Coleridge's 'caves of ice' (l. 36) and 'caverns measureless to man' (l. 4), and compare Shelley's 'secret chasms in tumult welling' with Coleridge's 'deep romantic chasm' (l. 12) and 'sacred river' (l. 26) that 'sank in tumult to a lifeless ocean' (l. 28).
123 *one majestic River* The river Rhone. Shelley sees the river as ultimately deriving from the glaciers in a natural cycle involving destructive and creative aspects.
127 *Mont Blanc... high* Shelley's imagination is still haunted by the mountain.
132 *none beholds them there* The key to the poem's subsequent excitement; if no one can see these things, yet they can be imagined, might that not offer the 'human mind's imaginings' (l. 143) a central role in constructing meaning?

The voiceless lightning in these solitudes
Keeps innocently, and like vapour broods
Over the snow. The secret strength of things
Which governs thought, and to the infinite dome 140
Of heaven is as a law, inhabits thee!
And what were thou, and earth, and stars, and sea,
If to the human mind's imaginings
Silence and solitude were vacancy?

139   *The secret strength of things* Shelley, moving beyond the term 'Power', purposefully does not identify this idea as 'Necessity'; it remains 'secret'. The rhyme between this line and 'human mind's imaginings' speaks eloquently of the poem's central theme.
141   *is . . . thee! SDN* reads 'is as a column, rests on thee'.
142–4   *And . . . vacancy?* The question is subtle. 'And' rather than 'But' implies that the poet knows his previous assertion has also involved 'the human mind's imaginings'; 'thou' is the Mountain, following on from its address as 'thee' in line 141; 'Silence and solitude' have already been evoked in previous lines, the former in lines 134–6, a reworking of lines 5–7 in Coleridge's 'Hymn before Sun-Rise': 'but thou, most awful Form! / Risest from forth thy silent Sea of Pines, / How silently!', the latter in lines 136–9. The poem's final word 'vacancy' implies a state of emptiness, lack of significance, but, it should be noted, one called into existence by 'imaginings'.

Prometheus Unbound, Act 1

Shelley published *Prometheus Unbound* in 1820. It is a 'lyrical drama in four acts' that describes Prometheus' resistance to Jupiter's tyranny and the overthrow of that tyranny when Demogorgon (representative of a force that presides over the cycles of history) pulls the tyrant down from his throne, an overthrow followed by evidences of change for the better in the human and cosmic spheres. If the work allegorizes Shelley's feelings and ideas about tyranny and reform, it functions as a complex allegory; much attention must be paid to the poem's internal verbal relations as Shelley develops associations, both positive and negative, round a cluster of words such as 'cave', 'air', 'sound' and 'breath'. His imagery can be multi-dimensional, fusing science and emotion in the description of love as a form of electricity or shaping volcanic descriptions into portents of social and political revolution.

At the core of the work are questions of perspective. At any moment, different possibilities, hopeful or despairing, present themselves. Central to Act 1, the only act included in this anthology, is Prometheus' wish to 'recall' (l. 59) 'The curse' (l. 58) he once inflicted on Jupiter. This wish both to revoke and remember the curse allows for an escape, on his part, from the cycle of mutual hatred which dominates the opening lines of the work. Intransigent opposition to Jupiter is necessary if tyranny is to be overthrown, yet Shelley suggests, too, the need not to remain 'eyeless in hate' (l. 9), a Miltonic phrase which the hovering syntax attributes to both parties. Once Prometheus has re-experienced the curse, by summoning up the Phantasm of Jupiter to repeat it, he is able, as in a session of psychoanalytical therapy, to work through and leave behind his desire for revenge against Jupiter. The rest of the act consists of two main sections; in one, Prometheus wards off temptations to despair, temptations orchestrated by Mercury, Jupiter's hand-wringing henchman; in the other, he receives comfort from Spirits of the Human Mind, who anticipate – though not without complications – a redeemed future.

Prometheus Unbound has a nuanced and complex way with precursor texts. It brings them to mind, only to rewrite them. It alludes to Aeschylus' *Prometheus Bound*, but it aligns the Greek dramatist's work with the Romantic poet's hope for change in post-revolutionary Europe. Shelley's lyrical drama searches past literature and culture for ideas and images that can help him communicate his own 'beautiful idealisms of moral excellence'. He is 'averse to a catastrophe so feeble as that of reconciling the Champion with the Oppressor of mankind' such as Aeschylus' lost play *Prometheus Unbound* was supposed to supply. Indeed, his play addresses various predecessors in a provocative epigraph at the head of the *Prometheus Unbound* volume, 'Audisne haec, Amphiarae, sub terram abdite?' (Do you hear this, Amphiaraus, hidden under the earth?). Amphiaraus was a King of Argos and a seer, favoured by Zeus who saved him in a battle by swallowing him up in the earth. The line quoted by Shelley is a line from Aeschylus' lost tragedy *Epigoni*, extant in Cicero's *Tusculan Disuptations*. In a notebook Shelley quotes the line below the words 'To the Ghost of Aeschylus'. To the degree that Aeschylus is among those addressed, Shelley is telling him that his own version of *Prometheus Unbound* will not seek to appease the 'Oppressor of mankind'.

At the same time, Shelley wished to reimagine a revolution shorn of the horrors and excesses which disfigured the French Revolution. Here the character of the hero, his mental state, is all-important. Like *The Prelude* and *The First Book of Urizen*, *Prometheus Unbound* is a Romantic retelling of *Paradise Lost*. Shelley chooses Prometheus rather than Satan as his hero, he tells us in his Preface, because the latter is more flawed than the former. Jupiter is associated through verbal echoes with Milton's God, a tyrannical figure, for Shelley as for Blake, and Prometheus shares with Milton's Satan, as Shelley reads *Paradise Lost*, qualities of 'courage and majesty and firm and patient opposition to omnipotent force'.

Prometheus needs to move beyond hatred and the thirst for revenge if he is to avert the cycle of revolt, bloodshed and restoration of tyranny evident in recent historical events. Shelley's work steeps itself in recent history, and yet it possesses, too, a remarkable generalizing sweep as it links (for example) the fate of the French Revolution to the abuse made of Christ's teaching by those who use religion to sanction violence; both serve as temptations to despair that the hero must experience yet resist. Shelley's idiom allows for recent political and historical upheavals to register as examples only. The present, for Shelley, is but the latest enactment of an ongoing fight between tyranny and freedom; he seeks imaginatively to resolve that fight and offer an imagined future free from strife through his ambitious rewriting of myth.

As a 'lyrical drama', *Prometheus Unbound* enacts its 'drama', at the heart of which is the contest between Jupiter and Prometheus, through poetic forms that aspire to the condition of music. Music is a central image for harmony throughout the work; the presence in the work of many lyrical forms bears witness to the longing for such harmony, and to Shelley's sense of the universe as alive with cosmic voices. Lyrical drama is, above all, a drama in which states of mind and orientations of consciousness matter supremely. This is not to say that Shelley has wholly abandoned the belief in Necessity apparent in *Queen Mab*. In that poem Shelley apostrophizes in this way: 'Spirit of Nature! all-sufficing Power, / Necessity! thou mother of the world!' (6. 197–8). He embraces Necessity precisely because, unlike the Christian God, it is indifferent to 'prayers or praises', 'the caprice / Of man's weak will' (6. 200, 200–1). And yet Necessity serves as the master of 'life, in multitudinous shapes, / Still pressing forward where no term can be' (6. 235–6). In *Prometheus Unbound*, Shelley still believes that things will happen because they must. The figure of Demogorgon is a riddle who seems to have a connection with the idea of Necessity; he tells Jupiter that he is 'Eternity – demand no direr name' (3. 1. 52). Larger forces, Shelley suggests, are at work in history.

Yet crucial to *Prometheus Unbound* is a strong conviction of the significance of mind, will and imagination. This conviction affects not only the portrayal of the hero in Act 1; it extends also to Shelley's developing grasp of the impact made by imaginative literature on readers. In his Preface he articulates his view, spelled out in *A Defence of Poetry*, that it is not the proper function of the poet to offer, in his poetry, 'a reasoned system on the theory of human life'; instead, poets should attempt to work on the imaginations of their readers. This stance does not mean that his poetry is at odds with 'a passion for reforming the world', but it does demand a greater sophistication than a merely propagandist poetics would countenance.

The inventiveness of Shelley's 'lyrical drama' means that it is suggestively open to different readings. In the first act, such inventiveness shows in the reworking of predecessors (see notes for more details) and in the interplay between blank verse and lyrical forms. The blank verse, in the opening speech, involves revisionary Miltonic echoes, as when Prometheus speaks of the fearful tribute paid to Jupiter of 'knee-worship, prayer and praise' (1. 6), recalling Satan's contemptuous reference to 'Knee-tribute yet unpaid, prostration vile' (*Paradise Lost*, 5. 782). The effect of the echo is to align Prometheus with Satan, and to suggest that in *Prometheus Unbound* Milton's Christian God has been reconfigured as a tyrant. Later in the same speech, Shelley produces a different kind of blank verse, one far more removed in its melodious and syntactical fluency from Milton's practice: 'The crawling glaciers pierce me with the spears / Of their moon-freezing chrystals; the bright chains / Eat with their burning cold into my bones' (31–3). Though the content alludes to pain, the lines have an assonantal beauty that allows us, very faintly, to discern the alternative, radiant vision about to emerge in the poem.

Shelley's lyrics are especially attuned to the way physical objects can allude to mental states. The Fourth Spirit tells how the poet, attentively meditating on the natural world, paradoxically does not 'heed nor see what things they be' (l. 746); they concern him in that they are materials from which he can shape 'Forms more real than living man' (l. 748). In so doing, the poet rebukes the misshaping of the Furies, which involves a parody of creative activity, as they take on form from their 'victim's destined agony' (1. 470). The ultimate truth may be 'imageless' (2. 4. 116), but Shelley's lyrics teem with images that strive to steer the reader's imagination in the direction of 'beautiful idealisms of moral excellence', while making clear that such a journey can easily be interrupted. Idealism's potential shipwreck lurks in every corner of the lyrical drama.

Text based on 1820, revised in the light of Mary Shelley's 1839 editions and the fair-copy manuscript in the Bodleian Mss. Shelley e. l, e. 2 end e. 3. (see *The Bodleian Shelley Manuscripts*, vol. IX, ed. Neil Fraistat, London: Taylor and Francis, 1991).

Audisne haec, Amphiarae, sub terram abdite?

PREFACE

The Greek tragic writers, in selecting as their subject any portion of their national history or mythology, employed in their treatment of it a certain arbitrary discretion. They by no means conceived themselves bound to adhere to the common interpretation or to imitate in story as in title their rivals and predecessors. Such a system would have amounted to a resignation of those claims to preference over their competitors which incited the composition. The Agamemnonian story was exhibited on the Athenian theatre with as many variations as dramas.

I have presumed to employ a similar licence. The *Prometheus Unbound* of Aeschylus supposed the reconciliation of Jupiter with his victim as the price of the disclosure of the danger threatened to his empire by the consummation of his marriage with Thetis. Thetis, according to this view of the subject, was given in marriage to Peleus, and Prometheus, by the permission of Jupiter, delivered from his captivity by Hercules. Had I framed my story on this model, I should have done no more than have attempted to restore the lost drama of Aeschylus; an ambition which, if my preference to this mode of treating the subject had incited me to cherish, the recollection of the high comparison such an attempt would challenge might welt abate. But, in truth, I was averse from a catastrophe so feeble as that of reconciling the Champion with the Oppressor of mankind. The moral interest of the fable, which is so powerfully sustained by the sufferings and endurance of Prometheus, would be annihilated if we could conceive of him as unsaying his high language and quailing before his successful and perfidious adversary. The only imaginary being resembling in any degree Prometheus is Satan; and Prometheus is, in my judgement, a more poetical character than Satan, because, in addition to courage, and majesty, and firm and patient opposition to omnipotent force, he is susceptible of being described as exempt from the taints of ambition, envy, revenge, and a desire for personal aggrandisement, which, in the Hero of *Paradise Lost,* interfere with the interest. The character of Satan engenders in the mind a pernicious casuistry which leads us to weigh his faults with his wrongs, and to excuse the former because the latter exceed all measure. In the minds of those who consider that magnificent fiction with a religious feeling it engenders something worse. But Prometheus is, as it were, the type of the highest perfection of moral and intellectual nature, impelled by the purest and the truest motives to the best and noblest ends.

This Poem was chiefly written upon the mountainous ruins of the Baths of Caracalla, among the flowery glades, and thickets of odoriferous blossoming trees, which are extended in ever widening labyrinths upon its immense platforms and dizzy arches suspended in the air. The bright blue sky of Rome, and the effect of the vigorous awakening of spring in that divinest climate, and the new life with which it drenches the spirits even to intoxication, were the inspiration of this drama.

The imagery which I have employed will be found, in many instances, to have been drawn from the operations of the human mind, or from those external actions by which they are expressed. This is unusual in modern poetry, although Dante and Shakespeare are full of instances of the same kind: Dante indeed more than any other poet, and with greater success. But the Greek poets, as writers to whom no resource of awakening the sympathy of their contemporaries was unknown, were in the habitual use of this power; and it is the study of their works (since a higher merit would probably be denied me) to which I am willing that my readers should impute this singularity.

Preface
Epigraph Audisne ... abdite? See Headnote for translation and provenance. The line is addressed in one of Shelley's notebooks 'To the Ghost of Aeschylus'; more generally, it throws the gauntlet down to other precursor poets, including Milton in *Paradise Lost* and Byron in *Manfred* (1817), a work which Shelley admired even as he dissented from what he saw as its pessimism.
Paragraph 2 *unsaying his high language* In fact, Prometheus does exactly this in the work's complex opening; after hearing his former curse, he says, 'It doth repent me: words are quick and vain' (1. 303). The function of language is always to the fore in *Prometheus Unbound.*
pernicious casuistry We wish to excuse Satan his crimes because of our indignation at his injuries; the result is a confused muddle. In the Preface to *The Cenci*, however, Shelley finds in the 'restless and anatomizing casuistry' provoked by the story of Beatrice a clue to the 'dramatic character' (p. 317) of her life. In *Prometheus Unbound* the hero may not quite be so free from fault as, here, Shelley asserts that he is.
Paragraph 3 *vigorous awakening of spring* One of the dominant metaphors in the second act is the idea of the arrival of spring.
Paragraph 4 *The imagery ... are expressed* Shelley alerts his readers to the degree to which his 'imagery' brings to the fore 'the operations of the human mind'. Mary Shelley's 'Note on *Prometheus Unbound*' in her 1839 edition of the poetry helpfully draws attention to Shelley's admiring comment in a notebook on a line from Sophocles which he renders as 'Coming to many ways in the wanderings of careful thought' and praises in these terms: 'What a picture does this line suggest of the mind as a wilderness of intricate paths, wide as the universe, which is here made its symbol'.

One word is due in candour to the degree in which the study of contemporary writings may have tinged my composition, for such has been a topic of censure with regard to poems far more popular, and indeed more deservedly popular, than mine. It is impossible that any one who inhabits the same age with such writers as those who stand in the foremost ranks of our own, can conscientiously assure himself that his language and tone of thought may not have been modified by the study of the productions of those extraordinary intellects. It is true that, not the spirit of their genius, but the forms in which it has manifested itself, are due less to the peculiarities of their own minds than to the peculiarity of the moral and intellectual condition of the minds among which they have been produced. Thus a number of writers possess the form, whilst they want the spirit of those whom, it is alleged, they imitate; because the former is the endowment of the age in which they live, and the latter must be the uncommunicated lightning of their own mind.

The peculiar style of intense and comprehensive imagery which distinguishes the modern literature of England, has not been, as a general power, the product of the imitation of any particular writer. The mass of capabilities remains at every period materially the same; the circumstances which awaken it to action perpetually change. If England were divided into forty republics, each equal in population and extent to Athens, there is no reason to suppose but that, under institutions not more perfect than those of Athens, each would produce philosophers and poets equal to those who (if we except Shakespeare) have never been surpassed. We owe the great writers of the golden age of our literature to that fervid awakening of the public mind which shook to dust the oldest and most oppressive form of the Christian religion. We owe Milton to the progress and development of the same spirit: the sacred Milton was, let it ever be remembered, a republican, and a bold inquirer into morals and religion. The great writers of our own age are, we have reason to suppose, the companions and forerunners of some unimagined change in our social condition or the opinions which cement it. The cloud of mind is discharging its collected lightning, and the equilibrium between institutions and opinions is now restoring, or is about to be restored.

As to imitation, poetry is a mimetic art. It creates, but it creates by combination and representation. Poetical abstractions are beautiful and new, not because the portions of which they are composed had no previous existence in the mind of man or in nature, but because the whole produced by their combination has some intelligible and beautiful analogy with those sources of emotion and thought, and with the contemporary condition of them: one great poet is a masterpiece of nature which another not only ought to study but must study. He might as wisely and as easily determine that his mind should no longer be the mirror of all that is lovely in the visible universe, as exclude from his contemplation the beautiful which exists in the writings of a great contemporary. The pretence of doing it would be a presumption in any but the greatest; the effect, even in him, would be strained, unnatural, and ineffectual. A poet is the combined product of such internal powers as modify the nature of others, and of such external influences as excite and sustain these powers; he is not one, but both. Every man's mind is, in this respect, modified by all the objects of nature and art; by every word and every suggestion which he ever admitted to act upon his consciousness; it is the mirror upon which all forms are reflected, and in which they compose one form. Poets, not otherwise than philosophers, painters, sculptors and musicians, are, in one sense, the creators, and, in another, the creations, of their age. From this subjection the loftiest do not escape. There is a similarity between Homer and Hesiod, between Aeschylus and Euripides, between Virgil and Horace, between Dante and Petrarch, between Shakespeare and Fletcher, between Dryden and Pope; each has a generic resemblance under which their specific distinctions are arranged. If this similarity be the result of imitation, I am willing to confess that I have imitated.

Let this opportunity be conceded to me of acknowledging that I have what a Scotch philosopher characteristically terms, 'a passion for reforming the world': what passion incited him to write and publish his book, he omits to explain. For my part I had rather be damned with Plato and Lord Bacon, than go to

---

Paragraph 5   *It is impossible . . . extraordinary intellects* Part of Shelley's response to an extremely hostile review of *The Revolt of Islam* which had appeared in the *Quarterly Review*, 21 (1819); it assailed Shelley for allegedly plagiarizing from Wordsworth. Shelley's notebook shows that he had Coleridge and Byron in mind.

Paragraph 6   *The great writers . . . to be restored* Shelley associates contemporary poetry with 'some unimagined change in our social condition' without explicitly ascribing to poetry or the 'social condition' a causal role. *Prometheus Unbound* seeks to imagine the grounds and nature of such an 'unimagined change'.

Paragraph 7   *A poet . . . but both* The sentence reveals Shelley's sense of the reciprocal dynamics involved in poetic creation between 'internal powers' and 'external influences'.

Paragraph 8   *Let this . . . publish this book* The 'Scotch philosopher' is Robert Forsyth and the quoted phrase is from his *Principles of Moral Science* (1805); Peacock uses it humorously in *Nightmare Abbey* (1818) in which he caricatures Shelley as the idealistic Scythrop Glowry, and Shelley is probably responding with equal good humour to Peacock here.

Heaven with Paley and Malthus. But it is a mistake to suppose that I dedicate my poetical compositions solely to the direct enforcement of reform, or that I consider them in any degree as containing a reasoned system on the theory of human life. Didactic poetry is my abhorrence; nothing can be equally well expressed in prose that is not tedious and supererogatory in verse. My purpose has hitherto been simply to familiarize the highly refined imagination of the more select classes of poetical readers with beautiful idealisms of moral excellence; aware that until the mind can love, and admire, and trust, and hope, and endure, reasoned principles of moral conduct are seeds cast upon the highway of life, which the unconscious passenger tramples into the dust, although they would bear the harvest of his happiness. Should I live to accomplish what I purpose, that is, produce a systematical history of what appear to me to be the genuine elements of human society, let not the advocates of injustice and superstition flatter themselves that I should take Aeschylus rather than Plato as my model.

The having spoken of myself with unaffected freedom will need little apology with the candid; and let the uncandid consider that they injure me less than their own hearts and minds by misrepresentation. Whatever talents a person may possess to amuse and instruct others, be they ever so inconsiderable, he is yet bound to exert them: if his attempt be ineffectual, let the punishment of an unaccomplished purpose have been sufficient; let none trouble themselves to heap the dust of oblivion upon his efforts; the pile they raise will betray his grave which might otherwise have been unknown.

DRAMATIS PERSONAE

PROMETHEUS.
DEMOGORGON.
JUPITER.
The EARTH.
OCEAN.
APOLLO.
MERCURY.
HERCULES.

ASIA.
PANTHEA. } Oceanides.
IONE.
The PHANTASM of JUPITER.
The SPIRIT of the EARTH.
The SPIRIT of the MOON.
SPIRITS of the HOURS.
SPIRITS. ECHOES. FAUNS.
FURIES.

Act I

SCENE.—*A ravine of icy rocks in the Indian Caucasus.* PROMETHEUS *is discovered bound to the precipice.* PANTHEA *and* IONE *are seated at his feet. Time, night. During the Scene, morning slowly breaks.*

Plato and Lord Bacon Intellectual heroes of Shelley, the former for his subtle imaginativeness and transcendent reach, the latter for his belief in enquiry.
Paley and Malthus William Paley, the author of *Evidences of Christianity* (1794), a work recommended to Shelley by his father and much disliked by the poet; Thomas Malthus, the author of *An Essay on the Principle of Population* (1798), a work which argued in direct contradiction to Godwin's notion of perfectibility that population increased at a rate that could not be matched by resources, and that, therefore (as interpreted by his ideological enemies, including Godwin and Shelley), famine and war were necessary means by which the growth of numbers were kept in check.
a systematical history Shelley comes closest to writing such a history in *A Philosophical View of Reform* (1819–20), composed about the time he was writing this section of the Preface.
Paragraph 9   *The having . . . have been unknown* Not merely a conventional formulation; the *Prometheus Unbound* volume longs for a state in which 'The world should listen', as 'To a Skylark' (l. 105) has it, and, correspondingly, the fear of not being listened to is a strong undercurrent in Shelley's work.
Act 1
Stage direction   *Indian Caucasus* The Hindu Kush, associated with the origins of civilization. Shelley's imagination links West and East in a harmonizing (rather than proto-imperialist) gesture.
During . . . breaks The slowly breaking morning has a symbolic resonance, suggestive of a long millennial day.

Prometheus. Monarch of Gods and Daemons, and all Spirits
But One, who throng those bright and rolling worlds
Which Thou and I alone of living things
Behold with sleepless eyes, regard this Earth
Made multitudinous with thy slaves, whom thou 5
Requitest for knee-worship, prayer, and praise,
And toil, and hecatombs of broken hearts,
With fear and self-contempt and barren hope;
Whilst me, who am thy foe, eyeless in hate,
Hast thou made reign and triumph, to thy scorn, 10
O'er mine own misery and thy vain revenge.
Three thousand years of sleep-unsheltered hours,
And moments aye divided by keen pangs
Till they seemed years, torture and solitude,
Scorn and despair,—these are mine empire: 15
More glorious far than that which thou surveyest
From thine unenvied throne, O Mighty God!
Almighty, had I deigned to share the shame
Of thine ill tyranny, and hung not here
Nailed to this wall of eagle-baffling mountain, 20
Black, wintry, dead, unmeasured; without herb,
Insect, or beast, or shape or sound of life.
Ah me! alas, pain, pain ever, forever!

No change, no pause, no hope! Yet I endure.
I ask the Earth, have not the mountains felt? 25
I ask yon Heaven, the all-beholding Sun,
Has it not seen? The Sea, in storm or calm,
Heaven's ever-changing Shadow, spread below,
Have its deaf waves not heard my agony?
Ah me! alas, pain, pain ever, forever! 30

The crawling glaciers pierce me with the spears
Of their moon-freezing chrystals; the bright chains
Eat with their burning cold into my bones.
Heaven's winged hound, polluting from thy lips
His beak in poison not his own, tears up 35
My heart; and shapeless sights come wandering by,

---

1 *Monarch* Jupiter.
1 *Daemons* In Plato's *Symposium*, translated by Shelley, beings intermediary between the divine and the mortal.
2 *One* Prometheus or, possibly, Demogorgon.
6 *knee-worship* For the Miltonic echo of *Paradise Lost* (hereafter *PL*), 5, l. 782, see Headnote.
7 *hecatombs* Large sacrifices.
8 *self-contempt* The opposite of what in 'Hymn to Intellectual Beauty' Shelley calls 'Self-esteem'; it involves an internalized sense of worthlessness, often the product of tyranny or indoctrination.
9 *eyeless in hate* The phrase, adapted from Milton, *Samson Agonistes* where Samson describes himself as 'Eyeless in Gaza at the mill with slaves' (l. 41), might be attached either to 'me' (that is, Prometheus) or to 'thou' (l. 10) (that is, Jupiter): the ambiguity suggests that Jupiter and Prometheus are locked in a system of mutual hate.

18–19 *Almighty . . . tyranny* Shelley's syntax is compressed; Jupiter would indeed be 'Almighty', had Prometheus not resisted him and therefore been condemned to his present sufferings.
20 *wall . . . mountain* Compare *Prometheus Bound*, l. 15: 'this bitter, bleak ravine'.
31–3 *The crawling . . . bones* The very sensuousness of these lines implies that Prometheus is beginning to move away from the mere iteration of 'pain' (as in ll. 23 and 30).
31 *spears* Recalls Christ's side being pierced by a spear after his death on the cross, one of many links between Christ and Prometheus established in the first act (see also l. 20 where Prometheus is 'Nailed' to the mountain as Christ was to the cross): see John 19: 34, 'But one of the soldiers with a spear pierced his side, and forthwith came there out blood and water'.

The ghastly people of the realm of dream,
Mocking me; and the Earthquake-fiends are charged
To wrench the rivets from my quivering wounds
When the rocks split and close again behind; 40
While from their loud abysses howling throng
The genii of the storm, urging the rage
Of whirlwind, and afflict me with keen hail.
And yet to me welcome is day and night,
Whether one breaks the hoar frost of the morn, 45
Or starry, dim, and slow, the other climbs
The leaden-coloured east; for then they lead
Their wingless, crawling Hours, one among whom
—As some dark Priest hales the reluctant victim—
Shall drag thee, cruel King, to kiss the blood 50
From these pale feet, which then might trample thee
If they disdained not such a prostrate slave.
Disdain? Ah no! I pity thee. What ruin
Will hunt thee undefended through wide Heaven!
How will thy soul, cloven to its depth with terror, 55
Gape like a hell within! I speak in grief,
Not exultation, for I hate no more,
As then, ere misery made me wise. The curse
Once breathed on thee I would recall. Ye Mountains,
Whose many-voiced Echoes, through the mist 60
Of cataracts, flung the thunder of that spell!
Ye icy Springs, stagnant with wrinkling frost,
Which vibrated to hear me, and then crept
Shuddering through India! Thou serenest Air,
Through which the Sun walks burning without beams! 65
And ye swift Whirlwinds, who on poised wings
Hung mute and moveless o'er yon hushed abyss,
As thunder, louder than your own, made rock
The orbed world—if then my words had power,
Though I am changed so that aught evil wish 70
Is dead within; although no memory be
Of what is hate—let them not lose it now!
What was that curse? for ye all heard me speak.

42 *The genii of the storm* The 'genii' personify forces at work in the natural world.
44–52 *And yet . . . slave* Shelley is adapting lines from *Prometheus Bound* 23–5 ('Glad you will be to see the night / Cloaking the day with her dark spangled robe; and glad / Again when the sun's warmth scatters the frost at dawn') to his hero's premonition of eventual triumph.
49 *As . . . victim* The simile betrays Prometheus; it suggests a connection between his longing for vengeance and religious tyranny.
53–9 *Disdain . . . recall* The drama's central 'reversal', placed daringly close to its opening. Prometheus' recoil from 'disdain' is captured in the language; he repeats 'Disdain' (l. 53) from the previous line, and revolts against the word's implications. Subsequent lines allow him both to imagine Jupiter's fall with some relish and to assert that he speaks 'in grief / Not exultation' (ll. 56–7). His assertion is credible precisely because Shelley suggests that hatred for Jupiter cannot be erased at a stroke.
59 *recall* Means to remember and to revoke, in context a fruitful ambiguity since it allows us to see Prometheus as he was (and to a degree still is) even as he is in the process of transcending his earlier self.
63 *vibrated* Quivered. The word appears to have been stressed on the first syllable in some poetry of the period, as in Coleridge's 'To William Wordsworth', 'When France in all towns lay vibrating' (l. 23), or Shelley's own 'Ode to Liberty', 'A glorious people vibrated again / The lightning of the nations' (ll. 1–2).
64–5 *Thou . . . beams* In this 'air' the sun's beams are not refracted.

First Voice (from the Mountains)

Thrice three hundred thousand years
   O'er the Earthquake's couch we stood:
Oft, as men convulsed with fears,
   We trembled in our multitude.

Second Voice (from the Springs)

Thunderbolts had parched our water,
   We had been stained with bitter blood,
And had run mute, 'mid shrieks of slaughter,
   Through a city and a solitude.

Third Voice (from the Air)

I had clothed, since Earth uprose,
   Its wastes in colours not their own,
And oft had my serene repose
   Been cloven by many a rending groan.

Fourth Voice (from the Whirlwinds)

We had soared beneath these mountains
   Unresting ages; nor had thunder,
Nor yon volcano's flaming fountains,
   Nor any power above or under
Ever made us mute with wonder.

First Voice

But never bowed our snowy crest
As at the voice of thine unrest.

Second Voice

Never such a sound before
To the Indian waves we bore.
A pilot asleep on the howling sea
Leaped up from the deck in agony,
And heard, and cried, 'Ah, woe is me!'
And died as mad as the wild waves be.

Third Voice

By such dread words from Earth to Heaven
My still realm was never riven:
When its wound was closed, there stood
Darkness o'er the day like blood.

---

74 *Thrice . . . years* The first line of a lyric in which nature is given a voice. As Mary Shelley puts it in her brilliant if at times arguable 'Note' to the poem, 'Shelley loved to idealize the real – to gift the mechanism of the material universe with a soul and a voice, and to bestow such also on the most delicate and abstract emotions and thoughts of the mind'. The quest for authentic voice, on the part of poet and hero, is close to the heart of the lyrical drama.

101–2 *there . . . blood* Again recalls the crucifixion; see Luke 23: 44: '. . . and there was a darkness over all the earth until the ninth hour'. The natural elements experienced the curse as a 'wound', yet a sublime one, that made subsequent 'silence . . . hell to us' (l. 106).

Fourth Voice

And we shrank back: for dreams of ruin
To frozen caves our flight pursuing
Made us keep silence—thus—and thus— 105
Though silence is as hell to us.

The Earth. The tongueless Caverns of the craggy hills
Cried, 'Misery!' then; the hollow Heaven replied,
'Misery!' and the Ocean's purple waves,
Climbing the land, howled to the lashing winds, 110
And the pale nations heard it, 'Misery!

Prometheus. I hear a sound of voices: not the voice
Which I gave forth. Mother, thy sons and thou
Scorn him, without whose all-enduring will
Beneath the fierce omnipotence of Jove, 115
Both they and thou had vanished, like thin mist
Unrolled on the morning wind. Know ye not me,
The Titan? he who made his agony
The barrier to your else all-conquering foe?
O rock-embosomed lawns and snow-fed streams, 120
Now seen athwart frore vapours, deep below,
Through whose o'ershadowing woods I wandered once
With Asia, drinking life from her loved eyes,
Why scorns the spirit which informs ye, now
To commune with me? me alone, who checked— 125
As one who checks a fiend-drawn charioteer—
The falsehood and the force of him who reigns
Supreme, and with the groans of pining slaves
Fills your dim glens and liquid wildernesses?
Why answer ye not, still? Brethren!

The Earth.   They dare not. 130

Prometheus. Who dares? For I would hear that curse again.
Ha, what an awful whisper rises up!
'Tis scarce like sound: it tingles through the frame
As lightning tingles, hovering ere it strike.
Speak, Spirit! from thine inorganic voice 135
I only know that thou art moving near
And love. How cursed I him?

---

112 *I hear a sound of voices* Prometheus and the Earth speak different languages, an image both of division and of the fact that the poem as a whole is searching for what later it calls 'A voice to be accomplished' (3. 3. 67).
117 *Know ye not me* Another echo of *PL*, this time of Satan's scornful question to Ithuriel and Zephon, the angels guarding Eden, 'Know ye not me? Ye knew me once no mate / For you, sitting where you durst not soar' (4. 828–9). Prometheus' tone is pleading as well as self-assertive.
121 *frore* Frozen.
122–3 *I wandered . . . eyes* Introduces Asia, Prometheus' female counterpart and the central figure in Act 2, in which she is both embodiment of love and beauty, and intellectual enquirer; the image of 'drinking love' suggests that love is as necessary to life as water.

126 *fiend-drawn charioteer* The image undergoes a positive makeover in 2. 4. where the chariots of the hours bringing the liberation of Prometheus are each drawn by 'A wild-eyed charioteer' (l. 132).
131 *Who dares . . . again* The lines and those following it again emphasize the difficulty of communication.
135 *inorganic* 'Not furnished with or acting by bodily or material organs'. Prometheus cannot trace the voice he hears to a bodily form.
137 *And love* Sometimes treated as a crux, the effect of 'And love' (meaning 'And that thou lovest') is affectingly simple after the communicative problems highlighted in previous lines. Though these problems persist, they gradually wane until at line 191, the Earth responds directly to Prometheus' plea.

The Earth. How canst thou hear
Who knowest not the language of the dead?

Prometheus. Thou art a living spirit; speak as they.

The Earth. I dare not speak like life, lest Heaven's fell King 140
Should hear, and link me to some wheel of pain
More torturing than the one whereon I roll.
Subtle thou art and good, and though the Gods
Hear not this voice, yet thou art more than God,
Being wise and kind: earnestly hearken now. 145

Prometheus. Obscurely through my brain, like shadows dim,
Sweep awful thoughts, rapid and thick. I feel
Faint, like one mingled in entwining love;
Yet 'tis not pleasure.

The Earth. No, thou canst not hear:
Thou art immortal, and this tongue is known 150
Only to those who die.

Prometheus. And what art thou,
O melancholy Voice?

The Earth. I am the Earth,
Thy mother; she within whose stony veins,
To the last fibre of the loftiest tree
Whose thin leaves trembled in the frozen air, 155
Joy ran, as blood within a living frame,
When thou didst from her bosom, like a cloud
Of glory, arise—a spirit of keen joy!
And at thy voice her pining sons uplifted
Their prostrate brows from the polluting dust, 160
And our almighty Tyrant with fierce dread
Grew pale, until his thunder chained thee here.
Then, see those million worlds which burn and roll
Around us: their inhabitants beheld
My sphered light wane in wide Heaven; the sea 165
Was lifted by strange tempest, and new fire
From earthquake-rifted mountains of bright snow
Shook its portentous hair beneath Heaven's frown;
Lightning and Inundation vexed the plains;
Blue thistles bloomed in cities; foodless toads 170
Within voluptuous chambers panting crawled;
When Plague had fallen on man and beast and worm,
And Famine; and black blight on herb and tree;
And in the corn, and vines, and meadow-grass,
Teemed ineradicable poisonous weeds 175
Draining their growth, for my wan breast was dry
With grief; and the thin air, my breath, was stained
With the contagion of a mother's hate

---

156 *Joy . . . frame* The simile works to make 'Joy' part of a physical process.
163 *see* Frequently the cue for visionary sights in the work.
165–9 *the sea . . . plains* When Prometheus was chained, the disaster was marked by earthquake-induced tempests, volcanic eruptions, storms and floods.

178 *contagion* Here 'contagious influence', that is, 'disease-spreading influence', but elsewhere 'contagion' can imply, albeit ambivalently, a capacity for good as when at 2. 3. 10 Asia speaks of 'The voice which is contagion to the world'.

Breathed on her child's destroyer; aye, I heard
Thy curse, the which, if thou rememberest not, 180
Yet my innumerable seas and streams,
Mountains, and caves, and winds, and yon wide air,
And the inarticulate people of the dead,
Preserve, a treasured spell. We meditate
In secret joy and hope those dreadful words 185
But dare not speak them.

    Prometheus.   Venerable Mother!
All else who live and suffer take from thee
Some comfort; flowers, and fruit, and happy sounds,
And love, though fleeting; these may not be mine.
But mine own words, I pray, deny me not. 190

    The Earth. They shall be told. Ere Babylon was dust,
The Magus Zoroaster, my dead child,
Met his own image walking in the garden.
That apparition, sole of men, he saw.
For know there are two worlds of life and death: 195
One that which thou beholdest; but the other
Is underneath the grave, where do inhabit
The shadows of all forms that think and live
Till death unite them and they part no more;
Dreams and the light imaginings of men, 200
And all that faith creates or love desires,
Terrible, strange, sublime and beauteous shapes.
There thou art, and dost hang, a writhing shade,
'Mid whirlwind-shaken mountains; all the Gods
Are there, and all the Powers of nameless worlds, 205
Vast, sceptred Phantoms; heroes, men, and beasts;
And Demogorgon, a tremendous Gloom;
And he, the Supreme Tyrant, on his throne
Of burning gold. Son, one of these shall utter
The curse which all remember. Call at will 210

191–218 *They shall... palace* Perhaps the moment at which the lyrical drama takes full possession of its own imaginative world, the passage seems to fuse Zoroastrian emphases on correspondences between the seen and the unseen with Platonic intuitions of an ideal world of which this world is a shadow. The blank verse – authoritative, grave and musical – has moved beyond the Miltonic cadences capably and purposefully mimicked in sections of the opening speech.

192–3 *The Magus... garden* Zoroaster's encounter with his own 'image' is seen as an extraordinary 'apparition' (l. 194) and associated with his occult powers as a mage and with his death.

195 *For... death* Shelley appears to mean that there are 'two worlds', one of 'life', the other of 'death', but the idea that there are 'two worlds', each of 'life and death', cannot be excluded.

196–202 *One... shapes* One world is beheld by Prometheus; 'the other' is located 'underneath the grave', a place where 'shadows' of thinking and living 'forms' wait to be reunited in death. Shelley's wording makes this place both a symbol of division and of reunion. It is especially significant that it contains human 'Dreams' and 'imaginings'. From Earth's perspective, these 'imaginings' seem 'light'; the force attached to them by Shelley is evident in the strength of line 201. It is as if the shadow-world bore the same relation to Prometheus' world as a work of art bears to reality.

202 *Terrible... shapes* Compare Edmund Burke on Milton's description of Death in *PL*: 'all is dark, uncertain, confused, terrible, and sublime to the last degree' (*A Philosophical Enquiry into the Origins of our Ideas of the Sublime and the Beautiful*, 1757). Shelley has added 'beauteous' to Burke's list.

207 *Demogorgon... Gloom* Demogorgon was interpreted by Mary Shelley and, effectively, Peacock in *Rhododaphne* (1818) as 'the Primal Power' and has been seen by others on the basis of his name's etymology as people-monster (demos-gorgon). Shelley's emphasis throughout is on his unknowable inaccessibility yet power.

208 *Supreme Tyrant* Jupiter.

    Thine own ghost, or the ghost of Jupiter,
    Hades or Typhon, or what mightier Gods
    From all-prolific Evil since thy ruin
    Have sprung, and trampled on my prostrate Sons.
    Ask, and they must reply: so the revenge   215
    Of the Supreme may sweep through vacant shades,
    As rainy wind through the abandoned gate
    Of a fallen palace.

      Prometheus.   Mother, let not aught
    Of that which may be evil, pass again
    My lips, or those of aught resembling me.   220
    Phantasm of Jupiter, arise, appear!

                Ione

    My wings are folded o'er mine ears:
      My wings are crossed over mine eyes:
    Yet through their silver shade appears,
      And through their lulling plumes arise,   225
    A Shape, a throng of sounds:
      May it be no ill to thee
    O thou of many wounds!
    Near whom, for our sweet sister's sake,
    Ever thus we watch and wake.   230

              Panthea

    The sound is of whirlwind underground,
      Earthquake, and fire, and mountains cloven;
    The Shape is awful like the sound,
      Clothed in dark purple, star-inwoven.
    A sceptre of pale gold,   235
      To stay steps proud, o'er the slow cloud,
    His veined hand doth hold.
    Cruel he looks, but calm and strong,
    Like one who does, not suffers wrong.

    Phantasm of Jupiter.   Why have the secret powers of this strange world   240
    Driven me, a frail and empty phantom, hither
    On direst storms? What unaccustomed sounds
    Are hovering on my lips, unlike the voice
    With which our pallid race hold ghastly talk
    In darkness? And, proud sufferer, who art thou?   245

---

212 *Hades* Zeus' brother, god of the underworld.
212 *Typhon* A Titan buried by Zeus underneath a volcano in the Bay of Naples.
217–18 *As rainy ... palace* The simile combines an account of the ineffectuality of any would-be revenge with an image of deposed power.
221 *Phantasm of Jupiter* The curse is spoken, not by Prometheus' phantasm, but Jupiter's; the suggestion is that the unregenerate Prometheus bears a resemblance to Jupiter.
229 *our sweet sister's sake* Ione refers to Asia; she and Panthea are her companions, but they also comfort Prometheus in his sufferings. Ione is characterized as more fearful and wondering, Panthea as bolder and more able to record what is happening.
239 *Like one ... wrong* The difference is between tyrant (one who 'does' wrong) and victim (one who 'suffers' wrong), but Shelley often implies that between the two verbs, of doing and of suffering, there is a strong link.
242–5 *What ... darkness?* Again, emphasis is placed on the oddness and difficulty of speech; in this work the struggle for accurate linguistic representation is itself a dramatic action.

Prometheus. Tremendous Image, as thou art must be
He whom thou shadowest forth. I am his foe,
The Titan. Speak the words which I would hear,
Although no thought inform thine empty voice.

The Earth. Listen! And though your echoes must be mute, 250
Grey mountains, and old woods, and haunted springs,
Prophetic caves, and isle-surrounded streams,
Rejoice to hear what yet ye cannot speak.

Phantasm. A spirit seizes me and speaks within:
It tears me as fire tears a thunder-cloud. 255

Panthea. See, how he lifts his mighty looks, the Heaven
Darkens above.

Ione. He speaks! O shelter me!

Prometheus. I see the curse on gestures proud and cold,
And looks of firm defiance, and calm hate,
And such despair as mocks itself with smiles, 260
Written as on a scroll . . . yet speak—O speak!

Phantasm

Fiend, I defy thee! with a calm, fixed mind,
  All that thou canst inflict I bid thee do;
Foul Tyrant both of Gods and Humankind,
  One only being shalt thou not subdue. 265
Rain then thy plagues upon me here,
Ghastly disease, and frenzying fear;
And let alternate frost and fire
Eat into me, and be thine ire
Lightning, and cutting hail, and legioned forms 270
Of furies, driving by upon the wounding storms.

Aye, do thy worst. Thou art omnipotent.
  O'er all things but thyself I gave thee power,
And my own will. Be thy swift mischiefs sent
  To blast mankind, from yon etherial tower. 275
Let thy malignant spirit move
Its darkness over those I love:
On me and mine I imprecate
The utmost torture of thy hate,
And thus devote to sleepless agony 280
This undeclining head while thou must reign on high.

248–9 *Speak . . . empty voice* The Phantasm's 'empty voice' allows Prometheus to see and hear his own former self.
258 *I see . . . cold* This 'seeing', which picks up on Panthea's 'See' in line 256, involves a sense that the 'curse' has taken visible form and imprinted itself 'on gestures proud and cold'.
262–301 *Fiend . . . time* The verse form used for the lyric consists of a stanza made up of an initial quatrain in alternately rhyming iambic pentameters, followed by three rhyming couplets, the first two of which are iambic tetrameters, the last of which consists of an iambic pentameter followed by an alexandrine. Shelley's handling of the form captures the speaker's 'calm, fixed mind' (l. 262) in its measured use of end-stopped lines, but it also intimates his hope of ultimate revenge which pulses, in particular, through the long last line of each stanza.
276 *Let . . . move* A parody of Genesis 1: 2, 'And the Spirit of God moved upon the face of the waters'.

> But thou, who art the God and Lord: O thou
> > Who fillest with thy soul this world of woe,
> To whom all things of Earth and Heaven do bow
> > In fear and worship: all-prevailing foe! 285
> I curse thee! let a sufferer's curse
> Clasp thee, his torturer, like remorse,
> Till thine Infinity shall be
> A robe of envenomed agony;
> And thine Omnipotence a crown of pain 290
> To cling like burning gold round thy dissolving brain.
>
> Heap on thy soul, by virtue of this Curse,
> > Ill deeds; then be thou damned, beholding good;
> Both infinite as is the universe,
> > And thou, and thy self-torturing solitude. 295
> An awful image of calm power
> Though now thou sittest, let the hour
> Come, when thou must appear to be
> That which thou art internally,
> And after many a false and fruitless crime 300
> Scorn track thy lagging fall through boundless space and time.

Prometheus. Were these my words, O Parent?

The Earth.   They were thine.

Prometheus. It doth repent me: words are quick and vain;
Grief for a while is blind, and so was mine.
I wish no living thing to suffer pain. 305

The Earth

> Misery, oh misery to me,
> That Jove at length should vanquish thee.
> Wail, howl aloud, Land and Sea,
> The Earth's rent heart shall answer ye.
> Howl, Spirits of the living and the dead; 310
> Your refuge, your defence lies fallen and vanquished.

First Echo

Lies fallen and vanquished?

---

289 *A robe ... agony* Alludes to the poisoned shirt of Nessus which tormented Hercules and drove him to his death.
290 *a crown ... pain* Alludes to the crown of thorns which Jesus was made to wear after being sentenced by Pilate to crucifixion (see Matthew 27: 29).
292–3 *Heap ... good* Milton explains that Satan was allowed by 'the will / And high permission of all-ruling Heaven' to pursue his 'own dark designs' in order that 'he might / Heap on himself damnation' (*PL*, 2. 211–12, 213, 214–15). Shelley regarded Milton's explanation as proving God's cruelty and in *A Defence of Poetry* attacks the 'alleged design of exasperating [Satan] to deserve new torments' (p. 692). Prometheus cursed Jupiter in terms that recall Milton's explanation of God's 'design'. For this he is implicitly blamed, as is Milton's God. At the same time, Shelley allows Prometheus to voice his previous longing for revenge even as the hero, aghast at his former words, wishes to deny that longing; the result is poetry of a complex power.
297–8 *let the hour / Come* The enjambment works to enact the coming of the hour.
302–5 *They ... pain* The very closeness of the rhyming suggests Prometheus' sense of the link yet difference between 'then' and 'now'.
306 *Misery* Earth mistakenly interprets Prometheus' expression of regret for surrender.

Second Echo

Fallen and vanquished!

Ione

Fear not: 'tis but some passing spasm,
    The Titan is unvanquished still. 315
But see, where through the azure chasm
    Of yon forked and snowy hill,
Trampling the slant winds on high
    With golden-sandalled feet, that glow
Under plumes of purple dye, 320
Like rose-ensanguined ivory,
    A Shape comes now,
Stretching on high from his right hand
A serpent-cinctured wand.

Panthea. 'Tis Jove's world-wandering herald, Mercury. 325

Ione

And who are those with hydra tresses
    And iron wings that climb the wind,
Whom the frowning God represses
    Like vapours steaming up behind,
Clanging loud, an endless crowd— 330

Panthea

These are Jove's tempest-walking hounds,
Whom he gluts with groans and blood,
    When charioted on sulphurous cloud
    He bursts Heaven's bounds.

Ione

Are they now led from the thin dead, 335
    On new pangs to be fed?

Panthea. The Titan looks as ever, firm, not proud.

First Fury. Ha! I scent life!

Second Fury.   Let me but look into his eyes!

Third Fury. The hope of torturing him smells like a heap
Of corpses to a death-bird after battle. 340

First Fury. Darest thou delay, O Herald? take cheer, Hounds
Of Hell: what if the Son of Maia soon
Should make us food and sport? Who can please long
The Omnipotent?

---

322 *A Shape* The word implies the need for interpretation and identification (subsequently supplied by Panthea at l. 325); the pattern is repeated with the arrival of the Furies (ll. 326–34). The beauty of Ione's description proves deceptive since Mercury comes at the torturing behest of Jupiter.
324 *A . . . wand* A caduceus, or snake-encircled staff, symbol of Mercury.

331 *Jove's . . . hounds* Shelley's Furies represent a reworking of the Roman Furies or Greek Eumenides, who in Aeschylus' *Oresteian Trilogy* pursue Orestes after he has killed his mother, Clytemnestra.
342 *Son of Maia* Mercury, whose mother was Maia, one of the Pleiades.

Mercury.   Back to your towers of iron,
And gnash beside the streams of fire and wail
Your foodless teeth! . . . Geryon, arise! and Gorgon,
Chimaera, and thou Sphinx, subtlest of fiends,
Who ministered to Thebes Heaven's poisoned wine,
Unnatural love, and more unnatural hate:
These shall perform your task.

First Fury.   Oh, mercy! mercy!
We die with our desire: drive us not back!

Mercury. Crouch then in silence.
                  Awful Sufferer,
To thee unwilling, most unwillingly
I come, by the great Father's will driven down,
To execute a doom of new revenge.
Alas! I pity thee, and hate myself
That I can do no more—aye from thy sight
Returning, for a season, Heaven seems Hell,
So thy worn form pursues me night and day,
Smiling reproach. Wise art thou, firm and good,
But vainly wouldst stand forth alone in strife
Against the Omnipotent; as yon clear lamps
That measure and divide the weary years
From which there is no refuge, long have taught,
And long must teach. Even now thy Torturer arms
With the strange might of unimagined pains
The powers who scheme slow agonies in Hell,
And my commission is to lead them here,
Or what more subtle, foul or savage fiends
People the abyss, and leave them to their task.
Be it not so . . . there is a secret known
To thee, and to none else of living things,
Which may transfer the sceptre of wide Heaven,
The fear of which perplexes the Supreme:
Clothe it in words, and bid it clasp his throne
In intercession; bend thy soul in prayer,
And like a suppliant in some gorgeous fane,
Let the will kneel within thy haughty heart;
For benefits and meek submission tame
The fiercest and the mightiest.

Prometheus.   Evil minds

---

345 *streams of fire and wail* Refers to two rivers in the underworld, Phlegethon and Cocytus (a river of tears); 'wail' is almost certainly a noun.
346 *Geryon* A monster with three heads.
346 *Gorgon* Medusa, whose head turned the onlooker to stone.
347 *Chimaera* A monster with lion's head, goat's body and serpent's tail.
347 *Sphinx* Winged monster of Thebes with a woman's head and lion's body.
349 *Unnatural . . . hate* The consequences of Oedipus' solving of the Sphinx's riddle were his marriage to his mother Jocasta ('Unnatural love') and the subsequent tragic events involving, for example, Oedipus' cursing of his sons ('unnatural hate').
352–80 *Awful . . . mightiest* One of the work's most thought-provoking creations, Mercury represents the intellectual conservative who throws in his lot with tyranny; Shelley suggests his 'self-contempt' especially in lines 356–60.
371 *secret* In the original Prometheus story, the 'secret' is that the offspring of Thetis will be greater than his father (Jupiter). But in Shelley's play the precise nature of the 'secret' which will overthrow Jupiter is never made clear; it involves a complex of forces.

Change good to their own nature. I gave all
He has; and in return he chains me here
Years, ages, night and day: whether the Sun
Split my parched skin, or in the moony night
The chrystal-winged snow cling round my hair: 385
Whilst my beloved race is trampled down
By his thought-executing ministers.
Such is the tyrant's recompense—'tis just:
He who is evil can receive no good;
And for a world bestowed, or a friend lost, 390
He can feel hate, fear, shame; not gratitude:
He but requites me for his own misdeed.
Kindness to such is keen reproach, which breaks
With bitter stings the light sleep of Revenge.
Submission, thou dost know, I cannot try: 395
For what submission but that fatal word,
The death-seal of mankind's captivity,
Like the Sicilian's hair-suspended sword
Which trembles o'er his crown, would he accept,
Or could I yield? Which yet I will not yield. 400
Let others flatter Crime, where it sits throned
In brief Omnipotence; secure are they:
For Justice, when triumphant, will weep down
Pity, not punishment, on her own wrongs,
Too much avenged by those who err. I wait, 405
Enduring thus, the retributive hour
Which since we spake is even nearer now.
But hark, the hell-hounds clamour: fear delay:
Behold! Heaven lowers under thy Father's frown.

Mercury. Oh, that we might be spared: I to inflict, 410
And thou to suffer! Once more answer me:
Thou knowest not the period of Jove's power?

Prometheus. I know but this, that it must come.

Mercury.   Alas!
Thou canst not count thy years to come of pain?

Prometheus. They last while Jove must reign; nor more, nor less 415
Do I desire or fear.

Mercury.   Yet pause, and plunge
Into Eternity, where recorded time,
Even all that we imagine, age on age,
Seems but a point, and the reluctant mind

381–2 *I gave ... has* Prometheus has endowed Jupiter with power (see also ll. 273–4).
387 *thought-executing ministers* Alludes to *King Lear*'s 'thought-executing fires' (3. 2. 4); as used by Shelley, the phrase may mean 'speedy as thought' and 'putting an end to thought'.
395 *Submission ... try* Compare *PL*, 4. 81–2, where Satan says that 'pardon' (4. 80) is available only 'by submission; and that word / Disdain forbids me'.
398 *Like ... sword* The sword hanging by a horse's hair over the head of Damocles by Dionysius the Elder, ruler of Syracuse, to show him what the life of a ruler was like.
406 *the retributive hour* Further evidence of Prometheus' trust in the inevitability of retribution for Jupiter.
410–11 *I ... suffer!* Mercury experiences a sense of being trapped on the wrong side in a conflict with Prometheus.
417 *recorded time* Compare *Macbeth* (5. 5. 21), 'To the last syllable of recorded time'.

  Flags wearily in its unending flight,   420
Till it sink, dizzy, blind, lost, shelterless;
Perchance it has not numbered the slow years
Which thou must spend in torture, unreprieved.

  Prometheus. Perchance no thought can count them, yet they pass.

  Mercury. If thou might'st dwell among the Gods the while,   425
Lapped in voluptuous joy?

  Prometheus.   I would not quit
This bleak ravine, these unrepentant pains.

  Mercury. Alas! I wonder at, yet pity thee.

  Prometheus. Pity the self-despising slaves of Heaven,
Not me, within whose mind sits peace serene,   430
As light in the sun, throned: how vain is talk!
Call up the fiends.

  Ione.   O sister, look! White fire
Has cloven to the roots yon huge snow-loaded cedar;
How fearfully God's thunder howls behind!

  Mercury. I must obey his words and thine: alas!   435
Most heavily remorse hangs at my heart!

  Panthea. See where the child of Heaven with winged feet
Runs down the slanted sunlight of the dawn.

  Ione. Dear sister, close thy plumes over thine eyes
Lest thou behold and die—they come, they come   440
Blackening the birth of day with countless wings,
And hollow underneath, like death.

  First Fury.   Prometheus!

  Second Fury. Immortal Titan!

  Third Fury.   Champion of Heaven's slaves!

  Prometheus. He whom some dreadful voice invokes is here,
Prometheus, the chained Titan. Horrible forms,   445
What and who are ye? Never yet there came
Phantasms so foul through monster-teeming Hell
From the all-miscreative brain of Jove;
Whilst I behold such execrable shapes,

---

420 *Flags wearily* The opening stresses convey the oppressive endlessness of the mental journey through eternity.
424 *Perchance* Prometheus picks up on Mercury's use of the same word (l. 422).
430–1 *Not . . . throned* An example of imagery expressing the 'operations of the human mind', assimilating to the poem's liberal cause a word, 'throned', associated with monarchy.
431 *how vain is talk!* The futility of language is a multi-faceted theme in Shelley; here it indicates Prometheus' double sense that debate with Mercury is a waste of breath, and that talk itself is cheap: what counts is the will's continued resistance.
436 *remorse* An emotion associated by Shelley with ineffectual guilt.

437–8 *See . . . dawn* Panthea's description momentarily reconceives Mercury in painterly terms, partly serving to highlight, by contrast, the hideousness of the Furies, but reminding us, too, of the different ways art can function; here, the lines serve as a deliberate form of 'aestheticization'.
444 *some dreadful voice* Again a 'voice' is heard before its meanings become clear; Shelley makes the process of communication strange partly to compel our engagement with the text. Even when Prometheus concedes, 'I know ye' (l. 459), he asks further questions about the Furies (ll. 461–2, 464).
448 *the . . . Jove* Jove's 'miscreative brain' results in parodies of true creations.

Methinks I grow like what I contemplate, 450
And laugh and stare in loathsome sympathy.

First Fury. We are the ministers of pain, and fear,
And disappointment, and mistrust, and hate,
And clinging crime; and as lean dogs pursue
Through wood and lake some struck and sobbing fawn, 455
We track all things that weep, and bleed, and live,
When the great King betrays them to our will.

Prometheus. O many fearful natures in one name,
I know ye; and these lakes and echoes know
The darkness and the clangour of your wings. 460
But why more hideous than your loathed selves
Gather ye up in legions from the deep?

Second Fury. We knew not that: Sisters, rejoice, rejoice!

Prometheus. Can aught exult in its deformity?

Second Fury. The beauty of delight makes lovers glad, 465
Gazing on one another: so are we.
As from the rose which the pale priestess kneels
To gather for her festal crown of flowers
The aerial crimson falls, flushing her cheek,
So from our victim's destined agony 470
The shade which is our form invests us round,
Else are we shapeless as our mother Night.

Prometheus. I laugh your power, and his who sent you here,
To lowest scorn. Pour forth the cup of pain.

First Fury. Thou thinkest we will rend thee bone from bone, 475
And nerve from nerve, working like fire within?

Prometheus. Pain is my element, as hate is thine;
Ye rend me now: I care not.

Second Fury.   Dost imagine
We will but laugh into thy lidless eyes?

Prometheus. I weigh not what ye do, but what ye suffer, 480
Being evil. Cruel was the Power which called
You, or aught else so wretched, into light.

Third Fury. Thou think'st we will live through thee, one by one,
Like animal life, and though we can obscure not
The soul which burns within, that we will dwell 485
Beside it, like a vain loud multitude
Vexing the self-content of wisest men:
That we will be dread thought beneath thy brain,
And foul desire round thine astonished heart,
And blood within thy labyrinthine veins 490
Crawling like agony?

450–1 *Methinks ... sympathy* The idea of the mind's susceptibility to 'sympathy', 'loathsome' here, ennobling elsewhere, is central to the work.
465–72 *The beauty ... Night* The Furies parody the process by which lovers delight in one another; they take their form from their 'victim's destined agony' (l. 470).

They exist in part as mental projections, as Shelley implies in line 493 when Prometheus speaks of 'The torturing and conflicting throngs within'.
483–91 *Thou ... agony?* The Fury's question is a taunt and a torment, but it also contains a concession that 'we can obscure not / The soul which burns within'.

Prometheus. Why, ye are thus now:
Yet am I king over myself, and rule
The torturing and conflicting throngs within,
As Jove rules you when Hell grows mutinous.

Chorus of Furies

From the ends of the earth, from the ends of the earth, 495
Where the night has its grave and the morning its birth,
    Come, come, come!
O ye who shake hills with the scream of your mirth
When cities sink howling in ruin; and ye
Who with wingless footsteps trample the sea, 500
And close upon Shipwreck and Famine's track
Sit chattering with joy on the foodless wreck;
    Come, come, come!
Leave the bed, low, cold, and red,
Strewed beneath a nation dead; 505
Leave the hatred, as in ashes
    Fire is left for future burning:
It will burst in bloodier flashes
    When ye stir it, soon returning;
Leave the self-contempt implanted 510
In young spirits, sense-enchanted,
    Misery's yet unkindled fuel;
Leave Hell's secrets half unchanted
    To the maniac dreamer: cruel
More than ye can be with hate 515
    Is he with fear.
    Come, come, come!
We are steaming up from Hell's wide gate,
And we burthen the blasts of the atmosphere,
But vainly we toil till ye come here. 520

Ione. Sister, I hear the thunder of new wings.

Panthea. These solid mountains quiver with the sound
Even as the tremulous air: their shadows make
The space within my plumes more black than night.

First Fury

Your call was as a winged car, 525
Driven on whirlwinds fast and far;
It rapt us from red gulphs of war.

Second Fury

From wide cities, famine-wasted;

---

490 *labyrinthine veins* Conveys a vivid sense of the body's many-veined capacity for suffering.
495–577 *From the ends . . . win* Through a series of lyrical metres (broken by four lines of blank verse from Ione and Panthea at ll. 521–4), the Furies torment Prometheus with a series of visions.
505 *a nation dead* France is likely to be in Shelley's mind.

506 *as in ashes* Parodies the image used at the end of 'Ode to the West Wind' of 'Ashes and sparks' (l. 67) waiting to be rekindled.
510–11 *Leave . . . sense-enchanted* The deft lyricism suggests that young idealists are especially vulnerable to disillusion.

Third Fury

Groans half heard, and blood untasted;

Fourth Fury

Kingly conclaves stern and cold,
Where blood with gold is bought and sold;

Fifth Fury

From the furnace, white and hot,
In which—

A Fury

Speak not—whisper not:
I know all that ye would tell,
But to speak might break the spell
Which must bend the Invincible,
   The stern of thought;
He yet defies the deepest power of Hell.

Fury

Tear the veil!

Another Fury

It is torn!

Chorus

The pale stars of the morn
Shine on a misery, dire to be borne,
Dost thou faint, mighty Titan? We laugh thee to scorn.
Dost thou boast the clear knowledge thou waken'dst for man?
Then was kindled within him a thirst which outran
Those perishing waters; a thirst of fierce fever
Hope, love, doubt, desire—which consume him for ever.
   One came forth of gentle worth.
   Smiling on the sanguine earth;
   His words outlived him, like swift poison
      Withering up truth, peace, and pity.
   Look where round the wide horizon
      Many a million-peopled city
Vomits smoke in the bright air.
Hark that outcry of despair!
'Tis his mild and gentle ghost
      Wailing for the faith he kindled.
Look again, the flames almost

---

530 *Kingly conclaves* Such as the Congress of Vienna which followed the defeat of Napoleon. Shelley's topical allusions cluster in this part of the act.
535 *to speak . . . spell* The Fury interrupts the lyrical flow, ushering in a new series of temptations, begun by a metrical key-change at line 539.
546 *One came forth* Christ.
548–9 *His words . . . pity* The furies point to the fate of Christ's words, often used to sanction forms of war and intolerance.

       To a glow-worm's lamp have dwindled:
       The survivors round the embers
         Gather in dread.
           Joy, joy, joy!   560
Past ages crowd on thee, but each one remembers,
And the future is dark, and the present is spread
Like a pillow of thorns for thy slumberless head.

Semichorus 1

Drops of bloody agony flow
From his white and quivering brow   565
Grant a little respite now:
See, a disenchanted nation
Springs like day from desolation;
To Truth its state is dedicate,
And Freedom leads it forth, her mate;   570
A legioned band of linked brothers,
Whom Love calls children—

Semichorus 2

          'Tis another's—
   See how kindred murder kin:
   'Tis the vintage-time for death and sin: 575
   Blood, like new wine, bubbles within;
      Till Despair smothers
The struggling world, which slaves and tyrants win.
         [*All the* FURIES *vanish, except one.*]

Ione. Hark, sister! what a low yet dreadful groan
Quite unsuppressed is tearing up the heart
Of the good Titan, as storms tear the deep,   580
And beasts hear the sea moan in inland caves.
Darest thou observe how the fiends torture him?

Panthea. Alas! I looked forth twice, but will no more.

Ione. What didst thou see?

Panthea.   A woeful sight: a youth
With patient looks nailed to a crucifix.   585

Ione. What next?

Panthea.   The heaven around, the earth below
Was peopled with thick shapes of human death,
All horrible, and wrought by human hands,
And some appeared the work of human hearts,
For men were slowly killed by frowns and smiles: 590

---

563 *Like . . . thorns* The image, in effect, seeks to make Christ and Prometheus types of one another; it suits the Furies to do so since they are convinced that the institution of Christianity has distorted the teachings of its founder.
567 *a disenchanted nation* As in line 28 of Coleridge's 'France: An Ode', a poem admired by Shelley, the phrase means a nation freed from false enchantment and refers to France at the outset of the Revolution.

573–7 *See . . . win* The second Semichorus, in brusque verbal brushstrokes, sketches recent history from a pessimistic liberal standpoint: it alludes to the French Revolution's descent into internecine violence and the Reign of Terror, and the despairing aftermath of the Napoleonic Wars, won by reactionary forces.

And other sights too foul to speak and live
Were wandering by. Let us not tempt worse fear
By looking forth: those groans are grief enough.

    Fury. Behold, an emblem: those who do endure
Deep wrongs for man, and scorn, and chains, but heap   595
Thousandfold torment on themselves and him.

    Prometheus. Remit the anguish of that lighted stare;
Close those wan lips; let that thorn-wounded brow
Stream not with blood; it mingles with thy tears!
Fix, fix those tortured orbs in peace and death,   600
So thy sick throes shake not that crucifix,
So those pale fingers play not with thy gore.
O horrible! Thy name I will not speak,
It hath become a curse. I see, I see
The wise, the mild, the lofty, and the just,   605
Whom thy slaves hate for being like to thee,
Some hunted by foul lies from their heart's home,
An early-chosen, late-lamented home,
As hooded ounces cling to the driven hind;
Some linked to corpses in unwholesome cells;   610
Some—hear I not the multitude laugh loud?—
Impaled in lingering fire: and mighty realms
Float by my feet, like sea-uprooted isles,
Whose sons are kneaded down in common blood
By the red light of their own burning homes.   615

    Fury. Blood thou canst see, and fire; and canst hear groans:
Worse things unheard, unseen, remain behind.

    Prometheus. Worse?

    Fury.   In each human heart terror survives
The ravin it has gorged: the loftiest fear
All that they would disdain to think were true: 620
Hypocrisy and custom make their minds
The fanes of many a worship, now outworn.
They dare not devise good for man's estate,
And yet they know not that they do not dare.
The good want power, but to weep barren tears.   625
The powerful goodness want: worse need for them.
The wise want love; and those who love want wisdom;
And all best things are thus confused to ill.
Many are strong and rich, and would be just,
But live among their suffering fellow-men   630

---

594 *Behold, an emblem* The Fury's wish to fixate Prometheus' sight on a despairing emblem is powerful. Yet Prometheus searches for a way of looking that moves beyond such emblems, and when such 'sights . . . shall be no types of things which are' (ll. 643, 645).
597–604 *Remit . . . a curse* Marks Prometheus' anguished refusal to see Christ as his 'double'. He admires him, but feels that he is hopelessly embroiled in his followers' misconstructions.
609 *ounces* The mountain panther or snow leopard.
618–31 *In each . . . what they do* The passage evokes with bleak power the hold over people's minds of an incapacity for positive change; it is among the moments in the work that show Shelley's deep understanding of human complicity. Mary Shelley may have been right to say that 'Shelley believed that mankind had only to will that there should be no evil, and there would be none', but she underestimates his grasp of how infinitely difficult it was for us so 'to will'. In this speech which left its mark on Yeats's 'The Second Coming', Shelley uses a bare, diagnostic blank verse to communicate the stand-offs and contradictions that check potential for change.

As if none felt: they know not what they do.

Prometheus. Thy words are like a cloud of winged snakes;
And yet I pity those they torture not.

Fury. Thou pitiest them? I speak no more! [*Vanishes.*]

Prometheus. Ah woe!
Ah woe! Alas! pain, pain ever, forever! 635
I close my tearless eyes, but see more clear
Thy works within my woe-illumed mind,
Thou subtle tyrant! Peace is in the grave.
The grave hides all things beautiful and good:
I am a God and cannot find it there: 640
Nor would I seek it: for, though dread revenge,
This is defeat, fierce King, not victory!
The sights with which thou torturest gird my soul
With new endurance, till the hour arrives
When they shall be no types of things which are. 645

Panthea. Alas! what sawest thou more?

Prometheus. There are two woes:
To speak and to behold; thou spare me one.
Names are there, Nature's sacred watch-words, they
Were borne aloft in bright emblazonry;
The nations thronged around, and cried aloud, 650
As with one voice, 'Truth, liberty, and love!'
Suddenly fierce confusion fell from Heaven
Among them: there was strife, deceit, and fear;
Tyrants rushed in, and did divide the spoil.
This was the shadow of the truth I saw. 655

The Earth. I felt thy torture, Son, with such mixed joy
As pain and virtue give. To cheer thy state,
I bid ascend those subtle and fair spirits,
Whose homes are the dim caves of human thought,
And who inhabit, as birds wing the wind, 660
Its world-surrounding ether: they behold
Beyond that twilight realm, as in a glass,
The future: may they speak comfort to thee!

Panthea. Look, sister, where a troop of spirits gather,
Like flocks of clouds in spring's delightful weather, 665
Thronging in the blue air!

---

631 *they ... do* Alludes to Christ's words on the Cross: 'Then said Jesus, Father, forgive them; for they know not what they do' (Luke: 23: 34). The Fury's allusion, arguably, invalidates the argument that it intends to clinch since it stirs a memory of Christ's forgiveness, and forgiveness (or pity) is a clue to Prometheus' overcoming of the temptation.
635 *Alas ... forever!* Echoes lines 23 and 30.
645 *no .. are* Glimpses a mode of seeing which leaves behind the language of 'types', anticipating the more self-sustaining lyricism of the second act.
646–55 *Alas ... I saw* Once more, the process of interpretation is dwelt on, as Prometheus sums up for Panthea the significance of his sights and the difficulty of using words to describe them, partly because it causes pain to speak about them, partly because abuse of language is among the sources of pain.
659–63 *Whose homes ... The future* The spirits of the human mind dwell in the 'dim caves of human thought' (l. 659); but they also inhabit 'Its [i.e. human thought's] world-surrounding ether' (l. 661), as though thought were surrounded by an air which we breathe. Beyond the 'twilight realm' (l. 662) of current ideological concerns, the spirits can 'behold' (l. 661), a word with a contemplative suggestiveness, 'The future'.
664 *gather* From this line-ending onwards, the verse falls into rhyme as Ione and Panthea anticipate the arrival of the comfort-bearing spirits.

Ione. And see! more come,
Like fountain-vapours when the winds are dumb,
That climb up the ravine in scattered lines.
And hark! is it the music of the pines?
Is it the lake? Is it the waterfall? 670

Panthea. 'Tis something sadder, sweeter far than all.

Chorus of Spirits

From unremembered ages we
Gentle guides and guardians be
Of Heaven-oppressed mortality;
And we breathe, and sicken not, 675
The atmosphere of human thought:
Be it dim, and dank, and grey,
Like a storm-extinguished day,
Travelled o'er by dying gleams;
  Be it bright as all between 680
Cloudless skies and windless streams,
  Silent, liquid, and serene;
As the birds within the wind,
  As the fish within the wave,
As the thoughts of man's own mind 685
  Float through all above the grave,
We make there our liquid lair,
Voyaging cloudlike and unpent
Through the boundless element:
Thence we bear the prophecy 690
Which begins and ends in thee!

Ione. More yet come, one by one: the air around them
Looks radiant as the air around a star.

First Spirit

On a battle-trumpet's blast
I fled hither, fast, fast, fast 695
'Mid the darkness upward cast.
From the dust of creeds outworn,
From the tyrant's banner torn,
Gathering round me, onward borne,
There was mingled many a cry— 700
'Freedom! Hope! Death! Victory!'

672–91 *From . . . in thee!* The metre is trochaic, shaping the lines into an optimistic lilt.
672 *unremembered ages* Ages that lie beyond memory; the phrase suggests the persistence of the spirits.
676 *The . . . thought* A central image in the work; the 'atmosphere' serves as a metaphor for states of political and spiritual health and sickness.
682 *liquid* Here and at line 687 the word means 'having the transparency, translucence, or brightness, of pure water'.
685–6 *As . . . grave* Comes close to comparing the spirits with themselves.
690 *prophecy* Implies Prometheus' eventual triumph.
694–701 *On . . . Victory!* T. S. Eliot was severe about such writing: '. . . in such lines, harsh and untunable, one is all the more affronted by the ideas, the ideas which Shelley bolted whole and never assimilated, visible in the catchwords of creeds outworn, tyrants and priests' (from *Selected Prose*, ed. Frank Kermode [London: Faber and Faber, 1975], p. 83). One retort is that the Spirit is bidding farewell to ideological 'creeds' which are themselves 'harsh and untuneable'. Within a few lines their fading (l. 702) gives way to a more musical 'sound beneath, around, above' (l. 704), which is 'the soul of Love' (l. 705). Indeed, the phrase 'creeds outworn' glancingly echoes Wordsworth's 'I'd rather be / A Pagan suckled in a creed outworn' ('The world is too much with us', ll. 9–10). Shelley may suggest that the older poet's wish to escape the present is reactionary rather than posing a positive alternative such as is hinted at in the Spirit's 'prophecy'.

Till they faded through the sky;
And one sound above, around,
One sound beneath, around, above,
Was moving; 'twas the soul of love;
'Twas the hope, the prophecy,
Which begins and ends in thee.

Second Spirit

A rainbow's arch stood on the sea
Which rocked beneath, immovably;
And the triumphant storm did flee,
Like a conqueror, swift and proud,
Between, with many a captive cloud,
A shapeless, dark and rapid crowd,
Each by lightning riven in half:
I heard the thunder hoarsely laugh.
Mighty fleets were strewn like chaff
And spread beneath a hell of death
O'er the white waters. I alit
On a great ship lightning-split,
And speeded hither on the sigh
Of one who gave an enemy
His plank, then plunged aside to die.

Third Spirit

I sate beside a sage's bed,
And the lamp was burning red
Near the book where he had fed,
When a Dream with plumes of flame
To his pillow hovering came,
And I knew it was the same
Which had kindled long ago
Pity, eloquence, and woe;
And the world awhile below
Wore the shade its lustre made.
It has borne me here as fleet
As Desire's lightning feet:
I must ride it back ere morrow,
Or the sage will wake in sorrow.

718–22 *I alit . . . die* Shelley sets this act of heroic self-sacrifice against the gleeful malevolence of a moment in Byron's *Manfred* in which a 'Second Voice' causes a shipwreck, saving only one person, 'A traitor on land, and a pirate at sea', who will 'wreak further havoc for me' (2. 3. 32, 33).

728–30 *the same . . . woe* An ancient idea that will be of service in the present. Shelley's radicalism looks for support to the past, especially the classical past.

Fourth Spirit

On a poet's lips I slept
Dreaming like a love-adept
In the sound his breathing kept;
Nor seeks nor finds he mortal blisses, 740
But feeds on the aerial kisses
Of shapes that haunt thought's wildernesses.
He will watch from dawn to gloom
The lake-reflected sun illume
The yellow bees i' the ivy-bloom, 745
Nor heed nor see what things they be;
But from these create he can
Forms more real than living man,
Nurslings of immortality!
One of these awakened me, 750
And I sped to succour thee.

Ione. Behold'st thou not two shapes from the east and west
Come, as two doves to one beloved nest,
Twin nurslings of the all-sustaining air,
On swift still wings glide down the atmosphere? 755
And hark! their sweet, sad voices! 'tis despair
Mingled with love and then dissolved in sound.

Panthea. Canst thou speak, sister? all my words are drowned.

Ione. Their beauty gives me voice. See how they float
On their sustaining wings of skiey grain. 760
Orange and azure deepening into gold:
Their soft smiles light the air like a star's fire.

Chorus of Spirits

Hast thou beheld the form of Love?

Fifth Spirit

As over wide dominions
I sped, like some swift cloud that wings the wide air's wildernesses,
That planet-crested shape swept by on lightning-braided pinions, 765
Scattering the liquid joy of life from his ambrosial tresses:
His footsteps paved the world with light; but as I past 'twas fading,
And hollow Ruin yawned behind: great sages bound in madness,
And headless patriots, and pale youths who perished, unupbraiding,
Gleamed in the night I wandered o'er—till thou, O King of sadness, 770
Turned by thy smile the worst I saw to recollected gladness.

737–51 *On a poet's . . . thee* Shelley's trochaic triplets express creativity's swift internalizing processes. The poet explores 'thought's wildernesses' (l. 742), a phrase which makes an unchartable *terra incognita* of thought, until he can create 'Forms more real than living man' (l. 748). The effect is to describe a Platonizing poetry.
754 *the all-sustaining air* A phrase suggestive of what is, in effect, a species of eco-poetry, in which the air we breathe serves as an image of our mental state.
759 *Their . . . voice* This time Ione is able to help Panthea; again, the difficulty of voice is to the fore, though here 'beauty' finds a satisfying idiom that heralds the lyrical style of later acts.
763–71 *As over . . . gladness* The metre of this complex lyric is iambic; the lines are 'fourteeners', though with a feminine rhyme at the end of each line. The effect is of a majestic yet disconcertingly bumpy ride, as love appears, paving 'the world with light' (l. 767), but leaving in his wake 'hollow Ruin' (l. 768). Shelley again focuses on the dangerous ease with which high ideals can turn to disillusion in the face of unwelcome historical experience.

Sixth Spirit

Ah, sister! Desolation is a delicate thing:
It walks not on the earth, it floats not on the air,
But treads with lulling footstep, and fans with silent wing
The tender hopes which in their hearts the best and gentlest bear, 775
Who, soothed to false repose by the fanning plumes above
And the music-stirring motion of its soft and busy feet,
Dream visions of aerial joy, and call the monster Love,
And wake, and find the shadow Pain—as he whom now we greet.

Chorus

Though Ruin now Love's shadow be, 780
Following him destroyingly
  On Death's white and winged steed,
Which the fleetest cannot flee,
  Trampling down both flower and weed,
Man and beast, and foul and fair, 785
Like a tempest through the air;
Thou shalt quell this horseman grim,
Woundless though in heart or limb.

Prometheus

Spirits! how know ye this shall be?

Chorus

In the atmosphere we breathe, 790
As buds grow red when snow-storms flee
  From spring gathering up beneath,
Whose mild winds shake the elder brake,
And the wandering herdsmen know
That the white-thorn soon will blow: 795
Wisdom, Justice, Love, and Peace,
When they struggle to increase,
  Are to us as soft winds be
To shepherd boys, the prophecy
Which begins and ends in thee. 800

Ione. Where are the Spirits fled?

Panthea.   Only a sense
Remains of them, like the omnipotence
Of music, when the inspired voice and lute
Languish, ere yet the responses are mute
Which through the deep and labyrinthine soul, 805
Like echoes through long caverns, wind and roll.

772–79 *Ah ... greet* A subtle lyric that addresses the state of 'Desolation' or 'disillusion'. The 'delicate' nature of 'Desolation' – a condition to which 'the best and gentlest' are especially vulnerable – is itself delicately caught, the rhythms never quite settling into regular iambic fourteeners until the final line in which the awakening from 'Love' to 'Pain' is described and enacted.

773–4 *It walks ... wing* The lines have a characteristic subtlety of suggestion; despite the negatives in line 773, Desolation appears to walk and to float, but we realize that its movements are internal, affecting 'tender hopes' (l. 775).

790 *atmosphere* Again this image is used to convey intimations of favourable change.

801–6 *Where ... roll* Ione and Panthea share a rhymed exchange to convey the aftermath of visionary experience.

805 *labyrinthine soul* Connects and contrasts with the earlier 'labyrinthine veins' (l. 490).

Prometheus. How fair these air-born shapes! and yet I feel
Most vain all hope but love; and thou art far,
Asia! who, when my being overflowed,
Wert like a golden chalice to bright wine   810
Which else had sunk into the thirsty dust.
All things are still: alas! how heavily
This quiet morning weighs upon my heart;
Though I should dream, I could even sleep with grief,
If slumber were denied not. I would fain   815
Be what it is my destiny to be,
The saviour and the strength of suffering man,
Or sink into the original gulph of things:
There is no agony, and no solace left;
Earth can console, Heaven can torment no more.   820

Panthea. Hast thou forgotten one who watches thee
The cold dark night, and never sleeps but when
The shadow of thy spirit falls on her?

Prometheus. I said all hope was vain but love: thou lovest.

Panthea. Deeply in truth; but the Eastern star looks white,   825
And Asia waits in that far Indian vale
The scene of her sad exile; rugged once
And desolate and frozen, like this ravine;
But now invested with fair flowers and herbs,
And haunted by sweet airs and sounds, which flow   830
Among the woods and waters, from the ether
Of her transforming presence—which would fade
If it were mingled not with thine. Farewell!

807–20 *How fair ... no more* Prometheus' speech marks a still point, one in which Earth's consolations and Heaven's torments (see l. 820) as his heterodox phrasing has it, leave him equally unmoved. The stage is set for the entrance of Asia, who embodies Prometheus' need and hope for 'love'.
808 *thou art far* The sound of 'far' picks up that of 'fair' in line 807, lending pathos to the line.
817 *The saviour ... man* It is noteworthy that Prometheus phrases this account of his role as something he hopes to assume; he has, we might feel, comes close to fulfilling it through his resistance and courage in the first act.
826 *far Indian vale* Panthea's use of 'far' takes the edge off the word by reminding Prometheus that Asia 'waits' for him.
830 *sweet airs and sounds* Crucial to the poetry of the second act.
832 *her transforming presence* Most vividly borne witness to in the lyrics of Act 2 scene 5.

Ode to the West Wind

Begun in late October 1819, the 'Ode to the West Wind', Shelley's most famous shorter poem, was published in *Prometheus Unbound, with Other Poems* (1820). It is accompanied by the following note:

This poem was conceived and chiefly written in a wood that skirts the Arno, near Florence, and on a day when that tempestuous wind, whose temperature is at once mild and animating, was collecting the vapours which pour down the autumnal rains. They began, as I foresaw, at sunset with a violent tempest of hail and rain, attended by that magnificent thunder peculiar to the Cisalpine regions.

The poem comes out of and fights against Shelley's despair at the state of English and European politics, and may represent his profoundest response to the Peterloo Massacre of August 1819, in which local yeomanry violently broke up a huge but peaceful demonstration in favour of parliamentary reform, in St Peter's Fields outside Manchester, killing at least 11 people and injuring several hundred others. It emerges, too, from Shelley's experience of critical neglect and hostility; he had recently read a cuttingly contemptuous review of *Laon and Cythna* in the *Quarterly Review* by an anonymous reviewer (in fact, John Taylor Coleridge, Coleridge's nephew, and like Shelley an Etonian) who wrote that Shelley was 'unteachable in boyhood, unamiable in youth, querulous and unmanly in manhood, – singularly unhappy in all three'. Shelley is likely to have felt that his words had been scattered, not 'among mankind' (l. 67), but on the stoniest of ground. His marriage, too, had endured considerable unhappiness, principally because of the deaths of two of his children, Clara who died in 1818 and William who died in 1819, triggering deep depression in Mary Shelley (pregnant again at the time of the poem's composition). Shelley, walking in a wood near the Arno, must have felt life was testing him and his optimistic beliefs to the limit.

Just before he composed the 'Ode', he wrote in a letter: 'Let us believe in a kind of optimism in which we are our own gods' (*SL*, vol. 2, p. 125). As Wordsworth had said in 'Resolution and Independence', 'By our own spirits are we deified'. Though the 'god' addressed and 'striven' (l. 51) with in the poem is the west wind, symbol of inspiration and secular equivalent to the Holy Spirit, it is the poet who succeeds in affirming the worth of his poetry 'by', as he puts it, 'the incantation of this verse' (l. 65). In his draft of the poem he scrawled in Greek, 'By my virtuous power I, a mortal, vanquish thee, a mighty god', and the sentiment captures the outcome of his prayer to and contest with the west wind.

As in the 'Hymn to Intellectual Beauty', Shelley appropriates rhetorical modes associated with traditional religious belief: invocation and prayer dominate the poem. Whereas the 'Hymn' stressed the inadequacy of language, in the Ode there is a heightened power of expression that is fully a match for the wind's 'unseen presence' (l. 2). The poem shows a masterful formal virtuosity. It consists of five sonnets, each sonnet being composed of four tercets and a couplet. The rhyme scheme is *terza rima*, the form used by Dante in the *Divina Commedia* and by Petrarch in his *Trionfi*. Later, in the unfinished 'The Triumph of Life' (1822) Shelley would use the form for a longer visionary narrative. Here he exploits its ability to look forward, the middle line of each tercet performing the role of a 'winged seed' (l. 7) bearing fruit in the rhymes of the next tercet; moreover, his final couplets continually achieve provisional resolutions.

Emotionally the poem fuses different feelings throughout, and owes its resonance to so doing. In the first section, Shelley compares and contrasts the powerful west wind with 'Thine azure sister of the Spring' (l. 9); depicted as 'moving everywhere' (l. 13), the west wind recalls an omnipresent Holy Spirit, yet it also evokes recollections of Hindu gods (such as those described in the writings of Sir William Jones) when it is depicted as 'Destroyer and Preserver' (l. 14). As in *Prometheus Unbound*, Shelley's words work on several levels at once: the phrasing admits of literal and metaphorical readings throughout. So the wind as an image for the agent and process of change will, the poet implicitly prays, 'destroy' corrupt regimes and 'preserve' the spirit of liberty. The compression of the writing marks an advance on the earlier use of seasonal imagery to portend political change used in *Laon and Cythna*, canto 9, stanzas 21–6, as when Cythna asserts, 'The blasts of autumn drive the winged seeds / Over the earth' (ll. 3649–50) and asks, 'O Spring, of hope, and love, and youth, and gladness / Wind-winged emblem! brightest, best and fairest! / Whence comest thou . . . ? (ll. 3658–60).

If the poem is a political poem, it is also about Shelley's desire to write a poetry that will prove transformative. Something of the potential cost of that desire can be sensed in the second section, where the poet turns his attention from the wind's action on the earth to its action in the air, comparing cirrus clouds running ahead of an oncoming storm to 'the bright hair uplifted from the head // Of some fierce Maenad' (ll. 20–1). The Maenads, followers of Bacchus, killed Orpheus, the archetypal poet, and Shelley may metaphorically suggest the sacrifice required of the poet as he opens his poem to the wind's energy and the violence it unleashes. The natural scene becomes 'a vast sepulchre' (l. 25) of which 'this closing night' (l. 24) is a 'dome' (l. 25) supported by the 'congregated might // Of vapours' (26–7). The writing, too, implies a poet on the lookout for comparisons and analogies: 'Loose clouds' call to mind 'Earth's decaying leaves' (l. 16), while the water-cycle daringly generates an image of sky and earth as a huge tree with 'tangled boughs' (l. 17) from which the leaf-like clouds are shaken.

In section 3, the poem turns its attention to the wind's agency in water. There is a change of key, the turbulence of section 2 giving way to a more reflective mood as the poem imagines 'The blue Mediterranean' (l. 30), and ancient civilizations built round it. Aesthetically seductive as 'old palaces and towers / Quivering within the wave's intenser day' (ll. 33–4) may be, the section presses beyond them, depicting in its second half the 'Atlantic's level powers' (l. 37) which obey the wind's dictates. These 'level powers' may suggest the 'levelling' embodied in America's fledgling democracy.

It is in the fourth section that the poet makes his delayed entrance in the poem, expressing his wish that he, too, could be subject to the wind, but conceding that his human consciousness distinguishes him from leaf, cloud and wave. This consciousness accounts for the fact of the poem's Jacob-like wrestling with the angel of the wind, and for the despair which he expresses briefly if tumultuously towards the end of the section, 'I fall upon the thorns of life! I bleed!'

(l. 54). The close of the section reclaims some dignity after this exclamation, reaffirming, in its final words, the fact that the poet is 'too like thee: tameless, and swift, and proud' (l. 56).

The final section explores the nature of that affinity. Shelley both pleads with and commands the wind, asking it to 'Make me thy lyre, even as the forest is' (l. 57), but tacitly recognizing in the very insistence of 'even as' that he cannot be in the same relationship with the wind as the natural world is. Though he urges total union between himself and the wind (ll. 60–1), he quickly assumes the upper hand as he tells the wind to 'Scatter' (l. 66) his 'words among mankind' (l. 67). The respective roles of poet and wind grow dizzyingly convoluted when the former asks the latter to 'Be through my lips to unawakened earth / The trumpet of a prophecy' (ll. 68–9). Is the wind using Shelley? Or is Shelley using the wind? Shelley does not write 'trumpeteer', which lends some support to the idea that it is 'through his lips', where 'through' means 'by virtue of' (as James Chandler points out in *England in 1819* [University of Chicago Press, 1998]), that the wind can disseminate his prophetic message. The element of 'fire', suggesting poetic inspiration, is to the fore in this section after references to earth, air and water in the first three sections. As in 'Mont Blanc', Shelley finishes the poem with a question, altered from the statement in the draft, 'When Winter comes Springs lags not far behind', and invites us to consider whether his seasonal analogy holds for the political and poetic spheres: in those spheres, does spring always follow winter? And yet, by holding his poem open to potential deconstruction, Shelley encourages a hard-worn but hopeful optimism.

1

O, wild West Wind, thou breath of Autumn's being,
Thou, from whose unseen presence the leaves dead
Are driven, like ghosts from an enchanter fleeing,

Yellow and black, and pale, and hectic red,
Pestilence-stricken multitudes: O, thou, 5
Who chariotest to their dark wintry bed

The winged seeds, where they lie cold and low,
Each like a corpse within its grave, until
Thine azure sister of the Spring shall blow

Her clarion o'er the dreaming earth, and fill 10
(Driving sweet buds like flocks to feed in air)
With living hues and odours plain and hill:

Wild Spirit, which art moving everywhere;
Destroyer and Preserver; hear, O, hear!

1   *O... being* Shelley uses apostrophe and alliteration to create a sense of wonder and awe.
2   *Thou... presence* 'Thou' is among the poem's crucial words, conferring on the wind not only a god-like 'being' but also a nature capable of being communed with by the poet.
2   *unseen presence* Compare the opening of 'Hymn to Intellectual Beauty', with its reference to 'some unseen Power' (l. 1).
2–3   *the leaves...fleeing* The leaves are passively 'driven' from the wind's 'unseen presence'; at the same time they are like 'ghosts' actively 'fleeing' from an 'enchanter'. In both cases the wind's power shows itself in its secondary effects.
4–5   *Yellow... multitudes* The four colours may suggest traditional race groupings; the 'Pestilence-stricken multitudes' shows a political awareness – here of the ravages of famine – at work.

6   *chariotest* The first verb showing the wind directly acting.
8   *like a corpse* The simile is deliberately misleading; the 'winged seeds' are not corpses, or if they are, they await resurrection.
9   *azure... Spring* The warm west wind of spring, traditionally masculine in Greek and Latin mythology; Shelley makes it feminine.
10   *clarion* A shrill war-trumpet, producing a rousing sound.
11   *Driving* Picks up on 'driven' in line 3.
13   *Wild... everywhere* A line vibrant with the verbal energy typical of Shelley, partly because of the ongoing present-tense implied by 'art moving'.
14   *Destroyer... Preserver* See Headnote.
14   *hear, O hear!* Has the ring of the Psalmist's pleading. Compare Psalm 102: 1, 'Hear my prayer, O Lord, and let my cry come unto thee'.

2

Thou on whose stream, 'mid the steep sky's commotion,   15
Loose clouds like earth's decaying leaves are shed,
Shook from the tangled boughs of Heaven and Ocean,

Angels of rain and lightning: there are spread
On the blue surface of thine airy surge,
Like the bright hair uplifted from the head   20

Of some fierce Maenad, even from the dim verge
Of the horizon to the zenith's height,
The locks of the approaching storm. Thou dirge

Of the dying year, to which this closing night
Will be the dome of a vast sepulchre,   25
Vaulted with all thy congregated might

Of vapours, from whose solid atmosphere
Black rain, and fire, and hail will burst: O, hear!

3

Thou who didst waken from his summer dreams
The blue Mediterranean, where he lay,   30
Lulled by the coil of his chrystalline streams,

Beside a pumice isle in Baiae's bay,
And saw in sleep old palaces and towers
Quivering within the wave's intenser day,

---

15 *stream* The primary sense is 'current', but the usual sense of 'flowing body of water' attaches to the word in the light of the surrounding imagery.
15–17 *commotion . . . Ocean* The feminine rhyme emphasizes the scene's 'commotion'.
16 *like earth's decaying leaves* The main point of comparison is that clouds are shed in a manner that brings to mind the shedding of leaves.
16–20 *shed . . . head* The same rhyme sounds in the same position as section 1, which has 'dead' (l. 2), 'red' (l. 4), and 'bed' (l. 6). Along with the unstoppable syntax, this repetition of rhyme helps to explain the effect of driving momentum. As in sections 1 and 3, the main verb of the poet's address ('hear') is held back till the section's last line.
18 *Angels . . . lightning* The phrase, in apposition to 'Loose clouds', exemplifies and sustains the poem's heterodox use of religious associations: Shelley uses the literal meaning of 'Angels', that is, 'messengers', but suggests, too, that the clouds are 'angels' in the sense of being 'attendant spirits'.
21 *Maenad* Female follower of Bacchus/Dionysus; possessed by the God, the Maenads or Bacchantes fell into trances during which their behaviour could be violent ('fierce').
22 *zenith's height* The zenith is the 'point of heavens directly above the observer'.
23 *The . . . storm* Shelley creates suspense and drama by holding back this phrase – effectively the sentence's subject – to the sentence's end. These 'locks' are higher clouds than the 'Loose clouds' (l. 16).
23 *dirge* A song of mourning sung at burials or at commemorations of the dead.
24 *this closing night* The use of 'this' puts us sharply in the present tense.
26 *Vaulted with all* This assonantal phrase helps to suggest that the night is a sepulchre built like a domed cathedral, whose congregation consists of a 'congregated might // Of vapours'.
27 *vapours* Clouds.
27–28 *from . . . burst* In 'A Volcano's Voice in Shelley' (*ELH* 24, 1957), G. M. Matthews quotes from Sir William Hamilton's account of the eruption of Vesuvius in 1794, an account involving clouds heaped in 'a gigantic and elevated column of the darkest hue over the mountain' and a subsequent rain of 'thunder-stones', in support of his general argument that Shelley often uses volcanic imagery to evoke revolutionary energies and with specific reference to these and surrounding lines in the Ode.
29–36 *Thou . . . them!* Shelley uses various devices to slow the poem down as he dwells on the calm sleepiness of the 'blue Mediterranean' and cultures surrounding it; they include the assonance of 'waken', 'Mediterranean' and 'lay' (sustained by the subsequent rhymes of 'bay' and 'day'); the 'lulling' liquid alliteration in lines 30–1; the use of initial stresses in lines 31 and 34 that prolong attention; and the conscious absorption in sensuous response (ll. 35–6).
32 *Beside . . . bay* Pumice is a porous lava and thus bears witness to a past volcanic eruption which has thrown up lava that has cooled and hardened. The bay of Baiae was a resort for the Romans, visited by the Shelleys on 8 December 1818. Shelley writes: 'We then coasted the bay of Baiae to the left in which we saw many picturesque & interesting ruins . . . from the boat the effect of the scenery was inexpressibly beautiful' (*Letters*, vol. 2, p. 61). In the letter and poem the power of nature to beautify is praised. The question whether such beauty is an aesthetic luxury that must be discarded in the wake of coming revolutionary change hovers over the poem.
34 *the wave's intenser day* The water gives 'intenser' form to that which it reflects.

All overgrown with azure moss and flowers
So sweet, the sense faints picturing them! Thou
For whose path the Atlantic's level powers

Cleave themselves into chasms, while far below
The sea-blooms and the oozy woods which wear
The sapless foliage of the ocean, know

Thy voice, and suddenly grow grey with fear,
And tremble and despoil themselves: O, hear!

4

If I were a dead leaf thou mightest bear;
If I were a swift cloud to fly with thee;
A wave to pant beneath thy power, and share

The impulse of thy strength, only less free
Than thou, O, Uncontrollable! If even
I were as in my boyhood, and could be

The comrade of thy wanderings over Heaven,
As then, when to outstrip thy skiey speed
Scarce seemed a vision; I would ne'er have striven

As thus with thee in prayer in my sore need.
Oh! lift me as a wave, a leaf, a cloud!
I fall upon the thorns of life! I bleed!

A heavy weight of hours has chained and bowed
One too like thee: tameless, and swift, and proud.

5

Make me thy lyre, even as the forest is:
What if my leaves are falling like its own!
The tumult of thy mighty harmonies

---

36 *the sense* The capacity for sensuous apprehension.
38 *Cleave themselves* As though anticipating the wind's desires.
40 *The ... ocean* Shelley's note reads: 'The phenomenon alluded to at the conclusion of the third stanza is well known to naturalists. The vegetation at the bottom of the sea, of rivers, and of lakes, sympathizes with that of the land in the change of seasons, and is consequently influenced by the winds which announce it.'
41 *grow ... fear* A fear possibly analogous to the 'fear of change' which 'Perplexes monarchs' at the sight of eclipse in *PL*, 1. 598, 599.
43–5 *If I ... wave* Shelley reminds us that the three previous sections have dealt, respectively, with the earth, the air and the sea.
47 *O, Uncontrollable!* The poem uses its formal control to suggest the 'Uncontrollable' nature of the wind.
51 *vision* Here, the word means something like a fantasy.

51 *striven* Like Jacob with the angel (Genesis 32: 24–9).
52 *As thus ... prayer* An affecting and crucial line that communicates the stress of the poet's striving with the wind through strongly accented monosyllables. 'As thus' refers to the poem we are reading, which gives immediacy to the poetic experience.
54 *the thorns of life* Possible sources include Keats, 'Sleep and Poetry', where he quarrels with poetry that merely 'feeds upon the burrs, / And thorns of life' (ll. 244–5). Shelley at this moment is (consciously) close to writing such a poetry.
57 *Make ... lyre* Alludes to the image of the Aeolian Harp used by Coleridge in his poem of that name.
58 *What ... own!* Shelley, with a desperate humour, reworks the imagery of leaves, to represent himself as a deciduous tree whose leaves are falling.

Will take from both a deep, autumnal tone, 60
Sweet though in sadness. Be thou, Spirit fierce,
My spirit! Be thou me, impetuous one!

Drive my dead thoughts over the universe
Like withered leaves to quicken a new birth!
And, by the incantation of this verse, 65

Scatter, as from an unextinguished hearth
Ashes and sparks, my words among mankind!
Be through my lips to unawakened earth

The trumpet of a prophecy! O, wind,
If Winter comes, can Spring be far behind? 70

60 *a deep, autumnal tone* For the tonality, compare Keats's 'To Autumn', written a few weeks before (Shelley would not have known the poem when writing his Ode), and the 'sober colouring' (l. 200) towards the close of Wordsworth's 'Ode: Intimations of Immortality'.
61 *Sweet* Contrasts with the use of 'sweet' at line 36. This sweetness is hard-won and coexists with 'sadness'.
61 *Spirit fierce* Recalls the 'fierce Maenad' of line 21.
63 *Drive* Now used as an imperative by the poet.
64 *a new birth* The manifold implications include the biographical fact that Mary Shelley was pregnant.
65 *incantation . . . verse* Again, 'this verse' plunges us into the present-tense immediacy of the poem; 'incantation' recalls the wind as 'enchanter' (l. 3), but this time the enchanter is the poet.
66–7 *Scatter . . . mankind!* Shelley's phrasing precludes a propagandist targeting of his 'words'; he asks that they be 'scattered'. 'Unextinguished' is a characteristic negative adjective that brings out how close to extinction the poet's hopes have been.
69–70 *O, wind . . . behind?* Rhetorical if applied only to the cycle of the seasons, the question is resonant with considerable doubt if applied to politics or poetic creativity.

Adonais, An Elegy on the Death of John Keats, Author of 'Endymion', 'Hyperion,' etc.

Adonais, Shelley's elegy for John Keats who died in Rome in February 1821, was written between April 1821 and June 1821, and published in Pisa in July 1821. Shelley was pleased with the first edition, which supplies our copy text; three substantive changes (in lines 72, 143, and 252) made by Mary Shelley in her 1839 edition of the poems, presumably with Shelley's authority, are given in the notes. Shelley regarded Keats as persecuted and driven to an untimely death by hostile reviews, especially the review of *Endymion* in the *Quarterly Review* (April 1818), in which the anonymous reviewer (John Wilson Croker) mocked Keats as 'a disciple of the new school . . . of Cockney Poetry' and jeered, 'our author . . . has no meaning'. Shelley's anger at Keats's treatment mirrors the anger he felt on his own behalf. The 'interposed stabs on the assassins of [Keats's] peace and of his fame' (*SL*, vol. 2, p. 297) are a crucial and polemical part of a poem described by Shelley as 'a highly wrought *piece of art*' (*SL*, 2, 294). This artistry shows in the poem's structure and wording. The poem works through feelings of grief and bitter resentment on Shelley's and his fellow-poet's account, and though it ultimately transforms those feelings in the splendour of the concluding stanzas it never wholly (to the poem's advantage) jettisons them. Even in these stanzas one can sense a kind of sublimated rage; in Shelley's own words, 'I have dipped my pen in consuming fire for his destroyers, otherwise the style is calm and solemn' (*SL*, 2, 300). Written in Spenserian stanzas, *Adonais* fulfils elegy's traditional task of lamenting and providing consolation, but it does so in highly original ways. The lament borrows conventions of pastoral elegy, deriving them from poets such as Bion, only to adapt them to Shelley's understanding of poetry as the product of 'the human mind's imaginings'. The 'flocks' (l. 75) mourning Keats are not sheep bemoaning the loss of their shepherd, as in traditional pastoral elegy, but his own 'quick Dreams' (l. 73), mental energies, at once creations of the poet and the 'Ashes and sparks' he has scattered 'among mankind', to borrow Shelley's wording from the close of 'Ode to the West Wind'. *Adonais* begins by respecting conventions, albeit in an idiosyncratic way, yet it quickly breaks new ground: Nature is shown ultimately to be indifferent to the loss of Keats, in stanzas 18–21 that celebrate the cyclical return of spring, but lament the apparent journey to extinction of human existence. 'Nought we know, dies. Shall that alone which knows / Be as a sword consumed before the sheath / By sightless lightning?' (ll. 177–9), asks Shelley. Is consciousness all that fails to return? The question demands answers. Before

Shelley supplies them in the poem's last section (stanzas 39–55), he stages two scenes of valediction. The first is the farewell of Urania, Muse of poetry, to her 'gentle child' (l. 235); she regrets his premature entrance into the literary lists, battling with hostile criticism which is figured as 'the unpastured dragon' (l. 238). In an anticipation of the final section, she alludes to 'the immortal stars' (l. 256), possibly including Keats in their number, but more evidently alluding to Byron, 'The Pythian of the Age' (l. 250). The second valedictory scene is the procession of poet-mourners in stanzas 30–5, in which Byron, Thomas Moore, Leigh Hunt and Shelley himself as a complexly self-tormented 'pardlike Spirit beautiful and swift' (l. 280) are imagined paying tribute to the dead poet.

In stanza 50, Shelley refers to a monument in honour of the Roman tribune, Caius Cestius, as 'flame transformed to marble' (l. 447). As Stuart Curran has argued, the poem 'reverses the magic formula' ('*Adonais* in Context', in *Shelley Revalued*, ed. Kelvin Everest [Leicester, UK: Leicester University Press, 1983], p. 178). In the final section, the marmoreal coldness of the opening gives way to a flaming out of Shelley's transforming desires. Adonais's weakness in the face of critics is forgotten; the *Quarterly* reviewer is dispatched as a 'noteless blot on a remembered name' (l. 327); and Adonais's post-mortal greatness is the subject of Shelley's finest writing in the poem. Here ideas of an afterlife for Adonais are gloriously asserted: Adonais, now no longer the weak mortal poet unable to endure the persecution of critics, lives again in various ways. If he is 'one with Nature' (l. 370) in a vision of pantheist absorption, he also, more neo-Platonically, assists 'the one Spirit's plastic stress' (l. 381). If he transcends time and history as part of the 'One' (l. 460), he also presides over the temporal, joining 'The splendours of the firmament of time' (l. 388). The language reworks Platonic and Christian images and ideas, but it locates trans-historical meaning in the enduring significance of great poetry. And yet the after-life, or 'abode where the Eternal are', 'Beacons' (l. 495) and beckons to Shelley with frightening literalness. Much of the poem's drama towards its close lies in the tension between the tug of that apparently post-mortal 'abode', attractive to Shelley, in part, because of his disillusion with 'cold mortality' (l. 486), and a residual instinct to cling to such mortality. The poem becomes highly personal; it is clear that Shelley, like his double in the procession of poet-mourners, is one 'Who in another's fate now wept his own' (l. 300).

Literary influences on Shelley's elegy include pastoral elegies by Bion and Moschus, Milton's *Lycidas* and Spenser's *Astrophel*. Dante's *Paradiso* comes to the fore in the poem's closing stanzas. But allusions, as often in Shelley, point up difference. Milton's consolation for the death of Lycidas is that of heavenly salvation for the drowned poet, achieved 'Through the dear might of him that walked the waves' (l. 173); Shelley's 'Heaven of song' (l. 413) is a self-created poetic fiction. In a similar way, Dante provides Shelley with metaphorical aid rather than metaphysical certainty. The poem, written shortly after the composition of *A Defence of Poetry*, makes claims for poetry comparable with those made by the essay; indeed, the following extract from *A Defence* comes close to defining the poem's final movement: 'what were our consolations on this side of the grave, and what were our aspirations beyond it, if Poetry did not ascend to bring light and fire from those eternal regions where the owl-winged faculty of calculation dare not ever soar?' (p. 696). At the poem's close, Shelley occupies a threshold state, half leaving behind 'cold mortality', drawn towards the beaconing 'soul of Adonais' (l. 494). He asserts a state of inspiration in the stanza's opening lines, 'The breath whose might I have invoked in song / Descends on me' (ll. 487–8), possibly alluding to the west wind in his Ode; like the 'leaves dead' in the Ode's first section, his 'spirit's bark' is 'driven' (l. 488), 'borne', as though subject to some power beyond his conscious will, 'darkly, fearfully, afar' (l. 492). Yet the poem stays this side, just, of the point where language is swallowed up by the silence of any absolute, and it is the poet as imperilled but courageous voyager who demands our attention as much as the goal of the voyage.

Αστήρ πρὶν μέν ἔλαμπες ενι ζώοισιν εώος.
Νυν δε θανῶν, λαμπεις ἔσπερος εν φθίμενοις.
Plato

PREFACE

Φάρμακον ἦλθε, Βίων, ποτι σον στομα, φάρμακον ἔιδες
Πῶς τευ τοῖς χέιλεσσι ποτεδραμε, κούκ εγλυκανθη;
Τις δὲ Θροτος τοσσοῦτον ἀνάμερος, ἢ κερκσαι τοι,
Ἡ δοῦναι λσλέοντι το φάρμακον; ἔκυυγεν ὠδαν.

Moschus, *Epitaph. Bion.*

It is my intention to subjoin to the London edition of this poem a criticism upon the claims of its lamented object to be classed among the writers of the highest genius who have adorned our age. My known repugnance to the narrow principles of taste on which several of his earlier compositions were modelled prove at least that I am an impartial judge. I consider the fragment of *Hyperion*, as second to nothing that was ever produced by a writer of the same years.

John Keats, died at Rome of a consumption, in his twenty-fourth year, on the——of——1821; and was buried in the romantic and lonely cemetery of the protestants in that city, under the pyramid which is the tomb of Cestius, and the massy walls and towers, now mouldering and desolate, which formed the circuit of ancient Rome. The cemetery is an open space among the ruins, covered in winter with violets and daisies. It might make one in love with death, to think that one should be buried in so sweet a place.

The genius of the lamented person to whose memory I have dedicated these unworthy verses, was not less delicate and fragile than it was beautiful; and where canker-worms abound, what wonder, if its young flower was blighted in the bud? The savage criticism on his *Endymion*, which appeared in the *Quarterly Review*, produced the most violent effect on his susceptible mind; the agitation thus originated ended in the rupture of a blood-vessel in the lungs; a rapid consumption ensued, and the succeeding acknowledgements from more candid critics, of the true greatness of his powers, were ineffectual to heal the wound thus wantonly inflicted.

It may be well said, that these wretched men know not what they do. They scatter their insults and their slanders without heed as to whether the poisoned shaft lights on a heart made callous by many blows, or one like Keats's composed of more penetrable stuff. One of their associates is, to my knowledge, a most base and unprincipled calumniator. As to *Endymion*; was it a poem, whatever might be its defects, to be treated contemptuously by those who had celebrated with various degrees of complacency and panegyric, *Paris*, and *Woman*, and a *Syrian Tale*, and Mrs Lefanu, and Mr Barrett, and Mr Howard Payne, and a long list of the illustrious obscure? Are these the men, who in their venal good nature, presumed to draw a parallel between the Rev. Mr Milman and Lord Byron? What gnat did they strain at here, after having swallowed all those camels? Against what woman taken in adultery dares the foremost of these literary prostitutes to cast his opprobrious stone? Miserable man! you, one of the meanest, have wantonly defaced one of the noblest specimens of the workmanship of God. Nor shall it be your excuse that, murderer as you are, you have spoken daggers, but used none.

The circumstances of the closing scene of poor Keats's life were not made known to me until the Elegy was ready for the press. I am given to understand that the wound which his sensitive spirit had received from the criticism of *Endymion* was exasperated by the bitter sense of unrequited benefits; the poor fellow seems to have been hooted from the stage of life, no less by those on whom he had wasted the promise of his genius, than those on whom he had

---

Preface
Epigraph Shelley translated these lines as follows: 'Thou wert the morning star among the living, / Ere thy fair light had fled; – / Now, having died, thou art as Hesperus, giving / New splendour to the dead.'
Preface The Greek is from Moschus' *Lament for Bion*, which translates: 'Poison, Bion, poison came to your lips, / and you took it. How could it touch / such lips without becoming nectar? / And what man on earth could be so vicious / as to mix poison and give it you / when you asked? He has poisoned music' (*Greek Pastoral Poetry*, trans. Anthony Holden [Harmondsworth, UK: Penguin, 1974]).
Hyperion Published in Keats's 1820 volume and praised by Shelley as being 'in the very highest style of poetry' (*Letters*, 2. 252–3).
cemetery of the protestants The Cimetero Acattolico in Rome; Shelley's son William was buried there (a fact which is alluded to in stanzas 49 and 51).
in love with death See Keats's 'Ode to a Nightingale': 'I have been half in love with easeful Death' (l. 52).
know not what they do See Luke 23: 34. One of a number of biblical allusions in the Preface turned ironically against those who disliked Keats's poetry, according to a cancelled draft of the Preface, solely because the poet was associated

with Leigh Hunt, William Hazlitt and 'other enemies of despotism & superstition'.
penetrable stuff Ultimately *Hamlet* 3. 4. 35; the phrase is also quoted by Byron in his 'English Bards and Scotch Reviewers' (l. 1050) in a passage relevant to *Adonais*.
One . . . calumniator Alludes to Robert Southey; Shelley mistakenly thought Southey was the author of a hostile review of *The Revolt of Islam* for the *Quarterly Review* in 1819.
Paris *Paris in 1815* (1817) by George Croly (who gave *Adonais* a vicious review).
Woman A poem (1810) by Eaton Stannard Barrett.
a Syrian Tale Ilderim: A Syrian Tale Part of *Eastern Sketches in Verse* (1816) by H. Galley Knight.
Mrs Lefanu Alicia Lefanu (1753–1817), author of *The Sons of Erin*, and apparently a sister of Sheridan.
John Howard Payne American dramatist who courted Mary Shelley after Shelley's death.
Rev. Henry Hart Milman Author and contemporary of Shelley at Eton and Oxford; Shelley thought (incorrectly) that he might have written the review in the *Quarterly Review* mentioned above, after his suspicions had moved away from Southey (see *SL*, 2, 298–9).
What gnat . . . camels? See Matthew 23:24: 'Ye blind guides, which strain at a gnat, and swallow a camel'.

lavished his fortune and his care. He was accompanied to Rome, and attended in his last illness by Mr Severn, a young artist of the highest promise, who, I have been informed, 'almost risked his own life, and sacrificed every prospect to unwearied attendance upon his dying friend.' Had I known these circumstances before the completion of my poem, I should have been tempted to add my feeble tribute of applause to the more solid recompense which the virtuous man finds in the recollection of his own motives. Mr Severn can dispense with a reward from 'such stuff as dreams are made of.' His conduct is a golden augury of the success of his future career— may the unextinguished Spirit of his illustrious friend animate the creations of his pencil, and plead against Oblivion for his name!

I

I weep for Adonais—he is dead!
O, weep for Adonais! though our tears
Thaw not the frost which binds so dear a head!
And thou, sad Hour, selected from all years
To mourn our loss, rouse thy obscure compeers,   5
And teach them thine own sorrow, say: with me
Died Adonais; till the Future dares
Forget the Past, his fate and fame shall be
An echo and a light unto eternity!

II

Where wert thou mighty Mother, when he lay,   10
When thy Son lay, pierced by the shaft which flies
In darkness? where was lorn Urania
When Adonais died? With veiled eyes,
'Mid listening Echoes, in her Paradise
She sate, while one, with soft enamoured breath,   15
Rekindled all the fading melodies,
With which, like flowers that mock the corse beneath,
He had adorned and hid the coming bulk of death.

Against . . . stone See John 8:7: 'He that is without sin among you, let him first cast a stone at her'.
you have spoken . . . none See *Hamlet* 3. 2. 366: 'I will speak daggers to her, but use none'.
The circumstances . . . press Shelley refers to a letter from the Rev. Robert Finch to John Gisborne, who passed it on to him.
Mr. Severn Joseph Severn (1793–1879), a painter and Keats's companion throughout his final months.
'such . . . made of' See *The Tempest* 4. 1. 156–7: 'We are such stuff / As dreams are made on'.
Poem
Title The title *Adonais*, pronounced as four equally weighted syllables, brings to mind two figures, as suggested by Earl Wasserman in *Shelley: A Critical Reading*. The first is Adonis. A beautiful young man and the lover of Aphrodite, Adonis was slain by a wild boar. He is associated with fertility rites that mark the return of spring. The second is Adonai, the Hebrew word for 'Lord'. Wasserman argues that Shelley's title presents a figure who transcends the limits of a fertility cult.
1–2 *I weep . . . Adonais!* See Bion's *Lament for Adonis*, lines 1–2: 'I mourn Adonis dead – loveliest Adonis – / Dead, dead Adonis' (Shelley's translation). The poem begins with a solemnity of address; it builds slowly from this point.
5 *compeers* Equals, peers. They are 'obscure' because, unlike the 'sad Hour' (l. 4), they have not been singled out ('selected', l. 4) for such duties of mourning.
8–9 *his fate . . . eternity!* The lines anticipate the consolation offered by the poem's conclusion; but, as yet, they are merely a conventional act of homage.
10 *mighty Mother* Urania, momentarily associated with Christ's mother by way of the reference to 'thy Son' (l. 11).
10–12 *Where . . . darkness?* See *Lycidas*, lines 50–1: 'Where were ye nymphs when the remorseless deep / Closed o'er the head of your loved Lycidas?'.
12 *Urania* Classical muse of astronomy, and also, more relevantly, the muse of sublime poetry for Dante and Milton (see *Purg.*, 29. 41–2 and *PL*, 7. 1–12). She assumes the place of Venus/Aphrodite in Shelley's reworking of the original myth of Adonis, a beautiful youth with whom Venus fell in love; he was killed by a wild boar.
17–18 *like flowers . . . death* The poetry itself at this stage is aware of the impulse to use words euphemistically to screen what Shelley calls, in a suddenly realistic phrase, 'the coming bulk of death'.
17 *corse* Corpse.

III

O, weep for Adonais—he is dead!
Wake, melancholy Mother, wake and weep!
Yet wherefore? Quench within their burning bed
Thy fiery tears, and let thy loud heart keep
Like his, a mute and uncomplaining sleep;
For he is gone, where all things wise and fair
Descend;—oh, dream not that the amorous Deep
Will yet restore him to the vital air;
Death feeds on his mute voice, and laughs at our despair.

IV

Most musical of mourners, weep again!
Lament anew, Urania!—He died,
Who was the Sire of an immortal strain,
Blind, old, and lonely, when his country's pride
The priest, the slave, and the liberticide
Trampled and mocked with many a loathed rite
Of lust and blood; he went, unterrified,
Into the gulf of death; but his clear Sprite
Yet reigns o'er earth; the third among the sons of light.

V

Most musical of mourners, weep anew!
Not all to that bright station dared to climb;
And happier they their happiness who knew,
Whose tapers yet burn through that night of time
In which suns perished; others more sublime,
Struck by the envious wrath of man or God,
Have sunk, extinct in their refulgent prime;
And some yet live, treading the thorny road,
Which leads, through toil and hate, to Fame's serene abode.

VI

But now, thy youngest, dearest one, has perished,
The nursling of thy widowhood, who grew,
Like a pale flower by some sad maiden cherished,
And fed with true love tears, instead of dew;
Most musical of mourners, weep anew!
Thy extreme hope, the loveliest and the last,
The bloom, whose petals nipped before they blew
Died on the promise of the fruit, is waste;
The broken lily lies—the storm is overpast.

19–27 *O . . . despair* The wish to 'weep for Adonais' is brought up against the fact of its apparent uselessness; the poetry checks its elegiac momentum in, say, the question 'Yet wherefore?' (l. 21).
25 *Deep* Abyss or pit – in effect, the grave.
29–36 *He died . . . light* These lines describe and praise Milton, isolated yet 'unterrified' after the Restoration, despite the threat to his life when former sympathizers with the Cromwellian cause were executed. He is the 'third among the sons of light' because he is, for Shelley, the greatest epic poet after Homer and Dante.

39–41 *happier they . . . perished* Lesser poets whose 'tapers' still 'burn', unlike greater poets whose works have been lost. The writing begins to look ahead to the conclusion in a line such as 38, with its anticipation of line 390, 'Like stars to their appointed height they climb'.
44–5 *some . . . abode* Again, the ending is anticipated (compare 'the abode where the Eternal are' (l. 495).
48–9 *Like a pale flower . . . dew* Alludes to Keats's 'Isabella' (1820).
51 *extreme* Utmost.

VII

To that high Capital, where kingly Death
Keeps his pale court in beauty and decay,
He came; and bought, with price of purest breath,
A grave among the eternal.—Come away!
Haste, while the vault of blue Italian day
Is yet his fitting charnel-roof! while still
He lies, as if in dewy sleep he lay;
Awake him not! surely he takes his fill
Of deep and liquid rest, forgetful of all ill.

VIII

He will awake no more, oh, never more!—
Within the twilight chamber spreads apace
The shadow of white Death, and at the door
Invisible Corruption waits to trace
His extreme way to her dim dwelling-place;
The eternal Hunger sits, but pity and awe
Soothe her pale rage, nor dares she to deface
So fair a prey, till darkness, and the law
Of mortal change, shall fill the grave which is her maw.

IX

O, weep for Adonais!—The quick Dreams,
The passion-winged Ministers of thought,
Who were his flocks, whom near the living streams
Of his young spirit he fed, and whom he taught
The love which was its music, wander not,—
Wander no more, from kindling brain to brain,
But droop there, whence they sprung; and mourn their lot
Round the cold heart, where, after their sweet pain,
They ne'er will gather strength, or find a home again.

X

And one with trembling hands clasps his cold head,
And fans him with her moonlight wings, and cries;
'Our love, our hope, our sorrow, is not dead;
See, on the silken fringe of his faint eyes,
Like dew upon a sleeping flower, there lies

---

55 *high Capital* Rome, where Keats died, and to which the poem will arrestingly return in stanza 48. Milton (*PL*, 1. 756) uses the phrase to describe Pandaemonium.
61 *as . . . lay* The simile is consciously illusory.
63 *liquid* Clear, undisturbed.
71–2 *law . . . maw* The rhyme is deliberately jolting; Shelley does not lose sight of the physical horror of death. 'Change' is an important word in the poem: at this stage, it marks human subjugation to death; at line 165, 'change and motion' are the signs of spring's rejuvenating effects; at line 341, with 'time' 'change' is that through which Adonais, now 'A portion of the Eternal . . . must glow'. The emphasis alters in the 1839 reading of line 72, which is: 'Of change, shall o'er his sleep the mortal curtain draw'. This reading consciously sustains euphemism.
73–81 *O . . . again* Once more, the possibility of rekindling is aroused, then denied. A comparable pattern of illusory revival followed by renewed awareness of death's finality occurs in stanza 12 (ll. 100–8).
80 *sweet pain* The 'pain' is 'sweet' because the 'Dreams' have been imbued by Adonais with poetic 'music' (l. 77).
84 *'Our love . . . dead'* See *Lycidas* line 166: 'For Lycidas your sorrow is not dead'.

A tear some Dream has loosened from his brain.'
Lost Angel of a ruined Paradise!
She knew not 'twas her own; as with no stain
She faded, like a cloud which had outwept its rain. 90

XI

One from a lucid urn of starry dew
Washed his light limbs as if embalming them;
Another clipped her profuse locks, and threw
The wreath upon him, like an anadem,
Which frozen tears instead of pearls begem; 95
Another in her wilful grief would break
Her bow and winged reeds, as if to stem
A greater loss with one which was more weak;
And dull the barbed fire against his frozen cheek.

XII

Another Splendour on his mouth alit, 100
That mouth, whence it was wont to draw the breath
Which gave it strength to pierce the guarded wit,
And pass into the panting heart beneath
With lightning and with music: the damp death
Quenched its caress upon his icy lips; 105
And, as a dying meteor stains a wreath
Of moonlight vapour, which the cold night clips,
It flushed through his pale limbs, and passed to its eclipse.

XIII

And others came . . . Desires and Adorations,
Winged Persuasions and veiled Destinies, 110
Splendours, and Glooms, and glimmering Incarnations
Of hopes and fears, and twilight Phantasies;
And Sorrow with her family of Sighs,
And Pleasure, blind with tears, led by the gleam
Of her own dying smile instead of eyes, 115
Came in slow pomp;—the moving pomp might seem
Like pageantry of mist on an autumnal stream.

XIV

All he had loved, and moulded into thought,
From shape, and hue, and odour, and sweet sound,
Lamented Adonais. Morning sought 120
Her eastern watchtower, and her hair unbound,
Wet with the tears which should adorn the ground,

---

94 *anadem* Garland worn as a headband.
100 *Splendour* See Dante's 'splendori', used in the *Paradiso* (e.g. 9. 13) and discussed in the *Convivio* 3. 14. 29–50, where 'splendour' is defined as reflected light.
107 *clips* 'Embraces' is the dominant sense, though 'cuts off' is another possible meaning.
116–17 *the moving . . . stream* Possibly alluding to Keats's 'To Autumn', which begins, 'Seasons of mists and mellow fruitfulness'.

118–20 *All . . . Adonais* At the close of the first of the poem's lamenting processions, these lines make clear that Adonais is being mourned for by his creations. Later, the procession of the fellow poets will follow, after Urania's lone lament. Shelley, at the poem's close, imagines both a fellowship of the Eternal and the solitariness of the living poet, now no longer a mourner but an intrepid quester.

Dimmed the aerial eyes that kindle day;
Afar the melancholy thunder moaned,
Pale Ocean in unquiet slumber lay, 125
And the wild winds flew round, sobbing in their dismay.

XV

Lost Echo sits amid the voiceless mountains,
And feeds her grief with his remembered lay,
And will no more reply to winds or fountains,
Or amorous birds perched on the young green spray, 130
Or herdsman's horn, or bell at closing day;
Since she can mimic not his lips, more dear
Than those for whose disdain she pined away
Into a shadow of all sounds:—a drear
Murmur, between their songs, is all the woodmen hear. 135

XVI

Grief made the young Spring wild, and she threw down
Her kindling buds, as if she Autumn were,
Or they dead leaves; since her delight is flown
For whom should she have waked the sullen year?
To Phoebus was not Hyacinth so dear 140
Nor to himself Narcissus, as to both
Thou Adonais: wan they stand and sere
Amid the drooping comrades of their youth,
With dew all turned to tears; odour, to sighing ruth.

XVII

Thy spirit's sister, the lorn nightingale 145
Mourns not her mate with such melodious pain;
Not so the eagle, who like thee could scale
Heaven, and could nourish in the sun's domain
Her mighty youth with morning, doth complain,
Soaring and screaming round her empty nest, 150
As Albion wails for thee: the curse of Cain
Light on his head who pierced thy innocent breast,
And scared the angel soul that was its earthly guest!

XVIII

Ah woe is me! Winter is come and gone,
But grief returns with the revolving year; 155
The airs and streams renew their joyous tone;
The ants, the bees, the swallows reappear;

132–5 *Since she . . . hear* Alludes to the myth of Echo and Narcissus: Echo was a nymph who fell in love with Narcissus; when her love was not returned by Narcissus, who was in love with his reflection, she wasted away until she became merely a voice (see Ovid, *Metamorphoses*, 3).
140–2 *To . . . Adonais* Apollo ('Phoebus') loved the youth Hyacinth, who was killed out of jealousy by Zephyrus and then metamorphosed into a flower by Apollo.
143 *drooping comrades* The subdued wit of 'drooping', applicable both to flowers and humans, is lost in the 1839 reading, 'faint companions'.
145–6 *Thy spirit's sister . . . pain.* Alludes to Keats's 'Ode to a Nightingale'; 'lorn' may allude to 'forlorn' in Keats's poem, lines 70, 71.
151 *Albion* England.
151 *the curse of Cain* Cain, the first murderer, was condemned by God to be 'a fugitive and a vagabond' (Genesis 4:12).

Fresh leaves and flowers deck the dead Seasons' bier;
The amorous birds now pair in every brake,
And build their mossy homes in field and brere; 160
And the green lizard, and the golden snake,
Like unimprisoned flames, out of their trance awake.

XIX

Through wood and stream and field and hill and Ocean
A quickening life from the Earth's heart has burst
As it has ever done, with change and motion, 165
From the great morning of the world when first
God dawned on Chaos; in its steam immersed
The lamps of Heaven flash with a softer light;
All baser things pant with life's sacred thirst;
Diffuse themselves; and spend in love's delight, 170
The beauty and the joy of their renewed might.

XX

The leprous corpse touched by this spirit tender
Exhales itself in flowers of gentle breath;
Like incarnations of the stars, when splendour
Is changed to fragrance, they illumine death 175
And mock the merry worm that wakes beneath;
Nought we know, dies. Shall that alone which knows
Be as a sword consumed before the sheath
By sightless lightning?—th' intense atom glows
A moment, then is quenched in a most cold repose. 180

XXI

Alas! that all we loved of him should be,
But for our grief, as if it had not been,
And grief itself be mortal! Woe is me!
Whence are we, and why are we? of what scene
The actors or spectators? Great and mean 185
Meet massed in death, who lends what life must borrow.
As long as skies are blue, and fields are green,
Evening must usher night, night urge the morrow,
Month follow month with woe, and year wake year to sorrow.

---

160 *brere* Archaic form of 'briar'.
161–2 *And . . . awake* Awakening occurs in the natural world, as if indifferent to the fact that Adonais cannot waken again; hence the later assertion at line 190.
163–71 *Through . . . might* The stanza announces and celebrates the 'quickening life' of spring; the syntax grows declarative and assertive, not broken and questioning, as in earlier stanzas. Questions, intensified in their probing by the revelation of nature's seeming indifference to human mortality, will return in the next two stanzas.
172–4 *The leprous . . . stars* The idea that flowers resemble incarnate stars is here, perhaps, merely a poetic conceit; but the final section of the poem sees Adonais, 'a pale flower' (l. 48) in life and death, transformed into a star.

177 *that alone which knows* Consciousness, the mind.
178–9 *as a sword . . . lightning* See Byron's *Childe Harold's Pilgrimage*, 3. 97, 'But as it is, I live and die unheard / With a most voiceless thought, sheathing it as a sword' (ll. 913–14), and his 'So we'll go no more a roving', 'For the sword outwears its sheath' (l. 5).
179 *sightless* Invisible, but also blind.
181–3 *Alas . . . . mortal!* Central lines, which show the poem's understanding of grief as both a form of love and itself subject to change and transience. They provoke further questions in lines 184–5 about the ultimate meaning of life, questions which are at the heart of Shelley's finest poetry and beat away restlessly throughout 'The Triumph of Life'.

XXII

He will awake no more, oh, never more! 190
'Wake thou,' cried Misery, 'childless Mother, rise
Out of thy sleep, and slake, in thy heart's core,
A wound more fierce than his with tears and sighs.'
And all the Dreams that watched Urania's eyes,
And all the Echoes whom their sister's song 195
Had held in holy silence, cried: 'Arise!'
Swift as a Thought by the snake Memory stung,
From her ambrosial rest the fading Splendour sprung.

XXIII

She rose like an autumnal Night, that springs
Out of the East, and follows wild and drear 200
The golden Day, which, on eternal wings,
Even as a ghost abandoning a bier,
Had left the Earth a corpse. Sorrow and fear
So struck, so roused, so rapt Urania;
So saddened round her like an atmosphere 205
Of stormy mist; so swept her on her way
Even to the mournful place where Adonais lay.

XXIV

Out of her secret Paradise she sped,
Through camps and cities rough with stone, and steel,
And human hearts, which to her aery tread 210
Yielding not, wounded the invisible
Palms of her tender feet where'er they fell:
And barbed tongues, and thoughts more sharp than they
Rent the soft Form they never could repel,
Whose sacred blood, like the young tears of May, 215
Paved with eternal flowers that undeserving way.

XXV

In the death chamber for a moment Death,
Shamed by the presence of that living Might,
Blushed to annihilation, and the breath
Revisited those lips, and life's pale light 220
Flashed through those limbs, so late her dear delight.
'Leave me not wild and drear and comfortless,
As silent lightning leaves the starless night!

---

195 *sister's song* The Echo (ll. 15–18) repeating Adonais' 'melodies' (l. 16).
198 *ambrosial* Heavenly
198 *fading Splendour* Urania.
208–16 *Out of . . . way* Urania's journey to Adonais is modelled on Venus' journey to Adonis in Bion. Compare, too, Shelley's translation of Plato's *Symposium*: 'For Love walks not upon the earth, nor over the heads of men, which are not indeed very soft' (James A. Notopoulos, *The Platonism of Shelley* [Durham, NC: Duke University Press, 1949], p. 435). Urania is compelled to walk over 'human hearts'.
212 *Palms* Soles of the feet.

Leave me not!' cried Urania: her distress
Roused Death: Death rose and smiled, and met her vain caress. 225

XXVI

'Stay yet awhile! speak to me once again;
Kiss me, so long but as a kiss may live;
And in my heartless breast and burning brain
That word, that kiss shall all thoughts else survive,
With food of saddest memory kept alive, 230
Now thou art dead, as if it were a part
Of thee, my Adonais! I would give
All that I am to be as thou now art!
But I am chained to Time, and cannot thence depart!

XXVII

'Oh gentle child, beautiful as thou wert, 235
Why didst thou leave the trodden paths of men
Too soon, and with weak hands though mighty heart
Dare the unpastured dragon in his den?
Defenceless as thou wert, oh where was then
Wisdom the mirrored shield, or scorn the spear? 240
Or hadst thou waited the full cycle, when
Thy spirit should have filled its crescent sphere,
The monsters of life's waste had fled from thee like deer.

XXVIII

'The herded wolves, bold only to pursue;
The obscene ravens, clamorous o'er the dead; 245
The vultures to the conqueror's banner true
Who feed where Desolation first has fed,
And whose wings rain contagion;—how they fled,
When like Apollo, from his golden bow,
The Pythian of the age one arrow sped 250
And smiled!—The spoilers tempt no second blow,
They fawn on the proud feet that spurn them as they go.

226–7 *Stay . . . live* Like the whole stanza, these lines are close to Bion ('Wait yet a while, Adonis – oh, but once, / That I may kiss thee now for the last time', Shelley's translation).
228 *heartless* Having lost heart.
234 *But . . . depart!* The alexandrine which ends the Spenserian stanza is used effectively here to express Urania's sense of being 'chained to Time'.
238 *the unpastured dragon* The hostile critic, responsible, in Shelley's view, for Keats's premature death; 'unpastured' means 'unfed'.

240 *mirrored shield* Alludes to Perseus' defence against Medusa, whose looks turned the beholder to stone.
250 *The Pythian of the age* Byron, who confronted the adverse reviewers of his *Hours of Idleness* (1807) volume in his satire 'English Bards and Scotch Reviewers' (1809) in a way that is compared to the slaying by Apollo of the serpent Python (Apollo 'known / As Pythian from that serpent overthrown', Ovid, *Metamorphoses*, 1).
252 *as they go* Altered to 'lying low' in Mary Shelley's 1839 edition.

XXIX

'The sun comes forth, and many reptiles spawn;
He sets, and each ephemeral insect then
Is gathered into death without a dawn, 255
And the immortal stars awake again;
So is it in the world of living men:
A godlike mind soars forth, in its delight
Making earth bare and veiling heaven, and when
It sinks, the swarms that dimmed or shared its light 260
Leave to its kindred lamps the spirit's awful night.'

XXX

Thus ceased she: and the mountain shepherds came
Their garlands sere, their magic mantles rent;
The Pilgrim of Eternity, whose fame
Over his living head like Heaven is bent, 265
An early but enduring monument,
Came, veiling all the lightnings of his song
In sorrow; from her wilds Ierne sent
The sweetest lyrist of her saddest wrong,
And love taught grief to fall like music from his tongue. 270

XXXI

Midst others of less note, came one frail Form,
A phantom among men; companionless
As the last cloud of an expiring storm
Whose thunder is its knell; he, as I guess,
Had gazed on Nature's naked loveliness, 275
Actaeon-like, and now he fled astray
With feeble steps o'er the world's wilderness,
And his own thoughts, along that rugged way,
Pursued, like raging hounds, their father and their prey.

253–61 *The sun . . . night.'* Urania offers an extended metaphor in which the 'sun' represents a great poet, giving rise to critics (the 'reptiles') and imitators ('each ephemeral insect'); when the great poet dies, he joins other great poets who have died ('immortal stars'). The stanza is important in the process of conferring greatness on Keats, for all the 'unfulfilled' (l. 397) nature of his career.
262 *mountain shepherds.* Fellow poets, as in other pastoral elegies, such as Lycidas with its 'woeful shepherds' (l. 165).
264 *Pilgrim of Eternity* Byron, who speaks in *Childe Harold*, 3. 70 of 'wanderers o'er Eternity / Whose bark drives on and on' (an image recalled in the final stanza of *Adonais*).
268 *Ierne* Ireland.
269 *The sweetest lyrist . . . wrong* Thomas Moore, author of *Irish Melodies*, a collection of lyrical poems (hence 'lyrist'), many of which bemoan Ireland's tragic history. For the phrasing, compare Shelley's 'To a Skylark': 'Our sweetest songs are those that tell of saddest thought' (l. 90).
271 *one frail Form* Shelley himself, or a version of him.
276 *Actaeon-like* Actaeon, out hunting, saw the goddess Diana naked; she punished him by turning him into a stag, after which he was chased and killed by his own hounds (Ovid, *Metamorphoses*, 3). In Shelley's use of the myth, the hounds are the poet's own 'thoughts' (l. 278).

XXXII

A pardlike Spirit beautiful and swift— 280
A Love in desolation masked;—a Power
Girt round with weakness;—it can scarce uplift
The weight of the superincumbent hour;
It is a dying lamp, a falling shower,
A breaking billow;—even whilst we speak 285
Is it not broken? On the withering flower
The killing sun smiles brightly: on a cheek
The life can burn in blood, even while the heart may break.

XXXIII

His head was bound with pansies overblown,
And faded violets, white, and pied, and blue; 290
And a light spear topped with a cypress cone,
Round whose rude shaft dark ivy tresses grew
Yet dripping with the forest's noonday dew,
Vibrated, as the ever-beating heart
Shook the weak hand that grasped it; of that crew 295
He came the last, neglected and apart;
A herd-abandoned deer struck by the hunter's dart.

XXXIV

All stood aloof, and at his partial moan
Smiled through their tears; well knew that gentle band
Who in another's fate now wept his own; 300
As in the accents of an unknown land,
He sung new sorrow; sad Urania scanned
The Stranger's mien, and murmured: 'who art thou?'
He answered not, but with a sudden hand
Made bare his branded and ensanguined brow, 305
Which was like Cain's or Christ's—Oh! that it should be so!

280–97 *A pardlike . . . dart* Shelley implies limitations in his self-portrait, but he also endows the 'pardlike Spirit' with an ongoing energy; his 'light spear', for instance, is entwined, by 'ivy tresses' 'Yet dripping with the forest's noonday dew'. It is as though this partial version of the self must be confronted before it can be transcended in favour of the more idealized version of Adonais which will follow.
280 *pardlike* A 'pard' is a leopard, sacred to Dionysus.
283 *superincumbent* Lying on, pressing down upon.
289 *pansies* Associated with thoughts, as in *Hamlet* 4. 5. 174 ('There is pansies, that's for thoughts').
291–2 *a light spear . . . grew* Suggests the 'thyrsus', or staff carried by Dionysus and his followers.
297 *A herd-abandoned . . . dart* See William Cowper's self-portrait, 'I was a stricken deer, that left the herd / Long since' (*The Task*, 3. 108–9; quoted from *The Complete Poetical Works*, ed. H. S. Milford [London, 1905]).

298 *partial* Prejudiced. The 'frail Form' takes Adonais' part against the hostile reviewers; his doing so is motivated by fellow-feeling (see l. 300).
306 *Cain's or Christ* In a letter to John Taaffe, Shelley commented: 'The introduction of the name of Christ as an antithesis to Cain is surely any thing but irreverence or sarcasm' (*SL*, 2, 306). A key word here must be 'antithesis'; Shelley is opposing Christ (the saviour of humankind) to Cain (the first murderer), but he implies that what they share is that they have both been driven from human society. He also implies the poet's ambivalent position, his 'brow' at once 'branded and ensanguined' (l. 305), wearing the mark of Cain (from one, hostile perspective), bloodied like Christ's from wearing a crown of thorns (from another, more sympathetic perspective).

XXXV

What softer voice is hushed over the dead?
Athwart what brow is that dark mantle thrown?
What form leans sadly o'er the white death-bed,
In mockery of monumental stone,
The heavy heart heaving without a moan?
If it be He, who, gentlest of the wise,
Taught, soothed, loved, honoured the departed one;
Let me not vex, with inharmonious sighs
The silence of that heart's accepted sacrifice.

XXXVI

Our Adonais has drunk poison—oh!
What deaf and viperous murderer could crown
Life's early cup with such a draught of woe?
The nameless worm would now itself disown:
It felt, yet could escape the magic tone
Whose prelude held all envy, hate, and wrong,
But what was howling in one breast alone,
Silent with expectation of the song,
Whose master's hand is cold, whose silver lyre unstrung.

XXXVII

Live thou, whose infamy is not thy fame!
Live! fear no heavier chastisement from me,
Thou noteless blot on a remembered name!
But be thyself, and know thyself to be!
And ever at thy season be thou free
To spill the venom when thy fangs o'erflow:
Remorse and Self-contempt shall cling to thee;
Hot Shame shall burn upon thy secret brow,
And like a beaten hound tremble thou shalt—as now.

XXXVIII

Nor let us weep that our delight is fled
Far from these carrion kites that scream below;
He wakes or sleeps with the enduring dead;
Thou canst not soar where he is sitting now.—
Dust to the dust! but the pure spirit shall flow
Back to the burning fountain whence it came,

---

312 *He* Leigh Hunt, who encouraged Keats and promoted his poetry.
319 *nameless worm* The anonymous reviewer of Keats's *Endymion* for the *Quarterly Review*.
327 *noteless* Without distinction.
336 *wakes or sleeps* Shelley returns to the idea of waking, now prepared to put something close to his full poetic authority behind the notion that Adonais has awoken; his more sceptical side inserts 'or sleeps', but he will take a less equivocal view in line 343. The phrase evokes Keats's 'Ode to a Nightingale', 'Fled is that music: – do I wake or sleep?' (l. 80).
337 *Thou ... now* See *PL*, 4, 828–9: 'Know ye not me? Ye knew me once no mate / For you, there sitting where ye durst not soar'.
338 *Dust to the dust!* The phrase echoes 'dust to dust' in the service for the Burial of the Dead.
338–9 *flow ... fountain* The enjambment on the *b* rhyme of the stanza (a key rhyme since it occurs four times in the Spenserian stanza) emphasizes the 'flowing' of the spirit.
339 *the burning fountain* The image of spirit as fire derives from Plotinus and the Platonic tradition. See Shelley's reference in 'On Christianity' to 'The unobscured irradiations from the fountain fire of all goodness' (Murray, p. 255).

A portion of the Eternal, which must glow 340
Through time and change, unquenchably the same,
Whilst thy cold embers choke the sordid hearth of shame.

XXXIX

Peace, peace! he is not dead, he doth not sleep—
He hath awakened from the dream of life—
'Tis we, who lost in stormy visions, keep 345
With phantoms an unprofitable strife,
And in mad trance, strike with our spirit's knife
Invulnerable nothings.—*We* decay
Like corpses in a charnel; fear and grief
Convulse us and consume us day by day, 350
And cold hopes swarm like worms within our living clay.

XL

He has outsoared the shadow of our night;
Envy and calumny and hate and pain,
And that unrest which men miscall delight,
Can touch him not and torture not again; 355
From the contagion of the world's slow stain
He is secure, and now can never mourn
A heart grown cold, a head grown grey in vain;
Nor, when the spirit's self has ceased to burn,
With sparkless ashes load an unlamented urn. 360

XLI

He lives, he wakes—'tis Death is dead, not he;
Mourn not for Adonais.—Thou young Dawn
Turn all thy dew to splendour, for from thee
The spirit thou lamentest is not gone;
Ye caverns and ye forests, cease to moan! 365
Cease ye faint flowers and fountains, and thou Air
Which like a mourning veil thy scarf hadst thrown
O'er the abandoned Earth, now leave it bare
Even to the joyous stars which smile on its despair!

XLII

He is made one with Nature: there is heard 370
His voice in all her music, from the moan
Of thunder, to the song of night's sweet bird;

---

344 *He . . . life* The line finds a definitive expression for the new vision, begun in the previous stanza and built on in the previous line, of the true meanings to be attached to the ideas of awaking and sleeping which have haunted the elegy.
347–8 *strike . . . nothings* The run-on accentuates the sense of 'unprofitable strife' (l. 346); it is noteworthy that Shelley speaks of 'our spirit's knife', a phrase suggestive of spiritual longing and unrest.
348 *'We' decay* The italicized pronoun shows how the tables have been turned since the grieving assertion earlier that '*He* will awake no more' (l. 190).

350 *Convulse . . . consume* The two verbs, bound together by assonance and alliteration, imply an intensifying process of misdirected emotional energy.
352 *He . . . night* Compare lines 336, 343, 344, 361, 370, 373 and 379 for similar constructions: declarative assertions governed by 'He' do much of the poetry's work in this section. The reader may hear the ringingly brave statements as possessing a kind of radiant but steeled bravado.
356 *the contagion . . . stain* Anticipates line 463.
372 *night's sweet bird* The nightingale.

He is a presence to be felt and known
In darkness and in light, from herb and stone,
Spreading itself where'er that Power may move 375
Which has withdrawn his being to its own;
Which wields the world with never wearied love,
Sustains it from beneath, and kindles it above.

XLIII

He is a portion of the loveliness
Which once he made more lovely: he doth bear 380
His part, while the one Spirit's plastic stress
Sweeps through the dull dense world, compelling there
All new successions to the forms they wear;
Torturing th'unwilling dross that checks its flight
To its own likeness, as each mass may bear; 385
And bursting in its beauty and its might
From trees and beasts and men into the Heaven's light.

XLIV

The splendours of the firmament of time
May be eclipsed, but are extinguished not;
Like stars to their appointed height they climb 390
And death is a low mist which cannot blot
The brightness it may veil. When lofty thought
Lifts a young heart above its mortal lair,
And love and life contend in it, for what
Shall be its earthly doom, the dead live there 395
And move like winds of light on dark and stormy air.

XLV

The inheritors of unfulfilled renown
Rose from their thrones, built beyond mortal thought,
Far in the Unapparent. Chatterton
Rose pale, his solemn agony had not 400
Yet faded from him; Sidney, as he fought
And as he fell and as he lived and loved

373 *He is... known* Compare Wordsworth's lines in 'Tintern Abbey', 'And I have felt / A presence that disturbs me with the joy / Of elevated thoughts' (ll. 94–6). Shelley's use of the passive voice makes Keats's 'presence' not simply dependent on one person's subjective response, and might be his way of outflanking Wordsworth even as he alludes to him.
375 *that Power* Again, Shelley is unspecific about the nature of a 'Power' which he imagines as possessing quasi-divine or neo-Platonic attributes.
381 *the one Spirit's plastic stress* See Coleridge's 'The Eolian Harp', line 47: 'Plastic and vast, one intellectual breeze'. In this and the previous stanzas, Shelley draws liberally on Wordsworth's and Coleridge's religious intuitions, but adapts them to his own fiction-making as he offers a series of 'beautiful idealisms' (Preface to *Prometheus Unbound*).
381–3 *while... wear* See Shelley's essay 'On the Devil, and Devils': 'But the Greek philosophers... accounted for evil by supposing that... God in making the world... moulded the reluctant and stubborn materials ready to his hand into the nearest arrangement possible to the perfect archetype existing in his contemplation' (David L. Clark, *Shelley's Prose*, Albuquerque: University of New Mexico Press, 1954, p. 266).
395–6 *the dead... air* Shelley follows the account of the enduring significance of great poets with a vivid description of their power to influence 'a young heart' (l. 393). As 'winds of light', the dead poets purvey inspiration; they 'live there', resurrected by those who have need of them.
397 *inheritors of unfulfilled renown* Those who died before receiving the recognition they deserved.
399 *the Unapparent* Shelley may have shaped his noun from *PL*, 7. 103 ('the unapparent deep') or Wordsworth's *The Excursion*, 9. 605 ('the unapparent fount of glory').
399 *Chatterton* Thomas Chatterton (1752–70), to whose memory Keats dedicated *Endymion*, died at the age of 17; he was, until recently, supposed to have committed suicide.
401 *Sidney* Sir Philip Sidney (1554–86), poet, soldier and courtier.

Sublimely mild, a Spirit without spot,
Arose; and Lucan, by his death approved:
Oblivion as they rose shrank like a thing reproved.

XLVI

And many more, whose names on Earth are dark
But whose transmitted effluence cannot die
So long as fire outlives the parent spark,
Rose, robed in dazzling immortality.
'Thou art become as one of us,' they cry,
'It was for thee yon kingless sphere has long
Swung blind in unascended majesty,
Silent alone amid an Heaven of song.
Assume thy winged throne, thou Vesper of our throng!'

XLVII

Who mourns for Adonais? oh come forth
Fond wretch! and know thyself and him aright.
Clasp with thy panting soul the pendulous Earth;
As from a centre, dart thy spirit's light
Beyond all worlds, until its spacious might
Satiate the void circumference: then shrink
Even to a point within our day and night;
And keep thy heart light lest it make thee sink
When hope has kindled hope, and lured thee to the brink.

XLVIII

Or go to Rome, which is the sepulchre
O, not of him, but of our joy: 'tis nought
That ages, empires, and religions there
Lie buried in the ravage they have wrought;
For such as he can lend,—they borrow not
Glory from those who made the world their prey;
And he is gathered to the kings of thought
Who waged contention with their time's decay,
And of the past are all that cannot pass away.

XLIX

Go thou to Rome,—at once the Paradise,
The grave, the city, and the wilderness;
And where its wrecks like shattered mountains rise,

---

404 *Lucan* The Roman poet (39–65 CE) and author of the *Pharsalia*; he committed suicide when his part in a conspiracy against Nero was discovered.
404 *by his death approved* The phrase probably distances Shelley from the view of Suetonius who accuses Lucan of having falsely incriminated his mother in a cowardly attempt to save himself.
407 *effluence* Literally 'flowing out'.
413 *an Heaven of song* Alludes to and adapts the Ptolemaic system, used by Dante, according to which there are a series of heavens.
414 *Vesper* Hesperus. See the poem's epigraph.
415–23 *Who . . . brink* The stanza addresses a 'Fond' (foolish and affectionate) double of the poet, who is advised to exercise his creative ability to imagine, and not to pursue a longing for post-mortal 'hope' beyond the 'brink' (expertly placed at the end of a long line and the stanza).
417 *pendulous* Suspended, oscillating.
424 *Or . . . Rome* Shelley has held back Rome since its earlier mention in stanza 7. Now he can bring its powerfully rendered history and meaning into connection with the poem's drive to exalt 'the kings of thought' (l. 430). See Shelley's letter (in December 1818): 'Rome is a city as it were of the dead, or rather of those who cannot die' (*SL*, 2, 59).

And flowering weeds, and fragrant copses dress
The bones of Desolation's nakedness
Pass, till the Spirit of the spot shall lead
Thy footsteps to a slope of green access
Where, like an infant's smile, over the dead, 440
A light of laughing flowers along the grass is spread.

L

And grey walls moulder round, on which dull Time
Feeds, like slow fire upon a hoary brand;
And one keen pyramid with wedge sublime,
Pavilioning the dust of him who planned 445
This refuge for his memory, doth stand
Like flame transformed to marble; and beneath,
A field is spread, on which a newer band
Have pitched in Heaven's smile their camp of death,
Welcoming him we lose with scarce extinguished breath. 450

LI

Here pause: these graves are all too young as yet
To have outgrown the sorrow which consigned
Its charge to each; and if the seal is set,
Here, on one fountain of a mourning mind,
Break it not thou! too surely shalt thou find 455
Thine own well full, if thou returnest home,
Of tears and gall. From the world's bitter wind
Seek shelter in the shadow of the tomb.
What Adonais is, why fear we to become?

LII

The One remains, the many change and pass; 460
Heaven's light forever shines, Earth's shadows fly;
Life, like a dome of many-coloured glass,
Stains the white radiance of Eternity,
Until Death tramples it to fragments.—Die,
If thou wouldst be with that which thou dost seek! 465

---

439 *a slope of green access* See Shelley's account of the Protestant Cemetery as 'a green slope near the walls, under the pyramidal tomb of Cestius . . . the most beautiful & solemn cemetery I ever beheld' (*SL*, 2, 59–60).
440 *like . . . smile* A restrained allusion to the fact that Shelley's son, William, who had died at the age of three in June 1819, was also buried in the Protestant Cemetery.
442 *grey walls* Of Rome.
444 *one keen pyramid* The tomb of Caius Cestius, a Roman tribune during the first century BCE.
451–9 *Here pause . . . become?* The poetry returns to the personal anguish and world-weariness, audible in stanzas 39 and 40, which have been temporarily played down in the magnificent stanzas of praise for the transformed Adonais. To the fore is the poet's suppressed grief for the death of his son; just behind this emotion is a veiled confession of domestic unhappiness. More generally, there is a wish to take shelter from 'the world's bitter wind', a wind at odds with 'The breath' that descends on him in the final stanza. The question in the last line of the stanza seems rhetorical, but the speaker's fear is evident.
460–4 *The One remains . . . fragments* For possible parallels, see Dante's *Paradiso* 29. 142–5: 'See now the height and breadth of the eternal worth, since it hath made itself so many mirrors wherein it breaketh, remaining in itself one as before', and Southey's *Thalaba* 5: 'The many-coloured domes / Yet wore one dusky hue'. The stanza recasts the previous stanza's desire to leave the world behind as a quasi-metaphysical opposition between the 'One' and 'the many', but attachment to the world of 'the many' glimmers through the writing: life's 'dome' has its 'many-coloured' attractions; its 'staining' is enriching as well as disfiguring; and the refusal yet again to end-stop the opening quatrain allows the trailing recognition that death's trampling destruction is close to being an act of vandalism.

Follow where all is fled!—Rome's azure sky,
Flowers, ruins, statues, music, words, are weak
The glory they transfuse with fitting truth to speak.

LIII

Why linger, why turn back, why shrink, my Heart?
Thy hopes are gone before: from all things here 470
They have departed; thou shouldst now depart!
A light is past from the revolving year,
And man, and woman; and what still is dear
Attracts to crush, repels to make thee wither.
The soft sky smiles,—the low wind whispers near: 475
'Tis Adonais calls! oh, hasten thither,
No more let Life divide what Death can join together.

LIV

That Light whose smile kindles the Universe,
That Beauty in which all things work and move,
That Benediction which the eclipsing Curse 480
Of birth can quench not, that sustaining Love
Which through the web of being blindly wove
By man and beast and earth and air and sea,
Burns bright or dim, as each are mirrors of
The fire for which all thirst, now beams on me, 485
Consuming the last clouds of cold mortality.

LV

The breath whose might I have invoked in song
Descends on me; my spirit's bark is driven
Far from the shore, far from the trembling throng
Whose sails were never to the tempest given; 490
The massy earth and sphered skies are riven!
I am borne darkly, fearfully, afar;
Whilst burning through the inmost veil of Heaven,
The soul of Adonais, like a star,
Beacons from the abode where the Eternal are. 495

---

469 *Why . . . Heart?* The question permits us to hear the poet's impulse to linger, turn back, and shrink, tying the line into a powerful knot of tensions.

477 *No . . . together* A bitter reference to the marriage service: See Matthew 19:6: 'What therefore God hath joined together, let not man put asunder'.

478–86 *That Light . . . mortality* For all the rejection of 'cold mortality', this stanza pays tribute, via Platonism and Dante, to forces at work in 'the Universe' that seek to bestow beauty and love upon a necessarily imperfect material world.

478 *That Light . . . Universe* See Dante, *Paradiso*, 1. 1–2 ('The All-mover's glory penetrates through the universe').

486 *Consuming . . . mortality* See Dante, *Paradiso* 33. 31–3, where St Bernard prays to Mary on Dante's behalf that 'thou do scatter for him every cloud of his mortality with prayers of thine, so that the joy supreme may be unfolded to him'.

487–95 *The breath . . . Eternal are.* The stanza focuses on the speaker's wish to undergo transformation. It might be read as expressing a longing for death, or as a suicide-wish, but it might also be read as a desire to undergo a going-out of the self, of the kind Shelley describes in *A Defence of Poetry*, and a movement towards other poets who, having undergone change, now enjoy a different order of being; they 'are', not in the sense that they have been reified or stilled, but because they are no longer striving to become, even as their new state of being will serve as a beacon for those who are so striving.

487 *The breath . . . song* Possibly alludes to the 'Ode to the West Wind'.

488–90 *my spirit's bark . . . given* See Dante, *Paradiso* 2. 1–6: 'O ye who in your little skiff, longing to hear, have followed on my keel that singeth on its way, turn to revisit your own shores; commit you not to the open sea; for perchance, losing me, ye would be left astray'.

Felicia Hemans, *née* Browne (1793–1835)

Felicia Hemans is among the most gifted and prolific of Romantic women poets. She enjoyed celebrity and fame in her lifetime (within the bounds of praise felt appropriate to accord to a women poet); but her work was felt by later generations to be sentimental and facile and fell into obscurity. As early as 1842, Elizabeth Barrett wrote to Mary Russell Mitford of Hemans that 'she always does seem to me a lady rather than a woman. . . . She is polished all over to one smoothness & one level, & is monotonous in her best qualities'.[1] Hemans herself felt that she had squandered her poetic gift through over-production caused by the need to support her family financially, writing close to her death, 'It has ever been one of my regrets that the constant necessity of providing sums of money to meet the exigencies of the boys' education, has obliged me to waste my mind in what I consider mere desultory effusions' (Wolfson, p. 521). Her family included a much-loved mother and Hemans's five sons by her husband, Captain Alfred Hemans. Hemans, born in Liverpool as Felicia Dorothea Browne, and Captain Hemans married in 1812, but Captain Hemans left for Rome in 1818 for his 'health' and never returned, nor did Hemans ever join him, despite her offer to do so in 1827 after her mother had died.

More recently criticism has discovered in Hemans a poet of very considerable significance. Her supposed sentimentality turns out to mask complex emotions. Whereas she was formerly seen in simplified terms as a poetic champion of the home and hearth, it is clear that she views the domestic as both vulnerable to threats and as potentially oppressive. Her poetry is full of female speakers who have experienced abandonment, lack of emotional fulfilment, sorrows caused by warfare. In *The Siege of Valencia: A Dramatic Poem* (1823), Hemans explores the conflict between a masculine code of honour and a vision, voiced by Elmina, of the futility of pursuing military glory. Hemans's historical backdrops vary ('The Forest Sanctuary', 1825, a long poem in Spenserian stanzas, describes 'the mental conflicts' of a Spanish Protestant in the sixteenth century), but her concerns recur, reaching memorable expression in *Records of Woman: With Other Poems* (1828). Dedicated to Joanna Baillie, the poet and dramatist, and author of *Plays on the Passions* (1798–1812), this volume presents, through an array of monologues, narratives and lyrics, a wide span of female voices and experiences.

It is in dramatic and lyrical poems in this and subsequent volumes that Hemans shows her poetic skills at their finest. These skills have much to do with the 'polished' quality disliked by Elizabeth Barrett, since such 'polish' bears witness to an endless process of self-aware mimicry in Hemans's work. That is not to accuse her of insincerity: merely to note that in (say) 'The Homes of England' she can both design an idealized myth of national harmony and admit that she is designing such a myth. These admissions or qualifications pervade her work, often signalled by shifts of style and tone, scratches in the stylistic polish, and syntactical breaks. Works such as 'The Graves of a Household' move between and hold in balance different temporal perspectives in ways that look ahead to Hardy's poems. Simultaneously the poetry affirms and laments, making it exceptionally hard to pigeonhole ideologically. Hemans, a poet of subtle tonal control, is capable of jolting surprises. So, at the end of 'The Graves of a Household', an exclamation concedes what seems unsayable, given the seemingly Christian orthodox terms of her poetry: the fear that there may be nothing beyond this life. Her work owes much to the example of other women writers; she addresses Mary Tighe in 'The Grave of a Poetess', projecting on to Tighe her own concerns with the tension between 'the woman's heart' (l. 51) and 'the poet's eye' (l. 52). But even more marked as literary influences are the works of the canonical male Romantic poets: Wordsworth, whom she knew and addresses in 'To Wordsworth' as a poet who 'Sees where the springs of living waters lie' (l. 28); Coleridge; and Byron and Shelley, both constant presences, at once admired and revised from a female viewpoint through intertextual dialogue.

Further Reading

Primary Texts

Records of Woman (1828).
The Forest Sanctuary: with Other Poems 2nd edn (1829).
Songs of the Affections (1830).
Felicia Hemans: Selected Poems, Letters, Reception Materials, ed. Susan J. Wolfson (Princeton, NJ: Princeton University Press, 2000).

---

1 Quoted from *Felicia Hemans: Selected Poems, Letters, Reception Materials*, ed. Susan J. Wolfson (Princeton, NJ: Princeton University Press, 2000), p. 590; hereafter Wolfson.

Secondary Texts

Paula R. Feldman, 'The Poet and the Profits: Felicia Hemans and the Literary Marketplace', *Keats-Shelley Journal* 46 (1997), pp. 148–76.

Angela Leighton, *Victorian Women Poets: Writing against the Heart* (London: Harvester Wheatsheaf, 1992).

Jerome J. McGann, *The Poetics of Sensibility: A Revolution in Literary Style* (Oxford: Oxford University Press, 1996).

Anne K. Mellor, *Romanticism and Gender* (New York: Routledge, 1993).

Marlon B. Ross, *The Contours of Masculine Desire: Romanticism and the Rise of Women's Poetry* (New York: Oxford University Press, 1989).

Nanora J. Sweet and Julie Melnyk (eds), *Felicia Hemans: Reimagining Poetry in the Nineteenth Century* (Basingstoke, UK: Palgrave, 2001).

Susan J. Wolfson, *Borderlines: The Shiftings of Gender in British Romanticism* (Stanford, CA: Stanford University Press, 2006).

Properzia Rossi

'Properzia Rossi' is one of the finest poems in what is, arguably, Hemans's best collection, *Records of Woman* (1828), a series of poems that explore female experience from the perspective of various characters. Of the volume Hemans wrote: 'I have put my heart and individual feelings into it more than any thing else I have written' (Wolfson, p. 498). In 'Arabella Stuart', Hemans represents 'the imagined fluctuations' of her heroine's 'thoughts and feelings' while imprisoned, and displays a psychologically astute lyricism in so doing. In 'Properzia Rossi' Hemans finds in her 'celebrated female sculptor' a means of using the form of dramatic monologue to articulate her feelings about the predicament of the female creator, awarded fame, but longing for love. Susan Wolfson draws attention in her edition of Hemans to Letitia Landon's comment in 'On the Character of Mrs Hemans's Writings', 'No emotion is more truly, or more often pictured in her song, than that craving for affection which answers not unto the call' (quoted Wolfson, p. 351). The poem captures in its use of risings and fallings of mood the speaker's pleasure in artistic creation, and yet her sense that she has been disappointed emotionally, a disappointment that might have prevented her from giving birth to 'creations of far nobler thought' (l. 63). Written in iambic pentameters, normally rhyming in couplets, occasionally interspersed with quatrain rhymes, the verse is full of expressive enjambments and strong caesurae, underscoring the dramatic power of the speaker's outpouring. Byron and Shelley are often called to mind, both through detailed echoes and larger thematic concerns, even if 'Properzia Rossi' gives a distinctively individual inflection to their emphases.

Properzia Rossi, a celebrated female sculptor of Bologna, possessed also of talents for poetry and music, died in consequence of an unrequited attachment.—A painting by Ducis represents her showing her last work, a basso-relievo of Ariadne, to a Roman knight, the object of her affection, who regards it with indifference.

---------Tell me no more, no more
Of my soul's lofty gifts! Are they not vain
To quench its haunting thirst for happiness?
Have I not lov'd, and striven, and fail'd to bind
One true heart unto me, whereon my own   5
Might find a resting-place, a home for all
Its burden of affections? I depart,
Unknown, though Fame goes with me; I must leave
The earth unknown. Yet it may be that death
Shall give my name a power to win such tears   10
As would have made life precious.

Headnote
Properzia Rossi A Bolognese sculptor (c. 1490–1530).
Ducis Louis Ducis, French painter (1775–1847). The painting to which Hemans referred was exhibited at the Paris Salon (1812–14).
Epigraph
7 *Its burden of affections* Hemans's phrasing edges towards the paradoxical as it plays a variation on Wordsworth's 'burthen of the mystery' (l. 39) in 'Tintern Abbey'.
7–9 *I depart . . . the earth unknown* 'Unknown', here, does not mean 'without reputation', but rather 'not fully understood and loved' – by 'One true heart' (l. 5).

I.

One dream of passion and of beauty more!
And in its bright fulfilment let me pour
My soul away! Let earth retain a trace
Of that which lit my being, though its race
Might have been loftier far.—Yet one more dream! 5
From my deep spirit one victorious gleam
Ere I depart! For thee alone, for thee!
May this last work, this farewell triumph be,
Thou, lov'd so vainly! I would leave enshrined
Something immortal of my heart and mind, 10
That yet may speak to thee when I am gone,
Shaking thine inmost bosom with a tone
Of lost affection;—something that may prove
What she hath been, whose melancholy love
On thee was lavish'd; silent pang and tear, 15
And fervent song, that gush'd when none were near,
And dream by night, and weary thought by day,
Stealing the brightness from her life away,—
While thou——Awake! not yet within me die,
Under the burden and the agony 20
Of this vain tenderness,—my spirit, wake!
Ev'n for thy sorrowful affection's sake,
Live! in thy work breathe out!—that he may yet,
Feeling sad mastery there, perchance regret
Thine unrequited gift. 25

II.

It comes,—the power
Within me born, flows back; my fruitless dower
That could not win me love. Yet once again
I greet it proudly, with its rushing train
Of glorious images:—they throng—they press—
A sudden joy lights up my loneliness,— 30

Text
2 *bright fulfilment* There is irony here in that a 'dream of passion and of beauty' (l. 1) can find 'fulfilment' in art (sculpture), but the artist cannot find 'fulfilment' emotionally.
3–4 *a trace... being* A possible echo of Shelley's 'The Triumph of Life', line 201, where Rousseau speaks of 'the spark with which Heaven lit my spirit'. Properzia can be seen as a Rousseau-like figure, suffering from earth's failure to provider her with 'purer nutriment' ('The Triumph of Life', l. 202). Hemans would have been able to read 'The Triumph of Life' in Shelley's *Posthumous Poems* (1824), edited by Mary Shelley.
5–6 *dream... gleam* A familiar rhyme in Romantic poetry (as in Wordsworth's 'Immortality Ode', ll. 56–7), here pointing towards the unstable nature of artistic triumph.
12–13 *a tone... affection* May rework a passage in Byron's *Childe Harold's Pilgrimage*, IV. 23. 202–7 (used by Hemans as the epigraph to 'The Spirit's Mysteries'), which speaks of 'things which bring / Back on the heart the weight which it would fling / Aside for ever' (ll. 202–4), such as 'A tone of music' (l. 205). Byron stoically endures such a 'tone'; Porphyria desires it. 'Tone' is a suggestive word in Romantic poetry, and the following *OED* definition may come closest to Hemans's meaning: 'A particular quality, pitch, modulation, or inflexion of the voice expressing or indicating affirmation, interrogation, hesitation, decision, or some feeling or emotion'.
14 *she* Properzia, imagining herself seen after death by 'Thou, lov'd so vainly!' (l. 9).
21 *my spirit, wake!* Compare Byron, 'On This Day I Complete My Thirty-Sixth Year', line 26: 'Awake, my Spirit!'
25–7 *It comes... love* The syntax of these lines suggests, in miniature, the ebb and flow (or, here, the flow and ebb) of the speaker's currents of feeling.

I shall not perish all!
                The bright work grows
Beneath my hand, unfolding, as a rose,
Leaf after leaf, to beauty; line by line,
I fix my thought, heart, soul, to burn, to shine,
Through the pale marble's veins. It grows—and now   35
I give my own life's history to thy brow,
Forsaken Ariadne! thou shalt wear
My form, my lineaments; but oh! more fair,
Touch'd into lovelier being by the glow
    Which in me dwells, as by the summer-light   40
All things are glorified. From thee my wo
    Shall yet look beautiful to meet his sight,
When I am pass'd away. Thou art the mould
Wherein I pour the fervent thoughts, th' untold,
The self-consuming! Speak to him of me,   45
Thou, the deserted by the lonely sea,
With the soft sadness of thine earnest eye,
Speak to him, lorn one! deeply, mournfully,
Of all my love and grief! Oh! could I throw
Into thy frame a voice, a sweet, and low,   50
And thrilling voice of song! when he came nigh,
To send the passion of its melody
Through his pierc'd bosom—on its tones to bear
My life's deep feeling, as the southern air
Wafts the faint myrtle's breath,—to rise, to swell,   55
To sink away in accents of farewell,
Winning but one, *one* gush of tears, whose flow
Surely my parted spirit yet might know,
If love be strong as death!

III.

              Now fair thou art,
Thou form, whose life is of my burning heart!   60
Yet all the vision that within me wrought,
    I cannot make thee! Oh! I might have given
Birth to creations of far nobler thought,
    I might have kindled, with the fire of heaven,
Things not of such as die! But I have been   65
Too much alone; a heart whereon to lean,
With all these deep affections, that o'erflow
My aching soul, and find no shore below;

31–3 *The bright . . . beauty* Enjambments (run-on lines) capture the 'unfolding' process of artistic creation.
35–7 *It grows . . . Ariadne!* 'It' turns out to be a sculpture of 'Ariadne', who was 'Forsaken' by Bacchus: the subject of Leigh Hunt's 'Bacchus and Ariadne'.
37 *thou* Ariadne.
45 *The self-consuming* The word 'self-consuming' sums up the speaker's sense of the cost of unspoken feeling. Compare John Clare, 'I am the self-consumer of my woes', line 3 of 'I Am' (composed in 1846).
49–59 *Oh! could I throw . . . death!* There is a parallel between this passage and Byron's *Childe Harold's Pilgrimage*, III. 97, where Byron wishes he could 'throw /

Soul, heart, mind, passions, feelings, strong or weak, . . . into *one* word' (ll. 907–8, 910). (Compare Properzia's '*one* gush of tears', l. 57.)
61–2 *Yet all the vision . . . thee!* The gap between originating 'vision' and final realization, a realization that cannot do justice to the original vision, occurs elsewhere in Romantic poetry, notably Shelley.
62–3 *I . . . Birth* Male poets also traditionally use this image of giving birth for artistic creation; in context, however, especially with the strong enjambment, Hemans recovers the full, biologically female nature of the image.
65–6 *But . . . alone* The brief assertion has, in context, a plangent effect.

An eye to be my star, a voice to bring
Hope o'er my path, like sounds that breathe of spring, 70
These are denied me—dreamt of still in vain,—
Therefore my brief aspirings from the chain,
Are ever but as some wild fitful song,
Rising triumphantly, to die ere long
In dirge-like echoes. 75

IV.

Yet the world will see
Little of this, my parting work, in thee,
   Thou shalt have fame! Oh, mockery! give the reed
From storms a shelter,—give the drooping vine
Something round which its tendrils may entwine,—
   Give the parch'd flower a rain-drop, and the meed 80
Of love's kind words to woman! Worthless fame!
That in *his* bosom wins not for my name
Th' abiding-place it ask'd! Yet how my heart,
In its own fairy world of song and art,
Once beat for praise!—Are those high longings o'er? 85
That which I have been can I be no more?—
Never, oh! never more; though still thy sky
Be blue as then, my glorious Italy!
And though the music, whose rich breathings fill
Thine air with soul, be wandering past me still, 90
And though the mantle of thy sunlight streams,
Unchang'd on forms, instinct with poet-dreams;
Never, oh! never more! Where'er I move,
The shadow of this broken-hearted love
Is on me and around! Too well *they* know, 95
   Whose life is all within, too soon and well,
When there the blight hath settled;—but I go
   Under the silent wings of peace to dwell;
From the slow wasting, from the lonely pain,
The inward burning of those words—'*in vain*,' 100
   Sear'd on the heart—I go. 'Twill soon be past.
Sunshine, and song, and bright Italian heaven,
   And thou, oh! thou, on whom my spirit cast
Unvalued wealth,—who know'st not what was given
In that devotedness,—the sad, and deep, 105
And unrepaid—farewell! If I could weep

74–5 *Rising . . . echoes* The syntax mimics a process of 'Rising' and falling.
86 *That . . . more?* Wordsworthian in cadence: it combines loss and hope, bringing into play echoes of 'Immortality Ode', line 9, 'The things which I have seen I now can see no more', and lines 184–5, 'the primal sympathy / Which having been must ever be'.
87 *Never . . . more* Compare Byron, *Don Juan*, I. 214, 1705, 'No more – no more – Oh! never more on me' and Shelley, 'Adonais', line 64: 'He will awake no more, oh, never more!'. In 'No More!', a later lyric, the poet describes the two words of the title as 'A dirge-like sound!' and makes them a refrain concluding each of the nine five-line stanzas.

96 *Whose . . . within* Possibly alludes to Hamlet's 'I have that within which passeth show' (1. 2. 85) and certainly takes us into one of Hemans's particular poetic spaces, psychic interiority.
100 *'in vain'* The 'inward burning' of these words is emphasized through the rhyme between 'vain' and 'pain'.
102 *bright Italian heaven* Compare Shelley, 'Adonais', line 59: 'the vault of blue Italian day'. The elegiac context of Shelley's poem is relevant to Hemans's passage ('"Twill soon be past', l. 101).
104 *Unvalued wealth* Hemans exploits the double meanings implicit in 'Unvalued', both that which is beyond valuation, because so precious, and that which is not properly recognized as valuable.

Once, only once, belov'd one! on thy breast,
Pouring my heart forth ere I sink to rest!
But that were happiness, and unto me
Earth's gift is *fame*. Yet I was form'd to be   110
So richly blest! With thee to watch the sky,
Speaking not, feeling but that thou wert nigh;
With thee to listen, while the tones of song
Swept ev'n as part of our sweet air along,
To listen silently;—with thee to gaze   115
On forms, the deified of olden days,
This had been joy enough;—and hour by hour,
From its glad well-springs drinking life and power,
How had my spirit soar'd, and made its fame
   A glory for thy brow!—Dreams, dreams!—the fire 120
Burns faint within me. Yet I leave my name—
   As a deep thrill may linger on the lyre
When its full chords are hush'd—awhile to live,
And one day haply in thy heart revive
Sad thoughts of me:—I leave it, with a sound,   125
A spell o'er memory, mournfully profound,
I leave it, on my country's air to dwell,—
Say proudly yet—"'*Twas her's who lov'd me well!*"

110–20 *Yet... dreams!* A powerful episode of imagined happiness, cut short by the awareness that it consists only of 'dreams'. 'Yet', to use Hemans's own conjunction in line 121, the poem concludes with a further imagining, a deferral to the future of the emotional fulfilment denied her in the present.

121 *I leave my name* The verb is repeated in lines 125 and 127, a repetition at once regretful and assertive.
128 "*'Twas... well!*" The poem ends with an imagined utterance, after the speaker's death, by the 'object of [Properzia's] affection', that acknowledges her fame and her love.

The Homes of England

The poem, written in eight-line stanzas which rhyme the second with the fourth lines, and the sixth with the eighth lines, demonstrates Hemans's impulse to write patriotic poetry yet to qualify that impulse. The poem appears to extol the virtues of 'England', a word appearing at the end of the refrain-like first line of each stanza. The epigraph from Scott's *Marmion* (IV. xxx) suggests that the poem might serve as a call to arms, yet the poem's pathos derives from its celebration of peace and tranquillity, qualities at odds with martial courage. The context of the epigraph is not without tension: an English page, Fitz-Eustace, admires the beauty of Scotland before a battle will occur (Flodden) that will result in the victory of the English. The reader must decide whether such tensions are subdued by the poem's vision, or whether they quietly complicate it. The overall effect of these first lines is to draw up different social ranks into the poem's unifying vision, a vision which includes 'stately Homes' (l. 1), 'merry Homes' (l. 9), 'blessed Homes' (l. 17), and 'Cottage Homes' (l. 25), until, in the final stanza, all these homes appear under the heading of 'free, fair Homes' (l. 33).

Arguably, the poem's celebration of hearth and home contains an elegiac element. A wistful fear can be heard in the second line's exclamation, 'How beautiful they stand!', as though Hemans feared that the houses might not stand forever. In this sense, the poem is a forerunner of Thomas Hardy's 'During Wind and Rain', in which a moment of value is set, in each stanza, against the knowledge of destruction. What in Hardy is explicit is only implicit in Hemans, hinted at in the attempt to find images of undying and endlessly repeated natural beauty (the deer and the swan in stanza 1), or of the perpetuating of story in song and book (stanza 2), or of a 'holy quietness' (l. 19) in stanza 3. The poem half-acknowledges that it is creating a myth, one of perpetually smiling cottages (stanza 4), or of 'hut and hall' (l. 34) conjoined in freedom. The fact that the poem ends with a plea for 'hearts of native proof' (l. 35) to defend this idealized England, and for the land to remain worthy of the 'child's glad spirit' (l. 39), may suggest a subliminal disquiet about the poem's myth. Or it may register the fact that national contentment and harmony are concepts that must include a readiness to 'guard each hallow'd wall' (l. 36). The poem was first published in *Blackwood's* 21 (April 1827), with a seven-line epigraph from Joanna Baillie's *Ethwald: A Tragedy* (1802): 'A land of peace, / Where yellow fields unspoil'd, and pastures green, / Mottled with herds and flocks, who crop secure / Their native herbage, nor have ever known / A stranger's stall, smile gladly. / See through its tufted alleys to Heaven's roof / The curling smoke of quiet dwellings rise'. Baillie's epigraph plays interestingly against the poem: Hemans, too, celebrates 'A land of peace', but, however quietly, she sees that 'peace' must be defended – which may mean war.

Text from *Records of Woman: With Other Poems*.

> Where's the coward that would not dare
> To fight for such a land?
> —Marmion

The stately Homes of England,
   How beautiful they stand!
Amidst their tall ancestral trees,
   O'er all the pleasant land.
The deer across their greensward bound   4
   Through shade and sunny gleam,
And the swan glides past them with the sound
   Of some rejoicing stream.

The merry Homes of England!
   Around their hearths by night,   10
What gladsome looks of household love
   Meet, in the ruddy light!
There woman's voice flows forth in song,
   Or childhood's tale is told,
Or lips move tunefully along   15
   Some glorious page of old.

The blessed Homes of England!
   How softly on their bowers
Is laid the holy quietness
   That breathes from Sabbath-hours!   20
Solemn, yet sweet, the church-bell's chime
   Floats through their woods at morn;
All other sounds, in that still time,
   Of breeze and leaf are born.

The Cottage Homes of England!   25
   By thousands on her plains,

---

3 *tall ancestral trees* Hemans's vision appears to be Burkean, even if the poem shows her consciously constructing a Burkean vision; the trees are 'ancestral', suggesting time-honoured links between past and present.
5 *greensward bound* Fiona Stafford points out an echo of Pope's 'January and May; or, the Merchant's Tale from Chaucer', line 621: 'The Knights so nimbly o'er the Greensward bound', and observes that this echo supports 'a sense of origin and gradual development' (*Starting Lines* [Oxford University Press, 2000], p. 205).
6 *shade . . . gleam* The detail may suggest, metaphorically, the mingled nature of English historical experience.
12 *ruddy light* Like 'rejoicing' (l. 8), 'ruddy' serves as a transferred epithet.
23–4 *All other . . . born* 'born' suggests not only 'carried' but also 'given life'.

They are smiling o'er the silvery brooks,
    And round the hamlet-fanes.
Through glowing orchards forth they peep,
    Each from its nook of leaves, 30
And fearless there the lowly sleep,
    As the bird beneath their eaves.

The free, fair Homes of England!
    Long, long, in hut and hall,
May hearts of native proof be rear'd 35
    To guard each hallow'd wall!
And green for ever be the groves,
    And bright the flowery sod,
Where first the child's glad spirit loves
    Its country and its God! 40

34 *Long, long* The opening two stresses form a spondee, and indicate the significance attached by Hemans to her aspiration.

40 *Its . . . God* The repetition of 'its' makes 'God' a possession of the child, who will conceive of God, in part, because of his or her experience of his 'country'.

The Spirit's Mysteries

The epigraph is taken from Byron, *Childe Harold's Pilgrimage*, IV. 23. 202–7; in line 205, Byron has 'summer's eve', not 'summer's breath'; in line 206, Byron has 'the wind', not 'a leaf', and he has 'shall wound', not 'may wound'. The poem, written in six-line stanzas of iambic pentameters, rhyming *ababcc*, meditates on the source of spiritual and imaginative intimations and presentiments in a manner that is Wordsworthian as much as Byronic. Byron is fascinated by the 'electric chain' of often painful emotional associations; Hemans, like Wordsworth in *The Prelude*, book 2 (not published until 1850), is intrigued and finally heartened in an explicitly Christian sense by the fact that we cannot trace our mental and imaginative experiences to their origins. Like Shelley in places (such as the 'Conclusion' to *The Sensitive Plant*), she draws comfort from human ignorance. Hemans's syntax exploits the capacity of the roomy six-line stanza to mimic the mind's process of reflection and self-questioning.

Text from *Records of Woman: With Other Poems*.

'And slight, withal, may be the things which bring
Back on the heart the weight which it would fling
    Aside for ever;—it may be a sound—
A tone of music—summer's breath, or spring—
    A flower—a leaf—the ocean—which may wound—
Striking th' electric chain wherewith we are darkly bound.'
                                    Childe Harold.

The power that dwelleth in sweet sounds to waken
    Vague yearnings, like the sailor's for the shore,
And dim remembrances, whose hue seems taken
    From some bright former state, our own no more;

1, 3 *waken . . . taken* The feminine rhyme lends a lilt to the lines in accord with their sense of coming upon 'mysteries'. Cleverly Hemans makes the second verb passive rather than active, transferring attention to 'some bright former state' (l. 4).

Is not this all a mystery?—Who shall say 5
Whence are those thoughts, and whither tends their way?

The sudden images of vanish'd things,
   That o'er the spirit flash, we know not why;
Tones from some broken harp's deserted strings,
   Warm sunset hues of summers long gone by; 10
A rippling wave—the dashing of an oar—
A flower scent floating past our parents' door;

A word—scarce noted in its hour perchance,
   Yet back returning with a plaintive tone;
A smile—a sunny or a mournful glance, 15
   Full of sweet meanings now from this world flown;
Are not these mysteries when to life they start,
And press vain tears in gushes from the heart?

And the far wanderings of the soul in dreams,
   Calling up shrouded faces from the dead, 20
And with them bringing soft or solemn gleams,
   Familiar objects brightly to o'erspread;
And wakening buried love, or joy, or fear—
These are night's mysteries—who shall make them clear?

And the strange inborn sense of coming ill, 25
   That ofttimes whispers to the haunted breast,
In a low tone which nought can drown or still,
   Midst feasts and melodies a secret guest;
Whence doth that murmur wake, that shadow fall?
Why shakes the spirit thus?—'tis mystery all! 30

Darkly we move—we press upon the brink
   Haply of viewless worlds, and know it not;
Yes! it may be, that nearer than we think
   Are those whom death has parted from our lot!
Fearfully, wondrously, our souls are made— 35
Let us walk humbly on, but undismay'd!

5–6 *Is . . . way?* The impulse to pose questions binds Hemans's practice firmly to that of Wordsworth and Shelley, in particular.

7–12 *The sudden . . . door* The stanza builds up a catalogue of examples; the main verb does not come until the end of stanza 3.

9 *Tones . . . strings* Hemans may be playing her own variation on Shelley's 'music by the night wind sent / Through strings of some still instrument', 'Hymn to Intellectual Beauty', lines 34–5.

11–12 *A rippling . . . door* At such a moment Hemans looks forward to a proto-Modernist fascination with the suggestiveness of images, bringing to mind T. S. Eliot or Virginia Woolf.

19 *far wanderings* The unexpected stress on 'far' and the near-assonance of 'far' and 'wand' illustrate how Hemans gives new life to familiar words.

20 *Calling* The antecedent could be the soul's 'wanderings' or the 'dreams'; the slight blur suits the subject of not quite grasping what is happening during 'night's mysteries' (l. 24).

25 *strange inborn sense* Again, Hemans's diction repays attention; the 'sense', though 'strange', is 'inborn'; we accept it as innate yet find it resists explanation.

30 *'tis mystery all* Compare Charles Wesley's very popular 'And can it be', written about 1738 – the second verse starts ''Tis mystery all'.

31 *Darkly we move* The opening stress-shift creates the effect of a key-change; the poem no longer asks questions; it tries to find tentative answers that are based on the hope that the 'mysteries' recorded in the poem correspond to genuine realities beyond our ken.

31 *brink* The word is placed deftly at the line-ending, as it is in Shelley's *Adonais*, l. 423.

32 *viewless worlds* Worlds that are invisible to us.

35 *Fearfully, wondrously* The interplay between the two adverbs sums up the mixture of feelings at the poem's heart. Compare Shelley, 'Adonais', line 492: 'I am borne darkly, fearfully, afar', and Psalm 139:14: 'I will praise thee; for I am fearfully and wonderfully made'?

          Humbly—for knowledge strives in vain to feel
             Her way amidst these marvels of the mind;
          Yet undismay'd—for do they not reveal
             Th' immortal being with our dust entwined?—   40
          So let us deem! and e'en the tears they wake
          Shall then be blest, for that high nature's sake.

38 *marvels ... mind* Hemans does not celebrate such mental 'marvels' in the spirit of an Enlightenment *philosophe*; she is, rather, impelled to affirm a very Wordsworthian awe before the mind's intimations of infinity.
41 *So let us deem!* The self-aware decision to choose a mode of apprehending reality is typical of Hemans.

42 *that high nature's sake* Seems to rework Wordsworth's lines in 'Ode: Intimations of Immortality', 149–50: 'High instincts before which our mortal nature / Did tremble like a guilty thing surprised'.

The Graves of a Household

The poem is written in ballad form, quatrains with alternating rhymes and four- and three-stress lines. It presents, in distilled terms, Hemans's recurrent concern with the sacredness of hearth and home, and her anxiety over its possible desecration at the hands of time, change and death. It builds towards a larger question about the end of life, about whether earth is, in fact, our only 'home', in which case we are doomed to the loss of the homes we carefully construct, or whether human beings can assert, with Wordsworth, that 'Our destiny, our nature, and our home / Is with infinitude, and only there' (*Prelude*, 1805, VI, 538–9). Where Wordsworth asserts, however, Hemans leaves a doubt hanging in the poem's air. The poem's control of tone is again remarkable, shifting from the seemingly sentimental opening to an altogether less comforting close. It moves from initial togetherness to subsequent apartness, before circling back to reminders of familial intimacy, until it breaks off to pose the final, unanswerable question (implicit in the exclamation with which the poem closes). The poem may recall Wordsworth's 'We Are Seven', as Susan Wolfson suggests (p. 429); Wordsworth's speaker also enumerates the scattering of her family, including the death of a sister and a brother, yet she refuses to accept the reality of death, affirming to the incredulous adult questioner that 'we are seven!' (l. 69). Hemans is less assured of the ultimate unreality of death.

Text is taken from *Records of Woman*.

          They grew in beauty, side by side,
             They fill'd one home with glee;—
          Their graves are sever'd, far and wide,
             By mount, and stream, and sea.

          The same fond mother bent at night   5
             O'er each fair sleeping brow;
          She had each folded flower in sight,—
             Where are those dreamers now?

          One, midst the forest of the west,
             By a dark stream is laid—   10
          The Indian knows his place of rest,
             Far in the cedar shade.

          The sea, the blue lone sea, hath one,
             He lies where pearls lie deep;

1, 3 *side ... far and wide* The poem's theme is caught in this rhyme.
8 *dreamers* In part, the word may suggest, because they 'dreamed' that childhood happiness would persist.
9 *One* Hemans uses this word repeatedly (see also ll. 13, 17, and 21) to bring out the disintegration of the family into isolated individuals.
9 *forest ... west* Probably alludes to Hemans's brother, Claude Scott Browne, who died in Kingston, Canada, in 1821.

> *He* was the lov'd of all, yet none 15
> O'er his low bed may weep.
>
> One sleeps where southern vines are drest
> Above the noble slain:
> He wrapt his colours round his breast,
> On a blood-red field of Spain. 20
>
> And one—o'er *her* the myrtle showers
> Its leaves, by soft winds fann'd;
> She faded midst Italian flowers,—
> The last of that bright band.
>
> And parted thus they rest, who play'd 25
> Beneath the same green tree;
> Whose voices mingled as they pray'd
> Around one parent knee!
>
> They that with smiles lit up the hall,
> And cheer'd with song the hearth,— 30
> Alas, for love! if *thou* wert all,
> And nought beyond, oh, earth!

20 *blood-red... Spain* Alludes to the Peninsular War in which Hemans's husband and two of her brothers fought.
25 *And... play'd* The line is busy with verbal life, bringing together the poem's main concerns. They who 'play'd' were first 'parted' and now 'rest' (in death).
28 *one parent knee* Hemans's mother died in 1827, an event which deeply affected the poet.
30 *hearth* A crucial word in Hemans's vocabulary, here rhyming with a possibly indifferent 'earth'. The sentence beginning at line 29 breaks off before finding a main verb.
31–2 *Alas... earth!* 'Love' would be cruelly disappointed, the poem suggests, if '*thou*' (that is, 'earth') were the final reality of life. There is a rhetorically effective and affecting use of apostrophe in the final two words, which appeal to 'earth' as if it were capable of response, even as the last two lines' exclamation worries that 'earth' is indifferent to human need.

The Image in Lava

Text from *Records of Woman*, where it appeared with the following note by Hemans: 'The impression of a woman's form, with an infant clasped to the bosom, found at the uncovering of Herculaneum'. Herculaneum was discovered in 1709, Pompeii in 1748; both places were destroyed by the volcanic eruption of Vesuvius in 79 CE.

Bodies were imprisoned in the lava. Hemans makes of one such group – a mother and baby – a virtual pieta that shows the undying nature of love, or, at least, what she hopes is love's undying nature, since the last line brings to the fore the strong element of hope underpinning Hemans's assertion that 'human love' (l. 37) is 'immortal' (l. 41). Working with her usual opposition between private and public, Hemans sets 'relics / Left by the pomps of old' (ll. 33–4) against 'this rude monument, / Cast in affection's mould' (ll. 35–6) – to the advantage of the latter. The poem uses a ballad-form, quatrains in alternating four- and three-stress lines, rhyming *abcb*, to articulate its shifting responses, often indicated by exclamations (see ll. 1, 4, 8, 13, 18, 20, 23, 31, 33, 37, 40, 41 and, crucially, 44). These exclamations do not wilfully hype up emotion; rather, they indicate stress-points, where the writer brings some new perspective to bear on her subject, as in line 20, where a fate worse than that suffered by mother and child is imagined, that of a parting where the mother 'might live and lose thee, precious one!' (l. 31).

> Thou thing of years departed!
> What ages have gone by,
> Since here the mournful seal was set
> By love and agony!

1 *Thou thing... departed!* The poem begins with an apostrophe addressed to the image in lava that recalls the address to the Grecian Urn at the start of Keats's Ode, but acknowledges that the object is less art-work than unnameable 'thing'.
4 *love and agony!* The doubling captures the emotional mixture at the poem's core.

Temple and tower have moulder'd, 5
    Empires from earth have pass'd,—
And woman's heart hath left a trace
    Those glories to outlast!

And childhood's fragile image
    Thus fearfully enshrin'd, 10
Survives the proud memorials rear'd
    By conquerors of mankind.

Babe! wert thou brightly slumbering
    Upon thy mother's breast,
When suddenly the fiery tomb 15
    Shut round each gentle guest?

A strange dark fate o'ertook you,
    Fair babe and loving heart!
One moment of a thousand pangs—
    Yet better than to part! 20

Haply of that fond bosom,
    On ashes here impress'd,
Thou wert the only treasure, child!
    Whereon a hope might rest.

Perchance all vainly lavish'd, 25
    Its other love had been,
And where it trusted, nought remain'd
    But thorns on which to lean.

Far better then to perish,
    Thy form within its clasp, 30
Than live and lose thee, precious one!
    From that impassion'd grasp.

Oh! I could pass all relics
    Left by the pomps of old,
To gaze on this rude monument, 35
    Cast in affection's mould.

Love, human love! what art thou?
    Thy print upon the dust
Outlives the cities of renown
    Wherein the mighty trust! 40

7–8 *And . . . outlast!* The poem moves into the terrain of the specifically female, 'woman's heart'.
10 *fearfully enshrin'd* A phrase that conveys the fear experienced by mother and child, and induced in the spectator, and surprises us with the religious suggestions of 'enshrin'd' (meaning 'enclosed in a shrine').
11 *Survives* A transitive verb, 'outlives'.
13 *brightly* This was 'calmly' in the poem's first publication in the *New Monthly Magazine* 20 (1827). 'Brightly' has an ironic pathos, given the imminence of 'the fiery tomb' (l. 15).
17 *A . . . fate* Compare Byron in '[Epistle to Augusta]', line 13: 'A strange doom was thy father's son'.

21 *Haply* Signals Hemans's movement into surmise, as does 'Perchance' in line 25; in both cases, the viewer constructs an emotional scenario which evidently involves a degree of projection.
36 *affection's mould* 'Mould' as in a sculptor's mould, and yet an irony flickers here since the 'mould' has been made by the volcanic lava and ash.
37 *Love, human love!* Compare Byron's 'Love, constant love' in *Don Juan*, 2. 209. 1669, where the tone is wryly flippant, in sharp contrast with the mood of Hemans's phrase.

412   *Felicia Dorothea Hemans (1793–1835)*

> Immortal, oh! immortal
> Thou art, whose earthly glow
> Hath given these ashes holiness—
> It must, it *must* be so!

41–4 *Immortal . . . so!* Hemans here does not (as she does at the end of 'The Graves of a Household') see the 'earthly' as potentially at odds with the 'Immortal'; it is the 'earthly glow' of love that confers 'holiness'. Yet the final line, with its repetition of 'must', concedes that the preceding assertion is simply that: an assertion.

Casabianca

'Casabianca' is among Hemans's most quoted (and mocked) poems, and its hero, the young Casabianca, has become a byword for doomed heroism. In her note to the poem, Hemans sets the scene: 'Young Casabianca, a boy about thirteen years old, son to the Admiral of the Orient, remained at his post (in the Battle of the Nile) after the ship had taken fire, and all the guns had been abandoned; and perished in the explosion of the vessel, when the flames had reached the powder'. The Battle of the Nile (1798) was among Nelson's most famous victories, and it is probably true, as Susan Wolfson asserts, that for Hemans 'To write about French heroics in a battle with England's premier military martyr-hero was a daring gambit' (p. 428). But Hemans did not publish the poem until many years after the battle and Nelson's death (in 1805), and her manner avoids anything that could be construed as 'anti-English'. In fact, though French, Casabianca displays a dedication to duty which an English audience would readily admire, and, indeed, Southey (as Wolfson notes, p. 428) speaks favourably of 'Casa-Bianca, and his son a brave boy, only ten years old' in his *Life of Horatio, Lord Nelson* (1813). At the same time, the boy's dedication to duty results in his total destruction, and the poem leaves one somewhere between admiration and perplexity at human behaviour in military conflict. Arguably, the poem examines the rule of the 'Father', a word used five times by Hemans (three times by the son) and suggests its implacable nature. (It may, thus, be interesting to set this poem against or alongside Blake's *The First Book of Urizen*.) It is written in 10 ballad stanzas, rhyming *abab*, moving between four- and three-stress iambic lines, the metre of, among other poems, Coleridge's 'The Ancient Mariner' some of whose meteorological effects may be recalled by Hemans in her eighth stanza.

Text from *The Forest Sanctuary: with Other Poems* (2nd edn., 1829).

> The boy stood on the burning deck
> Whence all but he had fled;
> The flame that lit the battle's wreck,
> Shone round him o'er the dead.
>
> Yet beautiful and bright he stood,   5
> As born to rule the storm;
> A creature of heroic blood,
> A proud, though child-like form.
>
> The flames rolled on—he would not go,
> Without his Father's word;   10
> That Father, faint in death below,
> His voice no longer heard.

1 *stood* The word is simple; in context, it speaks volumes about the boy's courage.
4 *Shone* Confers an angelic halo on the boy.
5 *Yet* A word used in its two different senses – as an adverb meaning 'still' and as a conjunction – at several key points in the poem: see lines 14, 18, 24.
6 *born . . . storm* Hemans makes him a commander, even a quasi-Byronic hero.

10, 12 *his . . . His* The fact that the first 'his' refers to the boy's wish to hear 'his Father's word', and the second to the Father's inability to hear 'His [that is, Casabianca's] voice' involves us grammatically in the boy's sense that their identities are inextricable.

He called aloud:—'Say, Father, say
   If yet my task is done?'
He knew not that the chieftain lay
   Unconscious of his son.

'Speak, Father!' once again he cried,
   'If I may yet be gone!
And'—but the booming shots replied,
   And fast the flames rolled on.

Upon his brow he felt their breath,
   And in his waving hair,
And looked from that lone post of death,
   In still, yet brave despair.

And shouted but once more aloud,
   'My Father! must I stay?'
While o'er him fast, through sail and shroud,
   The wreathing fires made way.

They wrapt the ship in splendour wild,
   They caught the flag on high,
And streamed above the gallant child,
   Like banners in the sky.

There came a burst of thunder sound—
   The boy—oh! where was he?
Ask of the winds that far around
   With fragments strewed the sea!—

With mast, and helm, and pennon fair,
   That well had borne their part—
But the noblest thing which perished there
   Was that young faithful heart!

---

19 *And'*—The boy's speech is interrupted by the voice of the 'booming shots'.
29–32 *They . . . sky* The writing is deliberately euphemistic, attributing to the 'wreathing fires' (l. 28) an implicit admiration for the boy's gallantry, but making clear the horrific reality underlying its figurative activity.

36 *fragments* Of the boy's body as well as of the boat.
39–40 *But . . . heart!* The ending conveys the poem's dual sense that the boy's fidelity to his father was 'noble', yet that it also involved his 'perishing'; it provokes larger questions about whether such heroism is warranted by such a cost.

The Lost Pleiad

The title alludes, as the poem's epigraph makes clear, to a line from Byron's 'Beppo' (1818), when Byron's narrator praises a beautiful woman glimpsed in youth, a face 'You once have seen, but ne'er will see again' (l. 104) and concludes the next stanza with a comparison between such a face and 'the lost Pleiad seen no more below' (l. 112). The 'lost Pleiad' is probably Merope, who hid because of shame at having married a mortal, Sisyphus. The poem may be applying to Byron's relative loss of fame his narrator's own lament or mock-lament. It serves, in fact, as proleptic elegy: Byron would die the year after the poem was first published. And yet the fact that, though 'A world sinks' (l. 24), 'yon majestic heaven / Shines not the less' (ll. 24–5) impels us 'to think on what *we* are' (l. 22; Hemans's italics). The nature of that self-contemplation is not spelled out, but its upshot may includes a characteristic blend of admiration and sadness. Our collective state is to be admired in that it can afford to lose sight of a remarkable individual with no apparent impact on the larger nature of things; yet there is pathos in the fact of such loss, a pathos clearer in the line's reading in its first publication in the *New Monthly Magazine* 8 (December 1823) (see note l. 22). The overall balance is a triumph of tonal control, achieved through Hemans's mastery of her five-line stanza, written in iambic pentameters, with a shortened trimeter in the third line, and rhyming *abbab*, a rhyme scheme that is used to communicate tos-and fros of feeling. The poem, a slightly wry version of the Romantic sublime, does not merely exclaim, 'How are the mighty fallen!'; it also asks questions about the aftermath of such a sense of sublimity.

Text from *The Forest Sanctuary* (1829).

'Like the lost Pleiad seen no more below.'
Byron

And is there glory from the heavens departed?—
  Oh! void unmark'd!—thy sisters of the sky
    Still hold their place on high,
Though from its rank thine orb so long hath started,
  Thou, that no more art seen of mortal eye!   5

Hath the night lost a gem, the regal night?
  She wears her crown of old magnificence,
    Though thou art exil'd thence—
No desert seems to part those urns of light,
  'Midst the far depths of purple gloom intense.   10

They rise in joy, the starry myriads burning—
  The shepherd greets them on his mountains free;
    And from the silvery sea
To them the sailor's wakeful eye is turning—
  Unchang'd they rise, they have not mourn'd for thee.   15

Couldst thou be shaken from thy radiant place,
  Ev'n as a dew-drop from the myrtle spray,
    Swept by the wind away?
Wert thou not peopled by some glorious race?
  And was there power to smite them with decay?   20

Why, who shall talk of thrones, of sceptres riven?—
  Bow'd be our hearts to think on what *we* are,
    When from its height afar
A world sinks thus—and yon majestic heaven
  Shines not the less for that one vanish'd star!   25

1 *And ... departed?* The fact that the poem opens with 'And', along with a question, suggests an ongoing dwelling on the departure of 'glory'.
2 *void unmark'd!* This theme of an unnoticed absence is central to the poem; the poet, of course, *is* marking the presence of a 'void'.
9 *No desert seems* 'Desert' means 'deserted space'; 'seems' suggests that all may not be as it appears.
11–15 *They rise ... for thee* This beautiful stanza concerns itself with the apparent indifference of nature to loss, the subject of other Romantic poems, including 'Adonais'. Hemans uses a series of indicative verbs (following the questions of stanzas 1 and 2) to convey the 'Unchang'd' (l. 15) face of things; the feminine rhyme of lines 11 and 14 supports a sense of cycles continuing, unaffected by loss, as does the repetition of 'rise' in lines 11 and 15.
11 *starry myriads* Set in marked contrast to the 'vanish'd star' (l. 25).
16–20 *Couldst ... decay?* Hemans returns to questions, aiming at a quasi-biblical grandeur of utterance.
21 *thrones ... riven?* Brings the poem's theme into connection with seismic political and historical events.
22 *Bow'd be our hearts* In the first printing, these words read, 'It is too sad'.
25 *one vanish'd star* The poem finishes by naming what has been lost, implying its secret wish to restore what has gone.

The Mirror in the Deserted Hall

The poem is written in quatrains, with three-stress lines in lines 1, 2 and 4 and a four-stress line in line 3; the metre is notionally iambic, but its many stress-shifts and additional syllables give it a lilting, wondering quality. The poem is a version of an *Ubi sunt?* (Where are they?) lament; it broods on the ephemerality of laughter, pleasure and physical beauty, but it draws from the vanishing of these things a consolation, first suggested by the haunting antepenultimate stanza in which the mirror reflects the stars and moon, then stated more explicitly in the final two stanza where Hemans moralizes her song. Again, Hemans relies on exclamation and question to inject drama into her lyric, though by the poem's end her rhetoric and syntax take on a 'solemn' (l. 32) if unstilted calm, reflected in the flowing enjambments found in many lines.

Text from *Songs of the Affections* (1830).

O, DIM, forsaken mirror!
How many a stately throng
Hath o'er thee gleam'd, in vanish'd hours
Of the wine-cup and the song!

The song hath left no echo; 5
The bright wine hath been quaff'd;
And hush'd is every silvery voice
That lightly here hath laugh'd.

Oh! mirror, lonely mirror,
Thou of the silent hall! 10
Thou hast been flush'd with beauty's bloom—
Is this, too, vanish'd all?

It is, with the scatter'd garlands
Of triumphs long ago;
With the melodies of buried lyres; 15
With the faded rainbow's glow.

And for all the gorgeous pageants,
For the glance of gem and plume,
For lamp, and harp, and rosy wreath,
And vase of rich perfume. 20

Now, dim, forsaken mirror,
Thou givest but faintly back
The quiet stars, and the sailing moon,
On her solitary track.

---

1 *O . . . mirror!* Addressing the mirror gives the poet ample scope for imagination. The use of 'forsaken' links the mirror with the many deserted figures who populate Hemans's poetry.
3 *vanish'd hours* 'Vanish'd' strikes the poem's key-note; as a verb it is repeated at line 12.
5 *The song . . . echo* The line is in an unrhymed position in the quatrain, a position which mimics its meaning; it has no 'echo'.
15–16 *With . . . glow* Compare Shelley's 'When the Lamp Is Shattered', especially lines 3–6: 'When the cloud is scattered / The rainbow's glory is shed. / When the lute is broken / Sweet tones are remembered not'. The first 12 lines of Shelley's poem served as the epigraph to Hemans's 'The Broken Lute' on its publication in *Blackwood's* (1828), despite Hemans's belated request to have Shelley's 'name omitted' because of her friends' objections to Shelley (see Wolfson, p. 496). Shelley's poem, like Hemans's, is concerned with aftermath and survival.
23–4 *The quiet . . . track* Hemans may be recalling, even alluding to, the description in Coleridge's 'The Ancient Mariner' of 'The moving Moon' (l. 263) accompanied by 'a star or two' (l. 266), immediately preceding the account of the 'water-snakes' (l. 273) that 'moved in tracks of shining white' (l. 274). In both cases awareness of the larger movements of the cosmos offers forms of release.

        And thus with man's proud spirit   25
        Thou tellest me 'twill be,
When the forms and hues of this world fade
        From his memory, as from thee:

        And his heart's long-troubled waters
        At last in stillness lie,   30
        Reflecting but the images
        Of the solemn world on high.

---

27 *When . . . fade* One among many examples of how Hemans inserts extra syllables in this poem's lines, here giving a speed to the line that suits its acceptance of the fading of worldly 'forms and hues'.

29 *And . . . waters* The extra syllable helps underscore 'long-troubled', itself a quietly surprising term, given that the mirror with which the heart is being compared has not been depicted, when full of the reflections of life, as 'troubled'. The poem's 'moral' means that one needs to reread earlier stanzas from a perspective where what seemed pleasures now seem troubles.

31 *but* Only.

John Keats (1795–1821)

Though the latest born of the great Romantic poets, John Keats was the first to die. Born 31 October 1795 to the head ostler at a suburban London stable (who had married the daughter of his employer and inherited the business), Keats died in Rome on 23 February 1821, at the age of 25. And his career was even briefer than these numbers suggest. 'Oh, for ten years, that I may overwhelm / Myself in poesy; so I may do the deed / That my own soul has to itself decreed', he had exclaimed in 'Sleep and Poetry' (1816), but in the event he barely had six years. Keats didn't begin writing poetry until 1814, and wrote no more after the summer of 1820 (significantly, both his first and last poems were imitations of Spenser). In fact, Keats's entire public career may be said to consist in the little more than four years between the appearance of his first published poem, the sonnet 'O Solitude' (*The Examiner*, May 1816) and the publication of *Lamia, Isabella, The Eve of St Agnes, and other Poems* (July 1820). Put in this painfully truncated context, Keats's achievement is all the more remarkable: the sonnets, the 'great odes', the romances, the epic visions for the *Hyperion* poems, and the celebrated letters were the productions of a poet who compressed his apprenticeship as well as his maturity into six overwhelming years.

Keats's brothers George and Tom were born in 1797 and 1799, and his sister Fanny in 1803. Shortly thereafter, their father died following a fall from a horse in 1804, and their mother remarried (leaving the four children in the care of their grandparents), before succumbing to tuberculosis in 1810. Throughout this period, Keats attended a progressive school in Enfield run by the Reverend John Clarke, whose son Charles Cowden Clarke, a teacher at the school, became an important mentor and friend. Cowden Clarke supported Keats's literary ambitions, and was a significant influence on his reading, introducing him to a great deal of Renaissance literature (including Tasso, Spenser and Chapman's Homer), music and the theatre. After the deaths of his parents, however, Keats left school at the urging of his guardian, and was apprenticed to Thomas Hammond, a surgeon and apothecary in nearby Edmonton. In 1815, he registered as a medical student at Guy's Hospital in London, and was granted a licence by the Court of Apothecaries in July 1816. Before the end of that year, however, Keats communicated to his guardian that he was resolved not to be a surgeon but a poet: 'I know that I possess Abilities greater than most Men, and therefore I am determined to gain my Living by exercising them'.[1]

1816 marked Keats's coming-of-age as a poet. In addition to appearing in print for the first time in Leigh Hunt's *Examiner* in May, Keats was later singled out by Hunt for his poetic promise (with the publication of 'On first Looking into Chapman's Homer' in December 1816), as one of three 'Young Poets' worthy of the reading public's attention. At the same time, he completed the rest of the 17 Italian sonnets which he was to include in his first volume, as well as 'Sleep and Poetry', the poetic programme-statement with which he concluded it. *Poems* was published in March 1817, with a dedicatory sonnet for Hunt. Though Keats here presents himself as seeing if he 'could please / With these poor offerings, a man like thee', he was already beginning to turn away from the influence exerted by Hunt. In commemorating the publication of Keats's first volume, they had wreathed one another with coronets of laurel and ivy (see Keats's 'On Receiving a Laurel Crown from Leigh Hunt'), but Keats was moving away from Hunt's sybaritic aesthetics toward something more severe and distinctly his own. (Ever wary of undue influence, Keats also that year turned down an invitation from Shelley to reside with him up the Thames from London at Marlow.)

During the same spring, Keats embarked on *Endymion*, a 'poetical romance' of more than 4,000 lines written in decasyllabic couplets. In his preface, Keats characterizes the poem as 'a feverish attempt, rather than a deed accomplished', before going on to castigate it further for its 'mawkishness', a result of having been written in a 'space of life' in which 'the soul is in a ferment, the character undecided, the way of life uncertain, the ambition thick-sighted'. Despite Keats's ambivalence regarding *Endymion*, the letters written soon after its completion in November 1817 demonstrate the degree to which Keats had matured as a poet in the course of his work on it. In a long meditation on the authenticity of the imagination in a letter to Benjamin Bailey, for example, Keats made the important observation that

> I am certain of nothing but of the holiness of the Heart's affections and the truth of the Imagination

---

1 *The Keats Circle: Letters and Papers 1816–1878*, 2 vols, ed. H. E. Rollins (Cambridge, MA: Harvard University Press, 1948) (hereafter *Keats Circle*), vol. 2, p. 307.

– What the Imagination seizes as Beauty must be truth – whether it existed before or not – for I have the same Idea of all our Passions as of Love they are all in their sublime, creative of essential Beauty.... The Imagination may be compared to Adam's dream [*Paradise Lost*, VIII, 452 ff] – he awoke and found it truth. I am the more zealous in this affair, because I have never yet been able to perceive how any thing can be known for truth by consequitive reasoning – and yet it must be.[2]

These are the critical concerns of the mature Keats, the poet who would eventually conclude the 'Ode on a Grecian Urn' with the cryptic dictum, '"Beauty is truth, truth beauty" – that is all / Ye know on earth, and all ye need to know'. Additionally, Keats's conviction here of the 'truth' of the imagination allies it with what he later terms the 'Life of Sensations' – that is, with intuitive perceptions which do not rely on reasoning or verifiable fact to insure them. (In another important letter from this period, also addressing the tension between imagination and reason, Keats characterizes as 'Negative Capability' that capacity 'when man is capable of being in uncertainties, Mysteries, doubts, without any irritable reaching after fact & reason'; *Letters*, vol. 1, p. 193.) Such an imaginative perception also enables the speaker of the 'Ode to a Nightingale' to lose all sense of himself sufficiently to sing himself (to 'fly to thee') into the nightingale's verdurous bower. And it is precisely such imaginative coups which constitute what Keats here terms the 'sublime', that faculty 'creative of essential beauty'.

Keats's reservations about *Endymion* were not merely seconded but vigorously superseded by the critics in the periodical press: soon after it was published in April 1818, *The Quarterly Review* and *Blackwood's Edinburgh Magazine* resumed their attacks on Keats and the 'Cockney School' (Hunt's radical Hampstead milieu) in the course of assailing the poem for its 'vulgarity' and 'idiocy'. Though the attacks gave rise to the posthumous speculation that Keats's health and well-being entered a terminal decline as a result (Byron went so far as to quip that 'poor Keats' had been 'snuffed out by an article'), the letters present a far more defiant perspective on a rapidly maturing poet. In a letter to his publisher, J. A. Hessey, in which he thanks all those who have sprung to his defence, Keats shifts the terms to assure him that

Praise or blame has but a momentary effect on the man whose love of beauty in the abstract makes him a severe critic on his own Works. My own domestic criticism has given me pain without comparison beyond what Blackwood or the [Edinburgh] Quarterly could possibly inflict. and also when I feel I am right, no external praise can give me such a glow as my own solitary reperception & ratification of what is fine.

(*Letters*, vol. 1, p. 373–4)

And in writing to his brother and sister-in-law during the same month (October 1818), he made the prophetic claim that '... the attacks made on me in Blackwood's Magazine and the Quarterly Review ... [are] a mere matter of the moment – I think I shall be among the English Poets after my death' (*Letters*, vol. 1, p. 394).

In the midst of the furore over *Endymion*, Keats made an important walking tour that summer of the English Lake District, Scotland and Ireland. Though the trip left his health seriously compromised (he returned with a chronically ulcerated throat), it also spurred him to take his vocation all the more seriously. As he wrote his brother Tom from the Wordsworthian neighbourhood of Windermere and Rydal, 'I shall learn poetry here and shall henceforth write more than ever, for the abstract endeavor of being able to add a mite to that mass of beauty which is harvested from these grand materials, by the finest spirits, and is put into etherial existence for the relish of one's fellows' (*Letters*, vol. 1, p. 301). Keats broke off his trip in August due to the condition of his throat and, upon his return to London, found his younger brother Tom dangerously ill with tuberculosis. Tom died on 1 December, at which point Keats halted work on *Hyperion* (which he had begun earlier that autumn) and moved into the Hampstead house of his friend Charles Armitage Brown. The other significant personal event from this period was the commencement of Keats's passionate love for Fanny Brawne, whom he met whilst nursing Tom that autumn. They arrived at an 'understanding' on 25 December 1818, but Keats's poverty, declining health and poetic ambition prevented the two of them from ever formalizing their engagement.

The autumn of 1818 also marks the beginning of Keats's *annus mirabilis*, a 12-month period from September 1818 through September 1819 in which he produced most of his mature work, and the bulk of that work upon which his reputation now rests: *Hyperion*, 'The Eve of St Agnes', 'La Belle Dame Sans Merci', the great odes of spring and fall 1819, a handful of brilliant sonnets, 'Lamia', and 'The Fall of

---

2   *The Letters of John Keats 1814–1821*, 2 vols, ed. H. E. Rollins (Cambridge, MA: Harvard University Press, 1958) (hereafter *Letters*), vol. 1, 184–5.

Hyperion'. The formal virtuosity of this work is as breathtaking as the other qualities we so readily associate with it – for example, the deliberate pacing of narrative movement in the Miltonic fragment of 'Hyperion'; the vividly sensuous imagery of 'The Eve of St Agnes', with its tapestried 'scene-painting'; the plangent refrains of 'La Belle Dame Sans Merci'; the 'vale of soul-making' that informs the 'Ode to Psyche'; the gustatory pleasures of 'Ode to a Nightingale' and 'To Autumn'; the troubling questions about the nature of 'truth' and 'beauty' on which the 'Ode on a Grecian Urn' closes; and the incantatory dream-vision of 'The Fall of Hyperion'. And the letters as well show Keats constantly pressuring the question of what it means to be a poet. In an important letter to Richard Woodhouse from the autumn of 1818, he goes to great lengths to define the 'character' of the poet:

As to the poetical character itself, (I mean that sort of which, if I am any thing, I am a Member; that sort distinguished from the wordsworthian or egotistical sublime; which is a thing per se and stands alone) it is not itself – it has no self – it is every thing and nothing – It has no character – it enjoys light and shade; it lives in gusto, be it foul or fair, high or low, rich or poor, mean or elevated – It has as much delight in conceiving an Iago [*Othello*] as an Imogen [*Cymbeline*]. What shocks the virtuous philosop[h]er, delights the camelion Poet. It does no harm from its relish of the dark side of things any more than from its taste for the bright one; because they both end in speculation. A Poet is the most unpoetical of any thing in existence; because he has no Identity – he is continually in for – and filling some other Body – The Sun, the Moon, the Sea and Men and Women who are creatures of impulse are poetical and have about them an unchangeable attribute – the poet has none; no identity – he is certainly the most unpoetical of all God's Creatures.
(*Letters*, vol. 1, pp. 386–7)

In delineating the poetical character in terms of gusto, Keats invokes another significant influence from this period – William Hazlitt. Keats had attended Hazlitt's lectures on the English poets in the winter of 1818, and here he seems to draw on that critic's earlier definition of gusto as 'power or passion defining any object' and as 'giving [the] truth of character from the truth of feeling'. It is precisely because poets have no identity, no character, themselves that they can so passionately render the 'truth' of another character. Or, as he formulated a similar claim in a letter from earlier in 1818, 'axioms in philosophy are not axioms until they are proved upon our pulses' (*Letters*, vol. 1, p. 279).

In February 1820, Keats coughed up blood, the first of a serious of haemorrhages that would culminate in his death a little over a year later. As Charles Armitage Brown recounts the night of 3 February 1820, Keats examined the drop of blood he found upon his bed sheet and summarily remarked, 'I know the colour of that blood; – it is arterial blood; – I cannot be deceived in that colour; that drop of blood is my death-warrant; – I must die' (*Keats Circle*, vol. 2, pp. 73–4). He spent much of the summer under the care of Leigh Hunt, before he was persuaded to travel to Italy in pursuit of a more agreeable climate. That same summer, his last volume, *Lamia, Isabella, The Eve of St Agnes, and other Poems* was published to much greater acclaim than either *Poems* or *Endymion*, with favourable notices in, among other places, *The Examiner* (Leigh Hunt), the *New Times* (Charles Lamb), and the *Edinburgh Review* (Francis Jeffrey). After arriving in Naples at the end of October, Keats proceeded to Rome (accompanied throughout by a young English painter, Joseph Severn), where he took rooms on the Piazza di Spagna, from which he wrote his last letter, to Charles Brown, taking his leave with the plangent words, 'I can scarcely bid you good bye even in a letter. I always made an awkward bow' (*Letters*, vol. 2, p. 360). He died on the evening of 23 February 1821 and was buried in the Protestant Cemetery. In the weeks immediately preceding his death, Keats had asked Severn for a tombstone without any kind of epitaph other than the words, 'Here lies one whose name was writ in water'; far more telling was his earlier, more confident proclamation that 'I shall be among the English poets after my death'.

Further Reading

Primary Texts

John Keats, *Poems* (London: C. and J. Ollier, 1817). (hereafter *1817*)

John Keats, *Endymion: A Poetic Romance* (London: Taylor and Hessey, 1818).

John Keats, *Lamia, Isabella, The Eve of St Agnes, and other Poems* (London: Taylor and Hessey, 1820). (hereafter *1820*)

Richard Monckton Milnes, *Life, Letters, and Literary Remains of John Keats*, 2 vols (London: Moxon, 1848). (hereafter *1848*)

The Poems of John Keats, ed. Ernest de Selincourt (London: Methuen & Co., 1905).

The Keats Circle: Letters and Papers 1816–1878, 2 vols, ed. H. E. Rollins (Cambridge, MA: Harvard University Press, 1948).

The Letters of John Keats 1814–1821, 2 vols, ed. H. E. Rollins (Cambridge, MA: Harvard University Press, 1958).

Keats: The Complete Poems, ed. Miriam Allott, Longman Annotated English Poets (London: Longman, 1970).

John Keats: Complete Poems, ed. Jack Stillinger (Cambridge, MA and London: Belknap Press of Harvard University Press, 1978).

John Keats, ed. Elizabeth Cook, The Oxford Authors (New York and Oxford: Oxford University Press, 1990).

Secondary Texts

Walter Jackson Bate, *John Keats* (Cambridge, MA: Harvard University Press, 1963).

Cleanth Brooks, 'Keats's Sylvan Historian: History Without Footnotes', in *The Well Wrought Urn* (New York: Harcourt Brace Jovanovich, 1974), pp. 151–66.

Charles and Mary Cowden Clarke, *Recollections of Writers* (London, 1878).

Robert Gittings, *John Keats* (London: Heinemann, 1968).

Geoffrey Hartman, 'Poem and Ideology: A Study of Keats's "To Autumn"', in *The Fate of Reading* (Chicago: University of Chicago Press, 1975), pp. 57–73.

William Hazlitt, *The Complete Works of William Hazlitt*, 21 vols, ed. P. P. Howe (London and Toronto: Dent, 1930–4).

Leigh Hunt, *Lord Byron and Some of His Contemporaries*, 2nd edn, 2 vols (London: Henry Colburn, 1828).

Leigh Hunt, *Imagination and Fancy* (London: Smith, Elder, & Co., 1844).

Leigh Hunt, *Periodical Essays, 1815–21*, ed. Greg Kucich and Jeffrey N. Cox, vol. 2 of *Selected Writings of Leigh Hunt*, 6 vols, gen. ed. Robert Morrison (London: Pickering and Chatto, 2003).

Leigh Hunt, *Later Literary Essays*, ed. Charles Mahoney, vol. 4 of *Selected Writings of Leigh Hunt*, 6 vols, gen. ed. Robert Morrison (London: Pickering and Chatto, 2003).

Charles Lamb, *The Works in Prose and Verse of Charles and Mary Lamb*, 2 vols, ed. Thomas Hutchinson (Oxford: Oxford University Press, 1908).

Marjorie Levinson, *Keats's Life of Allegory: The Origins of a Style* (New York and Oxford: Basil Blackwell, 1988).

Andrew Motion, *Keats* (New York: Farrar, Strauss, & Giroux, 1997).

Christopher Ricks, *Keats and Embarrassment* (New York and London: Oxford University Press, 1976).

Nicholas Roe, *John Keats and the Culture of Dissent* (Oxford: The Clarendon Press, 1997).

Jack Stillinger, *'The Hoodwinking of Madeline' and Other Essays* (Urbana: University of Illinois Press, 1971).

On First Looking into Chapman's Homer

Written in October 1816, this poem was first published by Leigh Hunt in *The Examiner*, 1 December 1816 and later collected in *Poems* (1817). Charles Cowden Clarke, Keats's friend and mentor from his schooldays at Enfield, recorded Keats's 'teeming wonderment' at his first introduction to Chapman's translation of Homer (rather than Pope's) and the composition of the poem in October 1816: 'when I came down to breakfast the next morning, I found upon my table a letter with no other enclosure than his famous sonnet.... We had parted ... at dayspring, yet he contrived that I should receive the poem from a distance of, may be, two miles by ten o'clock' (*Recollections*, pp. 128–30). Generally regarded as the most promising and finished of the short poems collected in the volume of 1817, 'On First Looking into Chapman's Homer' is arguably Keats's finest sonnet. In a variation on the Italian sonnet (two rhymes in the octave, three in the sestet), Keats only uses two rhymes in the last six lines (cf. Wordsworth, 'The world is too much with us'; for Keats's views on the challenges of writing sonnets in English, see 'If by dull rhymes our english must be chain'd', p. 442 below). With the turn comes a shift from the charted 'realms' of poetry to the uncharted possibilities of discovery (whether of a planet or an ocean), and with it the poem shifts into an entirely new register of imagery.

In the *Examiner* article, 'Young Poets' (P. B. Shelley, J. H. Reynolds and Keats), Hunt introduced Keats to the English reading public as a poet who 'has not yet published any thing except in a newspaper [*The Examiner*, May 1816]; but a set of his manuscripts was handed us the other day, and fairly surprised us with the truth of their ambition, and ardent grappling with Nature' (*Periodical Essays*, p. 75). Singling out this sonnet for especial praise, Hunt reprinted it in 1828 as an 'instance of a vein prematurely masculine' which 'completely announced the new poet taking possession' (*Lord Byron and Some of His Contemporaries*, vol. 2, p. 410), and again in 1844 in *Imagination and Fancy*, on the merits of its being 'epical in the splendour and dignity of its images, and terminating with the noblest Greek simplicity' (*Later Literary Essays*,

p. 109). George Chapman (1559–1634), poet, playwright and translator, published in 1614 *The Whole Works of Homer* (a copy of which had been lent to Cowden Clarke in 1816) and was admired by later English poets for the bravado and daring of his rendition. As Hunt writes, 'Chapman certainly stands upon no ceremony. He blows as rough a blast as Achilles could have desired to hear, very different from the soft music of a parade.... Mr. Keats's epithets of "loud and bold," showed that he understood him thoroughly' (*Lord Byron*, vol. 2, p. 412).

Text follows *1817*.

    MUCH have I travel'd in the realms of gold,
        And many goodly states and kingdoms seen;
        Round many western islands have I been
    Which bards in fealty to Apollo hold.
    Oft of one wide expanse had I been told   5
        That deep-brow'd Homer ruled as his demesne;
        Yet did I never breathe its pure serene
    Till I heard Chapman speak out loud and bold:
    Then felt I like some watcher of the skies
        When a new planet swims into his ken;   10
    Or like stout Cortez when with eagle eyes
        He star'd at the Pacific—and all his men
    Look'd at each other with a wild surmise—
        Silent, upon a peak in Darien.

4 *fealty to Apollo* Allegiance to Apollo, the Greek god of poetry.
5 *Oft* 'But' in *The Examiner*.
6 *demesne* 'domain'.
7 *pure serene* From the Latin, *serenus*, 'a clear or cloudless sky'; figuratively, the 'unruffled expanse of clear sky or calm sea' or 'calm brightness, quiet radiance'. A common usage by romantic poets: compare Coleridge, 'Hymn Before Sunrise in the Vale of Chamouni,' 'glittering through the pure serene' (l. 72); Byron, *Childe Harold's Pilgrimage*, 'Kissing, not ruffling, the blue deep's serene' (II, l. 70); and Henry Cary's 1814 translation of Dante, *Paradiso*, 'the pure serene / Of ne'er disturbed ether' (xix, 60–1). The line was 'Yet could I never judge what men could mean' in *The Examiner*.
8 *Chapman* See headnote above.
11–14 *Or like stout Cortez ... in Darien* Leigh Hunt comments:

> The men of Cortez staring at each other, and the eagle eyes of their leader looking out upon the Pacific, have been thought too violent a picture for the dignity of the occasion; but it is a case that requires the exception.... The last line ... makes the mountain part of the spectacle, and supports the emotion of the rest of the sonnet upon a basis of gigantic tranquillity.
> (*Lord Byron and Some of His Contemporaries*, vol. 2, p. 412)

11 *Cortez* Keats here mistakes Cortéz for Balboa, the Spanish conquistador who 'discovered' the Pacific Ocean in 1513. For the details of the expedition, Keats draws on William Robertson's *History of America* (1777), which he had read at Enfield.
13 *wild surmise* 'an idea formed in the mind ... that something may be true, but without certainty and on very slight evidence ...; a conjecture'. For Romantic poetry (especially that of Wordsworth and Keats), the surmise comes to designate both a mood (a hunch, a sense of possibility) and a mode (the formal investigation and presentation of the poet's conjecture). See headnote to 'Ode to a Nightingale' (p. 443).
14 *Darien* The isthmus of Darien, in Panama.

The Eve of St Agnes

Written in January–February 1819, and significantly revised in September 1819 (according to Keats's letters of 14 February and 5 September 1819, *Letters*, vol. 2, pp. 58, 157), 'The Eve of St Agnes' was published (with further revision) in 1820 in *Lamia, Isabella, The Eve of St Agnes, and Other Poems*. In an August 1819 letter to Benjamin Bailey, Keats refers to the poem as a tale based on the 'popular superstition' (*Letters*, vol. 2, p. 139) according to which virgins, by practising certain measures of divination (e.g. fasting, silence, sleeping in a supine position) on the eve of the feast of St Agnes (21 January), may be rewarded with a vision of their future husbands in a dream. Keats would have known this tradition from John Brand's *Observations on Popular Antiquities*, where he would have found this account of St Agnes:

St Agnes was a Roman virgin and martyr, who suffered in the tenth persecution under the Emperor Dioclesian, A. D. 306. She was condemned to be debauched in the public stews before her execution, but her virginity was miraculously preserved by lightning and thunder from Heaven. About eight days after her execution, her parents, going to lament and pray at her tomb, they saw a vision of angels, among whom was their daughter, and a lamb standing by her as white as snow, on which account it is that in every graphic representation of her, there is a lamb pictured by her side.

(*Observations on Popular Antiquities*, vol. 1, p. 21; 1841 edn)

On the feast day of St Agnes, two unshorn white lambs are specially blessed by the Pope during a pontifical high Mass in the Roman basilica of Sant'Agnese fuori le mura; afterward, their wool is woven by nuns into ecclesiastical vestments (see ll. 115–17 below). In a more profane context, it has also been suggested that the poem's depiction of erotic longing and consummation was inspired by the early stages of Keats's passion for Fanny Brawne.

Beyond Brand's *Observations*, the literary influences are many, including *Romeo and Juliet*, the novels of Ann Radcliffe, the romances of Walter Scott and Coleridge (respectively, *The Lay of the Last Minstrel* and 'Christabel'), and of course Spenser. The poem represents Keats's most sustained use of the Spenserian stanza (nine lines of iambic pentameter rhyming *ababbcbcc*, with the last line an Alexandrine), a stanza which allows for both narrative momentum and erotic languor, both luxuriousness of imagery and elongation of sound. When Hazlitt remarked in an 1818 lecture that 'Spenser was the poet of our waking dreams; and he has invented not only a language but a music of his own for them' (*Complete Works*, vol. 5, p. 44), he also managed to anticipate the radiant quality of Keats's imagery (e.g. the justly celebrated stanzas depicting Madeline in front of the casement, ll. 208–43) and the incantatory qualities of his own silvery language (e.g. the silent eloquence of Madeline's panting heart, compared to a tongueless nightingale, ll. 199–207).

After Keats revised the poem in September 1819, he showed it to his friend and admirer Richard Woodhouse (also the legal counsel to Keats's publishers, Taylor & Hessey), who promptly wrote to John Taylor that, in addition to numerous 'trifling alterations', there was also 'another alteration':

You know if a thing has a decent side, I generally look no further – As the Poem was originally written, *we* innocent ones (ladies & myself) might very well have supposed that Porphyro, when acquainted with Madeleine's love for him, & when 'he arose, Etherial flushed' [ll. 317–18 below] &c &c (turn to it) set himself at once to persuade her to go off with him, & succeeded & went over the 'Dartmoor black' (now changed for some other place [l. 351 below]) to be married, in right honest chaste & sober wise. But, as it is now altered, as soon as M. has confessed her love, P. instead winds by degrees his arm round her, presses breast to breast, and acts all the acts of a bonâ fide husband, while she fancies she is only playing the part of a Wife in a dream. This alteration is of about 3 stanzas; and tho' there are not improper expressions but all is left to inference, and tho' profanely speaking the Interest on the reader's imagination is greatly heightened, yet I do apprehend it will render the poem unfit for ladies, & indeed scarcely to be mentioned to them among the 'things that are'. – He says he does not want ladies to read his poetry: that he writes for men – & that if in the former poem there was an opening for doubt what took place, it was his fault for not writing clearly & comprehensibly – that he should despise a man who would be such an eunuch in sentiment as to leave a maid, with that Character about her, in such a situation: and should despise himself to write about it &c &c – and all this sort of Keats-like rhodomontade.

(*Letters*, vol. 2, p. 163)

In his response to Woodhouse regarding '[t]his Folly of Keats', Taylor wrote:

I don't know how the Meaning of the new Stanzas is wrapped up, but I will not be accessary . . . towards publishing any thing which can only be read by Men, since even on their Minds a bad Effect must follow the Encouragement of those Thoughts which cannot be rased without Impropriety. . . . Therefore . . . if he will not so far concede to my Wishes as to leave the passage as it originally stood, I must be content to admire his Poems with some other Imprint. . . .

(*Letters*, vol. 2, pp. 182–3)

When 'The Eve of St Agnes' was finally published in 1820, the offending stanza had been dropped (see note to l. 314 below). (The 1820 text is perhaps best understood as a composite of Keats's original and revised drafts of 1819, amended by the editing of Woodhouse and Taylor, then finally corrected in proof by Keats.) Keats's putative concerns regarding the poem's possible weaknesses in sentiment and description come up again, however, in another letter to Woodhouse. Characterizing 'Isabella, or the Pot of Basil' as 'what I should call were I a reviewer "A weak-sided Poem" with an amusing sober-sadness about it', Keats went on to observe, 'There is no objection of this kind to *Lamia* – A good deal to *St Agnes Eve* – only not so glaring' (*Letters*, vol. 2, p. 174).

Leigh Hunt, the poem's first and most consistent champion, felt otherwise. Long after distinguishing it as 'rather a picture than a story' in his review of the 1820 volume in the *Indicator* (2 August 1820; *Periodical Essays*, p. 288), Hunt reprinted the poem with his own commentary in *The London Journal* (21 January 1835), then again in *Imagination and Fancy* (1844). In his introductory comments there on Keats, Hunt wrote that 'Among his finished productions . . . the *Eve of St Agnes* still appears to me the most delightful and complete specimen of his genius. It stands mid-way between his most sensitive ones . . . and the less generally characteristic majesty of the fragment of *Hyperion*' (*Later Literary Essays*, p. 109). Hunt then closes with this accolade for Keats's 'sincerity and passion':

> Let the student of poetry observe, that in all the luxury of the *Eve of St Agnes* there is nothing of the conventional craft of artificial writers; no heaping up of words or similes for their own sakes or the rhyme's sake; no gaudy common-places; no borrowed airs of earnestness; no tricks of inversion; no substitution of reading or of ingenious thoughts for feeling or spontaneity; no irrelevancy or unfitness of any sort. All flows out of sincerity and passion. The writer is as much in love with the heroine as his hero is; his description of the painted window, however gorgeous, has not an untrue or superfluous word; and the only speck of a fault in the whole poem arises from an excess of emotion.
>
> (*Later Literary Essays*, p. 110)

Text follows *1820*, with variants from Woodhouse's transcript and Keats's suppressed revisions of September 1819.

I.

ST. Agnes' Eve—Ah, bitter chill it was!
The owl, for all his feathers, was a-cold;
The hare limp'd trembling through the frozen grass,
And silent was the flock in woolly fold:
Numb were the Beadsman's fingers, while he told   5
His rosary, and while his frosted breath,
Like pious incense from a censer old,
Seem'd taking flight for heaven, without a death,
Past the sweet Virgin's picture, while his prayer he saith.

1–9 *St Agnes' Eve . . . his prayer he saith* See Hunt's commentary on the imagery of this stanza:

> We feel the plump, feathery bird, in his nook, shivering in spite of his natural household warmth, and staring out at the strange weather. The hare cringing through the chill grass is very piteous, and the 'silent flock' very patient; and how quiet and gentle, as well as wintry, are all these circumstances, and fit to open a quiet and gentle poem! The breath of the pilgrim, likened to 'pious incense', completes them, and is a simile in admirable 'keeping', as the painters call it; that is to say, is thoroughly harmonious with itself and all that is going on. . . . There is no part of it unfitting. It is not applicable in one point, and the reverse in another.
>
> (*Later Literary Essays*, p. 111)

1 *bitter chill it was!* The sense of cold with which Keats begins is not merely a discrete detail but one of the most compelling facts and forces in the poem. The word 'chill' occurs three times (ll. 1, 113, 311), 'chilly' twice (ll. 235, 275) and 'cold' three times (ll. 2, 134, 378) – indeed, 'cold' is the last word of the poem ('among his ashes cold'). Even the light of the moon, which illuminates so many crucial passages, is 'chill', 'wintry' and 'pallid'. Warmth, in contrast, is less a material condition than a possibility, a prospect of human passion: the rich colours on Madeline's breast ('warm gules', l. 218) or Porphyro's heady anticipation in Madeline's otherwise chilly room ('his warm, unnerved arm', l. 280). As Hunt observes, 'There is to be no comfort in the poem, but what is given by love' (see note to l. 112).
2 *a-cold* Compare *King Lear*, 'Tom's a-cold' (III. iv. 56).
5 *Beadsman* 'one paid or endowed to pray for others; a pensioner or almsman charged with the duty of praying for the souls of his benefactors'.

II.

His prayer he saith, this patient, holy man; 10
Then takes his lamp, and riseth from his knees,
And back returneth, meagre, barefoot, wan,
Along the chapel aisle by slow degrees:
The sculptur'd dead, on each side, seem to freeze,
Emprison'd in black, purgatorial rails: 15
Knights, ladies, praying in dumb orat'ries,
He passeth by; and his weak spirit fails
To think how they may ache in icy hoods and mails.

III.

Northward he turneth through a little door,
And scarce three steps, ere Music's golden tongue 20
Flatter'd to tears this aged man and poor;
But no—already had his deathbell rung;
The joys of all his life were said and sung:
His was harsh penance on St. Agnes' Eve:
Another way he went, and soon among 25
Rough ashes sat he for his soul's reprieve,
And all night kept awake, for sinners' sake to grieve.

IV.

That ancient Beadsman heard the prelude soft;
And so it chanc'd, for many a door was wide,
From hurry to and fro. Soon, up aloft, 30
The silver, snarling trumpets 'gan to chide:
The level chambers, ready with their pride,
Were glowing to receive a thousand guests:
The carved angels, ever eager-eyed,
Star'd, where upon their heads the cornice rests, 35
With hair blown back, and wings put cross-wise on their breasts.

---

12 *meagre, barefoot, wan* Keats elsewhere uses similar groupings of epithets to produce the same cadence: compare *Endymion* 'lovelorn, silent, wan' (IV. 764) and 'Hyperion' 'nerveless, listless, dead' (I. 18). See also line 187.

14–18 *The sculptured dead . . . icy hoods and mails* Hunt suggests in *Imagination and Fancy* that Keats may have found in Cary's translation of Dante this image of sculptural figures as architectural columns:

> As, to support incumbent floor or roof,
> For corbel, is a figure sometimes seen,
> That crumples up its knees unto its breast;
> With the feign'd posture, stirring ruth unfeign'd
> In the beholder's fancy. . . .
>
> (*Purgatorio*, x, 119–23)

He further remarks, 'Most wintry as well as penitential is the word "aching" in "icy hoods and mails"; and most felicitous the introduction of the Catholic idea in the word "purgatorial". The very colour of the rails is made to assume a meaning, and to shadow forth the gloom of the punishment' (*Later Literary Essays*, p. 112).

16 *orat'ries* oratory; a small chapel or 'a place of prayer'.

21 *Flatter'd to tears* See Hunt, *Imagination and Fancy*:

> In this word 'flattered' is the whole theory of the secret of tears; which are the tributes, more or less worthy, of self-pity to self-love. . . . Yes, the poor old man was moved, by the sweet music, to think that so sweet a thing was intended for his comfort, as well as for others. He felt that the mysterious kindness of Heaven did not omit even his poor, old sorry case. . . . Hence, he found himself deserving of tears and self-pity, and he shed them, and felt soothed by his poor, old loving self.
>
> (*Later Literary Essays*, pp. 112–13)

26 *reprieve* here used figuratively, for 'respite' or 'redemption'.

27 *And . . . to grieve* In a manuscript copied by Woodhouse, there is an additional stanza at this point:

> But there are ears may hear sweet melodies,
> And there are eyes to heighten festivals,
> And there are feet for nimble minstrelsies,
> And many a lip that for the red wine calls,—
> Follow, then follow to the illumined halls,
> Follow me youth, and leave the eremite—
> Give him a tear—then trophied banneral
> And many a brilliant tasseling of the light,
> Shall droop from arched ways this high baronial night.

35 *cornice* ornamental moulding, just below the ceiling.

V.

At length burst in the argent revelry,
With plume, tiara, and all rich array,
Numerous as shadows haunting fairily
The brain, new stuff'd, in youth, with triumphs gay   40
Of old romance. These let us wish away,
And turn, sole-thoughted, to one Lady there,
Whose heart had brooded, all that wintry day,
On love, and wing'd St. Agnes' saintly care,
As she had heard old dames full many times declare.   45

VI.

They told her how, upon St. Agnes' Eve,
Young virgins might have visions of delight,
And soft adorings from their loves receive
Upon the honey'd middle of the night,
If ceremonies due they did aright;   50
As, supperless to bed they must retire,
And couch supine their beauties, lily white;
Nor look behind, nor sideways, but require
Of Heaven with upward eyes for all that they desire.

VII.

Full of this whim was thoughtful Madeline: 55
The music, yearning like a God in pain,
She scarcely heard: her maiden eyes divine,
Fix'd on the floor, saw many a sweeping train
Pass by—she heeded not at all: in vain
Came many a tiptoe, amorous cavalier,   60
And back retir'd; not cool'd by high disdain,
But she saw not: her heart was otherwhere:
She sigh'd for Agnes' dreams, the sweetest of the year.

---

37 *argent* silver or silvery, metallic; a further refinement of the 'silver, snarling trumpets' (l. 31).
39 *fairily* 'in a fairy-like manner', enchantingly.
46 *They told her how . . .* For details on the superstitions surrounding the eve of St Agnes's feast day, see the headnote above.
52 *couch supine* to lie on one's back, 'with upward eyes'.
54 *Of Heaven . . . that they desire.* In Keats's revisions to the poem in September 1819, he inserted a stanza here, in order (as Woodhouse wrote Taylor) 'to make the *legend* more intelligible, and correspondent with what afterward takes place, particularly with respect to the supper & the playing on the Lute' (*Letters*, vol. 2, p. 162).

'Twas said her future lord would there appear
Offering as sacrifice—all in a dream—
Delicious food even to her lips brought near;
Viands and wine and fruit and sugar'd cream,
To touch her palate with the fine extreme
Of relish: then soft music heard: and then
More pleasures followed in a dizzy stream

Palpable almost: then to wake again
Warm in the virgin morn, no weeping Magdalen.

For the 'pleasures' attendant upon Madeline's dream, see ll. 314–22 and note.
56 *yearning like a God in pain* Keats's gaping simile resonates with the language of pain in both the Hyperion poems: compare 'Hyperion: A Fragment', 'A living death was in each gush of sounds, / Each family of rapturous hurried notes, / That fell, one after one, yet all at once' (II, 281–3) and '. . . all the vast / Unwearied ear of the whole universe / Listened in pain and pleasure at the birth / Of such new tuneful wonder' (III, 64–7).
58 *sweeping train* See Keats's letter of 11 June 1820 to Taylor ('I do not use train for concourse of passers by but for Skirts sweeping along the floor'; *Letters*, vol. 2, pp. 294–5).
60 *cavalier* 'a courtly gentleman, a gallant'.
61 *high disdain* Compare Coleridge, 'Christabel', 'Each spake words of high disdain' (l. 416). On the possible influence of Coleridge's medieval romance on Keats's tale, see note to ll. 208–43.

VIII.

She danc'd along with vague, regardless eyes,
Anxious her lips, her breathing quick and short: 65
The hallow'd hour was near at hand: she sighs
Amid the timbrels, and the throng'd resort
Of whisperers in anger, or in sport;
'Mid looks of love, defiance, hate, and scorn,
Hoodwink'd with faery fancy; all amort, 70
Save to St. Agnes and her lambs unshorn,
And all the bliss to be before to-morrow morn.

IX.

So, purposing each moment to retire,
She linger'd still. Meantime, across the moors,
Had come young Porphyro, with heart on fire 75
For Madeline. Beside the portal doors,
Buttress'd from moonlight, stands he, and implores
All saints to give him sight of Madeline,
But for one moment in the tedious hours,
That he might gaze and worship all unseen; 80
Perchance speak, kneel, touch, kiss—in sooth such things have been.

X.

He ventures in: let no buzz'd whisper tell:
All eyes be muffled, or a hundred swords
Will storm his heart, Love's fev'rous citadel:
For him, those chambers held barbarian hordes, 85
Hyena foemen, and hot-blooded lords,
Whose very dogs would execrations howl
Against his lineage: not one breast affords
Him any mercy, in that mansion foul,
Save one old beldame, weak in body and in soul. 90

XI.

Ah, happy chance! the aged creature came,
Shuffling along with ivory-headed wand,
To where he stood, hid from the torch's flame,
Behind a broad hall-pillar, far beyond
The sound of merriment and chorus bland: 95
He startled her; but soon she knew his face,
And grasp'd his fingers in her palsied hand,

---

67 *timbrels* Tambourines; compare 'Ode on a Grecian Urn', 'What pipes and timbrels?' (l. 10).
70 *Hoodwinked with faery fancy* Characteristically Keatsian statement of the pleasures as well as dangers of the imagination. (See 'Ode to a Nightingale', '. . . the fancy cannot cheat so well / As she is famed to do', ll. 73–4). Affiliated with Spenser and faery-land, the imagination is celebrated for its power in colouring the events of daily life and thus investing them with new significance. That Madeline has been 'hoodwinked', however, not only suggests that she has succumbed to a certain thralldom of the imagination, but also anticipates the predicament awaiting her when she awakens, only to find her 'vision' before her (ll. 298 ff). See also *Romeo and Juliet*, 'We'll have no Cupid hoodwink'd with a scarf' (I. iv. 4).
70 *all amort* From the French, *à la mort*: 'to the death'. Figuratively, spiritless or dejected.
71 *lambs unshorn* See headnote above.
85–90 *For him . . . in soul* Compare Romeo's predicament in the mansion of the Capulets, as well as the role played by the nurse (*Romeo and Juliet*, I. iv. 5).
90 *beldame* 'aged woman'; sixteenth-century form of address for a nurse.
95 *bland* 'pleasing to the senses'.

Saying, 'Mercy, Porphyro! hie thee from this place;
They are all here to-night, the whole blood-thirsty race!'

XII.

'Get hence! get hence! there's dwarfish Hildebrand; 100
He had a fever late, and in the fit
He cursed thee and thine, both house and land:
Then there's that old Lord Maurice, not a whit
More tame for his gray hairs—Alas me! flit!
Flit like a ghost away.'—'Ah, Gossip dear, 105
We're safe enough; here in this arm-chair sit,
And tell me how'—'Good Saints! not here, not here;
Follow me, child, or else these stones will be thy bier.'

XIII.

He follow'd through a lowly arched way,
Brushing the cobwebs with his lofty plume, 110
And as she mutter'd 'Well-a—well-a-day!'
He found him in a little moonlight room,
Pale, lattic'd, chill, and silent as a tomb.
'Now tell me where is Madeline,' said he,
'O tell me, Angela, by the holy loom 115
Which none but secret sisterhood may see,
When they St. Agnes' wool are weaving piously.'

XIV.

'St. Agnes! Ah! it is St. Agnes' Eve—
Yet men will murder upon holy days:
Thou must hold water in a witch's sieve, 120
And be liege-lord of all the Elves and Fays,
To venture so: it fills me with amaze
To see thee, Porphyro!—St. Agnes' Eve!
God's help! my lady fair the conjuror plays
This very night: good angels her deceive! 125
But let me laugh awhile, I've mickle time to grieve.'

XV.

Feebly she laugheth in the languid moon,
While Porphyro upon her face doth look,
Like puzzled urchin on an aged crone
Who keepeth clos'd a wond'rous riddle-book, 130
As spectacled she sits in chimney nook.

---

111 *'Well-a—well-a-day!'* Compare Coleridge, 'Christabel', 'Ah, well-a-day!' (l. 264) and, in a similar cadence, '(ah woe is me!)' (l. 292).
112 *little moonlight room* See Hunt, *Imagination and Fancy*, 'The poet does not make his "little moonlight room" comfortable, observe. The high taste of the exordium is kept up. All is still wintry. There is to be no comfort in the poem, but what is given by love. All else may be left to the cold walls' (*Later Literary Essays*, p. 115).
115–17 *'Oh, tell me, Angela ... weaving piously.'* See headnote above.

120 *hold water in a witch's sieve* Compare *Macbeth*, 'But in a sieve I'll thither sail' (I. iii. 8).
124 *the conjuror plays* See headnote above. Conjurors were those who could summon spirits and constrain them to do their bidding. Whereas the mention of witches, elves and fays (ll. 120–1) suggested that Porphyro was in league with the otherworldly, so this casting of Madeline as a conjuror suggests that she may be capable of summoning up spirits.
125 *Good angels her deceive!* Angela hopes that Madeline will only have pleasant dreams, but the use of 'deceive' opens the way for Porphyro's ambiguous design.
126 *mickle* 'a great quantity or amount'.

But soon his eyes grew brilliant, when she told
His lady's purpose; and he scarce could brook
Tears, at the thought of those enchantments cold,
And Madeline asleep in lap of legends old. 135

XVI.

Sudden a thought came like a full-blown rose,
Flushing his brow, and in his pained heart
Made purple riot: then doth he propose
A stratagem, that makes the beldame start:
'A cruel man and impious thou art: 140
Sweet lady, let her pray, and sleep, and dream
Alone with her good angels, far apart
From wicked men like thee. Go, go!—I deem
'Thou canst not surely be the same that thou didst seem.'

XVII.

'I will not harm her, by all saints I swear,' 145
Quoth Porphyro: 'O may I ne'er find grace
When my weak voice shall whisper its last prayer,
If one of her soft ringlets I displace,
Or look with ruffian passion in her face:
Good Angela, believe me by these tears; 150
Or I will, even in a moment's space,
Awake, with horrid shout, my foemen's ears,
And beard them, though they be more fang'd than wolves and bears.'

XVIII.

'Ah! why wilt thou affright a feeble soul?
A poor, weak, palsy-stricken, churchyard thing, 155
Whose passing-bell may ere the midnight toll;
Whose prayers for thee, each morn and evening,
Were never miss'd.'—Thus plaining, doth she bring
A gentler speech from burning Porphyro;
So woful, and of such deep sorrowing, 160
That Angela gives promise she will do
Whatever he shall wish, betide her weal or woe.

133 *brook* In this instance, to check or forebear.
134–5 *Tears at the thought ... legends old.* In *Imagination and Fancy*, Hunt seizes on 'Tears' to develop his earlier explication of 'the whole theory of the secret of tears' (see note above to l. 21):

> He almost shed tears of sympathy, to think how his treasure is exposed to the cold; and of delight and pride, to think of her sleeping beauty, and her love for himself. This passage, 'asleep in the lap of legends old', is in the highest imaginative taste, fusing together the imaginative and the spiritual, the remote and the near. Madeline is asleep in her bed; but she is also asleep in accordance with the legends of the season; and therefore the bed becomes *their* lap as well as sleep's. The poet does not critically think of all this; he feels it: and thus should our young poets draw upon the prominent points of their feelings on a subject, sucking the essence out of them into analogous words, instead of beating about the bush for *thoughts*, and, perhaps getting clever ones, but not thoroughly pertinent, not wanted, not the best. Such, at least, is the difference between the truest poetry and the degrees beneath it.
> (*Later Literary Essays*, p. 116)

Also of note here is a similar imaginative coalescence in 'enchantments cold', a 'fusion' of Porphyro's singing (as incantation) and Madeline's earlier conjurations, which will be 'cold' as long as they are confined to a dream-vision.
138 *purple riot;* Keats's use of 'purple' invariably suggests imaginative and / or sensual excess: compare 'Isabella, or the Pot of Basil', 'Her silk had played in purple fantasies' (l. 370); 'Ode to a Nightingale' 'With beaded bubbles winking at the brim, / And purple-stained mouth' (ll. 17–18); and 'Lamia', 'That purple-lined palace of sweet sin' (II. 31).
140–62 *A cruel man ... weal or woe.* Compare the concern of Juliet's nurse regarding Romeo's schemes (*Romeo and Juliet*, II. iv. 164–88).
153 *beard* 'to oppose openly and resolutely, with daring or with effrontery'.
162 *betide her weal or woe* Regardless of the consequences for herself.

XIX.

Which was, to lead him, in close secrecy,
Even to Madeline's chamber, and there hide
Him in a closet, of such privacy   165
That he might see her beauty unespied,
And win perhaps that night a peerless bride,
While legion'd fairies pac'd the coverlet,
And pale enchantment held her sleepy-eyed.
Never on such a night have lovers met,   170
Since Merlin paid his Demon all the monstrous debt.

XX.

'It shall be as thou wishest,' said the Dame:
'All cates and dainties shall be stored there
Quickly on this feast-night: by the tambour frame
Her own lute thou wilt see: no time to spare,   175
For I am slow and feeble, and scarce dare
On such a catering trust my dizzy head.
Wait here, my child, with patience; kneel in prayer
The while: Ah! thou must needs the lady wed,
Or may I never leave my grave among the dead.'   180

XXI.

So saying, she hobbled off with busy fear.
The lover's endless minutes slowly pass'd;
The dame return'd, and whisper'd in his ear
To follow her; with aged eyes aghast
From fright of dim espial. Safe at last,   185
Through many a dusky gallery, they gain
The maiden's chamber, silken, hush'd, and chaste;
Where Porphyro took covert, pleas'd amain.
His poor guide hurried back with agues in her brain.

XXII.

Her falt'ring hand upon the balustrade,   190
Old Angela was feeling for the stair,
When Madeline, St. Agnes' charmed maid,
Rose, like a mission'd Spirit, unaware:
With silver taper's light, and pious care,
She turn'd, and down the aged gossip led   195
To a safe level matting. Now prepare,
Young Porphyro, for gazing on that bed;
She comes, she comes again, like ring-dove fray'd and fled.

---

169 *pale enchantment* As with 'enchantments cold' (l. 134), the phrase 'pale enchantment' underscores the lifelessness of the conjuration (contrasted with Porphyro's 'flushed', 'throbbing' presence, l. 318).
170–1 *Never on such night . . . all the monstrous debt.* Keats's allusion here is unclear; possibly a reference to Merlin's imprisonment by the Lady of the Lake.
173 *cates* 'edible delicacies'.
174 *tambour frame* Embroidery frame.
177 *catering* Angela refers here not so much to the 'cates and dainties' prepared for the feast, as to Porphyro's scheme 'to see her beauty unespied' (l. 166). Keats's phrasing here also anticipates the 'delicates' (l. 271) which Porphyro arranges for Madeline in her chamber, as well as the delicate stratagem he has undertaken.
179 *thou must needs the lady wed* Compare the Nurse's concern on Juliet's behalf (*Romeo and Juliet*, II. iv. 165–70).
185 *espial* 'the fact of being espied'; compare Byron, *The Corsair*, 'screened from espial by the jutting cape' (I, 601).
187 *silken, hush'd, and chaste* See note to l. 12.
188 *amain* 'exceedingly, greatly'.
189 *agues* Pronounced *a*-gues; figuratively, any fit of shaking or shivering.
198 *fray'd* 'afraid, frightened'; compare Spenser, *Faerie Queene*, 'like doves, whom the Eagle doth affray' (V. xii. 5). See also line 296.

XXIII.

Out went the taper as she hurried in;
Its little smoke, in pallid moonshine, died: 200
She clos'd the door, she panted, all akin
To spirits of the air, and visions wide:
No uttered syllable, or, woe betide!
But to her heart, her heart was voluble,
Paining with eloquence her balmy side; 205
As though a tongueless nightingale should swell
Her throat in vain, and die, heart-stifled, in her dell.

XXIV.

A casement high and triple-arch'd there was,
All garlanded with carven imag'ries

199–207 *Out went the taper . . . in her dell.* For Hunt, this stanza represents a triumph of minute observation:

> This [l. 200] is a verse in the taste of Chaucer, full of minute grace and truth. The smoke of the wax-taper seems almost as etherial and fair as the moonlight, and both suit each other and the heroine. But what a lovely line is the seventh about the heart 'Paining with eloquence her balmy side'! And the nightingale! How touching the simile! the heart a 'tongueless nightingale', dying in the bed of the bosom. What thorough sweetness, and perfection of lovely imagery! How one delicacy is heaped upon another! But for a burst of richness, noiseless, coloured, suddenly enriching the moonlight, as if a door of heaven were opened, read the stanza that follows.
> (*Later Literary Essays*, p. 118)

203 *No uttered syllable* If Madeline were to speak, she would break the spell ('My lady fair the conjuror plays', l. 124) which she hopes will produce a vision of the man she is to marry.

204 *her heart was voluble* Though Madeline cannot speak, her heart is both loud and eloquent – here evident in the pulsing cadence of 'her heart, her heart'.

205 *balmy* 'delicately and deliciously fragrant'; compare 'I stood tip-toe upon a little hill', 'a half heard strain, / Full of sweet desolation – balmy pain' (ll. 161–2).

206 *tongueless nightingale* In Ovid's telling of the myth of Procne and Philomela (*Metamorphoses*, vi), Philomela is deprived of her tongue after being raped by Tereus and eventually transformed into a nightingale, while her sister Procne is transformed into a swallow.

208–43 *A casement high . . . and be a bud again.* Perhaps the most frequently cited passage in the entire poem, ever since Charles Lamb's early review of the 1820 volume in *The New Times*:

> Such is the description that Mr Keats has given us, with a delicacy worthy of Christabel, of a high-born damsel, in one of the apartments of a baronial castle, laying herself down devoutly to dream on the charmed Eve of St Agnes; and like the radiance, which comes from those old windows upon the limbs and garments of the damsel, is the almost Chaucer-like painting, with which this poet illumines every subject he touches. We have scarcely anything like it in modern description. It brings us back to ancient days, and 'Beauty making beautiful old rhymes' [Shakespeare, *Sonnets*, 106. 3].
> (*Works*, vol. 1, p. 257)

Citing 'ancient days', Chaucer, and Coleridge's medieval romance, Lamb alerts us to the influence of literary medievalism on Keats's own 'romance' at the same time as he provides another set of terms (notably painting, description and illumination) for Keats's own influence on a later generation of post-Romantic poets and painters, including Tennyson, William Holman Hunt, William Morris and D. G. Rossetti. Whether described as making pictures out of words or turning words into pictures, Keats's 'scene-painting' illuminates the texture of the poem, much as the moon (in this passage) allows Porphyro to gaze upon his beloved. Though the moonlight is cold, the colours are warm and precipitate the description of Madeline's 'warmed jewels', 'fragrant boddice', and 'rich attire' (ll. 228, 229, 230). (See also Hunt, who further remarked that 'Keats is no half-painter. . . . He feels all as he goes. In his best pieces, every bit is precious; and he knew it, and laid it on as carefully as Titian or Giorgione'; *Lord Byron and Some of His Contemporaries*, vol. 1, p. 429.)

208 *casement* Frame forming a window. Throughout Keats's poetry, the casement represents a multitude of 'romantic' possibilities; see for example 'Ode to Psyche', 'A bright torch, and a casement ope at night' (l. 66) and 'Ode to a Nightingale', 'Charm'd magic casements, opening on the foam / Of perilous seas, in faery lands forlorn' (see ll. 69–70 and note).

> Of fruits, and flowers, and bunches of knot-grass, 210
> And diamonded with panes of quaint device,
> Innumerable of stains and splendid dyes,
> As are the tiger-moth's deep-damask'd wings;
> And in the midst, 'mong thousand heraldries,
> And twilight saints, and dim emblazonings, 215
> A shielded scutcheon blush'd with blood of queens and kings.
>
> ### XXV.
>
> Full on this casement shone the wintry moon,
> And threw warm gules on Madeline's fair breast,
> As down she knelt for heaven's grace and boon;
> Rose-bloom fell on her hands, together prest, 220
> And on her silver cross soft amethyst,
> And on her hair a glory, like a saint:
> She seem'd a splendid angel, newly drest,
> Save wings, for heaven:—Porphyro grew faint:
> She knelt, so pure a thing, so free from mortal taint. 225
>
> ### XXVI.
>
> Anon his heart revives: her vespers done,
> Of all its wreathed pearls her hair she frees;
> Unclasps her warmed jewels one by one;
> Loosens her fragrant boddice; by degrees
> Her rich attire creeps rustling to her knees: 230
> Half-hidden, like a mermaid in sea-weed,
> Pensive awhile she dreams awake, and sees,
> In fancy, fair St. Agnes in her bed,
> But dares not look behind, or all the charm is fled.
>
> ### XXVII.
>
> Soon, trembling in her soft and chilly nest, 235
> In sort of wakeful swoon, perplex'd she lay,

210 *knot-grass* 'common weed in waste ground, with numerous intricately-branched creeping stems, and small pale pink flowers'.
215 *emblazonings* 'armorial or heraldic decorations'.
216 *A shielded scutcheon . . . queens and kings* See Hunt, *Imagination and Fancy*: 'Could all the pomp and graces of aristocracy, with Titian's and Raphael's aid to boot, go beyond the rich religion of this picture, with its "twilight saints", and its scutcheons, "*blushing* with the blood of queens"'? (*Later Literary Essays*, p. 118). An escutcheon is a shield or shield-shaped surface on which a coat of arms is depicted.
218 *gules* 'red, as one of the heraldic colours'; here, in stained glass. See Hunt, *Imagination and Fancy*, 'How proper as well as pretty the heraldic term *gules*, considering the occasion. "Red" would not have been a fiftieth part as good. And with what elegant luxury he touches the "silver cross" with "amethyst", and the fair human hand with "rose-colour", the kin of their carnation!' (*Later Literary Essays*, p. 119).
219 *boon* Blessing, favour.
222 *glory* 'Aura or aureole'.

224 *Save wings, for Heaven* See Hunt, *Imagination and Fancy*:

> The lovely and innocent creature, thus praying under the gorgeous painted window, completes the exceeding and unique beauty of this picture, – one that will for ever stand by itself in poetry, as an addition to the stock. It would have struck a glow on the face of Shakespeare himself. He might have put Imogen [*Cymbeline*] or Ophelia [*Hamlet*] under such a shrine.
> (*Later Literary Essays*, p. 118)

226 *vespers* Evening prayers.
228 *warmed jewels* See Hunt, *Imagination and Fancy*: 'How true and cordial the *warmed* jewels, and what matter of fact also, made elegant, in the rustling downward of the attire; and the mixture of dress and undress, and of the dishevelled hair, likened to a "mermaid in seaweed"'! (*Later Literary Essays*, p. 119).
236 *perplex'd she lay* Madeline's state of perplexity – her inability to determine what she sees – proceeds from the entangled crossing of waking and sleeping states in the preceding lines: 'pensive awhile she dreams awake, and

Until the poppied warmth of sleep oppress'd
Her soothed limbs, and soul fatigued away;
Flown, like a thought, until the morrow-day;
Blissfully haven'd both from joy and pain; 240
Clasp'd like a missal where swart Paynims pray;
Blinded alike from sunshine and from rain,
As though a rose should shut, and be a bud again.

XXVIII.

Stol'n to this paradise, and so entranced,
Porphyro gazed upon her empty dress, 245
And listen'd to her breathing, if it chanced
To wake into a slumberous tenderness;
Which when he heard, that minute did he bless,
And breath'd himself: then from the closet crept,
Noiseless as fear in a wide wilderness, 250
And over the hush'd carpet, silent, stept,
And 'tween the curtains peep'd, where, lo!—how fast she slept.

XXIX.

Then by the bed-side, where the faded moon
Made a dim, silver twilight, soft he set
A table, and, half anguish'd, threw thereon 255
A cloth of woven crimson, gold, and jet:—
O for some drowsy Morphean amulet!
The boisterous, midnight, festive clarion,
The kettle-drum, and far-heard clarionet,
Affray his ears, though but in dying tone:— 260
The hall door shuts again, and all the noise is gone.

---

sees, / In fancy' (ll. 232–3) and 'In sort of wakeful swoon' (l. 236). At once awake and asleep (as in the 'Ode to a Nightingale', 'Do I wake or sleep?', l. 80), Madeline is here bewildered by her own imagination. Compare Coleridge, 'Christabel', 'With open eyes (ah woe is me!) / Asleep, and dreaming fearfully, / Fearfully dreaming . . .' (ll. 292–4).

237 *poppied warmth of sleep* Poppied: drugged or drowsy. Compare 'Sleep and Poetry', 'Sleep, quiet with his poppy coronet' (348) and *Endymion*, 'A little onward ran the very stream / By which he took his first soft poppy dream' (IV, 785–6).

235–43 *Soon, trembling . . . and be a bud again.* According to Hunt *(Imagination and Fancy)*, 'perhaps the most exquisite [stanza] in the poem':

> Can the beautiful go beyond this? I never saw it. And how the imagery rises! flown like a *thought* – blissfully haven'd – clasp'd like a missal in a land of *Pagans*: that is to say, where Christian prayer-books must not be seen, and are, therefore, doubly cherished for the danger. And then, although nothing can surpass the preciousness of this idea, is the idea of the beautiful, crowning all –
>
> Blinded alike from sunshine and from rain,
> As though a rose should shut, and be a bud again.
>
> Thus it is that poetry, in its intense sympathy with creation, may be said to create anew, rendering its words more impressive than the objects they speak of, and individually more lasting; the spiritual perpetuity putting them on a level (not to speak it profanely) with the fugitive compound.
> (*Later Literary Essays*, p. 119)

241 *Paynims* Non-Christians, habitually used with reference to Muslims; a common epithet in the romances of Southey, Scott and Byron. See Scott, *Lay of the Last Minstrel*, 'For Paynim countries I have trod' (II. xii) and Byron, *Childe Harold's Pilgrimage*, 'And traverse Paynim shores, and pass Earth's central line' (I. xi).

244 *paradise* To be understood here as a metaphorical pleasure garden or bower of bliss, a potential site of *l'amour passion*. Compare *Endymion*, '. . . such a paradise of lips and eyes, / Blush-tinted cheeks, half-smiles, and faintest sighs' (I, 618–19).

257 *Morphean amulet!* Morpheus is the Greek god of dreams; hence a charm to induce sleep.

258–9 *festive clarion . . . far-heard clarionet* A 'clarionet' is the diminutive of 'clarion', or trumpet.

260 *Affray* 'frighten'; see note to l. 198 above.

XXX.

And still she slept an azure-lidded sleep,
In blanched linen, smooth, and lavender'd,
While he from forth the closet brought a heap
Of candied apple, quince, and plum, and gourd; 265
With jellies soother than the creamy curd,
And lucent syrops, tinct with cinnamon;
Manna and dates, in argosy transferr'd
From Fez; and spiced dainties, every one,
From silken Samarcand to cedar'd Lebanon. 270

XXXI.

These delicates he heap'd with glowing hand
On golden dishes and in baskets bright
Of wreathed silver: sumptuous they stand
In the retired quiet of the night,
Filling the chilly room with perfume light.— 275
And now, my love, my seraph fair, awake!
Thou art my heaven, and I thine eremite:
Open thine eyes, for meek St. Agnes' sake,
Or I shall drowse beside thee, so my soul doth ache.'

XXXII.

Thus whispering, his warm, unnerved arm 280
Sank in her pillow. Shaded was her dream
By the dusk curtains:—'twas a midnight charm
Impossible to melt as iced stream:
The lustrous salvers in the moonlight gleam;
Broad golden fringe upon the carpet lies: 285
It seem'd he never, never could redeem
From such a stedfast spell his lady's eyes;
So mus'd awhile, entoil'd in woofed phantasies.

XXXIII.

Awakening up, he took her hollow lute,—
Tumultuous,—and, in chords that tenderest be, 290

---

266 *soother* A combination of 'smoother' and 'more soothing'.
267 *tinct* 'tinged'. See Hunt, *Imagination and Fancy*: 'Here is delicate modulation, and super-refined epicurean nicety! "Lucent syrops tinct with cinnamon" make us read the line delicately, and at the tip-end, as it were, of one's tongue' (*Later Literary Essays*, p. 120).
268 *Manna . . . argosy transferred* 'Manna' is to be understood here in an extended sense as a rare delicacy, an exotic fruit from afar; see *Endymion*, 'And here is manna pick'd from Syrian trees' (II, 452). An 'argosy' is a merchant ship of significant proportions.
269–70 *From Fez . . . cedared Lebanon* Fez is in northern Morocco. The ancient Central Asian city of Samarkand (now in Uzbekistan) was famous for its silks; Lebanon was likewise renowned for its cedars. Though Madeline's room is decidedly 'chilly' (ll. 235, 275) and confined, the exotic Levantine locales of the delicacies here on display further embellish the 'paradise' into which Porphyro has stolen. As was the case with the 'wintry moon' setting in relief the warmth of the gules on Madeline's breast (ll. 217–18), however, they finally serve only to underscore the abiding contrast between warmth and cold at work throughout the poem.
276 *seraph* A member of the seraphim, a class of angel distinguished by the fervour of their love (as opposed to cherubim, distinguished for their knowledge).
277 *eremite* 'a recluse, hermit'; compare 'Bright Star!', 'Like nature's patient, sleepless eremite' (l. 4).
279 *so my soul doth ache* A characteristically Keatsian affiliation of pleasure and pain – here, the taunting pain of Porphyro's proximity to the object of his desire. Compare *Endymion*, 'What! dost thou move? dost kiss? O bliss! O pain!' (II, 773); see also 'Ode on Melancholy', '. . . and aching Pleasure nigh, / Turning to poison while the bee-mouth sips' (ll. 23–4).
280 *unnerved* Weak, listless.
288 *entoiled in woofed phantasies* Ensnared in woven imaginings.

He play'd an ancient ditty, long since mute,
In Provence call'd, 'La belle dame sans mercy:'
Close to her ear touching the melody;—
Wherewith disturb'd, she utter'd a soft moan:
He ceased—she panted quick—and suddenly   295
Her blue affrayed eyes wide open shone:
Upon his knees he sank, pale as smooth-sculptured stone.

XXXIV.

Her eyes were open, but she still beheld,
Now wide awake, the vision of her sleep:
There was a painful change, that nigh expell'd   300
The blisses of her dream so pure and deep
At which fair Madeline began to weep,
And moan forth witless words with many a sigh;
While still her gaze on Porphyro would keep;
Who knelt, with joined hands and piteous eye,   305
Fearing to move or speak, she look'd so dreamingly.

XXXV.

'Ah, Porphyro!' said she, 'but even now
Thy voice was at sweet tremble in mine ear,
Made tuneable with every sweetest vow;
And those sad eyes were spiritual and clear: 310
How chang'd thou art! how pallid, chill, and drear!
Give me that voice again, my Porphyro,
Those looks immortal, those complainings dear!
Oh leave me not in this eternal woe,
For if thou diest, my Love, I know not where to go.'   315

XXXVI.

Beyond a mortal man impassion'd far
At these voluptuous accents, he arose,
Ethereal, flush'd, and like a throbbing star

---

292 *'La belle dame sans mercy* See below, headnote to 'La Belle Dame Sans Merci'.
296 *affrayed* 'alarmed'; see note to l. 198 above.
298–9 *Her eyes were open ... her sleep* See note to l. 236 above.
300–3 *There was a painful change ... many a sigh* In a trajectory reminiscent of numerous of Keats's mature poems (see especially 'Ode to a Nightingale'), Madeline is here reawakening to the harsh light of reality after her hiatus in a dream-state. Having swooned and, through dreaming, flown away (ll. 235–9), Madeline was 'Blissfully havened both from joy and pain' (l. 240) under the power of a 'steadfast spell' (l. 287); now she is obliged to confront just how 'pallid, chill, and drear' (l. 311) things appear once she is wide awake and lamenting 'No dream, alas! alas! and woe is mine!' (l. 328). Compare 'Sleep and Poetry', 'The visions all are fled – the car is fled / Into the light of heaven, and in their stead / A sense of real things comes doubly strong' (ll. 155–7).
306 *dreamingly* 'as if in a dream'.
314–22 *Oh, leave me not ... frost-wind blows* In Keats's September 1819 revisions, he more sensuously presents Porphyro's 'melting' into Madeline's 'wild dream':

See while she speaks his arms encroaching slow
Have zon'd her, heart to heart—loud loud the dark winds blow!
For on the midnight came a tempest fell
More sooth for that his quick rejoinder flows
Into her burning ear:—and still the spell
Unbroken guards her in serene repose.
With her wild dream he mingled as a rose
Marryeth its odour to a violet.
Still, still she dreams; louder the frost-wind blows. . . .

For Woodhouse's concern that these lines would 'render the poem unfit for ladies', see headnote above.
317 *voluptuous* 'of or pertaining to ... the gratification of the senses; luxuriously sensuous'. For Keats, more comprehensively a term of self-indulgent excess, whether of the senses or of the emotions; see *Endymion*, 'And, with a blind voluptuous rage, I gave / Battle . . .' (III. 611–12) and 'we might die; / We might embrace and die: voluptuous thought!' (IV. 758–9).
318–19 *Ethereal ... deep repose* Compare *Romeo and Juliet*, '. . . cut him out in little stars, / And he will make the face of heaven so fine / That all the world will be in love with night . . .' (III. ii. 22–4).

Seen mid the sapphire heaven's deep repose;
Into her dream he melted, as the rose
Blendeth its odour with the violet,—
Solution sweet: meantime the frost-wind blows
Like Love's alarum pattering the sharp sleet
Against the window-panes; St. Agnes' moon hath set.

XXXVII.

'Tis dark: quick pattereth the flaw-blown sleet:
'This is no dream, my bride, my Madeline!'
'Tis dark: the iced gusts still rave and beat:
'No dream, alas! alas! and woe is mine!
Porphyro will leave me here to fade and pine.—
Cruel! what traitor could thee hither bring?
I curse not, for my heart is lost in thine,
Though thou forsakest a deceived thing;—
A dove forlorn and lost with sick unpruned wing.'

XXXVIII.

'My Madeline! sweet dreamer! lovely bride!
Say, may I be for aye thy vassal blest?
Thy beauty's shield, heart-shap'd and vermeil dyed?
Ah, silver shrine, here will I take my rest
After so many hours of toil and quest,
A famish'd pilgrim,—saved by miracle.
Though I have found, I will not rob thy nest
Saving of thy sweet self; if thou think'st well
To trust, fair Madeline, to no rude infidel.'

XXXIX.

'Hark! 'tis an elfin-storm from faery land,
Of haggard seeming, but a boon indeed:
Arise—arise! the morning is at hand;—
The bloated wassaillers will never heed:—
Let us away, my love, with happy speed;
There are no ears to hear, or eyes to see,—
Drown'd all in Rhenish and the sleepy mead:
Awake! arise! my love, and fearless be,
For o'er the southern moors I have a home for thee.'

---

320 *melted* Here in the most sensuous and figurative sense, 'to be "dissolved" in ecstasy' (hence potentially more 'profane' than Keats's use of 'mingled' in the rejected lines; see note to ll. 314–22 above).

322–4 *Solution sweet . . . moon hath set.* With the blowing of the frost-wind and the setting of the moon, the lovers' idyll comes to an end and they are confronted with the dangers of remaining in the castle.

325 *flaw-blown sleet* Compare Cary's translation of Dante, *Inferno*, 'Large hail, discolour'd water, sleety flaw / Through the dun midnight air stream'd down amain' (vi. 9–10).

333 *A dove forlorn . . . unpruned wing* See note to l. 198 above.

336 *Thy beauty's shield . . . vermeil dyed?* See Hunt, *Imagination and Fancy*: 'With what a pretty wilful conceit the costume of the poem is kept up in this line about the shield! The poet knew when to introduce apparent trifles forbidden to those who are void of real passion, and who, feeling nothing intensely, can intensify nothing' (*Later Literary Essays*, p. 122).

339 *pilgrim* Compare Romeo and Juliet's first exchange, in which he characterizes himself and his lips as 'blushing pilgrims' (*Romeo and Juliet*, I. v. 93–110).

342 *infidel* See note to l. 241 above. This stanza's use of 'vassal', 'pilgrim' and 'infidel' all draws on the vocabulary of the medieval romance.

343 *elfin* Common Spenserian usage; compare 'La Belle Dame Sans Merci', 'She took me to her elfin grot' (l. 29).

344 *haggard* 'wild, unreclaimed'.

346 *wassailers* Revellers.

349 *Rhenish* Wine from the Rhine valley.

XL.

She hurried at his words, beset with fears,
For there were sleeping dragons all around,
At glaring watch, perhaps, with ready spears—
Down the wide stairs a darkling way they found.— 355
In all the house was heard no human sound.
A chain-droop'd lamp was flickering by each door;
The arras, rich with horseman, hawk, and hound,
Flutter'd in the besieging wind's uproar;
And the long carpets rose along the gusty floor. 360

XLI.

They glide, like phantoms, into the wide hall;
Like phantoms, to the iron porch, they glide;
Where lay the Porter, in uneasy sprawl,
With a huge empty flaggon by his side:
The wakeful bloodhound rose, and shook his hide, 365
But his sagacious eye an inmate owns:
By one, and one, the bolts full easy slide:—
The chains lie silent on the footworn stones;—
The key turns, and the door upon its hinges groans.

XLII.

And they are gone: ay, ages long ago 370
These lovers fled away into the storm.
That night the Baron dreamt of many a woe,
And all his warrior-guests, with shade and form
Of witch, and demon, and large coffin-worm,
Were long be-nightmar'd. Angela the old 375
Died palsy-twitch'd, with meagre face deform;
The Beadsman, after thousand aves told,
For aye unsought for slept among his ashes cold.

353   *dragon* Dragoon? Here, presumably a formidable man-at-arms.
355   *darkling* Elizabethan formulation for dark, obscure; compare 'Ode to a Nightingale, 'Darkling I listen' (l. 51).
357   *chain-drooped lamp* Compare Coleridge, 'Christabel', 'The lamp with twofold silver chain / Is fastened to an angel's feet' (ll. 182–3).
358   *arras* 'tapestry'.
365   *wakeful bloodhound* compare the 'mastiff bitch' in Coleridge, 'Christabel'.
375–6   *Angela the old . . . meagre face deform;* See Woodhouse's 19 September 1819 letter to Taylor: '[Keats] has altered the last 3 lines to leave on the reader a sense of pettish disgust, by bringing Old Angela in dead stiff & ugly. – He says he likes that the poem should leave off with this Change of Sentiment – it was what he aimed at, & was glad to find from my objections to it that he had succeeded' (*Letters*, vol. 2, pp. 162–3).
378   *ashes cold* In closing the poem on the word 'cold' (prominent as well in the first stanza), Keats further distances the reader from the warmth associated only with the lovers, now 'fled away into the storm' (l. 371) at the same time as he entombs the romance in its medieval frame ('ages long ago', l. 370) amidst 'ashes cold'.

La Belle Dame Sans Merci

Written in April 1819 (see Keats's journal-letter to George Keats and his wife Georgiana, 14 February–3 May 1819, where a draft of the poem appears under the heading for 21 April; *Letters*, vol. 2, pp. 95–6), 'La Belle Dame Sans Merci' was published by Leigh Hunt in *The Indicator*, 10 May 1820 over the signature 'Caviare'. When first published in *The Indicator*, Keats's ballad included a number of archaisms and an important stanzaic transposition (in both instances generally regarded as compromising the poem and presumably introduced by Hunt), as well as an important introductory comment by Hunt:

Among the pieces printed at the end of Chaucer's works, and attributed to him, is a translation, under this title, of a poem of the celebrated Alain Chartier, Secretary to Charles the Sixth and Seventh. It was the title which suggested to a friend the verses at the end of the present number. We wish Alain could have seen them. He would have found a Troubadour air for them, and sung them. . . . The union of the imaginative and the real is very striking throughout, particularly in the dream. The wild gentleness of the rest of the thoughts and of the music are alike old; and they are also alike young; for love and imagination are always young, let them bring with them what times and accompaniments they may.

(Hunt, *Periodical Essays*, pp. 257–8)

In addition to Chartier's poem (ca. 1424), additional possible sources and influences include Dante's account of Paolo and Francesca in *Inferno*, V, Chaucer's *The Knight's Tale*, various Spenserian enchantresses in *The Faerie Queene* (e.g. Duessa, Phaedria, and the false Florimel in, respectively, books I, II, and III–IV), Shakespeare's *Pericles*, Burton's rendering of erotic melancholy in *The Anatomy of Melancholy*, Browne's *Britannia's Pastorals*, numerous traditional ballads (especially 'Thomas the Rhymer') and Chatterton's neo-medieval 'songes'. Of these, Phaedria's enchantment of Cymochles (*Faerie Queene*, II. vi. 2–18) and the ballad-tradition informing 'Thomas the Rhymer' are the most significant: while the former is replete with a sensuousness of tone, imagery and atmosphere appropriate to romance, the latter provides Keats with the form and language of a mysterious ballad. And in both instances, it is a fatal enchantress who, 'in language strange', sings the knight into a state of thralldom. (In taking as its premise the destructive power of human passion, 'La Belle Dame Sans Merci' thus stands in dramatic opposition to 'The Eve of St Agnes', with its celebration of felicitous love). Written in a ballad stanza with heavily accented last lines (alternating tetrameter and trimeter lines rhyming *abcb* in which the fourth line often has three stressed and only one unstressed syllable), Keats further draws on the conventions of the ballad tradition in his dramatic use of incremental repetition, refrain and the supernatural. When Keats's cancellations in the journal-letter are restored (all noted below), the ballad becomes even more macabre and unsettling, with the renewed emphasis on death and the withering away of the afflicted knight; Hunt's emendations, on the other hand, generally undo the ominous, haunting tone of the poem.

Text follows Keats's journal-letter of 14 February–3 May (entry for 21 April 1819), with cancellations from the journal-letter and variants from the *Indicator* text of 1820; for the full *Indicator* text, see Hunt, *Periodical Essays*, pp. 259–60.

> O what can ail thee knight at arms
>   Alone and palely loitering?
> The sedge has withered from the Lake
>   And no birds sing!
>
> O what can ail thee knight at arms   5
>   So haggard and so woe begone?
> The squirrel's granary is full
>   And the harvest's done.
>
> I see a lilly on thy brow
>   With anguish moist and fever dew,   10

Title 'The Beautiful Woman without Mercy'. Derived, according to Leigh Hunt, from Alain Chartier's Provençal air 'La Belle Dame Sans Merci'. See 'The Eve of St Agnes', 'He played an ancient ditty, long since mute, / In Provence called "La belle dame sans mercy"' (ll. 291–2).

1–2 *O what can ail thee . . . palely loitering?* See Chaucer, *The Knight's Tale* (ll. 1363–6):

> His eyen holwe and grisly to biholde,
> His hewe falow and pale as asshen colde,
> And solitarie he was and evere allone,
> And waillynge all the nyght, and makynge his mone.

1 *knight at arms* The *Indicator* text has 'wretched wight', a common creature (often implying commiseration) and a common Spenserian usage.

3 *sedge* 'various coarse grassy, rush-like or flag-like plants growing in wet places'.

4 *And no birds sing!* De Selincourt suggests an echo here of William Browne, *Britannia's Pastorals*, 'Within the shady woods / Let no bird sing!' (II. i. 244–5; *Poems of John Keats*, p. 527). Compare also Shakespeare, *Sonnets*, 78, 'Bare ruin'd choirs, where late the sweet birds sang' (l. 4).

9–11 *I see a lilly . . . a fading rose* Both common emblems of physical beauty, the lily ('Ladie of the flowring field'; *Faerie Queene*, II. vi. 16) and the rose are in Spenserian terms associated respectively with sanctity (Christian) and passion (variously construed). Taken together, they contribute here to the imagery of love and nature.

9 *a lilly* 'death's lilly' in the journal-letter.

10 *anguish moist* Compare Hunt, *Story of Rimini*, 'And pale he stood, and seem'd to burst all o'er / Into moist anguish never felt before' (IV. 64–5).

> And on thy cheeks a fading rose
> Fast withereth too—
>
> I met a Lady in the Meads
>   Full beautiful, a faery's child
> Her hair was long, her foot was light 15
>   And her eyes were wild—
>
> I made a Garland for her head,
>   And bracelets too, and fragrant Zone:
> She look'd at me as she did love
>   And made sweet moan— 20
>
> I set her on my pacing steed
>   And nothing else saw all day long
> For sidelong would she bend and sing
>   A faery's song—
>
> She found me roots of relish sweet 25
>   And honey wild and manna dew
> And sure in language strange she said
>   'I love thee true'—
>
> She took me to her elfin grot
>   And there she wept and sigh'd full sore 30
> And there I shut her wild wild eyes
>   With kisses four.

11 *a fading rose* 'death's fading rose' in the journal-letter.
13–48 *I met a Lady . . . no birds sing* The lady or 'belle dame' described from this point forward resembles both the 'Queen of fair Elfland' in 'Thomas the Rhymer' and various enchantresses (most notably Phaedria) in *The Faerie Queene*; see the headnote above for more details.
13 *I* With this line, the ballad shifts persona from the literary 'I' of lines 1–12 which depicted the knight at arms in the present tense (e.g. 'I see a lilly on thy brow') to the balladic 'I' of the knight at arms himself as he recounts his travails in the past tense (e.g. 'I met a lady in the Meads').
13 *Meads* Meadows; 'Wilds' in the journal-letter.
17–24 The *Indicator* text transposes these two stanzas.
17 *I made a Garland for her head* Compare Spenser, *Faerie Queene*, 'Sometimes her head she fondly would aguize [array] / With gaudie girlonds' (II. vi. 7) and 'Girlonds of flowres sometimes for her fair hed / He fine would dight' (III. vii. 17).
18 *fragrant Zone* 'a girdle or belt . . . any encircling band', here made from flowers. Compare William Collins, 'Ode on the Poetical Character', 'Her baffled Hand with vain Endeavour / Had touch'd that fatal Zone to her denied' (ll. 15–16); both poets allude to Spenser's narrative of the cestus or girdle of Venus (*Faerie Queene*, IV. v. 1–6), the chief attribute of the 'faire Florimell' (though temporarily usurped by the false Florimell).
20 *And made sweet moan* Murmured sweetly; compare 'Ode to Psyche', 'Nor virgin choir to make delicious moan' (l. 30) and 'So let me be thy choir and make a moan' (l. 44). See also Chaucer, *The Knight's Tale* (note to ll. 1–2 above) and Burton's citation of Homer's Bellerophon (*Iliad*, III), 'That wandered in the woods sad all alone, / Forsaking men's society, making great moan' (*Anatomy of Melancholy*, pt I, sect III).

23 *sidelong would she bend* 'sideways would she lean' in *Indicator*.
26 *And honey wild and manna dew* 'honey dew' in the journal-letter. Compare Coleridge, 'Kubla Khan', 'For he on honey-dew hath fed' (l. 53) and Spenser, *Faerie Queene*, 'Did raine into her lap an hony dew' (III. xi. 31). See also *Endymion*, 'Amid his pains / He seemed to taste a drop of manna-dew, / Full palatable, and a colour grew / Upon his cheek . . .' (I. 765–8).
29 *elfin grot* Grotto, 'cave or cavern, esp. one which is picturesque, or which forms an agreeable retreat'; another echo of Spenser. See also 'Thomas the Rhymer':

> 'And see ye not that bonny road,
> That winds about the fernie brae?
> That is the road to fair Elfland,
> Where thou and I this night maun gae.' (ll. 49–52)

(A 'brae' is a 'steep bank bounding a river valley'.)
30 *and sigh'd full sore* This is 'and there she sighed' in the journal-letter and 'gazed and sighed deep' in *Indicator*. Compare Spenser, *Faerie Queene*, 'And sigh full sore, to heare the miserie' (IV. viii. 64).
31 *wild wild* 'wild sad' in *Indicator*. This is a characteristically Keatsian use of repetition to create a sense of overabundance: compare 'Ode to Psyche', 'O happy, happy dove' (l. 22); 'Ode on a Grecian Urn', 'Ah, happy, happy boughs . . . / / More happy love, more happy, happy love!' (ll. 21, 25); 'Ode on Melancholy', 'And feed deep, deep upon her peerless eyes' (l. 20).
32 *With kisses four* See Keats's journal-letter of 14 February–3 May 1819:

  And there she lulled me asleep
    And there I dream'd—Ah Woe betide!
  The latest dream I ever dreamt   35
    On the cold hill side.

  I saw pale kings and Princes too
    Pale warriors, death pale were they all;
  They cried 'La belle dame sans merci
    Thee hath in thrall.'   40

  I saw their starv'd lips in the gloam
    With horrid warning gaped wide
  And I awoke and found me here
    On the cold hill's side

  And this is why I sojourn here   45
    Alone and palely loitering;
  Though the sedge is wither'd from the Lake
    And no birds sing—

Why four kisses – you will say – why four because I wish to restrain the headlong impetuosity of my Muse – she would have fain said 'score' without hurting the rhyme – but we must temper the Imagination as the Critics say with Judgment. I was obliged to choose an even number that both eyes might have fair play: and to speak truly I think two apiece quite sufficient – Suppose I had said seven; there would have been three and a half a piece – a very awkward affair – and well got out of on my side. . . .
           (*Letters*, vol. 2, p. 97)

In *Thomas the Rhymer*, Thomas's seven-year servitude to the Queen of Elfland is secured once 'he has kissed her rosy lips, / All underneath the Eildon Tree' (ll. 23–4).

33 *there she lulled me asleep* Compare Spenser, *Faerie Queene*, '. . . soone he slumbred, fearing not be harm'd, / The whiles with a loud lay she [Phaedria] thus him sweetly charm'd' (II. vi. 14) and 'By this she had him lulled fast a sleepe' (II. vi. 18).

39 *They* 'Who' in *Indicator*.
40 *thrall* 'bondage, servitude, captivity'; alternatively, 'one whose liberty is forfeit; a captive'. Compare Keats's 'Calidore: A Fragment', 'so he gently drew / his warm arms, thrilling now with pulses new, / From their sweet thrall' (ll. 101–3) and his 'I cry your mercy, pity, love – aye love', 'Withold no atom's atom or I die, / Or living on perhaps, your wretched thrall' (ll. 10–11). Thrall is a common Spenserian usage; see *Faerie Queene*, 'Or weaknesse is to sinfull bands made thrall' (I. viii. 7) and 'him that witch hath thralled to her will' (II. i. 54). See also Cary's 1814 translation of Dante, '. . . we read of Lancelot, / How him love thrall'd' (*Inferno*, v. 124–5).
41 *gloam* 'twilight'; from 'gloaming', 'the dusky light of evening'.
43 *With horrid warning gaped wide* 'All tremble warning wide agape' in the journal-letter.
45 *why I sojourn here* 'why I wither here' in the journal-letter.

Ode to Psyche

The 'Ode to Psyche' was written late April 1819 (see Keats's journal-letter to George and Georgiana Keats of 14 February–3 May 1819, where a draft of the poem appears under the heading for 30 April; *Letters*, vol. 2, pp. 106–8), and published in 1820. Writing to George and Georgiana Keats on 30 April 1819, Keats prefaced his transcription of the 'Ode to Psyche' thus:

The following Poem – the last I have written is the first and the only one with which I have taken even moderate pains – I have for the most part dash'd of[f] my lines in a hurry – This I have done leisurely – I think it reads the more richly for it and will I hope encourage me to write other thing[s] in even a more peaceable and healthy spirit. You must recollect that Psyche was not embodied as a goddess before the time of Apuleius the Platonist who lived afteir [*sic*] the Agustan [*sic*] age, and consequently the Goddess was never worshipped or sacrificed to with any of the ancient fervour – and perhaps never thought of in the old religion – I am more orthodox [than] to let a hethen [*sic*] Goddess be so neglected –
        (*Letters*, vol. 2, pp. 105–6)

Keats had previously taken up the myth of Cupid and Psyche in 'I stood tip-toe upon a little hill' (ll. 141–50), and his treatment here is indebted to its retelling in Apuleius' *The Golden Ass* (trans. William Adlington, 1566). According to this version, Psyche was so beautiful that Venus became jealous of her and sent Cupid to make her fall in love with a hideous creature. Instead, Cupid took her as his lover, installed her in a palace, where he only visited her at night and forbade her to look at him. When she hid a lamp to see him, however, a drop of oil fell upon him and he abandoned her, leaving Psyche to complete a series of impossible tasks set by Venus. After many travails and suffering, Psyche was granted immortality by Jupiter and reunited with Cupid – hence 'too late' to be a properly revered member 'of all Olympus' faded hierarchy'. 'Psyche' is Greek for 'soul', and her sufferings have often been read as an allegory for the soul's journey through this life. Earlier in the same journal-letter in which he transcribed the ode, Keats wrote at length about our human world not as a 'vale of tears' but much more grandly as a 'vale of Soul-making':

> Call the world if you Please 'The vale of Soul-making' Then you will find out the use of the world (I am speaking now in the highest terms for human nature admitting it to be immortal which I will here take for granted for the purpose of showing a thought which has struck me concerning it) I say '*Soul making*' Soul as distinguished from an Intelligence – There may be intelligences or sparks of the divinity in millions – but they are not Souls till they acquire identities, till each one is personally itself. I[n]telligences are atoms of perception – they know and they see and they are pure, in short they are God – how then are Souls to be made? ... Do you not see how necessary a World of Pains and troubles is to school an Intelligence and make it a soul? A Place where the heart must feel and suffer in a thousand diverse ways!
> (*Letters*, vol. 2, pp. 102–3)

The 'Ode to Psyche' is one of the five 'great odes' of the spring of 1819 and anticipates or echoes any number of the themes and tensions which are considered throughout 'Ode to a Nightingale', 'Ode on a Grecian Urn', 'Ode to Melancholy', and 'Ode on Indolence', as well as 'To Autumn': dreaming (in opposition to seeing), waking (in opposition to sleeping), imagination (in opposition to reality), human thought (in opposition to inhuman thoughtlessness), feigning (as artifice, in opposition to the real) and numerous other variations on Keats's preoccupation in these odes with *poeisis* (as making, in opposition to aesthetic objects). Unlike the later odes of spring 1819, the form of the 'Ode to Psyche' is much less regular, consisting in irregular verse-paragraphs (three in the letter and four in the 1820 volume), rather than the 10-line stanza that Keats later develops. The result is a more Pindaric poem, not merely in form but in feeling as well, producing something of a crisis-poem, as the persona (via a series of impassioned apostrophes to Psyche) first laments what she does not have in terms of worship and adoration, then corrects this imbalance through the operations of his own 'fond believing lyre' and 'all the gardener Fancy e'er could feign'.

Text follows *1820*, with variants from Keats's journal-letter of 14 February–3 May (entry for 21 April 1819).

    O GODDESS! hear these tuneless numbers, wrung
        By sweet enforcement and remembrance dear,
    And pardon that thy secrets should be sung
        Even into thine own soft-conched ear:
    Surely I dreamt to-day, or did I see   5
        The winged Psyche with awaken'd eyes?
    I wander'd in a forest thoughtlessly,
        And, on the sudden, fainting with surprise,
    Saw two fair creatures, couched side by side
        In deepest grass, beneath the whisp'ring roof   10
    Of leaves and trembled blossoms, where there ran
        A brooklet, scarce espied:
    'Mid hush'd, cool-rooted flowers, fragrant-eyed,
        Blue, silver-white, and budded Tyrian,
    They lay calm-breathing on the bedded grass;   15
        Their arms embraced, and their pinions too;
        Their lips touch'd not, but had not bade adieu

1–2   *O Goddess ... remembrance dear* Compare Milton, 'Lycidas', ll. 3–7, especially the cadences of 'bitter constraint, and sad occasion dear' (l. 6).
4   *soft-conched ear* Resembling a shell.
7   *thoughtlessly* Indolently. Compare 'Ode on Indolence', '... leave my sense / Unhaunted quite of all but – nothingness?' (ll. 19–20).
14   *Tyrian* Purple, 'in reference or allusion to the purple or crimson dye anciently made at Tyre from certain molluscs'.

> As if disjoined by soft-handed slumber,
> And ready still past kisses to outnumber
> At tender eye-dawn of aurorean love:
> The winged boy I knew;
> But who wast thou, O happy, happy dove?
> His Psyche true!
>
> O latest born and loveliest vision far
> Of all Olympus' faded hierarchy!
> Fairer than Phœbe's sapphire-region'd star,
> Or Vesper, amorous glow-worm of the sky;
> Fairer than these, though temple thou hast none,
> Nor altar heap'd with flowers;
> Nor virgin-choir to make delicious moan
> Upon the midnight hours;
> No voice, no lute, no pipe, no incense sweet
> From chain-swung censer teeming;
> No shrine, no grove, no oracle, no heat
> Of pale-mouth'd prophet dreaming.
>
> O brightest! though too late for antique vows,
> Too, too late for the fond believing lyre,
> When holy were the haunted forest boughs,
> Holy the air, the water, and the fire;
> Yet even in these days so far retir'd
> From happy pieties, thy lucent fans,
> Fluttering among the faint Olympians,
> I see, and sing, by my own eyes inspired.
> So let me be thy choir, and make a moan
> Upon the midnight hours;
> Thy voice, thy lute, thy pipe, thy incense sweet
> From swinged censer teeming;
> Thy shrine, thy grove, thy oracle, thy heat
> Of pale-mouth'd prophet dreaming.
>
> Yes, I will be thy priest, and build a fane

20 *eye-dawn of Aurorean love* Compare Milton, 'Lycidas', 'Under the opening eye-lids of the morn' (l. 26); Aurora is the goddess of the dawn.
21 *winged boy* Cupid. A common Spenserian phrasing (see *Faerie Queene*, I. i. 47).
24–67 *O latest born ... warm Love in!* Presented as one verse paragraph in Keats's letter of April 1819.
24–5 *O latest born ... faded hierarchy!* Compare 'Hyperion', 'For 'tis the eternal law / That first in beauty should be first in might' (I. 228–9).
25 *Olympus' faded hierarchy!* Olympus was the classical abode of the gods in Greek mythology.
26 *Phoebe's Sapphire-regioned star* Phoebe is an alternative name for Diana or Artemis, goddess of the moon; hence bright, radiant.
27 *Vesper* Venus, the evening star.
28–35 *though temple thou hast none ... prophet dreaming* Compare Milton, 'On the Morning of Christ's Nativity', ll. 173–80.
30 *delicious moan* Compare 'La Belle Dame Sans Merci', 'And made sweet moan' (l. 20).
35 *pale-mouthed prophet* Compare Milton, 'On the Morning of Christ's Nativity', 'No nightly trance, or breathed spell, / Inspires the pale-ey'd Priest from the prophetic cell' (ll. 179–80).
37 *fond believing lyre* A stringed instrument resembling a small harp; ancient attribute of lyric poetry. That the lyre should be 'fond' and 'believing' suggests not only that those who play it believe in their song but, more disconcertingly, that its song may after all be 'idle' or 'false' – compare Milton, 'Lycidas', 'Ay me, I fondly dream! / Had ye been there ... for what could that have done?' (ll. 56–7).
41 *lucent fans* 'shining wings'. Psyche was often represented with the wings of a butterfly, as if to suggest the lightness of the soul.
42 *faint Olympians* See line 25 and note. In Keats's reading, by the time of Psyche's deification, the 'faded hierarchy' of the Olympian gods was such that (according to Keats, as cited above in the headnote) Psyche 'was never worshipped or sacrificed to with any of the ancient fervour – and perhaps never thought of in the old religion'.
44–9 *So let me ... prophet dreaming* Compare Keats's letter of April 1819 (cited above in the headnote): 'I am more orthodox than to let a hethen goddess be so neglected'.

>   In some untrodden region of my mind, 50
> Where branched thoughts, new grown with pleasant pain,
>   Instead of pines shall murmur in the wind:
> Far, far around shall those dark-cluster'd trees
>   Fledge the wild-ridged mountains steep by steep; 55
> And there by zephyrs, streams, and birds, and bees,
>   The moss-lain Dryads shall be lull'd to sleep;
> And in the midst of this wide quietness
>   A rosy sanctuary will I dress
> With the wreath'd trellis of a working brain, 60
>   With buds, and bells, and stars without a name,
> With all the gardener Fancy e'er could feign,
>   Who breeding flowers, will never breed the same:
> And there shall be for thee all soft delight
>   That shadowy thought can win, 65
> A bright torch, and a casement ope at night,
>   To let the warm Love in!

50 *fane* 'temple'; here, rhyming suggestively with 'feign' (see note to l. 62 below).

62 *all the gardener Fancy e'er could feign* In Renaissance discussions of the poetic imagination (e.g. George Puttenham, *The Arte of English Poesie*, 1589), it is a common conceit to represent 'fancy' as a gardener who can improve and embellish ('dress') all of the materials with which he works; hence the ability of 'Fancy' to 'feign', to form or fashion.

66 *and a casement ope at night* Compare 'Ode to a Nightingale', line 69 and note.

66–7 *A bright torch . . . warm Love in!* As observed in the headnote, Cupid only visited Psyche under cover of darkness, and did not permit her to see him. When Psyche one night hid a lamp in the hope of finally looking at her lover, a drop of oil from the lamp woke him, after which he abandoned her.

If by dull rhymes our english must be chain'd

This sonnet was most likely composed between 30 April and 3 May 1819, according to the evidence in Keats's long journal-letter of 14 February–3 May 1819, but not published until 1848 in Milnes's *Life, Letters, and Literary Remains of John Keats*. The last of Keats's experimental sonnets, it is prefaced in the letter with a long comment:

> Incipit altera Sonneta [Here begins another sonnet]. – I have been endeavouring to discover a better sonnet stanza than we have. The legitimate [Italian] does not suit the language over-well from the pouncing rhymes – the other kind [English] appears too elegiac – and the couplet at the end of it has seldom a pleasing effect – I do not pretend to have succeeded – it will explain itself –
> (*Letters*, vol. 2, p. 108)

Keats suggests here that while he is not satisfied with the sounds and 'pouncing' rhymes of the Italian sonnet (beginning with two quatrains rhyming *abbaabba*), which work better in a romance language than in English, neither is he pleased with the logic of the English sonnet, with its reliance on three elegiac quatrains (*ababcdcdefef*) and a couplet. In this attempt to contrive a sonnet 'more interwoven and complete' in order to 'fit the *naked foot* of Poesy' (emphasis added), Keats loosely divides 14 lines into four tercets (*abcabdcabcde*) and, drawing on the last two lines of this 12-line unit, a concluding quatrain (*dede*). The resulting structure underscores not merely Keats's unchaining of the sonnet from its standard forms, but also his innovative garlanding of his own rhyme sounds, such that the *d*-rhymes assert that 'Poesy' 'be' 'free' – very much the theme as well as the technique of the sonnet. As is the case in Wordsworth's 'Nuns fret not', Keats plays here with the seeming restrictions and formal limitations of the sonnet (140 syllables stretched out over 14 lines and a grid of rhyme) in order to liberate himself (and the English language) from 'dull rhymes' and 'constrained' metres. To this end, he relies throughout on a rewoven rhyme scheme, various metrical substitutions, and vigorous enjambment.

Text follows Keats's journal-letter of 14 February–3 May (entry for 3 May 1819).

If by dull rhymes our english must be chain'd
And, like Andromeda, the Sonnet sweet,
Fetter'd in spite of pained Loveliness;
Let us find out, if we must be constrain'd,
Sandals more interwoven and complete   5
To fit the naked foot of Poesy;
Let us inspect the Lyre and weigh the stress
Of every chord and see what may be gained
By ear industrious and attention meet,   10
Misers of sound and syllable no less,
Than Midas of his coinage, let us be
Jealous of dead leaves in the bay wreath Crown;
So if we may not let the Muse be free,
She will be bound with Garlands of her own.

2 *Andromeda* In Greek myth, the daughter of Cassiopeia, who offended the gods by boasting that her daughter was more beautiful than they. Consequently, Andromeda was chained to a rock on the sea-shore until her rescue by Perseus; see Ovid, *Metamorphoses*, IV. 663–752.
3 *Fetter'd* 'bound with chains or shackles' (especially at the feet); figuratively, 'hampered by disadvantageous conditions'. Beginning the line with a trochee, Keats ironically unbinds it from the conventional iambic pattern. See lines 5, 10, 12 and 13 for additional trochaic substitutions.
5–6 *Sandals . . . naked foot of Poesy* Keats plays here on the convention of metrical 'feet', which he is in fact trying to refit to the patterns of English. In closing the sonnet's first sentence at the end of line 6, Keats disregards the convention of doing so at the end of the either the first or second quatrain – thus 'interweaving' a more 'complete' sonnet.

7 *Lyre* Ancient attribute of lyric poetry; see note to 'Ode to Psyche', line 37.
8–9 *what may be gained / By ear industrious* In enjambing lines 8–9, Keats overrides the conventional distinction between the second and third quatrain of the English sonnet and, even more dramatically, that between the octave and the sestet in an Italian sonnet. In doing so, he disrupts the reader's sense of the form's conventional logic and thus may be said to free the reader as well.
11 *Midas* The second of Keats's allusions to Ovid's *Metamorphoses*, underscoring his attempts here to 'transform' the sonnet. Midas was a legendary king of Phrygia who, after having entertained a companion of Dionysus, was granted one wish. He wished that everything he touched should turn to gold (which he later came to regret when he was unable to eat). See Ovid, *Metamorphoses*, XI. 100–93.

Ode to a Nightingale

Written May 1819, most likely the second of Keats's odes of 1819, and first published in *Annals of the Fine Arts* (July 1819), the 'Ode to a Nightingale' was collected in *Lamia, Isabella, The Eve of St Agnes, and other Poems* (1820). The well-known anecdote concerning the composition of this famous ode first appeared in Charles Armitage Brown's *Life of John Keats* (1841):

In the spring of 1819 a nightingale had built her nest near my house. Keats felt a tranquil and continual joy in her song; and one morning he took his chair from the breakfast-table to the grass-plot under a plum-tree, where he sat for two or three hours. When he came into the house, I perceived he had some scraps of paper in his hand, and these he was quietly thrusting behind the books. On inquiry, I found those scraps, four or five in number, contained his poetic feeling on the song of our nightingale. The writing was not well legible; and it was difficult to arrange the stanzas on so many scraps. With his assistance I succeeded, and this was his 'Ode to a Nightingale', a poem which has been the delight of everyone.

(*Keats Circle*, vol. 2, p. 65)

Regardless of Brown's factual accuracy, his recollections and Keats's letters from the spring of 1819 represent it as having been a particularly felicitous period, personally as well as poetically. The 14 February–3 May journal-letter, for instance, contains transcriptions of six sonnets, a comic narrative, stanzas in imitation of Spenser, 'La Belle Dame sans Merci', the 'Song of the Four Fairies', and 'Ode to Psyche' – a remarkable demonstration of Keats's formal virtuosity in the spring of his poetic *annus mirabilis*. And a letter to Fanny Keats, also from May 1819, not only anticipates certain phrasings from the ode (especially from the second stanza), but captures as well a sense of arcadian promise:

O there is nothing like fine weather, and health, and Books, and a fine country, and a contented Mind, and Diligent-habit of reading and thinking, and an amulet against the ennui – and, please heaven, a little claret-wine cool out of a cellar a mile deep – with a few or a good many ratafia cakes – a rocky basin to bathe in, a strawberry bed to say your prayers to Flora in, a pad nag to go you ten miles or so. . . .

(*Letters*, vol. 2, p. 56)

In embarking upon a sustained lyric address to an iconic songbird, Keats would have been able to draw on a range of poetic precedents: Milton, 'O nightingale, that on yon bloomy spray' and *Paradise Lost*, 3, 38–40; Charlotte Smith, 'To a Nightingale' and 'On the Departure of the Nightingale; (both collected in *Elegiac Sonnets*); Coleridge, 'To the Nightingale' and 'The Nightingale: A Conversation Poem'. (Coleridge lurks in the margins of the ode in an altogether different fashion as well, for he and Keats walked several miles together on Sunday 11 April 1819, discoursing on 'a thousand things', including 'Nightingales, Poetry – on Poetical sensation – Metaphysics – Different genera and species of Dreams – Nightmare . . .',

Letters, vol. 2, p. 88–9.) Though not titularly addressed to a nightingale, two other lyrics also resonate here, perhaps more poignantly than any of the above: Wordsworth's 'To the Cuckoo' and 'The Solitary Reaper'. Each of these lyrics contrasts one voice with one or two others, and it is precisely the sort of comparison (or competition) between human voice and the 'wandering voice' of birdsong that propels Keats's ode as it investigates the surmise that the 'viewless wings of poesy' may indeed transport one into a region of song. As noted above ('On First Looking into Chapman's Homer', l. 13 and above), the surmise is a critical rhetorical form for romantic lyric poets, one which in Keats's ode constitutes a bower of sorts, a privileged space somewhere between the desolation of human mortality and the allure of the nightingale's immortal song, in which the poet may stand 'half in love with easeful Death'.

This is the first of Keats's odes to employ the distinctive 10-line stanza that returns throughout the rest of the odes written in the spring of 1819. Rhyming *ababcdecde*, it appears to comprise the quatrain of an English sonnet and the sestet of an Italian sonnet.

Text follows *1820*, with variants from *Annals*.

1.

My heart aches, and a drowsy numbness pains
  My sense, as though of hemlock I had drunk,
Or emptied some dull opiate to the drains
  One minute past, and Lethe-wards had sunk:
'Tis not through envy of thy happy lot,   5
  But being too happy in thine happiness,—
    That thou, light-winged Dryad of the trees,
      In some melodious plot
  Of beechen green, and shadows numberless,
    Singest of summer in full-throated ease.   10

2.

O, for a draught of vintage! that hath been
  Cool'd a long age in the deep-delved earth,

1–4 *My heart aches . . . Lethe-wards had sunk* Numerous critics have suggested that Keats here draws on Horace, *Epodes*, xiv, ll. 1–4: *Mollis inertia cur tantam diffuderit imis / oblivionem sensibus, / Pocula Lethaeos ut si ducentia somnos / arente fauce traxerim* . . . ('. . . why soft indolence has diffused as great forgetfulness over my inmost senses as if with parched throat I had drained the bowl that brings Lethean sleep . . .'; Loeb edn).

1 *drowsy numbness pains* Keats regularly affiliates pain with ecstatic happiness and numbness with the difficulty of writing. For the former, see the 'Ode to Melancholy' and its articulation of 'aching pleasure nigh' (l. 23); for the latter, see Keats's letter to Benjamin Bailey of 25 May 1818, in which he complains, 'I have this morning such a Lethargy that I cannot write . . . my hand feels like lead – and yet it is [an] unpleasant numbness it does not take away the pain of existence' (*Letters*, vol. 1, p. 287).

2 *hemlock* Here, not life-threatening, but used medicinally as a powerful sedative.

4 *Lethe-wards* In Greek mythology, Lethe was one of the five rivers of the underworld, associated with forgetfulness and oblivion.

11–20 Compare Keats's 1818 verses 'Hence burgundy, claret, and port' for a lyrical celebration of the pleasures of wine and their association, for Keats, with summer and things Arcadian.

11 *vintage* Metonymy for 'wine', which in turn generates the synaesthetic 'tasting' of texture, colour, motion, sound and heat (ll. 13–14).

> Tasting of Flora and the country green,
>   Dance, and Provençal song, and sunburnt mirth!
> O for a beaker full of the warm South,
>   Full of the true, the blushful Hippocrene,
>   With beaded bubbles winking at the brim,
>   And purple-stained mouth;
>   That I might drink, and leave the world unseen,
>   And with thee fade away into the forest dim:

3.

> Fade far away, dissolve, and quite forget
>   What thou among the leaves hast never known,
> The weariness, the fever, and the fret
>   Here, where men sit and hear each other groan;
> Where palsy shakes a few, sad, last gray hairs,
>   Where youth grows pale, and spectre-thin, and dies;
>   Where but to think is to be full of sorrow
>   And leaden-eyed despairs,
>   Where Beauty cannot keep her lustrous eyes,
>   Or new Love pine at them beyond to-morrow.

4.

> Away! away! for I will fly to thee,
>   Not charioted by Bacchus and his pards,
> But on the viewless wings of Poesy,
>   Though the dull brain perplexes and retards:
> Already with thee! tender is the night,
>   And haply the Queen-Moon is on her throne,
>   Cluster'd around by all her starry Fays;
>   But here there is no light,

---

13 *Flora* See Keats's 1 May 1819 letter to Fanny Keats (cited in the headnote above).

15 *beaker full of the warm South* Metonymy for 'wine from the South'.

16 *Hippocrene* Spring and fountain on Mount Helicon, sacred to the Muses and supposedly capable of inspiring those who drank from it.

23 *the weariness, the fever, and the fret* Compare Wordsworth, 'Lines Written a Few Miles Above Tintern Abbey', 'when the fretful stir / Unprofitable, and the fever of the world, / Have hung upon the beatings of my heart' (ll. 53–5).

26 *Where youth grows pale, and spectre-thin, and dies* Keats's younger brother Tom died of tuberculosis in December 1818, at the age of 19. See also Wordsworth, *The Excursion*, 'While man grows old, and dwindles, and decays; / And countless generations of mankind / Depart; and leave no vestige where they trod' (IV. 760–2).

29–30 *Where beauty . . . beyond tomorrow* Compare 'Ode on Melancholy', 'She dwells with Beauty – Beauty that must die; / And Joy, whose hand is ever at his lips / Bidding adieu' (ll. 22–3).

31–3 *Away! . . . wings of Poesy,* The speaker here repudiates the sedative effects of hemlock and wine in favour of poetry (more comprehensively, the poetic imagination) as the means of 'transport' from the painful mortality of the 'here' to the immortal 'there' represented by the nightingale in its song.

32 *Bacchus and his pards* Roman god of the vine, habitually attended by leopards and panthers ('pards').

33 *viewless wings* 'invisible wings'; compare Coleridge, 'Reflections on Having Left a Place of Retirement', 'Long-listening to the viewless sky-lark's note' (l. 19).

36 *haply the Queen-Moon is on her throne* Haply: 'perhaps'; another indication of the mode of surmise that characterizes the poem throughout, as the persona here wonders aloud whether the moon, and her attendants ('her starry fays'), witness his ecstatic union with the nightingale. For 'the Queen-moon', see Coleridge, 'To the Nightingale', 'How many wretched Bards address *thy* name, / And hers, the full-orb'd Queen that shines above' (ll. 7–8).

37 *fays* A Spenserian usage for 'faeries'. Compare Keats's 'Imitation of Spenser', 'And on his back a fay reclined voluptuously' (l. 18) and 'To J. H. Reynolds Esq.', 'The windows as if latch'd by fays and elves' (l. 50).

38–50 *But here . . . on summer eves* Both the darkness of the evening and the pleasure the speaker takes in the darkness recall Coleridge's 'The Nightingale: A Conversation Poem':

> You see the glimmer of the stream beneath,
> But hear no murmuring; it flows silently,
> O'er its soft bed of verdure. All is still,
> A balmy night! and though the stars be dim,
> Yet let us think upon the vernal showers
> That gladden the green earth, and we shall find
> A pleasure in the dimness of the stars.
>   (ll. 5–11)

Save what from heaven is with the breezes blown
    Through verdurous glooms and winding mossy ways.   40

5.

I cannot see what flowers are at my feet,
    Nor what soft incense hangs upon the boughs,
But, in embalmed darkness, guess each sweet
    Wherewith the seasonable month endows
The grass, the thicket, and the fruit-tree wild;   45
    White hawthorn, and the pastoral eglantine;
        Fast fading violets cover'd up in leaves;
        And mid-May's eldest child,
    The coming musk-rose, full of dewy wine,
    The murmurous haunt of flies on summer eves.   50

6.

Darkling I listen; and, for many a time
    I have been half in love with easeful Death,
Call'd him soft names in many a mused rhyme,
    To take into the air my quiet breath;
Now more than ever seems it rich to die,   55
    To cease upon the midnight with no pain,
        While thou art pouring forth thy soul abroad
        In such an ecstasy!
    Still wouldst thou sing, and I have ears in vain—
        To thy high requiem become a sod.   60

7.

Thou wast not born for death, immortal Bird!
    No hungry generations tread thee down;
The voice I hear this passing night was heard
    In ancient days by emperor and clown:
Perhaps the self-same song that found a path   65

---

40 *verdurous* 'flourishing thick and green'; compare Cary's 1814 translation of Dante, 'So Four animals, each crown'd with verdurous leaf' (*Purgatorio*, xxix, 89) and Coleridge, 'The Nightingale', lines 6–7 (cited in note to ll. 38–50).

43 *in embalmed darkness, guess each sweet* Darkness steeped in the balmy incense of the bower into which the speaker has sung himself, and in which he now attempts to conjecture the sensual pleasure with which he is surrounded. In this stanza and the next two, the speaker articulates an imaginative freedom reassuringly at odds with the 'here' of stanza 3, characterized by 'the weariness, the fever and the fret' of the human condition.

46–50 *White hawthorn . . . summer eves.* Compare *A Midsummer Night's Dream*:

    I know a bank whereon the wild thyme blows,
    Where oxslips and the nodding violet grows
    Quite overcanopied with luscious woodbine,
    With sweet musk-roses and with eglantine. . . .
        (II. i. 249–52)

51 *Darkling* 'dark, obscure'; compare Milton, *Paradise Lost*, '. . . the wakeful Bird / Sings darkling, and in shadiest Covert hid / Tunes her nocturnal note' (3. 38–40; noted by Keats in his edition of Milton).

55 *rich* Keats regularly uses 'rich' to characterize intensity of experience, whether sensual or emotional; compare *Endymion*, 'Rich with a sprinkling of fair musk-rose blooms' (I. 19), and 'Ode on Melancholy', 'some rich anger' (l. 18).

56 *to cease upon the midnight* Compare Keats's 'Why did I laugh to-night?', 'Yet could I on this very midnight cease' (l. 11).

60 *requiem* 'dirge or solemn chant for the repose of the dead'; here to be understood proleptically, for the speaker remains but 'half in love with easeful Death', only imagining that 'Now more than ever seems it rich to die'.

62 *generations* See note to l. 26; compare Wordsworth, *The Excursion*, IV. 760–2.

65 *the self-same song* Song is to be understood here metonymically as 'voice'; compare Wordsworth, 'To the Cuckoo', '. . . shall I call thee Bird, / Or but a wandering Voice?' (ll. 3–4) and '. . . thou art to me / No Bird; but an invisible Thing, / A voice, a mystery' (ll. 14–16).

Through the sad heart of Ruth, when, sick for home,
  She stood in tears amid the alien corn;
    The same that oft-times hath
    Charm'd magic casements, opening on the foam
Of perilous seas, in faery lands forlorn.   70

8.

Forlorn! the very word is like a bell
  To toll me back from thee to my sole self!
    Adieu! the fancy cannot cheat so well
    As she is fam'd to do, deceiving elf.
Adieu! adieu! thy plaintive anthem fades   75
  Past the near meadows, over the still stream,
    Up the hill-side; and now 'tis buried deep
      In the next valley-glades:
    Was it a vision, or a waking dream?
Fled is that music:—Do I wake or sleep?   80

66 *Ruth* Ruth left her native land of Moab to accompany her mother-in-law Naomi to Bethlehem, and worked as a gleaner in the fields after the reapers had passed (Ruth 2: 1–3). In his 1818 lecture 'On Poetry in General' (collected as part of the *Lectures on the English Poets*), William Hazlitt observes that 'The story of Ruth . . . is as if all the depth of natural affection in the human race was involved in her breast' (*Works*, vol. 5, p. 16). See also Wordsworth's 'The Solitary Reaper', in which the speaker, reflecting on the reaper's 'melancholy strain', claims that 'No Nightingale did ever chaunt / So sweetly to reposing bands / Of Travellers in some shady haunt, / Among Arabian sands' (ll. 9–12).
68–70 *The same . . . fairy lands forlorn* Leigh Hunt singles out these lines for their mystery and imaginative power:

> You do not know what the house is, or where, nor who the bird. . . . But you see the window, open on the perilous sea, and hear the voice from out the trees in which it is nested, sending its warble over the foam. The whole is at once vague and particular, full of mysterious life. You see nobody, though something is heard; and you know not what of beauty or wickedness is to come over that sea.
> (*Imagination and Fancy*, p. 344)

69 *magic casements* There is throughout Keats's writing a fascination with the 'Romantic' possibilities intimated by windows, windowpanes, and thresholds; see, for instance, 'Ode to Psyche', '. . . and a casement ope at night, / To let the warm Love in!' (ll. 66–7); 'To J. H. Reynolds Esq.', 'The windows as if latch'd by fays and elves – / And from them comes a flash of light / As from the Westward of a summer's night' (ll. 50–2); and Keats's letter to Fanny Keats of 13 March 1819, 'I should like the window to open onto the Lake of Geneva – and there I'd sit and read all day like the picture of somebody reading' (*Letters*, vol. 2, p. 46). And of course the central scene in 'The Eve of St Agnes', the two stanzas depicting Madeline at her prayers, beginning 'A casement high, and triple-arched there was' (ll. 208 ff).

70 *forlorn* First 'utterly lost', then 'desolate'. In repeating the closing word of the preceding stanza, the poem shifts abruptly from imagined faery lands (the Romantic reverie of stanzas 4 to 7) to the desolate reality of the here-and-now (the speaker's 'sole self'). In doing so, the poem reveals that it is finally not the song of the nightingale but the language of human poetry (pointedly, the tolling of the word 'forlorn') that has greater sway over the Keatsian poet. (Compare Wordsworth's use of 'forlorn' in relation to imaginative vision, 'The world is too much with us', ll. 9–14.)
73–7 *Adieu! . . . Up the hill-side* Compare Charlotte Smith, 'On the Departure of the Nightingale', 'Sweet poet of the woods! – a long adieu! / Farewel, soft minstrel of the early year' (ll. 1–2).
73–4 *fancy . . . deceiving elf* The fancy, or poetic imagination, is here castigated both because it 'cheats' (beguiles and deceives) us – and because it does not do so well enough for us to fail to realize that we have been deceived.
77 *up the hill-side* Compare Wordsworth, 'The Solitary Reaper', 'And, as I mounted up the hill, / The music in my heart I bore, / Long after it was heard no more' (ll. 29–31).
79 *Was it a vision, or a waking dream?* Compare 'Ode to Psyche' 'Surely I dreamt to-day, or did I see / The winged Psyche with awakened eyes?' (ll. 5–6). Whereas the earlier ode opens with a question as to the speaker's dream-state, the latter closes with essentially the same dilemma, thus leaving unresolved the status of the poet's 'waking dream'. Compare Hazlitt's 1818 lecture 'On Chaucer and Spenser' (also collected in *Lectures on the English Poets*), where he remarks that 'Spenser was the poet of our waking dreams; and he has invented not only a language but a music of his own for them' (*Works*, vol. 5, p. 44; see above, headnote to 'The Eve of St Agnes').
80 *Do I wake or sleep?* Repeating the poem's decisive concluding query, the speaker encapsulates the tension in the poem between the 'here' of wakeful, everyday reality, where 'but to think is to be full of sorrow', and the imagined 'there' of 'embalmed darkness' in the nightingale's pastoral bower.

Ode on a Grecian Urn

Written May 1819, this is most likely the third of Keats's odes of 1819. It was first published in *Annals of the Fine Arts* (January 1820), and collected in *Lamia, Isabella, The Eve of St Agnes, and other Poems* (1820). In an 1845 letter to the publisher Edward Moxon, B. R. Haydon accounted for the publication of this ode and the previous in the *Annals of the Fine Arts*:

> The ode to the Nightingale, & to a Grecian Urn were first published in the Annals as well – as he repeated both to me in the Kilburn meadows, in his recitative tone of melancholy voice just after he had composed them. I begged a copy for the Annals as I wrote many things in the work – and there they appeared at my request before the[y] came out in a Volume.
> (*Keats Circle*, vol. 2, p. 142)

There are indeed a number of abiding similarities with the 'Ode to a Nightingale', including this ode's further development of the 10-line stanza rhyming *ababcdecde* (now with a decasyllabic eighth line), which becomes standard for the two remaining odes of spring 1819. The 'Ode on a Grecian Urn' similarly confronts the difference between the idealized realm of the aesthetic (here, the 'still', 'unravished' urn) and the more vulnerable, temporal underpinnings of lived human experience. With this division comes an acute awareness of the differences between the powers of lyric poetry and other forms of art (here, the urn as a 'Sylvan historian' seemingly better equipped than poetry, or 'our rhyme', to reveal its 'tale'). Finally, as is the case with 'Nightingale', the ode is organized along similar lines of a seeming departure from, then return to quotidian human reality, attendant upon the persona's recognition of the limitations of the work of art and the value of 'breathing human passion', however painful.

In Hazlitt's writing on Greek statuary (with which Keats may well have been conversant), he makes two observations strikingly similar to Keats's own (see l. 28 below), regarding the distance between the ideal aesthetic object and 'breathing human passion'. In 'On Gusto' (1816), he observes:

> The gusto in the Greek statues is of a very singular kind. The sense of perfect form nearly occupies the whole mind, and hardly suffers it to dwell on any other feeling. It seems enough for them *to be*, without acting or suffering. Their forms are ideal, spiritual. Their beauty is power. By their beauty they are raised above the frailties of pain or passion; by their beauty they are deified.
> (*Works*, vol 4, p. 79)

Two years later, in a lecture 'On Poetry in General', Hazlitt elaborates his point that Greek statues are 'marble to the touch and to the heart'.

> They have not an informing principle within them. In their faultless excellence they appear sufficient to themselves. By their beauty they are raised above the frailties of passion or suffering. By their beauty they are deified. But they are not objects of religious faith to us, and their forms are a reproach to common humanity. They seem to have no sympathy with us, and not to want our admiration.
> (*Works*, vol. 5, p. 11)

While Keats does not have in mind one particular urn, he was familiar with Greek statuary (compare 'On Seeing the Elgin Marbles') and did make a drawing of one particular vase, known as the Sosibios vase. Keats's archetypal urn here seems to depict three 'interwoven' scenes: Arcadian revelry and pursuit (stanza 1); a piper, a lover and a maiden (stanzas 2 and 3); and a sacrificial ritual (stanza 4). While the poet concedes that the urn, addressed at the outset as a 'Sylvan historian', may be able to 'express / A flowery tale more sweetly than our rhyme', he increasingly underscores what the figures on the urn can *not* do – to wit, realize their passion. Finally, in the last stanza, he denounces the urn's 'silent form' as but a 'Cold Pastoral' as he turns away in conclusion from 'marble men and maidens' to human sorrows and human truths.

Text follows *1820*, with variants from *Annals*.

1.

THOU still unravish'd bride of quietness,
Thou foster-child of silence and slow time,

---

1 *Thou still unravished bride of quietness* In this initial apostrophe to the urn as a 'still unravished bride of quietness', the critical word is 'still', which denotes 'quiet' (which serves to ironize the throwing-forth of the speaker's voice, since a silent urn cannot respond to this summons), 'as yet' (as in not yet ravished), and 'ever'. The urn's status as both quiet and untouched simultaneously points out its strengths and anticipates its weaknesses: it is intact and inviolate, yet will ever remain a 'silent form' (see l. 44).

Sylvan historian, who canst thus express
   A flowery tale more sweetly than our rhyme:
What leaf-fring'd legend haunts about thy shape   5
   Of deities or mortals, or of both,
      In Tempe or the dales of Arcady?
   What men or gods are these? What maidens loth?
What mad pursuit? What struggle to escape?
   What pipes and timbrels? What wild ecstasy?   10

2.

Heard melodies are sweet, but those unheard
   Are sweeter; therefore, ye soft pipes, play on;
Not to the sensual ear, but, more endear'd,
   Pipe to the spirit ditties of no tone:
Fair youth, beneath the trees, thou canst not leave   15
   Thy song, nor ever can those trees be bare;
      Bold Lover, never, never canst thou kiss,
   Though winning near the goal—yet, do not grieve;
She cannot fade, though thou hast not thy bliss,
   For ever wilt thou love, and she be fair!   20

3.

Ah, happy, happy boughs! that cannot shed
   Your leaves, nor ever bid the Spring adieu;
And, happy melodist, unwearied,
   For ever piping songs for ever new;
More happy love! more happy, happy love!   25
   For ever warm and still to be enjoy'd,
      For ever panting, and for ever young;
All breathing human passion far above,

---

3 *Sylvan historian* As noted above in the headnote, the urn may be considered an historian because it tells a story – in other words, because it sets forth a more linear *narrative* than 'our rhyme', which operates according to the conventions of *lyric*. 'Sylvan' denotes an association with a wood or woods (i.e. a pastoral habitat and conventions), as suggested by the 'leaf-fringed legend [that] haunts about thy shape' (l. 5).
5–10 *What leaf-fringed legend . . . What wild ecstasy?* The litany of questions here again ironizes the quietness of the urn, since none of the questions is or ultimately can be answered by this 'foster-child of silence'.
7 *Tempe or the dales of Arcady* Classical loci celebrated in antiquity for their pastoral beauty; Tempe (a valley in Thessaly) was renowned for its cool climate; Arcady (Arcadia) was the mythological home of pastoral shepherd-poets.
9 *What mad pursuit?* This was 'what love, what dance?' in *Annals*.
10 *timbrels?* 'percussive musical instrument, similar to a tambourine'.
13 *sensual ear* The ear of the physical senses.
14 *ditties* 'short simple songs'.
15–20 *Fair youth . . . and she be fair!* As was the case in the closing sestet of the first stanza, the speaker again interrogates the urn and exposes the liabilities of its perfection. Though the lover will love for ever and the fair maid's beauty will never fade, neither will they ever know the 'bliss' of a shared 'kiss'. In *never* realizing their passion, the lovers will *ever* remain unsatisfied.
19–20 *She cannot fade . . . and she be fair!* Compare 'Ode to a Nightingale' for the opposing representation of mortal love and beauty, 'Where Beauty cannot keep her lustrous eyes, / Or new Love pine at them beyond tomorrow' (ll. 29–30).
21 *Ah, happy, happy boughs* Compare 'Ode to Psyche', 'O happy, happy dove' (l. 22) and 'Ode to a Nightingale', ''Tis not through envy of thy happy lot, / But being too happy in thine happiness' (ll. 5–6). The repetition of 'happy' also reiterates the structure of 'never, never' in the preceding stanza.
24–7 *For ever piping . . . for ever young* As is also the case in l. 20, the insistent repetition of 'for ever' recalls the ambiguities of 'still' in the opening line. Though the melodist will be piping songs 'for ever' and the lovers will be young 'for ever', none will be able to experience passion – hence all will remain 'for ever' unravished.
28 *All breathing human passion far above* See headnote above for Hazlitt's observations on the distance between impervious Greek statuary and frail human passion.

>   That leaves a heart high-sorrowful and cloy'd,
>   A burning forehead, and a parching tongue.   30
>
>   4.
>
>   Who are these coming to the sacrifice?
>   To what green altar, O mysterious priest,
>   Lead'st thou that heifer lowing at the skies,
>   And all her silken flanks with garlands drest?
>   What little town by river or sea shore,   35
>   Or mountain-built with peaceful citadel,
>   Is emptied of this folk, this pious morn?
>   And, little town, thy streets for evermore
>   Will silent be; and not a soul to tell
>   Why thou art desolate, can e'er return.   40
>
>   5.
>
>   O Attic shape! Fair attitude! with brede
>   Of marble men and maidens overwrought,
>   With forest branches and the trodden weed;
>   Thou, silent form, dost tease us out of thought
>   As doth eternity: Cold Pastoral!   45
>   When old age shall this generation waste,
>   Thou shalt remain, in midst of other woe

29 *high-sorrowful* Keats regularly forms compounds with 'high', often to designate heightened emotional or imaginative states; compare 'Fancy', 'high-commissioned send her' (l. 27) and 'Lamia', 'Thou smooth-lipp'd serpent, surely high inspired!' (I. 83).

31–40 *who are these ... can e'er return* Compare 'To J. H. Reynolds Esq.', 'The sacrifice goes on; the pontif knife / Gloams in the sun, the milk-white heifer lows, / The pipes go shrilly, the libation flows' (ll. 20–2). Here for the third time, the speaker's interrogation of the urn exposes the urn's fundamental silence (in this instance, as silent as the empty town's empty streets).

34 *flanks* This was 'sides' in *Annals*.

40 *desolate* Compare Keats's use of 'forlorn' in 'Ode to a Nightingale' (ll. 70, 71). As in the earlier ode, this word marks a nadir (or furthest reach of the poet's imagining a realm alternative to the human), from which it will now return upon the mortal and the present, characterized though they are by transience and pain.

41 *Attic* 'of or pertaining to Attica, or its capital Athens' (i.e. of or pertaining to classical Greece); hence, 'marked by simple and refined elegance, pure, classical'. Compare 'On First Seeing the Elgin Marbles' regarding 'Grecian grandeur' (I. 12).

41 *brede* Poetical archaism denoting 'anything plaited, entwined, or interwoven'; compare 'Lamia', 'Spoilt all her silver mail, and golden brede' (1, 158), and Collins, 'Ode to Evening', 'With brede etherial wove' (l. 7).

42 *overwrought* 'overlaid' and 'overelaborated', suggesting that the urn's pure shape is not merely overlaid with its patterns but that these patterns are themselves overdone.

44 *tease us out of thought* Compare 'To J. H. Reynolds Esq.':

>   Things cannot to the will
>   Be settled, but they tease us out of thought.
>   Or is it that Imagination brought
>   Beyond its proper bound, yet still confined,—
>   Lost in a sort of Purgatory blind,
>   Cannot refer to any standard law
>   Of either earth or heaven?
>   (ll. 76–82)

Keats suggests here that the urn 'teases[s] us out of thought' precisely because it is a 'silent form': had it been able to respond to – let alone answer – any of the questions posed throughout the ode, we would not now be ' out of thought', whether thoughtless (confused) or beyond thought (because in a realm of imaginative vision).

45 *Cold Pastoral!* The speaker's most succinct statement of his ambivalence regarding the urn. As a pastoral, the urn offers a conventionally nostalgic image of a lost Arcadian way of life; if this image is 'cold', however, it would seem to deny the very comfort it promises (consider its 'cold' distance from and denial of 'All breathing human passion', l. 28).

> Than ours, a friend to man, to whom thou say'st,
> 'Beauty is truth, truth beauty,'—that is all
> Ye know on earth, and all ye need to know. 50

49–50 *'Beauty is truth . . . ye need to know.* This reads 'Beauty is Truth, Truth Beauty.—That is all / Ye know on Earth, and all ye need to know.' in the *Annals*. The absence of quotation marks containing 'Beauty is truth, truth beauty' in the *Annals* (and in four early transcripts) has heightened the confusion surrounding these two lines. With or without them, there are potentially three ways (at least) to consider the apostrophic structure of this cryptic pronouncement: (1) the urn to the reader ('ye . . . on earth'); (2) the poet to the urn (as aesthetic object); and (3) the poet to the figures on the urn. When construed as an address from the urn to the reader (perhaps the most plausible claim, given that the urn has just been addressed in the preceding line as 'thou'), this aphorism seems to revisit (if not resolve) certain moments in the second stanza (esp. ll. 15–20) regarding the seeming eternity of the piper's melodies and the fair maiden's beauty. For other formulations by Keats regarding the aesthetic and imaginative union between 'beauty' and 'truth', see his letters of December 1817–January 1818: 'What the imagination seizes as Beauty must be truth'; '[t]he excellence of every Art is its intensity, capable of making all disagreeables evaporate, from their being in close relationship with Beauty & Truth'; 'I never can feel certain of any truth but from a clear perception of its Beauty' (*Letters*, vol. 1, pp. 184, 192, vol. 2, p. 19).

Ode on Melancholy

The fourth of Keats's 1819 odes, the 'Ode on Melancholy' was probably written in May 1819 (subsequently published in *1820*). Though the shortest of the odes, it is both the most tightly constructed (formally as well as logically) and the most succinct in its articulation of several motifs which resound throughout the odes: the sorrow that attends intense passion, the transience of beauty and the necessarily intertwined relations between pain and pleasure. The speaker begins the first stanza negatively, exhorting the reader what *not* to do when overcome with melancholy: do not turn to Lethe nor to wolf's-bane nor nightshade, for these suicidal remedies will serve only to 'drown the wakeful anguish of the soul', an anguish which emerges later as integral to the pleasure of melancholy. Rather, as the speaker advises in the second stanza, indulge the melancholy, 'glut thy sorrow' and 'feed deep', for with melancholy comes a heightened perception of beauty, however transient. The third stanza then aligns melancholy and delight in a series of images connecting pleasure and pain, valorizing those who feel both most intensely, and postulating in conclusion that true happiness is always con-nected with sorrow and grief. As Keats writes in a letter from the spring of 1819, simultaneously preoccupied with indolence (see headnote to 'Ode on Indolence') and melancholy:

This is the world – thus we cannot expect to give way many hours to pleasure – Circumstances are like Clouds continually gathering and bursting – While we are laughing the seed of some trouble is put into the wide arable land of events – while we are laughing it sprouts [it] grows and suddenly bears a poison fruit which we must pluck – Even so we have leisure to reason on the misfortunes of our friends; our own touch us too nearly for words.
(*Letters*, vol. 2, p. 79)

The literary history of melancholy – variously understood as pensive sadness on the one hand, and overbearing, suicidal gloom on the other – is a rich one, including works as formally divergent as Burton's epic *Anatomy of Melancholy* (which Keats was reading in the spring of 1819) and Milton's lyric *Il Penseroso*, Cowper's *The Task* and Charlotte Smith's *Elegiac Sonnets*. Throughout the odes of 1819, Keatsian melancholia may be heard not merely in this ode (in which the bursting of 'Joy's grape' ultimately requires one to 'taste the sadness' of melancholy's sovereign might, ll. 28–9), but also in the speaker's unavoidable consciousness of 'the weariness, the fever, and the fret' even while listening to the nightingale's rapturous melody, or in the painful recognition in the 'Ode on a Grecian Urn' that transience is the necessary price of human beauty and human passion.

Text follows *1820*.

452 John Keats (1795–1821)

1.

No, no, go not to Lethe, neither twist
    Wolf's-bane, tight-rooted, for its poisonous wine;
Nor suffer thy pale forehead to be kiss'd
    By nightshade, ruby grape of Proserpine;
Make not your rosary of yew-berries,   5
    Nor let the beetle, nor the death-moth be
        Your mournful Psyche, nor the downy owl
A partner in your sorrow's mysteries;
    For shade to shade will come too drowsily,
        And drown the wakeful anguish of the soul.   10

2.

But when the melancholy fit shall fall
    Sudden from heaven like a weeping cloud,
That fosters the droop-headed flowers all,
    And hides the green hill in an April shroud;
Then glut thy sorrow on a morning rose,   15
    Or on the rainbow of the salt sand-wave,
        Or on the wealth of globed peonies;
Or if thy mistress some rich anger shows,
    Emprison her soft hand, and let her rave,
        And feed deep, deep upon her peerless eyes.   20

3.

She dwells with Beauty—Beauty that must die;

---

1 *No, no, go not to Lethe* The abruptness of the first line (and its repeated negatives) may be understood as a response to an abandoned opening stanza (see the mention of Lethe in the last line below):

> Though you should build a bark of dead men's bones,
> And rear a phantom gibbet for a mast,
> Stitch creeds together for a sail, with groans
> To fill it out, blood-stained and aghast;
> Although your rudder be a dragon's tail
> Long severed, yet still hard with agony,
> Your cordage large uprootings from the skull
> Of bald Medusa, certes you would fail
> To find the Melancholy – whether she
> Dreameth in any isle of Lethe dull.

With the speaker's negative injunctions here ('no . . . neither . . . nor . . . not . . .' and so forth), he is directing the reader away from the gothic excesses of the cancelled stanza and toward a more nuanced view of melancholy.
1 *Lethe* In Greek mythology, one of the five rivers of the underworld, associated with forgetfulness and oblivion.
2 *Wolf's-bane* Otherwise known as aconitum, the roots of which are poisonous; in legend, an important ingredient in witches' magic potions.
4 *nightshade, ruby grape of Proserpine* Nightshade, or belladonna, has toxic purple berries, leaves, and roots; Prosperpine was the Roman goddess of the underworld.

5 *yew-berries* Conifer with mildly toxic berries, commonly planted in or surrounding burial grounds.
6 *death-moth* A Mediterranean moth, the Death's Head moth, distinguishable by a skull-shaped pattern on its back.
7 *mournful Psyche* See headnote above to 'Ode to Psyche'.
11–20 *But when . . . peerless eyes.* The rhetorical structure of the second stanza ('But . . . Then') further exhorts the reader not to flee from melancholy but to embrace it – not to turn from it as somehow mind-numbing but to embrace it as revivifying – for it is only with the 'glutting' of one's sorrow that one can fully experience beauties as various as, say, a rose or a peony, the sun glinting off the sand, or the passion of a lover.
18 *rich* Sumptuous, replete with possibility; compare 'Ode to a Nightingale', 'Now more than ever seems it rich to die' (l. 55).
20 *deep, deep* Characteristically Keatsian use of repetition to create a sense of overabundance; compare 'Ode to Psyche', 'O happy, happy dove' (l. 22) and 'Ode on a Grecian Urn', 'Ah, happy, happy boughs . . . / / More happy love, more happy, happy love!' (ll. 21, 25).
21 *She dwells with Beauty – Beauty that must die* In opening the third and concluding stanza, the speaker directly aligns melancholy with beauty (thus completing the revalorization of melancholy begun in the second stanza); initiates the metaphor of the dwelling (consummated in the 'temple of Delight', l. 25); and underscores the transience of beauty (its melancholy truth).

  And Joy, whose hand is ever at his lips
   Bidding adieu; and aching Pleasure nigh,
   Turning to poison while the bee-mouth sips:
  Ay, in the very temple of Delight   25
   Veil'd Melancholy has her sovran shrine,
    Though seen of none save him whose strenuous tongue
  Can burst Joy's grape against his palate fine;
   His soul shall taste the sadness of her might,
    And be among her cloudy trophies hung.   30

22–3 *Joy . . . Bidding adieu* As with 'Beauty' above, so is 'Joy' transient. To understand joy is to understand its imminent departure or (ll. 28–9 below) its integration with sadness. Compare 'Ode to a Nightingale', 'Adieu! adieu! Thy plaintive anthem fades' (l. 75), in which Keats similarly initiates the ode's denouement by marking the irreconcilable difference between the (melancholy) pleasures of the imagination (here, Beauty, Joy, Pleasure, Delight) and 'the world', in which 'Circumstances are like Clouds continually gathering and bursting' (*Letters*, vol. 2, p. 79, cited above in headnote).
23 *aching Pleasure* Compare 'Ode to a Nightingale', 'My heart aches' (l. 1). Here as elsewhere (e.g. 'glut thy sorrow'), the modalities of pleasure and pain are never mutually exclusive, but are habitually characterized in terms of one another.

Ode on Indolence

Written in the spring of 1819 (likely in March, given evidence in the *Letters*), the 'Ode on Indolence' was omitted from *1820* and not published until 1848 in Milnes's *Life, Letters, and Literary Remains of John Keats*. In the same journal-letter to George and Georgiana Keats (14 February–03 May 1819) in which Keats transcribes the 'Ode to Psyche' and glosses his definition of melancholy, he gives a long account on 19 March of his indolent temper:

> This morning I am in a sort of temper indolent and supremely careless: I long after a stanza or two of Thomson's Castle of indolence [James Thomson's 'The Castle of Indolence' (1748)] – my passions are all asleep from my having slumbered till nearly eleven and weakened the animal fibre all over me to a delightful sensation about three degrees on this side of faintness – if I had teeth of pearl and the breath of lillies I should call it languor – but as I am I must call it Laziness – In this state of effeminacy the fibres of the brain are relaxed in common with the rest of the body, and to such a happy degree that pleasure has no show of enticement and pain no unbearable frown. Neither Poetry, nor Ambition, nor Love have any alertness of countenance as they pass by me: they seem rather like three figures on a greek vase – a Man and two women – whom no one but myself could distinguish in their disguisement. This is the only happiness; and is a rare instance of advantage in the body overpowering the Mind
>   (*Letters*, vol. 2, pp. 78–9)

In both the letter and the ode, Keatsian indolence is not merely a sense of languor or laziness but of insensibility and a general want of feeling: 'My passions are all asleep . . . pleasure has no show of enticement and pain no unbearable frown'. Keats thought of this poem as particularly representative of his '1819 temper' and appears to have regarded it highly, as evidenced in his 9 June 1819 letter to Sarah Jeffrey, in which he remarks that 'You will judge of my 1819 temper when I tell you that the thing I have most enjoyed this year has been writing an ode to Indolence' (*Letters*, vol. 2, p. 116). Keats's readers have habitually disagreed. Numerous critics have suggested that Keats's preoccupation at this time with indolence carried over into the production of an indolent poem: unlike the impassioned apostrophes and energetic versification which characterize the other odes of spring 1819, there is here almost no dramatic tension or engagement between the persona and the three allegorical figures on the urn representing Love, Ambition and Poesy. (As Keats writes in his journal-letter, these figures have no 'alertness of countenance as they pass me by'.) Though these 'shadows' pass no fewer than three times, the speaker never once engages them – unlike, say, earlier addresses to Psyche, the nightingale, the scenes on an earlier urn, or the imagined melancholic. The contrast with 'Ode on a Grecian Urn' is the most arresting: whereas the speaker of the earlier ode impetuously and repeatedly interrogated the urn – 'Thou still unravished bride of quietness, / Thou foster-child of silence and slow time' – here the speaker is from the outset resolutely passive – 'One morn before me were three figures seen'. Though generally considered inferior to the five 'great odes' of 1819 (all of which were published in 1819 or 1820), the 'Ode on Indolence' does like them deploy the full 10-line stanza first adopted in 'Ode on a Grecian Urn' and in fact bears numerous similarities in poetic diction to both this ode and the 'Ode to a Nightingale'.

  Text follows *1848*.

'They toil not, neither do they spin.'

1

One morn before me were three figures seen,
   With bowed necks, and joined hands, side-faced;
And one behind the other stepp'd serene,
   In placid sandals, and in white robes graced:
They pass'd, like figures on a marble urn,   5
   When shifted round to see the other side;
      They came again; as when the urn once more
Is shifted round, the first seen shades return;
And they were strange to me, as may betide
   With vases, to one deep in Phidian lore.   10

2

How is it, shadows, that I knew ye not?
   How came ye muffled in so hush a masque?
Was it a silent deep-disguised plot
   To steal away, and leave without a task
My idle days? Ripe was the drowsy hour;
   The blissful cloud of summer-indolence   15
      Benumb'd my eyes; my pulse grew less and less;
Pain had no sting, and pleasure's wreath no flower.
   O, why did ye not melt, and leave my sense
      Unhaunted quite of all but—nothingness?   20

3

A third time pass'd they by, and, passing, turn'd
   Each one the face a moment whiles to me;
Then faded, and to follow them I burn'd
   And ached for wings, because I knew the three:
The first was a fair maid, and Love her name;   25
   The second was Ambition, pale of cheek,
      And ever watchful with fatigued eye;
The last, whom I love more, the more of blame
   Is heap'd upon her, maiden most unmeek,—
      I knew to be my demon Poesy.   30

Epigraph Matthew 6: 28: 'Consider the lilies of the field, how they grow; they toil not, neither do they spin'.
5 *like figures on a marble urn* See Keats's journal-letter entry for 19 March 1819 (cited in headnote above).
10 *Phidian* Phidias, Greek architect and sculptor (5th century BCE), was responsible for the adornment of the Parthenon (including the Elgin Marbles).
11 *How is it, shadows, that I knew ye not?* Unlike the urgent, impassioned apostrophes in the other odes of spring 1819 (most especially 'Ode to a Nightingale' and 'Ode on a Grecian Urn'), the questioning throughout this stanza reveals the persona's general idleness and indifference – or (as Keats puts it in the journal-letter of March 1819), his 'Laziness'.
12 *masque* Variant of 'mask'; an elaborate form of court entertainment combining drama, music, song, dance and spectacle, and involving masked figures representing allegorical entities (here, Love, Ambition, and Poesy). Keats doubly distances Love, Ambition, and Poesy – at once figures on an urn and figures in a masque – from the waking, human 'world' of the speaker.
18 *Pain had no sting, and pleasure's wreath no flower* Keatsian indolence; see his journal-letter entry for 19 March 1819 (cited in headnote above).
20 *nothingness* See Keats's journal-letter entry for 19 March 1819, 'I do not know what I did on Monday – nothing – nothing – nothing – I wish this was any way extraordinary' (*Letters*, vol. 2, p. 77).
24 *ached for wings* Compare 'Ode to a Nightingale', 'My heart aches' (l. 1) and 'I will fly to thee, / / . . . on the viewless wings of Poesy' (ll. 31, 33). Unlike the earlier ode, the speaker here is too indolent to address or resolve this shortcoming.

4

They faded, and, forsooth! I wanted wings:
  O folly! What is Love? and where is it?
And for that poor Ambition—it springs
  From a man's little heart's short fever-fit;
For Poesy!—no,—she has not a joy,—
  At least for me,—so sweet as drowsy noons,
    And evenings steep'd in honied indolence;
O, for an age so shelter'd from annoy,
  That I may never know how change the moons,
    Or hear the voice of busy common-sense!

5

A third time came they by;—alas! wherefore?
  My sleep had been embroider'd with dim dreams;
My soul had been a lawn besprinkled o'er
  With flowers, and stirring shades, and baffled beams:
The morn was clouded, but no shower fell,
  Though in her lids hung the sweet tears of May;
    The open casement press'd a new-leaved vine,
    Let in the budding warmth and throstle's lay;
O shadows! 'twas a time to bid farewell!
    Upon your skirts had fallen no tears of mine.

6

So, ye three ghosts, adieu! Ye cannot raise
  My head cool-bedded in the flowery grass;
For I would not be dieted with praise,
  A pet-lamb in a sentimental farce!
Fade softly from my eyes, and be once more
  In masque-like figures on the dreamy urn;
    Farewell! I yet have visions for the night,
And for the day faint visions there is store;
  Vanish, ye phantoms, from my idle spright,
    Into the clouds, and never more return!

31 *I wanted wings* See note to l. 24 above.
34 *fever-fit* Compare 'Ode to a Nightingale', 'The weariness, the fever, and the fret' (l. 23) and '... Beauty cannot keep her lustrous eyes, / Or new Love pine at them beyond tomorrow' (ll. 29–30). As elsewhere in Keats's poetry, human passion is characterized first and foremost by its transience.
42 *embroider'd* Compare 'Ode on a Grecian Urn', 'With brede / Of marble men and maidens overwrought' (ll. 41–2).
47–8 *The open casement ... throstle's lay* Compare 'Ode to Psyche', 'and a casement ope at night, / To let the warm Love in!' (ll. 66–7) and 'Ode to a Nightingale', '... magic casements, opening on the foam / Of perilous seas in fairy lands forlorn' (ll. 69–70 and note). As in the earlier odes, the casement here figures a threshold of 'Romantic' possibilities – 'Let in the budding warmth and throstle's lay'.
48 *throstle's lay* Song of the thrush, a reclusive songbird known for its haunting melodies.
49 *farewell!* As is the case at the outset of the ode when the speaker first addressed the three figures (see note to l. 11), so here he begins to take leave of them without any apparent urgency – 'Upon your skirts had fallen no tears of mine'. The indolence of the poem is thus apparent not merely in its versification but prominently in its tone.
51 *adieu!* Compare 'Ode to a Nightingale', 'Adieu! adieu! Thy plaintive anthem fades' (l. 75). As in the earlier ode, Keats here formally initiates the concluding stanza by taking leave of and re-establishing a degree of critical distance between himself and his subject.
55 *Fade softly* Compare 'Ode to a Nightingale', '... fade away into the forest dim – / Fade far away, dissolve ...' (ll. 20–1) and 'Thy plaintive anthem fades' (l. 75).
56 *masque-like figures* See note to line 12.
57 *Farewell!* See note to line 51. In banishing the figures (now 'phantoms'), Keats's speaker repudiates them much as was the case at the end of 'Ode to a Nightingale'. Similarly, he positions himself somewhere between waking and sleeping ('I yet have visions for the night, / And for the day faint visions there is store').

To Autumn

Written in late September 1819 (probably 19–21 September, on the basis of letters to J. H. Reynolds and Richard Woodhouse), the ode 'To Autumn' was first published in *1820*. Writing to Reynolds from Winchester on 21 September 1819, Keats rhapsodized over the beauty of the season:

> How beautiful the season is now – How fine the air. A temperate sharpness about it. Really, without joking, chaste weather – Dian skies – I never lik'd stubble fields so much as now – Aye better than the chilly green of the spring. Somehow a stubble plain looks warm – in the same way that some pictures look warm – this struck me so much in my sunday's walk that I composed upon it. I hope you are better employed than in gaping after weather. I have been at different times so happy as not to know what weather it was – No I will not copy a parcel of verses. I always somehow associate Chatterton with autumn.
>
> (*Letters*, vol. 2, p. 167)

The Sunday in question fell on the 19th of September, and in a second letter of the 21st (to Woodhouse), Keats copied out 'To Autumn' ('You like Poetry better – so you shall have some I was going to give Reynolds'; *Letters*, vol. 2, pp. 170–1), the last of the 'great odes' of 1819. While similar to the odes of the spring in both form (here adding an extra line to the 10-line stanza and varying the rhyme scheme accordingly) and a thematic preoccupation with the tensions between pleasure and pain, between imagined worlds and the 'real world' in which we ultimately must live, this final ode differs significantly in tone and overall mood. Rather than the impassioned apostrophes of, say, 'Ode to a Nightingale' and 'Ode on a Grecian Urn', 'To Autumn' is far more descriptive of landscape and setting (not as backdrop but, rather, as process and maturation), and resorts to apostrophic address only in the second stanza. If the impassioned music of the versification (to paraphrase Wordsworth) renders the majority of the spring odes Pindaric in tone, 'To Autumn' may be said to be resolutely Horatian: meditative, calm and poised. This balance is perhaps most succinctly stated at the outset of the third stanza: after the initial yearning for something alternative to autumn ('Where are the songs of spring? Aye, where are they?'), a yearning already qualified by the second question, the speaker reassuringly affirms, 'Think not of them, thou hast thy music too'. Rich with allusion to Thomson, Chatterton, Coleridge and Keats's own verse, 'To Autumn' gathers up the fruits of the *annus mirabilis* of 1819 at the same time as it anticipates the sensuous, sonorous poetry of Tennyson and Stevens.

Text follows *1820*.

1.

    S<small>EASON</small> of mists and mellow fruitfulness,
        Close bosom-friend of the maturing sun;
    Conspiring with him how to load and bless
        With fruit the vines that round the thatch-eves run;
    To bend with apples the moss'd cottage-trees,   5
        And fill all fruit with ripeness to the core;
        To swell the gourd, and plump the hazel shells
    With a sweet kernel; to set budding more,
        And still more, later flowers for the bees,
        Until they think warm days will never cease,   10
        For Summer has o'er-brimm'd their clammy cells.

---

1 *Season of mists and mellow fruitfulness* Compare Thomson, 'Autumn', 'These roving mists that constant now begin' (l. 736); see also Wordsworth, *The Excursion*, 'And mellow Autumn, charged with bounteous fruit, / Where is she imaged?' (V. 400–1). The mellowness of autumn not only suggests its 'maturing sun' (l. 2), the warmth of stubble plains (see the letter to Reynolds cited in the headnote above), and the 'oozings' of the cider press (ll. 21–2) but, in terms of the sounds and consequent tone of the poem, both the long vowels and the alliterative reliance on the double-'l' that together create the 'fruitfulness' of the poem: 'fill', 'swell', 'o'er-brimmed', 'furrow', 'winnow', 'swallows' – to name but a few.

5–11 *To bend . . . their clammy cells.* The images of bounteousness in these lines are very much a product of the transitive verbs ('bend', 'fill', 'swell', 'plump') that suggest the weight and the process of the harvest ripening, as well as the promise of future fruit ('still more').

7 *plump* Compare *Endymion*, 'Ere a lean bat could plump its wintery skin' (IV. 377).

11 *o'er-brimmed their clammy cells* Compare *Endymion*, '. . . every sense / Filling with spiritual sweets to plenitude, / As bees gorge full their cells' (III. 38–40). Regarding the language of fullness throughout this stanza, see note to line 1 above. Compare Tennyson, 'The Lotos-Eaters', 'Lo! sweeten'd with the summer light, / The full-juiced apple, waxing over-mellow, / Drops in a silent autumn night' (ll. 77–9).

2.

Who hath not seen thee oft amid thy store?
    Sometimes whoever seeks abroad may find
Thee sitting careless on a granary floor,
    Thy hair soft-lifted by the winnowing wind;   15
Or on a half-reap'd furrow sound asleep,
    Drows'd with the fume of poppies, while thy hook
        Spares the next swath and all its twined flowers:
And sometimes like a gleaner thou dost keep
    Steady thy laden head across a brook;   20
    Or by a cyder-press, with patient look,
        Thou watchest the last oozings hours by hours.

3.

Where are the songs of Spring? Ay, where are they?
    Think not of them, thou hast thy music too,—
While barred clouds bloom the soft-dying day,   25
    And touch the stubble-plains with rosy hue;
Then in a wailful choir the small gnats mourn
    Among the river sallows, borne aloft
        Or sinking as the light wind lives or dies;
And full-grown lambs loud bleat from hilly bourn;   30
Hedge-crickets sing; and now with treble soft

12–22 *Who hath not seen . . . hours by hours* The personification of autumn throughout this stanza draws on a variety of pastoral (more specifically, georgic) representations of the season as a woman carrying out the rural chores attendant upon the harvest. Compare the opening of Thomson's 'Autumn': 'Crown'd with the sickle and the wheaten sheaf, / While *Autumn*, nodding o'er the yellow plain, / Comes jovial on' (ll. 1–3).

15 *winnowing wind* Winnowing is 'to expose (grain or other substances) to the wind or to a current of air so the lighter particles . . . are separated or blown away'.

17–18 *Drowsed . . . poppies* Historically, poppies were planted in and along cornfields, and have long been associated with sleep; compare Keats, 'Sleep and Poetry', regarding 'Sleep' as a 'Wreather of poppy buds and weeping willows' (l. 14). In an earlier draft, Keats writes 'Dosed with red poppies; while thy reaping hook / Spares for some slumbrous minutes the next swath'; in the letter of 21 September 1819, Keats has 'Dased' for 'Drowsed'.

17 *thy hook* A reaper's hook, used for cutting corn and grains (see note above to ll. 17–18).

19 *gleaner* One who gleans, 'to gather or pick up ears of corn which have been left by the reapers'.

22 *hours by hours* Keats's repetition here of 'hours' underscores the plurality of 'oozings' over which Autumn watches and dozes, as if 'warm days will never cease' (l. 10). It also marks yet another instance of his dramatic use of repetition throughout the odes: compare 'Ode to Psyche', 'O happy, happy dove' (l. 22), 'Ode on a Grecian Urn', 'Ah, happy, happy boughs . . . / / More happy love, more happy, happy love!' (ll. 21, 25) and 'Ode on Melancholy', 'She dwells with Beauty – Beauty that must die' (l. 21).

23–33 *Where are the songs of spring? . . . twitter in the skies.* Whereas the spring has 'songs' – set compositions, now finished – the autumn is said to have 'music' – a fine art at the intersection of the beauties of form and the articulation of emotions, seemingly less bound than the temporal restraints demarcating spring. That the music is furthermore that of (among many voices) a 'wailful choir' of mourning gnats and the wind which 'lives or dies' further underscores Keats's location of beauty at the intersection of pain and pleasure, living and dying, the temporal (human) and the atemporal (art). Though the language of this stanza anticipates silence and darkness, it lingers and closes with anticipation in the 'gathering swallows'.

25 *barred clouds bloom* Keats's use of 'bloom' as a transitive verb is unusual, and may be understood here in the sense of 'to give a bloom to; to colour with a soft warm tint or glow'; alternatively, it may also be understood as a poetic substitution for the substantive 'bloom', 'the delicate powdery deposit on fruits . . . when fresh-gathered'. Suggesting the promise of youth, 'bloom' also stands here in paradoxical relation to the 'soft-dying day'. Regarding 'barred', compare Coleridge, 'Dejection: An Ode', 'those thin clouds above, in flakes and bars' (l. 31).

26 *stubble-plains* Regarding the warmth and beauty of a stubble plain, see Keats's 21 September 1819 letter to Reynolds (cited above in the headnote).

28 *sallows* Willows; compare 'I stood tip-toe . . .', 'the o'erhanging sallows' (l. 67).

31 *Hedge-crickets* Associated for Keats with both summer and winter; compare the sestet (ll. 9–14) of 'On the Grasshopper and the Cricket':

    The poetry of earth is ceasing never.
    On a lone winter evening, when the frost
    Has wrought a silence, from the stove there shrills
    The cricket's song, in warmth increasing ever,
    And seems to one in drowsiness half lost,
    The grasshopper's among some grassy hills.

The red-breast whistles from a garden-croft;
And gathering swallows twitter in the skies.

31–3 *and now with treble soft... twitter in the skies.* With 'now', the speaker locates the poem's denouement in a 'garden-croft' ('piece of enclosed ground... adjacent to a house') as the robin 'whistles' and the swallows 'twitter' at the same time as the lambs and crickets continue to bleat and sing. Compare Coleridge, 'This Lime-Tree Bower My Prison', 'now the bat / Wheels silent by, and not a swallow twitters' (ll. 56–7); see also Wallace Stevens, 'Sunday Morning', '... in the isolation of the sky, / At evening, casual flocks of pigeons make / Ambiguous undulations as they sink, / Downward to darkness, on extended wing' (ll. 117–20).
33 *gathering swallows* Compare Thomson, 'Autumn', 'When Autumn scatters his departing gleams, / Warned of Approaching Winter, gathered, play / The swallow-people' (ll. 836–8).

Bright star, would I were stedfast as thou art

Written in 1819 (presumably October–November, along with additional lyrics inspired by Fanny Brawne, including 'The day is gone and all its sweets are gone', 'What can I do to drive away' and 'I cry your mercy, pity, love – aye love'), this sonnet was published 27 September 1838 in *The Plymouth and Devonport Weekly Journal*. Unlike 'On First Looking into Chapman's Homer', which employs a variation on the 'legitimate' Italian sonnet, Keats here uses the 'illegitimate' English sonnet (as is also the case in 'The day is gone...' and 'I cry your mercy...'), with its reliance on four rather than two rhymes in the octave, to articulate his passion for Fanny. The rhetorical force of feeling comes to the fore with the turn: the decisive stress on the first syllable of line 9, followed by the spondee in the second foot, announce the speaker's resolution to retain the vigilance of the star while abjuring its distance from the human. There is a revealing parallel to lines 1–6 in Keats's letter to Tom Keats of 25–7 June 1818, describing a tour of the Lake District, in which he writes of Windermere that:

> ... the two views we have had of it are of the most noble tenderness – they can never fade away – they make one forget the divisions of life; age, youth, poverty and riches; and refine one's sensual vision into a sort of north star which can never cease to be open lidded and stedfast over the wonders of the great Power.
>
> (*Letters*, vol. 1, p. 299)

Text follows *1848*.

    Bright star, would I were stedfast as thou art—
        Not in lone splendor hung aloft the night,
    And watching, with eternal lids apart,
        Like nature's patient, sleepless eremite,
    The moving waters at their priestlike task   5
        Of pure ablution round earth's human shores,
    Or gazing on the new soft-fallen mask
        Of snow upon the mountains and the moors;
    No—yet still stedfast, still unchangeable,
        Pillow'd upon my fair love's ripening breast,   10
    To feel for ever its soft swell and fall,
        Awake for ever in a sweet unrest,
    Still, still to hear her tender-taken breath,
    And so live ever—or else swoon to death.

4 *eremite* 'a recluse, hermit'. Compare 'The Eve of St Agnes', 'And now, my love, my seraph fair, awake! / Thou art my heaven, and I thine eremite' (ll. 276–7).
6 *ablution* 'the washing of the body as a religious rite' (as anticipated by 'priestlike' in the preceding line).
13 *Still, still* Whereas 'still' in line 9 underscores the attributes of the star which the speaker was adopting for himself ('steadfast... unchangeable'), here the force of 'Still, still' (a spondee) indicates a further accretion of these qualities, as in 'ever more and more' or 'invariably'.
14 *swoon* 'to fall into a fainting fit'. In Keats's lexicon, habitually associated with erotic allure and the loss of individual volition. Compare several representative usages in *Endymion*: 'Now indeed / His senses had swooned off' (I. 397–8) and 'Oh, he had swooned / Drunken from pleasure's nipple' (II. 868–9).

Letitia Elizabeth Landon (L. E. L.) (1802–38)

Letitia Landon is among the most intriguing poets of the Romantic period, a poet who makes a fascinating parallel with Felicia Hemans, with whom she enjoyed great popularity in the 1820 and 1830s. Like Hemans, Landon, under the enigmatic and curiosity-arousing initials 'L. E. L.', sold many copies of her published volumes and appeared regularly in the gift books and literary annuals of the day. Both women lost male figures at significant stages in their lives, Hemans her husband who left her, Landon her father, an army agent fallen on hard times, who died in 1824. Both wrote to support themselves and their families, Hemans her mother and sons, Landon her mother and younger brother. If Hemans writes of home and hearth, and their vulnerability to destruction, Landon takes as her obsessive topic the twinned subject of 'poetry and erotic love', in the words of Jerome McGann and Daniel Riess.[1] Hemans's characteristic tone is one of sadness sweetened by transcendental longing; Landon's one of tragic, sometimes sardonic fatality leavened by desire for escape. Hemans, though aware of the perils of fame, was shielded from the metropolitan literary world and enjoyed respect and admiration: Wordsworth speaks of her in his 'Extempore Effusion upon the Death of James Hogg' as 'that holy Spirit, / Sweet as the spring, as ocean deep' (ll. 37–8; quoted from Wu, *Romanticism: An Anthology*, 3rd edn). Landon was exposed to rumour and scandal that besmirched her name, first in connection with her literary mentor, William Jerdan, editor of *The Literary Gazette*. Rumours of relationships (almost certainly innocent) with other men, including Edward Bulwer-Lytton, Daniel Maclise, the portrait painter, and William Maginnis, contributor to *Frazer's Magazine*, resurfaced after her engagement to John Forster, the future biographer of Charles Dickens, an engagement which Landon broke off after Forster questioned her about letters to Maginnis. In her essay, published in 1835, entitled 'On the Character of Mrs. Hemans's Writings', Landon writes with great insight and fellow-feeling, and yet awareness of difference. She notes that Hemans expresses a 'yearning for affection – unsatisfied, but still unsubdued' (*SW*, p. 180), and the reader may feel that here Landon is looking in a mirror; many of her finest poems speak of this yearning. She has a keen sense of Hemans's hidden sorrows, but she comments, too, that 'Mrs Hemans was spared some of the keenest mortifications of a literary career. She knew nothing of it as a profession which has to make its way through poverty, neglect, and obstacles: she lived apart in a small, affectionate circle of friends' (*SW*, p. 183). Landon's autobiographical investment is clear at this point of the essay, and it was to escape such 'mortifications', in part, that in 1838 she married George Maclean, governor of the British-ruled Gold Coast in West Africa. The newly wed couple sailed to the Gold Coast on 5 July and Landon arrived on 16 August of 1838.[2] A few months later, on 15 October, Landon was found dead in her room, apparently clutching an empty bottle of diluted prussic acid, used medicinally at the time.

Whether Landon's death was the result of accident, murder or suicide has been much debated. Like Shelley's death by drowning in July 1822, Landon's confirmed the quasi-mythic status she constructed in her poems, and both enjoyed and endured as a woman. Landon owes much to the example of earlier Romantics as she prepares a face to meet the reader's gaze. 'On Wordsworth's Cottage, near Grasmere Lake' (published posthumously in 1839) contrasts the 'sunny respite' offered by Wordsworth's poetry with 'the feverish dream' of the poet's own experience; other poems allude to Byron and Shelley with particular persistence (as recorded in our notes), often to play a variation on their themes. Her major volumes of poetry – *The Improvisatrice* (1824), *The Troubadour* (1825), *The Golden Violet* (1826), *The Venetian Bracelet* (1829), and *The Vow of the Peacock* (1835), as well as her work from 1831 as editor of and contributor to the annual *Fisher's Drawing Room Scrap-Book* – gave the reading public what it wished, lashings of sentimental melancholy. As the reviewer for *The Literary Magnet* of *The Improvisatrice* noted, a touch mordantly, 'Her poetical breathing appears to proceed from a soul, whose very essence is love; and seared hearts – withered hopes – broken lutes – blighted flowers – music and moonlight, sing their melancholy changes through all her verses' (*SW*, p. 295). But Landon's work also shows an increasing ability to demystify romance, an ability evident from the start of her career and indicated by the first two of the four poems we have included. The figure of the poet trapped both by social convention and her own artistic myth emerges in her finest work, poems such as 'Lines of Life' or the longer

---

1 *Letitia Elizabeth Landon: Selected Writings*, ed. Jerome McGann and Daniel Riess (Peterborough, ONT: Broadview, 1997), p. 22; hereafter *SW*.
2 See *The Poetical Works of Letitia Elizabeth Landon (L. E. L)*, ed. William B. Scott [the Pre-raphaelite painter and poet], with an Introductory Memoir (London: Routledge, 1880), p. xiv.

'A History of the Lyre' (published in *The Venetian Bracelet*). In this last poem, the male narrator encounters 'Eulalie', one of Landon's most memorable self-fashionings, a female poet capable of improvising inspired verses. Eulalie tells of the suffering imposed by the search for fame: 'The way grows steeper, obstacles arise, / And unkind thwartings from companions near' (ll. 164–5). She describes, affectingly, the conventional modes of happiness prescribed for women, domestic love and happiness, and speaks of her apartness from them, cut off by her unchosen 'gift' (l. 202). In these outpourings Landon is at once confessional and artful, carefully constructing a version of her self likely to appeal. In her awareness of emotion as potentially affected 'affect', Landon is a poet capable of stripping the masks away from dissimulation and contrivance, as in 'Lines of Life'. At the same time, the question, 'Why write I this?' (l. 73), in this poem haunts her work, and the struggle for an answer (true fame? spiritual betterment?) can be traced in her finest poems. As an artist, Landon is capable of improvised flow, but also terse candour; her management of metre is never so adroit that it stifles a living if consciously artificial poetic voice. Her work underwent unjustified neglect for many decades; only recently, thanks to the work of such critics as Angela Leighton and Jerome McGann, is it receiving the attention it deserves. We have focused in detail on a few poems, in the hope that attention to their arresting emotional dynamics will help in the process of recovering a proper sense of Landon's literary value.

Further Reading

Primary Texts

The Improvisatrice and Other Poems (1824). Available in Woodstock Books facsimile edn., intro Jonathan Wordsworth (Poole, 1996).

The Troubadour; Catalogue of Pictures, and Historical Sketches (1825).
The Venetian Bracelet . . . and Other Poems (1829).
Fisher's Drawing Room Scrap-Book, 1838 (1837).
Life and Literary Remains of L. E. L., 2 vols (London: Colburn, 1841)
The Poetical Works of Letitia Elizabeth Landon (L. E. L), ed. William B. Scott, with an Introductory Memoir (London: Routledge, 1880)
Letitia Elizabeth Landon: Selected Writings, ed. Jerome McGann and Daniel Riess (Peterborough, ONT: Broadview, 1997)

Secondary Texts

Angela Leighton, *Victorian Women Poets: Writing Against the Heart* (Hemel Hempstead, UK: Harvester, 1992).
Angela Leighton and Margaret Reynolds (eds), *Victorian Women Poets: An Anthology* (Oxford: Blackwell, 1995), pp. 39–42.
Jerome McGann, *The Poetics of Sensibility: A Revolution in Poetic Taste* (Oxford: Oxford University Press, 1996).
Daniel Riess, 'Laetitia Landon and the Dawn of English Post-Romanticism', *Studies in English Literature* 36 (1996), pp. 807–27.
Duncan Wu, *Romantic Women Poets: An Anthology* (Oxford: Blackwell, 1997), pp. 593–8.

Lines Written under a Picture of a Girl Burning a Love-Letter

The poem was published as one of the 'Fragments' in *The Improvisatrice and Other Poems* (1824), which was received with great critical acclaim. The title poem dwells on the figure of the female poet inspired to spontaneous outpourings of poetry, a figure who derives, as *The Literary Magnet* 2 (1824) noted, from 'the Corinne of Madame De Stael' (*SW*, p. 295). An artfully literary construction, she seems, like many of Landon's speakers, to be a mask that allows the poet to speak emotional truths; her themes include 'Love's long catalogue of tears' (l. 108), a potent subject in Landon's work. 'Lines Written under a Picture . . .' gives compact and distilled expression to the poet's conviction that 'love's history' (l. 12) involves enchantment followed by suffering. Love, poetry and the trajectory of human life are analogues of one another in Landon; in writing about love, composed of fatal power and necessary pain, she articulates a vision of experience that seems, like T. S. Eliot's Tiresias in *The Waste Land*, to have foresuffered all. The poem has as its epigraph a rhyming couplet in iambic pentameters, followed by three quatrains of iambic tetrameters, each quatrain rhyming *abab*. The overall effect is, thus, close to that of a Shakespearean sonnet, except that the final couplet opens the poem. The 'lines' of the epigraph's opening refer to the handwriting in the letter, but bring the 'lines' of a poem to mind. Not that the poem overtly speaks about the 'impassioned heart's fond communing'; rather, in its spareness and decisiveness, it suggests a complicated mood. The speaker wishes to burn the letter, not because her relationship with the letter-writer is over, but because of her desire that no one else's gaze 'Should dwell upon one thought of thine' (l. 4). But as the letter burns, it erases even 'thy name' (l. 8) and acts as a portent of 'love's history' (l. 12). The poem uses a series of measured assertions, all of which imply will and control, only to juxtapose them with the discovery that love is likely to obey its own predestined and unhappy plot; purpose (caught in the march of the iambic feet) belongs less to the speaker than to the course of love, destined unsettlingly not to run smooth. A further juxtaposition is the fact that the obliteration of the letter accompanies the emergence of the poem. It is as though poetry is born out of love's despair.

> The lines were filled with many a tender thing,
> All the impassioned heart's fond communing.
>
> I TOOK the scroll: I could not brook
>   An eye to gaze on it, save mine;
> I could not bear another's look
>   Should dwell upon one thought of thine.
> My lamp was burning by my side,   5
>   I held thy letter to the flame,
> I marked the blaze swift o'er it glide,
>   It did not even spare thy name.
> Soon the light from the embers past,
>   I felt so sad to see it die,   10
> So bright at first, so dark at last,
>   I feared it was love's history.

1 *scroll* The word refers to the rolled-up letter; it has a suggestion of something significant, like a prophecy.
1 *took . . . brook* The internal rhyme tells of the speaker's impatient decisiveness.

8, 10, 12 *I marked . . . I felt . . . I feared* The progression from seemingly detached observation, to feeling, to fear constitutes the drama of the poem.

A Child Screening a Dove from a Hawk. By Stewardson

Published as one of the 'Poetical Sketches of Modern Pictures' in *The Troubadour; Catalogue of Pictures, and Historical Sketches* (1825), which supplies our copy-text, the poem responds to a painting by Thomas Stewardson, a pupil of George Romney. The poem is only 12 lines in length, consisting of three quatrains, each of alternating tetrameters and trimeters, each rhyming *abcb*. But, a song about innocence engulfed by experience, it contains, amid its terseness, much shifting of tones. In the painting Landon has found an image not only for her sense that 'Ever amid the sweets of life / Some evil thing must be' (ll. 7–8), but also for the human instinct to 'moralize' (l. 9) in exactly the way she has just done in the second stanza. The poem does not merely lament the likely fact that 'That dove will die, that child will weep' (l. 5). In fact, it underplays the opportunities for sentimental response, beginning with an almost sardonic, twice-repeated 'Ay' (ll. 1, 2) in what is less an instruction to the child than a spectator's comment. As Jerome McGann and Daniel Riess suggest, 'the poem succeeds through its ironic appropriation of the hawk's point of view' (*SW*, p. 25). 'Yet I misdoubt' in line 3 indicates that the screening is likely to be unsuccessful, for all the efforts of 'thy trembling hand'. In the second stanza, Landon begins by assuming that loss and sorrow are inevitable, but quickly questions whether this is the case: 'Is this their destinie?' (l. 6). 'Destinie' brings into play the notion of fate, a notion both supported by and backed away from in the next two lines. If they appear to support the idea that 'amid the sweets of life / Some evil thing must be', they do not quite endorse the concept of 'destinie'. The third stanza returns to the opening 'Ay', only this time to turn a sardonic eye on the poem's speaker, 'Ay, moralize, – is it not thus / We've mourn'd our hope and love?' (ll. 9–10). Moralizing, the lines intimate, is our natural way of coping with the need to 'mourn', and the lines make clear, too, that 'We' have had experiences of the death of 'hope and love'. The final lines adopt a more impassioned tone, opening with an exclamatory 'Alas!' that asserts 'there's tears for every eye, / A hawk for every dove!' (ll. 11–12). These lines may seem merely to restate in intensified form the moralized message which concludes stanza 2. In fact, they restore a sense of the unaccommodated, pre-moralized reality of sorrow and destruction: each 'eye' will know 'tears'; every 'dove' has waiting for it 'A hawk'. Moralizing, painting, and, implicitly, poetry itself: all run the risk of distracting our attention from pain and loss.

462 *Letitia Elizabeth Landon (1802–38)*

AY, screen thy favourite dove, fair child,
    Ay, screen it if you may,—
Yet I misdoubt thy trembling hand
    Will scare the hawk away.

That dove will die, that child will weep,—   5
    Is this their destinie?
Ever amid the sweets of life
    Some evil thing must be.

Ay, moralize,—is it not thus
    We've mourn'd our hope and love?   10
Alas! there's tears for every eye,
    A hawk for every dove!

1 *Ay* McGann and Riess suggest that Landon enjoys 'Wordplays that call attention to the relations' among 'the romantic "I," the assenting "Ay," and the gazing eye' (*SW*, p. 24). See also the first two lines of 'Lines Written Under a Picture . . .'.
2 *if you may* Implies that the child 'may' be powerless to 'screen' the dove.
3 *misdoubt* Have misgivings (whether).
4 *scare* A word that enters the child's frame of mind (that is, 'scaring away' the hawk is just how the child would think of its efforts) before the sudden pulling away to a long perspective in the next line, which refers to 'that child'.
11 *there's tears* Grammatically, this should be 'there are', but 'there's' does much to give the impression of a mind cutting through to the core of the matter.

Lines of Life

'Lines of Life' takes its punning title from Shakespeare's sonnet 16, line 9 (see *SW*, p. 275) and draws our attention to its own existence as a collection of 'lines'. The poem, published in *The Venetian Bracelet . . . and Other Poems* (1829), which supplies our copy-text, consists of 27 quatrains, each of alternating tetrameters and trimeters, each rhyming *abcb*. Lines 1–48, in particular, speak of the poet's complicity in a social system which has encouraged repression and dissimulation. Lines 49 to the end protest, with moments of faint-heartedness, against society's 'fetters' (l. 48): they articulate Landon's 'loftier mood / Of generous impulse, high resolve' (ll. 50–1), a mood which she claims underpins her poetry. Poetry, she argues, following Byron's lead in *Childe Harold's Pilgrimage*, canto 3, stanza 6, gives her release from a 'worthless' (l. 82) mundane self. 'What am I? Nothing. But not so art thou, / Soul of my thought, with whom I traverse earth' (ll. 50–1), wrote Byron. Landon also asks, 'what am I?' (l. 81), coming up with an unflattering answer, before she asserts, 'song has touch'd my lips with fire' (l. 85). Bleak as is its analysis of 'life's weary chain' (l. 90), the poem is not wholly pessimistic because of the high valuation it places on 'hallow'd words' (l. 91). Perhaps Landon's most evidently Romantic trait is her exaltation of art, even if that exaltation recognizes that poetry exacts a high price from its creator. The poem has a compelling power, deriving, in part, from the poet's longing that it will be her 'words' (l. 96), her 'song' (l. 100), which will influence posterity. And yet the final note of affirmation allows for the fact that appeals to posterity involve awareness that the appellant will experience 'The silence of the dead' (l. 106). 'I care not' (l. 107), writes Landon, with, it seems, as much exhausted indifference as triumphant disdain. The poem manages to sound as though it comes from confessional depths, an effect deriving from skilled manipulation of rhetorical effects: the use of the first person in a calculatedly declarative way in each stanza from the second to the tenth; a taut control of diction, able to distinguish between past 'timidness' (l. 7) and present 'caution' (l. 8); and the sparing use of suggestive images, such as the comparison between unacknowledged 'feelings' and 'wrecks / In the unfathom'd main' (ll. 23–4).

Orphan in my first year's, I early learnt
To make my heart suffice itself, and seek
Support and sympathy in its own depths.

WELL, read my cheek, and watch my eye,—
  Too strictly school'd are they,
One secret of my soul to show,
  One hidden thought betray.

I never knew the time my heart
  Look'd freely from my brow;
It once was check'd by timidness,
  'Tis taught by caution now.

I live among the cold, the false,
  And I must seem like them;
And such I am, for I am false
  As those I most condemn.

I teach my lip its sweetest smile,
  My tongue its softest tone;
I borrow others' likeness, till
  Almost I lose my own.

I pass through flattery's gilded sieve,
  Whatever I would say;
In social life, all, like the blind,
  Must learn to feel their way.

I check my thoughts like curbed steeds
  That struggle with the rein;
I bid my feelings sleep, like wrecks
  In the unfathom'd main.

I hear them speak of love, the deep,
  The true, and mock the name;
Mock at all high and early truth,
  And I too do the same.

I hear them tell some touching tale,
  I swallow down the tear;
I hear them name some generous deed,
  And I have learnt to sneer.

I hear the spiritual, the kind,
  The pure, but named in mirth;
Till all of good, ay, even hope,
  Seems exiled from our earth.

And one fear, withering ridicule,
  Is all that I can dread;
A sword hung by a single hair
  For ever o'er the head.

Epigraph Presumably composed by Landon herself, the seemingly artless blank verse makes a marked contrast with the groomed and artful quatrains of the poem proper.
1 *Well* Compare Coleridge's openings to 'This Lime-Tree Bower My Prison' and 'Dejection: An Ode'.
9, 11 *false* The repetition suggests the poet's feeling of entrapment within 'falsity'.
16 *Almost* The word indicates a residue of self-worth in the speaker.

17–18 *I pass . . . say* The syntax, holding back 'Whatever I would say', mimes the speaker's care in social situations.
21–4 *I check . . . main* Checked thoughts resemble 'curbed steeds', but repressed feelings are like lost ships; the distinction is alive to different kinds of self-censoring.
30 *I . . . tear* 'swallow' effectively enacts a physical repression of feeling.
39–40 *A sword . . . head* The sword of Damocles (see note on Shelley, *Prometheus Unbound*, 1. l. 398, p. 364).

We bow to a most servile faith,
    In a most servile fear;
While none among us dares to say
    What none will choose to hear.

And if we dream of loftier thoughts,
    In weakness they are gone;
And indolence and vanity
    Rivet our fetters on.

Surely I was not born for this!
    I feel a loftier mood
Of generous impulse, high resolve,
    Steal o'er my solitude!

I gaze upon the thousand stars
    That fill the midnight sky;
And wish, so passionately wish,
    A light like theirs on high.

I have such eagerness of hope
    To benefit my kind;
And feel as if immortal power
    Were given to my mind.

I think on that eternal fame,
    The sun of earthly gloom,
Which makes the gloriousness of death,
    The future of the tomb—

That earthly future, the faint sign
    Of a more heavenly one;
—A step, a word, a voice, a look,—
    Alas! my dream is done.

And earth, and earth's debasing stain,
    Again is on my soul;
And I am but a nameless part
    Of a most worthless whole.

Why write I this? because my heart
    Towards the future springs,
That future where it loves to soar
    On more than eagle wings.

The present, it is but a speck
    In that eternal time,
In which my lost hopes find a home,
    My spirit knows its clime.

41–4 *We . . . hear* Landon switches here from 'I' to 'We'. Having established her unhappy loneliness in 'social life' (l. 19), she generalizes her predicament.
54 *And wish . . . wish* The cadence here has a new openness to feeling, caught in the 'passionate' repetition of 'wish'.
58 *benefit my kind* Compare Shelley's desire to love 'all human kind' in the last line of 'Hymn to Intellectual Beauty'.
65 *That earthly future* The first run-on from stanza to stanza in the poem, capturing the poet's sudden fervour, soon to be temporarily dampened (see l. 68).
71–2 *And . . . whole* Parodies Romantic pantheism of the kind expressed by Wordsworth in 'Tintern Abbey' and Byron in parts of the third canto of *Childe Harold's Pilgrimage*.
73 *Why write I this?* An example of the Romantic impulse to dramatize the act of writing, a means of drawing attention to the perilous but significant sense-making undertaken in and by the very poem we are reading.

Oh! not myself,—for what am I?—
    The worthless and the weak,
Whose every thought of self should raise
    A blush to burn my cheek.

But song has touch'd my lips with fire,   85
    And made my heart a shrine;
For what, although alloy'd, debased,
    Is in itself divine.

I am myself but a vile link
    Amid life's weary chain;   90
But I have spoken hallow'd words,
    Oh do not say in vain!

My first, my last, my only wish,
    Say will my charmed chords
Wake to the morning light of fame,   95
    And breathe again my words?

Will the young maiden, when her tears
    Alone in moonlight shine—
Tears for the absent and the loved—
    Murmur some song of mine?   100

Will the pale youth by his dim lamp,
    Himself a dying flame,
From many an antique scroll beside,
    Choose that which bears my name?

Let music make less terrible   105
    The silence of the dead;
I care not, so my spirit last
    Long after life has fled.

---

85 *touch'd ... fire* A much-used phrase to describe the onset of inspiration that derives from Isaiah 6: 6–7 (the context is relevant to Landon's poem): 'Then flew one of the seraphims unto me, having a live coal in his hand, which he had taken with the tongs from off the altar: And he laid it upon my mouth, and said, Lo, this hath touched thy lips; and thine iniquity is taken away. and thy sin purged.'

89–90 *I ... chain* One of a number of echoes of Byron's *Childe Harold's Pilgrimage*, canto 3, in which the poet expresses his dislike of being 'A link reluctant in a fleshly chain' (stanza 72, l. 685).

93–104 *My first ... name?* Landon expresses her longing for fame in a series of questions.

95 *Wake* The usually unaccented first syllable here takes an emphatic and appropriate stress.

Felicia Hemans

Landon admired Felicia Hemans and wrote about her with striking empathy in her essay, published in 1835, 'On the Character of Mrs. Hemans's Writings' and in an earlier elegy, 'Stanzas on the Death of Mrs. Hemans'. Both works anticipate the concerns of 'Felicia Hemans', published in 1837 in *Fisher's Drawing Room Scrap-Book, 1838*, from which we derive our copy-text. 'Stanzas', full of allusions to Hemans's work, notes 'thy song is sorrowful, / Its beauty is not bloom' (ll. 41–2) and moves on to speak of the woman behind the poem, 'Ah! dearly purchased is the gift, / The gift of song like thine' (ll. 49–50). The element of fellow-feeling is evident here, and in the essay, which, pondering the question, 'what is a poetical career?' asserts: 'But never can success repay its cost' (*SW*, p. 184). The sense that Hemans purchased fame 'too dearly' ('Felicia Hemans', l. 33) is the more affecting for covertly voicing Landon's own mixed feelings about her poetic career.

'Felicia Hemans' consists of five stanzas, each of 16 lines, rhyming *ababcdcdefefghgh*, in a strictly alternating pattern of feminine and masculine rhymes. The pattern corresponds to the poem's mingled effect of affirmation and sadness, loss and compensation, admiration and self-projection. Echoes of other Romantic poems saturate the piece. McGann and Riess speak of Landon as the producer of 'self-consciously quotational writing' (*SW*, p. 23), a shrewd observation that invites us to see the poet as investing in, and yet at a knowing distance from, a repertoire of Romantic attitudes. In this poem, the consequence is to throw into keen relief the change of stance in the third and fourth stanzas, in which Landon investigates what lies below the surface of an admired poem: 'We say,' she remarks, her first line mimicking the tone of a responsive reader, 'the song is sorrowful, but know not / What may have left that sorrow on the song' (ll. 41–2). These and subsequent lines in the third stanza open up a gap between the finished artistic product and the life that lies behind the poetry. 'Yet', muses Landon in the fourth stanza, the very ability to move between surface and depth, defines 'mind in woman' (l. 49). The stanza gives a gendered inflection to familiar Romantic conceptions. In 'Dejection: An Ode', Coleridge speaks of the 'inanimate cold world allowed / To the poor loveless ever-anxious crowd' (ll. 51–2); for Landon, in a variation on this theme, the gifted woman possesses 'a keener feeling / Than those around, the cold and careless, know' (ll. 51–2).

The word 'know' and its cognate forms are crucial to the poem. The first stanza celebrates Hemans's poetic bequest, her ability both to find words for feelings and to create a new fund of perceptions, 'A beauty known but from thy breathing there' (l. 12). In the second stanza, Landon comments that 'By its immortal verse is language known' (l. 22). What can be a hackneyed, even a comic rhyme, that between 'poet' (l. 21) and 'know it' (l. 23), takes on a surprising seriousness in this context. The stanza speaks, too, of the widespread knowledge of Hemans's work, extending to America. But in the third stanza, Landon attends to what we 'know not' (ll. 35, 41). In the fourth stanza, however, she emphasizes that women poets such as Hemans do have access to a special kind of knowledge. In an allusion to Romantic Prometheanism, Landon implicitly claims for 'the woman's heart' (l. 56) a heroism comparable to that which inspires the protagonists of poems such as Byron's 'Prometheus' and Shelley's *Prometheus Unbound*: 'The fable of Prometheus and the vulture, / Reveals the poet's and the woman's heart' (ll. 55–6). The final stanza plays a further variation on the painful knowledge versified in 'Dejection: An Ode'. Coleridge declares that 'we receive but what we give' (l. 47). Hemans, according to Landon, desired 'The beautiful' (l. 67), 'But only from [herself] its being drew' (l. 68): proof both of the imagination's indomitable creative power and of the recalcitrant nature of this 'harsh world' (l. 70). The poem's fluency and skill are characteristic, as is its sense that 'song' and 'sorrow' are inextricable.

> No more, no more—oh, never more returning,
>   Will thy beloved presence gladden earth;
> No more wilt thou with sad, yet anxious, yearning
>   Cling to those hopes which have no mortal birth.
> Thou art gone from us, and with thee departed,   5
>   How many lovely things have vanished too:
> Deep thoughts that at thy will to being started,
>   And feelings, teaching us our own were true.
> Thou hast been round us, like a viewless spirit,
>   Known only by the music on the air;   10
> The leaf or flowers which thou hast named inherit
>   A beauty known but from thy breathing there:
> For thou didst on them fling thy strong emotion,
>   The likeness from itself the fond heart gave;
> As planets from afar look down on ocean,   15
>   And give their own sweet image to the wave.

1 *No more, no more* See Heman's poem, 'No More!'
3–4 *No more . . . birth* Landon might be describing the 'yearning' evident in a poem such as Hemans's 'The Spirit's Mysteries' (p. 407).
8 *And . . . true* Our feelings are confirmed when we find them expressed in Hemans's poetry.
9–11 *spirit . . . inherit* The rhyme between 'spirit' and 'inherit' is central to Romantic poetry, fascinated by questions to do with the spirit's inheritance.

15–16 *As planets . . . wave* A reworking of Shelley's more sombre image in 'Alastor', 'His wan eyes / Gaze on the empty scene as vacantly / As ocean's moon looks on the moon in heaven' (ll. 200–2), Landon's lines imply the need of the self to confer 'strong emotion' (l. 13) if the natural is to have any meaning.

And thou didst bring from foreign lands their treasures,
    As floats thy various melody along;
We know the softness of Italian measures,
    And the grave cadence of Castilian song.
A general bond of union is the poet,
    By its immortal verse is language known,
And for the sake of song do others know it—
    One glorious poet makes the world his own.
And thou—how far thy gentle sway extended!
    The heart's sweet empire over land and sea;
Many a stranger and far flower was blended
    In the soft wreath that glory bound for thee.
The echoes of the Susquehanna's waters
    Paused in the pine-woods words of thine to hear;
And to the wide Atlantic's younger daughters
    Thy name was lovely, and thy song was dear.

Was not this purchased all too dearly?—never
    Can fame atone for all that fame hath cost.
We see the goal, but know not the endeavour
    Nor what fond hopes have on the way been lost.
What do we know of the unquiet pillow,
    By the worn cheek and tearful eyelid prest,
When thoughts chase thoughts, like the tumultuous billow,
    Whose very light and foam reveals unrest?
We say, the song is sorrowful, but know not
    What may have left that sorrow on the song;
However mournful words may be, they show not
    The whole extent of wretchedness and wrong.
They cannot paint the long sad hours, passed only
    In vain regrets o'er what we feel we are.
Alas! the kingdom of the lute is lonely—
    Cold is the worship coming from afar.

Yet what is mind in woman but revealing
    In sweet clear light the hidden world below,
By quicker fancies and a keener feeling
    Than those around, the cold and careless, know?
What is to feed such feeling, but to culture
    A soil whence pain will never more depart?
The fable of Prometheus and the vulture,

---

20 *Castilian* Spanish. In her essay on Hemans, Landon writes: 'Mistress both of German and Spanish, the latter country appears to have peculiarly captivated her imagination' (*SW*, p. 180).

21 *A general . . . poet* Compare Wordsworth, Preface to *Lyrical Ballads* (1802), 'the Poet binds together by passion and knowledge the vast empire of human society' (R. L. Brett and A. R. Jones, eds, *Lyrical Ballads* [London: Methuen, 1963], p. 259).

29 *the Susquehanna's waters* A river in America, on the banks of which the young Coleridge and Southey proposed to establish their Pantisocratic community.

40 *unrest* Possibly recalling Shelley's line, 'And that unrest which men miscall delight' ('Adonais', l. 354).

41–2 *We . . . song* Though the sorrowful life-experience may remain unknown, Landon does connect the 'sorrowful' song with a real experience 'Which may have left that sorrow on the song'. To this extent, she espouses an expressive, even confessional view of poetry, as when, in her essay on Hemans, she writes: 'I believe that no poet ever made his readers feel unless he had himself felt' (*SW*, p. 175).

46 *vain . . . are* Landon may suggest that such 'regrets' are 'vain', in part, because they do not fully do justice to 'what we are'; only the poetry does that, yet the poetry cannot emerge without the toil and distress described in the stanza.

53 *culture* A verb, meaning to 'cultivate'.

Reveals the poet's and the woman's heart.
Unkindly are they judged—unkindly treated—
   By careless tongues and by ungenerous words;
While cruel sneer, and hard reproach, repeated,
   Jar the fine music of the spirit's chords.   60
Wert thou not weary—thou whose soothing numbers
   Gave other lips the joy thine own had not.
Didst thou not welcome thankfully the slumbers
   Which closed around thy mourning human lot?

What on this earth could answer thy requiring,   65
   For earnest faith—for love, the deep and true,
The beautiful, which was thy soul's desiring,
   But only from thyself its being drew.
How is the warm and loving heart requited
   In this harsh world, where it awhile must dwell.   70
Its best affections wronged, betrayed, and slighted—
   Such is the doom of those who love too well.
Better the weary dove should close its pinion,
   Fold up its golden wings and be at peace;
Enter, O ladye, that serene dominion,   75
   Where earthly cares and earthly sorrows cease.
Fame's troubled hour has cleared, and now replying,
   A thousand hearts their music ask of thine.
Sleep with a light the lovely and undying
   Around thy grave—a grave which is a shrine.   80

58 *careless tongues* Compare 'evil tongues' in Wordsworth's 'Tintern Abbey', l. 132, itself an echo of *Paradise Lost*, 7. 26.
60 *Jar* Takes an expressive stress at the start of the line.
70 *harsh world* Compare the hero's request in *Hamlet* that Horatio should 'in this harsh world draw thy breath in pain / To tell my story' (5. 2. 290–1).
75 *serene dominion* Seeking a space free from care for the dead poet, Landon echoes Shelley's *Prometheus Unbound* at its most transformative, Asia singing of her journey at the end of Act 2 (scene 5, ll. 85–6): 'Meanwhile thy spirit lifts its pinions / In music's most serene dominions'.
79 *light* Followed by a comma in the 1839 reprinting, from which we have taken the semi-colon at the end of line 74. But the comma in line 79 is unnecessary. Landon's meaning is that 'the lovely and undying' 'Sleep with a light' 'Around thy grave'.

Index of Titles and First Lines

Adonais, An Elegy on the Death of John Keats 381
Ah! Sun-flower 36
'Ah Sun-flower! weary of time' 37
Alastor; Or, The Spirit of Solitude 318
'And is there glory from the heavens departed?' 414
Anecdote for Fathers, Shewing how the practice of Lying may be taught 79
'A slumber did my spirit seal' 123
'Ay, screen thy favourite dove, fair child' 462

'Behold her, single in the field' 169
'Be the proud Thames, of trade the busy mart!' 14
'Bob Southey! You're a poet – poet Laureate' 257
Bright star, would I were stedfast as thou art 458
'Bright star, would I were stedfast as thou art –' 458

Casabianca 412
Child Screening a Dove from a Hawk, A. By Stewardson 461
Chimney Sweeper, The 27
Christabel 205
Clod and the Pebble, The 31
Composed upon Westminster Bridge, Sept. 3, 1803 161
Crystal Cabinet, The 71

Dejection: An Ode 234
Don Juan, Canto I 263
Don Juan, Dedication 256

'Earth has not any thing to shew more fair' 161
'Earth, ocean, air, beloved brotherhood!' 321
Ecchoing Green, The 22
Elegiac Stanzas, Suggested by a Picture of Peele Castle in a Storm, Painted by Sir George Beaumont 170
'Enslav'd, the Daughters of Albion weep; a trembling lamentation' 42
Eolian Harp, The. Composed at Clevedon, Somersetshire 175
[Epistle to Augusta] 246
'Ere on my bed my limbs I lay' 232
Eve of St Agnes, The 421
Expostulation and Reply 102

Felicia Hemans 465
First Book of Urizen, The 50
'Five years have passed; five summers, with the length' 105
Fly, The 34
Fountain, The, A Conversation 126
France: An Ode 224
Frost at Midnight 221

Graves of a Household, The 409

'Hear the voice of the Bard!' 31
Holy Thursday (Songs of Experience) 32
Holy Thursday (Songs of Innocence) 28
Homes of England, The 405
Hymn to Intellectual Beauty 338

Idiot Boy, The 91
If by dull rhymes our english must be chain'd 442
'If by dull rhymes our english must be chain'd' 443
'If from the public way you turn your steps' 130
'I have a boy of five years old' 79
'I heard a thousand blended notes' 81
'I loved Theotormon' 42
'I love thee, mournful, sober-suited Night!' 17
Image in Lava, The 410
'In distant countries I have been' 89
Inscription for an Ice-House 4
'In the sweet shire of Cardigan' 77
Introduction (Songs of Experience) 30
Introduction (Songs of Innocence) 21
'In Xanadu did Kubla Khan' 186
'Is this a holy thing to see' 33
'It is an ancient Mariner' 190
'It is the first mild day of March' 75
'I took the scroll: I could not brook' 461
'I travel'd through a Land of Men' 69
'It seems a day' 128
'I wander through each charter'd street' 38
'I want a hero: an uncommon want' 263
'I was angry with my friend' 40
'I was thy Neighbour once, thou rugged Pile!' 170
'I weep for Adonais – he is dead!' 384

Kubla Khan 183

La Belle Dame Sans Merci 436
Lamb, The 24
Last of the Flock, The 88
Lines of Life 462
Lines written a few miles above Tintern Abbey, on revisiting the banks of the Wye during a Tour, 13 July, 1798 105
Lines written at a small distance from my House, and sent by my little Boy to the Person to whom they are addressed 75
Lines written in early Spring 81
Lines Written under a Picture of a Girl Burning a Love-Letter 460
Little Black Boy, The 25
'Little Fly' 34
'Little Lamb, who made thee?' 24
'Lo, a shadow of horror is risen' 51
London 37
Lost Pleiad, The 413
'Love seeketh not Itself to please' 32
'Low was our pretty Cot: our tallest Rose' 178

Mental Traveller, The 68
Michael, A Pastoral Poem 129
'Midway the hill of Science, after steep' 6
Mirror in the Deserted Hall, The 415
'Monarch of Gods and Daemons, and all Spirits' 353
Mont Blanc. Lines written in the Vale of Chamouni 342
'Much have I travel'd in the realms of gold' 421
'My heart aches, and a drowsy numbness pains' 444
'My mother bore me in the southern wild' 26
'My pensive Sara! thy soft cheek reclined' 176
'My Sister – my sweet Sister – if a name' 247

Nightingale, The, A Conversation Poem, April, 1798 228
'No cloud, no relique of the sunken day' 229
'No more, no more – oh, never more returning' 466
'No, no, go not to Lethe, neither twist' 452
Nurse's Song 29
Nutting 128

Ode (from 1815 entitled 'Ode: Intimations of Immortality from Recollections of Early Childhood') 162

Ode on a Grecian Urn 448
Ode on Indolence 453
Ode on Melancholy 451
Ode to a Nightingale 443
Ode to Psyche 439
Ode to the West Wind 376
'O, dim, forsaken mirror!' 415
'Of the primeval Priest's assum'd power' 51
'O Goddess! hear these tuneless numbers, wrung' 440
'Oh there is blessing in this gentle breeze' 141
'One dream of passion and of beauty more!' 402
'One morn before me were three figures seen' 454
On First Looking into Chapman's Homer 420
'On some rude fragment of the rocky shore' 13
'O Rose thou art sick' 33
'O what can ail thee knight at arms' 437
'O, wild West Wind, thou breath of Autumn's being' 378

Pains of Sleep, The 232
'Piping down the valleys wild' 22
Poison Tree, A 39
Prelude, The, 1805, Book 1 140
'Press'd by the Moon, mute arbitress of tides' 17
Prometheus Unbound, Act I 348
Properzia Rossi 401

Reflections on Having Left a Place of Retirement 177
Resolution and Independence 156
Rights of Woman, The 3
Rime of the Ancient Mariner, The 187
'River, that rollest by the ancient walls' 252
Ruined Cottage, The 110

'Season of mists and mellow fruitfulness' 456
'She dwelt among th'untrodden ways' 123
Sick Rose, The 33
Simon Lee, The Old Huntsman, With an incident in which he was concerned 76
Slumber did my spirit seal, A 123
Solitary Reaper, The 169
Song: 'She dwelt among th'untrodden ways' 122
Sonnet I ['The partial Muse, has from my earliest hours'] 11
Sonnet VII: On the departure of the nightingale 12
Sonnet XII: Written on the sea shore. – October, 1784 13
Sonnet XXX: To the River Arun 14
Sonnet XXXII: To Melancholy 15
Sonnet XXXIX: To Night 16

Sonnet XLIV: Written in the church-yard at Middleton in Sussex 17
Spirit's Mysteries, The 407
'St. Agnes' Eve – Ah, bitter chill it was!' 423
Stanzas to [Augusta] 243
Stanzas to the Po 251
Strange fits of passion I have known 121
'Strange fits of passion I have known' 122
'Stranger, approach! within this iron door' 5
'Sweet poet of the woods – a long adieu!' 12

Tables Turned, The; An Evening Scene, on the same subject 103
'The awful shadow of some unseen Power' 339
'The boy stood on the burning deck' 412
'The everlasting universe of things' 343
'The Frost performs its secret ministry' 222
'The Maiden caught me in the Wild' 72
'The partial Muse, has from my earliest hours' 11
'The power that dwelleth in sweet sounds to waken' 407
'There is a thorn; it looks so old' 82
'There was a roaring in the wind all night' 157
'There was a time when meadow, grove, and stream' 162
'The stately Homes of England' 406
'The Sun does arise' 23
'The world is too much with us; late and soon' 160
'They grew in beauty, side by side' 409
This Lime-Tree Bower My Prison 180
Thorn, The 82
'Though the day of my destiny's over' 244
'Thou still unravish'd bride of quietness' 448

'Thou thing of years departed!' 410
''Tis eight o'clock, – a clear March night' 92
''Tis the middle of night by the castle clock' 207
To Autumn 456
To Mr. S. T. Coleridge 6
'Twas on a Holy Thursday, their innocent faces clean' 29
''Twas summer and the sun was mounted high' 110
Two April Mornings, The 124
Tyger, The 34
'Tyger, Tyger, burning bright' 35

'Up! up! my friend, and clear your looks' 104

Visions of the Daughters of Albion 40

'Well! If the Bard was weather-wise, who made' 235
'Well, read my cheek, and watch my eye' 463
'Well, they are gone, and here must I remain' 181
'We talk'd with open heart, and tongue' 126
'We walk'd along, while bright and red' 124
'When latest Autumn spreads her evening veil' 16
'When my mother died I was very young' 28
'When the voices of children are heard on the green' 30
'Why William, on that old grey stone' 102
World is too much with us, The 160

'Ye Clouds! that far above me float and pause' 225
'Yes, injured Woman! rise, assert thy right!' 3